The Mimetic Evolution of the Court of Justice of the EU

Leonardo Pierdominici

The Mimetic Evolution of the Court of Justice of the EU

A Comparative Law Perspective

palgrave
macmillan

Leonardo Pierdominici
Dipartimento di scienze giuridiche
Alma Mater Studiorum - Università of Bologna
Bologna, Italy

ISBN 978-3-030-47863-6 ISBN 978-3-030-47864-3 (eBook)
https://doi.org/10.1007/978-3-030-47864-3

Cover credit: G. de Chirico, Il grande metafisico, 1917—Archivart/Alamy Stock Photo

This Palgrave Macmillan imprint is published by the registered company Springer Nature Switzerland AG
The registered company address is: Gewerbestrasse 11, 6330 Cham, Switzerland

Acknowledgments

This book is a revised version of the PhD dissertation which I wrote and defended at the European University Institute of Florence. I am grateful to the whole EUI Community and the Italian Ministry of Foreign Affairs for having granted me the best possible environment for doctoral studies.

Special thanks are due to those who helped and inspired me in the first steps of my academic career, in Bologna and Florence: Susanna Mancini, Miguel Poiares Maduro, Loïc Azoulai. Without their guidance, I would have been lost.

I owe a huge debt of gratitude to Giuseppe Martinico: a passionate academic, a mentor, a friend.

I would like to thank Bruno de Witte and Laurent Pech who, as members of my PhD jury, gave me detailed and thoughtful comments which I tried to address in subsequent work.

This book was written in many different locations. My thanks go to the administrative staff of the Universities that hosted me: the EUI, the University of Michigan, the Alma Mater Studiorum–Università di Bologna.

Along this journey, I greatly benefitted from discussions with many colleagues, and in particular with Samo Bardutzky, Francesco Biagi, Lidia Bonifati, Carlo Maria Cantore, Giacomo Delledonne, Giacomo Di Federico, Federico Fabbrini, Elena Ferioli, Filippo Fontanelli, Kasia Granat, Daniel Halberstam, Neil Komesar, Enrico Legnini, Andrea Lollini, Leandro Mancano, Zurab Matcharadze, Alessandro Martinuzzi,

François-Xavier Millet, Francesco Paniccià, Francesca Raimondo, Bosko and Milena Tripkovic.

All my other friends in Bologna, Florence, Macerata deserve credit as well.

The book is dedicated to my family.

CONTENTS

CHAPTER 1

Introduction

This book aims to offer new perspectives in the legal study of the Court of Justice of the European Union (CJEU), by reversing some traditional ones. In the multidisciplinary field of European studies, the Court of Justice has mainly been analysed in the light of its central role in the process of continental integration: i.e. the central role of the Court and its case law *for the evolution* of the EU legal order.[1] Moreover, the CJEU has been traditionally studied by specialists for its important role as an *agent* of comparative law: i.e. as the quintessential example of a supranational court which is a "natural" user of comparative material and comparative analysis of law.[2]

On the contrary, my proposal is to study the *evolution of the Court* itself, rather than that of the EU legal order in its judge-made dimension. The evolution of jurisprudence and interpretative activity of the CJEU will constitute a background of my research, but not its principal focus. Rather, my monograph will address as its main topic of study the *structure* and the *organization* of the Court itself, taken as an institution: and it will do so by looking at several institutional aspects of its structure and organization, selected and constructed as a complete range of symptomatic figures of judicial institutionalization.

I will approach this analysis through a comparative lens, not, however, through a review of the comparative method employed by the Court's judges, but rather by showcasing how the development and the institutional evolution of the CJEU happened through a selective internalization

L. Pierdominici, *The Mimetic Evolution of the Court of Justice of the EU*, https://doi.org/10.1007/978-3-030-47864-3_1

of comparative influences. This process took place in such a way that the Court's institutionalization can be considered *mimetic*: that is, able to engage and internalize the solicitations which came from EU Member States influences of different legal traditions and responding to global challenges in relation to the increasing role of the international forms of judicial review and the international judicial review bodies. Thus, I will look at the comparative influences in the Court's institutional evolution: to demonstrate—in a slogan—how the institutional development of the CJEU has been *culturally* influenced in order to be *functionally* efficient.

1.1 The Structure

The CJEU has often been described as "arguably the most powerful international court" in the world[3] and as the protagonist of a strong dynamic of "self-empowerment".[4] Historically, the basis of this analysis has been on doctrinal aspects of the Court's activity: to name a few, the revolutionary use of its procedures, the interpretative methods it adopted, and the substantive detachment it shaped from the loose forms of traditional international law. The evolution of the power of the Court has been traditionally studied through an analysis of its powerful, innovative doctrinal choices and of its capacity to shape the evolution of EU law.[5] However, the Court's success and its process of "self-empowerment" have never been measured against its intrinsic adaptive capacity as an organization vis-à-vis the peculiar plural environment in which it has acted. "It is widely accepted that the Court of Justice has played—and continues to play—a key role as the motor of European integration"[6] is a classic adage framed in a telling Aristotelian jargon. In fact, EU integration is a motion process, and the CJEU played the role of its *primum movens*. But in such Aristotelian terms, the question arises whether the CJEU is an *unmoved mover* of the motion of integration—from which an initial movement derives, but which is not moved by others, already perfectly done and with no sign of becoming—or is a living institution that made its way not only by fostering but also by adapting to the different stages of a progressive integration. In other words: it is well-known that the studies of European integration—which is, in itself, a process—are a *locus amoenus* of evolutionary theories (also in the legal perspective) focusing on the transformation of political inter-institutional relationships.[7] But how much of the successful evolution of an institution, of its "self-empowerment", its gain of authority and legitimacy, is based on the capacity to engage and internalize the solicitations to its structure and organization? This works aims to provide answers to this question and highlight this parallel and equally important aspect in the evolution of the CJEU.[8]

In this respect, the objective of my study is to highlight the way in which an increasingly important and increasingly debated judicial body like the CJEU, traditionally not a priority of EU institutional reform, has changed over time and evolved through positive law amendments and the will of the *Herren der Verträge*, but also, and decisively, through wise and often spontaneous recalibrations of institutional characteristics. It is commonplace to argue that "comparative insights have certainly informed the text of the Treaties and the design of the European institutions",[9] but the academic literature did not go beyond scarce or anecdotal remarks on this point; similarly, the high degree of autonomy of the EU judicial system—that has even been defined as a form of "judicial self-government"—is a broad and relevant yet "largely understudied phenomenon".[10] The proposed book aims at filling these gaps in the literature.

The analysis will be structured as follows: after an introduction to the research and its situation in the tradition of European and comparative studies, five chapters will look at five different *specific* but *central* and *paradigmatic* aspects of the structural, organizational and institutional development of the Court in the decades since its foundation. In a kind of logical order of institutionalization, I will look first of all at a historical reconstruction of the genesis of the CJEU, since the times of its foundation, to highlight how the design of the Court and its powers was heavily influenced by the existing judicial forms present in the higher courts of the Member states at that time, which thus constituted the first important and established comparative models, and "naturally" influenced the first negotiators and players in the field. I will also emphasize also how, in shaping the ECJ, domestic models of judicial review prevailed over original forms of international judicial review, which were taken into account. Then, the work will analyse what logically follows in structuring and organizing a court: thus, the appointment of its members, its human resources. It will highlight how the system of selection of the CJEU's judges, advocates general and personnel has been for several decades a neglected and even mysterious topic, covered by the traditional and taken-for-granted discretion of the States in the selection of international judges; but that the situation has decisively changed with a new procedure established pursuant to Article 255 TFEU introduced by the Lisbon Treaty. In this change as well, comparative influences were essential: a certain specific and apt model of selection was adopted, in conformity with international trends, and it is proving to be so apt to influence national models in turn. The following chapter, again in order of logic problematisation in the structuring of the Court, would analyse the problem of transparency in the works of the CJEU, considered as a "deliberative institution",[11] both in the traditional terms of its discussed modalities of internal deliberation and in the new terms of the openness of its judicial activities and proceedings (a theme recently raised by scholars for the first time).[12] In both senses, comparative influences were crucial. The next step would be to investigate the modalities and techniques of docket control and the problems of allocation of judicial activity and resources by the CJEU. These problems are essential for the actual work of the Court, that has often considered "victim of its own success"[13] especially in terms of an increasing overload of cases, and they are often influenced by tensions that originate from the Member States and their legal cultures, on the point of the very conceptualisation of what docket control can and should mean, by the different approaches of common law and civil law countries to the question of the abstractness of the preliminary ruling procedure of Article 267 TFEU,[14] or by the various exigencies coming from different contexts with regard to the CJEU's action. The last chapter will look at the stylistic modalities of the decisions of the CJEU, considering them as the final product, the output, of the structure and organization of the institution, directly influenced by these latter as well as stratified cultural aspects. Some final remarks will conclude the work, summing up the results of the analysis, and further reflecting on the idea of *mimetism*—the capacity of the CJEU, as a supranational institution, to evolve by facing several organizational challenges and by solving them through a selective internalization of internal and external comparative lessons. *Mimetism* will be examined as both a phenomenological and methodological concept, with particular importance in the supranational setting.

1.2 Some Key-Concepts: Autonomy, Authority, Mimetism

The work will not be a mere description of the (per se significant) institutional evolution of the CJEU. On the contrary, it aims at looking at such evolution in connection with the institutional success of the Court and its "self-empowerment" moves. In this respect, some key-concepts will constitute the common thread of the analysis.

The first is the concept of *autonomy* of the Court. Its institutional evolution has always happened with a distinctive dose of self-determination, of autonomous negotiation: in a certain sense, this is an institutional aspect which is coupled with the well-known *autonomous* nature of EU law, described as an ambition to "self-referentiality"[15] (often, the Court's calls to the autonomy of EU law also appeal to its own autonomy).[16] The autonomy of the Court is also the logical premise for the particular forms of institutional evolution and selective internalization of comparative influences I will describe throughout the work. It is relevant to reflect on this specific autonomous nature of the Court since it is peculiar for a judicial institution, and it is also very much a characteristic of the most recent debates on its structure and organization. Not only the CJEU is not an unmoved mover of the EU integration, and it is an institution able to evolve; but it is essential to notice that it has been capable of evolving autonomously, often with a hefty dose of independence from political powers—making itself a bearer and responsible of its own choices and positions. One can notice this unique institutional feature in several organizational aspects: the power enshrined in Article 281 TFEU in relation to possible amendments to its Statute; the unique self-determination inherent in Article 253 TFEU in relation to the "Rules of Procedure of the Court of Justice"; the historical importance of *cercles de discussion* composed of Court's members in every tentative reform; in certain sense, even the exacerbated debate which recently led to the last institutional reform of the General Court.

The second key-concept is the *authority* of the Court. The work will try to assess a specific aspect of the "social expectations" that the CJEU has been forced and able to confront in its diachronic evolution; and I will determine how and to what extent it was able to shape and feed its authority by using institutional and discursive resources to induce deference on all the actors of its special, so-called "supranational" environment, in particular by the internalization of national models and comparative challenges. Therefore, in looking at the aforementioned *specific* but *central* and *paradigmatic* aspects of the structural, organizational and institutional development of the Court, I will try to reflect on how evolution in the structure and the organization of the Court fed its authoritative position in the EU legal space, and therefore on how such evolution is part of its authority's development.[17] In doing so, I will look at the employment of several of the "institutional and discursive resources" scholars described as at the disposal of international courts, and therefore, in particular, "traits" of its human capital, judges, "features of the judicial process", and some specific aspects of "the appeal of the outcome".[18]

The third key-concept is ***mimetism***. As said, through the research, it is possible to look at a specific trait of the supranational institutionalization: the capacity of the CJEU, as a supranational institution, to evolve by facing several organizational challenges and by solving them through a selective internalization of internal and external comparative lessons. I argue that this is a peculiar aspect of how the story of the CJEU, in itself an evolutionary story,[19] developed. The judicial apparatus of the European Union faced the same challenges in terms of legitimacy, functionality, enlargement, resources as the EU as an international organization evolving and transforming into something more (and maybe something *other*). What I aim to demonstrate is that one of the "efficient secrets"[20] of this evolution's success has been the capacity to progressively internalize the solicitations which came from the influences of the different legal traditions of the Member States of the EU (of course with increasing strain as the EU grew dimensionally) and also able to respond to global challenges concerning the increasing role of the international forms of judicial review and the international judicial review bodies. The idea of mimesis is borrowed from well-known sociological and philosophical studies, that describe it as a natural trait of the evolution of animals, humans, languages and institutions.[21] It is useful to understand that evolutions do not happen in a vacuum, but in social spaces filled with gestures, ideas, forms, models, already stratified. *Tabula rasa* is a fictional status,[22] and a relationship between "who comes before" and "who comes next" naturally emerges,[23] and this is what mimesis is all about. While its effects can grow either in the form of co-operation or in the form of rivalry,[24] the causes triggering mimesis are always "utilitarian".[25] Mimesis is a form of a naturally utilitarian search for models that can guarantee more probable advantages[26]: an interesting heuristic for studies in comparative law and institutional organization, especially when dealing with supranationalisation. Indeed, it is in this vein that the Court evolved in its institutional structure and organization by selectively internalizing certain forms. This happened with a decisive role of specific comparative influences. The functional evolution was critical for the Court to increase its authority in an increasingly plural setting and arrived with a dynamic of self-empowerment, often autonomously from other powers.

Such a multipronged phenomenon, which I will analyse in a vast series of case studies, can only be intended as, and read only through, a syneresis of two historical-comparative approaches. By looking at how different comparative influences have faced and have been internalized by the structure and organization of the Court of Justice, a better understanding of the institution's functional evolution will be possible, to notice how it has been able to develop and to increase in authority within a dynamic of self-empowerment, often autonomously from other powers. In this sense, through the proposed analysis I aim to demonstrate—in a slogan—how institutional development of the CJEU has been *culturally* influenced in order to be *functionally* efficient.

The proposed research is qualitative and doctrinal in nature, and aims at being a veritable exercise of theory building through causal inference[27]: it is constructed around some key-concepts that will be elucidated by offering causal explanations for observed phenomena. The idea is to look at some *specific* but *central* and *paradigmatic* aspects of the structural, organizational and institutional development of the Court: these case studies are chosen as "prototypical cases",[28] in such a way to highlight their common features to test my arguments' validity, and presented in a technical/logical order of institutionalization. The first observation will be the historical genesis of the CJEU, its role and powers; then its composition, and therefore at the appointment of its judges, advocates general and personnel; then its deliberation, in terms of modalities and transparency; then the modalities of allocation of judicial activity and resources by the Court, and its techniques of docket control; finally the stylistic modalities of its decisions, and therefore the final product, the output, of the structure and organization of the institution.

The common thread in this multifaceted analysis will be to highlight certain standard features in the institutional evolution of the Court: an often autonomous evolution, or made of an ample degree of autonomous judicial choices, led to strengthening the authority of the Court, through a selective internalization of comparative influences and institutional forms. In this respect, the analysis will nourish itself of comparative legal history, reflections on the particular sort of legal transplants one can trace at the supranational level, and a comparative study of the underlying European legal cultures. In this way, it will try to shed light on something peculiar about the supranational institutionalization of the EU, precisely what I intend when I talk of *mimetism* as a syneresis of different traditional comparative analysis, the cultural and the functional. In particular, the research will try to demonstrate, as said, how the institutional development of the CJEU has been *culturally* influenced in order to be *functionally* efficient. In doing so, a reflection on the specialty of classic comparative methods when transposed in the supranational setting will be natural.

1.3 The Situation of the Research

The inspiration for the proposed analysis of the institutional evolution of the European Court of Justice comes from the state of the different disciplines involved. Its natural background is in certain specific trends of comparative and European legal studies.

The first background of the research is the current discovery, or rediscovery, of historical studies of EU Law. European studies are, by force of circumstances, a relatively young discipline despite their increasingly specific and problematic variety. Still, it is possible to describe, in the considerable amount of relevant literature, the genealogical stratification of the scholarship, at least in specific areas as well as in terms of broad trends. If one focuses on European law, on the Court of Justice as well as its activity and role, in particular, it is possible to argue that after its first years firmly (and traditionally) in the hands of international lawyers,[29] the field of research has been invaded (and probably conquered)[30] by a so-called *constitutionalist* doctrine. These two—the international and the constitutionalist—were contrasting (or opposite?) scholarly trends but also two different visions of the project of European integration, and of the role of the Court. They implicate, as it has been written, different epistemological dimensions and “a query about what integration stands for (the descriptive dimension), how it is to be explained and construed (the explanatory dimension), and eventually what it should stand for (the normative dimension)”.[31] In this respect, the shift between the two schools of thought was based, as well known, on a different understanding of the premises and consequences of the important founding layers of the European legal construct: in particular, since the first years, of the principles of direct effect and primacy of EU law. In this sense, the *constitutionalist* doctrine changed the terms of the theoretical discussion (especially since the eighties and prompted by the original inspirations of the Schuman Declaration and the comparative work of Eric

Stein)[32] by putting at its centre certain devices which were direct products of the early, "glorious"[33] days of the European Court of Justice. In turn, this led the social sciences to "discover European constitutionalism"[34] (and EU constitutional lawyers to discover social sciences) so that a big stream of scholarship based on political science heuristics flourished within the realm of the EU, often with the explicit and specific purpose of exploring (or sometimes by minimizing the importance of)[35] "the systemic implications of the doctrines and the dynamics of the constitutional conversation"[36] mostly about primacy and direct effect. In this sense, political science scholars not only went on arguing about the possibility of spill-over effects of the integration project from the economic sector to others (the typical foundational discourse)[37] but started to translate the classic (traditionally *national*) concerns of federalism's regulatory state, power aggregation and the distributive choices in modern society at the supranational level (not taking constitutionalism as "the object of inquiry but its condition").[38] Moreover, "a second and more direct engagement of political science with constitutionalism"[39] arose by directly taking constitutionalism and dynamics as an object in and of itself worthy of analysis. Through this avenue, the European Court, its doctrines and its interactions with other actors—Community institutions, national courts, the bar, and so on—became a central concern to political science with extraordinarily important results. Of course, it was quite automatic to bring the conceptual and methodological insights developed in judicial studies in national contexts to this inquiry in addition to all of the discipline's conceptual and theoretical tools to analyse the Court of Justice as a "normal" institutional and political actor. From this approach, an acute sensibility emerged of how the Court had managed to empower both itself and the other supranational institutions through its case law but also a hitherto unknown wave of criticism for its supposed departure "from acceptable (normative) and accepted (empirical) interpretative standards".[40]

These critical remarks can be depicted nowadays as a new orthodoxy[41]; but at the time (and by using social science heuristics) stating that the Court could "get it wrong" or making it meaningful to ask whether the Court's rulings were accepted rather than acceptable, or treating the Court as a political actor and openly introducing the question of judicial politics, or bringing relevance to whom the actual judges were (rather than treatment as a disembodied institutional voice), or highlighting in print the existence of a critical discourse among academics who were not, however, ready to go to print, actually broke "a whole series of taboos".[42] The new critical wave could also be read, in Kuhn's epistemological terms,[43] as an under-stress test for the constitutional paradigm (as happened with the internationalist paradigm), famously described by Martin Shapiro as the picture of "...the Community as a juristic idea; the written constitution as a sacred text; the professional commentary as a legal truth; the case law as the inevitable working out of correct implications of the constitutional text; and the constitutional court as a disembodied voice of right reason and constitutional theology".[44] From that turning point, critical studies flourished in the EU's legal studies landscape. Legal scholars championed a new wave of "reconsideration" "begun by the mid-1990s",[45] "prompted partly by the design of the Maastricht Treaty, which kept the ECJ out of two of the three pillars, and by the famous Maastricht judgment of the German Constitutional Court",[46] and led in particular to the new refined pluralist theories.[47] However, important critical studies not only flourished on the core assumptions but also by questioning the affirmed empirical conclusions of the new paradigm. For instance, questioning the notion that national judiciaries and member states had accepted the new European rule of law by documenting the extent to which they "contained justice",[48] or emphasizing the deeper and more legitimate legal roots of European integration that rest on simple administrative delegation from national institutions,[49] or with a "new Bourdieu-based sociological" approach[50] exploring how and to what extent European constitutionalism—including the academic variant—merely constituted an attempt of self-empowerment of jurists and was, in fact, no more than an ordinary process of *juridification*.[51] Last among these new avenues of research—while some renowned scholars in the field still question the full explanatory power of the constitutionalist school[52]—is one of the most interesting critical approaches to EU legal studies that have just emerged in the last few years. It promises new inspiration and new perspectives of research for the present work as well. The "new historical analyses of the roots and nature of European public law"[53] are admittedly part of the most recent wave of critical studies.[54] Also, as (natural) "latecomers to the field"[55] and undoubtedly inspired by theoretical elements in precedent explanations, historians came into play in EU studies with the explicit plan to reflect, through new documentary and oral evidence and a different methodology, on the "constructing and deconstructing" of "'Constitutional' European Law".[56] The basic assumption of this "movement" is that "'Constitutional' European law did not flow naturally from the Treaties of Rome". Instead, it was somehow "artificially" (if not ideologically) constructed and chosen over other plausible alternatives. The idea is to use historiographical heuristics not only in the Braudel's *longue durée* tradition of small stories that need to be told to understand a large-scale phenomenon such as European integration but also to generally bring the analysis into such artificial construction and "into the machine room of law",[57] to understand better the process through which Europe has been "lawyered".[58] In this sense, this emerging trend aims at responding to the classic constitutionalist narrative that—although finely detailed by one of its main proponents in a comparative perspective with the political dimension of the integration process[59]—is still widely promoted as the story of a key actor: the European Court of Justice. Through its case law, it built a constitutionalized, proto-federal legal order for the continent by successfully managing to persuade national courts to act as European courts.[60] As a result, by the early 1990s, a genuine federalized rule of law existed in the new European Union. In addition to the majority of the aforementioned social science approaches, the "new historians" are first of all offering empirical details for a revisionist interpretation of the nature of the constitutional practice, at least to explain once and for all how this was caused by a combination of historical factors, including the agency of the Legal Service of the Commission, a transnational alliance involving European institutions, and a transnational network of pro-European jurists, academics, national administrations, courts and legal elites in general (some original resistance notwithstanding). Enlarging the scope of European constitutional narrative in its institutional terms is likely to be causing the "new historians" also to provide new inspiration and new material to put the European Court of Justice and the European judicial architecture under the spotlight. This happens not only by repeatedly stressing the role of promotion in the so-called constitutionalization of the Treaties[61] but also by reflecting again, as in the first political science wave, on structural/organizational questions about the Court including its nature and preferences, the independence of its judges coming from the Member States, or the relationship between the Court and its national counterparts.[62] This can be done by producing new, reliable and qualitatively rich information about the internal workings of the Court and its interaction with its various interlocutors and by offering at least tentative tests allowing us to adjudicate among competing hypotheses, and propose new hypotheses, inductively informed by the Court's historical practice.

All this renewed interest poses again, in diachronic/evolutionary terms, important questions about the legitimacy and the authority of the Court of Justice in relation to its capacity of development and its interactions.[63] This is the first contextual scenario within which I wish to situate my research.

The second background of the research is in the current discovery, or re-discovery, of debates on the legitimacy and authority of international judicial review bodies. The idea of a renewed focus on the everlasting problem of the legitimacy and the authority of the Court of Justice can also be contextualized under the temporal aspect. The European Court can be depicted, after all, as the standard-bearer of the global phenomenon of empowerment of international judicial institutions—a phenomenon that is nowadays at the centre of many debates and has been considered as "one of the dominant features of the international legal order of the past two decades".[64] As it is well known, a common, insightful narrative of the internationalist doctrine in this respect has been to describe an incipient "fragmentation" of the international legal order in an archipelago of different legal norms and regimes, often with their institutional entourages and dedicated tribunals.[65] However, because of the increasing importance of such international bodies and international judicial bodies in particular "as lawmakers",[66] and beyond a simple proto-typical "role of settling disputes",[67] a broad debate has been recently raised about their sources and forms of *legitimacy* and *authority*. The discussion on the legitimacy of adjudicatory bodies is far from being new or original. On the contrary, the debates on the courts' role, especially in constitutional legal orders, related process of adjudication and democratic grounds, and the proper balance of power between the judiciary and the political process, have filled libraries for centuries with an overwhelming body of literature on almost every imaginable aspect of the so-called domain of 'judicial policymaking'. Often, these debates focus on concepts which are difficult to grasp or substantiate, such as the "legitimacy" of judicial bodies—recently defined as "one of the most unspecified concepts in political theory and social science"[68]—or are shaped in broad, quasi-sociological terms so that it becomes easy to label them far from the real and everyday practice of these institutions. After all, a legitimacy crisis is a rare, if not extraordinary phenomenon for today's institutions. However, the legitimacy argument is still present in the academic discussion on courts, and the transposition of these sensitivities at the supranational/international level brings something new and interesting to the debate. First, the canonical lamentation based on the static notion of the "counter-majoritarian difficulty"[69] is difficult to apply, or at least is not applied automatically beyond the state, since the canonical concepts of the *trias politica* and the division of powers à la Montesquieu (which are the logic bases for such a critical argument) are not applicable either. As it is known, at the supranational/international level, the concept of "institutional balance"[70] is often preferred as an analytical tool for the arising institutional frictions and this is particularly true within the context of the European Union. Consequently, the problem of finding a sort of indirect democratic legitimation for the practice of judicial review becomes even more difficult and, therefore, intriguing. When removed from its genealogical mythology by a Constitution to its special enforcer (be it a specialized Constitutional Court or an apex Supreme Court), the super-legitimacy is blurred in the realm of international agreements, and the similar canonical justification of the ever-present possibility of the political powers to overturn the judicial *dicta* becomes weakened by the different decision-making circuits in place. This also leads to recalibration within the debate and recently leads to strong and persuasive proposals for the substitution of the confusing discussions around the concept of *legitimacy* with a more circumstantiated approach based on the concepts of *authority* and *authoritativeness* of (international) judicial bodies. A recent symposium was devoted in particular to the problem of "International Courts and the Quest for Legitimacy",[71] and focused on how "change in quantity" of the activity and importance of international courts and tribunals "has come with a change in quality",[72] in addition to the enlargement of significant functions of these bodies beyond mere "settlement of disputes".[73] This includes, repeating the original terms employed, the stabilization of normative expectations, the direct production of law, the control as well as the legitimization of the powers exercised by other actors. Such point of view feeds the proposal of the concepts of *authority* and *authoritativeness* as better heuristic devices for the study of the institutional position of contemporary apical judicial bodies—that goes beyond certain political science approaches which focus simply on the rationality and the opportunity of the delegation of powers within the international realm. The creation of international judicial review institutions is studied by applying, first of all, the classic *principal-agent* scheme. There are indeed numerous plausible reasons why actors, and especially international actors, create institutions that confer authority and submit to such authority being exercised over them.[74] As it has been well explained by now affirmed *law and politics* scholars,[75] incentives for such a delegation, and even for a toleration of a certain degree of unpredictability or leeway, come with the expectation of certain instrumental gains—particularly "when an agent is expected to undertake specific and possibly repetitive tasks more efficiently or effectively".[76] Because of the precise dynamics of empowerment of these institutions, considering this as an established phenomenon of the last decades (and primarily with the European Court of Justice), the proposal has been to assess the authority by going beyond simple, static act of delegation of power and its more or less opportunistic rationality, by trying to consider its establishment in diachronic terms.

In fact, the idea of *authority* should be defined by following the historical account by Hannah Arendt[77] "in *contradistinction* to coercion by force and persuasion through arguments", and therefore, in analysing a judicial institution, "in contradistinction" to both the simple, apparent legal obligation to justify decisions as well as the only consequent execution moment of these decisions. These two moments—posing a justified decision and then executing it—are natural phenomena where the general authority of a legal order is the ability to posit and have certain decisions respected more than measuring a specific judge's authority. Judicial bodies' special *authority* rests in something different or something further, precisely because it is defined as being based "on a moment of voluntary recognition that separates it from coercion" (a fact for every example of international judicial review). It is also different from persuasion "in the sense that it can prompt conforming behaviour even in the absence of substantive agreement"[78] (the challenge these institutions are forced to face). It has been said that such a notion of authority involves in itself both the vertical element of hierarchy and the horizontal element of voluntary adhesion—building a particular relationship of cognition and recognition between legal subjects.[79] In this vein, international judicial bodies' authority "grows and is stabilized through the dynamics of discursive construction".[80] These dynamics surely include the (more or less) rational, "foundational" moment of the delegation of powers but also include a phase of construction, adding a minimal degree "of wanting to obey"[81] (voluntary recognition) to the initial rational calculation.[82] They also consist of a series of "discursive resources" that international courts "can themselves use to further add to their authority".[83] Such a phase of construction concerns what specially distinguishes and sustains authority and therefore "not individual recognition in the specific case of its exercise but its social recognition—social belief in its legitimacy",[84] often framed in terms of "culturally and historically conditioned", and stratified, "expectations".[85] In contrast to power, authority is said to be "traditional" in character.[86] It has its roots in the past, which it continues to use to boost its claims in the present. It refers to past practice but "independently of their content, within bounds",[87] but is also "like law, eternally in the state of becoming".[88] Some scholars conceptualize these questions by describing the existence of "different layers of authority",[89] and suggest that a first layer concerns whether an institution is considered functionally necessary to achieve common goods and the competence of such an institution to take certain measures. However, a second layer concerns the proper and socially accepted exercise of such authority. In this light, I will try to assess a specific aspect of the "social expectations" that the European Court of Justice has been forced and able to confront in its diachronic evolution; and I will assess how and to what extent it was able to shape and feed its authority by using "institutional and discursive resources to induce deference" on all the actors of its special, so-called "supranational" environment, in particular by the internalization of national models and comparative challenges. Therefore, I will try to reflect on how the evolution in the structure and the organization of the Court fed its authoritative position in the EU legal space, and therefore on how such evolution is part of its authority's development. In doing so I will list and analyse several of the "institutional and discursive resources" scholars described as at the disposal of international courts, and therefore, in particular, "traits" of its human capital, judges, "features of the judicial process", and some specific aspects of "the appeal of the outcome",[90] in terms of functions performed.

The third background of the research, complementing the previous ones, is in the current discovery (or de-discovery) of debates on the construction of the supranational legal order as a plural legal space influenced by national forms: as an experiment of *unitas in diversitate*. This is a speciality of the context within which the Court of Justice of the EU operates that any meaningful EU legal studies research needs to take into account. In studying the institutional evolution of the European Court of Justice, I will analyse how influences from other experiences created a decisive impact on the construction of a *sui generis* supranational institution. In particular, I will focus on the challenges and the influences coming from the EU Member States legal orders. In doing so, I will follow a certain trend of the last season of EU scholarship aimed at a discovery (or re-discovery) of debates on the cultural legal diversity in the supranational project and how the inherent diversity from which they stem influences the construction of common supranational institutions. Like all debates of the kind, this is usually shaped around the phrase *unitas in diversitate*. As it is well known, this was the "fortunate" motto of the "otherwise unfortunate Draft Constitutional Treaty",[91] equally notorious for not being replicated in the Lisbon Treaty. This can be said to articulate something very peculiar and foundational about the EU and its aims and principles. In a nutshell, it points to the necessary equilibrium between the competing forces of legal unity and legal diversity within the European Union legal order and at the Union's declared intention to "respect", also in legal terms, "the national and regional diversity [of the Member States] and at the same time bring the common cultural heritage to the fore".[92] The emergence of these cultural concerns, usually developed precisely around the trinomial *unitas—diversity—identity*, is not new. Such an approach, which departs from and complements the prototypical functional understandings of the EU, has been the subject of intellectual debates ever since the early 1950s.[93] After all, the traditional puzzle remains between the nature of the European Union as "the most extensive and developed example of supranational political integration based on voluntary cooperation in the world",[94] fraught with essentially universalistic fundamental values basic to the whole project of integration, and the historical differentiation in Europe among political entities with different histories and traditions in which "(t)he territorial nation state has been the predominant political framework and actor with considerable overlap between territorial, political, legal, administrative, economic, social and cultural boundaries".[95] Therefore, we are talking about a well-stratified debate, coessential to a political-legal definition of Europe and its projection in both the past and the future.[96] It is becoming more and more common to state, in academic conversations, that "(t)oday, we find ourselves in a legal, psychological, and discursive universe different from the one 15 years ago",[97] in another renewed phase of the European integration and of the European discourse (and the emergence of the multifaceted Eurocrisis cannot but confirm such change):[98] and the debate on *unitas* and *diversitas* surely denotes, in its actualized terms, a new or renewed scholarly approach in the field of EU *legal* studies. In my view, it includes a new interest in the overlapping of a European legal culture of possible autonomous nature over different national legal cultures and traditions and the research on the inspiration drawn by the former from the latter. Is the institutional nature of European institutions *sui generis*, as often stated for the substance of its legal fabric? Is it influenced by the examples of the national legal cultures and by their influences on the activity of EU institutions, and by their interrelations? Was the EU legal space influenced by comparative material only in its substantive traits, or also in its institutional ones? And can the institutional evolution of the European Court of Justice be described in these terms? It is commonplace to argue that "comparative insights have certainly informed the text of the Treaties and the design of the European institutions",[99] but the academic literature did not go beyond scarce or anecdotal remarks on the point. The proposed perspective is the application in the EU realm of basic lessons of comparative law methodology, and in particular of one of its masters, H. Patrick Glenn, who in his general works devoted to "legal traditions of the world",[100] repeatedly insisted on the idea of such traditions as "information", and not mere "action".[101] By this maxim, he wanted to stress the idea of an ever "changing presence of the past" in the legal practice[102] and counteract the bias of considering the recall of legal tradition as the link to actions devoid of thought or mindless habits which should be—and ultimately can be—stripped away by the application of choices based on pure reason. On the opposite, he has always argued that legal traditions are arsenals of information available to individuals, institutions or societies as they make choices for themselves since, in these choices, both rationality and context are necessarily comprised. No legal setting can be entirely rational (or context-neutral) because, without context, there would be nothing for rationality to act upon. Conversely, no legal setting can be completely irrational (or completely context-specific) because even the act of preserving and transmitting a tradition involves performing rational operations upon it.[103] The usual ground of application of such cultural sensitivities is substantive law. This is true for the classics of comparative law of the last century, shaped by debating private law and its historical origins, its familiarities as well as its developments.[104] This is also true in EU scholarship, where refined works have been devoted to the problem of the so-called "Europeanisation" of law(s). This phrase was precisely used and known to label a new narrative in EU legal studies: the idea of looking at the legal phenomenon in the supranational setting as a unitary instrumental *agent* of integration as well as a diverse object of the integrative process. The foundational study that championed the first approach, and notoriously glorified the legal lever as a genuine "engine" for the construction of a "Community of law", was the *Integration Through Law* project.[105] In this fundamental work, law was portrayed as an *agent* and, therefore, as a relatively independent (though artificially constructed) variable that influences other key dimensions of the integration process. In turn, this influences the legal orders of the Member States.[106] Legal integration denoted in this sense is equivalent to integration *through* law because "even if law is not the main catalyst of change in the integration process, many changes are greatly conditioned by legal and institutional elements" in the EU sphere.[107] The *unitas* aspect was also clearly put into action as the cause and the effect of a genuine political model that linked law and politics with judicial adjudication and integration.[108] This amounted to a genuine "science of government" of EU polity, cross-sector knowledge capable of "both of seizing the 'system' (a 'legal order') of the institutions, positions and groups that make up 'Europe', and of evaluating its functioning with regard to a specifically legal rationality",[109] with tangible effects on ample areas of national substantive law. On the contrary, new studies on the Europeanisation of law wanted to create "a new narrative"[110] by focusing on the dimension of law as an *object* of European integration. In this sense, law is studied not as an independent variable, but as a dependent one, constituting a relatively autonomous field of integration and cultural explication alongside politics, economics, etc.[111] Here, legal integration is particularly studied as the integration *of* laws, that is, the reciprocal adaptation of state legal systems in (relation to) a European legal system that aims at the gradual removal of differential treatment. The privileged perspective is the binary, osmotic process through which the law produced by the European Union and its "autonomous" legal order (agent) has an impact on and changes the law(s) of national legal orders (objects) and is in turn changed by this process of interpretation, application and implementation. Furthermore, the *diversitas* element of the conundrum is put under the spotlight. The different national legal systems of the EU Member States are the *objects* to be integrated, so to be moved closer or harmonized. This idea/*project* necessarily implicates the diversity of legal cultures that these different systems represent. In turn, they also have an effect and an influence on the *agent* in a process that is no longer unidirectional, but mutual. The concept of *Europeanization* is, in a certain sense, the recognition of the importance of the underlying structures and identities of the Member States for the real success of the project of integration.[112] It has been aptly described as a heuristic "post-ontological character, being concerned with what happens once EU institutions are already in place and produce their effects".[113] It includes the complexity of our contemporary understanding of the problems of the European project by bringing "even more to the debate than classical theories of integration do on their own".[114] Intergovernamentalism[115] and neo-functionalism[116] focus upon "both formal and functional relationship at the EU level" and adopt a "'top-down' approach"[117]; Europeanization focuses on the layer of "(P)rocesses of (a) construction (b) diffusion and (c) institutionalization of formal and informal rules, procedures, policy paradigms, styles, 'ways of doing things' and shared beliefs and norms which are first defined and consolidated in the making of EU decisions and then incorporated in the logic of domestic discourse, identities, political structures and public policies".[118] This brings the national and domestic level into the mix,[119] and "seeks to problematize the interaction between the levels in a more reflexive, circular way".[120]

Looking not only at substantive law, but also at the institutional dimension as well as an EU institution like the Court of Justice through this prism is particularly interesting since it reminds us that the strong institutionalization of the European communities as an international law experiment[121] did not occur in a vacuum. Quite the opposite, it occurred by overlapping with pre-existing legal forms in a continent with the oldest legal traditions. In this institutional sense, the *Integration through law* approach is still alive and looks at the important efforts of uniformity and the potential of construction of a single "political imagination"[122] through the construction of a "symbolic arsenal of cultural mythology",[123] which was not confined in the immediate visible signs and "cultural artefacts" such as "flag, anthem, Europe day, motto and Jean Monnet prizes" but also "embodied" in documents such as "the EU Charter of Fundamental Rights, the Constitutional Treaty and, above all, the jurisprudence of the European Court of Justice",[124] and in general in the various cross-sectoral sources of law produced by the European Union and its institutions. But it must be reminded that the experience of institutionalization and search for common European institutional forms was also in itself an experiment of legal *unitas in diversitate*, constantly under stress with the changes and the developments of the European Union in size and in power. The following pages will attempt to analyse this phenomenon.

1.3.1 Mimetism *as a Potential Link Between Cultural Studies and Functionalism in Supranational Law*

In summary, the current, parallel, insightful debates on the new historical studies on the European Union, the establishment of its legal order and the perspectives linked to a renewed appreciation of the European federal-like nature of *unitas in diversitate* especially applied to the different legal cultures, as well as the broad ongoing discussion on the authority and the legitimacy of international judicial review bodies, all suggest a study like the one I propose. It is timely to take a fresh look at the *institutional* evolution of the CJEU, in terms of its structure and organization, precisely in the light of the new historical material and with attention to the influences from the judicial forms of the Member States as well as their legal cultures and from the comparative conversation of the legitimacy and authority of international judicial review. Again, my thesis is that through this type of reconstruction, it is possible to highlight a peculiar aspect of how the story of the Court of Justice, in itself an evolutionary story,[125] evolved in a *mimetic* way. The judicial apparatus of the European Union faced the same challenges in terms of legitimacy, functionality, enlargement, resources as the EU as an international organization evolving and transforming into something more (and maybe something *other*). I will scrutinize them in the following chapters. But what I aim to demonstrate is that one of the "efficient secrets"[126] of this evolution's success—since it has become commonplace to talk of the ECJ as a "*victim of its own success*"[127]—has been the capacity to progressively internalize the solicitations which came from the influences of the different legal traditions of the Member States of the EU (of course with increasing strain as the EU grew dimensionally) and also be able to respond to global challenges in relation to the increasing role of the international forms of judicial review and the international judicial review bodies.

As said, traditional legal forms are arsenals of information available to operators and institutions, living of the ever-changing presence of the past, that cannot be obliterated, that naturally inform every legal setting.[128] In every evolutive process, a relationship between what comes before and what comes next naturally emerges[129]; and the construction of such a relationship is naturally utilitarian,[130] inspired by the search for models that can guarantee more probable advantages.[131] And in fact, certain specific traits of the institutional evolution of the Court can be appreciated only through comparative research, for a variety of reasons.

The first reason stipulates that if the *situation* of the research I tried to perform in the previous pages is correct, all the relevant scholarly trends are involved in comparative analysis. The internationalist/constitutionalist diatribe is, by definition, comparative and in search of a *tertium comparationis* for the European Union. Therefore, the results of the diatribe diverge precisely in finding a sort of "*sui generis*", relatively incomparable nature of the EU, or on the opposite by positioning it, in several respects, in the widening disciplinary field of comparative constitutional law.[132] In this sense, the *Integration through Law* research project—the first organic study of law as an agent and object of European integration that I analysed previously—focused more than 25 years ago on the triggered gradual process of *convergence* in the European Member States that was supposed to lie at the heart of an emerging European identity. It also investigated "those legal doctrines, institutions, mechanism and procedures, which could shed light on this dual aspect of the law",[133] in a way that was considered instrumental to achieving "a degree of convergence in at least some aspects of human behaviour basic to social life" as "sine qua non for productive and peaceful coexistence of peoples, indeed, for their very survival".[134] Therefore, it first aimed to demonstrate the functioning and the ultimate attended results of this mutual conditioning of legal structure and political process in which "while law is a product of the polity, the polity is also to some extent the creature of the law".[135] This led to a powerful use of comparative law science, and in particular external comparisons with the United States of America and other federal-like systems, intended as a deeper understanding of the *functionalist* power of law.[136]

On the other hand, the rethinking of the *unitas in diversitate* component in the European project and European law, in particular,[137] was only raised in the academic debate later on,[138] but is again comparative in nature. Its aim is not to address, in classic *functional* terms as in the old Florentine project, what law could do in a context of increasing integration, but question the functional determinist narratives by a comparative *cultural* study to understand what were the inherent limits of a harmonizing project. Not by chance, its critical approach has been coupled with historical and sociological perspectives.[139]

The context in which the "New Historians" work is naturally comparative as well. Recent historical research has shown that members of the legal establishment, both at the national and supranational levels, drew not only on public international law, i.e. a treaty between sovereign states but also upon domestic sources of law to inspire their constitutional innovations—providing new precious insights that I will try to contextualize further. But they also go beyond by contributing to the comparative law tradition in the wake of the Watsonian inspiration.[140] In seeking to demonstrate that "legal systems are not hermetically sealed and self-contained and that, in addition to formally recognized sources of law, such as constitutions, statutes, and judicial precedent, it is necessary to include foreign law as a major and constant source of legal decisionmaking",[141] they also show "which legal networks of scholars, lawyers, and judges have shaped the European constitutional practice"[142]; they trace the upward transfers of domestic rules that shape EU law as a relatively autonomous legal sphere, in which one "can detect the creation of a European legal consciousness, not a coherent doctrinal apparatus detached from society, but rather competing and conflicting approaches to legal concepts, judicial techniques, and social values that through compromises or unintended consequences shape the current European constitutional practice".[143] In this light, they provide different case studies of resistance versus acceptance. Interestingly, the new historical research can be considered as a transposition of the classic comparative transplant literature[144] in the relatively novel domain of supranational law: particularly when it tries to shed some light on the causal question with evidence on the incentives and actors that prompted the transfer of elements of domestic law into supranational law. Most of this classic literature has examined the horizontal transfer of rules and models between national legal systems. When it looks into the impact of international law, it has focused on the *downward* transfer of law into national systems as a consequence of international agreements or other forms of international pressure and the extent to which reception has been successful or unsuccessful.[145]

Comparative law—historically but, strangely, nowadays as well—has generally neglected to analyse the *upward* transfer of domestic rules and models into the legal frameworks of regional and international systems of governance. The new historians can be considered, in this respect, as inspirational multidisciplinary innovators. Their research focuses on such upward transplants and seeks to provide evidence, through their specific methodology, of the importance of domestic legal rules in inspiring the institutional framework of the emerging supranational legal system of European governance. As it has been noted with the globalization of law and politics, this new form of transplantation can be expected to become increasingly common, and therefore this new trend launched in Europe can be expected to have relevance for tracing the genesis of the numerous systems of international courts and lawmaking that have come afterward.[146]

Consequently, and finally, there is the broad debate on the new forms of international judicial review, in which the inquiry in the normative basis and the functionality of the relevant institutions is always framed in terms of (1) reconstruction of the different actual forms and (2) creation of optimal, prototypical models. The comparative nature of the discussion is inherent to the method itself. This was also emphasized by the suggestions of leading scholars to export certain general institutional principles applying to the CJEU (and according to this view, calling for some reforms in its organization) in all the different forms of international judicial review bodies.[147]

Therefore, my project will try to merge these different but interrelated inspirations and their comparative approaches. The analysis will nourish itself of comparative legal history, reflections on the special sort of legal transplants one can trace at the supranational level, and a comparative study of the underlying European legal cultures. In this way, it will also shed light on something peculiar about the supranational institutionalization of the EU, precisely what I intend when I talk of *mimetism* as a syneresis of different comparative analysis. There are, notoriously, two traditional approaches to comparative law: the *functional* and the *culturalist*. We can consider the first as the conventional methodology of comparative study—the "epicentre of comparative method of law"[148]—postulated by masters such as Zweigert and Kötz.[149] It has always aimed at explaining legal instruments and institutions—in classical Durkheimian terms—through their usefulness for society by highlighting their inherent teleology, their importance for social engineering, and their capacity to adapt to different contexts.[150] The second is a general category used by scholars to indicate all those other approaches that aimed at differentiating from the functional method and, in doing so, focused on the decisive importance of "context", and not of the *telos*, for the evolution and the comprehension of law as a social phenomenon.[151] In this sense, the category is described precisely as composed of comparative legal history, the study of legal transplants and the comparative study of legal cultures as the "three main current approaches other than functionalism", and as the approaches that can be more sensitive to the specificities of the different legal environments.[152] Usually, these two major schools of thought have been kept separate as antithetical—as describing two different points of departure and two different agendas of research. It is nonetheless interesting to notice, as I will attempt to show, that these two perspectives can naturally and meaningfully merge together in the evolutionary studies of the supranational legal context. In particular, the following pages will try to show how the capacity of the Court of Justice of the EU, as a supranational institution, to evolve by facing several organizational challenges and by solving them through an internalization of internal and external comparative lessons (coming therefore by the examples of its own Member states and from the international debate) amounts to one of the decisive, resolutive features of its own story of success. I argue that this occurred in a *mimetic* fashion. The Court evolved into its institutional structure and organization by selectively internalizing certain forms. This happened with a decisive role of specific comparative influences. The functional evolution was decisive for the Court to increase its own authority in an increasingly plural setting and arrived with a dynamic of self-empowerment, often autonomously from other powers.

Such a multipronged phenomenon, which I will analyse in a vast series of case studies, can only be intended as, and read only through a syneresis of the two historical comparative approaches. By looking at the way in which different comparative influences have faced and internalized by the structure and organization of the Court of Justice, a better understanding of the institution's functional evolution will be possible. I will study the *cultural* influences in the institutional development of the CJEU as building block of its *functional* efficiency. Through the prism of institutional organization, in this sense, I will try to study what has already been highlighted by some as a peculiar specificity of the European system. In a work dealing with the interaction of supranational and national substantive laws, Azoulai wrote some years ago that "(L)e système communautaire est non seulement capable de *résister aux pressions exercées de l'extérieur* par les systèmes nationaux (…) mais, bien plus, il est capable de *les utiliser jusqu'à les transformer en facteurs d'organisation*".[153] Such words describe something peculiar in the nature of the European legal system—notoriously suspended between its birth "at the crossroads of national legal traditions"[154] and its aspiration to an *autonomous* nature, to "self-referentiality".[155] They describe something relevant also from the institutional point of view. These attributes are openly reminiscent of the work of biophysicist and philosopher Henri

Atlan, who studied, in particular, the processes of natural and social organization and auto-organization. It was Atlan who described every process of auto-organization as a costant dynamic of disorganization and reorganization, as a process of condensation of complexity halfway between the *functional* and *structural*, "resulting from a succession of retrieved disorganizations, followed each time by a re-establishment at a level of more variety and less redundancy".[156] In this process of condensation of complexity that is both functional and structural, a decisive role is said to be played by its context. The surrounding environment changes continuously, in a manner "neither predetermined nor magic". The living system which, being able to integrate "the errors" in its organization, "is able to react in such a way (...) to be modified in a beneficial way, or in a way that at least preserves its further survival".[157] Such process of condensation of complexity, both functional and structural, can also be observed, I will try to show, in the *mimetic* institutional, organizational evolution of a supranational institution, the European Court of Justice, in which specific external forms of institutional structure and organization, often culturally influenced, became functional factors of organization for the development of the institution and the growth of its authority.

After all, "(L)egal orders are actually formed from acts of understanding and interpretation in the process of practical legal life", in which "various systemic legal formations (international, supranational, and national legal systems)" intertwine in a process of "constant interaction and mutual influence". A call for a study of such "dynamic of law", which "cannot be represented as either an isolated immanent process or as a quality of a passive sphere of external influences", has been launched, by referencing to the need to study both the "synchronic and diachronic aspects" of such a dialogical evolution.[158] In this vein, an invitation to expand the boundaries of the comparative research (both methodologically and dimensionally) was also issued, according to which to a classic horizontal comparison, which "compares legal systems or institutions belonging to the same level, both national (e.g. for comparative constitutional law) and international level (e.g. comparing international institutions)",[159] a vertical comparison should be also be added: a comparison between systems, or legal institutions, which "do not belong to the same level".[160] Such a multidimensional approach—as a way to deal with the problem of the "comparative methodology and pluralism in legal comparison in a global age"—would be needed to expand the comparative research in a "top-down" manner to study the context of the *internalization* of international norms and regulations by national legal orders, whereby national law is required to incorporate international concepts into the domestic legal system.[161] The same expansion could also be directed in a "bottom-up" vertical comparison to analyse "the transposition of legal concepts, or the ideas behind them, from national to international level",[162] or the incorporation of national principles by international standards.[163]

The processes of globalization or regionalization (primarily as a fundamental paradigm) and the process of Europeanisation are the first potential scopes of application of such multidimensional expansion since they are, according to many, "challenging the mechanical understanding of methodology" in legal studies.[164] The proposed diachronic analysis of the structural and organizational aspects of the European Court of Justice will be a perfect case study for the analysis of a successful, autonomous, but culturally influenced legal evolution of a supranational institution, and it will try to test all these methodological assumptions. Comparativism is described by its contemporary theorists as not merely the description of "the common and the difference, commensurability and incommensurability, but their proportional correlation"[165]: the analysis of my hypothesized *mimetic* evolution can be precisely seen as an appraisal of such interrelation between *unitas* and *diversitas*, *functional* and *contextual*, within their possible correlation.

A syneresis of the two historical comparative approaches, functional and culturalist, will be needed for such this endeavour. Such syneresis is not only implied in classic reflections which saw the conceptual apparatus of comparative law as "supranational in character",[166] but also invoked remarks by scholars who recently embarked on reflections on the role of legal culture in the comparative study of the EU system. It has been recently noted[167] that although the local specificities and the associated "cultural argument" have been deployed "in the specific European context (…) most often (…) in opposition to the possibility of achieving more legal Europeanisation", and in antithesis to the "edification of a community" and the construction of a "common legal culture", a more refined use of the "legal cultures" sensitivity, applied in the supranational environment, cannot but merge such an approach with a functional evolutionary one. In this respect, a fundamental distinction has been suggested between an external and internal dimension of legal culture, also intended as a distinction between the broad societal and more specific professional ideas of legal culture, linked to the way that legal operators think about the law.[168] The often idealized societal perception of legal *culturalism* leads to the design of separated, fractured *families* of legal development[169] with scarce or no permeability, while a more realist appraisal of the higher degree of homogeneity within the professional legal operators,[170] who are also the actual actors of legal development, makes us think about differences as an arsenal or toolkit of solutions that can be used for functional purposes. As the new historiographical and sociological literature on the legal construction of the European Communities has demonstrated,[171] such degree of homogeneity was very much present (and still is) in the process of integration and institutionalization, facilitating a functional—i.e. utilitarian—osmosis of *unitas* and *diversitas*.

Utilitarianism, as said, is a feature of mimesis, intended as a search for models that can guarantee more probable advantages: this has to do with the authority of institutions, in the multidimensional terms stipulated, and sometimes with the autonomy of them, when the functional modalities of evolution are spontaneous, self-driven. This is particularly the case for the Court of Justice, as I will try to explain: the autonomy of the EU judicial system—even defined as a form of "judicial self-government"—is considered as a broad and relevant yet "largely understudied phenomenon",[172] and the research will try to shed some light on it.

1.4 The Work Plan

I will undertake the task described by selecting some *specific* but *central* and *paradigmatic aspects* of the structural, organizational and institutional development of the Court in the decades since its foundation.

In the next second chapter, I will propose a historical reconstruction of the genesis of the Court of Justice, since the times of its foundation and later when it was a small tribunal for the litigation among six Member states of the (then) European Coal and Steel Community and Economic Community. In this context, I will highlight how a significant inspiration for the design of the Court and its powers came about from the well-known and already-established judicial forms present in the higher courts of the Member states at that time. After all, these were already important and established comparative models and naturally influenced the first negotiators and players in the field. But I will also emphasize also how there were already other visions at the time which did not prevail: particularly, taking inspiration from the (then) known forms of international judicial review.

After this first essentially historical introduction on the foundation of the Court, I will present my case studies in a kind of technical/logical order of institutionalization.

In the third chapter, I will focus, therefore, on what logically follows in structuring and organizing a court: thus, on the appointment of its members, its human resources. The system of appointment of the European Court of Justice's judges, advocate generals and personnel has been for several decades a neglected and even mysterious topic, covered by the traditional and taken-for-granted discretion of the States in the selection of international judges. But the situation, as it is well known, has recently changed with a new procedure established pursuant to Article 255 TFEU introduced by the Lisbon Treaty. If it is still beyond a doubt that "from whatever point of view, including that of national courts",[173] members of the Court enjoy a high degree of recognition and expertise-derived legitimacy, a new discussion on the point is also timely in relation to a comparative analysis of judicial appointments in the different Member States that tell us of rather different systems of selection and composition of judicial bodies—with clear implications on the perception of related epistemic communities. This must be related to an important aspect that is under constant discussion on the CJEU's composition: the recurring theme of disconnection from national judicial practice, also in terms of expertise and understanding of the reality of national adjudication systems.

In the fourth chapter, following the order of a logic problematization in the structuring of the court, I will analyse the problem of transparency in the works of the CJEU, considered as a "deliberative institution",[174] both in the traditional terms of its discussed modalities of internal deliberation and in the new terms of the openness of its judicial activities and proceedings (a theme recently raised by scholars for the first time).[175] In this former sense, a reflection will be attempted on the questions arising from the duty of collegiality of the Court and the lack of dissenting opinions—a judicial feature present in several Member states, and to which their lawyers are used—and often invoked for the CJEU in academic commentaries. Particular attention will be given to the peculiar role of the Advocate General in this perspective. A comparative law study of the different options in the Member States and international courts will lead us to some thoughts on how much this is relevant for both the quality of the legal reasoning of the Court and for the direct connection, through full disclosure of all the different arguments and interpretative options on EU law, with the different culturally influenced epistemic communities of the Member States. It will be possible to notice that if the Court has not properly changed throughout its evolution in such a traditional sense, it has placed itself at the forefront of the new mentioned trend of internal openness, the one related to administrative transparency, albeit with discussed modalities.

In the fifth chapter, the next step will be to investigate the modalities and techniques of docket control and the problems of allocation of judicial activity and resources by the CJEU. These problems are essential for the actual work of the Court, often considered "victim of its own success"[176] especially in terms of an increasing overload of cases. However, they are often influenced by tensions that originate from the Member States and their legal cultures, on the point of the very conceptualization of what docket control can and should mean; by the different approaches of common law and civil law countries to the question of the abstractness of the preliminary ruling procedure of Article 267 TFEU[177]; or by the various exigencies coming from different contexts with regard to the CJEU's action. Therefore, I will investigate how the different contexts of the single Member states and judges' different backgrounds influence the use of the fundamental preliminary reference procedure. It will be also important to highlight that the very idea of the existence of techniques of docket control and selection of cases, while entirely accepted in some national legal cultures, is unfamiliar and somehow repudiated for others. After all, this is also becoming a relevant problem for other international judicial bodies, precisely because of their recent growth in role and size.[178] I will look at how the Court evolved by a selective choice of so-called neutral solutions to the problem of docket control, precisely because of influence in this perspective by the diverse nature of its counterparts.

In the sixth and final chapter, an analysis of the stylistic modalities of the decisions of the CJEU will follow, considering them as the final product, the output, of the structure and organization of the institution, directly influenced by these latter as well as cultural aspects. As it is well known, the Court has been widely criticized for its apodictic, cryptic, Cartesian judgements,[179] of French derivation,[180] which also make large use of formulaic language.[181] I will try to explain how much this has a lot to do with a cultural stratification in the Court's activity, and therefore, to what extent the style of the court is culturally shaped. Furthermore, I will try to show how much this has to do with the success of the Court in its dialogical relationship with Members States courts, which are often speaking a "different language"[182] for stratified cultural reasons. It also has profound consequences for the simplicity of these different national courts to undertake relationships with the CJEU, and, indirectly but very importantly, for the successful, coherent and uniform application of EU law in all the Member States, a matter of classic but increasing concern among scholars.[183] In this sense, I will talk of the style of the Court as shaped by its machinery as *fabrique du droit*,[184] and inherent plurality and diversification of the EU legal order.

Some final remarks will conclude my work, summing up the results of the analysis, and further reflecting on the idea of *mimetism* as both a phenomenological and methodological concept.

Notes

1. The amount of relevant literature is so huge that even a reasonable summary would be impossible. Paradigmatic and influential works in this respect are, inter alia: M. Lagrange, The Court of Justice as a Factor in European Integration, in 15 American Journal of Comparative Law, 1966–1967, p. 709; A.W. Green, Political Integration by Jurisprudence, A.W. Sijthoff 1969; H.G. Schermers, The European Court of Justice: Promoter of European Integration, in 22 The American Journal of Comparative Law, 1974, p. 444; R. Lecourt, L'Europe des juges, Bruylant 1976; E. Stein, Lawyers, judges, and the making of a transnational constitution, in 75 American Journal of International Law, 1981, p. 1; H. Rasmussen, On Law and Policy in the European Court of Justice: A Comparative Study in Judicial Policymaking, BRILL 1986; A.M. Burley, W. Mattli, Europe before the Court: A Political Theory of Legal Integration, in 47 International Organization, 1993, p. 41; G. Garrett, The Politics of Legal Integration in the European Union, in 49 International Organization, 1995, p. 171; W. Mattli, A.M. Slaughter, Law and Politics in the European Union: A Reply to Garrett, in 49 International Organization, 1995, p. 183; R. Dehousse, The European Court of Justice. The Politics of Judicial Integration, Macmillan 1998; L.M. Poiares Maduro, We the Court: The European Court of Justice and the European Economic Constitution, Hart 1998; A. Arnull, The European Union and Its Court of Justice, 1st ed., Oxford 1999; M. Shapiro, The European Court of Justice, in P. Craig, G. de Búrca (eds.), The Evolution of EU Law, 1st ed., Oxford University Press 1999, p. 321;

L. Neville Brown, T. Kennedy, The Court of Justice of the European Communities, 5th ed., Sweet & Maxwell 2000; H.G. Schermers, D.F. Waelbroeck, Judicial Protection in the European Union, 6th ed., Kluwer Law 2001; G. de Búrca, J.H.H. Weiler (eds.), The European Court of Justice, OUP 2001; D. Sarmiento, Poder Judicial e integración europea. La construcción de un modelo jurisdiccional para la Unión, Thomson Civitas 2004; A. Stone Sweet, The European Court of Justice, in P. Craig, G. de Búrca (eds.), The Evolution of EU Law, 2nd ed., OUP 2011, p. 121; M. Adams, H. de Waele, J. Meeusen, G. Straetmans (eds.), Judging Europe's Judges: The Legitimacy of the Case Law of the European Court of Justice, Hart 2013; M. Dawson, B. de Witte, E. Muir (eds.), Judicial Activism at the European Court of Justice, Edward Elgar 2013; T. Horsley, The Court of Justice of the European Union as an Institutional Actor. Judicial Lawmaking and its Limits, CUP 2018. Recent reviews can be found in recent overview, see A. Stone Sweet, The European Court of Justice and the Judicialization of EU governance, in 5 Living Reviews in European Governance, 2010, available at the website http://www.europeangovernance-livingreviews.org/Articles/lreg-2010-2/ (accessed 2 March 2020); and T. Horsley, Reflections on the Role of the Court of Justice as the 'Motor' of European Integration: Legal Limits to Judicial Lawmaking, in 50 Common Market Law Review, 2013, p. 931.

2. See *inter alia* A. Bredimas, Comparative Law in the Court of Justice of the European Communities, in 32 The Yearbook of World Affairs, 1978, p. 320; P. Pescatore, Le recours, dans la jurisprudence de la Cour de justice des Communautés européennes, à des normes déduites de la comparaison des droits des Etats Membres, in Revue internationale de Droit comparé, 1980, p. 337; M. Hilf, The Role of Comparative Law in the Jurisprudence of the Court of Justice of the European Communities, in A.L.C. De Mestral et al. (eds.), The Limitation of Human Rights in Comparative Constitutional Law, Les éditions Tvon Blais 1986, p. 549; Y. Galmot, Reflexions sur le recours au droit compare par la Cour de justice des Communautés européennes, in Revue française de droit administratif, 1990, p. 261; J. Mertens de Wilmars, Le droit comparé dans dans la jurisprudence de la Cour de justice des Communautés européennes, in Journal des Tribunaux, 1991, p. 37; T. Koopmans, The Birth of European Law at the Crossroads of Legal Traditions, in 39 American Journal of Comparative Law, 1991, p. 493; C.N. Kakouris, Use of the Comparative Method by the Court of Justice of the European Communities, in 6 Pace International Law Review, 1994, p. 267; K. Lenaerts, Interlocking Legal Orders in the European Union and Comparative Law, in 52 International and Comparative Law Quarterly,

2003, p. 873; F. van der Mensbrugghe, L'utilisation de la méthode comparative en droit européen, Presses universitaries de Namur 2003; T. von Danwitz, The Rule of Law in the Recent Jurisprudence of the ECJ, in 37 Fordham International Law Journal, 2014, p. 1311; G. Alpa, Comparazione e diritto straniero nella giurisprudenza della Corte di Giustizia dell'Union europea, in 32 Contratto e impresa, 2016, p. 879; K. Lenaerts, The European Court of Justice and the Comparative Law Method, in 25 European Review of Private Law, 2017, p. 297; F. Jacobs, Comparative Law and European Union Law, in M. Reimann, R. Zimmermann (eds.), The Oxford Handbook of Comparative Law, 2nd ed., OUP 2019, chapt. XIX; and G. de Vergottini, Diritto costituzionale comparato, CEDAM 2019, pp. 61–68.

3. In this sense, very recently, H. Brady, Twelve things everyone should know about the European Court of Justice, paper of the Centre for European Reform, 42/2014, p. 7.
4. See e.g. H. Rasmussen, On Law and Policy in the European Court of Justice: A Comparative Study in Judicial Policymaking, BRILL 1986; A.M. Burley, W. Mattli, Europe Before the Court: A Political Theory of Legal Integration, in 47 International Organization, 1993 p. 41; J.H.H. Weiler, A Quiet Revolution. The European Court of Justice and its Interlocutors, in 26 Comparative Political Studies 1994, p. 510; G. Garrett, The Politics of Legal Integration in the European Union, in 49 International Organization, 1995, p. 171; A. Grimmel, Judicial Interpretation or Judicial Activism? The Legacy of Rationalism in the Studies of the European Court of Justice, in 18 European Law Journal, 2012, p. 518.
5. See the various contributions to L. Azoulai, L.M. Poiares Maduro (eds.), The Past and Future of EU Law. The Classics of EU Law Revisited on the 50th Anniversary of the Rome Treaty, Hart 2010, precisely as a close inspection of all the great, revolutionary, doctrinal choices of the Court of Justice.
6. T. Horsley, Reflections on the Role of the Court of Justice as the 'Motor' of European Integration: Legal Limits to Judicial Lawmaking, in 50 Common Market Law Review, 2013, p. 931.
7. For an authoritative legal perspective on the point see J.H.H. Weiler, The Transformation of Europe, in 100 Yale Law Journal, 1991, p. 2403.
8. In this sense, by European Court of Justice, CJEU, ECJ, or sometimes just CJ, I will refer to the apical Court within the general institution placed in Luxembourg. I will clarify when my analysis will also take into account the General Court and the Civil Service Tribunal (whose genesis will be described in Chapter 6 of the book).
9. A. Bakardjieva Engelbrekt, Comparative Law and European Law: The End of an Era, a New Beginning, or Time to Face the Methodological Challenges?, in 61 Scandinavian Studies in Law, 2015, p. 88.

10. A. Alemanno, L. Pech, Thinking Justice Outside the Docket: A Critical Assessment of the Reform of the EU's Court System, in 54 Common Market Law Review, 2017, 54: pp. 129, 130.
11. J. Ferejohn, P. Pasquino, Constitutional Courts as Deliberative Institutions: Towards an Institutional Theory of Constitutional Justice, in W. Sadurski (ed.), Constitutional Justice, East and West, Kluwer Law International 2002, p. 21.
12. A. Alemanno, O. Stefan, Openness at the Court of Justice of the European Union: Toppling a Taboo, in 51 Common Market Law Review, 2014, p. 97.
13. T. Koopmans, La procédure préjudicielle - victime de son succès?, in F. Capotorti, C. Ehlermann (eds.), Du droit international au droit de l'integration - Liber amicorum Pierre Pescatore, Nomos Verlagsgesellschaft 1987, p. 347.
14. See G. Davies, Abstractness and Concreteness in the Preliminary Reference Procedure, in N. Nic Shuibhne (ed.), Regulating the Internal Market, Edward Elgar Publishing 2006, p. 210.
15. In the words of R. Barents, The Autonomy of Community Law, Kluwer Law International 2004, who provides a full and rich appraisal of the phenomenon.
16. See the critical points issued by the Court itself in the much discussed Opinion 2/13, of 18 December 2014 (ECLI:EU:C:2014:2454).
17. See on the idea of a "changing authority" of the Court R.D. Kelemen, The Court of Justice of the European Union: Changing Authority in the Twenty-First Century, in K.J. Alter, L.R. Helfer, M.R. Madsen (eds.), International Court Authority, OUP 2018, chapt. 10.
18. I. Venzke, Understanding the Authority of International Courts and Tribunals: On Delegation and Discursive Construction, in 14(2) Theoretical Inquiries in Law, 2013, p. 382, at 404.
19. See F.G. Jacobs, The Evolution of the European Legal Order, in 41 Common Market Law Review, 2004, p. 303, and *Id.*, The European Court of Justice: Some Thoughts on Its Past and Its Future, in 2 The European Advocate, 1994–1995, p. 2.
20. To echo the historical phrase of W. Bagehot, The English Constitution, Oxford University Press 1867, reprinted 2001, at p. 44 at 48.
21. *Inter alia*, R. Girard, Mensonge romantique et verité romanesque, Grasset 1961, E. Auerbach, Mimesis: The Representation of Reality in Western Literature, Princeton University Press 1953, Walter Benjamin, "On the Mimetic Faculty," trans. by Edmund Jephcott, in Selected Writings: Volume 2, Part 2, 1931–1934, ed. by Michael W. Jennings, Howard Eiland, and Gary Smith (Cambridge, MA and London England: The Belknap Press of Harvard University Press), 720, G. Mormino, Per una teoria dell'imitazione, Raffaello Cortina editore, 2016, Y. Mény

(ed.), Les politiques du mimétisme institutionnel: la greffe et le rejet, L'Harmattan 1993.

22. J.J. Rousseau, Discorso sulle scienze e le arti, in *Id.*, Scritti politici, Laterza 1994, p. 7; S. Pinker, The Blank Slate, Penguin 2002.
23. G. Mormino, Per una teoria dell'imitazione, *op. cit.*, 81.
24. V. Gallese, The Two Sides of Mimesis: Girard's Mimetic Theory, Embodied Simulation and Social Identification, in 16 Journal of Consciousness Studies, 2009, p. 21; G. Mormino, Per una teoria dell'imitazione, *op. cit.*, 81 et seq.
25. G. Mormino, Per una teoria dell'imitazione, *op. cit.*, 82–83.
26. *Ivi*, 84–85.
27. R. Hirschl, The Question of Case Selection in Comparative Constitutional Law, in 53 American Journal of Comparative Law, 2005, pp. 125, 131–132.
28. *Ivi*, 142–143.
29. See on this, *inter alia*, the reflections of J.H.H. Weiler, Journey to an Unknown Destination. A Retrospective and Prospective of the European Court of Justice in the Arena of Political Integration, in 31 Journal of Common Market Studies, 1993, p. 417, at 433 *et seq.*, and A. Grilli, Le origini del diritto dell'Unione europea, Il Mulino 2009, at p. 63 *et seq.*
30. M. Avbelj, The Pitfalls of (Comparative) Constitutionalism for European Integration, Eric Stein Working Paper 1/2008, available at the website: http://ssrn.com/abstract=1334216 (accessed 2 March 2020).
31. In the words of M. Avbelj, Questioning EU Constitutionalisms, in 9/1 German Law Journal, 2008, p. 1, at 1.
32. J.H.H. Weiler, J. Trachtman, European Constitutionalism and Its Discontents, in 17 Northwestern Journal of International Law & Business, 1997, p. 354, at 361–362.
33. See C. Lyons, Flexibility and the European Court of Justice, in G. de Bùrca, J. Scott (eds.), Constitutional Change in the EU, Hart Publishing 2000, p. 95, at 108.
34. J.H.H. Weiler, J. Trachtman, European Constitutionalism and Its Discontents, *op. cit.*, at 363.
35. I refer to the studies of intergovernamentalist inspiration, such as those of S. Hoffman, The European Sisyphus. Essays on Europe, 1964–1994, Boulder: Westview Press 1995; A. Moravcsik, The Choice for Europe: Social Purpose and State Power from Messina to Maastricht, Cornell University Press 1998; and P.L. Lindseth, Power and Legitimacy: Reconciling Europe and the Nation-State, Oxford University Press 2010.
36. J.H.H. Weiler, J. Trachtman, European Constitutionalism and Its Discontents, *op. cit.*, at 373.

37. And the substance of the debate among the so called neofunctionalist and intergovernamentalist schools of thought: see in this respect, the classic E.B. Haas, The Uniting of Europe: Political, Social, and Economic Forces, 1950–1957, Stanford University Press 1958, and S. Hoffman, The European Sisyphus. Essays on Europe, 1964–1994, *op. cit.*; A. Moravcsik, The Choice for Europe: Social Purpose and State Power from Messina to Maastricht, *op. cit.*
38. J.H.H. Weiler, J. Trachtman, European Constitutionalism and Its Discontents, *op. cit.*, at 365.
39. *Ibidem.*
40. J.H.H. Weiler, J. Trachtman, European Constitutionalism and Its Discontents, *op. cit.*, at 366.
41. J.H.H. Weiler, Hjalte Rasmussen - Nemo propheta in patria sua, in H. Koch, K. Hagel-Sørensen, U. Haltern, J.H.H. Weiler (eds.), Europe. The New Legal Realism—Essays in Honour of Hjalte Rasmussen, Djøf Forlag 2010, p. xiii.
42. J.H.H. Weiler, J. Trachtman, European Constitutionalism and Its Discontents, *op. cit.*, at 366.
43. T. Kuhn, The Structure of the Scientific Revolutions, University of Chicago Press 1962.
44. M. Shapiro, Comparative Law and Comparative Politics, in 53 Southern California Law Review, 1980, p. 537, at 538.
45. M. Rasmussen, Rewriting the History of European Public Law: The New Contribution of Historians, in 28/5 American University International Law Review, 2013, p. 1187, at 1195.
46. *Ivi*, at 1195.
47. *Ivi*, at 1196.
48. L. Conant, Justice Contained: Law and Politics in the European Union, Cornell University Press 2002.
49. P.L. Lindseth, Power and Legitimacy: Reconciling Europe and the Nation-State, *op. cit.*
50. M. Rasmussen, Rewriting the History of European Public Law: The New Contribution of Historians, *op. cit.*, at 1196.
51. A. Vauchez, The Force of a Weak Field: Law and Lawyers in the Government of the European Union (For a Renewed Research Agenda), in 2 International Political Sociology, 2008, p. 128; A. Vauchez, B. de Witte (eds.), Lawyering Europe. European Law as a Transnational Social Field, Hart 2013.
52. B. De Witte, The European Union as an International Legal Experiment, *op. cit.*
53. In the words of M. Rasmussen, Rewriting the History of European Public Law: The New Contribution of Historians, *op. cit.*
54. *Ivi*, at 1197.

55. *Ibidem.*
56. M. Rasmussen, Constructing and Deconstructing 'Constitutional' European Law: Some Reflections on How to Study the History of European Law, in H. Koch, K. Hagel-Sørensen, U. Haltern, J.H.H. Weiler (eds.), Europe. The New Legal Realism—Essays in Honour of Hjalte Rasmussen, *op. cit.*, p. 639.
57. *Ivi*, at 649.
58. In the words of A. Vauchez, B. de Witte (eds.), Lawyering Europe. European Law as a Transnational Social Field, *op. cit.*; see also F. Nicola, B. Davies, EU Law Stories. Contextual and Critical Histories of European Jurisprudence, CUP 2017.
59. J.H.H. Weiler, The Transformation of Europe, *op. cit.*, at 2403.
60. See the profound analysis of M. Claes, The National Courts' Mandate in the European Constitution, Hart Publishing 2006.
61. The "making of a transnational constitution" depicted by E. Stein, Lawyers, judges, and the making of a transnational constitution, *op. cit.*
62. These are the examples made by P. Pollack, The New EU Legal History: What's New, What's Missing?, in 28 American University International Law Review, 2013, p. 1257.
63. See, recently, M. Adams, H. de Waele, J. Meeusen, G. Straetmans (eds.), Judging Europe's Judges: The Legitimacy of the Case Law of the European Court of Justice, *op cit.*; M. Dawson, B. de Witte, E. Muir (eds.), Judicial Activism at the European Court of Justice, *op cit.*
64. A. von Bogdandy, I. Venzke, Beyond Dispute: International Judicial Institutions as Lawmakers, in 12 German Law Journal, 2011, p. 979.
65. In the terms notoriously described by G. Hafner, Risks Ensuing from Fragmentation of International Law, in Official Records of the General Assembly, 55th Session, Supplement No. 10 (A/55/10), annex, the Report of the Study Group on Fragmentation of International Law', doc. A/CN.4/L.644, based on the outline prepared by the Chairman of the Study Group, M. Koskenniemi, on The Function and Scope of the *lex specialis* Rule and the Question of Self-contained Regimes', available at the website www.un.org/law/ilc/sessions/55/fragmentation_outline.pdf (accessed 2 March 2020) and the Report of the Study Group on Fragmentation of International Law: Difficulties Arising from the Diversification and Expansion of International Law; ON Doc. A/CN.4/L.663/Rev. 1; and by M. Koskenniemi, P. Leino, Fragmentation of International Law. Postmodern Anxieties?, in 15 Leiden Journal of International Law, 2002, p. 553.
66. A. von Bogdandy, I. Venzke, Beyond Dispute: International Judicial Institutions as Lawmakers, *op cit.*, at 979 and 983.
67. *Ivi*, at 979.

68. J.H.H. Weiler, Epilogue: Judging the Judges—Apology and Critique, in M. Adams, H. de Waele, J. Meeusen, G. Straetmans (eds.), Judging Europe's Judges. The Legitimacy of the Case Law of the European Court of Justice, *op. cit.*, at 235.
69. Coined, as well known, by A.M. Bickel, The Least Dangerous Branch. The Supreme Court at the Bar of Politics, Yale University Press 1986.
70. J.P. Jacqué, The Principle of Institutional Balance, in 41 Common Market Law Review, 2004, p. 383.
71. International Courts and the Quest for Legitimacy, Hebrew University of Jerusalem/Tel Aviv University Faculty of Law, Jerusalem-Tel Aviv, 3–4 June 2012, now published in Theoretical Inquiries in Law, Volume 14, Issue 2, July 2013.
72. I. Venzke, Understanding the Authority of International Courts and Tribunals: On Delegation and Discursive Construction, in 14(2) Theoretical Inquiries in Law, 2013, p. 382.
73. *Ibidem.*
74. *Ivi*, at 388–389.
75. A.T. Guzman, International Tribunals: A Rational Choice Analysis, in 157 University of Pennsylvania Law Review, 2008, p. 171; L.H. Helfer, A.M. Slaughter, Why States Create International Tribunals: A Response to Professors Posner and Yoo, in 93 California Law Review, 2005, p. 899.
76. I. Venzke, Understanding the Authority of International Courts and Tribunals: On Delegation and Discursive Construction, *op. cit.*, at 382.
77. H. Arendt, What is Authority?, in Ead., Between Past and Future: Six Exercises in Political Thought, Meridian 1963.
78. I. Venzke, Understanding the Authority of International Courts and Tribunals: On Delegation and Discursive Construction, *op. cit.*, at 383.
79. L. Azoulai, Les fondements de l'autorité de l'Union, in L. Azoulai, L. Burgorgue-Larsen (eds.), L'autorité de l'Union européenne, Burylant 2006, p. 5.
80. I. Venzke, Understanding the Authority of International Courts and Tribunals: On Delegation and Discursive Construction, *op. cit.*, at 383.
81. *Ivi*, at 386.
82. In the words of M. Weber, Economy and Society: An Outline of Interpretive Sociology, University of California Press 1978.
83. I. Venzke, Understanding the Authority of International Courts and Tribunals: On Delegation and Discursive Construction, *op. cit.*, at 384.
84. *Ivi*, at 397.
85. B. Lincoln, Authority: Construction and Corrosion, University of Chicago Press 1994.
86. I. Venzke, Understanding the Authority of International Courts and Tribunals: On Delegation and Discursive Construction, *op. cit.*, at 399.

87. *Ivi*, at 398.
88. *Ivi*, at 409, with reference to R. von Jhering, The Struggle for Law, 2nd ed., Callaghan 1915, p. 13.
89. M. Zürn, M. Binder, M. Ecker-Ehrhardt, International Authority and Its Politicization, in 4 International Theory 2012, p. 69, at 83.
90. I. Venzke, Understanding the Authority of International Courts and Tribunals: On Delegation and Discursive Construction, *op. cit.*, at 404.
91. C. Joerges, Unity in Diversity as Europe's Vocation and Conflicts Law as Europe's Constitutional Form, LEQS Paper No. 28/2010, at p. 1.
92. Treaty on the Functioning of the European Union, Title XIII, Article 167(1), previously in Treaty the European Union, Title XII, Article 151(1).
93. See F. Cerutti, Towards the Political Identity of the Europeans. An Introduction, in F. Cerutti, E. Rudolph (eds.), A Soul for Europe, Vol. 1: A Reader, Peeters 2001, p. 1.
94. J. Olsen, Unity and Diversity—European Style, ARENA Working Paper No. 24/2005, at p. 14.
95. *Ibidem.*
96. In these terms P.G. Monateri, Il problema di una definizione di Europa: una questione di teologia politica?, in 1 Rivista critica del diritto privato, 2005, p. 3.
97. U. Haltern, On Finality, in A. von Bogdandy, J. Bast (eds.), Principles of European Constitutional Law, Hart Publishing 2010, p. 209.
98. See in this respect A.J. Menéndez, The Existential Crisis of the European Union, in 5 German Law Journal, 2013, p. 453.
99. A. Bakardjieva Engelbrekt, Comparative Law and European Law: the End of an Era, a New Beginning, or Time to Face the Methodological Challenges?, in 61 Scandinavian Studies in Law, 2015, p. 88.
100. H.P. Glenn, Legal Traditions of the World, Oxford University Press 2014.
101. *Ibidem*, at p. 12 *et seq.* in particular. See also *Id.*, The Capture, Reconstruction and Marginalization of 'Custom', in 45 American Journal of Comparative Law, 1997, p. 613.
102. *Ibidem.*
103. *Ivi*, at p. 17 *et seq.*
104. See in this sense the recent reconstructive reflections in A. Riles (ed.), Rethinking the Masters of Comparative Law, Hart Publishing 2001, and P.G. Monateri, Geopolitica del diritto: genesi, governo e dissoluzione dei corpi politici, *op cit.*
105. M. Cappelletti, M. Seccombe, J.H.H. Weiler (eds.), Integration Through Law. Europe and the American Federal Experience, vol. 1. Methods, Tools and Institutions, De Gruyter 1986.

106. D. Augenstein, Identifying the European Union: Legal Integration and European Communities, in *Id.* (ed.), Integration through Law Revisited. The Making of the European Polity, Ashgate 2012, p. 161.
107. R. Dehousse, J.H.H. Weiler, The Legal Dimension, in *Eid.* (eds.) The Dynamics of European Integration, Pinter Publishers 1990, p. 242, at 246.
108. A. Vauchez, The Force of a Weak Field: Law and Lawyers in the Government of the European Union (For a Renewed Research Agenda), *op cit.*, at 134.
109. *Ibidem.*
110. See J. Hendry, The Double Fragmentation of Law: Legal System-Internal Differentiation and the Process of Europeanization, in D. Augenstein (ed.), Integration through Law Revisited. The Making of the European Polity, *op. cit.*, p. 233, in particular at 236 *et seq.*
111. D. Augenstein, Identifying the European Union: Legal Integration and European Communities, *op. cit.*, at 161.
112. See J. Hendry, Unitas in Diversitate: on Legal Cultures and the Europeanisation of Law, PhD dissertation, European University Institute, 2009, available at the website https://cadmus.eui.eu/handle/1814/12045 (accessed 2 March 2020) at pp. 40–41.
113. Belonging the concept of integration "to the ontological stage of research": see on all this C. Radaelli, Whither Europeanization? Concept Stretching and Substantive Change, European Integration online Papers (EIoP), 2000, at p. 6.
114. *Ibidem.*
115. A. Moravcsik, Preferences and Power in the European Community: A Liberal Intergovernmentalist Approach, in 31 Journal of Common Market Studies, 1993, p. 473.
116. E.B. Haas, The Uniting of Europe: Political, Social, and Economic Forces, 1950–1957, *op. cit.*
117. See J. Hendry, Unitas in Diversitate: on Legal Cultures and the Europeanisation of Law, *op. cit.*, at 40–41.
118. C. Radaelli, Whither Europeanization? Concept Stretching and Substantive Change, *op. cit.*, at 4.
119. S.S. Andersen, The Mosaic of Europeanization. An Organizational Perspective on National Recontextualization, ARENA Working Papers No. 04/11, in particular at p. 7 *et seq.*
120. See J. Hendry, Unitas in Diversitate: on Legal Cultures and the Europeanisation of Law, *op. cit.*, at 41.
121. As recently famously defined by B. De Witte, The European Union as an International Legal Experiment, *op cit.*
122. U. Haltern, On Finality, *op cit.*, at 209.
123. *Ibidem.*

124. *Ibidem.*
125. See F.G. Jacobs, The Evolution of the European Legal Order, in 41 Common Market Law Review, 2004, p. 303, and *Id.*, The European Court of Justice: Some Thoughts on its Past and its Future, in 2 The European Advocate, 1994–1995, p. 2.
126. To echo the historical phrase of W. Bagehot, The English Constitution, Oxford University Press 1867, reprinted 2001, at p. 44 at 48.
127. T. Koopmans, La procédure préjudicielle - victime de son succès?, in F. Capotorti, C. Ehlermann (eds.), Du droit international au droit de l'integration - Liber amicorum Pierre Pescatore, Nomos Verlagsgesellschaft 1987, p. 347.
128. H.P. Glenn, Legal Traditions of the World, *op. cit.*
129. G. Mormino, Per una teoria dell'imitazione, *op. cit.*, 81.
130. *Ivi*, at 82–83.
131. *Ivi*, 84–85.
132. See M. Avbelj, The Pitfalls of (Comparative) Constitutionalism for European Integration, *op cit.*, and the rich reflections of R. Schütze, From Dual to Cooperative Federalism. The Changing Structure of European Law, OUP 2009.
133. M. Cappelletti, M. Seccombe, J.H.H. Weiler (eds.), Integration Through Law. Europe and the American Federal Experience—A General Introduction, in *Eid.* (eds.), Integration Through Law. Europe and the American Federal Experience, vol. 1. Methods, Tools and Institutions, *op cit.*, at p. 15.
134. M. Cappelletti, Foreword to the Florence Integration Project Series, in M. Cappelletti, M. Seccombe, J.H.H. Weiler (eds.), Integration Through Law. Europe and the American Federal Experience, vol. 1. Methods, Tools and Institutions, *op cit.*, p. III, at VI.
135. D. Augenstein, M. Dawson, Introduction. What Law for What Polity? 'Integration Through Law' in the European Union, in D. Augenstein (ed.), Integration Through Law Revisited. The Making of the European Polity, *op. cit.*, p. 1, at 1.
136. R. Michaels, The Functional Method of Comparative Law, in M. Reimann, R. Zimmerman (eds.), The Oxford Handbook of Comparative Law, Oxford University Press 2006, p. 339.
137. A. von Bogdandy, European Law Beyond 'Ever Closer Union'—Repositioning the Concept, Its Thrust, and the ECJ's Comparative Methodology, in 22 European Law Journal, 2016, p. 591.
138. N. Walker, Legal Theory and the European Union: A 25th Anniversary Essay, in 25 Oxford Journal of Legal Studies, 2005, p. 581.
139. See, as major recent examples, the works by Antoine Vauchez and Morten Rasmussen cited throughout this dissertation.

140. A. Watson, Legal Transplants: An Approach to Comparative Law, University Press of Virginia 1974.
141. F. Bignami, Rethinking the Legal Foundations of the European Constitutional Order: The Lessons of the New Historical Research, in 28 American University International Law Review, 2013, p. 1311, at 1321.
142. F. Nicola, Critical Legal Histories in EU Law, in 28 American University International Law Review, 2013, p. 1173, at 1183.
143. *Ibidem.*
144. See at least A. Watson, Legal Transplants. An Approach to Comparative Law, *op. cit.*; O. Kahn-Freund, On Uses and Misuses of Comparative Law, in 1 Modern Law Review, 1974, p. 1; E. Stein, Uses, Misuses - and Non-Uses of Comparative Law, in 2 Northwestern Law Review, 1977, p. 198; E.M. Wise, The Transplants of Legal Patterns, in 38 American Journal of Comparative Law, 1990, p. 1; P. Legrand, The Impossibility of Legal Transplants, in 4 Maastricht Journal of European and Comparative Law, 1997, p. 111; F. Schauer, The Politics and Incentives of Legal Transplantation, in J. Nye Jr., J. Donahue (eds.), Governance in a Globalizing World, Brookings Institution Press 2000, p. 253; G. Teubner, Rechtsirritationen: Zur Koevolution von Rechtsnormen und Produktionsregimes, in G. Dux, F. Wetz (eds.), Moral und Recht im Diskurs der Moderne: Zur Legitimation gesellschaftlicher Ordnung, Leske + Budrich 2001; and the reconstructions by W. Twining, Diffusion of Law: a Global Perspective, in 49 Journal of Legal Pluralism & Unofficial Law, 2004, p. 1, and J.W. Cairns, Watson, Walton, and the History of Legal Transplants, in 41 Georgia Journal of International and Comparative Law, 2013, p. 637. See also, for specific reflections on transplants in comparative public law, V. Perju, Constitutional Transplants, Borrowing and Migrations, in M. Rosenfeld, A. Sajo (eds.), Oxford Handbook of Comparative Constitutional Law, Oxford University Press 2012, p. 1306, and G. Frankenberg, Comparative Law as Critique, Elgar 2016, and for a reflection on the EU realm, P.G. Monateri, La circolazione dei modelli giuridici e le sue conseguenze per l'Unione europea, in A.M. Petroni (ed.) Modelli giuridici ed economici per la Costituzione europea, Il Mulino 2001, p. 87.
145. F. Bignami, Rethinking the Legal Foundations of the European Constitutional Order: The Lessons of the New Historical Research, *op. cit.*, at 1323.
146. *Ibidem.*
147. A. von Bogdandy, The European Lesson for International Democracy. The Significance of Articles 9 to 12 EU Treaty for International Organizations, in 23 European Journal of International Law, 2012.

148. In the words of A.E. Platsas, The Functional and the Dysfunctional in the Comparative Method of Law: Some Critical Remarks, in 12.3 Electronic Journal of Comparative Law, 2008, p. 1, at 1.
149. See the classic K. Zweigert, H. Kötz, An Introduction to Comparative Law, Clarendon Press 1998, at 34: "The basic methodological principle of all comparative law is that of functionality".
150. See the reflections by R. Michaels, The Functional Method of Comparative Law, *op cit.*, at 344–345.
151. See A.E. Platsas, The Functional and the Dysfunctional in the Comparative Method of Law: Some Critical Remarks, *op. cit.*, at 3.
152. See R. Michaels, The Functional Method of Comparative Law, *op cit.*, at 339–340.
153. L. Azoulai, Les garanties procédurales en droit communautaire, PhD dissertation, European University Institute, 2000, available at the website https://cadmus.eui.eu/handle/1814/4550 (accessed 2 March 2020), at 115.
154. See for this definition T. Koopmans, The Birth of European Law at the Crossroads of Legal Traditions, *op. cit.*, p. 493.
155. In the words of R. Barents, The Autonomy of Community Law, Kluwer Law International 2004, who provides a full and rich appraisal of the phenomenon.
156. H. Atlan, Entre le cristal et la fumée. Essai sur l'organisation du vivant, Editions du Seuil 1979, at 63 (personal translation).
157. *Ivi*, at 72.
158. See for all these reflections M.A. Damirli, Comparative Law Hermeneutics: Cognitive Possibilities, in 5 Journal of Comparative Law, 2010, p. 65, at 67.
159. R. Scarciglia, Comparative Methodology and Pluralism in Legal Comparison in a Global Age, in 6 Beijing Law Review, 2015, p. 42, at 45.
160. *Ibidem*; see also the classic analysis by R. Dehousse; Comparing National and EC Law: The Problem of the Level of Analysis, in 42 The American Journal of Comparative Law, 1994, p. 687.
161. A. Momirov, A. Naudé Fourie, Vertical Comparative Law Methods: Tools for Conceptualizing the International Rule of Law, in 2 Erasmus Law Review, 2003, p. 291, at 295.
162. *Ivi*, at 296; R. Scarciglia, Comparative Methodology and Pluralism in Legal Comparison in a Global Age, *op. cit.*, at 45.
163. H.E. Chodosh, Comparing Comparisons: In Search of Methodology, in 84 Iowa Law Review, 1999, p. 1025, at 1038 in particular.
164. J. Husa, The Method Is Dead, Long Live the Methods! European Polynomia and Pluralist Methodology, in 5 Legisprudence, 2011, p. 249,

at 252; R. Scarciglia, Comparative Methodology and Pluralism in Legal Comparison in a Global Age, *op. cit.*, at 45.

165. A.D. Tikhomirov, Philosophical Problems of Legal Comparativistics, in 5 Journal of Comparative Law, 2010, p. 159, at 169.
166. K. Zweigert, H. Kötz, An Introduction to Comparative Law, *op. cit.*, at 73 *et seq.*; see on this also A.V. Tkachenko, Functionalism and the Development of Comparative Law Cognition, in 5 Journal of Comparative Law, 2010, p. 71, at 76–77 in particular.
167. G. Comparato, New Voices: Challenging Legal Culture, in 7 European Journal of Legal Studies, 2014, p. 5, at 16–17 in particular.
168. *Ibidem*, with reference to L.M. Friedman, The Legal System. A Social Science Perspective, Russell Sage Foundation, 1975, at p. 223.
169. See on the usual instrumentality of such a design P.G. Monateri, Geopolitica del diritto: genesi, governo e dissoluzione dei corpi politici, *op. cit.*
170. Often "authoritatively created through legal education": see G. Comparato, New Voices: Challenging Legal Culture, *op. cit.*, at p. 17.
171. See in particular A. Vauchez, The Force of a Weak Field: Law and Lawyers in the Government of the European Union (For a Renewed Research Agenda), *op. cit.*; A. Vauchez, B. de Witte (eds.), Lawyering Europe. European Law as a Transnational Social Field, *op. cit.*; and M. Rasmussen, Constructing and Deconstructing 'Constitutional' European Law: Some reflections on how to study the history of European law, *op. cit.*
172. A. Alemanno, L. Pech, Thinking Justice Outside the Docket: A Critical Assessment of the Reform of the EU's Court System, in 54 Common Market Law Review, 2017, 54: pp. 129, 130.
173. M Bobek, Of Feasibility and Silent Elephants: The Legitimacy of the Court of Justice through the Eyes of National Courts, in M. Adams, J. Meeusen, G. Straetmans, H. de Waele (eds.) Judging Europe's Judges: The Legitimacy of the Case Law of the European Court of Justice Examined, *op. cit.*, p. 197, at 227.
174. J. Ferejohn, P. Pasquino, Constitutional Courts as Deliberative Institutions: Towards an Institutional Theory of Constitutional Justice, in W. Sadurski (ed.), Constitutional Justice, East and West, Kluwer Law International 2002, p. 21.
175. A. Alemanno, O. Stefan, Openness at the Court of Justice of the European Union: Toppling a Taboo, in 51 Common Market Law Review, 2014, p. 97.
176. T. Koopmans, La procédure préjudicielle - victime de son succès?, *op. cit.*

177. See G. Davies, Abstractness and Concreteness in the Preliminary Reference Procedure, in N. Nic Shuibhne (ed.) Regulating the Internal Market, Edward Elgar Publishing 2006, p. 210.
178. See for some reflections on point, generally, K.J. Alter, Delegation to International Courts and the Limits of Recontracting Political Power, in D. Hawkins, D.A. Lake, D. Nielson, M.J. Tierney (eds.), Delegation and Agency in International Organizations, Cambridge University Press 2006, p. 312.
179. J.H.H. Weiler, Epilogue: The Judicial Après Nice, in J.H.H. Weiler, G. de Burca, The European Court of Justice, *op. cit.*, at p. 225.
180. M. Lasser, Judicial Deliberations. A Comparative Analysis of Judicial Transparency and Legitimacy, Oxford University Press 2004.
181. L. Azoulai, La fabrication de la jurisprudence communautaire, in P. Mbongo, A. Vauchez (eds.), Dans la fabrique du droit européen. Scènes, acteurs et publics de la Cour de justice des Communautés européennes, Bruylant 2009, p. 153.
182. J.H.H. Weiler, Epilogue: The Judicial Après Nice, *op. cit.*, at 225.
183. See S. Prechal, National Courts in EU Judicial Structures, in 25 Yearbook of European Law, 2007, p. 429, at 432–433, and M. Bobek, Of Feasibility and Silent Elephants: The Legitimacy of the Court of Justice through the Eyes of National Courts, *op. cit.*, at 200 *et seq.*
184. P. Mbongo, A. Vauchez (eds.), Dans la fabrique du droit européen. Scènes, acteurs et publics de la Cour de justice des Communautés européennes, *op. cit.*, inspired by the seminal work of B. Latour, La fabrique du droit. Une ethnographie du Conseil d'Etat, La Découverte & Syros 2002.

CHAPTER 2

The Foundation and Structuring of the Powers of the Court

As said, to first describe the comparative influences' potentiality of internalization via the structure and organization of what is nowadays the Court of Justice of the European Union, I will look back at its foundation at the time of the negotiations of the first Communities' Treaties. In this chapter, I will revise, in light of the new historical legal research and an analysis of the first specialized literature on EU legal affairs, the foundation of the common judicial body. First, I will study how some precise choices set the path for its significant development, discarding other opposite proposals based on typically—at the time—weak international adjudicative forms. I will also do so by recalling the recent political science and comparative law literature that teaches us how the incentives, actual motivations for creating a court and assigning to it specific roles in a federal or international context are both typical and recurring.[1] These were all at the centre of the debate at the time. I will then describe how the actual form of the original Court was not only chosen against different models but also naturally influenced by the already well-known and established judicial forms of its original Member States in its more decisive features. I argue that the internalization of these forms, tools and powers is literally at the basis of the success of the Court in the following years. This is also exemplified by the other phenomenon of internalization relating to the Dutch debate on the direct effect of international norms, which I analyse in the last part.

L. Pierdominici, *The Mimetic Evolution of the Court of Justice of the EU*, https://doi.org/10.1007/978-3-030-47864-3_2

2.1 Choice of Form: The Original Debate on the Creation of a Court for the European Communities

As it is very well known, the actual European Union has its antecedents and historic premises in the old European Communities born in the 1950s with the coagulation of the meaningful and noble intentions of the original six Member states Belgium, France, West Germany, Italy, the Netherlands and Luxembourg. The idea of a *direct continuity* between such stratified communitarian projects holds true in terms of the original political inspirations, against the ever common and simplistic narrative depicting, even today, European integration as an original economic project which slowly transformed into a political project.[2] But such an idea of *direct continuity* is also undoubtedly right for the basic institutional design of supranational organizations. The primitive European Coal and Steel Community, born with the Treaty of Paris of 1951, was run by four institutions: a High Authority composed of independent appointees from the different States, a Common Assembly composed of national parliamentarians, a Special Council consisting of national ministers, and a Court of Justice. All these would ultimately form the blueprint for today's European Commission, European Parliament, the Council of the European Union, and my main object of study, the Court of Justice of the European Union (formerly known as European Court of Justice). The European Coal and Steel Community was joined by two other similar organizations in 1957 (along with the Treaty of Rome). These are the European Economic Community and European Atomic Energy Community, with whom it shared its membership and some institutions, particularly the common assembly and the judicial arm still represented by a unified Court of Justice. In 1967, all its institutions were merged with that of the European Economic Community, including both the High Authority (merged with the Commission) and the Councils. In 1973, the progressive enlargements of the Communities began, initiating a continuum that is still in progress and that is now grouping—after the Treaty of Maastricht of 1992, the expiration of the Treaty of Paris in 2002 and the absorption of ECSC activities and resources, and the Treaty of Lisbon of 2007—27 Member states under the formally unified framework of an all-encompassing European Union.

In this unique compound of meta-objectives with even spiritual and messianic dimensions,[3] precise and powerful political visions as well as both symbolic and substantive economic tools, and thus two remarkable strands—the functional and the idealist, pragmatism and values—combined, some features have been considered by the scholars as directly comparable with other international or federal regulatory regimes.

First of all, certain trends and spill-over effects are characterizing every experiment of economic integration, regardless of form and stage, according to what I discussed above. Every project of economic integration calls for the unification of economic policies between different states through the partial or full abolition of tariff and non-tariff restrictions on trade taking place among them. In turn, this is meant to lead to lower prices for distributors and consumers with the goal of increasing the combined economic productivity of states. In this sense, as one of the major scientists applied to these studies theorized,[4] as economic integration increases, the barriers of trade between markets diminish, with different degrees categorized in several stages.[5] Supranational common markets, with their free movement of economic factors across national borders, naturally generate demand for further integration, not only economically (via monetary unions) but also politically and somehow socially. Thus, economic communities naturally tend to evolve into political unions over time. This has been studied in depth, focusing particularly on the possible shift of independent power from intergovernmentally negotiated decisions by member states to a more complex system of independent supranational institutions by the various functionalist and intergovernamentalist political scientists.[6] But it has also been the main focus of comparative lawyers exploring the fundamental double role of law in these contexts of integration, as both an agent and an object, as explained in the introduction. It is worthy to recall that this same field of research was explored from different perspectives: and therefore by explaining, in a classic functionalist sense, how much and to what extent the legal lever could induce, or even force, integration; and on the other hand, how much and to what extent the complex dimensions of the legal phenomenon, taken as inherently and etymologically "traditional", could be irritated, could react and resist to this project of integration. These different approaches, as said, needed two different uses and two different methodologies of comparative research.

But there is also another important aspect that led the scholars to draw direct comparisons between the European Communities before, the European Union afterward and other international or federal regulatory regimes. As anticipated, we are talking about the institutional design problem of these transnational integration projects. In particular, an important literature emphasized how much these projects tend to face the need for *collective action* over some sets of mutually agreed policies among the relevant set of states. Quite typically, whatever the substance of the common regulatory regime (liberalization of trade, environmental standards, promotion of human rights and *a fortiori* an ambitious mixture of each), all the participant entities rationally perceive a benefit from mutual adherence with the proposed regulatory regime's rules. However, at the same time, they have no incentives to comply with unilaterally. Quite the opposite, their individual "better-off" situation would consist of freeriding policy while everyone else is following the rules.[7]

This obvious but elucidating theorization explains the rational basis for the construction of common institutions. These are usually common *fora* of political nature for the coordination of policies and their implementation, which can also foster the creation of systems of *reputation record* and *punishment*, in the classic form of retaliation.[8] But these are also (and always more) judicial bodies, considered as the more effective and reliable monitoring compliance systems. The choice for their establishment has been depicted as perfectly rational in terms of comparative constitutional engineering[9] and comparative institutional analysis.[10] Even though a taxonomy of the various integrative projects vary considerably when considering their systems of "legalization of dispute resolution",[11] ranging from "least legalistic treaties without independent third-party review" to the most legalistic agreements "with standing tribunals that can be petitioned by a wide array of litigants and that issue binding decisions with direct effect on national law",[12] a certain preference for fully fledged and stable tribunals can be easily traced with an inclination directly proportional to the complexity of the regulatory system and the number of interested parties.

The principal rational explanation for the establishment of these courts is to build a reliable monitoring system while simultaneously decreasing the costs of compliance for state governments. Once an agreement is signed, every possible change in domestic political, social and economic contexts faced by a government could constitute the incentive to defect from the regime's rules, precisely by presenting an immediate cost in terms of political popularity. This undermines the regulatory regime and its necessarily longer-term rationality. In this sense, as it has been said in rather explicative and iconic political jargon, the common judicial bodies come to play a double role. First, they configure a so-called *fire-alarm mechanism* by constituting the institutionalized venue in which a state brings a challenge, making both the challenged state and the third-party one(s) aware of the conflict. Second, they act as an *information clearinghouse* by being a venue in which these states then argue, following certain prototypical forms, over the challenge, thus channelling both the existence and the resolution of conflicts as well as the negotiations and the information exchanged accordingly.[13] All this could also be performed by other kinds of institutions, as stated earlier. But the more complex the regulatory system, and the higher the number of the interested entities, the more the existence of an independent, third-party judicial body becomes rational and desirable according to this model. Additionally, it is relevant to note that the centrality of the common court as an institutionalized venue for contestation and as a deliberative forum, according to the two roles mentioned above, has often been, purposively or not, emphasized by allowing other actors—usually "private individuals, firms, special interests, or subnational governments"[14]—to have standing before it. In turn, this leads to several joint consequences, usually considered in institutional design. It increases the probability of effective monitoring, decreases the cost in time and resources of governments for the identification of possible violations and advance challenges, and also tends to increase the quantity, variety and quality of the arguments put before the court.

The historical research recently devoted to the negotiations of the European Communities in the 1950s can show us how much these models built by political scientists and comparative lawyers hold in the case of the structuring European integration project since the beginning. This coincidence could be considered a truism, since these heuristic models are built retrospectively and often use the European Communities as primary benchmark. But the historiography on the structuring of the Communities gives us valuable insights into the original positions taken in negotiations, the positions of opposite nature, and in the rationale of these and final choices. It is possible today, in light of more recent heuristic models, to contextualize these choices by first explaining the original inspirations that shaped the Court as now we know it, and conversely, how the judicial arm of the European Communities and Europe itself, without its actual contribution, might have been if other paths were followed.[15]

The first reference in this respect is to the inspired negotiations that led to the establishment of the European Coal and Steel Community in the very early 1950s. As it is well known, the Schuman Declaration of May 9, 1950, fraught as it was of political visions and clear substantive recipes, barely included one short paragraph directly mentioning the institutional setting considered as apt for the "*mise en œuvre*"[16] of the integration project. The creation of a "common High Authority entrusted with the management of the scheme (…) composed of independent persons appointed by the governments, giving equal representation",[17] was since the beginning announced as the first and obvious step for the solution of the described *collective action* questions. But the same paragraph of the Declaration, again in perfect coincidence with what I discussed, pointed out a certain agnosticism when it came to the subject of the monitoring system. It merely stated that future "(A)ppropriate measures" would be provided "for means of appeal against the decisions of the Authority".[18] The appearance of "incompletely theorized agreement"[19] of this last clause is not deceptive. Recent historical research[20] tells us that the first (four) draft versions of the Schuman Declaration—Jean Monnet and three influent lawyers, Paul Reuter, Etienne Hirsch, and Pierre Uri, supported the work of Robert Schuman—did not even contain a reference to the problem of judicial review in the ECSC settlement. In this sense, the perception is that, in the primitive discussion for the project, a unique and simple coordination and monitoring system of political nature, as the High Authority, was considered enough for the complexity of the regulatory regime of the ECSC. After all, the Community was at the time "simply" coordinating and liberalizing the market of coal and steel products among only six Member states.

A reference to a proper system of judicial review only came about with the elaboration—or rather, with the "correction"[21]—of the fifth version of the Declaration. But again, this was merely another proof of the internal debate and particularly the fact that the drafters took several options into account, evaluating the pros and cons for the enforcement of the envisaged regulatory regime. Interestingly enough, the provisional amendment which made its appearance in the fifth, sixth and seventh traceable versions of the Schuman Declaration provided that the decisions of the new supranational Authority "*ne seront révisables que par appel devant la Cour permanente de Justice Internationale*".[22] Therefore, this hypothesized a direct delegation to the Court of The Hague established some five years before.[23] Such a tentative solution can be considered as the temporary emersion of the will to prefigure an independent monitoring system while simultaneously externalizing it to an already-established institution that is not formed merely by judges from the member states. The idea was probably aimed at simplifying the organization of the Community while increasing hypothetical costs in terms of reputation for freerider parties. But that solution could have problems too and this is crystal clear for any trained lawyer half a century later. An externalization would have also implied the lack of any control on the role of the judicial body as an *information clearinghouse*, on the deliberative forms as well as the substance of the arguments put before it, on the decisive design of the standing rights and thus on the development of EU law as an "autonomous" legal order. In any case, this first hypothesis of delegation emerged in early negotiations is nowadays the mere evidence that an internal debate occurred. It was rapidly discarded and the historical eighth and final version, as said, was drafted in the classic open-ended language of compromise, calling for future "(A)ppropriate measures". But the debate on the proper judicial review system to be designed for the ECSC was simply in its infancy. Other relevant elements recently came, for instance, from the disclosure of internal French negotiations leading to the Conference of Paris of June 21, 1950, in direct continuity with the works leading to the Declaration of the 9 May. The same aforementioned diplomatic consultants and particularly Paul Reuter and Pierre Uri worked to refine the position of France, especially on the point of the institutional setting. Again, the design of the High Authority and thus the central executive branch and its powers were under the spotlight. But in light of the Declaration, which after all, without clarifying any detail, already called for some "means of appeal against the decisions of the Authority", the discussion was extended to a tentative complete envisaging of such means. In this context, the first proposal was a kind of division in three layers of the grounds for appeal and competent institutions. A first complaint was envisaged as being directly addressable to the High Authority, eventually forced to revise a contested decision and approve it by a majority of two thirds.[24] A second, consequent complaint was imagined as addressable, on grounds of economic *opportunity*, to a special "*haut collège arbitral*" (or "*collège des médiateurs*"[25]) of three members, chosen by the then highest personalities of the international legal order.[26] A third complaint, on grounds of breach of the law of the Treaty and abuse of power ("*contre les excès de pouvoirs*"),[27] was still imagined as addressable to the International Court of Justice of The Hague.[28]

This written evidence of internal discussion notwithstanding, the scenery had already changed and was simplified by the Conference of Paris. On June 21, 1950, Jean Monnet spoke of two appeal procedures in his overall presentation for the national delegations.[29] On June 24, 1950, a draft version of the ECSC Treaty, prepared by the French consultants, was circulated among the other representatives describing a mere double-track system in its Articles 7 and 8. The involvement of the International Court of Justice was discarded. A first instance of re-examination in front of the High Authority was again foreseen and again asking for a revision and an approval by a majority of two thirds, but with the decisive extension of the standing rights to private firms and companies—at least with regard to decisions and recommendations directly and individually applicable to their cases. An important clarification was also provided about the second foreseen layer of appeals. The original idea of an "*haut collège arbitral*" evolved in the form of a "*Cour d'arbitrage* ad hoc" to be addressed by States and, in restrictive cases, by private firms and companies on three different grounds ranging from the breach of the law of the Treaties (where judgements would have been binding *inter partes*) to the threats for the full-employment policies and the equilibrium of the balance of trade of single States (in such cases, the Court would have acted merely as a mediator and with recommendations to the High Authority).[30] It was also clear from this text that the French delegation envisaged such *Cour d'arbitrage* not as a permanently sitting body but as conveneable ad hoc, if necessary, and without professional components.

In this sense, the French position on the ECSC institutional setting, despite some uncertainties, was clear. The idea was, in coherence with the original inspiration of the French founding fathers, to make of the High Authority the real engine of the integration project, with important but not decisive nor central opportunities for the judicial review of its decisions. It was for the Authority to overcome, at least the physiology and the numerically large part of the possible *collective action* problems of the regulatory regime. An independent monitoring system was considered useful only in extreme, pathological cases. Therefore, the idea was not to establish a permanent Court for the new European Community but to use the two forms of international judicial review already known: either an externalization to the International Court of Justice or the ad hoc creations of arbitral bodies. According to the new documentary research, in this original position there were also direct comparative influences. In particular, it is reported[31] that Jean Monnet himself feared for possible obstacles or even a paralysis of the central leading activity of the High Authority coming from the role of "*gouvernement des juges*" of a hypothetical permanent judicial review body. In this, the critical remarks of the French master of comparative law Édouard Lambert were directly echoed: his book of some decades earlier, named "*Le gouvernement des juges et la lutte contre la législation sociale aux États-Unis*",[32] precisely denounced the pervasive role of the judicial review of legislation made by the US Supreme Court, and therefore the supposed perils of a stable and powerful judicial institution, in a (at the time) vaguely comparable *federal* system, and had a high resonance in the public debate.[33]

Interestingly enough, the positions of the other national delegations that also convened at the Conference of Paris were influenced by similarly based yet somehow opposite evaluations. While the French Planning Commissioner Monnet was worried about the possible obstacles to the full executive power of the High Authority, and thus for a dilution of the adequate regulatory capacity of the Community, all the other delegations showed concern for a potentially uncontrolled expansion of the common supranational executive branch.[34] In the case of the Belgian, Dutch and Luxembourgish delegations, representing the "small" states of the original Community, the major will was—not by chance—to create some kind of filter for possible pervasive decisions of the High Authority threatening the "vital interests"[35] of a state, or "incompatible with its sovereignty".[36] Again, the creation of a *Cour d'arbitrage*, composed of ministers of economic affairs of the Member states (and of a judge of the International Court of Justice as president),[37] was vaguely envisioned by these parties in form of a special monitoring system of clear political (and national) nature. But the real strong opposition to the original French plan came from the German delegation and, interestingly enough, from the American consultants involved in these preliminary works. Already in the context of a special *Comité des juristes* convened in the mid-July of 1950, composed of the legal experts of each delegation, and leading to the drafting of an important "*Mémorandum sur les institutions*",[38] the idea of designing a first layer of appeals by entrusting the High Authority of a second reading was definitely discarded. As it has been underlined,[39] the American consultants of the German delegation explicitly warned that forcing the High Authority always to reconsider its own decisions posed a severe threat to its prestige. A similar argument was used, *a fortiori*, for the proposal of the small states of a *Cour d'arbitrage* of political nature and directly linked to the nation states. Furthermore, the more the negotiations went on, the more the complex and plural institutional setting of the *communauté* was defined—at least in its basic structure and envisaging a *Conseil* and an *Assemblée* along with the supranational common executive—the more the case for a permanent, independent court became stronger. This position for a structured institution was championed, first of all, by Walter Hallstein, the German law professor who was the head of his delegation (and, as it is well known, would then become the president of the European Commission). In the prodromes of the second round of negotiations in Paris, he spoke directly of an expected "considerable edifying function" of a stable judicial body, "guardian of the objectivity of the High Authority".[40] Some years later, he also envisaged how such an institution would foster the necessary "'organic interpretation' also determined by the wide-reaching objective of the Common Market",[41] showing a significant dose of foresight. Already at the time of the negotiations, the German delegation had a clear vision "to create a Federal Court similar to the new German Bundesverfassungsgericht that would ensure the development of a European Rechtsstaat", and of the extent to which this, over time, "would create a European consciousness and thus play a role similar to the American Supreme Court".[42] Two main technical aspects were therefore strongly proposed: the need to prefigure the Court as holding exclusive rights to interpret the Treaty, to develop a uniform jurisprudence; and the opportunity to offer private litigants, initially mainly firms and associations of firms, the option to instigate proceedings before the Court to check the legality of the decisions and acts of the High Authority. This provided the double purpose of giving them a right to appeal against any supranational decision directly addressed to them (and on which national courts were incompetent) and at the same time, through the private action, "spurring the development of a uniform legal system".[43] An analogue position was taken by the American consultants of the US High Commissioner in Germany, John McCloy (himself a well-reputed lawyer), Robert Bowie, George Ball and David Bruce. They directly referred to their federal model, severely criticizing any idea of appeals based on the economic merits or the opportunity of a case. Furthermore, they pleaded for the institution of a strong permanent court, which, as in the explicit example of the US Supreme Court, could surely give the risk "*de voir les juges permanents réinterpréter, au fil des années, le traité et les intentions de ses auteurs*",[44] yet ensured better benefits, in particular relation to a consistent interpretation of a necessarily evolving common law.[45] On this basis, also given these direct "American" influences on Monnet, with which there was an open and informal dialogue,[46] an agreement was reached during the summer of 1950 by all the delegations. Despite a last tentative of the French delegation (in the Article 25 of the draft version of the ECSC Treaty of the November 8, 1950) to not design the role of the judges of the Court as full-time—with the parallel delegation to future agreements in the Council for an amendment—the final draft version of the November 27, without any further postponement, provided for a permanent and stable Court of Justice for the first European Community.

2.2 Design of Powers of the Court and National Influences

Comparative influences were not only visible in the original debate on the creation of the Court and what I called "the choice of the form" of institutionalization. The same phenomenon of internalization was very much present in the design of the powers of the Court. In fact, in the case of diplomatic negotiations, it is quite typical to use comparative material from national legal forms and international models that are already known. This material is employed as an inspiration for the construction of political positions, and sometimes for the reaffirmation and exportation of national solutions.[47] As noticed, the negotiations leading to the Treaty of Paris made no exception. In any case, I have also tried to show in the previous paragraph how, in the negotiations of the European Coal and Steel Community and its institutional setting, and in particular in the structuring of its judicial review system, the use of this external inspiration was complicated (and made more interesting in retrospective) by a series of factors. First, we now have both the documental/historiographic evidence to trace these debates as well as the political science heuristics to understand and highlight their rationale. Second, it is relevant for my purposes to underline that the inspirational trajectories of the different delegations were mixed and complicated, and ranged from the adherence to their own national experiences (as in the German case) to proposals based on critical visions of different external models (the US federal judicial architecture in particular, feared by Monnet and taken as a basis by the Germans and their American consultants), and of the different kinds of international organizations, with only political bodies or ad hoc arbitral tribunals. But the most interesting part of this retrospective comes when one approaches the actual forms taken by the Court of Justice of the ECSC, as eventually established, and the changes it underwent with the new negotiations leading to the Treaty of Rome and the new Communities. In fact, in these cases, the comparative conversation did not come simply as an exchange of statements of intent, or in the form of abstract constitutional engineering. On the contrary, it was directly substantiated in the actual powers exercised by the Court, its forms and its relationships with other actors and institutions.

2.2.1 *The "Administrative" Competences*

It is a commonplace in the literature to say that French judicial administrative forms strongly influenced the Court.[48] And even though the original French position on the proper nature of the Court was, as said, based on different premises, this is true for several reasons. But it is also commonplace to say that "the birth of European law" occurred "at the crossroads of legal traditions",[49] and an analysis of the powers conferred to the original versions of the Court of Justice will also substantiate this thesis in this particular "architectural" sector. It has been recently written, precisely by one of the 'new historians' studying the development of European law, that the best way "to characterise the new Court" in its original setting is to consider it "(E)ssentially (…) an innovative mix between at least three legal traditions".[50] In its real forms, it would be possible to identify "several features of a classic international Law, including the downside that there was no effective legal system of addressing the non-compliance of member states"; "important tasks of administrative law (…) (M)odelled on the French *Conseil d'Etat*", principally in the control of the legality of the actions of the High Authority; and finally, according to "the ambition of Hallstein and the German delegation to create a Federal Court similar to the American Supreme Court or the new *Bundesverfassungsgericht*", only met certain features with limited success of "what could be termed functional constitutionalism".[51] It is easy to understand—again retrospectively and therefore being familiar with the evolution that the European Court of Justice and the EU legal order had in the last decades—the basis for such a reconstruction. But apart from a relatively deceptive or non-technical use of the ever-problematic term "legal tradition",[52] this can only be accepted through a more specific contextualization while taking into account the single legal tools employed as well as their background.

Ironically, one can notice that in seeking the model upon which the Court of the ECSC had been based, the various governments and parliaments at the time entered into an interesting and symbolic multiple exercise of chauvinism—described at the time by the scholars as a "patriotic dispute".[53] In the French National Assembly, M. Coste-Floret, the *rapporteur* of the Foreign Affairs Commission, stated in a rather direct fashion: "If I wish to define this new organ in a single word, I would say that it is a *Conseil d'Etat*".[54] He based such an apodictic reconstruction on the observations that "(t)he principles of our French public law are the basis of the Protocol that regulates the working of the Court of Justice. The principles that govern the composition and working of the *Conseil d'Etat* have passed into the Treaty (...) The *avocats généraux* are essentially the Government commissaires of the *Conseil d'Etat* (...) In cases to be brought before the Court there is found in express terms in the Treaty the classic distinction in French public law between appeals of annulment and appeals in pleine jurisdiction".[55] This contention was also replicated by speakers in the *Conseil de la République*[56] and by the Report of the French Delegation.[57] Interestingly, a similar reference was made in the debates of the Luxembourgish Parliament, when it was stated that "(t)he Court of Justice is organised upon the model of the French *contentieux administratif* which in principle only controls the legality and not the advisability of a measure".[58] However, in the Belgian *Exposé des Motifs*[59] it was affirmed that the nature and the role of the Court were predominantly administrative (*de haute jurisdiction administrative*), but it was then described as "similar in many respects to that of our Conseil d'Etat", and also comparable, "in so far as it decides certain private interests, to the Mixed Arbitral Tribunals set up by the peace treaties in Belgium after the 1914 war".[60] In the Netherlands, we find it stated that many members of the Parliament "believed that the Court of the Coal and Steel Community to be nearly the same in competence as the Supreme Court of the United States"[61]; an impression coupled nonetheless with the skepticism of other representatives declaring "(t)he Court of Justice" as "considerably less important in the Community than ... the Netherlands' Supreme Court in our country".[62]

Apart from these general depictions, focusing on the question of the Court's powers (we will go through all the other mentioned organizational and structural aspects in the following chapters), I already explained how the logical turn to an administrative-like system of judicial review for the European Court came from the early negotiations after the Schuman

Declaration. In particular, it stemmed from the position of the German request to allow private firms to institute proceedings against decisions and acts of the High Authority against the fierce opposition, particularly from the Benelux representatives, who used the argumentation—which will become typical when discussing in some fundamental controversies, a decade after, the primacy and the direct effect of EC law[63]—according to which such a system would have undermined the authority of national courts and was, in any case, "unnecessary because the respective governments could bring the grievances of national firms to the High Authority and the Court".[64] While it is well known that the rise of the worldwide phenomenon of judicial review in the last two centuries was linked to the role of *arbitration*—in a general sense—played by courts in federal contexts,[65] in the at-the-time under-defined supranational context of the European Union the prevalence of a position similar to the Benelux countries' would have meant nothing more than the establishment of a real, technical system of *arbitration*, left to pure political will and thus to the political discretion of national governments. The idea to leave the door open to some private right of standing in front of the Court was based originally in the ECSC legal setting on the idea of the possibility of a direct contestation (as said, vaguely proposed also on grounds of *opportunity*) of the High Authority commerce-linked measures. But once such a proposal eventually managed to find its way and its proclamation—for the different reasons and with the various inspirations described—what were the real references for the design of the actual powers of the Court?

At a first glance, the German expansive request fit well with the nature of an administrative system of French derivation and thus with the establishment of specific tools for the defence of the private citizen against abuses of the public entity and of a right for firms to institute proceedings against decisions which the High Authority had directed towards them specifically. But the first provision defining the competence of the Court was Article 31 of the ECSC Treaty, with its general ambiguity. It contained a sort of broad institutional mandate, which is still in place today "to ensure the respect of law in the interpretation and application of the Treaty and the rules laid down for the implementation thereof": "*La Court assure le respect du droit dans l'interpretation et l'application du présent Traité et des regles d'exécution*". This rule has been famously described, also decades later and in the light of the evolution of the European law, as a "quizzical" one.[66] It seems to entrust the Court of Justice, and to have entrusted it already at the time, of that typical '*nomophylactic*' function of supreme courts and therefore to depict it a *φυλαξ*, a 'guardian', of the uniform interpretation of the law and coherence of the legal order to which it belongs. But in doing so, as it has been written, "its implication seems to be that the treaty assumes the existence of a Community legal order"[67]: it took it for granted, already at the time, remaining in any case "silent on the substance of such a legal order", in terms of its "sources of law or (...) legal principles", "relationship between Community rules and national legislation", definition of "any human right or civic liberty".[68] Such a detachment between the scope of the institutional mandate and the definition of the field of application of the Court was still striking for a commentator writing in the early 1990s as Tim Koopmans—who, again retrospectively, explained it for "historical reasons", linked to an idea of complete political integration on multiple levels which at the time seemed closer, and feasible in a relatively short time. It is suggested that it was in the diplomatic perspective of a rapid completion of full European political integration that Article 31 was sketched and suggested in the provisions of the Treaty. But this broad, supreme mandate was probably even odder for commentators in the 1950s since it somehow appeared *ex abrupto* after the negotiations. It can surely be traced back to the positions wondering for the Luxembourg Court a leading supervisional role similar to the US Supreme Court. However, it opened the path for some suggestive opposite interpretations in the first academic accounts.

Interestingly enough, the academic conversation soon after the enactment of the provision pointed to the articles' meaning as "open to several interpretations".[69] Again, this anticipated a fundamental debate solved only in the following decades in problematizing the question "whether the words "shall ensure the respect of law" are to be taken as meaning that the Court is to be guided by the general principles of international law" or rather "the phrase has a more restricted sense and merely implies that in the interpretation and application of the Treaty, the Court is to be bound by recognised rules of interpretation and that the application of the Treaty shall be subordinate to the law as set out in the Treaty thus interpreted".[70] It is particularly interesting to note that the perspective was seemingly inverted at the time. The use of all canonical rules of interpretation by the Court of Justice—an autonomous and discretionary use of them which would have led, in the following years, to the autonomization of European law itself[71]—was considered a "*restricted*" option vis-à-vis the subordination of the interpretation and application of Community law to the established general international law principles, even though the solution of leaving the Court free to refer to "general principles", or "its own notion of what is right and just", or "what the authors of a Treaty would have intended"[72] was already presented as "generally accepted".[73] The other option of interpretation, at least generically discussed in this sense, was the possibility to hold the mandate of Art. 31 "either to grant a power to the Court to interfere ex officio" at least in some kind of situation "where it finds one of the organs of the Community interpreting or applying the Treaty unlawfully",[74] or to merely define the Court's own duty in respect of interpretation and application after its jurisdiction had been invoked. This latter option, and the idea of Art. 31 as a mandate for the ordering of the Community only when requested by a litigant, were in any case invoked by the Treaty with little doubt and were after all very much in line with all the provisions following and specifying Art. 31.

After four Articles 32 (32, 32a, 32b, 32c) devoted to the composition of the new Court—in which in any case some direct traces of French influences were found already by the first commentators[75] (as said earlier, I will study this aspect in detail in the next chapter)—the ECSC Treaty structured the jurisdiction of the Court in terms of grants of rights of recourse and of prerequisites for appealing to it. As it is well known, these grants of rights were acknowledged originally, following the preparatory works, to the Member States, the Council, the High Authority, in a typical *arbitral* vein; but they were also acknowledged to enterprises and their associations and, on certain specific occasions,[76] also to individuals.

The first relevant category, also for my research, is the actions of annulment. Article 33, paragraph 1 of the ECSC Treaty allowed the Court to give judgements upon appeals brought by one of the Member States or by the Council seeking to have a decision or recommendation of the High Authority annulled. Moreover, its second sentence added the power of the Court, in certain specific circumstances, to take High Authority's assessment of the situation into consideration, resulting from the economic facts and conditions in the light of which the decision or recommendation was made. Furthermore, Article 33 paragraph 2 allowed enterprises and associations to bring appeals against decisions or recommendations "concerning" or "affecting" them, "under the same conditions" as appeals may be brought under par. 1. What were these conditions? Article 33 can be considered—and has been considered[77]—as an incorporation into the ECSC Treaty of the same four grounds of appeal that had for long, already at the time, been recognized as grounds upon which administrative acts may be challenged before the French administrative jurisdictions and particularly before and according to the *Conseil d'Etat*. It was, notoriously, the highest French administrative tribunal to progressively construct, *ex nihilo*, the essential parameters for the judicial control of the administrative activity in civil law countries—inspiring all the other similar jurisdictions of the Continent.[78] It was actually in the same year of the first negotiations leading to the Schuman Declaration and the ECSC Treaty that, with the grand arrêt 17 février 1950, n° 86949, *Ministre de l'agriculture c/Dame Lamotte*,[79] the *Conseil* structured the possibility of such a control as a "*principe général du droit*", a general principle of law. This coincidence is relevant, one can argue, since the definition itself of the possibility of such a control as a "general principle" is based on the traditional, stable definition of the grounds of appeal upon which administrative acts may be challenged, the definition of four relevant grounds in this respect, and the famous distinction between grounds involving the "external legality" of acts—the incompetence of the agent and the vices of form or procedure—and grounds involving the "internal legality" of acts—the violation of the law and the *détournement de pouvoir*.

Article 33 of the ECSC Treaty is the exact transposition of these traditional grounds as defined specifically by the *Conseil d'Etat* in the newborn supranational context. Not only: it is the transcript in supranational positive law of judge-made tools which were not written elsewhere in the positive law of the Member states, not in French law, nor even in other comparable environments like the Italian administrative law where, in any case, the relevant categories were inspired by the French prototypes but used to differ (at least in their labels) in several respects.[80] Art. 33 provided that "(T)he Court shall have jurisdiction in actions brought by a Member State or by the Council", or by "(U)ndertakings or the associations referred to in Article 48 ... under the same conditions" to have decisions or recommendations of the High Authority declared "void on grounds of lack of competence, infringement of an essential procedural requirement, infringement of this Treaty or of any rule of law relating to its application, or misuse of powers". The categories forged by the French administrative judges were therefore transposed in their exact wording in the text of the Treaty. But, as typical for such comparative transplants, especially in such an "upward" move to the new supranational context, there were some frictions even noted by early commentators at the time.

It is, in fact, to be noted that:

- The category of "*incompetence*", the term applied to actions performed by an agent outside the defined limits of his legal powers, has been naturally included. But although a notion of clear *ultra vires* action gives rise to no uncertainty, yet as the powers conferred upon the High Authority by the ECSC Treaty were in such wide terms, it was already submitted at the time that difficulties in particular cases may occur,[81] especially when considering that the Community, according to the original Article 2, was empowered by broad mandates to work for "economic expansion", for the "development of employment", the "raising of the standards of living in member countries".
- The category of "violation of substantial procedural requirements"—consisting of the omission or incomplete or irregular accomplishment of a substantive procedural requirement to which an act of administrative nature is subject, either by the law or by rules, or inherently from its nature—is of course strictly dependent on a definition of what procedural requirements are to be held substantial. In a newly born legal setting, this was questionable and open to developments. It was surely the case, in the original Community setting, of all the articles in which the Treaty required the High Authority to consult either the Council or the at-the-time Consultative Committee before it made a decision or recommendation. A failure to do so would have amounted to grounds for annulment. The same solution was generally agreed, since the beginning,[82] for the cases in which the advice had been taken but not been adequately considered. But this aspect is linked to a dimension that is extraneous surely for the French paradigmatic system and also to the majority of the other Member States and legal orders.[83] The transposition of these vices for the scrutiny of all "decisions and recommendations", also of "general" and therefore normative[84] nature could be problematic when such acts did not set out the reasons that prompted the High Authority to take them, as required by Art. 15, par. 1 of the Treaty. The motivation of acts of administrative nature was the physiology of all the national legal orders of the Community; not so for the motivation of acts of normative nature, that would have become, nonetheless, a specific features of the EC legal order.[85]
- The "violation of the law" occurs when an administrative decision, although taken according to the legal requirements, is nevertheless in contradiction—entirely or in part—to other provisions of the law.

In the transposition of this category, a conflict of interpretations arose upon the exact scope of these words once put in context with the ECSC, and therefore on the distinction of two different levels of norms, since the negotiations. The Treaty itself used the words "a violation of the Treaty and of any rule of law concerning its application": "*violation du Traité ou de toute règle de droit relative à son application*". Accordingly, the Report of the French Delegation made the same expansive vein explicit, stating that "(I)t was necessary to add to the violation of the terms of the Treaty itself, violation of rules made for its application and, if the case should occur, other relevant texts, such as international conventions, as well as the general principles of law. All of these are covered by the wording in article 33".[86] But according to some early commentators from a common law background, it was "submitted that the strict wording of sentence 1 in Art. 33 does not appear to support the wide meaning given to it by the French delegation, for reference is made in the sentence only to "the Treaty" and the additional rules of law mentioned are only those concerning the Treaty's application—and thus one must assume that other rules of law are to be excluded"[87]; while for some others the transposition should have gone so far to design a "Court, following the practice of the French Conseil d'Etat, ... able to annul a decision not only for a violation of the letter of the Treaty," but equally for a breach of its "spirit".[88]

- The "*détournement de pouvoir*" has been historically defined as occurring when an agent performs an act for a purpose other than that which was presupposed when the related power was granted. Therefore, this vice of an administrative act has been historically based in its French judge-made definition on the "turning away" of a necessarily discretionary power from its correct use, not directly violating any provision of the law, but "twisting—*détourner*—a legal power from the purpose for which it has been granted to make it serve ends that were not intended".[89] In fact, this was the line that Prof. Reuter followed when he stated in the aftermath of the approval that "under this definition will fall those acts which aim at a purely personal or national interest, when the Treaty requires that the act must be in the common interest of the Community".[90] In its report, the French Delegation also stated that "the notion of *détournement de pouvoir*, in particular, has been clearly understood and willingly—*facilement*—accepted by our foreign partners".[91]

This could be the case, but the practice of the first cases brought at the Court in the first years of activity clearly shows a certain degree of friction in the transposition, and the risk of a category "lost in translation" in the supranational context. The applicants—especially in the form of private companies and associations—were somehow prompted to expand the conception of "*détournement*", since only by proving such misuse of powers they were admitted to opposing regulatory measures. And, not by chance, such an expansive reading particularly came about by Italian plaintiffs. For instance, in the case 2/54,[92] the representative of the Italian Government declared that "*(I)l y a toujours détournement de pouvoir lorsque la Haute Autorité contrevient au Traité dans l'exercice du pouvoir qu'il lui confère*" (Rec. 1, p. 21); in the subsequent case 3/54,[93] the Italian plaintiff, the Associazione Industrie Siderurgiche Italiane (ASSIDER), presented the "*injustice manifeste*" and the "*illogisme*" of the opposed decision of the Authority as cases of *détournement* of its *pouvoir*. This can be explained, in comparative terms, if one observes the different development of the judge-made grounds of administrative litigation in the Italian legal order. The local category of "*sviamento di potere*", literally corresponding to the *détournement*, is nothing more than one of the different modalities of the "*eccesso di potere*", which includes the "*injustice manifeste*" and the "*incohérence manifeste*" as well. Therfore, within the Italian context, the *eccesso di potere* is an autonomous ground of appeal, including *détournement* and others *species*, alongside the basic "*incompetenza*" and "*violazione di legge*"; in France, it is a general concept including all the four vices transposed in the European context.[94]

The events of the construction of Article 33 clearly show the phenomenon of upward transfer from national forms to supranational powers, while additionally explaining how the image and the practice of the European Court of Justice as an inherently "comparative" Court—in terms of its activity and its methodology[95]—is also firmly based on the original aspects of the structure and the organization of the Court and is often a consequence of them. In this respect, the grounds of appeal of Art. 33 are a perfect example, particularly in the interpretation of the *détournement de pouvoir*. In fact, after the structuring of the powers of the Court, and the design of ground of appeal for the annulment actions reminiscent of the French paradigm, it was noted that the Court had to quickly face an interpretative "attack" to these categories based on different national legal cultural premises. Consequently, the response of the Court was, in the case 3/54 itself, an exhaustive analysis made by the Advocate General Maurice Lagrange of the concept of *détournement de pouvoir* in all six Member States, anticipated by the clear statement of intention according to which "*(L)a notion de détournement de pouvoir n'a évidemment pas été inventée par les auteurs du Traité et, pour essayer de se former une opinion sur ce que doit être le détournement de pouvoir dans l'application du Traité, opinion nécessairement révisable d'ailleurs et perfectible au fur et à mesure des développements de la jurisprudence, il faut d'abord savoir ce qui en est dans le droit respectif de nos six pays*", and opposing a strict "Franco-Beneluxienne"[96] conceptualization to the similar but not overlapping Italian and German interpretations. In that particular case the Court had no reason to take a side in the interpretative *querelle*: but, already in the subsequent case 6/54,[97] it used the formula "*(E)lle aurait usé de ses pouvoirs (...) dans un but autre que celui en vue duquel ceux-ci lui ont été conférés*", therefore adhering to the "Franco-Beneluxienne" concept and thus to the opinions according to which "*vouloir maintenant, dans le droit de la Communauté, ranger sous la rubrique du détournement de pouvoir des cas qui relèvent en France du moyen de violation de la loi, équivaudrait à écarter délibérément la volonté des auteurs du Traité quant à l'étendue des pouvoirs de contrôle conférés par eux à la Cour*"[98] (a doctrinal opinion to which Lagrange made explicit reference in its conclusions in the case 3/54). The solution of the specific case of the *détournement* was also confirmed again some years later in the case 15/57[99]; but, more importantly, the method of the judicial comparative interpretation, prompted by the original inherently comparatively influenced structure of powers of the Court, became more and more used also to fill the gaps in the institutional design of the Treaty,[100] or to define other autonomous concepts of European law.[101]

In any case, Article 33 was not the only example of this hybrid genetic nature of the powers of the newborn Court. A further example of the extent to which "French procedural law has been copied"[102] was found and stigmatized with such explicit terms by the early commentators in the Treaty's subsequent Article 34. Following an annulment of a decision or recommendation of the High Authority, that Authority is itself required to take the measures to carry out the decision of annulment, "so that its duty is in no way superseded by the Court".[103] Also in here, the Report of the French Delegation pointed out that the solution was directly taken from the formula of the *Conseil d'Etat* so that the High Authority, as any public administration in that legal system, was "put back, as far as possible … into the situation where it would have been if the annulled decision had not been passed".[104] But also the creation of a procedure of plenary appeal—"*de pleine juridiction*"—alongside the actions for annulment in which the European judge would exercise "all his customary judicial powers",[105] and therefore would be free to examine every aspect of the case—whether of "law" or "fact"—and would be competent to rule on the monetary issues of the litigation (*e.g.* through an award of damages) was considered to be "borrowed from French administrative law".[106] Of course, the reference was to cases in which the Court acts in matters of quasi-contractual (Aquilian) or noncontractual liability, "which in France, when applied to administrative actions, means liability of public authorities *(la responsabilité de la puissance publique)*".[107] The same Article 40, in providing for compensation in case of injury caused during the delivery of tasks based on the Treaty by the Community, was based on the distinction rooted in French administrative law between a fault of service—*faute de service*—and personal fault—*faute personelle*—and therefore to the "*assez tenue, assez délicate à faire*"[108] distinction between faults to be imputed to the agent and those to be imputed to the administration. Its two first paragraphs precisely mirrored such a traditional distinction.[109] However, these three examples of division of labour between the Court and the administrative authority could still be considered the results of the adoption of a system of administrative jurisdiction of every sort. The phenomenon of upward transfer of national judicial forms in the supranational setting is even more evident when the crucial position of the preliminary reference procedure is taken into account.

2.2.2 Transformation of the Preliminary Reference Procedure

What is more relevant to my purpose is, in fact, the other great example of upward fertilization of the structure of the European Court's powers: the evolution of the preliminary reference procedure. The fundamental importance of this instrument for the construction of the European legal (and political)[110] architecture is well known nowadays. It has been used more and more throughout the years whenever a national court or tribunal refers a question of European law to the European Court of Justice for a preliminary ruling so as to enable the national court, upon receiving that ruling, to decide the case before it. Questions of EU law arise in cases before the courts of different Member States. The function of such a clever procedural tool is to ensure uniform interpretation and validity of EU law across all the Member States. It is well known that already Alexis de Tocqueville, in his magisterial study on the construction of a federal "Democracy in America", highlighted that "The object of the creation of a Federal tribunal was to prevent the courts of the States from deciding questions affecting the national interests in their own department, and so to form a uniform body of jurisprudence for the interpretation of the laws of the Union. This end would not have been accomplished if the courts of the several States had been competent to decide upon cases in their separate capacities from which they were obliged to abstain as Federal tribunals".[111] In this sense, the European solution for a correct and uniform application of a common law has been special, and primarily based on the institute I am discussing: the CJEU itself characterizes the preliminary reference procedure as constructed around the co-operation between national courts and Luxembourg.[112] However, it is the CJEU that controls this co-operation and sets its terms. In its 'dialogue' with national courts, it has the upper hand and has succeeded in co-opting national courts into an EU federal judicial system, at the same time placing the individuals, European citizens, in the relevant position of monitors and enforcers of Community obligations vis-à-vis the Member States (according to the so called the "Private-Attorney-General Model").[113] In this respect, scholars have written of an "ingenious" construction, leading to a fundamental "habit of obedience" in Member States.[114] In the fifth chapter, I will further discuss the evolution of this mechanism and these features, particularly relating to certain specific structural and organizational aspects of the dialogical relationship it creates between the European Court and national judges.

But the analysis of the preliminary reference procedure is also important in this research concerning its genetic moment and its infancy. The procedural tool has been particularly important in strengthening the role of the European Court of Justice as a veritable supreme court of the supranational organization, according to the perspective and political will of certain delegations. However, its original role in the ECSC Treaty was different from what it became in the subsequent Treaty of Rome, and thus in the context of the European Economic Community legal order. Article 41 of the ECSC Treaty laid down that only the newborn European Court was competent ("shall have sole jurisdiction") to decide as a preliminary question upon the validity of the "*délibérations*" of the High Authority and the Council in cases where a controversy brought before a national tribunal had put that validity into issue. Interestingly enough, it is possible to say that it was "not created to satisfy German demands for a uniform interpretation of European law",[115] as the principle of legality of Article 3 and Article 31 itself would have demanded. Instead, proposed again by Maurice Lagrange as head of the French delegation, the article had the simple primary purpose of clarifying the division of labour between national courts and the new European Court in addition to their spaces of jurisdiction.

In fact, what is evident for today's analyst is the "restrictive character"[116] of the provision, a character which retrospectively, is considered "surprising" by scholars.[117] It structured an exclusive competence of the Court, "*en vue d'éviter que les juridictions nationales se prononcent dans des questions mettant en cause la Communauté*",[118] on matters of *validity* of acts of the supranational institutions. But it completely omitted, within the "*questions mettant en cause la Communauté*", the problem of the allocation of the competence of *interpretation* of European law. The study of the preliminary works for the ECSC Treaty shows how the provision of Art. 41 was an addition made to its "Chapter IV—The Court" as a completion of Article 40, which—as previously stated—in the context of the discipline for the disputes arising from the fault of the agents of the Community, was all devoted to the allocation of jurisdiction between the European Court and "national courts of tribunal".[119] In this vein, Article 40 provided that "the Court shall have jurisdiction to order pecuniary reparation from the Community, on application by the injured party, to make good any injury caused in carrying out this Treaty by a wrongful act or omission on the part of the Community in the performance of its functions" (par. 1); that "(T)he Court shall also have jurisdiction to order the Community to make good any injury caused by a personal wrong by a servant of the Community in the performance of his duties", according to the Staff Regulations or the Conditions of Employment applicable to them (par. 2); and, finally, that "(A)ll other disputes between the Community and persons other than its servants to which the provisions of this Treaty or the rules laid down for the implementation thereof do not apply shall be brought before national courts or tribunals" (par. 3). This precise allocation was entirely based on the principle according to which the European Court "*connaît de tout ce qui concerne l'application du traité et ne connaît que de cela*".[120] And that same rationale—a strict *actio finium regundorum* between the jurisdiction of the European Court and of the national tribunals to avoid conflicts of jurisdiction—was at the basis of the prototypical form of preliminary reference procedure. That is, the demand was to prevent that national courts could take over the task of ruling on the *validity* of supranational measures and therefore to declare these latter void without the possibility of the supranational judicial arm to opine.

Thus, a certain degree of centralization was already present in the ECSC Treaty; but it did not include, and probably it did not need, a centralization of the '*nomophylactic*' function of interpretation of European law to boost its uniformity and the coherence of the legal order. As it is known, this decisive element was added by the Treaty of Rome in the construction of the "new" European Court of Justice of the European Economic Community. But here again, a closer look into the dynamics of this construction can also give us a new perspective on the relative influences in coherence with the purposes of the present research. Among the scholars, there is little doubt on the institutional continuity between the Court of the European Coal and Steel Community of the first part of the 1950s and the subsequent common judicial arm of the new Communities born with the Treaties of Rome of 1957. It was explicitly decided, following the creation of the European Economic Community and EURATOM, that a single court would have dealt with legal disputes arising under all three Communities[121] though the methods of taking legal action differed in each one.[122] And it was the same Court, already established in Luxembourg, in the same location and with the same personnel, by force of the Treaty of Paris, to take over the tasks and the powers prescribed by the new intergovernmental agreements.[123] However, such continuity did not come as an obvious result. For the second time in quick succession, it was by no means clear at the beginning of a round of diplomatic negotiations (this time, leading to the Treaties of Rome) how the institutional structure of the two communities would look like and, again, "whether it would include a Court".[124] In fact, in its first years, the European Court's activity was surely characterized, as described, by certain peculiar aspects of scientific interest. But its activity was unremarkable in quantitative terms considering the small caseload—the Court only pronounced 27 judgements and almost all concerned the annulment of decisions under articles 33 and 35—and the weakness of article 41, and was not politically visible or "marked by any pronounced activism".[125] But it is important to note that—as a constant feature in the history of European integration, made up of a series of developmental stages and setbacks—the negotiations started not many months after the defeat of the European Defence Community Treaty in the French National Assembly, and also that, since a team of renowned lawyers was involved, certain Court's moves to gradually strengthen "some of the constitutional features"[126] of the Treaty of Paris did not go unnoticed among the diplomatic parts. This happened with the efforts to make it easier for private litigants to go to Court by blurring the distinction between general decisions and those directed towards a particular firm[127]; and concerned the already clear twist according to which—while it had been expected that the Court should control the High Authority—the weakness of the latter meant that it focused instead on protecting the Community against the transgressions of the member states.[128] Therefore, there was common consciousness among the six governments that a new step in the field of European integration would have to use economic leverage again; and diplomats were all wary of unduly ambitious political schemes. But still, there were different perspectives on how to frame the legal and institutional setting. This new irresolution was first of all reflected in the Spaak Report, which said relatively little on the institutional aspects of the project.[129] But it was also made clear by the confrontation—well documented by the new historical research[130]—between the French delegation, which was not openly able to support "a connection between the ECSC assembly and court, and the two projected Communities",[131] due to the widespread internal skepticism with regard to supranational institutions in the national legislature, and the other five teams, "dominated by pro-Europeans",[132] representing governments that to a varying degree wished to maintain a minimum of political coherence among the various efforts of European integration and considered the institutional infrastructure as an essential way to accomplish this. In a note submitted to the head of delegations on September 11, 1956, the proposal to altogether remove the court came onto the table again by the French *Conseiller politique* of the Foreign Minister George Vedel. In his view, most legal cases in the new Communities would have been technical in nature, and were better suited for submission to a Court of Arbitrage constituted by professional experts.[133] But a fierce German high-level internal debate has also been reported. According to the documentary evidence,[134] the local Ministry of Economics wanted to remove the Court and the Assembly from the European institutional edifice as well, though the Foreign Ministry rejected this view and argued that the ECJ was indispensable as a stabilizer of the Communities.

The lack of consensus on the destiny of the ECJ meant that it was removed from the agenda of the meeting of the head of delegations in October 1956 and such disagreement on the institutional system was only overtaken after the meeting between German Chancellor Konrad Adenauer and French Prime Minister Guy Mollet in November 1956. Having been granted important economic concessions and in the spirit of the general Franco-German agreement to bring the negotiations to a successful end, the French government accepted the inclusion of the Court and the Assembly among the institutions of the new communities as long as these were not strengthened by gaining any new competences—thus endangering the ratification of the treaties in the National Assembly.[135] But here was the point: after the emergence of such common general political will, with France eventually accepting one Assembly and one Court to be shared by all three Communities—also emphasizing in this respect the aspect of continuity—on the condition that the powers of these two institutions were not strengthened, the turn was then for the specialized *Groupe de rédaction*, established in 1956, to draft the Treaties and forge the relative institutional clauses translating into positive commands of supranational law this compromise. It is reported that, while all of the major institutional questions were decided at the political level and by the heads of delegation, the Committee was given a relatively free hand with regard to the ECJ.[136] Moreover, we know that it was not only composed of leading jurists from each of the European jurisdictions, with direct and autonomous knowledge in the field resulting from the different background experiences, but also—as one can historically learn from the precious Pierre Pescatore's direct written testimony[137]—composed in such a way to reflect the intergovernmental positions—so that "all members except the French wanted to push as far as they possibly could in the direction of strong European institutions",[138] including in this promotion the "constitutional features of the Court".[139]

This precious and peculiar combination resulted in an interesting compromise. In some respects, in delineating the new institutional setting, the Committee even curbed the competences of the ECJ, negating the doctrinal developments of the early 1950s. In particular, the widened access of private litigants that the ECJ had contributed to in its previous case law[140] was compressed in the new Article 173,[141] reaffirming the need for an optimization of the sources of controversies—thus writing a new important chapter of a long story still debated up to recent times.[142] However, it is possible to say that overall the *Groupe* strengthened the Court's powers by not meeting the conditions agreed with the French delegation for its approval, stressing the *constitutional* features of the supranational judicial competences, and being influenced by the decisive example coming from a national legal culture. The most important novelty stemming from the new draft was the development of the system of preliminary references from national courts to the European Court of Justice, going well beyond the narrow construction of Article 41 of the Treaty of Paris and the division of labour and jurisdiction in hearing of the *validity* of supranational acts. In fact, Article 177 of the Treaty of Rome of the European Economic Community came to include the new competence of the Court to rule on the *interpretation* of European law that has proved to be decisive for the construction of the European constitutional architecture in the following decades. As it is well known, Article 177 was not an invitation to the Court of Luxembourg to evaluate whether national law conflicted with European law, nor was it to evaluate the application of any resulting national or supranational law directly to the facts of a case in front of a judge. How to apply national law was explicitly beyond the jurisdiction of the Court, even if this was precisely how the article would eventually be used.[143] Instead, Article 177 was designed for the aforementioned '*nomophylactic*' function to make sure that next to a centralization of the competence to rule on its validity, the interpretation of European law could become uniform throughout the Community through a specific tool. This was not achieved and not politically achievable by structuring the European Court as an appellate jurisdiction in hierarchical relationship with the national tribunals (which is the typical position of such '*nomophylactic*' bodies).

However, from a historical perspective, new research reveals how a solution and a proper tool were found in the arsenal of the internal legal cultures of the continent. It is reported in both old and recent sources[144] that the proposal for the enlargement of the scope of Article 177 EEC, in relation to Article 41 ECSC, came in fact from Nicola Catalano, the Italian *Avvocato dello stato*, and later judge at the European Court itself, who was sitting in the *Groupe* representing the Italian Republic together with the President and diplomat Roberto Ducci. He produced in the *Groupe de rédaction* the text proposing a preliminary ruling mechanism which also extended to questions of interpretation. This is now commonly and explicitly linked to the fact that he already "knew preliminary references from the Italian Constitutional system",[145] on which he relied. Perfect parallelism with a national paradigm can be made, similar to the one made on the grounds of the action of annulment. It is perhaps less explicit, but once one draws attention to the temporal contingencies, it is possible to argue that there is a likely convergence of rationales. The Italian Constitutional Court started its functions a few months before the negotiations at the castle of Val Duchesse in 1956; but its structure and powers were already discussed and defined some years before with the Constitutional Law n. 1 of 1948 and with the ordinary Law n. 87 of 1953. With these instruments, in the wake of the explosion of the phenomenon of the constitutional adjudication in the aftermath of Second World War,[146] a so-called *mixed* system of constitutional jurisdiction was established, well-debated in the Italian Constitutional Assembly[147] and then in the legal academia since its inception,[148] and therefore well known in its procedural shrewdness by Catalano. The Italian Republic had the willingness to create a system of adjudication in which ordinary national laws could be confronted and censored for their coherence with a hierarchically superior norm of constitutional nature. For doing so, two were the main comparative historical models at the time: the so-called *diffuse* model traditionally evolved in the United States of America already in the nineteenth century, a context in which every ordinary judge can rule on the constitutionality of a norm brought before her and eventually disapply it (and in which the importance and the prescriptivity of such judgement augment with the importance of the judge, until the final stage of the Supreme Court)[149]; and a so-called *centralized* model, according to the Kelsenian scheme of the 1920s[150]—a context in which a central, unique and specialized court has the monopoly over the judgements of constitutional adjudication and is directly reached by different categories of claimants according to special rules on their standing rights. But, as it is well known today, Italy as well as Germany—the two prominent examples of the new wave of the judicial review after the war—established so-called *mixed* models, particularly regarding the issue of access to the constitutional adjudicative body. Focusing on the solution offered by the Italian Law n. 87 of 1953, one notes that a central, unique and specialized Constitutional Court was set up with the monopoly over the judgements of constitutional adjudication; but every single judge, every jurisdiction, every *court or tribunal* of the Italian legal order was entrusted with the power to hear a question on the constitutionality of a law from the parties of the case or to raise it autonomously, and, after having evaluated on the relevance and the "not manifestly unfoundedness" of the question, to suspend the judgement before itself and send the question to the specialized Court. As it is well known, this system was iconically labelled before its actual implementation by Calamandrei, a major jurist who worked directly on the point in the Italian Constituent Assembly, as the "service of antechamber" of the Constitutional Court—making every ordinary judge a "porter" of this latter.[151] Therefore, since the beginning, it was directly meant as the construction of an *incidental* system of control on the compatibility between two different layers of norms, by including an active role of both the ordinary judges—before and after the constitutional judgement—and specialized ones. It is therefore not a surprise that this system has also prompted the construction, by the Italian Constitutional Court, of special techniques of interpretation and judgements not confined merely to the binary option of upholding a norm or striking it down for constitutional reasons (according to the Kelsenian paradigm of the "negative legislator").[152] It has fed a context of peculiar "dialogue" between the specialized Court of constitutional adjudication and the judges of single, concrete cases, in which, for instance, questions of constitutionality are often discarded if the norms under scrutiny can be then interpreted and applied as the Court suggests in the same judgements of dismissal (so-called "*sentenze interpretative di rigetto*").[153]

The transformation of the European preliminary ruling in Article 177 of the Treaty of Rome was based on the same dynamics. Catalano himself, in his academic writings of the early 1960s, explicitly recognizes such powerful inspiration drawn from incidental systems of constitutionality control.[154] The national judge, in the original model of the ECSC Treaty, had a rather limited "European mandate"[155]: it was nothing more than a simple *paper-pusher* who necessarily had to strip herself of the competence to rule on the validity of supranational acts in order to prevent conflicts of jurisdiction. In this perspective, the new system of the Treaty of Rome designed something new and different from the pure alternative between the competence of two different bodies (as in the *pure* systems of constitutional adjudication). The judge became involved in a much more complex and fruitful relationship built around the task of *interpretation* of European laws. The model structured a *mixed* system for such an interpretative enterprise. The ordinary judge of every national jurisdiction was provided with a direct mandate to hear and interpret questions of European law. Only in cases of serious doubts on the interpretation was the mechanism of centralization to be activated through the procedural tools of a preliminary cognition on the matter by the judge, a conditioned reference, and an *incidental* judgement issued by the specialized Court. This is precisely the essence of a mixed system of constitutional adjudication such as the Italian model, which today we know was discussed by the drafters of the Treaty following the input of Catalano. The much-discussed label of the national judge as "European judge" *par excellence*, as the natural judge of European law,[156] is therefore derived by the inherent rationale of such a *mixed* system of adjudication and reminiscent of the Calamandrei's idea of a "service of antechamber" for a central Court (actually, it is understandable as a development of that already-established model). It is on this solid basis that the famous dynamics of "self-empowerement" of both national and supranational judge, as described by Weiler,[157] were constructed. The era of the Court's "incremental search for a role"[158] came to an end, and started the glorious days of the Court. As it is well known, the national judges, especially in tribunals of first instance,[159] increasingly sought a direct dialogue with the European Court of Justice over the interpretation of European law—empowering it but simultaneously entrusting themselves with an indirect power of judicial review and power of adjudication of constitutional significance.

2.3 Different Perspective, Same Dynamics: The Establishment of the Doctrines of Primacy and Direct Effect

Apart from all the previously mentioned fundamental procedural devices, another substantial "efficient secret"[160] in the construction of this dialogical relationship was, of course, the establishment of the judicial doctrines of primacy and direct effect.[161] I am not talking here, in strict terms, of the design of conferred powers of the Court or generally of its structure and organization. But I am referring, as it is well known, to principles that are believed to constitute the foundation of the effectiveness of the Community legal order, to play the role of pillars of its constitutional nature, to even embody the actual transfer of constitutional power to Europe.[162] They were the building blocks on which the powers of the European Court—and particularly the just discussed preliminary reference power—were firmly constructed. Therefore, in concluding this chapter, it is interesting to note that in the establishment of decisive functional principles such as primacy and direct effect, which shaped European law in the next decades, a tribute was again paid to the decisive interplay between the original constitutional settings of the national Member States and the incipient forms of the supranational architecture.[163] Albeit not in connection to positivized competences of the Court, in this case one can also see how the constitutional structures of the Member States have decisively informed the ECJ's powers. Therefore, I will discuss the point to illustrate another relevant phenomenon of upward fertilization that is useful for reflecting on the idea of *mimetic* evolution of the supranational setting.

Historical research in the last years was devoted to the unexplored "complexity and mutuality between national constitutional reform 'towards' Europe and the development of European integration in the 1950s".[164] With increasing attention, some scholars focus on how the first constitutional debates internal to the Member States shaped, and produced (through the mentioned upward transfer of forms and problems), the construction of the original European legal system. This is already reflected in the Italian debates on a mixed system of constitutional adjudication, transferred as seen, *mutatis mutandis*, in the negotiations at the castle of Val Duchesse of 1956 and in the drafting of the new Article 177 of the Treaty of Rome from the basis of Article 41 of the ECSC Treaty.

But according to some authors,[165] it is, even more, the case of Dutch constitutional reforms discussed and implemented between 1950 and 1956. These were part of the set of constitutional reforms that were put in place, in different degrees, across all the six Member States of the original European Communities to comply with the new challenges of the relationship between legal orders. Provisions on the interaction between the national and international legal orders were to be found in the new constitutions of France, Germany and Italy. For example, the German *Grundgesetz* authorized the federal state to transfer sovereign powers to (similarly democratic) international organizations, whereas the French 1946 constitution and the Italian 1947 constitution stated that national sovereignty could be limited when needed (generally) for the international organization and defence of peace. Separately, Belgium and Luxembourg undertook similar constitutional reforms aimed at preparing their national constitutions for the expansion of international and European co-operation.[166] However, in this context, only the Netherlands chose to recognize direct importance and authority to cogent international law and did so in light of an interesting, particularly explicit and timely debate. The Dutch 1953 constitutional reform "not only fully authorised the transfer of legislative, administrative and judicial competences to international organizations",[167] as directly or indirectly done by all the other Members; but, driven by the same reading of the Dutch legal tradition that inspired the discussions on sovereignty and the transfer of competences, the reform also produced provisions on the primacy and direct effect of international law that went far beyond the constitutions of other European countries—so to be considered as the factor which "paved the way for an early wave of preliminary references (Article 177 EEC) to the European Court of Justice".[168]

This argument is not merely the result, as in other cases, of a deductive analysis of the relevant "formants".[169] It is also supported, one could say, by empirical data. The historical research on the Dutch reform not only tells us how and to what extent—in one of the only six original Member States—the theoretical and practical problems inherent in recognition of primacy and direct effect of international law were abundantly discussed in a way that was undoubtedly well-known years later by the first European Court's judges. It also highlights how debates of the early 1950s shaped the "constitutional practice"[170] of the following years since eight of the first eleven referrals to the European Court of Justice came precisely from the Netherlands.

In what terms was this seminal debate undertaken? Essentially, it already ran parallel to the ECSC negotiations and the initiatives for a European Defence Community (EDC) and a European Political Community (EPC). A first Dutch "Committee concerning the co-operation between government and parliament with regard to foreign affairs" (the so-called "Van Eysinga Committee") was established in The Hague in May 1950, "ten days after the French foreign minister, Robert Schuman, announced his plans for a new European Coal and Steel Community (ECSC)",[171] and presented its report in July 1951. This was the first of three bodies expected to recommend comprehensive constitutional reforms. After a recent debacle over a Benelux treaty in 1949 on the harmonization of duties, with the Committee's works a clarification of the role of the parliament in Dutch foreign policy formation was sought and eventually found in a modernization of the relevant constitutional clauses and recalibration of institutional powers.[172] A collateral debate went on in a second constitutional committee active in 1950, the "Van Schaik Committee" (presided over by the minister for constitutional affairs J. R. H. van Schaik), which was responsible for a more general modernization of the nineteenth-century Dutch constitution. This focused on the proposal of a new constitutional provision on international organizations explicitly stating that certain competences could be transferred to "organizations of international law". In particular, the debate was between scholars who argued for the need for such explicit clause and those who, on the contrary and from the perspective of legal precedent, thought that a constitutional clause was not necessary for the transfer of competences to international organizations. This last position was based on a historical reading of the Dutch legal tradition. Such transfers with no explicit constitutional mandate were found to have already taken place in the early nineteenth century such as in the empowerment of the 1816 Central Commission for the Navigation of the Rhine with judicial authority on a river crucial for Dutch trade, or the installation of the Permanent Court of Arbitration in 1899. In those cases, a constitutional provision was not found to be needed. The same applied to the transfer of often far-reaching decision-making authority to organizations such as the UN Security Council after 1945. These precedents were supported by the fact that earlier proposals for constitutional regulation of such transfers had never found much support. In the early twentieth century, Dutch constitutional committees had discussed the constitutionality of these transfers and although a special constitutional provision had been proposed in 1912, no reform followed. The government eventually included the Van Schaik proposal for a provision on the transfer of competences in its constitutional amendment bill, recognizing both the dramatic rise in international co-operation and symbolic value.

What is remarkable is that, driven by the same aforementioned historical reading of the Dutch legal tradition that inspired the discussions on sovereignty and the transfer of competences, the constitutional reform of 1953 also produced direct provisions on the primacy and direct effect of international law that went far beyond the constitutions of other European countries. Interestingly, in the Van Eysinga Committee, these were merely introduced as a side issue to the main question about the new ratification procedure. It was argued in the same vein as the general debate that both primacy and direct effect were already part of Dutch legal practice, pointing to the fact that in 1906 the Hoge Raad (the Supreme Court of the Netherlands) had acknowledged that international law could bind individuals. This step was also taken in other jurisdictions including in Belgium in 1925.[173] Therefore, having already touched the problem of the "direct effect" of international provisions, the Hoge Raad did not (at the time) settle the question of whether international law had *primacy* over conflicting national law. This question would be in any case explicitly disputed in the inter-war period. For instance, as Van Leeuwen has pointed, this happened in the 1937 annual meeting of the Dutch lawyers association (Nederlandse Juristenvereniging: NJV) and how "only a small majority of prominent legal scholars voted in favour of the proposition that treaty law 'binding in the national sphere' should be given priority over national law whether antecedent or subsequent".[174] From its part, the Hoge Raad avoided explicitly adjudicating on the matter and tried to "interpret away" any possible conflict between treaty law and posterior national legislation.[175] However, it is relevant to notice that its "temporary partner", the *High Court on Special Justice Concerning the Second World War* (*Bijzondere raad van cassatie*), made a clear move recognizing the supremacy of international law in a 1949 ruling.[176] Despite the split doctrinal opinion and the uncertain practice, the Van Eysinga Committee, in the person of its President, kept on arguing that the only purpose of its 1950 proposal was to lay down what had already been settled in Dutch doctrine.

After a first round of discussions, the new constitutional provision on primacy still had the support of a large majority of both the Van Eysinga Committee and the Van Schaik Committee, but the government decided to leave the contested clause out of its constitutional amendment bill—fearing that the legislative would be powerless against a judicial interpretation of a treaty which might not always fit the intended results of the original negotiations. Regardless, such a primacy clause was reintroduced in an amendment to the government bill by P. J. S. Serrarens, leader at the time of the Dutch European Movement who would also soon become Dutch judge at the ECJ in Luxembourg; and, labelled precisely as "Serrarens amendment", defended primarily as a political choice. Serrarens pointed out the fact that earlier frameworks of international co-operation had failed precisely for the lack of proper enforcement more than for bad intention or bad design. The primacy of treaty law would also apply to the decisions of international organizations; and by this Serrarens and his fellow MPs were open in their desire to prompt, by an explicit national constitutional provision introducing the possibility of enforcing these decisions, a first step in strengthening international regimes and particularly the incipient European communities.[177] An explicit debate followed, even pointing to the optimal institutional allocation of powers for a more uniform application of international law. Opponents to the amendment objected to the consequences of the amendment for the balance of powers in the Dutch system and argued that the legislature, not the courts, would be the best guarantee of a consistent application of international law, as it met and co-ordinated regularly with its international counterparts. Serrarens responded with the fear that legislatures might still ultimately choose to defend national interests whereas courts were, in theory, impartial and rejected comparisons with the clause on constitutional review, whereas the legislature was perfectly capable of keeping the Dutch constitution in mind when preparing new law. The vast amount of written and unwritten international law was an entirely different matter and thus new laws might, unintentionally, diverge from previous international arrangements.

Therefore, the problem was incredibly well investigated in several different aspects. Eventually, the pro-Europeans won the vote in the Chamber of Representatives, passing the Serrarens amendment; new open discussions followed in the Senate, where the government chose to defend the latest amendment to rescue the rest of the bill. By the spring of 1953, the obligatory second reading of the constitutional amendment was finished. Thus, after three years of discussion "on Dutch traditions and European ambitions",[178] the provisions on the "anyone binding force" and primacy of treaty law were fixed in the constitution. Therefore, from 1953 onwards, the Dutch constitution stipulated in its Articles 65[179] and 66[180] that international law bound Dutch citizens and companies without having to be transformed into national legislation (it was "binding on anyone" or, as it would later be translated, it had "direct effect") and that it should have primacy over contrary national legislation.

Further proof of the consciousness of the move comes from the fact that the story of Dutch constitutional provisions laying the groundwork for path-breaking ECJ jurisprudence did not even end there, with the formal adoption of these two important constitutional articles. In 1956, a small yet crucially important revision described by the executive as simply technical was still to come. The reforms of 1953 had just come to light when a new debate on possible constitutional amendments came to the fore: in particular, under the form of first problems with the new ratification procedure, and scholarly criticism precisely on "the terminology and consequences of the new provisions on direct effect and primacy".[181] A general revision of the constitution was already scheduled for 1956. Thus the government decided to tackle these "technical" problems by creating a new third committee, led by the professor of constitutional and international law R. Kranenburg. Its mandate precluded a wholesale reconsideration of the 1953 reform, but the Kranenburg Committee eventually limited the 1953 reform by placing a crucial condition on the primacy of international law, again reminiscent of all the technical debates which would then be followed in EC law: namely, they argued that international law only possessed primacy in the Dutch legal order if it were of a *self-executing nature*. Although the 1956 constitutional amendment limited the primacy of international law in the Netherlands—not without further political ado on the coherence with the traditional openness of the Dutch legal order and the previous Serrarens amendment—this provision would still produce quite considerable consequences for the development of European law.[182] Now that the Dutch constitution stipulated the self-executing nature of treaties and decisions of international organizations in order for them to become binding in the national legal order, the question of whether the incipient forms of European law were of self-executing nature became a core question for Dutch courts and was abundantly debated yet again. Therefore, it is impossible to think that jurists and practitioners in the following years, including those of the European Communities' circle, could be unaware of it.

In a creative 1962 ruling, the Hoge Raad would explicitly make a call for references to the European Court of Justice in order to clarify the "intention" behind certain treaty provisions.[183] As a consequence of this ruling—and of the initiative of a group of pro-European lawyers who engaged in a series of test cases strategically—a "steady stream of Dutch preliminary references to Luxembourg" emerged.[184] The second of these cases, filed in the name of the Dutch transport company, NV Algemene Van Gend en Loos, provided the Luxembourg judges with what would eventually proved to be a fundamental question in the development of the European legal architecture, but very much in the spirit of the internal debate just described. That is, whether Article 12 of the EEC Treaty, entailing a negative obligation to refrain from introducing new customs duties, was self-executing. Not by chance, the Dutch and the Belgian governments tried to prevent the Court from making statements by arguing that the questions were purely of internal constitutional law, on which it had no jurisdiction.[185] But when the Court of Justice ruled that Article 12 was indeed self-executing, because the Treaties of Rome intended to create a "new legal order in international law", its interpretation not only found a solution for the controversy at hand, but also established the principle of direct effect for all the European member states—even if, unlike the Dutch, their national constitutions had not known direct effect in the past.[186] Thus, a cornerstone of European constitutional practice was laid, with essential general scope, but also firmly based on specific internal contingencies.

As already noted, it is relevant to highlight that statistically, eight of the first eleven referrals came from the Netherlands. Therefore, in the long term, it is possible to argue that the Dutch 1953 and 1956 constitutional reforms would leave a crucial mark on the history of European integration. And they did it in two interrelated ways. For the Netherlands, the constitutional reforms were part of a long tradition of limited national sovereignty, commonly symbolized by Hugo Grotius or the 1922 constitutional clause on the peaceful settlement of conflicts through international law.[187] This tradition, in particular, was reflected in the far-reaching constitutional reforms on the transfer of competences to international organizations and the ratification of treaties deviating from the constitution. Both reforms were readily accepted by the Dutch political and legal elites, who—explicitly and willingly choosing the European path—reaffirmed the perception of an existing tradition of partial sovereignty. The debate on the Dutch constitutional reforms, or more specifically the second provision of 1956 that limited the primacy of international law to self-executing provisions, prompted Dutch courts to turn to the European Court of Justice asking for an interpretation of the 1957 EEC Treaty. Creating the occasion for a wave of preliminary references to Luxembourg, the Dutch constitution reform thus definitively incited the crucial 1963 ruling of the ECJ in *Van Gend en Loos*. So began the constitutional practice of European law, again with a decisive influence shaped by the internal Member States' practice. As stated, it also had a decisive impact on how the powers of the European Court of Justice could be performed throughout the decades.

2.4 The Original Choices in the Establishment of the Court of Justice as a Form of Improvement of Its Authority

From the analysis conducted throughout this chapter, it is possible to draw some first conclusions on the ability of the Court of Justice to evolve from an institutional point of view. I tried to show how the same idea of the establishment of a permanent European Court of Justice and then the structuring of its specific decisive powers—and even the first functional principles it happened to develop in its early jurisprudence decisively—were all based on the capacity of institutional internalization of specificities coming from external influences. In hindsight, this has been decisive for the improvement of the Court's authority in several respects.

It is self-evident that the supranational legal order as we know it today could not have reached the current level of development without a stable judicial body as eventually decided in the early 1950s by adopting one specific solution and by discarding competing solutions proposed by certain national delegations. Even more decisively, it is well known that the actual powers eventually conferred to the Court—all based, as said, on national influences—proved crucial in the evolution of the institution's role in its legal order. This is the case of its "administrative" powers, all modelled after the French public judiciary, that allowed it to play a central role as arbitrator among the various actors of the Community. This is, even more, the case for the preliminary reference jurisdiction, based on the Italian mixed system of constitutional adjudication, which was notoriously a crucial instrument for the construction of many of the supranational constitutional doctrines,[188] and the subjectivation of the Treaties by empowering the individual as an agent of Community law with a view to enhance effectiveness and legitimacy of it.[189] The same direct link with the authority-building of the ECJ is evident when looking at how internal constitutional debates shaped the first fundamental doctrinal tenets of EU constitutional law.

Already in the early years of the Court, when its structure was debated and under revision (in the passage from the ECSC to the Treaty of Rome), a wise calibration in the powers of the Court came from the selective internalization of national forms: those were the first utilitarian moves in its institutional evolution, which proved to be decisive choices to make the European Court of Justice emerge as a key actor of the supranational legal order.

Notes

1. See for instance G. Maggi, The Role of Multilateral Institutions in International Trade Cooperation, in 89 American Economic Review, 1999, p. 190; C.J. Carrubba, Courts and Compliance in International Regulatory Regimes, in 67 Journal of Politics, 2005, p. 669; M. Gilligan,

L. Johns, B.P. Rosendorff, Strengthening International Courts and the Early Settlement of Disputes, 54 Journal of Conflict Resolution, 2010, p. 5; L. Johns, Strengthening International Courts: The Hidden Costs of Legalization, University of Michigan Press 2011.

2. See the direct critical remarks by J.H.H. Weiler, On the Distinction between Values and Virtues in the Process of European Integration, paper of the Institute for International Law and Justice, International Legal Theory Colloquium Spring 2010, available at the website http://iilj.org/courses/documents/2010Colloquium.Weiler.pdf (accessed 2 March 2020), at pp. 1–2, with reference to N.D. Jaibi, W. Landolsi, L'Union européenne: d'une Communauté Economique à une Communauté de Citoyens, in R. Ben Achour, S. Laghmani (eds.), Les droits de l'Homme: une nouvelle cohérence pour le droit international?, Pedone 2008, p. 249, at 250: "*C'est de cette dynamique que procède le passage d'une Communauté économique à une Communauté de citoyens. C'est-à-dire d'une Communauté qui repose sur la réalisation d'un Marché commun, dans lequel la libre circulation des personnes (en tant qu'agents économiques), des marchandises, des services et des capitaux est garantie à une Communauté de citoyens, c'est-à-dire une Communauté d'individus appartenant à une Union politique fondée sur les principes – ou pour reprendre la terminologie retenue par le Traité de Lisbonne – de valeurs de liberté, de démocratie, du respect des droits de l'Homme et des libertés fondamentales, ainsi que l'Etat de droit. Autrement dit, c'est de cette dynamique que procède le passage d'une intégration négative à une intégration positive*". See also the organic reflections in A. Grilli, Le origini del diritto dell'Unione europea, *op. cit.*, at 37 *et seq.*; A. Williams, The Ethos of Europe. Values, Law and Justice in the EU, Cambridge University Press 2010; J. Dickson, P. Eleftheriadis (eds.), Philosophical Foundations of European Union Law, Oxford University Press 2012; D. Kochenov, G. de Búrca, A. Williams, Europe's Justice Deficit?, Hart Publishing 2015.
3. J.H.H. Weiler, The Political and Legal Culture of European Integration: An Exploratory Essay, in 9 International Journal of Constitutional Law, 2011, p. 678.
4. B. Balassa, The Theory of Economic Integration, Homewood 1961.
5. The degree of economic integration has been typically categorized by the literature into seven stages: preferential trading area, free trade area, customs union, common market, economic union, economic and monetary union, complete economic integration, differing one with the other in the degree of unification of economic policies, with the highest one being the completed economic integratio union of the states, which would most likely involve political integration as well.
6. See Note 37 in Chapter 1.

7. C.J. Carrubba, A Model of the Endogenous Development of Judicial Institutions in Federal and International Systems, 71 Journal of Politics, 2009, p. 55; C.J. Carrubba, M.J. Gabel, Courts, Compliance, and the Quest for Legitimacy in International Law, in 14 Theoretical Inquires in Law, 2013, p. 505.
8. C.J. Carrubba, M.J. Gabel, Courts, Compliance, and the Quest for Legitimacy in International Law, *op. cit.*, at 516.
9. G. Sartori, Comparative Constitutional Engineering: An Inquiry into Structures, Incentives and Outcomes, New York University Press 1994.
10. N. Komesar, Imperfect Alternatives: Choosing Institutions in Law, Economics, and Public Policy, University of Chicago Press 1994.
11. C.J. Carrubba, M.J. Gabel, Courts, Compliance, and the Quest for Legitimacy in International Law, *op. cit.*, at 510.
12. *Ivi*, at 511.
13. *Ibidem.*
14. *Ivi*, at 518.
15. See for a contextualisation of the ECJ in the post-war proliferation of international courts and tribunals A. Arnull, Me and My Shadow: The European Court of Justice and the Disintegration of European Union Law, in 31 Fordham International Law Journal, 2007, p. 1174.
16. A. Boerger-De Smedt, La Cour de Jusitice dans les négociations du traité de Paris instituant la CECA, in 2 Journal of European Integration History, 2008, p. 7, at 10.
17. R. Schuman, Declaration of May 9th 1950, available at the website http://europa.eu/about-eu/basic-information/symbols/europe-day/schuman-declaration/ (accessed 2 March 2020).
18. *Ibidem.*
19. According to the definition given by C.R. Sunstein, Practical Reason and Incompletely Theorized Agreements, in 51 Current Legal Problems, 1998, p. 267.
20. A. Boerger-De Smedt, La Cour de Justice dans les négociations du traité de Paris instituant la CECA, *op. cit.*, at 10.
21. *Ibidem.*
22. *Ibidem.*
23. *Ibidem*, making reference to FJM, AMG 2/3/8, Haut-commissariat de la République de France en Allemagne "Exposé de M. Monnet devant le Conseil de la Haute Commission Alliée, Petersbourg, 23 mai 1950", Godesberg, 24.05.1950.
24. A. Boerger-De Smedt, La Cour de Justice dans les négociations du traité de Paris instituant la CECA, *op. cit.*, at 11, making reference to FJM, AMG 2/4/4a, [Note concernant la HAUTE AUTORITÉ], sn, sd [mai/juin 1950]; FJM, AMG 2/4/7, [De Uri à Monnet] "Schéma de

traité", 07.06.1950; FJM, AMG 2/4/16, P. Reuter "Observations sur le schéma de traité" (article 6), 14.06.1950.

25. *Ibidem*, making reference to FJM, AMG 2/4/3, Reuter à Monnet [Projet d'un schéma de traité, 16.05.1950; FJM, AMG 2/4/4a, [Note concernant la Haute Autorité], sn, sd [mai/juin 1950]; FJM, AMG 2/4/8, Uri "Schéma de traité. Recours contre les décisions de la Haute Autorité", 12.06.1950; FJM, AMG 2/4/16, P. Reuter "Observations sur le schéma de traité", 14.06.1950.
26. The secretary general of the United Nations, the president of the International Court of Justice, and the director of the International Labour Organization.
27. A. Boerger-De Smedt, La Cour de Justice dans les négociations du traité de Paris instituant la CECA, *op. cit.*, at 10–11.
28. *Ivi*, at 11, making reference to FJM, AMG 2/4/3, Reuter à Monnet [Projet d'un schéma de traité, 16.05.1950; FJM, AMG 2/4/4a, [Note concernant la Haute Autorité], sn, sd [mai/juin 1950] et FJM, AMG 2/4/8, Uri "Schéma de traité. Recours contre les décisions de la Haute Autorité", 12.06.1950.
29. *Ibidem.*
30. *Ibidem.*
31. *Ibidem*, with reference to FJM, Interview of M. Lagrange by A. Marès, Paris, 23 September 1980.
32. E. Lambert, Le gouvernement des juges et la lutte contre la législation sociale aux État-Unis: l'expérience américaine du contrôle judiciare de la constitutionnalité des lois, M. Giard & Cie edition 1921.
33. See on this point A. Grilli, Moloch politico o governo dei giudici? Gli albori dell'Europa comunitaria, in P. Maffei, G.M. Varanini (eds.), Honos alit artes. Studi per il settantesimo compleanno di Mario Ascheri - Vol. III Il cammino delle idee dal medioevo all'antico regime. Diritto e cultura nell'esperienza europea, Firenze University Press 2014, p. 227.
34. *Ibidem.*
35. "*Intérêts vitaux*", according to A. Boerger-De Smedt, La Cour de Justice dans les négociations du traité de Paris instituant la CECA, *op. cit.*, at 13, with reference to Archives du Ministère des Affaires étrangères belge (AMAE/B), Dos.gén. CECA 5216, Projet de traité réalisant le Plan Schuman. Principales dispositions à prévoir, s.d.; Réunion du Plan Schuman – 7 juin 1950 (délégations belgo-luxembourgeoise et néerlandaise).
36. "*Incompatible avec sa souveraineté*": *ibidem.*
37. *Ivi*, at 15.
38. AEL/AE, doc. 11349, "Premier avant-projet. Mémorandum sur les institutions de la proposition du 9 mai", 1st August 1950.

39. A. Boerger-De Smedt, La Cour de Justice dans les négociations du traité de Paris instituant la CECA, *op. cit.*, at 16–17.
40. *Ivi*, at 17, with reference to PAAA/Abt.2, SFSP, dos.62, "Protokoll über die Zusammenkunft der deutschen Delegation mit H. Monnet in Houjarray ... 2.7.50".
41. M. Rasmussen, Constructing and Deconstructing 'Constitutional' European Law: Some reflections on how to study the history of European law, *op. cit.*, at 644, with reference to Bundesarchiv. (BA) Nachlass Walter Hallstein, Koblenz, Bestand N 1266, 919, Speech by Walter Hallstein at Haus Rissen, Institut für Wirtschafts- und Sozialpolitik, Hamburg-Rissen, 29 July 1958.
42. M. Rasmussen, The Origins of a Legal Revolution—The Early History of the European Court of Justice, in 2 Journal of European Integration History, 2008, p. 77, at 83.
43. *Ivi*, at 84.
44. A. Boerger-De Smedt, La Cour de Justice dans les négociations du traité de Paris instituant la CECA, *op. cit.*, at 17.
45. *Ibidem*, with reference to FJM, AMG 4/6/6, B[all] "Memorandum of suggestions regarding article 8 of proposed working paper", 04.07.1950.
46. *Ibidem*.
47. See on the typical practical functions of comparative law G. de Vergottini, Diritto costituzionale comparato, CEDAM 2013, at p. 34 *et seq*.
48. See on the point D. Tamm, The History of the Court of Justice of the European Union Since its Origin, in A. Rosas, E. Levits, Y. Bot (eds.), The Court of Justice and the Construction of Europe: Analyses and Perspectives on Sixty Years of Case-Law—La Cour de Justice et la Construction de l'Europe: Analyses et Perspectives de Soixante Ans de Jurisprudence, T.M.C. Asser Press 2013, p. 9, at 17.
49. T. Koopmans, The Birth of European Law at the Crossroads of Legal Traditions, *op. cit.*, at 493.
50. M. Rasmussen, The Origins of a Legal Revolution—The Early History of the European Court of Justice, *op. cit.*, at 85.
51. *Ibidem*; see also J.M. Galabert, The Influence of the Conseil d'État Outside of France, in 49 International and Comparative Law Quarterly, 2000, p. 700, and J. Wilson, Jurisconsultes et conseillers d'État: aux origines de l'ordre juridique communautaire, in 14 Journal of European Integration History, 2008, p. 35.
52. See, *inter alia*, the reflections by M. Van Hoecke, M. Warrington, Legal Cultures, Legal Paradigms and Legal Doctrine: Towards a New Model for Comparative Law, in 47 The International and Comparative Law Quarterly, 1998, p. 495, and A. Somma, Giochi senza frontiere. Diritto comparato e tradizione giuridica, in 8 Ars Interpretandi, 2003, p. 317.

53. D.G. Valentine, The Court of Justice of the European Coal and Steel Community, Martinus Nijhoff 1955, at p. 9.
54. *Assemblée Nationale*, Official Reports, 1951, p. 8855, col. 1.
55. *Ibidem*, also declaring that "*it is upon the principles of our public law that this Court will develop its precedents*". For critical remarks on these points see D.G. Valentine, The Court of Justice of the European Coal and Steel Community, *op. cit.*, at 9.
56. M. Carcasonne, Official Reports, 1952, p. 715, col. 1.
57. R.D.F., p. 32, quoted also by D.G. Valentine, The Court of Justice of the European Coal and Steel Community, *op. cit.*, at 9.
58. M. Biever, Compte rendu, 1951–1952, col. 1611.
59. Sénat de Belgique, Session ordinaire, 1950–1951, no. 369, p. 14.
60. By a law dated 25 May, 1928, these Tribunals were empowered to determine certain private Belgian interests: their decisions were executory in Belgium provided that they were stamped by the agent général of the Belgian Goverment appointed to the Mixed Tribunal.
61. Voorlopig Verslag, no. 2228, no. 7, 1951–1952, par. 8, p. 69, col. 1.
62. Eerste Kamer, Official Reports, 1952, p. 211, col. 1.
63. See on this, recently, M. Rasmussen, Revolutionizing European law: A History of the Van Gend en Loos Judgement, in 12 International Journal of Constitutional Law 2014, p.136, at 156 *et seq.*; but, already, and authoritatively, P. Pescatore, Van Gend en Loos, 3 Feburary 1963—A View From Within, in L. Azoulai, L.M. Poiares Maduro (eds.), The Past and Future of EU Law. The Classics of EU Law Revisited on the 50th Anniversary of the Rome Treaty, *op. cit.*, p. 3.
64. M. Rasmussen, The Origins of a Legal Revolution—The Early History of the European Court of Justice, *op. cit.*, at 84.
65. See recently on this S.G. Calabresi, J. Owens, The Origins of Judicial Review, Northwestern Public Law Research Paper No. 14-05, available at the website http://ssrn.com/abstract=2391457 (accessed 2 March 2020).
66. T. Koopmans, The Birth of European Law at the Crossroads of Legal Traditions, *op. cit.*, at 495.
67. *Ibidem.*
68. *Ibidem.*
69. D.G. Valentine, The Court of Justice of the European Coal and Steel Community, *op. cit.*, at 56.
70. *Ibidem.*
71. See extensively on the point R. Barents, The Autonomy of Community Law, *op.cit.*
72. D.G. Valentine, The Court of Justice of the European Coal and Steel Community, *op. cit.*, at 57.
73. *Ivi*, at 56.
74. *Ibidem.*

75. *Ibidem.*
76. Art. 66, par. 5.2 of the Treaty.
77. See the coinciding statements by D.G. Valentine, The Court of Justice of the European Coal and Steel Community, *op. cit.*, at 71; T. Koopmans, The Birth of European Law at the Crossroads of Legal Traditions, *op. cit.*, at 493; J. Rivero, Le problème de l'influence des droits internes sur la Cour de Justice de la Communauté Européenne du Charbon et de l'Acier, in 4 Annuaire français de droit international, 1958, p. 295.
78. See the reconstruction by D. de Pretis, La giustizia amministrativa, in G. Napolitano (ed.), Diritto amministrativo comparato, Giuffrè 2007.
79. CE Ass 17 février 1950, *Ministre de l'Agriculture c/Dame Lamotte.*
80. J. Rivero, Le problème de l'influence des droits internes sur la Cour de Justice, *op. cit.*, at 303–304.
81. D.G. Valentine, The Court of Justice of the European Coal and Steel Community, *op. cit.*, at 73.
82. A. Antoine, La Court de Justice de la C.E.C.A., in 6 Révue Génerale de Droit International Public, 1953, p. 234; D.G. Valentine, The Court of Justice of the European Coal and Steel Community, *op. cit.*, at 74.
83. S. Boccalatte, La motivazione della legge. Profili teorici e giurisprudenziali, CEDAM 2008, especially at 191 *et seq.*
84. See for the use of this definition, *ex multis*, T. Hartley, The Foundations of European Community Law, 6th ed. Oxford University Press 2007, at p. 368.
85. See specifically C. Hen, La motivation des actes des institutions communautaires, in 13 Cahiers de Droit Européen, 1977, p. 54; A. Vedaschi, Istituzioni europee e tecnica legislativa, Giuffrè 2001, especially at p. 75 *et seq.* and 133 *et seq.*
86. D.G. Valentine, The Court of Justice of the European Coal and Steel Community, *op. cit.*, at 74.
87. *Ivi*, at 75.
88. A. Antoine, La Court de Justice de la C.E.C.A., *op. cit.*, at p. 236.
89. E. Leferrière, Traité de la Jurisdiction Administrative et les Recours Contentieux, Berger-Levrault 1896, II, at p. 548.
90. D.G. Valentine, The Court of Justice of the European Coal and Steel Community, *op. cit.*, at 75.
91. *Ivi*, at 76.
92. Judgement of 21 December 1954, Italy / ECSC High Authority (2/54, ECR 1954–1956, p. 37).
93. Judgement of 11 February 1955, Assider / ECSC High Authority (3/54, ECR 1954–1956, p. 63).
94. J. Rivero, Le problème de l'influence des droits internes sur la Cour de Justice, *op. cit.*, at 304.

95. On the idea of the European judge as an quintessentially comparatist judge see the reflections by P. Pescatore, Le recours dans la jurisprudence de la Cour de justice des Communautés européennes, à des normes déduites de la comparaison des droits des Etats membres, in 32 Revue international de droit comparé, 1980, p. 337; J. Mertens de Wilmars, Le droit comparé dans la jurisprudence de la Cour de Justice des Communautés Européennes, in 110 Journal des Tribunaux, 1991, p. 37; C.N. Kakouris, Use of the Comparative Method by the Court of Justice of the European Communities, in 6 Pace International Law Review, 1994, p. 267; K. Lenaerts, Interlocking Legal Orders in the European Union and Comparative Law, in 52 International & Comparative Law Quarterly, 2003, p. 873; L.M. Poiares Maduro, Interpreting European Law: Judicial Adjudication in a Context of Constitutional Pluralism, in 1 European Journal of Legal Studies, 2007, p. 1, especially at 5 *et seq.*; J. Bengotxea, Multilingual and Multicultural Legal Reasoning. The European Court of Justice, in A.L. Kjær, S. Adamo (eds.), Linguistic Diversity and European Democracy, Ashgate 2011, p. 97.
96. J. Rivero, Le problème de l'influence des droits internes sur la Cour de Justice, *op. cit.*, at 305.
97. Judgement of 21 March 1955, Netherlands / ECSC High Authority (6/54, ECR 1954–1956, p. 103).
98. In the words of E. Steindorff, Le recours pour excès de pouvoir dans le droit de la Communauté européenne du charbon et de l'acier, Klostermann 1952, directly cited by Advocate General Lagrange in its Opinion.
99. Judgement of 12 June 1958, Compagnie des hauts fourneaux de Chasse / ECSC High Authority (15/57, ECR 1957–1958, p. 211).
100. See e.g. Judgement of 17 December 1970, Einfuhr- und Vorratsstelle für Getreide und Futtermittel / Köster (25/70, ECR 1970 p. 1161), "*fondamental pour le système législatif de la Communauté*" according to P. Pescatore, Le recours dans la jurisprudence de la Cour de justice des Communautés européennes, à des normes déduites de la comparaison des droits des Etats membres, *op. cit.*, at 340, that decided on the regime of normative execution of Council regulations with explicit reference, at par. 6, to "the legal concepts recognized in all the Member States".
101. See the notorious Judgement of 12 July 1957, Algera and others /Common Assembly (7/56, 3/57 to 7/57, ECR 1957–1958, p. 39), that decided on the possibility of annullment or withdrawal of Communitarian individual administrative measures by recognizing the existence "*d'un problème de droit administratif, bien connu dans la jurisprudence et la doctrine de tous les pays de la Communauté*", and explicitly solving it "*en s'inspirant des règles reconnues par les législations, la doctrine et la jurisprudence des pays membres*".

102. D.G. Valentine, The Court of Justice of the European Coal and Steel Community, *op. cit.*, at 71.
103. *Ibidem.*
104. D.G. Valentine, The Court of Justice of the European Coal and Steel Community, *op. cit.*, at 87.
105. M. Lagrange, The Court of Justice as a Factor in European Integration, *op.cit.*, at 712.
106. *Ibidem.*
107. *Ibidem.*
108. P. Duez, G. Debreyere, Traité de Droit Administratif, Dalloz 1952, at p. 694.
109. "Article 40 Subject to the provisions of the first paragraph of Article 34, the Court shall have jurisdiction to assess damages against the Community, at the request of the injured party, in cases where injury results from a fault involved in an official act of the Community in execution of the present Treaty. It shall also have jurisdiction to assess damages against any official or employee of the Community, in cases where injury results from a personal fault of such official or employee in the performance of his duties. If the injured party is unable to recover such damages from such official or employee, the Court may assess an equitable indemnity against the Community. All other litigation between the Community and third parties, other than that relating to the application of the provisions of the present Treaty and implementing regulations, shall be brought before the national tribunals."
110. In the recent iconic words of J.H.H. Weiler, The political and legal culture of European integration: An exploratory essay, *op. cit.*, at 690, "(T)he secret of the principle of the rule of law in the legal order of the European Union is that genius process of preliminary references and preliminary rulings". It is after all telling that all the Court of Justice's judgements considered as "classics" and fundamental tenets of the EU legal order in a well-known recent publication, L. Azoulai, L.M. Poiares Maduro (eds.) The Past and Future of EU Law. The Classics of EU Law Revisited on the 50th Anniversary of the Rome Treaty, *op. cit.*, were given under the preliminary reference procedure.
111. A. de Tocqueville, Democracy in America, Vol. 1, Chapter 8, available at the website https://www.gutenberg.org/files/815/815-h/815-h.htm (accessed 2 March 2020).
112. See for instance what held in C-393/98 Judgement of 22 February 2001, Gomes Valente (C-393/98, ECR 2001 p. I-1327) ECLI:EU:C:2001:109, at 17: "According to case-law that is well established, that obligation to refer is based on cooperation, with a view to ensuring the proper application and uniform interpretation of Community law in all the Member States, between national courts, in their

capacity as courts responsible for the application of Community law, and the Court of Justice [...] and it is particularly designed to prevent a body of national case-law that is not in accordance with the rules of Community law from being established in any Member State...".

113. Again in the recent authoritative words of J.H.H. Weiler, The political and legal culture of European integration: An exploratory essay, *op. cit.*, at 691, "the preliminary reference procedure is, overwhelmingly, a device for judicial review of member state compliance with their obligations under the treaties. It is ingenious for two reasons: First, it deploys individuals, vindicating their own rights, as the monitors and enforcers of Community obligations vis-à-vis the member states. It has been called the private-attorney-general model. And second, it deploys national courts. The judgement is spoken through the mouths of member state courts. The habit of obedience associated with national law is, thus, attached to European law. The gap between the rule of law and the rule of international law is narrowed, even closed".
114. *Ibidem.*
115. M. Rasmussen, The Origins of a Legal Revolution—The Early History of the European Court of Justice, *op. cit.*, at 84.
116. A. Boerger-De Smedt, La Cour de Justice dans les négociations du traité de Paris instituant la CECA, *op. cit.*, at 29.
117. *Ibidem.*
118. *Ibidem.*
119. M. Rasmussen, The Origins of a Legal Revolution—The Early History of the European Court of Justice, *op. cit.*, at 84: "The predecessor of the famous article 177 of the EEC Treaty, article 41, which introduced a system of preliminary references in the ECSC, allowing the Court to pronounce its judgement on the validity of European law, was interestingly enough not created to satisfy German demands for a uniform interpretation of European law. Proposed instead by Lagrange, it had the sole purpose of clarifying the division of work between national courts and the new European Court". See also, accordingly, A. Boerger-De Smedt, La Cour de Justice dans les négociations du traité de Paris instituant la CECA, *op. cit.*, at 29–30.
120. Archives historiques des communautés européennes (Florence), Fonds Uri, dos. 37/2, Lagrange, "Élaboration de l'exposé des motifs" (s.d.), as quoted by A. Boerger-De Smedt, La Cour de Justice dans les négociations du traité de Paris instituant la CECA, *op. cit.*, at 29.
121. M. Rasmussen, The Origins of a Legal Revolution—The Early History of the European Court of Justice, *op. cit.*, at 87.
122. R. Dehousse, The European Court of Justice: The Politics of Judicial Integration, *op. cit.*, at 5.

123. See A. Grilli, Le origini del diritto dell'Unione europea, *op. cit.*, at Chapter 5; D. Tamm, The History of the Court of Justice of the European Union Since its Origin, *op. cit.*, at 17 *et seq.*
124. M. Rasmussen, The Origins of a Legal Revolution—The Early History of the European Court of Justice, *op. cit.*, at 86.
125. *Ibidem.* It is interesting to note that Art. 41 ECSC was actually never applied: see M. Lagrange, The Court of Justice of the European Communities from the Schuman Plan to the European Union, in Mélanges Fernand Dehousse. Vol. 2, la construction européenne, Éditions Labor 1979, pp. 127, 132, «(F)inally, the Treaty of Paris does not provide for references for a preliminary ruling, merely for assessment of the validity of acts (Article 41). That possibility has never actually been used, perhaps because individuals and their legal advisers were unaware of it or because the disputes were resolved in other ways».
126. *Ivi*, at 85.
127. D.G. Valentine, The Court of Justice of the European Coal and Steel Community, *op. cit.*, at 87.
128. See the reflections by C. Penera, The Beginnings of the Court of Justice and its Role as a Driving Force in European Integration, in 1 Journal of European Integration History, 1995, p. 111, at 118–122; see also, accordingly, H. Rasmussen, On Law and Policy in the European Court of Justice: A Comparative Study in Judicial Policymaking, *op. cit.*, at pp. 208–213.
129. See P.H. Spaak, Rapport des chefs de delegation aux Ministres des Affaires Etrangeres /Report of the Heads of Delegation to the Ministers of Foreign Affairs (21 April 1956), available at the website http://aei.pitt.edu/996/1/Spaak_report_french.pdf (accessed 2 March 2020).
130. M. Rasmussen, The Origins of a Legal Revolution—The Early History of the European Court of Justice, *op. cit.*, at 86; A. Boerger-De Smedt, La Cour de Justice dans les négociations du traité de Paris instituant la CECA, *op. cit.*, at 10.
131. M. Rasmussen, The Origins of a Legal Revolution—The Early History of the European Court of Justice, *op. cit.*, at 86.
132. *Ibidem*: for example Carl Friedrich Ophüls, Jean-Charles Snoy, Lambert Schaus, Lodovico Benvenuti (heads of delegation) and Spaak (Belgian Foreign Minister), all of whom had participated in one or more of the intergovernmental negotiations on the European Coal and Steel Community, the European Defence Community and the European Political Community during the 1950s.
133. M. Rasmussen, The Origins of a Legal Revolution—The Early History of the European Court of Justice, *op. cit.*, at 87.
134. *Ibidem.*
135. *Ibidem.*

136. M. Rasmussen, The Origins of a Legal Revolution—The Early History of the European Court of Justice, *op. cit.*, at 88.
137. The great Luxembourgish jurist, and future judge of the Court, was in fact a the time acting as legal advisor of the Foreign Ministry of Luxembourg; and later in time he wrote about his personal experience in P. Pescatore, Les Travaux du 'Groupe Juridique' dans la négociation des Traités de Rome, in 34 Studia Diplomatica, 1981, p. 159.
138. M. Rasmussen, The Origins of a Legal Revolution—The Early History of the European Court of Justice, *op. cit.*, at 88.
139. *Ibidem.*
140. See on this C.J. Mann, The Function of Judicial Decision in European Economic Integration, Brill Academic Publishers 1972, p. 75 *et seq.*
141. The Court of Justice itself referred to the perceived intentions of the authors of the Treaty in this respect, in the case Judgement of 14 December 1962, Confédération nationale des producteurs de fruits et legumes and others /Council of the EEC (16/62 and 17/62, ECR 1962 p. 471, at 478: "the system (…) established by the Treaties of Rome lays down more restrictive conditions then does the ECSC Treaty for the admissibility of applications for annulment by private individuals". See in this respect the reconstruction by H. Rasmussen, Why Is Article 173(2) Interpreted Against Private Plaintiffs, in 5 European Law Review, 1980, p. 112.
142. See for instance, recently, I. Pernice, The Right to Effective Judicial Protection and Remedies in the EU, in A. Rosas, E. Levits, Y. Bot (eds.), The Court of Justice and the Construction of Europe: Analyses and Perspectives on Sixty Years of Case-Law—La Cour de Justice et la Construction de l'Europe: Analyses et Perspectives de Soixante Ans de Jurisprudence, *op. cit.*, p. 381.
143. See under Chapters 5 and 6 of this study for some more reflections on the point, and B. de Witte, The Preliminary Ruling Dialogue: Three Types of Questions Posed by National Courts, in B. de Witte, J. Mayoral, U. Jaremba, M. Wind, K. Podstawa (eds.), National Courts and EU Law: New Issues, Theories and Methods, Elgar 2016, p. 15, for a recent taxonomical reconstruction.
144. See originally A. Trabucchi, L'effet erga omnes des décision préjudicielles rendues par la Cour de justice des Communautés européennes, in 10 Revue trimestrielle de droit européen, 1974, p. 56, and Lord Mackenzie-Stuart, Elogio funebre del sig. Nicola Catalano ex membro della Corte - udienza solenne 18 ottobre 1984, in Compendio delle attività della Corte di giustizia delle comunità europee 1984–1985 e udienza solenni 1984–1985, pp. 139–140; and recently, in the historical literature, M. Rasmussen, The Origins of a Legal Revolution—The Early History of the European Court of Justice, *op. cit.*, at 89, A. Grilli, Le

origini del diritto dell'Unione europea, *op. cit.*, at 65 *et seq.*, D. Tamm, The History of the Court of Justice of the European Union Since its Origin, *op. cit.*, at 17.

145. M. Rasmussen, The Origins of a Legal Revolution—The Early History of the European Court of Justice, *op. cit.*, at 89; see also A. Arnull, The Court of Justice Then, Now and Tomorrow, in M. Derlen, J. Lindholm (eds.), The Court of Justice of the European Union: Multidisciplinary Perspectives, Hart Publishing 2018, p. 1, at 4.
146. See on this M. Cappelletti, Il controllo giudiziario di costituzionalità delle leggi nel diritto comparato, Giuffrè 1968.
147. See as a recent reconstruction of the rich debate U. de Siervo, L' istituzione della Corte costituzionale in Italia: dall'Assemblea costituente ai primi anni di attività della Corte, in P. Carnevale, C. Colapietro (eds.), La giustizia costituzionale fra memoria e prospettive. A cinquant'anni dalla pubblicazione della prima sentenza della Corte costituzionale, Giappichelli 2008, p. 49.
148. See *inter alia* C. Mortati, La Corte costituzionale ed i presupposti per la sua vitalità, in Iustitia, 1949, p. 69; G.G. Stendardi, La corte costituzionale: il giudizio di legittimità costituzionale delle leggi, Giuffrè 1955; P. Curci, La Corte costituzionale: composizione, attribuzioni, funzionamento, Giuffrè 1956; and, already with a comparative approach, M. Cappelletti, La giurisdizione costituzionale delle libertà. Primo studio sul ricorso costituzionale (con particolare riguardo agli ordinamenti tedesco, svizzero e austriaco), Giuffrè 1955.
149. This system is the result of a well-known historical evolution, and of a basic sillogistic interpretation going from the higher value of the constitutional norms to the necessary existence of a power of judicial review based on those, recently summarized by B. Barbisan, Il mito di *Marbury v. Madison* e le origini della giustizia costituzionale negli Stati Uniti, Il Mulino 2008.
150. See the seminal H. Kelsen, La garantie juridictionnelle de la Constitution (la Justice constitutionnelle), in 35 Revue du droit public et de la science politique, 1928, p. 197.
151. P. Calamandrei, La Corte costituzionale e il processo civile, in F. Carnelutti et al. (eds.), Studi in onore di Enrico Redenti nel XL anno del suo insegnamento, Giuffrè 1951, at pp. 199 and 203 in particular.
152. H. Kelsen, General Theory of Law and State, Harvard University Press 1945, at pp. 268–269.
153. See for an updated taxonomy M. Bellocci, T. Giovannetti (eds.), Il quadro delle tipologie decisorie nelle pronunce della Corte costituzionale. Quaderno predisposto in occasione dell'incontro di studio con la Corte costituzionale di Ungheria. Palazzo della Consulta, 11 giugno 2010, available at the website http://www.cortecostituzionale.

it/documenti/convegni_seminari/STU%20219_Tipologia_decisioni.pdf (accessed 2 March 2020).

154. N. Catalano, Manuale di diritto delle Comunità europee, Giuffrè 1962, pp. 97–98.
155. See, for a recent reconstruction on the point, M. Claes, The National Courts' Mandate in the European Constitution, *op. cit.*
156. See Lord Slynn of Hadley, What Is a European Community Law Judge?, in 52 Cambridge Law Journal, 1993, p. 234.
157. See for instance J.H.H., A Quiet Revolution: The European Court of Justice and Its Interlocutors, *op. cit.*, at 518 *et seq.* in particular.
158. As per the apt definition by S. Saurugger, F. Terpan, The Court of Justice of the European Union and The Politics of Law, Palgrave Macmillan 2017, p. 11.
159. See the analysis by M. Broberg, N. Fenger, Preliminary References to the European Court of Justice, 2nd ed. Oxford University Press 2014, Chapter 2 and 3.
160. See on the phrase Note 132 above.
161. See on this J.H.H. Weiler, Journey to an Unknown Destination. A Retrospective and Prospective of the European Court of Justice in the Arena of Political Integration, *op. cit.*, at 425; see also K.J. Alter, Establishing the Supremacy of European Law: The Making of an International Rule of Law in Europe, Oxford University Press 2001, p. 47.
162. See J.H.H. Weiler, In Defense of the Status Quo: Europe's Constitutional Sonderweg, in Id., M. Wind (eds.), European Constitutionalism Beyond the State, Cambridge University Press 2003, p. 7, at 7–8.
163. In interplay with the specific legal philosophies of some of the early supranational judges, as made clear by recent literature: see e.g. E. Stein, Lawyers, Judges and the Making of a Transnational Constitution, *op. cit.*, A. Vauchez, The Force of a Weak Field: Law and Lawyers in the Government of the European Union (For a Renewed Research Agenda), *op. cit.*, A. Vauchez, B. de Witte (eds.), Lawyering Europe: European Law as a Transnational Social Field, *op. cit.*, and recently W. Phelan, The Revolutionary Doctrines of European Law and the Legal Philosophy of Robert Lecourt, in 28 The European Journal of International Law, 2017, p. 935.
164. K. Van Leeuwen, On Democratic Concerns and Legal Traditions: The Dutch 1953 and 1956 Constitutional Reforms 'Towards' Europe, in 21 Contemporary European History, 2012, p. 357, at 358.
165. *Ibidem.*
166. See also on this point, in the recent literature A. Albi, J. Ziller (eds.), The European Constitution and National Constitutions: Ratification and Beyond, Kluwer Law International 2006; M. Claes, The Europeanisation of National Constitutions in the Constitutionalisation of Europe:

Some Observations Against the Background of the Constitutional Experience of the EU-15, in 3 Croatian Yearbook of European Law and Policy, 2007, p. 1; F. Hoffmeister, Constitutional Implications of EU Membership: A View from the Commission, in 3 Croatian Yearbook of European Law and Policy, 2007, p. 59.

167. K. Van Leeuwen, On Democratic Concerns and Legal Traditions, *op. cit.*, at 362.
168. See M. Rasmussen, Revolutionizing European Law: A History of the Van Gend en Loos Judgement, *op cit.*, at 146–147.
169. In the sense of elements of a dynamic approach to comparative law, focusing on law as a social activity: a formant of the law is, according to the lesson of R. Sacco, Legal Formants: A Dynamic Approach to Comparative Law, in 39 American Journal of Comparative Law, 1991, p. 1, a group, a type of personnel, or a community, institutionally involved in the activity of creating law.
170. K. Van Leeuwen, On Democratic Concerns and Legal Traditions, *op. cit.*, at 372.
171. *Ivi*, at 359.
172. A tacit approval procedure, very similar in practice to the oversight principle in delegated law-making of France, Germany and Italy, was established, according to which parliament was allowed thirty days to demand a ratification debate before a treaty was ratified tacitly.
173. See H. Bribosia, Report on Belgium, in A.M. Slaughter, A. Stone Sweet, J.H.H. Weiler (eds.), The European Court and National Courts, Doctrine and Jurisprudence: Legal Change in Its Social Context, *op. cit.*, p. 3.
174. K. Van Leeuwen, On Democratic Concerns and Legal Traditions, *op. cit.*, at 367.
175. It did so especially in two rulings on the Rhine Navigation Treaty on 17 December 1934: Nederlandse Jurisprudentie (1935), 5 and 11; Fleuren, Een ieder verbindende bepalingen, 126–7.
176. Bijzondere Raadvan Cassatie, 12th January 1949, NJ (1949), 87.
177. K. Van Leeuwen, On Democratic Concerns and Legal Traditions, *op. cit.*, at 367.
178. *Ibidem.*
179. "Artikel 65: *Binnen het Koninkrijk geldende wettelijke voorschriften vinden geen toepassing, wanneer deze niet verenigbaar zou zijn met overeenkomsten, die hetzij vóór, hetzij na de totstandkoming der voorschriften zijn bekend gemaakt overeenkomstig artikel 66*", translation from H.F. van Panhuys, The Netherlands Constitution and International Law, in 47 American Journal of International Law, 1953, p. 537, at 540: "Legal provisions in force within the Kingdom shall not apply if the application should be incompatible with agreements which have

been published in accordance with article 66 either before or after the enactment of the provisions".

180. "Artikel 66: *De wet geeft regels omtrent de bekendmaking van overeenkomsten. De overeenkomsten verbinden een ieder, voorzover zij zijn bekend gemaakt*", translation from H.F. van Panhuys, The Netherlands Constitution and International Law, *op. cit.*, at 540: "Rules with regard to the publication of agreements shall be laid down in the law. Agreements shall be binding on anyone insofar as they will have been published".
181. K. Van Leeuwen, On Democratic Concerns and Legal Traditions, *op. cit.*, at 370, with reference to F.J.F.M. Duynstee, Grondwetsherziening 1953: De nieuwe bepalingen omtrent de buitenlandse betrekkingen in de Grondwet, Kluwer 1954; H.F. van Panhuys, De regeling der buitenlandse betrekkingen, in 28 Preadvies, p. 1.
182. The new article 65 (in 1956 renumbered 66) stated: "*Binnen het Koninkrijk geldende wettelijke voorschriften vinden geen toepassing, wanneer deze toepassing niet verenigbaar zou zijn met een ieder verbindende bepalingen van overeenkomsten, die hetzij vóór, hetzij na de totstandkoming der voorschriften zijn aangegaan*", translation from H.F. van Panhuys, The Netherlands Constitution and International Law: A Decade of Experience, in 58 American Journal of International Law, 1964, p. 88, at 107: "Legislation in force within the Kingdom shall not apply if this application would be incompatible with provisions of agreements which are binding upon anyone and which have been entered into either before or after the enactment of such legislation".
183. HR, 18 May 1962, NJ (1965), 115.
184. K. Van Leeuwen, On Democratic Concerns and Legal Traditions, *op. cit.*, at 372. See also M. Rasmussen, Constructing and Deconstructing 'Constitutional' European Law: Some reflections on how to study the history of European law, *op. cit.*, at 648; A. Vauchez, The Transnational Politics of Judicialisation: Van Gend en Loos and the Making of EU Polity, in 16 European Law Journal, 2010, p. 1.
185. F.C. Mayer, Van Gend en Loos: The Foundation of a Community of Law, *op. cit.*, at 18.
186. Judgement of 5 February 1963, Van Gend en Loos / Administratie der Belastingen (26/62, ECR 1963, p. 1).
187. See on this L.F.M. Besselink, The Constitutional Duty to Promote the Development of the International Legal Order, in 34 Netherlands Yearbook of International Law, 2003, p. 89.
188. See Note 119 in this chapter.
189. L.M. Poiares Maduro, We the Court: The European Court of Justice and the European Economic Constitution, *op. cit.*, at 9; F.C. Mayer, Van Gend en Loos: The Foundation of a Community of Law, *op. cit.*

CHAPTER 3

The Appointment of Members of the Court

In exploring the structuring process of every court in a kind of logic succession—once ideally founded the institution and defined, as seen, its powers—the following step, according to the roadmap recalled in the introduction, is an analysis of its composition. In fact, in following this logic order of institutionalization, I will now look at the choice of the European Court of Justice's members. This is another relevant case study in my perspective since, in the recent past, clear evidence has emerged on the capacity of the structure and the organization of the Court to change as influenced by the external and internal legal environments.

The selection of judges for international judicial bodies has been traditionally considered as one of the significant examples of completely opaque fields of study. The relative designations have often been made behind closed doors[1]; the power of the states to select their nominees is usually depicted as inherently *ab-solutus*, free from any legal constraint.[2] A sign of this institutional configuration is also the historical lack of academic attention to the point. It is a trend that has in part changed only in recent times.[3] Interestingly, this aspect is coupled with an equally rare political debate typically generated.[4] Such broad disillusion is also very present in comparative law research: in fact, it has been famously said that in terms of structure and rules of internal functioning—and mainly focusing on judicial selection—each international court should be considered as "an island",[5] i.e. an independent and self-contained regime with no common traits with the other fragments[6] of the legal world. As will be

L. Pierdominici, *The Mimetic Evolution of the Court of Justice of the EU*, https://doi.org/10.1007/978-3-030-47864-3_3

explained, at the national level some more evident tendencies have been definable. Also in this respect, it was common in the literature to understand the nominations to supreme/constitutional courts as a by-product of a nation's general rules for the appointment of ordinary judges—imbued with the same rationale but also very much influenced and modified by the inherent political traits of the relative choices.[7] After all, in this respect, the ultimate goal is different. While in selecting judges for national general courts, especially district and appellate courts, the ability researched is to strictly observe black-letter law, correctly apply it, and provide expert interpretation of highly specific legal provisions, the task of constitutional and international courts as well as their judges is to correct failures and deficiencies in the law and national practices, by focusing more on the principles and values on which a legal system rests. In this sense, it will also be interesting to notice whether and to what extent the selection of the judges of the Court of Justice of the European Union, sometimes depicted as a supranational constitutional court,[8] evolved in one direction or the other. All the trends mentioned are going through a process of change at a broad comparative level: mostly, the evolution seems to be in the sense of a capture, through different *legal* means, of the essential *political* dimension inherent in the choices for appointees.

Indeed, there is a strong connection between national sovereignty and international judicial selection. Evidence of this is given by what should be the starting point of any analysis on the topic: that no rules of general application have been promulgated on the functioning of international courts. This is the first meaning of the idea of these courts as islands, with their own systems of governance and rules, including for the selection of judges. However—and this should be kept in mind—despite their differences, these courts do have one point in common. States have always been much concerned about how international judges are appointed because those appointments have been seen as something that affects their national sovereignty. So, when read within a logic of institutionalization, this field becomes crucial. As will be explained, the relationship between these two poles (national sovereignty and international judicial selection) will gain different equilibria depending on different approaches to the subject matter of the present chapter.

The aim of these pages is thus to:

1. Look back at the rationale behind the rise of judicial selection models by paying particular attention to the United States' example as a laboratory for historical construction. This will be crucial for recalling a first taxonomy proposed by scholars in this field (meritocratic systems, elective systems and appointive systems) born for certain precise and relevant reasons;
2. Identify patterns of apical courts selections[9] as an explanation of the translation of the mentioned systems in different environments and of the adaptive transformation of their rationale;
3. Deal with the selection of the CJEU's judges, framing this part of the chapter in light of the dialectic between what Von Bogdandy and Venzke labelled as a "liberal supranational" approach vis-à-vis the alternatives of the historical "pure intergovernmentalism" and the most modern tendencies to a "cosmopolitan" approach.[10]

For that to happen, a historical/evolutive approach will be followed, consistent with the other chapters. It will be maintained that coherently with what will be detected at the national and international levels, the need to reform the appointment process of the CJEU was pushed up in the European agenda from two separate sides: the European Parliament's political initiatives in the 1980s and 90s and the activity of some official judicial Reflection groups. All these channels promoted a reform very much in line with comparative trends and wrote a new chapter of institutional internalization by the European Court of paradigms and pressures coming from external and internal legal environments. The evolution has without a doubt fostered the institution's authority: evidence is also in the influence the supranational changes had in turn in the national settings, as will be seen in the last part of the analysis.

3.1 Selection of Judges: Comparative Trends at the National and International Level and Their Rationale

3.1.1 The Historical Rise of Judicial Selection Models

It is common in the literature to place the problem of the judicial appointment processes in the context of an institutional balance to be sought between judicial *independence* and *accountability*. This is a common trait of the debates on national selection of ordinary judges, national selection of judges for supreme or constitutional jurisdictions and international judges. As scholars have emphasized, the nature of the institutional balance between independence and accountability differs "according to the particular form of judicialization and the political system in which it occurs"[11]: these are live issues, subject to change, in all the relevant environments.[12] Broadly speaking, one can define the concept of judicial *independence* as the apparent need that in order to perform her functions effectively—and therefore to be considered legitimate and authoritative by the parties of the case—the judge is expected to adjudicate impartially, according to the rules of the legal system, *sine spe ac metu*, without expectation of benefits or fear of reprisals.[13] Therefore, judges must be personally and professionally equipped to resolve legal disputes impartially, particularly in terms of a certain detachment from the leverage of political powers: there is a need to shield them from outside influence. At the same time, such independence cannot be considered as absolute, in any legal system. Judges are in any case constrained by, and should follow, existing law, procedures and practices; they are not free to act perversely or for ulterior motives. Inevitably, they find themselves under controls of either a judicial or administrative nature and therefore subject to some forms of *accountability* in relation to the law, political powers and the public at large. In a nutshell, this is what has been described as the "conundrum of the apparently insoluble tension between judicial independence and judicial accountability".[14] It is evident that the institutional settings provided to solve or to manage it can differ. Of course, the problem of the initial selection of adequate candidates for a judicial position does not exhaust the issues involved in the balance of these two principles. Several other aspects should be considered, including at least their promotion or renewals, the organization of the administration of the court system, the judges' non-judicial activities, the working conditions including salary and pensions systems, the complaints and disciplinary sanctions (including protection of the position).[15]

The initial selection of human resources themselves is nonetheless of fundamental importance. This was already reflected in the first modern theorizations on the definition of a *judiciary branch* as a *third* power opposed to the others. It is well known that the Alexander Hamilton, in the Federalist paper no. 78 proceeding "to an examination of the judiciary department of the proposed government", emphasized as the first point of his analysis "(T)he mode of appointing the judges", even before icastically defining them as "the least dangerous" branch, with "no influence over either the sword or the purse". He clearly stated that the problem of the selection of judges "is the same with that of appointing the officers of the Union in general (...) According to the plan of the convention, all judges who may be appointed by the United States are to hold their offices during good behavior; which is conformable to the most approved of the State constitutions and among the rest, to that of this State. Its propriety having been drawn into question by the adversaries of that plan, is no light symptom of the rage for objection, which disorders their imaginations and judgements. The standard of good behavior for the continuance in office of the judicial magistracy, is certainly one of the most valuable of the modern improvements in the practice of government. In a monarchy it is an excellent barrier to the despotism of the prince; in a republic it is a no less excellent barrier to the encroachments and oppressions of the representative body. And it is the best expedient which can be devised in any government, to secure a steady, upright, and impartial administration of the laws". In this respect, Hamilton warned that if the periodic power to select judges were given "to the people, or to persons chosen by them for the special purpose, there would be too great a disposition to consult popularity, to justify a reliance that nothing would be consulted but the Constitution and the laws".

The Hamiltonian reflection, deeply rooted in historical analysis, can also be considered as a prototypical comparative taxonomy, ranging from the original monarchic forms of state of the old continent to the new republican forms of *trias politica*. Nonetheless, it is well known that in Europe, and the civil law countries in particular, the traditional conception of the judges as public servants and experts and devoted servants of the state has dominated; for a long time, this has not been made urgent or justified a developed scholarly reflection on the matter.[16] In fact, the first doctrinal categorizations came at the national level and from American scholarship, by both jurists and political thinkers. They were prompted by the great deal of diversity that is verified in the federal structure of the United States, where the existence of a federal layer of courts, and then the legislative autonomy of each State in the internal organization of justice in its own legal order, historically led to a proliferation of systems of selection, quite often different from one another.

Since the times of the Hamiltonian teachings, a variety of systems of selection were accumulated and stratified, for precise historical reasons. As Hamilton observed, at the birth of the nation, most states provided the appointment of judges. The passage from a purely appointive system, modelled and inherited from the English monarchic tradition, to a prototypical *elective* system was advocated at a later stage, particularly by the *Jacksonian* movement in the early XIX century. It was considered the best way to expand public participation in government and to end its "monopoly" led by social elites, according to the general political platform of the movement.[17] In 1832, Mississippi became the first state to establish an entirely elective judiciary. New York followed in 1846, and many states followed soon thereafter. Every state that joined the Union between 1846 and 1958 adopted constitutions that provided for elective judiciaries. During the same period, Michigan (1850), Pennsylvania (1850), Virginia (1850) and Maryland (1851) amended their constitutions to provide for the election of part or all of their judges. By the time of the Civil War, 22 out of 34 states elected their judges.

On the other hand, the diffusion of so-called *non partisan elections* or of a *merit system* was detectable, at a later moment, as a precise reaction to the distortions led by the first wave of elections. The criticism was mainly aimed at the opportunity of a judiciary directly implicated with political affiliation, with a complex system of electoral campaigns, and with the correlated problems of fundraising.[18] In fact, in American history, it was not long before a backlash occurred. Two factors were considered to motivate change. First, political parties quickly arrived at complete control over the election of judicial candidates and the retention of judges in partisan elections. In local historiography, early judicial elections are today described as working out "as a de facto system of appointment".[19] Also, the legal literature of the time was rich with harsh criticism: "It is one of our most absurd bits of political hypocrisy that we actually talk and act as if our judges were elected whenever the method of selection is, in form, by popular election. In a great metropolitan district (…), where we have a typical long ballot and the party machines are well organized and powerful, our judges, while they go through the form of election, are not selected by the people at all. They are appointed. The appointing power is lodged with the leaders of the party machines. These men appoint the nominees".[20] Second, a selection system according to which judges are asked to become politicians in order to ascend to the bench eroded public confidence in the judiciary. In a notable speech before the American Bar Association in 1906, Roscoe Pound stated that "(p)utting courts into politics and compelling judges to become politicians, in many jurisdictions has almost destroyed the traditional respect for the bench".[21] New political debates followed, led in particular by the critical bar associations, to restore public confidence in the courts that had been lost in part because of the political nature of judicial elections.

The result of this first early open debate on the proper balance between independence and accountability and of a consequent stratification of institutional solutions was the definition (and stratification) of three basic models of selection: the *appointive system*, the *elective system* and the *merit selection system*, also known as *Missouri plan*. These all started to coexist, and still coexist in the United States, before constituting the models which later spread elsewhere in the vast majority of constitutional democracies.

In pure terms, the *appointive* system is nothing more than the traditional method of nomination in which political authorities make both the candidacies and the final decisions on the appointments. This is, again in pure terms (although historically occurred), an obvious maximization of the profile of *accountability* of judges vis-à-vis the political powers at the expense of a severe threat to their *independence*. As seen, the first sequential historical modification was the change for *elective systems* in which the political community—the citizens—directly choose judges through a vote among candidates. In this respect, a first further internal diversification in the category arose on the point of candidacies. The first examples of elective judges were directly associated with political parties and held regular campaigns for fundraising and the aggregation of consensus. As said previously, modifications later occurred leading to several examples of so-called *non-partisan elections*, with candidates listed on the ballot with no label designating any party affiliation. In this sense, a tentative shift in the accountability system was clear by linking the judges directly with a broad electorate and not with political authorities. This solution was also clearly addressed to reinvigorate the idea of independence from any other power. The dynamics of "capture" of judges' elections by the political parties eventually frustrated both goals and led to a first form of corrections with tentatively non-partisan elections.

The second type of correction within the institutional balance came some decades later with *Missouri Plan*, as previously said. If the turn to judicial elections was initially meant to allow voters to elect judges, in the wake of a political platform for democratization by the end of the nineteenth century, political corruption became, in fact, the paramount problem. In coherence with the suggestions of American Judicature Society—a national, non-partisan organization formed by a group of judges and lawyers in 1913 in the US precisely to react to the corruption problems and to push for a qualified, independent judiciary and ensure fairness in the US justice system—a recalibration of the selection systems was proposed based on merit more than on accountability.[22] The idea of choosing judges by using a non-partisan merit selection process as a correction of the elective system was proposed within this context. In 1940, the state of Missouri was the first to adopt what formally went under the name of "Nonpartisan Selection of Judges Court Plan", and it is now often referred to as a "merit selection" system or the "Missouri Plan". It was publicly discussed and approved by the voters in the same years; and in 1945, this method became part of Missouri's State Constitution.

In general terms, the *merit selection system* combined aspects of both the appointment and election methods to select judges, using a merit-based evaluation system. Under the plan, when a judicial vacancy occurs, applicants meeting the qualifications for the judgeship may apply. An independent, non-partisan judicial selection commission is set to review the applications, to interview the applicants and to compile a list of the most qualified candidates. The commission then forwards a list of suitable names to the political authorities responsible for the final choice. In this sense, the political power is still sovereign in its decision, but restrained by an external evaluation made by a specialized, independent body. In Missouri's original model, the intention of restraining the political discretion was also very well exemplified by the provision of a term (of sixty days) to appoint a candidate from the list: in the case of the governor not making a selection within the term, the independent commission itself was entrusted with the power to make the selection, thus countering the danger of instrumental inertias. The plan borrowed from the election systems the provision according to which newly appointed judges must stand for so-called *retention* in the next general election after serving a specific period in office. If a majority of voters opposed retention, the judge was removed from office and the selection process started again.

Of course, this institutional solution presented several advantages once compared to historical predecessors. It confined the direct intervention by political authorities, confirming the need for accountability, in the first and the last phases of selection, and it entrusted the voters of the final word in the course of action. At the same time, it included clear elements based on merit—the only ones that the continental European systems based on public *concours* evaluate—in the crucial, central phase.

Not only were clear qualifications for the candidates set by the political will in advance—after all, this was also possible in the appointive or elective systems. It limited the political discretion of the final phase to a choice among already filtered, shortlisted appointees, chosen according to their qualifications by an independent, non-partisan, special commission. In this sense, the filter of this particular body worked as a basis and a guarantee for the independence of the final candidate, in any case leaving its nomination to the political process.

Thus, as the prototypical discretionary appointive system in continental Europe inherited from the *ancien régime* was simply replaced by a system of public *concours*—in which the merit-based element of the system was based on a selection through exams[23]—the American states' "laboratories"[24] created a stratification of institutional solutions. The *Missouri plan,* then adopted with some modifications in various other contexts, became famous as a successful mix of all the historical elements previously traceable in the institutional balance: merit, lack of political affiliation, representativity, transparency, link to the final political discretion as well as accountability, and protection of independence.[25] Hence, a final taxonomy has been proposed by scholars in this respect.[26] Together with pure "*meritocratic*" systems of selection (based on the choice, through a competition, of specialized public officials),[27] more or less pure *elective* systems (with direct or indirect political affiliations), more or less pure *appointive* systems (with more or less ample direct discretion of the political authorities), the emergence of a group of so-called mixed, hybrid systems, modelled after the *Missouri plan*, has been historically detected.

3.1.2 Models of Apical Court Selections, in Europe and at the International Level

The original American historical development created technical solutions widely exported in different systems. Given the taxonomy that I just described (i.e. between the elective, meritocratic and appointive systems), the emergence of a fourth, hybrid category is particularly relevant if one moves from the original level of the selection of national ordinary judges to the level of the selection of constitutional and international ones. It also becomes particularly relevant if one analyses these aspects not only taxonomically, but in my usual evolutionary, diachronic terms. It was soon clear that a different balance needs to be stricken between judicial independence and accountability when talking of ordinary trial courts on the one hand and the highest courts of review on the other. As already mentioned, judges in top review courts—under this category one can refer to both municipal apical and international bodies—are reaching "decisions that often have far-reaching social and political implications",[28] and they are ***naturaliter*** involved in choices of constitutional significance, often implicating failures or inconsistencies in the fabric of the legal order and focusing more on the principles and values on which a legal system rests. Therefore, a greater emphasis has always been placed in their appointment process, precisely on the point of the inherent political sensitivity and accountability. The case for such procedures as public interviews or confirmation hearings for court judges—designed to provide the public with knowledge about the values and attitudes of these influential decision-makers—became much more critical and much more persuasive at every apical court level.

After all, as it has been argued, the potential threat to judicial independence is reduced at this level.[29] Judges in top courts have often reached the top of their careers and are not looking for promotions. They are better able to withstand pressure from their selectors once on the bench. Moreover, where judges are called upon to decide between competing ideologies, values or policies which underlie the law, the notion of independence as mere impartiality (as between parties) becomes problematic, if not blurred. Is it realistic to require that the appointment systems select judges who are impartial when judging between one set of values and another, in the same way as they must be impartial when deciding between one party on trial and another? The justification for the participation in some form of the elected branches of government in the appointments process of the highest ranks of the judiciary (or of particular types of judges not officially ranked in the judiciary)[30] has thus been historically reasonable. Yet, it is precisely at this level of courts that the highest calibre of judges is needed, and considerable damage would be done to the legal system if the selection of candidates based on partisan political affiliation rather than skills and abilities undermines the quality and the prestige of the judicial college. The challenge that the appointment processes for top review courts face, more than in ordinary selection procedures, "is to ensure that the democratic legitimacy of the judiciary is maintained without introducing a form of politicization that reduces the quality of the judges appointed and transforms judges into politicians in wigs".[31]

In this sense, the search for the elusive balance between independence and accountability in top judicial appointment processes has led to substantive reforms in many contexts. And, as the literature has remarked, the adoption of judicial appointment commissions can be considered as a major trend: even more significantly, scholars highlight that it looks "likely to become the most popular selection system of the twenty-first century".[32] Throughout common law and civil systems alike, the use of commissions is increasingly being explored as a solution to the difficult problem of achieving a balance between independence and accountability in top judicial selection. Canada, South Africa, Scotland, England and Wales, as well as many civil law systems in Europe now use some form of commission.[33] To describe the trend, mention can be made here of the recently established English Judicial Appointments Committee,[34] Swedish Judicial Committee[35] and Slovenian Judicial Council.[36] For the supreme jurisdictions, as described above, deviating systems can sometimes be used. This includes the restricted selection commission for the UK Supreme Court[37] or the twelve members of the German *Richterwahlausschuss* that scrutinize prospective *Bundesverfassungsgericht* judges,[38] still confirming the application of the model. Quorums and voting rules are not always evident but appear to vary, with the majority decisions presumably being a recurring feature. For regular judicial functions, these commissions ordinarily invite applications, go through the files, stage interviews with prospective candidates and draw up a list of suitable candidates.[39] The high strength in the use of judicial appointment commissions is in fact in their adaptability, which allows them to be shaped to meet the particular requirements of each system.[40]

Even more importantly for my analysis, the mentioned adaptability of the mixed/hybrid system based on independent selection commissions, which allows them to be shaped to meet the particular requirements of each system, has also proved decisive in the evolution of the selection of international judiciary. There have been remarkable debates over the last years on the undeniable growing importance of the international judiciary. One of the most widely resonant has been the sharp division between thinkers Eric Posner and John Yoo on the one hand, and Laurence Helfer and Anne-Marie Slaughter on the other, over the appropriate role of judicial independence in the international courts.[41] Some have characterized this as being a divergence of opinion between two ideal types of international judges—those who act as "trustees" and those who see themselves as "agents"[42] of the governments, with all the clear institutional consequences these different configurations can hint at. About the international judicial selection process, these alternative positions are relevant to many vital questions, including whether and to what extent states should have complete discretion in nominating their candidates, the appropriate selection criteria for international judges and whether the judicial election process should be insulated from the election processes of other political appointments in international organizations. These and other issues are often informed by views as to the correct balance between state and supranational autonomy/sovereignty. And they are, in turn, underpinned by familiar, if sometimes unarticulated, normative assumptions about the appropriate boundaries of the power of judges versus politicians. In this sense, the typical normative discussions on the legitimacy of judicial review vis-à-vis the political process have seen a revival.

Here again, the scarcity of academic research on the topic has often been underlined.[43] Though the limited, often anecdotal evidence that exists about the way judges are appointed to international courts, and their usual personal professional prestige, do not lead to serious concerns about the integrity and ability of selected judges. What is less clear, as synthesized with a witticism, is "whether able and independent judges have been appointed because of, or in spite of, the selection processes"[44] through which the appointments take place. Empirical research by Erik Voeten on the decision-making of national governments concerning international judicial appointments has identified a range of various motivations for the selection of different candidates: "(g)overnments are neither simply picking the best qualified candidate nor are they singularly obsessed with limiting sovereignty costs, although both motivations are sometimes important".[45] Voeten's research highlights the importance of factors other than those represented in schematic dichotomy merit/affiliation, such as the desire on the part of states to signal a credible commitment to the international legal order and the role of political patronage.

In going into a more detailed analysis, one cannot but start from the notation that the number of international courts and international judges has risen significantly in the last two or three decades, although it remains obviously low when compared to domestic legal systems. The first international court, the Central American Court of Justice was established in 1907 but it was short-lived. The next international court was the Permanent Court of International Justice, found in 1922 and based in The

Hague. The creation of the International Court of Justice then followed in 1946, as the "principal judicial organ of the United Nations".[46] Until the late 1950s, the International Court of Justice and its fifteen judges had a virtual monopoly on the judicial resolution of international disputes. The situation today is undoubtedly changed. Beyond the ICJ, there is nowadays a so-called fragmented space with a wide range of international and regional courts dealing with a variety of subject matters, including free trade, international criminal law, human rights and the law of the sea.[47] Among significant recent developments, in 2002 the International Criminal Court (ICC) was established in The Hague (its eighteen judges were elected in 2003), while, at the time of writing, new regional courts are being established in the Caribbean area[48] and in Africa.[49] According to the typical international dispute resolution scheme, the judges of these various courts and tribunals are supplemented by the appointment of ad hoc judges whereby, in several international courts, a state involved in a case may appoint a judge if it has no national members on the bench[50]—in the same vein as arbitrators sitting on arbitral tribunals established to deal with a particular case. More recently, the Security Council has mandated the establishment of pools of ad litem judges for the ad hoc criminal tribunals for the former Yugoslavia and for Rwanda to assist those tribunals in dealing with their caseload within a reasonable period.[51]

Such appointments can add complexity to the issues of judicial selection and judicial independence. In any case, the starting point for any analysis on the topic is that no rules of general application have been promulgated on the functioning of international courts. As previously said, it is common to say that, to a certain extent, each body is an island[52] with its system of governance and rules, including the selection of judges. However, these courts do have one point in common: states have always been much concerned about which international judges are appointed, and how. This is understandable. As already noticed in advance, if states set up courts and entrust them with functions over their mutual controversies, they inevitably lose *a degree* of control over what that body does. The kind of control they lose is different from the similar problem faced with delegation to domestic/municipal courts. The legal questions facing the latter are in any case treated, before and after the judicial pronunciation, according to the internal democratic cycle: political decision-making, judicial intervention, possible overturn by a reinforced majority. This is often not the case for international controversies, at least in terms of facility of the overturning. An international court, an independent international court, necessarily extends its independence to relations with the states which created it, and which may then become direct parties in cases before it.

Scholars have pointed two significant ways in which, in this peculiar context, governments seek to influence international courts: by controlling the budget of the institution itself and by deciding who will sit in the court as a judge.[53] Financial and human resources: the appointment process and the independence of the court are once again closely connected. State concerns about the judicial selection process, so interrelated in their interests and sovereignty, have been evident from the very beginning of the short history of international courts. The first efforts to move beyond the model of international adjudication via mere ad hoc arbitration with the establishment of a permanent international court (a movement replicated, as seen, in the negotiations for setting up the ECJ) were during the Hague Peace Conference of 1899. It notably failed because states were unable to agree on the modalities of selection for a representative group of judges. At the time, around fifty states participated in the negotiations. The issue, on the contrary, did not arise for the Central American Court of Justice in 1907: there were only three state parties, so each could have a judge in a sort of "direct" form of "representation". In 1922, the Permanent Court of International Justice (PCIJ) became the first international court in which the number of judges was to be smaller than the number of state parties, with an evident *caesura* with the principle of direct representation of national sovereignty and national interests. The same situation is also detectable in the International Court of Justice, where fifteen judges sit on a court that is nowadays open to more than 180 states. Already in the early period of the establishment of international courts and tribunals, it was recognized by commentators that the "proper manning" of the courts, and their successful functioning, could only be assured if careful scrutiny was exercised when the actual selection of judges was made.[54] But states were very clear in their wish to use full control and in considering that their freedom should not be limited. An amusing anecdote comes via the story of Manly Hudson, judge and president of the Permanent Court of International Justice. In 1944, he planned to review the existing applicable rules. His clear conclusion was the following: "No absolute disqualifications can be said to exist in general international law to restrict the freedom of States, though the literature of the nineteenth century evidenced some disposition to list such qualities as infancy and insanity as barring a person's selection".[55]

The typical way in which the constitutive instruments of the various international and regional courts set rules on the judicial selection is essentially by establishing specific criteria to be fulfilled by individual members, while additional considerations or requirements are often imposed as regards the bench as a whole. About the qualifications of individual international judges, recurring but quite neutral criteria include: high moral character/integrity, possession of qualifications required in their respective countries for appointment to highest judicial office, or status of jurisconsults of recognized competence in international law, demonstrated expertise in area of law relevant to the court in question (i.e. trade, human rights, law of the sea, etc.). With regards to considerations to be taken into account in the composition of an international bench *as a whole*, while in some contexts geographic representation requirements are unnecessary as the college is composed of one judge nominated or appointed by each participating state, relevant provisions requiring some considerations for representation of different geographic areas and different legal systems or different legal cultures are easy to find.[56]

In this, one finds symbolized the first, *ex ante* explanation of the strong connection between national sovereignty and international judicial selections. It is reflected in the initial criteria for the selection and the composition of the judiciary bodies. According to the famous rationalization offered by Christian Tomuschat, these criteria are ultimately linked to the need for international courts to "be able effectively to discharge their functions".[57] If every court entrusted with judicial responsibilities "must be large enough to process all the cases brought before it", it must also keep, on the other hand, "a sufficient degree of internal cohesion". It cannot be blown up to the size of a parliamentary body, losing its unity and messing its jurisprudence in contradictions and inconsistencies. Consequently, "even if it may be desirable at the international level to provide for one judge per each State participating in a scheme of judicial settlement of disputes",[58] this (disputable) wish can be undoubtedly feasible in certain regional organizations but cannot be granted in all circumstances. According to Tomuschat, this functional analysis is preferable to simple, rough readings based on pure instrumental arguments. "No reasonable government", in fact, would "expect that 'its' judge on the bench should act as a kind of defence lawyer for the protection of a presumed national interest", if not at the price of a marginalization of the judge herself by her peers and the consequent logical exclusion of any reasonable influence as "forceful champion of the legitimate aspirations"[59] of her own country. "Realistically speaking", the national affiliation and representation of the judge would serve two other primary functions. First of all, it helps the college in the understanding of the often inevitable national background of international disputes. If issues arise which are closely connected with the domestic legal system of one of the parties concerned, no one else can better offer a proper understanding of the national backdrop than a qualified professional grown from the system concerned (with no incontrovertible results, but certainly with great persuasive force). Secondly but consequently, once one considers, as said, that international judicial bodies as rational monitoring system decreasing the costs of compliance to mutual regulatory schemes for states' governments, it is also rational that "states – which means governments and their peoples – must be able to trust that their legitimate concerns are taken into account with the requisite care". In this sense, the presence of one's "own" judge enhances each state's confidence in the scheme. "If justice were meted out exclusively by foreigners, the perception would spread that the relevant scheme had a discriminatory character", or even "as some kind of neo-colonial usurpation of the basic political rights of the people".[60] A national judge is suited to allay such fears and also to make known in the international college both the technicalities of each legal system and, in some sense, the political sensitivities and the possible social results of judicial decisions—not under the form of veto powers or undue influence—but only by making sure that a broad principle of international cooperation guides the relevant decision-making process.

Thus, once one rationalizes the otherwise puzzling idea of the need for "representation" in judicial bodies, and contextualizes in this sense the tension between judicial independence and judicial accountability at the international level, it is possible to better understand the evolution in the selection process at a comparative international level and put it in parallel with the trend detected at the national level. In fact—in the context of that same recent general debate that was mentioned in the introduction about the legitimacy and the democratic justification of the growing authority of international courts—renowned scholars have suggested a direct parallel between the kind of democratic legitimacy to which these courts can aspire and the evolution of their human resources selection. In particular, Von Bogdandy and Venzke, in their *comparative international* investigation,[61] distinguish three possible answers to the problem of the independence/accountability conundrum, as declined when "peoples that are subject to a court's jurisdiction do not constitute a single people",[62] and "there is no" a single "institutional sovereign".[63]

The approach Von Bogdandy and Venzke describe firstly, also in historical terms, is the most obvious, and linked to the *absolute* nature of national sovereignty. What they call a first model, the "*intergovernmental approach*", traces the authority of international courts and their judges simply to the will of their founding father, the unitary states, and in particular to the states' governments as prominent representatives in international law (in coherence with the "full powers" clauses of art. 7 of the Vienna Convention on the law of the treaties).[64] In this view, the selection of judges (according to the previously mentioned rationales) forms a genuine part of foreign politics, and therefore remains an *absolute* prerogative of the executive. They are "masters" of the relevant treaties and therefore masters also of the selection procedures, seen as pure implementation with no possibility of external intervention whatsoever, but only of self-containment in the form of previously established criteria to be fulfilled. This approach indeed informs most of the procedures still in place for electing international judges. As it has been said, and as will be analyzed in detail in the next paragraph, "it amounts to a sad irony in world history" that this procedure has endured "in rare purity", and until recently, with regard to the selection of judges of the European Court of Justice, "the one court that has contributed to overcoming classical international law more than any other".[65] This major paradigm of "*intergovernmental approach*" is still found nowadays by scholars in the Statute of the International Court of Justice, given the importance of the institution, even though there are undoubtedly some elements of hybridization in it "to insulate nominations from political influence",[66] (at least in pure terms). In fact, within this context, according to art. 3 of the ICJ Statute, the designation of each of the fifteen judges is formally filtered by so-called "national groups" sitting in the Permanent Court of Arbitration or (in the case of countries not represented within the latter) by national groups appointed specifically for this purpose. At least three months before the date of the election, the Secretary-General of the United Nations calls these national groups to designate four candidates within a specified period, including a maximum of two nominees from the same nationality as the national group. Although no detailed regulations exist giving binding instructions to the states about how to proceed in the process of screening and evaluating candidates, art. 6 of the Statute of the Court even recommends each national group "consult with its highest court of justice, its legal faculties and schools of law and its national academies and national sections of international academies devoted to the study of law". The lists of candidates are then sent to both the Assembly and the Security Council: individual applicants are evaluated and elected by these two bodies according to the possession of the broad and general requirements set out in art. 2 of the Statute of the ICJ, asking for judges of "high moral character", who should either "possess the qualifications required in their respective countries for appointment to the highest judicial offices" or "be jurisconsults of recognized competence in international law". These criteria are almost universally considered as too vague by scholars[67]; and empirical research has evidenced how the selections are not actually based on individual evaluations of single candidates but almost only on geographical considerations on the opportunity of the composition of the bench (with the establishment of a conventional pro quota system for each continent).[68] In this vein, the procedure can still clearly be considered as "*intergovernmental*", according to Von Bogdandy and Venzke's taxonomy, for several concurring reasons. There are undoubtedly certified "strong vested interests of governments in controlling the nomination process in order to influence the composition" of the court (as usual, and natural); and, "(A)t a practical level", for ICJ appointments "states will most likely be actively involved in campaigning for a candidate to succeed, and therefore want to ensure that a candidate is politically acceptable and 'electable'".[69] But the decisive factor is that no practical, scrutinized/enforced limits are placed on the exercise of those sovereign interests, given the vague criteria for the appointment and the only formal role of the vote in the two international *fora* involved (the UN Assembly and the Security Council), entrusted with a simple formal consent. In particular, it is important to note that the candidacies are not subject to any supervision by any independent committee or subcommittee inside the Assembly so that there is no real evaluation of the quality of the candidates and their independence. This is coupled with the lack of transparency in the work of national groups (subject, in fact, entirely to governmental directives).[70]

So, the historical forms verified nowadays as "*intergovernmental approaches*" to the problem of democratic legitimation and composition of the international courts are in any case hybrid forms, with some kinds of limits (although weak) to the pure expression of sovereign interests by the executives.

Therefore, when scholars build two other categories for their proposed taxonomy, they do so based on further and more stringent differentiations. Interestingly, they particularly look at the presence of effective limits posed to the national executives and to the different institutions which can be entrusted of such a counter-balance role.

Von Bogdandy and Venzke label "*liberal approaches*"—as second models in their taxonomy—the examples of international institutions in which the basic "division of domestic and foreign politics that characterizes the traditional intergovernmental approach"[71] is no more accepted. Such categorical distinction should be considered, after all, "increasingly less plausible in the wake of the globalization of many spheres of life". The liberal approach would then be recognizable where the procedures for choosing "senior domestic and international judges" align; and in particular, where there is "a prominent role for domestic parliaments" in the selection procedures or, in any case, a more penetrating scrutiny made at the international level, also through independent ad hoc bodies, on the effective choices made at national level. In this sense, the pure discretion of national governements would be effectively contained, and the liberal values that should be expressed at the national level would imbue the international institutions. The historical example in this respect is to be found in the International Criminal Court. Its Statute was adopted in 1998 to create, as it is well known, the first permanent court established to try individuals accused of committing crimes of genocide, crimes against humanity and severe violations of the laws of war. In contrast to the International Court of Justice, also as a historical antecedent, the Statute of the ICC provides detailed guidance as to the individual qualifications of its eighteen judges as well as criteria and guidance for their nomination and election. It provides an interesting alternative: it allows the nomination procedure to follow either the ICJ procedure or, explicitly (Article 36), the procedure used for the appointment of national superior court judges. States are also required, in any case, to provide precise information on how the candidate they have nominated meets the criteria laid down by the Statute. These stringent criteria include "established competence" and experience in criminal law and procedure, or in "relevant areas of international law such as international humanitarian law and the law of human rights". Moreover, it is remarkable that until 2010 these criteria were scrutinized by the Assembly of State Parties (the general management oversight and legislative body of the court system):

previous discussions as to whether there should be some type of specialized screening body to provide more information on candidates to guide states and to assess them (as proposed by member states such as the United Kingdom)[72] did not lead to tangible results. But in December 2010 an *Independent Panel on International Criminal Court Judicial elections* was established, under the pressure and with the sponsorship sponsored of the "Coalition for the International Criminal Court", a group of NGOs aiming to promote the nomination and election of the most highly qualified officials through fair, merit-based and transparent processes. This panel is now entrusted with the task of issuing a report containing an assessment of each judicial candidate as "Qualified" or "Not Qualified" after the closing of the nomination period and in advance of each judicial elections; and the official "Reports of the Advisory Committee on Nominations of Judges" in the ICC Assembly of States Parties also proves a clear osmosis between the opinions of the Independent Panel and the final results of the ICC selective process.[73] From this example it becomes clear that the elements of important hybridization already traced at the national level, under the form of independent panels constituted by honourable professionals and responsible of an independent screening of the new candidacies, are taking place more and more at the international level—and with growing results.

Von Bogdandy and Venzke then add a third category, which they label the "*cosmopolitan approach*" to the legitimation and the selection of judges.[74] Of course, this would be similar to the "*liberal*" approach as far as it creates a set of credible limits to the pure sovereign will of national executives. But the democratic legitimization and the balance between independence and accountability of international judges in this model are created through a stronger reliance—not on the national bodies—but directly on the international/supranational *fora* and their institutions, as possibly veritable direct factors of democratization. The *cosmopolitan* element would rest here in the detachment between the national and international level, and in considering this latter as an autonomous, independent space in which citizens—through their direct tools of control—can be the "ultimate reference point in the justification of public authority".[75] The practical element of such a process of evolution of old sovereign schemes in the selection of international judges would be the central and active role of international/supranational assemblies, replacing in this sense the executives but also the legislatures of the nation states.

A "cautious expression" of such development in the judicial selection processes is to be found, according to Von Bogdandy and Venzke themselves, in how the election of judges to the European Court of Human Rights is evolving through the role of the Parliamentary Assembly of the Council of Europe. The nowadays ECtHR full college is composed of 47 judges (one per member state) "of high moral character", and with "the qualifications required for appointment to high judicial office or (...) jurisconsults of recognised competence". The selection of these human resources is a two step process composed of a first, national phase, which leads to transmitting a list of three candidates and a second, supranational phase to scrutinize it and arrive to the final election. The relevant *cosmopolitan* trend in this respect is in that all the reforms occurred—explicitly aimed at making the process of appointment "reflect the principles of democratic procedure, the rule of law, non-discrimination, accountability and transparency",[76] and at "the need for maintaining the independence of the judges and preserving the impartiality and quality of the Court"[77]—have been taking place in the "Strasbourg phase" and have been autonomously led by the Parliamentary Assembly of the Council of Europe. In particular, from 1996 onwards, the Parliamentary Assembly has started to think about possible improvements of its own procedures; and this notably resulted in a request for standardization of the curricula of national candidates to better assess them and in the emergence of the practice of candidate interviews, made by a special *Sub-committee of the Assembly's Committee on Legal Affairs and Human Rights*. After the dissatisfaction of the 1998 round of elections—in terms of substantial internal difference among the national procedures for candidacies and lack of transparency, inadequate qualifications of some candidates and lack of gender balance—a new set of reforms was prompted yet again by the Permanent Assembly. These resulted in the Assembly's Recommendation 1649 (2004), which tried to set rules on the transparency of the calls for interest, gender balance, qualifications and the linguistic knowledge of candidates[78]; and in the Assembly's Resolution 1646 (2009), which stressed the need for states to make explicit their internal selection procedures and highlighted the need for satisfactory level of linguistic knowledge by the candidates.[79] This unprecedented supranationally-led evolution culminated, first of all, in "a positive politicization of the election process", when the Assembly even "rejected a member state's list of candidates because it did not include any female candidate".[80] Second, in 2010, an *Advisory Panel of Experts on Candidates for Election as Judge to the European Court of Human Rights* was established: an independent body composed of seven experts, appointed by the Committee of Ministers of the Council of Europe but sitting in individual capacity, and entrusted with the tasks of screening the candidacies and consequently informing the States/Contracting Parties and the Parliamentary Assembly of its deliberations—i.e. a panel which adds its work to that of supranational representative body, without substituting its selection. It is interesting to note that, here again, the institutional solution of an independent screening panel is replicated, in the particularly advanced context of a supranationally/cosmopolitan inspired development.

3.2 Selection of Judges in Luxembourg: Liberal Supranationalism as a Reaction to Pure Intergovernmentalism?

Interestingly, the question of the appointment of the members of the Court of Justice of the European Union can be put in the context I have tried to sketch in the previous pages. In particular, it can be read as the paradigm of an evolution from a system devoted to the pure intergovernmental *raisons d'État* to the expression of a kind of *liberal supranationalism*: an evolution developed in the wake of what comparatively registered both at the national and the international level. The few scholars who analytically pointed to the problem of the international judicial selection proposed, in addition to all the previously mentioned heuristic tools, a historical division. As said earlier, a critical step in the early twentieth century was the move from an international judiciary system made of ad hoc tribunals, where states directly appointed adjudicators for specific disputes, to the establishment of the first permanent international dispute settlement bodies. As also seen, the previous unsettled model of adjudication was also proposed by some of the negotiating parties in the original context of the European Coal and Steel Community and afterward, even in the negotiations of the European Economic Community Treaty. However, the European Communities definitely followed the second path, becoming one of the most prominent examples of the mentioned fundamental change in the nature of international adjudication.

However, the European Court of Justice was not paradigmatic of a second significant move. The shift in the institutional nature of international adjudication also gradually led, in several contexts, to the acceptance of the appointment of non-national judges, selected by international intergovernmental bodies, based on criteria related to individual qualities and regional (or other) criteria of representation. A crucial distinction arose (which still affects judicial selection processes today) between "full representation courts", where each state has a judge of its nationality on the court permanently, and "selective representation courts", where there are fewer seats than the number of states that are parties to the court's statute.[81] Obviously, in the latter type of courts, a choice has to be made between candidates from different states, thus giving rise to a higher degree of competition in which political influences, among other factors, can and do hold stay.

But there is an additional consequence to mention about this ideal partition. In "selective representation courts", such as the International Court of Justice, the International Criminal Court or the International Tribunal for the Law of the Sea (ITLOS), precise procedures tend to be established for the nomination of candidates and their election by the relevant intergovernmental bodies: in most cases these procedures are in the governing statutes, or alternatively or additionally they come via accepted conventions. In "full representation courts", on the other hand, the historical tendency in general terms has been little procedural guidance and even less external supervision on the choice of judges.[82] The states, as contracting parties, were in these contexts guaranteed through the perspective of an almost absolute sovereign exercise in their appointment, and therefore had no incentive to negotiate binding rules for the other parties, also to be applied for them.

This is the case for the European Communities' judicial body in its early decades. As already mentioned, Von Bogdandy and Venzke described it as "a sad irony in world history"[83] that an almost unfettered *intergovernmental approach* has endured "in rare purity", and until recently, with regard to the selection of judges of the European Court of Justice, "the one court that has contributed to overcoming classical international law more than any other". All the characteristic elements of what I define an *intergovernmental approach* to international judicial appointments were reified in the European Communities and the European Union, at least until very recently, until the Treaty of Lisbon and 2010. Traditionally, the members of the ECJ have always been appointed by "common accord of the Member States", without any formal assessment of their appropriateness being made at the supranational level. Since the ECSC Treaty, no mention has been made of any specific machinery or rules for nominating candidates, or, most of all, about their nationality, so that in theory, members of the Court could always be drawn from persons of nationality other than that of any one of the Member States.[84]

In fact, an established convention has always been in charge according to which every state nominates one judge for six years, with partial re-election every three years and the possibility of renewable mandates. As the recent historical research has demonstrated to us,[85] the most tangible *intergovernmental* aspect—the very principle according to which every Member State directly nominates one judge—was probably a natural and perhaps automatic principle to apply in the original context of six contracting entities: but, in any case, it was the result of open negotiations among those entities. During the prodromes of the European Coal and Steel Community, and also later during the negotiations of the Treaty of Rome, such an equation was the proposal of the French delegation.[86] As already highlighted, the French delegation originally argued for an old-fashioned system of supranational European adjudication, modelled after ad hoc arbitral tribunals nominated for single controversies. While this last proposal for an unsettled status of the Court of Justice decisively failed, the French proposal for selecting its judges prevailed, particularly against the representatives of the German delegation. The same historical research on the Communities' origins tells us that these latter made explicit their concern that a procedure dominated by the Member States might jeopardize the independence of the newly established EU judicial institution.[87]

In the resulting context, based on the "common accord of the Member States", if for some scholars "fears of political pressure gradually dissipated",[88] it is a fact that the Member States have traditionally enjoyed extensive discretionary powers in choosing their candidates for judicial office at the Court of Justice and the later established Court of first instance. Until the Treaty of Lisbon, no nominee was ever officially rejected, although at least in theory the governments of the Member States could have refused, in the internal negotiations, to grant their "accord" to a nomination.[89] Such a broad discretion was the result of an explicit mutual agreement among States and the consequent formal, un-effective mutual limits posed in a context of clear "full representation". The ECSC Treaty of Paris merely stated that judges were to be chosen from persons "offering every guarantee of independence and competence",[90] without even mentioning the need for specific legal training. At least a couple of actual nominees in the early days of the European Court were not technically trained as lawyers; on the contrary, as anecdotally narrated by today's scholars with a certain curiosity,[91] some of them were secondary school teachers who became trade unionists[92] or civil servants with an economic training.[93] In the recent words of one of the recent *chroniqueurs* of the history of European integration, "if the first nominations sometimes appeared to be quite far from, if not the legal realm, then at least the judicial function, the professional qualifications of the Court's members were heterogeneous, to say the least".[94]

The impression of a tribunal based on the pure and simple representation of national wills is also corroborated by the fact that—unlike in the context of other international court such as the ICJ, where Article 9 of the Statute asks the judges to represent "the main forms of civilization and the principal legal systems of the world"—no principles of representativity were even sketched for the ECJ, leaving full discretion to the executives.

In all, this can be easily read as the founding fear that a certain lack of judicial independence, also highlighted by the technical shortcomings of the candidates, was in balance with stressed accountability at least researched by the Member States. And this assumption can be corroborated if one juxtaposes and compares the thoughts of those who claim that, in this respect (and as seen), "fears of political pressure gradually dissipated",[95] with the ideas of the authors who, on the other hand, speculate on the ever-present strong political significance of these nominations. For instance, Karen J. Alter's work in the 1990s on the European Court of Justice notoriously found that national nominations to the Court were governed by a variety of political considerations "including party affiliation and political connections".[96] Her work was aimed at explaining how an "unusually influential international court"[97] managed "to escape member states control"[98]; but this did not imply a denial of the influence sought by the states and by their internal dynamics. Indeed, in some ways it was a reaffirmation of the problem of the possible "unusual" influence of the governments. Historically, it has always been "in the muffled atmosphere of ministerial cabinets and diplomatic meetings, sheltered from the public gaze",[99] that the members of the ECJ were appointed. But this grey nature of the nominations did not deprive them of political salience. In the famous reading offered by J.H.H. Weiler, the national appointments were not only sources of formal legitimation of the Court,[100] but also, at the empirical level, the sign of acceptance of its practices by governments. At least by "the 1970s and 1980s ... when any misconceptions about the 'least dangerous branch' would have already been dispelled", consequences could be drawn by the fact that they "eschewed any possible temptation at obvious 'court packing' or 'jurisdiction stripping'", and clearly nominated "most appointees ... with a past reputation of a general accord with the constitutional and material construct of the European Court of Justice".[101]

In this game, a role was inevitably played by a sort of mutual trust not only in relation to the Court, but also among the national governments. In here as well, the importance of factors other than those represented in schematic dichotomy merit/affiliation, such as the desire on the part of states to signal a credible commitment to the international legal order and the role of political patronage, played a role. But while this could be seen—as far as one can tell concerning a procedure which was far from transparent—as a positive dynamic for the overall quality of the judicial college, the same could not be said about the temporal nature of the judges' mandate. As it has always been renewable, the system of appointment gave national authorities leverage to apply pressure on the single members, and this has ever raised some concern for their independence.[102]

In any case, for a long while, another typical, if indirect, element of the *intergovernmental approach* to judicial selections has been detectable in the Court of Justice' case: the "startling"[103] little amount of academic attention on the matter that clashed with the prominent place of the Court within the European Union and in European law scholarship since the beginning of the integration process.[104] The reasons for the change and the evolution that the ECJ judicial appointment procedure experienced are not investigated very much in depth by the literature, and are rather to be found in the legislative history on the point—and in the contextual institutional setting—than in doctrinal speculation. As seen and in coherence with the evolutions at the national and international levels, it is essential to note that the need to reform the appointment process was in fact pushed up the European agenda from two separate sides.

First, pressure came from the European Parliament's political initiative. In the 1980s and early 1990s, the assembly demanded that the Council choose half of the Luxembourg judges and the Parliament choose the other half, or as an alternative that every judicial nominee be subjected to parliamentary assent.[105] In official publications, the Court of Justice had previously rejected bolder propositions for opening up the procedure to full parliamentary scrutiny by involving separate hearings of all nominees by a parliamentary committee.[106] In this sense and according to the comparative categories already exposed, one can say that the road to a real *cosmopolitan* reform of the European Union judicial selection process has been attempted under the guidance or with the envisioned central role of the European Parliament, as the unique body entrusted with a direct democratic/popular legitimation and therefore as the only institution able to imbue such legitimation on other bodies. Not by chance, this was also the solution suggested by the *rapport Spinelli* in 1984,[107] and then replicated in other Parliaments' resolutions in which the centrality of the assembly for the CJ judicial appointments was always envisaged.[108] But this bold step, modelled after the national selection processes in charge in the United States of America and tentatively transposed, eventually failed, as said, in international contexts such as the European Convention for Human Rights system.

Certain reflection groups with a strong participation of ECJ judges constituted the second source of pressure on the need for reform. These made reform proposals ahead of recent Treaty amendments. In particular, it was with the much-discussed Ole Due Report of 2000[109] that the creation of a judicial selection panel was first mooted, as an independent entity composed of highly qualified jurists to be established to give independent opinions on the national nominations. Furthermore, a complete discussion was held in the *Cercle de discussion* on the Court of Justice at the Convention on the Future of Europe (2002–2003), despite the alleged lack of debate in the context of Intergovernmental Conferences on the court when compared to other institutions.[110] In fact, the very idea of creating a Court with a restricted composition was openly debated and actually gathered certain sympathy from important then-members[111] as a way to enhance the effectiveness of the working methods and internal cohesion; such an innovative proposal would have broken the axiom of the "full representation court" system, inevitably calling for revolutionary changes in the selection of human resources, but it was discarded precisely by recalling the virtues of the principle of one judge per member state, also in terms of "the representation of all the legal traditions".[112]

Consequently, an examination of a full range of possible new procedures of selection (considered as directly applicable *rebus sic stantibus*) was undertaken. With a simple reaffirmation of then Art. 223 TCE on the nomination "by common accord of the governments of the Member

States", the *Cercle* discussed the idea of entrusting the Council of the powers of nomination in detail, to make, in their intention, the act of appointment theoretically amenable to judicial control[113]; with the idea, again, of associating the European Parliament in the procedure, "*par un avis ou avis conforme*",[114] and with or without the task of a direct audition of candidates. From both the minutes of the works in the *Cercle* and the Convention, and the words of the first commentators,[114] it is clear that the establishment of an independent "*comité d'évalutation*" was proposed as a "*contrepartie*" both "*au mantien du système actuel*" and to the opposite idea, preferred by the majority in the *Cercle*, of a major involvement of the Council.

A definite will emerged to establish a "*filtre*" to check and offer explicit guarantees on the "*qualité professionelle*" of the candidates, without leaving absolute leeway to the states but also without centralizing the definitive choices at the supranational level. This was a clear purpose of the institutional reformers, pursued without even being precise on the composition of such an independent panel,[116] or on the possibility for the states to nominate single or multiple candidates.[117] The only clarified detail—already discussed since the beginning and again in an explicit spirit of compromise—was on the opportunity of offering the Parliament the power to design a candidate in the panel, once decided not to take a clear step in the affiliation of the assembly in direct selection decisions. This was the element resulting from previous negotiations, which provided more significant roles for the assembly. The suggestion of a "*consultation obligatoire*" of an independent committee was then formalized in Article III-357 of the abortive Constitutional Treaty and subsequently ended up without any additional debate in the Treaty of Lisbon that entered into force on December 1, 2009.

Such a Panel is now prescribed and regulated by Article 255 of the Treaty on the Functioning of the European Union. It was officially established on March 1, 2010, pursuant to a decision of the Council of 25 February 2010.[118] The decision laying down the panel's operating rules was adopted simultaneously.[119] In line with the terms of Article 255 TFEU, both decisions were taken on the initiative of the President of the Court of Justice. The Panel comprises seven persons chosen from former members of the Court of Justice and the General Court, members of national supreme courts and lawyers of recognized competence, one of whom, as per the original idea, is proposed by the European Parliament. In the five years since its establishment, its works have been the object of a particular form of transparency in the form of official Reports published every year by the body itself[120] and, often, based on those, of first critical academic commentaries.[121]

The most critical remarks on the experiences of its early years of operation have been pointed to the only partial transparency of the actual functioning of the Panel. Point 6 of the operating rules in the Council Decision 2010/124/EU of 25 February 2010 mandates that Member State governments, once they have chosen their nominee as European judge, shall send their proposal to the General Secretariat of the Council. The proposal is then forwarded to the President of the Panel. If it wishes, the Panel can request that governments submit additional information or other materials on the candidatures, but it owns no self-standing powers of investigation and is thus dependent on their cooperation. After conducting the necessary analysis (including a possible interview), its members draft a collective opinion on the merits of the proposed candidate, which is communicated to the representatives of the Member State government. Unless the procedure is devoted to the renewal of the mandate of a Judge or an Advocate General, the interview of the candidate by the Panel constitutes, in practice, the centrepiece of the entire course of action. Point 7 of the Panel's operating rules explicates this key feature ("Except where a proposal relates to the reappointment of a Judge or Advocate-General, the panel shall hear the candidate"), adding that "the hearing shall take place in private". Suggestions to open up these sessions to the broader public have also been advanced during the negotiations of the Discussion Circle on the Court of Justice at the European Convention, but were ultimately rejected with a view to the protection of the candidates' privacy.

In addition to this, according to Point 5 of the operating rules, "all deliberations of the Panel", with no exception, "shall take place *in camera*". Once the Panel members have formulated their reasoned opinion on the candidate's suitability, this "shall be forwarded to the Representatives of the Governments of the Member States". Point 8 allows, if so desired, that the Presidency of the Council call upon the Panel's President to present the decision before the Member States' representatives meeting within that context. It has been inferred by the Panel itself, in its first composition, that a combined reading of these last rules implies that, apart from this previous case, the opinion ought to remain confidential.[122] In this sense, it would also seem to constitute a third-party document under the Union's general transparency rules, and under Article 4 of Regulation 1049/2001: therefore, the Council is bound to refuse access to a document where disclosure would undermine the privacy and integrity of individuals, in particular with regard to the protection of personal data.[123] Indeed, the Panel has concluded from this provision, in conjunction with the judgement of the Court in the *Bavarian Lager* case,[124] that its opinions on individual candidates could be principally qualified as personal data, so that their content, therefore, should not be disseminated to a broader audience.[125] The overriding rationale forms the desire to protect the candidates' reputation. Equally, it is thought that more openness here might discourage potential candidates from letting their name go forward.[126]

Scholars belittle the anxiety for a full transparency of what used to be, until a few years ago and in general comparative terms, a rather obscure phenomenon by highlighting that—by way of compensation—the Panel has decided to publish periodic reports on its activities[127]; that the various talks and publications by its members are thought to offer sufficient additional insight on its working methods and ordinary proceedings[128]; and that, in several ways, one can find further information on the nominations, given that no secrecy surrounds the governments' nominations to the panel, so that whenever a second candidate is put forward, everyone will understand that the first candidate did not make the grade. Moreover, since the Member States are obliged to submit all candidatures to the General Secretariat of the European Council and unsuccessful candidates can be traced online with relative ease, scholars have noticed that candidates are easily identifiable anyway.[129]

However, referring to specific works in this field, and apart from these particular points, one can tackle the overall diffuse, and understandable, criticism on the transparency of the system with the findings of my previous investigation on the comparative panorama of solutions for international judicial appointments, and the EU legislative history on the point (especially of the last decade of negotiations). It is clear from my reconstruction how the evolution in the appointment of the EU judges was significant, going from a completely obscure, *intergovernmental approach* to a functioning system of supranational filtering of candidates. But the reform undertaken was born and clearly evolved as a compromised solution. The idea of setting up an independent panel as a filter for national selections was already in place for some years for the Civil Service Tribunal of the European Union, so that the solution was already in the arsenal of tested solutions and well known to the drafters of the reform.[130] Also, as suggested by some scholars,[131] there is clear indication to be taken from the timing of the change. The fact that the idea made its appearance against a rather different background in the late 90s, being formalized by the Due Report,[132] was then discussed within the context of the EU formal constitutionalization experiment,[133] and then simply replicated at the end of the decade, makes one think about the institutional pressure that reformers identified in those circumstances. And it is evident that if the *ancien régime* was usually justified because of the mutual trust among governments in the selections of their judicial "representatives", and the principle that every Member State nominates one judge that survived multiple rounds of enlargement of the European Union, a decisive role must have been played by the catalyzation of the concerns provoked by the last decade's Eastern enlargements. The often suggested lack of trust in the sovereign procedures of the new Eastern Member States for the selection of their supranational candidate judges is the phenomenon usually indicated as the basis of the adoption of a new filter.

As found by scholars, "the advisory committee, in the form of the Article 255 TFEU Panel, had the decisive appeal of reforming, without radically changing, the existing arrangements".[134] The aim was clearly to guarantee objectivity in ensuring the competence of the nominated judges when a simple, unruled mutual trust seemed to be no more effective. But if "the creation of the panel provided for in Article 255 TFEU … to advise on appointments to the Court of Justice and General Court is part of a broader trend that interlinks with similar changes at the national level of EU Member States, and at the level of international and regional tribunals", as also recognized by commentators,[135] a proper contextualization tells us that the institutional choice made took the form of a compromise both vis-à-vis possibile comparative models and in terms of nature of prefigured supranational control over the sovereign choice of states. A pure, *cosmopolitan approach*—based on a centralization on the supranational institutions, for instance with an active role of the European Parliament as proposed in several ways—was explicitly discarded, at least in the actual phase of integration. A median solution, with the establishment of a soft check by a supranational independent panel, was considered sufficient. It leaves the exercise of sovereign prerogatives to governments but also creates a credible institutional setting for the control of their choices, and their coherence with those *liberal* values which are at the basis of the judicial selection choices of every Member State at its national level. To do so, a purely advisory mechanism, with simple "fact-finding prerogatives" and a kind of "pedagogical mission",[136] like the one provided in Article 255 TFEU, was established.

As seen with my taxonomy on models of international judicial selection, a *liberal* approach lies behind this choice, aimed at a sort of osmosis between the values and the procedures affirmed at the national level and their projection and control at the supranational level. Not even a form of *elective retention*, as per the prototypical form of *merit selection* procedures, was considered: not in the hands of the voters, and this can be considered as obvious in a supranational setting, but not even by the Parliament in an indirect move of representative confirmation. Quite the opposite, the original critical form of governmental renewal was left untouched, stressing the compromised nature of the solution once more. And the success of the indirect, pedagogical mission of such a form of *liberal* selective system—respecting the values that the States apply in their selection at the internal national level, with no full intrusion in their selection powers and no centralization—is proved by the first empirical evidence after some years from the reform. Not only the first public (even though anonymous) internal Reports of the Panel confirm both the need and functioning of this filtering system, since, far from being a paper tiger, it has indeed already produced a good number of negative opinions,[137] and has therefore effectively helped in the streamlining of selections. After all, this is the first and foremost objective of the reform. But, as some authors have recently highlighted,[138] there is also a sort of spillover effect to be registered at the national level which reinforces, I argue, the idea of an osmotic relationship based on liberal values in the selection criteria and processes, according, as usual for the phenomena I observe in this work, to both upward and downward transfers. The members of the Panel based on art. 255 TFEU are said to have taken particular account, in their first screenings (at least in the case of candidatures for a first term of office), of the following criteria: (1) the essential reasons which led the government to propose the candidate; (2) the letter from the candidate explaining the reasons for the application; (3) a bibliographic list of works (if any) published by the candidate; (4) the text of other recent publications, of which the candidate is the author, written in or translated into English or French (5) information on the national procedure that led to the candidate being selected.[139] And whenever any of these elements are not included in the dossier submitted, the standard practice of the Panel, recognized in the Activity Reports,[140] has been to ask the government of the Member State concerned to supplement the information. This includes information on the national procedures of selection. And in this sense, the Panel is, therefore, more and more performing an analysis of the candidate's suitability, in terms of legal and language expertise, professional experience and so on, coupled with an analysis of the suitability of those national procedures. The Panel operationalizes the criterion of "judicial independence" by insisting on a formalized national procedure that can guarantee both the independence and the relevant qualifications of candidates. To that effect, Member States should inform the Panel, for instance, "whether there was a public call for applications, whether a national selection committee was set up, and if so how the national selection committee was made up and what it recommended"[141]: and this also leads to an indirect exam of these techniques as constitutive elements of the candidacy exam.[142]

In turn, this indirect exam may have been responsible for the introduction of new procedures in several Member States, precisely in the last years. If national methods for the selection of national judges were, according to the *liberal* approach, the model for the selection at the international and at the European level, the new EU mechanism is found to have fostered, in turn, new and more open national procedures for candidates as EU judges and advocates general. According to recent research on the point, whereas in the 1990s within the vast majority of EU Member States the internal selection of supranational candidates was mostly an informal and diffused process, usually neither stipulated in law nor transparent, as of 2013 only very few countries from the proposed selection displayed these features.[143] Dumbrovský, Petkova, Van Der Sluis have explained that "mixed-type" selection with the involvement, of independent Advisory Committees have been put in place in the Netherlands, Finland, Germany, Austria, UK, Bulgaria, Slovenia, Croatia, the Czech Republic, Slovakia and Poland[144]; and listed only Spain, Italy and Greece as sticking to pure governmental, opaque nominations.[145] It is interesting to note in this respect that also Italy, meanwhile, has adopted in 2018 the system of open selective procedure to identify the new two candidates as judges to be submitted to the Council of the European Union, by explicitly referring to the criteria developed by Article 255 TFEU Panel and even defining a model of curriculum to be presented according to the supranational indications.[146]

3.3 The Evolution of Judicial Appointments as a Form of Improvement of the Court's Authority

From the analysis conducted throughout this chapter, it is possible to draw meaningful conclusions on the ability of the Court of Justice to evolve throughout the decades from an institutional point of view. The reform finally adopted with the Treaty of Lisbon (but already discussed earlier in several settings), which introduced an independent supranational panel for the screening of the national candidate European judges, is decisive in the improvement of the Court's authority in several respects.

First of all, the reform is a shield against the absolute discretionary role of Member States' in the selection of the Court's main human resources. And in forging this shield, the reform provides for an indirect increase of the Court's influence in the selection process[147]: according to Article 255 TFEU, its President presents a proposal for the operating rules of the Panel and for its composition, which the governments of the Member States so far have followed,[148] so that commentators have talked of a factual right of co-determination.[149] Moreover, Article 255 TFEU provides for the presence of former members of the Court in the Panel, fostering the *esprit de corps* in the selection process.

One can easily see in the analysis above the institutional capability of the European Court to evolve by internalizing a model that is now widespread at a comparative level, both in national and international settings. As said, the possibility of an independent screening as a filter of sovereign political choices of selection is the quintessential element of a so-called "liberal approach"[150] to the solution of the judges' independence/accountability conundrum.

The adoption of such a model can be easily depicted as a utilitarian move in mimetic terms, as stipulated. It is easy to understand how it improves the authority of the Court, not only from the inherent quality of the Court's composition, but also from the perspective of its external image—in a self-empowerment move that is typical, as I argue, of the institutional evolution of the Court across decades. The selected model was a compromise between other more radical options, and was criticized by some commentators.[151] Still, it was the model ostensibly suggested by Court's members in the various debates occurred, preferences of other institutions' (such as the EU Parliament) notwithstanding. It preserves the power and the image of the Court, at the same time avoiding open political pressures on the appointments as it is often the case for the EU Court of Auditors.[152]

This last is not, unfortunately, just a theoretical point. As observed, the annual reports published by Article 255 Panel admit that the primary interest of the body is currently in assessing linguistic capacities and above all specialistic competence in the field of EU law of the candidates. This is of course rational in ordinary times. But nowadays, in the era of so-called democratic backsliding in various Member States of the Union,[153] it is not dystopic to think to a possible role of the Panel in screening the independence of the candidates vis-à-vis the political preferences of their Member States' governments: after all, certain critical episodes already emerged in the past at the national level,[154] and it is well known that one of the most evident symptoms of said democratic backsliding is precisely the attack on the independence of the judiciary by governments.[155] It is a specific merit of the compromise solution inherent in the adopted model not to leave to political discretion, neither at the national nor at the supranational level, crucial decisions of the kind.

In this perspective, the success in the evolutionary model is even more visible from the element I touched upon in the last part of the chapter. As typical in the osmotic idea of the "liberal approach" described by Von Bogdandy and Venzke, the reform in the appointment system was so strong and decisive that, in its actual dynamics, it was not only influenced by existing procedures in Member States for other candidates, but has come to influence, in turn, the respective national procedures for the European candidates, and it is aimed at influencing. Precisely with reference to the practice of some Member States to restrict the independence of the national judges, the Court of Justice has recently issued a much-discussed line of cases that opened the door to the conversion of EU values as standards for the organization of the national judiciary, thanks to both a creative interpretation of Article 19(1) TEU and the firm reference to Article 2 TEU and judicial independence.[156] It seems that such an interpretative approach can be coupled with the institutional role of Article 255 Panel in structuring a federal-like system where supranational controls on the discretionary national choices are legitimized: in this respect, the Court ends up playing a central, though indirect, role, which again increases its authority.

Notes

1. R. Mackenzie, P. Sands, International Courts and Tribunals and the Independence of the International Judge, in 44 Harvard International Law Journal, 2003, p. 272, at 277–278.
2. *Ibidem.*
3. K. Malleson, Introduction, in K. Malleson, Peter H. Russell (eds.), Appointing Judges in an Age of Juducial Power: Critical Perspectives from around the World, University of Toronto Press 2007, p. 3.
4. *Ibidem.*
5. R. Mackenzie, P. Sands, Judicial selection for International Court: Towards Common Principles and Practices, in K. Malleson, Peter H. Russell (eds.), Appointing Judges in an Age of Juducial Power: Critical Perspectives from around the World, *op. cit.*, p. 216. See in the same sense, and with the same image, D. Terris, C.P.R. Romano, L. Swigart, The International Judge: An Introduction to the Men and Women Who Decide the World's Cases, Oxford University Press 2007, p. 104.
6. To echo the notorious phrase by M. Koskenniemi, P. Leino, Fragmentation of International Law? Postmodern Anxieties, in Leiden Journal of International Law, *op. cit.*
7. G. Gee, The Persistent Politics of Judicial Selection: A Comparative Analysis, in A. Seibert-Fohr (ed.), Judicial Independence in Transition, Springer 2012, p. 121 *et seq.*; J. Bell, Judiciaries within Europe: A Comparative Review, Cambridge University Press 2010, at p. 15 *et seq.*
8. See among the many, in the literature in English, F.G. Jacobs, Is the Court of Justice of the European Communities a Constitutional Court?, in D.M. Curtin, D. O'Keeffe (eds.), Constitutional Adjudication in European Community and National Law, Butterworth 1992, p. 25; A. Arnull, A Constitutional Court for Europe?, in 6 Cambridge Yearbook of European Legal Studies, 2003–2004, p. 1; B. Vesterdorf, A Constitutional Court for the EU?, in 4 International Journal of Constitutional Law, 2006, p. 607; L. Azoulai, The Future Constitutional Role of the European Court of Justice, in J. Baquero Cruz, C. Closa (eds.), European Integration From Rome to Berlin, Peter Lang 2009, p. 229.
9. Intended as top domestic review courts and international courts, which, as I will explain further in the next paragraphs, tend to have similar problems of selection and therefore similar procedures for recruiting their staff.
10. A. Von Bogdandy, I. Venzke, In Whose Name? An Investigation of International Courts' Public Authority and Its Democratic Justification, in 23 European Journal of International Law, 2012, p. 7.
11. K. Malleson, Introduction, *op. cit.*, p. 4.

12. M. Andenas, D. Fairgrieve, Judicial Independence and Accountability: National Traditions and International Standards, in G. Canivet, M. Andenas, D. Fairgrieve (eds.), Independence, Accountability and the Judiciary, British Institute of International and Comparative Law 2006, p. 3.
13. C. Guarnieri, D. Piana, Judicial Independence and the Rule of Law: Exploring the European Experience, in S. Shetreet, C. Forsyth (eds.), The Culture of Judicial Independence: Conceptual Foundations and Practical Challenges, Martinus Nijhoff–Brill Publishers 2012, p. 113.
14. A. Paterson, The Scottish Judicial Appointment Board: New Wine in Old Bottles?, in K. Malleson, Peter H. Russell (eds.), Appointing Judges in an Age of Juducial Power: Critical Perspectives from around the World, *op. cit.*, p. 13, at 14.
15. M. Andenas, D. Fairgrieve, Judicial Independence and Accountability: National Traditions and International Standards, *op. cit.*, at 8.
16. See the general reflections by J.H. Merryman, The Civil Law Tradition, Stanford University Press 2007, p. 34 *et seq.*; R.C. van Caenegem, Judges, Legislators and Professors: Chapters in European Legal History, Cambridge University Press 1987, p. 131 *et seq.*
17. M. Tushnet, The Constitution of the United States of America: A Contextual Analysis, Hart 2009, p. 125. See also C. Nelson, A Re-evaluation of Scholarly Explanations for the Rise of the Elective Judiciary in Antebellum America, in 37 American Journal of Legal History, 1993, p. 190, at 191–192: "Delegates [to state constitutional conventions] branded the appointive system 'a relic of monarchy' and the 'last vestige of aristocracy'; some delegates referred to 'the immortal Jackson,' and there was much talk of the need to make the judiciary 'consonant with our theory of government".
18. See the historical reconstruction by T.R. Phillips, The Merits of Merit Selection, in 32 Harvard Journal of Law and Public Policy, 2009, p. 67, at 71 *et seq.*
19. J.W. Hurst, The Growth of American Law: The Law Makers, Little Brown and Company 1950, at 133, as also quoted by J. Goldschmidt, Merit Selection: Current Status, Procedures, and Issues, in 49 University of Miami Law Review, 1994, p. 1, at 6.
20. A.M. Kales, Methods of Selecting and Retiring Judges, in 11 Journal of the American Judicature Society, 1928, pp. 133, 134–135.
21. R. Pound, The Causes of Popular Dissatisfaction with the Administration of Justice, in 40 American Law Review, 1906, p. 729, at 748.
22. See T.R. Phillips, The Merits of Merit Selection, *op. cit.*, at 76 *et seq.*
23. See P.H. Russell, Judicial Recruitment, Training, and Careers, in P. Cane, H. Kritzer, The Oxford Handbook of Empirical Legal Research, Oxford University Press 2010, p. 522, at 536.

24. According to the definition popularized by Justice Louis Brandeis in New State Ice Co. v. Liebmann, 285 U.S. 262 (1932).
25. See the reflections of K. Malleson, The New Judiciary: The Effects of Expansion and Activism, Ashgate 1999, at pp. 140–151.
26. K. Malleson, Introduction, *op. cit.*, pp. 3–4 *et seq.*; see also S.A. Akkas, Appointment of Judges: A Key Issue of Judicial Independence, in 16 Bond Law Review, 2004, p. 1.
27. M.L. Volcansek, Appointing Judges the European Way, in 34 Fordham Urban Law Journal, 2006, p. 363.
28. K. Malleson, Introduction, *op. cit.*, p. 5.
29. *Ibidem.*
30. This is the formal status, in some legal orders, of constitutional courts' judges.
31. K. Malleson, Introduction, *op. cit.*, p. 6.
32. *Ibidem.*
33. See for details already The role of the Judicial Service Commission: proceedings. Multilateral meeting organized by the Council of Europe jointly with the General Council of the Judiciary of Spain, Council of Europe Press 1995.
34. Formally a non-departmental public body which was created on 3 April 2006 through the Constitutional Reform Act 2005: see on its activity, in comparative perspective, J.L. Maute, English Reforms to Judicial Selection: Comparative Lessons for American States, in 34 Fordham Urban Law Journal, 2007, p. 387.
35. The *Domarnamnden*, an independent committee composed of senior judges and lawyers: the constitutional reforms in force since January 2011 now require candidates for permanent roles to publicly apply to it.
36. See for details A.M. Mavcic, Guarantees of Independence of the Judiciary: the Slovenian Experience, paper presented at the International Judicial Reform Symposium, 2–3 April 2012, Ankara, Turkey, available at the website http://www.concourts.net/lecture/Ankara%202012_1_.pdf (accessed 2 March 2020).
37. See on this S. Turenne, Constitutional Adjudication and Appointments to the UK Supreme Court, in S. Shetreet (ed.), The Culture of Judicial Independence, Brill 2014, p. 396, at 406.
38. See for details on the German procedures J. Bell, Judiciaries within Europe: A Comparative Review, *op. cit.*, at 127.
39. See H. de Waele, Not Quite the Bed That Procrustes Built? Dissecting the System for Selecting Judges at the Court of Justice of the European Union, in M. Bobek (ed.), Selecting Europe's Judges, Oxford University Press 2015, p. 41.
40. K. Malleson, Introduction, *op. cit.*, at 7.

41. E.A. Posner, J.C. Yoo, Judicial Independence in International Tribunals, in 93 California Law Review, 2005, p. 1.
42. L.R. Helfer, A.M. Slaughter, Why States Create International Tribunals: A Response to Professors Posner and Yoo, *op.cit.*
43. R. Mackenzie, K. Malleson, P. Martin, P. Sands, Introduction, in R. Mackenzie, K. Malleson, P. Martin, P. Sands, Selecting International Judges: Principle, Process, and Politics, Oxford University Press 2010, p. 2.
44. *Ibidem.*
45. E. Voeten, The Politics of International Judicial Appointments, in 9 Chicago Journal of International Law, 2009, p. 389.
46. See Chapter XIV of the Charter of the United Nations, available at the website http://www.un.org/en/documents/charter/chapter14.shtml (accessed 2 March 2020).
47. See Note 65 in Chapter 1 for references.
48. The Caribbean Court of Justice (CCJ).
49. Most notably the African Court on Human and Peoples' Rights and the East African Court of Justice.
50. R. Mackenzie, P. Sands, Judicial Selection for International Courts: Towards Common Principles and Practices, in K. Malleson, Peter H. Russell (eds.), Appointing Judges in an Age of Judicial Power. Critical Perspectives from around the World, *op. cit.*, p. 216.
51. R. Mackenzie, P. Sands, International Courts and Tribunals and the Independence of the International Judge, *op. cit.*, at 274.
52. See above for the reference to R. Mackenzie, P. Sands, Judicial Selection for International Courts: Towards Common Principles and Practices, *op. cit.*, p. 216; and D. Terris, C.P.R. Romano, L. Swigart, The International Judge: An Introduction to the Men and Women Who Decide the World's Cases, *op. cit.*, p. 104.
53. R. Mackenzie, P. Sands, Judicial Selection for International Courts: Towards Common Principles and Practices, *op. cit.*, p. 216.
54. *Ivi*, at 217.
55. M.O. Hudson, International Tribunals: Past and Future, Carnegie Endowment for International Peace and Brookings Institution 1944, at p. 34.
56. Paradigmatic in this respect is the Statute of the International Court of Justice, which mandates, under articles 3 and 9, that the ICJ judges should represent "the main forms of civilization and (…) the principal legal systems of the world".
57. C. Tomuschat, National Representation of Judges and Legitimacy of International Jurisdictions: Lessons from ICJ to ECJ?, in I. Pernice, J. Kokott, C. Saunders (eds.), The Future of the European Judicial System in a Comparative Perspective, Nomo Vertlag 2006, p. 183, at 183.

58. *Ibidem.*
59. *Ibidem.*
60. *Ivi*, at 184.
61. A. Von Bogdandy, I. Venzke, In Whose Name? An Investigation of International Courts' Public Authority and Its Democratic Justification, *op. cit.*
62. *Ivi*, at 37.
63. J. Crawford, J. McIntyre, Judicial Impartiality and the International Judiciary, in S. Shetreet, C. Forsyth (eds.), The Culture of Judicial Independence: Conceptual Foundations and Practical Challenges, *op. cit.*, at p. 190.
64. "Article 7 Full powers. 1. A person is considered as representing a State for the purpose of adopting or authenticating the text of a treaty or for the purpose of expressing the consent of the State to be bound by a treaty if: (a) he produces appropriate full powers; or (b) it appears from the practice of the States concerned or from other circumstances that their intention was to consider that person as representing the State for such purposes and to dispense with full powers. 2. In virtue of their functions and without having to produce full powers, the following are considered as representing their State: (a) Heads of State, Heads of Government and Ministers for Foreign Affairs, for the purpose of performing all acts relating to the conclusion of a treaty; (b) heads of diplomatic missions, for the purpose of adopting the text of a treaty between the accrediting State and the State to which they are accredited; (c) representatives accredited by States to an international conference or to an international organization or one of its organs, for the purpose of adopting the text of a treaty in that conference, organization or organ".
65. A. Von Bogdandy, I. Venzke, In Whose Name? An Investigation of International Courts' Public Authority and Its Democratic Justification, *op. cit.*, at 37.
66. R. Mackenzie, K. Malleson, P. Martin, P. Sands, The Nomination Process, in *Eid.*, Selecting International Judges: Principle, Process, and Politics, Oxford University Press 2010, at p. 65.
67. *Ibidem.*
68. P. McAuliffe, Selecting International Judges: Principle, Process, and Politics, in 11 International Criminal Law Review, 2011, p. 359.
69. R. Mackenzie, K. Malleson, P. Martin, P. Sands, The Nomination Process, *op. cit.*, at p. 65.
70. P. McAuliffe, Selecting International Judges: Principle, Process, and Politics, *op. cit.*, at 359.
71. A. Von Bogdandy, I. Venzke, In Whose Name? An Investigation of International Courts' Public Authority and Its Democratic Justification, *op. cit.*, at 34.

72. See R. Mackenzie, K. Malleson, P. Martin, P. Sands, The International Court of Justice and the International Criminal Court in Historical Context, in *Eid.*, Selecting International Judges: Principle, Process, and Politics, *op. cit.*, at 21.
73. See for instance http://www.icc-cpi.int/iccdocs/asp_docs/ASP12/ICC-ASP-12-23-ENG.pdf, pp. 3–4.
74. A. Von Bogdandy, I. Venzke, In Whose Name? An Investigation of International Courts' Public Authority and Its Democratic Justification, *op. cit.*, at 35.
75. *Ibidem.*
76. As per the Recommendation 1649 (2004) of the Parliamentary Assembly of the Council of Europe concerning "Candidates for the European Court of Human Rights", paragraph 3.
77. As per the objective No. 8 stated at the High Level Conference on the Future of the European Court of Human Rights, 19 February 2010, in the so called Interlaken Declaration, available at the website https://wcd.coe.int/com.instranet.InstraServlet?command=com.instranet.CmdBlobGet&InstranetImage=2045095&SecMode=1&DocId=1547616&Usage=2 (accessed 2 March 2020).
78. Available at the website http://assembly.coe.int/CommitteeDocs/2010/20100504_ajdoc12rev.pdf (accessed 2 March 2020).
79. Available at the website http://assembly.coe.int/nw/xml/XRef/Xref-XML2HTML-en.asp?fileid=17704&lang=en (accessed 2 March 2020).
80. A. Von Bogdandy, I. Venzke, In Whose Name? An Investigation of International Courts' Public Authority and Its Democratic Justification, *op. cit.*, at 35.
81. E. Voeten, The Politics of International Judicial Appointments, *op. cit.*, at 410–402.
82. See R. Mackenzie, K. Malleson, P. Martin, P. Sands, The International Court of Justice and the International Criminal Court in Historical Context, *op. cit.*, at p. 8.
83. A. Von Bogdandy, I. Venzke, In Whose Name? An Investigation of International Courts' Public Authority and Its Democratic Justification, *op. cit.*, at 37.
84. T. Kennedy, Thirteen Russians! The Composition of the European Court of Justice, in A.I.L. Campbell, M. Voyatzi (eds.), Legal Reasoning and Judicial Interpretation of European Law: Essays in honour of Lord Mackenzie-Stuart, Trenton Publishing 1996, p. 69.
85. A. Boerger-De Smedt, La Cour de Justice dans les négociations du traité de Paris instituant la CECA, *op. cit.*, at 19 *et seq.*; see also J.M. Sauvé, Le rôle du comité 255 dans la sélection du juge de l'Union, in A. Rosas, E. Levits, Y. Bot (eds.), The Court of Justice and the Construction of Europe: Analyses and Perspectives on Sixty Years of Case-law - La Cour

de Justice et la Construction de l'Europe: Analyses et Perspectives de Soixante Ans de Jurisprudence, *op. cit.*, p. 99, at 100.

86. A. Boerger-De Smedt, La Cour de Justice dans les négociations du traité de Paris instituant la CECA, *op. cit.*, at 20–21; D. Tamm, The History of the Court of Justice of the European Union Since Its Origin, *op. cit.*, at 16 *et seq.*
87. *Ibidem*; see also T. Dumbrovský, B. Petkova, M. Van Der Sluis, Judicial Appointments: The Article 255 TFEU Advisory Panel and Selection Procedures in the Member States, in 51 Common Market Law Review, 2014, p. 455, at 458.
88. T. Dumbrovský, B. Petkova, M. Van Der Sluis, Judicial appointments: The Article 255 TFEU Advisory Panel and selection procedures in the Member States, *op. cit.*, at 458.
89. *Ibidem.*
90. Art 32 of the Treaty Establishing the European Coal and Steel Community: "Article 32. The Court shall be composed of seven judges, appointed for six years by agreement among the governments of the member States from among persons of recognized independence and competence. A partial change in membership of the Court shall occur every three years, affecting alternatively three members and four members. The three members whose terms expire at the end of the first period of three years shall be designated by lot. Judges shall be eligible for reappointment. The number of judges may be increased by unanimous vote of the Council on proposal by the Court. The judges shall designate one of their number as President for a three-year term".
91. H. de Waele, Not Quite the Bed That Procrustes Built? Dissecting the System for Selecting Judges at the Court of Justice of the European Union, *op. cit.*, p. 24.
92. This is the case of Petrus Josephus Servatius Serrarens, first Dutch judge of the ECSC Court despite its lack of any legal training.
93. This is the case of Jacques Rueff, first French judge of the ECSC Court and of the Court of the European Communities.
94. A. Cohen, Ten Majestic Figures in Long Amaranth Robes': The Formation of the Court of Justice of the European Communities, in A. Vauchez, B. de Witte (eds.), Lawyering Europe, *op. cit.*, at 30.
95. T. Dumbrovský, B. Petkova, M. Van Der Sluis, Judicial appointments: The Article 255 TFEU Advisory Panel and selection procedures in the Member States, *op. cit.*, at 458.
96. K.J. Alter, Who Are the 'Masters of the Treaty'?: European Governments and the European Court of Justice, in *Ead.*, The European Court's Political Power: Selected Essays, Oxford University Press 2009, p. 109.
97. *Ibidem.*
98. *Ivi*, at 110.

99. R. Dehousse, The European Court of Justice: The Politics of Judicial Integration, *op. cit.*, at 14.
100. J.H.H. Weiler, Journey to an Unknown Destination: A Retrospective and Prospective of the European Court of Justice in the Arena of Political Integration, *op. cit.*, at 424.
101. *Ivi*, at 426.
102. See the remarks by J.H.H. Weiler, Epilogue: Judging the Judges—Apology and Critique, in M. Adams, H. de Waele, J. Meeusen, G. Straetmans (eds.), Judging Europe's Judges: The Legitimacy of the Case Law of the European Court of Justice, *op. cit.*, p. 235.
103. T. Dumbrovský, B. Petkova, M. Van Der Sluis, Judicial appointments: The Article 255 TFEU Advisory Panel and selection procedures in the Member States, *op. cit.*, at 456.
104. On the social recruitment of the early ECJ in the 1950s and 1960s see A Cohen, 'Ten Majestic Figures in Long Amaranth Robes': The Formation of the Court of Justice of the European Communities, *op. cit.*, the only other recent accounts on appointments at the ECJ being D. Siebert, Die Auswahl der Richter am Gerichtshof der Europäischen Gemeinschaften: zu der erforderlichen Reform des Art. 167 EGV, Taschenbuch 1997, and S.J. Kenney, The Members of the Court of Justice of the European Communities, in 5 Columbia Journal of European Law, 1999, p. 101.
105. F.G. Jacobs, The Member States, the Judges and the Procedure, in Institut D'Études Européennes. Université Libre de Bruxelles (ed.), La Cour de Justice des Communautés Européennes, Éditions de l'Université de Bruxelles 1981, p. 11.
106. Report of the Court of Justice on certain aspects of the application of the Treaty on European Union (Luxembourg, May 1995), paragraph 13, available at the website http://www.cvce.eu/content/publication/2003/4/2/3644862f-2e8f-4170-9616-e573a41b61c5/publishable_en.pdf (accessed 2 March 2020): "(…) the Court considers that a reform involving a hearing of each nominee by a parliamentary committee would be unacceptable. Prospective appointees would be unable adequately to answer the questions put to them without betraying the discretion incumbent upon persons whose independence must, in the words of the treaties, be beyond doubt and without prejudging positions they might have to adopt with regard to contentious issues which they would have to decide in the exercise of their judicial function".
107. Projet de traité instituant l'Union européenne sur le site du CVCE. Retranscription du Bulletin des Communautés européennes. Luxembourg: Office des publications officielles des Communautés européennes. Février 1984, n° 2, available at the website http://www.cvce.eu/obj/projet_de_traite_instituant_l_union_europeenne_14_fevrier_1984-fr-0c1f92e8-db44-4408-b569-c464cc1e73c9.html (accessed 2 March 2020).

See Article 30: «La Cour de justice assure le respect du droit dans l'interprétation et l'application du présent traité et de tout acte adopté en vertu de celui-ci. 2. *Les membres de la Cour sont nommés pour moitié par le Parlement et pour moitié par le Conseil de l'Union. Au cas où le nombre des membres serait impair, le Parlement en nomme un de plus que le Conseil.* 3. L'organisation de la Cour, le nombre et le statut de ses membres et la durée de leur mandat sont régis par une loi organique qui détermine également la procédure et les majorités requises pour leur nomination. Jusqu'à l'entrée en vigueur de cette loi, les dispositions pertinentes des traités communautaires et les mesures prises pour leur mise en œuvre s'appliquent à la Cour de justice de l'Union. 4. La Cour arrête son règlement de procédure» (emphasis added).

108. See e.g. the resolution of 22 November 1990 (rapport Martin), in which it was proposed to nominate the judges «pour 12 ans par le Conseil avec l'avis conforme du Parlement européen»; the resolution of 16 September 1993, according to which «les membres de la CJCE devraient être élus par le Parlement européen et le Conseil, selon une procédure uniforme à définir, pour un mandat de 9 ans non renouvelable»; the resolution of 10 February 1994 (rapport Herman), proposing judges «nommés par le Parlement, à la majorité des membres qui le composent et par le Conseil, pour un mandat de 9 ans non renouvelable. Les modalités de cette nomination sont précisées par une loi organique»; the resolution of 13 March 1996 (rapport Dury – Maij-Weggen), again suggesting that «il conviendrait de renforcer le rôle du Parlement européen, l'avis conforme étant prévu pour les nominations à la Cour des comptes et à la CJCE». See for an extended analysis of these positions see G. Garzòn Clariana, Le Parlement européen dans le développement de la CJCE, in N. Colneric, D. Edward, J.P. Puissochet, D.R. Colomer (eds.), Une Communauté de droit Festschrift per Gil Carlos Rodríguez Iglesias, Berliner Wissenschafts-Verlag 2003, p. 21.
109. Report by the Working Party on the Future of the European Communities' Court System for the European Commission, January 2000, available at the website http://ec.europa.eu/dgs/legal_service/pdf/due_en.pdf (accessed 2 March 2020).
110. R. Passos, Le Système juridictionnel de l'Union, in G. Amato, H. Bribosia, B. de Witte (eds.), Genèse et destinée de la Constitution européenne, Bruylant 2007, p. 565, at 565.
111. *Ivi*, at 584: the President of the Court of the time, Gil Carlos Rodriguez Iglesias, expressed his favour for the proposal, together with then members M.M. Vitorino, Floch, Mme Azevedo, Lord Maclennan.
112. CONV 573/03, (CERCLE I-7) du 21 février 2003. See on this point again R. Passos, Le Système juridictionnel de l'Union, *op. cit.*, at 584.
113. R. Passos, Le Système juridictionnel de l'Union, *op. cit.*, at 584.

114. *Ibidem.*
115. *Ivi*, at 585.
116. *Ibidem.*
117. *Ivi*, at 586.
118. 2010/125/: Council Decision of 25 February 2010 appointing the members of the panel provided for in Article 255 of the Treaty on the Functioning of the European Union.
119. 2010/124/: Council Decision of 25 February 2010 relating to the operating rules of the panel provided for in Article 255 of the Treaty on the Functioning of the European Union.
120. However, at the time of writing, the last Report published online seems to be the "Third Activity Report of the Panel Provided for by Article 255 of the Treaty on the Functioning of the European Union" of the end of 2013, available at the website http://curia.europa.eu/jcms/upload/docs/application/pdf/2014-02/rapport-c-255-en.pdf (accessed 2 March 2020).
121. See for example T. Dumbrovský, B. Petkova, M. Van Der Sluis, Judicial appointments: The Article 255 TFEU Advisory Panel and selection procedures in the Member States, *op. cit.*; A. Peri, La selezione dei giudici della Corte di giustizia. Poteri e limiti del comitato ex. Art. 255 TFUE, in 4 Diritto Pubblico Comparato ed Europeo, 2012, p. 1472; organically and in a comparative perspective, M. Bobek (ed.), Selecting Europe's Judges, *op. cit.*; and, as views from within, coming from members of the first appointed Panel, Lord Mance, Judges judged, in European Advocate (Journal of the Bar European Society), 2012, p. 2; J.M. Sauvé, Le rôle du comité 255 dans la sélection du juge de l'Union, *op. cit.*
122. See the first "Activity report of the panel provided for by Article 255 of the Treaty on the Functioning of the European Union", available at the website http://register.consilium.europa.eu/doc/srv?l=EN&f=ST%206509%202011%20INIT (accessed 2 March 2020), at pp. 5–6; on the point, see also H. de Waele, Not Quite the Bed That Procrustes Built? Dissecting the System for Selecting Judges at the Court of Justice of the European Union, *op. cit.*, at 21.
123. Regulation 1049/2001 of the European Parliament and of the Council of 30 May 2001 regarding public access to European Parliament, Council and Commission documents [2001] OJ L145/43.
124. C-28/08 P Judgement of 29 June 2010, Commission/Bavarian Lager (C-28/08 P, ECR 2010 p. I-6055) ECLI:EU:C:2010:378.
125. Lord Mance, The Composition of the European Court of Justice, talk given to the United Kingdom Association for European Law on 19th October 2011, available at the website http://ukael.org/past_events_46_1935078262.pdf (accessed 2 March 2020), at pp. 19–20.

126. J.M. Sauvé, Le rôle du comité 255 dans le sélection du juge de l'Union, *op. cit.*, p. 116.
127. H. de Waele, Not Quite the Bed that Procrustes Built? Dissecting the System for Selecting Judges at the Court of Justice of the European Union, *op. cit.*, at 38.
128. *Ivi*, at 39.
129. T. Dumbrovský, B. Petkova, M. Van Der Sluis, Judicial appointments: The Article 255 TFEU Advisory Panel and selection procedures in the Member States, *op. cit.*, at 461.
130. See 2005/151/EC, Euratom: Council Decision of 18 January 2005 appointing members of the Committee provided for in Article 3(3) of Annex I to the Protocol on the Statute of the Court of Justice.
131. See T. Dumbrovský, The European Court of Justice after the Eastern Enlargement: An Emerging Inner Circle of Judges, paper presented at the EUSA Twelfth Biennial Conference, Boston, March 2011, available at the website http://papers.ssrn.com/sol3/papers.cfm?abstract_id=2551211 (accessed 2 March 2020) and the reflections by M. Bobek, Epilogue: Searching for the European Hercules, in *Id.* (ed.), Selecting Europe's Judges, *op. cit.*, p. 279. The same point was also suggested by L. Pech, The CJEU at 60: Still Fit for Purpose?, paper presented at the 50th anniversary jubilee conference of the Common Market Law Review "Current Challenges for EU Law—New Views, New Inspirations", 26–27 April 2013, Noordwijk, Netherlands.
132. See Note 109 in this Chapter.
133. See the reflections above, and the references to R. Passos, Le Système juridictionnel de l'Union, *op. cit.*
134. T. Dumbrovský, B. Petkova, M. Van Der Sluis, Judicial appointments: The Article 255 TFEU Advisory Panel and selection procedures in the Member States, *op. cit.*, at 459.
135. *Ivi*, at 456.
136. A. Alemanno, How Transparent Is Transparent Enough? Balancing Access to Information versus Privacy in Judicial Selection, in M. Bobek (ed.), Selecting Europe's Judges, *op. cit.*, p. 202, at 220–221.
137. The last published "Report of the Panel Provided for by Article 255 of the Treaty on the Functioning of the European Union", of the end of 2013, available at the website http://curia.europa.eu/jcms/upload/docs/application/pdf/2014-02/rapport-c-255-en.pdf (accessed 2 March 2020), at p. 9, describes 7 of the 67 opinions delivered since the panel started working as unfavourable, with no unfavourable opinions were delivered on candidatures for the renewal of a term of office, so that "22% (7 out of 32) of the opinions on candidatures for a first term of office were unfavourable".

138. T. Dumbrovský, B. Petkova, M. Van Der Sluis, Judicial appointments: The Article 255 TFEU Advisory Panel and selection procedures in the Member States, *op. cit.*, at 455–448.
139. All criteria explicitly enumerated in the second "Activity report of the panel provided for by Article 255 of the Treaty on the Functioning of the European Union", of December 2012, available at the website http://register.consilium.europa.eu/doc/srv?l=EN&f=ST%205091%202013%20INIT (accessed 2 March 2020), at p. 8.
140. *Ibidem*: "Whenever any of these elements, bar the last one, are not in the dossier forwarded to the panel, the panel automatically requests it".
141. *Ivi*, at 9: "Since the start of its work, the panel has requested information on the national selection procedure whenever this information was not provided directly by the Member State proposing the candidature. The purpose of the request is to know whether there was a call for applications, whether an independent body had decided on the merits, i.e. the professional merits of the candidature chosen with regard to the post to be filled, or whether any other selection procedure offering at least equivalent guarantees, such as choice of the candidate by a Member State's highest court, had been used. Lastly, it wishes to know what conclusions the government drew from such a procedure, if it exists".
142. *Ibidem*, admittedly: "a national selection procedure, even a very comprehensive and credible procedure, cannot, of course, by itself constitute grounds for considering as suitable a candidature deemed unsuitable by the panel. The existence of a national selection procedure can nonetheless help the panel overcome any doubts it may harbour following its examination of the dossier and/or the hearing of the candidate. In other words, the existence of a national procedure enabling the merits of candidates to be assessed in an independent and objective manner may, when in the eyes of the panel a candidature has certain weak points, work in the candidate's favour as the panel's doubts and questions can be put aside by the panel's justified trust in the national procedure".
143. T. Dumbrovský, B. Petkova, M. Van Der Sluis, Judicial appointments: The Article 255 TFEU Advisory Panel and selection procedures in the Member States, *op. cit.*, p. 466 e ss.; S. Spáč, Recruiting European Judges in the Age of Judicial Self Government, in German Law Journal, 2018, p. 2077 e ss.
144. T. Dumbrovský, B. Petkova, M. Van Der Sluis, Judicial appointments: The Article 255 TFEU Advisory Panel and selection procedures in the Member States, *op. cit.*, at 466 *et seq.*
145. *Ibidem.*
146. D.P.C.M. in G.U. 4a serie speciale del 9 ottobre 2018, n. 80, announcing an open procedure «volta all'individuazione delle proposte del Governo italiano da sottoporre al Consiglio dell'Unione europea per il rinnovo del mandato di due giudici del Tribunale dell'Unione europea».

147. C. Krenn, Self-Government at the Court of Justice of the European Union: A Bedrock for Institutional Success, in 19 German Law Journal, 2018, p. 2007, 2018, with reference to A. Alemanno, How Transparent is Transparent Enough? Balancing Access to Information against Privacy, in M. Bobek (ed.), Selecting Europe's Judges, *op. cit.*, at 204 (talking of "some embryonic form of unintended judicial self-government") and T. Dumbrovský, B. Petkova, M. Van Der Sluis, Judicial appointments: The Article 255 TFEU Advisory Panel and selection procedures in the Member States, *op. cit.*, at 481–482 (who speak of the potential for a "subtle move" in the direction of judicial self-government).
148. As also suggested by C. Krenn, Self-Government at the Court of Justice of the European Union: A Bedrock for Institutional Success, at 2018, good examples are the cases of the first and second panesl proposed by then-President Skouris, on which see respectively Council of the European Union, Recommendation concerning the composition of the panel provided for in Article 255 TFEU, Doc 5932/10 JUR 57 INST 26 COUR 13 (February 2, 2010), available at the website https://register.consilium.europa.eu/doc/srv?l=EN&f=ST%205932%202010%20INIT, and its approval without discussion by Council Decision of 25 February 2010 appointing the members of the panel provided for in Article 255 of the Treaty on the Functioning of the European Union (2010/125/EU), and Council of the European Union, Recommendation concerning the composition of the panel provided for in Article 255 TFEU, Doc 16858/13 JUR 600 INST 638 COUR 92 + ADD (December 4, 2013) and its approval without discussion as an A-item by Council Decision of 11 February 2014 appointing the members of the panel provided for in Article 255 of the Treaty on the Functioning of the European Union (2014/76/EU).
149. U. Karpenstein, Artikel 255 AEUV, in E. Grabitz, M. Hilf, M. Nettesheim (eds.), Das Recht der Europäische Union, Verlag C.H. Beck, 2017, nn. 11–12.
150. A. Von Bogdandy, I. Venzke, In Whose Name? An Investigation of International Courts' Public Authority and Its Democratic Justification, *op. cit.*, at 34.
151. See the interesting reflections by N. Tsereteli, H. Smekal, The Judicial Self-Government at the International Level—A New Research Agenda, in German Law Journal, 2018, p. 2137.
152. See on this point N. Barkaia, C. Iglesias, H. Nahr, R. Tesei, Watching the Guardians. The European Court of Auditors in Light of Transparency, Paper of the College of Europe Transparency Group 2017/20818, available at the website http://transparency.eu/wp-content/uploads/2018/04/ECA_Transparency-Group-CoE-17-18.pdf (last access 2 March 2020).

153. *Ex multis* see the reflections by L. Pech, K.M. Scheppele, Illiberalism within: Rule of Law Backsliding in the EU, in Cambridge Yearbook of European Legal Studies, 2017, p. 3, and G. Halmai, The Possibility and Desirability of Rule of Law Conditionality, in Hague Journal of the Rule of Law, 2018, p. 1.
154. T. Dumbrovský, B. Petkova, M. Van Der Sluis, Judicial appointments: The Article 255 TFEU Advisory Panel and selection procedures in the Member States, *op. cit.*, 476.
155. See European Commission, Reasoned proposal in accordance with Article 7(1) of the Treaty on European Union regarding the rule of law in Poland, COM(2017) 835 final, 20 December 2017, especially at paragraph 173 e ss.; se also in general terms D. M. Gibler, K.A. Randazzo, Testing the Effects of Independent Judiciaries on the Likelihood of Democratic Backsliding, in American Journal of Political Science, 2011, p. 696.
156. The reference is of course to the line of cases started with Judgement of 27 February 2018, Associação Sindical dos Juízes Portugueses (C-64/16) ECLI:EU:C:2018:117.

CHAPTER 4

The Deliberation of the Court and Its Transparency

In this chapter, I will look at how the European Court of Justice chose a specific institutional arrangement to strengthen its authority throughout the decades, also in terms of its activity of deliberation and transparency. In particular, it will be highlighted that this aspect corresponds to both classic and new forms of institutional organization. Crucial to the topic are both the old traditional debate on the forced collegiality of the Court's decision, the absence of the possibility of dissenting opinions, the role of the Advocates General, and the brand new debate on the possibility of access, by thirds, to Court documents.

The connection with the authority of the Court as an institution is again evident. Courts are by force of nature exemplary deliberative institutions.[1] They are set up, entrusted with powers and composed with their selected members to perform certain functions. To do so, they necessarily perform as *fora* "in which reasons, explanations, and justifications are both expected and offered for coercive state policies".[2] Their authority, after all, is supposed to rest in large part on the qualities of judicial reasoning and thus on reasons linking court decisions to legal or moral authority. This is commonly traced to the fact that courts are institutions lacking democratic credentials and often lacking direct means to implement their decisions. So, deliberation, the duty to corroborate with reasons and the possibility for the public to externally check how decisions are taken seem especially valuable (and familiar) aspects of judging.

L. Pierdominici, *The Mimetic Evolution of the Court of Justice of the EU*, https://doi.org/10.1007/978-3-030-47864-3_4

After all, what kind of deliberation is asked of courts? What kind of transparency is required, and why? Since the basic Aristotelian teachings, the general understanding of deliberation focuses on an effectual requirement: deliberation, and public deliberation in particular, shall aim at critically evaluating and perhaps changing goals or preferences. Through deliberation, "people come to recognize and embrace reasons for action that they may not have understood previously".[3] Furthermore, in public deliberation, the kinds of goals or preferences that agents might be expected to bring to the forum are especially likely to be subject of undertaking a process of evaluation and revision since—at least within a liberal legal system—private and public purposes, individual and political interests, must fit together in complex ways. In any case, whether goals or purposes actually change as a result of deliberation, or remain open to revision, the way that deliberation changes or reinforces goals or purposes is by giving reasons or arguments and by making explicit and open to access and check both those and possibly the base material. In this sense, deliberation is participating in the process of reasoning about public action. This entails being open to reasons—being willing to alter your preferences, beliefs or actions if convincing reasons are offered to do so—and being willing to base attempts to persuade others on giving reasons rather than threatening coercion or duplicity.

Courts, in this sense, are institutions particularly expected to perform their deliberative tasks. As scholars have noted, the most directly democratic institutions, in the sense of closeness to the people, such as parliaments (or, logically before, even the electoral proceedings), are subject to relatively scarce expectations in this respect, or even "are not expected to be deliberative at all". They are, indeed, often "surrounded with impediments to deliberation" and publicity, and are not asked to give particular reasons or motivation to their *dicta*[4]; whereas the least democratic decision-making institutions are expected to take the form of more or less pure *fora* of public reason. This is so for several interrelated reasons. Deliberation or reasoning, as already suggested, might be regarded as a substitute for more direct democratic legitimacy, which—as also seen in the previous pages[5]—judges of almost all types notoriously lack. This is also relevant from the point of view of the need to persuade the public to follow or comply with authoritative decisions. And it can be compared to the somewhat opposite tendency, at least in "western democratic traditions", to consider the imposition of deliberative requirements on already majoritarian action as "anti-democratic or elitist",[6] where good reasons and deliberations have been (and should have been) already scrutinized in advance by the votes of citizens and their representatives. With regard to majoritarian action, it is often said that "(R)easons, in a democracy, shouldn't get counted twice".[7] On the other hand, one should consider the natural (desirable) insulation of every judicial body from the direct political circuit and therefore the need to "count" their reason at least once (since it is not done in advance), and the specific sensible role of supreme, constitutional and international judiciaries in this respect. Using the same pun, one can say that in the case of apical judiciaries, there is a specific, relatively high value of such a count. The more risk of taking patently counter-majoritarian decisions against the will of a democratically elected body,[8] the more these are expected to be made with particular safeguards of transparency.

Public policies and sovereign choices—the essential core business of supreme, constitutional and international courts—take place within a hierarchy of norms, especially when involving moral and constitutional norms that appropriately limit democratic choices. When engaged in regulating the boundaries between such norms and democratic choices, giving reasons and deliberation is thus crucially important. After all, what is being contemplated in such regulation is telling the people or their representatives that a particular policy or a certain sovereign choice is not legitimate and/or may not be permitted. Therefore, apical courts are especially burdened with deliberative expectations in precisely those areas where constitutional values and choices may be at stake. The legislature, insofar as it acts as a constitutional interpreter, would face similar deliberative expectations but not when it is engaged in making policies of the kind that are safely within the bounds of ordinary constitutional acceptability.

But there is even something more to say—as it has been argued[9]—with regard to international adjudicatory bodies' deliberation. Undoubtedly, these not only "exercise public authority in deciding legal disputes"[10]; but they do not operate as parts of proper polities that include functioning political legislatures and the expression of a proper general will through deliberative means. Nonetheless, they can easily and strongly go against the decisions of political powers. This aspect profoundly changes the relationship between law and politics, decouples the judicial interpretative tasks from the direct relation with parliamentary politics and the political circuit in general, and modifies—at the end of the day—the quintessential distinction between legislative law creation and judicial law-application, by petrifying the former ("once an international agreement is in place, it is largely withdrawn from the grasp of its individual makers").[11] It also does so by giving more and more importance to judicial decisions. As it has been forcefully said, international judicial decisions "enjoy an exceptional standing in traditional semantic disputes about what the law is"[12] in the international realm.

In light of all this, it is no surprise that scholars also tend to discuss more and more the authority and legitimacy of courts, particularly international courts, in relation to the modalities of their "cognition and decision".[13] In this sense, high courts, unlike other political institutions, do not merely make orders or decisions known in different means. They are expected to publish acceptable rationales for their assertions: arguments that others—whether or not their interests have been vindicated—can be expected to respect, embrace or eventually contest at the political level. In this sense, the expectation that courts explain their holdings has been effectively portrayed as a *deliberative* expectation in two ways.[14] The first, as previously said, is reminiscent of Rawls' idiom and conceptualizes the judicial arguments as "public reasons for action - reasons of a kind each of us can be expected to embrace from our own moral vantage point".[15] From here, the importance of the plausible, understandable nature of those reasons, which in some normative sense are offered to become *our own* reasons for action. Second, from an institutional point of view, since courts are naturally collegial institutions, their reasons are reached through an internal process of deliberation, guided by the particular court's decision-making norms. These norms feed shared expectations on the courts' behaviour and external understandability: for instance, on the point whether they will publish a single opinion or multiple opinions will be released as well. In this sense, a court's published reasoning is placed on a grey scale within a normative framework ranging from a commitment to consensus-seeking to free majoritarian expression.

By making their reasons and processes of deliberation known, courts are providing indirect democratic justifications for public actions. At the same time, they are making "the working out of democratic principles in new circumstances, and in particularities of specific cases" explicit[16]: and, in this sense, in doing so, deliberative judges may enhance the powers of democratically elected agents by offering them "a more flexible and intelligent system to implement and refine their own legislation and public ordinances".[17] Judicial adjudication and its public nature also have an *efficiency*-enhancing effect, directly linked to fostering court's authority in legal systems: judicially provided reasons allow others—state officials, other judges, lawyers, ordinary citizens, etc.—to anticipate the implications of the current decision for future cases; they play a predictive or coordinating role in addition to the mere justificatory one, permitting society as a whole to more effectively coordinate actions and achieve important common purposes.

In basic procedural terms, these indirect democratic and efficiency/authority enhancing effects are conceptually mirrored in a sort of dual direction of judicial justifications within the two functions they perform. First of all, they are traditionally due to complying with the expectations of participants in the process. The parties of a controversy are involved in how a case is handled and require the court to deal with the arguments that they introduce. This cooperative treatment of the matter in dispute is not confined to questions of fact or evidence but—against the widespread understanding of the principle *jura novit curia*—also extends to questions of law. But judicial justifications are also addressed, in a broader sense, to the "epistemic communities"[18] of reference of any court, so that judicial decisions are placeable at the same time "within the general context of justifying public authority".[19] The open discussion of interests and competing positions are part of the social basis of democracy that feeds the democratic public as well as processes of social integration. Judgements of courts are part of this and may generate democratic potentials if only they are embedded in normative discourses "of a certain quality".[20]

These dual directions and double functions are what has led more and more scholars to not only assess the modalities of "cognition and decision" of courts but, in doing so, to use parameters such as the openness, "the publicness and transparency"[21] of courts' procedures and deliberations, in evaluating their legitimacy and their exercise of authority. One can find a certain paradox here, which is also defining the evolutive trends that I am talking about in this chapter as the more uncertain. Traditionally, arguments based on the protection of the authority and the impartiality of the courts were considered as promoting a certain opposite "closeness" of the judicial deliberations. The authoritative court, in this primordial perspective, was the closed one, capable of speaking with one loud voice irrespective of the modalities of internal deliberations and maintaining them secret. The idea of widening the access to courts' *interna corporis* as a tool for enhancing efficiency, effectiveness, public confidence in the judicial system, fair administration of justice and eventually authority came—or, better, is coming—only at a later time. What one can call the second direction of judicial deliberations—aimed at the public's perception of the judiciary and judicial decision-making, at promoting public confidence in the judiciary, allowing the public to access judicial proceedings and records, encouraging judges to act fairly, consistently and impartially, allowing the public, in a word, to "judge the judge"—comes as a disputed, late spillover of the general phenomenon of strengthening the right of access of the citizen to information held by public authorities and to assure "transparency".

As the witticism goes, "(T)o work effectively, it is important that society's (…) process satisfy the appearance of justice (…) and the appearance of justice can best be provided by allowing people to observe it".[22] Clearly, this aspect as well is involved with the proper institutional setting to hold the judiciary accountable without compromising its independence; and, in tackling such a question, some scholars make a relevant distinction in this regard between more "traditional" forms of (hard) accountability, and more modern, "*soft accountability*".[23] Hard accountability for the judiciary entails that judges can only be indirectly scrutinized and held answerable for their professional functioning. Traditional forms of control such as mechanisms of the appeal system, procedures of recruitment, appointment, promotion, permanent education, disciplinary action and so on are relevant in this sense. Hard accountability methods are purposively designed to be aloof, not to compromise judicial independence.[24] On the other hand, soft accountability deals with the openness and representation of the judiciary in a more direct way. This type of accountability has to do with procedural transparency, representation and sensitivity towards different interests and "needs of a changing social environment".[25] This is a two-way process according to which courts need to open up to the public, enter into a dialogue with other agents and social parts, while at the same time being more sensitive to values and the needs of the community. In this sense, it could be broadly labelled as *social* accountability.[26] Soft accountability is by no means a new concept for the judiciary but the increase of soft accountability instruments such as a more open complaints processes and a more open attitude regarding access to information and deliberation are indicative of a trend in which the relative instruments are used to answer growing public pressure for greater social accountability regarding the judiciary.

The chapter will investigate these issues and is structured as follows: In light of the mentioned coordinates, first I will look at the classic form of institutional organization attached to the idea of openness and transparency, in addition to the debate on the forced collegiality or the possibility of dissenting opinions as modalities of judicial deliberation. I will study the comparative trends in this respect and link them to the institutional reality of the CJEU. I will then turn my attention to a new form of institutional organization and a new idea of openness and transparency: the possibility of access, by thirds, to Court document, as a measure to increase its soft accountability. In this sense, I will look at the relevant incipient comparative trend and at how the CJEU has evolved accordingly.

4.1 Openness as Access to Deliberation: Comparative Remarks

Concepts such as openness and transparency are more often invoked than defined.[27] Nonetheless, as previously said, there is undoubtedly a typical meaning traditionally attached to the idea of judicial "openness": I am referring to the possibility of having access not only to the official or officious documental output of the courts, i.e. the official judgements, but rather to the modalities of their internal deliberation as collegial institutions and therefore to the confrontation of different opinions and solutions (if any) to the cases at hand. In particular, I refer to the modalities of the decision of the judicial college and, specifically, the possible public knowledge of the different positions of judges: therefore, to the disclosure (official, not unofficial) of assents and dissents in the college, as well as subjective imputation of the dissents (indication of who dissented).[28] Judicial openness has often been intended in this sense and only in this sense, not only because the aspects related to the access to judicial documents constitute a new and unexplored field of study but also because, on the contrary, a dense historical stratification of institutional solutions has been registered concerning individual judicial opinions at the comparative level. And while the problem has declined in different ways at the comparative level, it has also been discussed and singularly solved in the EU judicial system.

National and international approaches to the disclosure of judicial opinions have always varied widely. A whole range of options can be traced, and different solutions have been adopted in different systems: from the historical practice of *seriatim* opinions—still followed by the Supreme Court of the United Kingdom—whereby each member of the college taking part in the deliberations makes explicit her opinion separately before publishing them in sequence, to the criminalization of violations of the secrecy of deliberations, interpreted as forbidding the publication of judges' individual opinions and votes and as an obligation of collegiality. Such diverging approaches find different justificatory reasons in literature, leading to a discussion "that, according to some, has now become a matter of faith more than of reason".[29] A sort of tralatitious taxonomy presents individual opinions as a specificity of common law systems and international law judicial bodies, leaving civil law systems to their long-established principle of secrecy of court deliberations.

However, this common understanding is no longer realistic, given the numerous hybridizations.[30] First, many civil law countries, also of great representativeness as will be seen, do allow judges sitting in their supreme and constitutional courts to publish separate opinions. Furthermore, if the prohibition against separate opinions usually implies the secrecy of deliberations, and the two principles are usually used as synonyms, the opposite is not necessarily true, and many legal systems adopt the principle of secrecy of deliberations (meaning that these are held *in camera* and that the discussions that take place among the judges remain secret) while allowing for the publication of separate opinions.[31] Thus, conceptually, the secrecy of internal debates does not necessarily exclude the possibility of publishing individual opinions and therefore of shedding light on judicial deliberation *ex post*. The main theoretical arguments in favour and against separate opinions have been widely discussed. It is interesting, of course, to notice how they are differently declined in the various contexts and therefore in the various kinds of judicial bodies as well as in the different legal systems they are part of.

In historical terms, the principle of secrecy of deliberations and the concealment of individual votes are based primarily on the traditional view of the role of judges as a *bouche* declaring the will of the political power, the King. Since the King could not be wrong and thus could not but have one and only one will, judgements were—or at least had to seem—unanimous.[32] This view can be coupled with the idea of tracing the origins of secrecy of deliberations back to the culture of secrecy deriving from the entanglement between State and religion: even in secular State such as France, judges used to and still take the traditional oath to "religiously" preserve the secrecy of deliberations.[33] Historical arguments have subsequently been rationalized and supported by more modern reasons. In particular, the already discussed necessary independence of the judge, especially in its external aspect (independence from possible sources of pressure coming from outside the court), is considered as calling for a "shield" to mask—behind the secrecy of individual opinions and the collegiality—the personal understandings of the single component. In this way, members of the bench cannot and do not have to calculate the potential consequences of their decisions, also within the singular professional field, and are free to decide following their conscience and not be tempted towards instrumental positions. This argument is particularly valuable whenever judges are appointed or reappointed with a decisive, tangible role of political forces (as is the case for many constitutional and all international judges), also to preserve an appearance of independence of the judicial institution as such. Particularly in the case of international judges, as said, nationality is in a shared understanding an essential factor in determining their vote: rightly or wrongly,[34] international judges are assumed to be particularly loyal to the State that appointed them for both concerns on their career or initial national selections based on their sentiments and restrained conduct. Therefore, a prohibition of separate opinions is decisive to break inertia leading to a pernicious principal–agent relation between nations and appointees.

Another typical argument against the publication of separate opinions is the need to safeguard the authority of judgements. In this sense, being open and showing the existence of substantial disagreement inside the college of decision-makers would be detrimental for the public image of the judiciary and could undermine its authoritativeness. The transparency on the possible reasons for alternative solutions to certain controversies would encourage to call into question the validity of the judgement and refuse to enforce it or appeal against it whenever possible. The tendency to a sort of individualization of justice would also be part of this criticism.[35] In this respect, a further contextualization can be done by pointing to the level of establishment of the institution. There are well-established courts and there are courts whose authority is shaking, because they are newly born or institutionally weak for other reasons. Powerful courts could well afford the adoption of separate opinions without being afraid of possible contestations to their authority. Newly established or intrinsically flimsy institutions would need to demonstrate, towards the outside, a systemic (although fictitious) cohesion—thus needing to mask dissents. As will be seen, for some, this was the original reason why separate opinions were not allowed at the European Court of Justice when it was a new and feeble institution bound to apply a completely new and technical set of legislation.[36] Interestingly, scholars have also argued that the admissibility of dissents at the European Court of Human Rights risked initially constituting a factor weakening its authority vis-à-vis the nation states, putting the Court's survival itself at risk.[37]

The argument alluding to the safeguard of the authority of judgements is sometimes also declined in the sense of the need to ensure that the final judicial decisions adopted are unambiguous. They should give a definitive answer to a specific legal question and in this sense solve a controversy with no purpose in opening a discussion about the best possible or a coexistent interpretation[38] with the relative risks for legal certainty. Legal certainty is what is mainly at stake here. While some actors tend to give it the highest value (e.g. claimants, or practitioners), others do not (e.g. scholars, who are more interested in increasing the level and quality of the theoretical debate over a certain legal issue). And in terms of contextualization, in some settings, when dealing with cases of value or constitutional significance, pluralism of solutions can be preferable over certainty while in others, when dealing with controversies affecting economic operators, the other way around holds. In this sense, it is already evident that the case of the CJEU, given its variegated case law, is halfway between these two paradigms.

Lastly, practical considerations are often raised against separate opinions since they would hamper the celerity of proceedings and an appropriate internal organization, also in terms of cohesion, of the courts,[39] and since they would imply additional financial burdens. These last economic considerations are particularly relevant in the peculiar case of institutions, such as national tribunals in multilingual States or the CJEU itself, that might be required to publish their acts in more than one official language. In these institutions, allowing for individual opinions would represent a considerable burden in terms of time and resources since it would require their translation into all official languages.[40]

As already mentioned, in terms of arguments in favour of separate opinions, the common understanding of their practice as a typical trait of common law systems comes from the historical evolution from the British tradition of deciding *seriatim* (each judge adopting and publishing his own full decision with no majority opinion) to the practice of joining separate opinions to a majoritarian one in the US Supreme Court.[41] But scholars have also explained that historically, many civil law systems were not strangers to breaches of the principle of secrecy of deliberations and the fiction of unanimous judicial bodies: several examples of an early emergence of dissents in Continental Europe could be found in the Spanish legal tradition, in the pre-Napoleonic Italian States, and pre-united Germany,[42] sometimes allowing for the publication of such separate opinions.[43]

In coherence with the paradoxical ambivalence I already discussed, the need to preserve the independence of judges is often presented as both a compelling argument against the publication of separate opinions and an argument in favour of the practice. In fact, in some readings, the possibility of issuing individual opinion safeguards judges' *internal* independence as a form of freedom of expression and in the form of autonomy and integrity from other members of the bench.[44] The external aspect of independence, and therefore the risk of undue influence over judges, would not be a sufficient argument to ban separate opinions, also for the disproportionality between the means used and the objectives pursued.[45]

The idea of ensuring authority and clarity is also a recurring ambivalent argument for both supporting and contesting the admissibility of separate opinions. Authors who favour the publication of separate opinions argue that authority should not rest on secrecy, especially if somewhat fictitious, but on quality of deliberations; and judges and observers tend to agree that dissents can, and often do, improve the quality of the final judgement, and in general of legal reasoning beyond the details of the case at hand[46] in the "chain novel" sense.[47] A carefully drafted and circulated dissent can improve the quality of the judgement by forcing the others to deal with the arguments of the dissenters, soon or in the future. In some cases, dissenting opinions may even be drafted, circulated, and never published, if a certain argument is eventually dealt and inserted in the reasoning.[48] In any case, dissents can thus play an essential role in the future development of the law: in some cases, they may eventually become the majority opinion or influence it, constituting the means for an ideal dialogue with future and lower courts.[49] Authority would also be measured in the need for judicial bodies to be "not only authoritarian but also authoritative",[50] and therefore to issue amply explained and fully reasoned decisions: in this sense, separate opinions would also serve as a legitimating factor for the majority—proving to have carefully considered, even though ultimately rejected, all the possible arguments.[51]

Moreover, not only the idea of a forced unanimity, based on the assumption of only one correct interpretation of the law and judicial reasoning as a legal syllogism,[52] is increasingly considered obsolete; but nowadays it is common sense that it can be detrimental to the quality of a court's judgements by compelling the members to try and reach a compromise at all cost—often at the expense of the rational coherence and clarity of the final output due to the need to include certain statements or reasons or views just to satisfy all the judges sitting on the bench, at least partially.[53] In hindsight, the need to preserve collegiality in the decision-making process is another twofold argument. Indeed, while some fear that judges, once given the possibility of writing their own individual statement, will no longer fully engage in the internal deliberations with a view of reaching a common decision or at least a common understanding, some experiences seem to prove the contrary. In many States where separate opinions have been introduced, this has not fostered a less cooperative attitude of the judges: for example, this is the case of Germany, a paradigmatic civil law country which introduced dissents at the level of the Bundesverfassungsgericht,[54] but where these are only used when it is truly impossible to come to an agreement between the judges.[55] At least in legal cultures where judges feel a strong duty of loyalty to their institution, the introduction of dissenting opinions does not necessarily weaken the collegiality of the deliberations.[56]

With a clear focus on the binomial democracy/transparency, it is also relevant to notice that in many jurisdictions, judgements are formally issued "in the name of the people", recalling that the power exerted by judges comes from the people. However, if judges in several contexts cannot enjoy a direct democratic legitimation, it is their decision-making process that must become more transparent, allowing for internal criticism.[57] This is also an important aspect for courts that enjoy powers of scrutiny over sovereign choices of political powers, such as constitutional and international jurisdictions: and in fact, the need for a transparent, open exercise of power is also an argument applied for the CJEU in the EU governance context.[58] Such democratic potential is also visible in the role of dissents fostering an ideal dialogue—not only between courts of the present and future—but also between courts, political powers, and practitioners. Separate opinions explicit additional and alternative arguments that lawyers or lower courts can adapt and translate into new legal reasoning; they may suggest new developments and interpretations to legislators; or they can generally attract public attention and push political powers to reform certain contested fields of law.[59] Separate opinions are part of the ongoing inter-institutional dialogue[60] and "help improve its quality and quantity".[61]

If traditional arguments for and against the practice of separate opinions show us no prominent reasons either in favour or against their publication, there is nonetheless a remarkable comparative phenomenon to notice. A certain growing trend towards permitting judges to publish concurring and dissenting opinions has been noticed by scholars,[62] which is particularly visible among the EU Member States and international courts. This is triggering a renewal of the debate at the EU level over the opportunity to prioritize publicity over secrecy also in this aspect of judicial activities, symbolized here as well by an official Study of the European Parliament on the point which explicitly aims at reopening the debate on the EU judicial architecture with a view towards comparative practice.[63]

Among the European Member States, some still prohibit such openness in judicial deliberation. However, even in those contexts, formal discussions about the possibility of reform take place, not only in academic quarters but often with the involvement and encouragement of the judicial institutions themselves. For instance, in Italy, judges are not allowed to publish individual opinions: the principle of the secrecy of deliberations and individual opinions applies both for ordinary judges and in the specialized Constitutional Court. But while the new law on judges' civil liability of 1988, applicable at all levels, somewhat relaxed such principle,[64] it is important to notice that the extension of the ban to constitutional rulings was never completely undisputed. Discussions on its opportunity took place during the Parliamentary debate leading to the adoption of the law on the functioning of the Constitutional Court,[65] and it has subsequently been challenged several times, with early influential academic works[66]; draft bills were presented in Parliament,[67] and some seminars were held at the Court itself to obtain information about the practice of other courts.[68] France and Belgium adhere to the principle of the secrecy of deliberations, which has been explicitly interpreted in both contexts as prohibiting the publication of individual opinions. The Belgian Court of Cassation has recognized the secrecy of deliberations as a principle of Belgian law and recently confirmed that judges are bound to preserve it[69] in coherence with the punishment of any violation according to Art. 458 of the local criminal code.[70] The French *Conseil d'État* recognized the same principle as a characteristic of French public law, prohibiting even to label a court's decision as "unanimous" since this would amount to a revelation of the individual vote of each of the members.[71] The secrecy of deliberations is still proscribed and forms part of the oath that judges must take when taking up judicial functions. It is also considered as binding not only on ordinary judges but also on the members of the *Conseil Constitutionnel*.[72] The principle of secrecy is also explicitly stated for the specialized Luxembourgish and Maltese constitutional courts, and in the diffuse system of judicial review in the Netherlands.[73] Lastly, but equally notable, Austria strictly adheres to the obligation of collegiality both in the ordinary and in the constitutional judiciaries; yet here again, dissenting judges are allowed, but simply recorded and kept secret, so that only higher courts (in the case of ordinary courts) and colleagues have access to the relative registers.[74] However, this tradition of secrecy has not gone unchallenged and since the 1960s scholars have repeatedly called it into question, and many authors seem to support reform, while the Constitutional Court, on the whole, is against such a change.[75]

Unlike the mentioned cases, which nowadays can be considered as exceptions despite significantly involving many original Members of the European Communities, twenty of the actual EU Member States embrace the institution of separate opinions in some form for ordinary or constitutional functions. Interestingly, several of them do so after relatively recent reforms. While most of the original Member States mandate, and mandated, the full collegiality of courts at the time, Germany—another EC founding part—is the quintessential example of a country following the civil law tradition but allowing constitutional judges to issue separate opinions. But this phenomenon took place over the years. Historically, Germany has not always adhered to the principle of secrecy. Only since the XIX century this has become a general rule for ordinary judges.[76] When the Federal Constitutional Tribunal was founded, separate opinions were not foreseen, although a discussion was held on the point and a formal proposal that would have granted minority judges the right to publish their dissent was rejected,[77] on the ground that "the trust in justice and especially in constitutional justice was not yet sufficiently developed (…) to preclude the possibility in litigation with political aspects that public reactions (…) may result if, in litigation involving political issues, a judge himself asserted that it would have been possible to decide otherwise".[78] However, dissenting opinions emerged through practice. The Tribunal took office in 1951 and already in some cases since 1952, the Court made the numerical results of the voting public, breaching the appearance of unanimity while still keeping the identity and the reasons of minority judges secret; later in 1952, there was the first case of dissenting opinion attached to the formal judgement, which fostered doubts about its formal validity.[79] In 1966, a decision was taken with a 4 to 4 vote for the first time and the court decided to incorporate the views of both groups of judges in judgement. In 1967, the Second Section (Senat) of the Court established the practice of revealing the number of yes and no votes. As a result, a new case of parity happened in 1969, eventually leading to the modification of the statute on the Bundesverfassungsgericht proposed by the Federal Government.[80] In its current text, as amended in 1970, the law explicitly grants minority judges the right to publish their separate opinion (*Sondervotum*).[81] Interestingly, while this right was initially used extensively,[82] a compromise between secrecy and widespread use of dissents was then struck, since the court is now known for its traditional efforts in reaching a common solution and an unanimous decision, and for the use of separate opinions only when such efforts do not succeed, for more coherence and transparency in the deliberations.[83]

The States that joined the European Communities in 1973 were in one way or the other all familiar with the practice of separate opinions. Denmark, which follows the tradition of diffuse judicial review, was familiar with a system of anonymous dissenting opinions, mentioned at least for their existence in the official judgement since 1930.[84] Since the 1950s, it adopted a full-fledged regime of open dissenting for all the collegiate courts of the legal order, including the Supreme Court.[85] Ireland is the rare case in which the Constitution itself explicitly prohibits the publication of separate opinions in certain constitutional matters[86]; but, in any case, as a common law system, it has always provided ordinary judges and judges of the Supreme Court (when exerting ordinary jurisdiction) with the possibility to issue separate opinions (in some cases, through the *seriatim* procedure).[87] In the United Kingdom, as mentioned, judges' decisions were traditionally issued *seriatim* through separately published individual opinions and decisions then taken by majority. This is true for historical reasons, traced back to the modalities of adjudication of the House of Lords, whose members enjoyed the full right to express their opinion freely.[88] In 1966, before the accession to the European Communities (also for the Judicial Committee of the Privy Council where dissents were originally not allowed), a reform was undertaken so that at least a single minority opinion was admitted.[89] The tradition now also continues within the context of the new Supreme Court which issues *seriatim* decisions even when it decides cases based on the Human Rights Act and the compatibility of UK legislation with the ECHR and the ECtHR's jurisprudence.[90]

In Greece, which joined the EEC in 1981, constitutional review is diffuse and the publication of dissenting opinions (although anonymous) is, exceptionally, even mandated by the Constitution (Article 93.3) regardless of the type of adjudication (constitutional or ordinary) or institution.[91] The same trend of openness was established in both Portugal and Spain. In the case of Portuguese, a long-established tradition allowed both constitutional and ordinary judges to deliver a dissenting[92]; the debate and the institutional choice for the *voto vencido* (literally, defeated vote) was renewed with Article 42(4) of Law 28/1982, some years before the EC accession, in particular for the members of the Constitutional Tribunal.[93] In Spain, again a quintessential civil law country, the tradition of secrecy has never been followed to the same extent as France, and the practice of the so-called *voto reservado* (dissenting judges could have their vote recorded in a separate secret register) was maintained in the Code of Civil Procedure and the Code of Criminal Procedure until recently. Furthermore, the Constitution of 1978 explicitly provides for the publication of dissenting opinions in the context of judgements of the *Tribunal Constitucional* (Art. 164)[94]; and subsequently, but before the EC accession, the possibility of adopting separate opinions was also extended to ordinary courts.[95]

With the exposure to nordic and eastern legal experiences, this European trend towards openness was even more evident. In fact, in Sweden and Finland, which joined in 1995, the diffuse judicial review systems unquestionably allow judges to publish separate opinions whether exerting ordinary or constitutional jurisdiction.[96] And then, nearly all the legal systems interested in the massive EU enlargement of the last decade (in the two phases of 2004 and 2007) were and are familiar with the practice. This is true for the Czech Republic, which introduced it shortly after the division of Czechoslovakia with the law on the Constitutional Court of June 1993[97]; and for Slovakia, which initially adhered to the Czechoslovak tradition of secrecy of deliberations, but first applied the corrective of a registration of the dissent, and then, since 2000, fully embraced published separate opinions.[98] Estonia, considered by local jurists as a paradigm,[99] allows the publication of judicial dissents in nearly all its judiciary; in particular, according to the Constitutional Review Court Procedure Act,[100] separate opinions can be attached to final judgements and opinions on the interpretation of the Constitution (performed, in the diffuse system of judicial review, by a special section of the Supreme Court). In Latvia and Lithuania, which on the contrary are centralized systems with separate Constitutional courts, traces of the practice were already in the early regulations of the 1990s soon after independence, and further reforms have expanded its use.[101] The Hungarian Constitutional Court, created in 1990, followed the German model and consequently constitutional judges were soon allowed to deliver their individual opinions, published together with the final judgement.[102] The Polish Constitutional Tribunal, created in 1982 by constitutional amendment, had its powers established in the *Constitutional Tribunal Act* of 1997, which details the rules applicable to dissenting opinions.[103] The same is true for the case of judges in the Slovenian Constitutional Court with the detailed Constitutional Court Act and the Rules of Procedure of the Court.[104] Even in Cyprus, where there is an unsettled system according to which the Supreme Court currently also exercises constitutional jurisdiction, notwithstanding the constitutional provisions that foresee a separate constitutional court, judges are allowed to publish dissenting opinions.[105] Finally, after the fall of the Communist regime also Romania and Bulgaria adopted centralized systems of judicial review and set up a constitutional court. The first, modelled in the 1989 Constitution after the Italian and French models, did not initially contemplate separate opinions but these were introduced soon after.[106] The second, created in 1991, had dissenting and concurring opinions expressly mentioned in the Regulations on the Organization of the Activities of the Constitutional Court.[107]

These data are capable of breaking several traditional assumptions on the diffusion of the form of openness of judicial deliberations discussed. They go against outdated common understanding regarding cultural roots, supposedly only linked to common law systems; they go against the idea that separate opinions are an exception to the general rule of secrecy of individual votes, while the panorama of the practices in the EU Member States is the opposite.

And the strong trend in the diffusion of this openness practice is only confirmed by an examination of the international jurisdictions—the other points of reference for comparative remarks and influences over the CJEU—so that many authors conclude that the permissive rule is a general principle of international law.[108] In large part of international courts, the possibility for the members to detach themselves from the college choices constitutes an unchallenged tradition. International judges are commonly granted, for the rationales I already analysed above, the right to issue individual opinions, which are attached to the judgement of the majority and often carry considerable importance.

Rules of the kind apply both in prototypical international courts, such as the International Court of Justice, and in regional institutions like the European Court of Human Rights; only exceptionally individual opinions are limited in these contexts.[109] For instance, judges at the International Court of Justice, including ad hoc judges if appointed, have the power to publish separate opinions: and such configuration was directly borrowed by the direct institutional predecessor, the Permanent Court of International Justice. The real discussion on the opportunity of such openness in deliberation happened in the 1920s, at the time of the latter's establishment, and the major point debated was the opportunity to grant the right of public dissenting to all judges, or except those having the nationality of States concerned in the dispute at hand. This exception reflected, here again, a common understanding that I already investigated: the idea that national judges would always feel compelled to side and issue separate opinions in favour of their State. In the end, it was rejected, not to create disparities among those sitting on the bench, and the final decision was to allow all judges to publish dissenting opinions.[110] The rule was then translated in the Statute of the ICJ (Art. 57), expressly allowing separate opinions: an option which is frequently used by the members, since according to a recent study, until 2005 the Court had rendered a total of 243 judgements with no less than 1017 individual opinions attached.[111] This plethora of separate reasoning surely sheds light on the ICJ's deliberation details, often clarify the majority judgement, and is deemed capable of fostering the development of international law[112]; at the same time, it is interesting to notice that empirical and statistical research show a remarkable trend on the part of national judges (and even more so, ad hoc judges) to publish dissenting opinions whenever the decision is against their national State, therefore confirming certain original concerns. However, no serious contestations have been raised about the practice in recent years.[113] The European Convention of Human Rights expressly describes separate opinions as a possibility for its Court: Article 45(2) of the Convention clarifies that "if a judgment does not represent, in whole or in part, the unanimous opinion of the judges, any judge shall be entitled to deliver a separate opinion". The principle is replicated and further explained in the *Rules of Court* of the EctHR (Rule 74(2)), which foresee the possibility of "separate opinion, concurring with or dissenting from that judgment, or a bare statement of dissent", with a sort of graduation and discretion in the explication of transparency.[114] In practice, dissenting opinions have been extensively used[115] and fostered the development of the Court's interpretation of the Convention, especially when dealing with certain specific features of its jurisprudence, such as the search for a common "European consensus" or the need to adopt an evolutionary interpretation of a certain rule, by anticipating, in some cases, subsequent developments in the Court's case law.[116] However, the possibility of issuing separate opinions has also had negative outcomes, especially leading to allegations that States have tried to pressure their national judges. Notably, an amendment of the rules concerning the appointment of judges was adopted to meet these concerns: they are now elected for a longer but non-renewable term.[117] This detail will also be important for my reflections on the CJEU's reality. The rules on dissenting opinions at the ECtHR have also been substantially reproduced in similar regional institutions such as the Interamerican Court of Human Rights and the African Court on Human and People's Rights.[118] Moreover, it is to be noted that all existing international criminal tribunals allow their members to publish separate opinions. Articles 23(2) of the Statute of the ICTY and 22(2) of the Statute of the ICTR both read "the judgment shall be rendered by a majority of the judges of the Trial Chamber and shall be delivered by the Trial Chamber in public. It shall be accompanied by a reasoned opinion in writing, to which separate or dissenting opinions may be appended". The question was in this respect significantly debated at the time of the negotiation of the Statute of the International Criminal Court since the initial project, drafted by the UN International Law Commission in 1994, explicitly excluded the possibility of publishing individual opinions not to affect the authority of the newly established Court negatively. But here again, the final decision overturned these concerns, also by relying on the views expressed by judges of the ICTY and ICTR and their positive appreciation of the role of individual opinions.[119] As a result, the Rome Statute—famously considered as a unique blend of the civil law and common law traditions—also does allow the publication of the views of both majority and minority judges. Therefore, probably one of the few and most notable exceptions to the principle of full transparency and openness in the international tribunal and arbitrary bodies can only be found in the *Understanding on rules and procedures governing the settlement of disputes* annexed to the WTO Agreement. But in this context as well, not only individual opinions can be issued by panellists, and must just remain anonymous (Articles 14 and 17); also, scholars often highlight the facility to trace back opinions to the substantial author, so that the rule can only partly preserve the independence of panellists from possible external pressure.[120]

4.2 Openness as Access to Deliberation: The Debate for the European Court (also with Reference to the Advocates General and Their Opinions)

4.2.1 Old and New Debates on the Adoption of Dissenting Opinions in Luxembourg

The Court of Justice of the European Union follows the tradition of secrecy of deliberations and apparent unanimity that initially prevailed, as seen, in the six founding Member States. Article 35 of the CJEU Statute provides that "(T)he deliberations of the Court of Justice shall be and shall remain secret"; and the "secrecy of the deliberations of the Court" is further mentioned in Articles 2, 10 and 13 of the act, also as an obligation of every single member.

Notably, the possibility of allowing the publication of separate individual opinions was initially discussed, but in the end, the proposal was rejected.[121] In this narrow perspective, one cannot say that a positive institutional *evolution* occurred over time: but some interesting reflections can be made about today's peculiar institutional solution and the possibility of changes in the future—also in light of the new principles inserted in the Treaties and their impact on other aspects of the institutional "transparency" of the Court.

A first significant source of knowledge is in the recent historical reconstruction of the debate's origins. The opportunity to introduce separate opinions in Luxembourg was already discussed in the negotiations of the Court of Justice of the European Coal and Steel Community in 1950.[122] In particular, this happened at a second stage of the negotiations within the context of a broader discussion on mandates of Court's judges and specifically on their duration. Historical evidence says that the matter was debated soon after the problem of whether to constitute lifelong mandates for the judges or to define their shorter duration, and as a logical consequence of this first problem.[123] I already referred to how the duration of judicial mandates and the possibility for them to express their individual position against the collegiality are crucial aspects for their independence. It is also relevant to recall that at the beginning there was not even a clear idea on the number of judges that were to compose the ECSC Court and then on their appointment process, so that, for a certain period in the negotiations, even the idea that the seventh judge member could be elected as a "*représentant des syndicats ouvriers*"—by the trade unions active in the coal and steel business—took place. It was only later that the mentioned equilibrium of national representativity was reached.[124]

Put in this perspective, one can understand more of the initial ideas on the deliberation of the Court. The principle of the judges' independence was stated in Article 32 of the Treaty of Paris but not thoughtfully inserted into a strict frame of norms to protect it. The much-discussed system of short term appointment and reappointment of judges comes directly from this climate and these original discussions. The intention was to both acknowledge "their rightful role" of discretion to governments[125] and foresee "*conversations d'ensemble*" over appointments of members of the High Authority (a political body) and of the Court (an independent one)—together.[126] These original sensitivities—which saw in the judicial appointments choices of political nature, and sorts of bargaining chips in a larger balance of representation—made impossible to accept the German and Belgian proposals for long terms (9 years) or lifelong mandates against the French idea of renewable and relatively short mandates. The same original, political sensitivities were also very significant in the idea—discussed and rapidly discarded at this stage of negotiations and with such problems on the table—to allow separate opinions. It would have been utterly unthinkable to give judges of no clear representativity (as they were conceptualized at that stage) the possibility to express their singular view and make the internal dynamics of such undetermined collegiality explicit. It is in this sense that Nicola Catalano, renowned negotiator of the time, then member of the ECSC legal service and judge of the Court itself, wrote years later that the opposite idea—to impose the secrecy of deliberation with the purpose to assure the autonomy of the judges—would lead to the final decision of the delegates with apparent reference to comparative solutions.[127]

This influential and historical background shaped the structure and organization of the European Court throughout the decades. A reform in this respect has never been realized. Still, several speculations have taken place. More transparency and the adoption of separate opinions have been repeatedly suggested by leading scholars and practitioners over the years, often with explicit reference to the level of attained *maturity* of the EU legal order. Among many, Grainne de Búrca[128] and J.H.H. Weiler[129] have suggested the shift at the turn of the new millennium, and this last author recently renewed his argument.[130] Rasmussen has used the point to emphasize the inertial but reformable tendency of the Court of Justice towards "(P)oor Reasonings and the Complete Non-transparency of *Willensbildung*".[131] Perju has recently published a refined plea "toward a discursive turn in European law", as a means and a contribution to a positive "politicization" of European law.[132] All these opinions are coherent with a notorious prediction made by Gordon Slynn, former Advocate General and then judge at the Court of Luxembourg in the 1980s, according to which the introduction of separate opinions was a project for our present century and not for the last one.[133]

Actually, in terms of legal basis, scholars have even speculated on the fact that, in purely abstract terms, it is not the reading of the mentioned numerous rules of the CJEU Statute concerning the secrecy of deliberations (Articles 2, 10, 13 and 35) that directly forbid the publication of dissents, but their interpretation.[134] The principle of secrecy inserted may be after all intended as merely prohibiting judges from reporting what happens during *in camera* deliberations, as in other national contexts,[135] and not from making known, afterwards, their opinion in a written form. In the same context—interestingly, here again an official Study commissioned by the European Parliament—not only it is suggested that the second interpretation prevailed in the European Court possibly "as a consequence of the influence of the continental tradition"[136]; but also that, to allow for the publication of separate opinions, legislative reform could not even be necessarily required, if not to provide a more transparent legal basis for a practice possibly applicable *rebus sic stantibus*.

New reflections were then prompted by the inclusion of the new Article 1 TEU and Article 15 TFEU in the fabric of the Treaty of Lisbon. The first, Article 1 TEU, states the general obligation of the European Union—and thus its institutions, bodies, offices and agencies—towards "decisions (...) taken as openly as possible to the citizen".[137] The second, more specifically, provides that to promote good governance and to ensure the participation of civil society, the Union—and thus all its institutions, bodies, offices and agencies—shall conduct its work as openly as possible, providing all the possible forms of transparency, active cooperation and communication between institutions and the public typically entailing access to information. Even in this sense, speculations were offered on the capability of such promises to change the status quo. The value of transparency, explicitly reaffirmed in the text of the Treaties, could be easily interpreted, after all, as an argument for the preference of openness over secrecy for judicial deliberations. And this could be linked—as is the case of the whole debate on Articles 1 TEU and 15 TFEU—with the overall process of democratization of the European Union.[138]

Still, some realistic notations are in order. The first to be made is a formal one. By virtue of the exception of Article 15(3) TFUE, the reaffirmed values of openness and transparency are legally applicable to the Court of Justice only when it is exerting administrative function, and technically not in its purely judicial functions. So, a simple extension of the principle of openness to the CJEU as provided by the Treaty of Lisbon is undoubtedly not set to change (according to this current interpretation) the actual situation alone. Even though the combined reading of the new Article 1 TEU and Article 15 TFEU has the potential to give rise to significant changes in the way the Court interacts with the public (as will be explained *in extenso* in dealing with the second dimension of openness of judicial activities) it does not question the *raison d'être* of the principle of secrecy of collegiate deliberations per se, nor ensure the overall openness of the Court's proceedings.[139] But there are also other reasons why it appears improbable that the CJEU (and the Member States) may decide in the near future to amend the Statute and embrace, in the short term, any practice of individual, separate or dissenting opinions. Public access to the deliberations may indeed allow the public—more than judgements fictionally written by a unanimous choir of voices—to grasp information from the debate that members of the bench had on particular points of law. This would be particularly interesting and important in the development of EU law. But in the context of the EU, there are specific concerns on the serenity of legal proceedings and possibility of external pressure on judges. All the arguments traditionally linked to the secrecy of judicial deliberation are still well present, and debated, at the CJEU's level, and their presence makes the commentators think that the debate about separate opinions will never advance until they remain alive.[140]

Introducing dissenting opinions could inevitably lead the CJEU to move away from the actual forced cooperative method it has hitherto followed. Today, the practice of Luxembourg provides that the Rapporteur of every single case prepares a note that can serve as a basis for the judgement. Then all members who sit in the same chamber and disagree can also submit their notes explaining their position. Not only these documents, as will be seen, are without a doubt inaccessible for the public. But if substantial disagreements emerge, discussions simply go on to try to reach an agreement on a common text. When a consensus eventually cannot be reached and a vote is taken, the outvoted judges continue to take part in the drafting of the text of the judgement, suggesting improvements in light of her position. Consequently, the final outcome will be, in fact, a genuinely collegiate judgement.[141] But, as observed with acumen,[142] if "(A) camel is said to be a horse designed by a committee", the risk will always be to have "camel" judgements, which may cloak an inability to reach a clear decision, in which diverging views are in some ways all included. In the end, it is unclear which one prevails.[143] These concerns are even enhanced by the apodictic, cryptic, Cartesian[144] argumentative style of the Court of Justice (on which I will elaborate further in the sixth chapter), accused in turn of making its judicial reasoning even less intelligible.

Again, some authors fear that allowing judges to deviate from the majority's opinion might lead to ignoring the views of dissenters and marginalize them at the time of drafting the judgement—resulting in less cooperation in the improvement of the reasoning and radicalization of minoritarian positions.[145] This concern for a cooperative method of deliberation and thoughtful and consensual decision can be counterbalanced, as seen, with those empirical experiences (especially in national contexts and where separate opinions are a new tool) in which there is a practice of efforts made to ensure that no dissent is published, by taking into account, as far as possible, the views of the minority. In this sense, it would be difficult to predict whether allowing for separate opinions at the CJEU would lead to their actual use, given that, of course, they would not be obligatory and there are significant differences in terms of legal cultures of the judges in addition to different compositions in which the Court can be convened.

The typical argument made in *legal* terms against individual opinions, which has also been consistently cited concerning the CJEU, is the potential threat to the authority of the Court's judgements. If, as said, according to some authoritative opinions the EU legal order is mature enough to be confronted with a public debate and even a politicization of some of its features,[146] according to some others it is still too young and fragile to allow for public dissents that might weaken it. This argument assumes various relevant dimensions at the supranational level. In one sense, maturity could be measured against the readiness of States, as sovereign masters of the Treaties, to see national judges voting against national interests, or to accept the legitimacy/authority of the Court once its (apparent) unanimity is no longer veiling the existence of internal dissents and alternative (but equally valid) solutions to the legal issues at stake.[147] Moreover, given the specificity of the EU federal judicial architecture and the complex interactions between the CJEU and national courts, especially in the context of the preliminary ruling procedure, allowing the publication of separate opinions might have unforeseen consequences: a more discursive, analytic and conversational style associated with more transparency could foster the dialogue with national courts; but conversely, it could also undermine their perception of (and their respect for) the authority of the CJEU by ordinary judges. In this sense, there would be a risk for the most precious and protected assets of the EU legal system: the (decent level of) uniform application of EU law throughout the territories of all the Member States' jurisdictions, the fundamental objective of what I often called the nomophylactic function of the Court of Justice. After all, as it has been noted by an actual member of the Court, dissent could also amount to dangerously unveiling—in the continuous comparative effort of the Court in the construction of a common supranational law—whether certain national traditions have more power and more weight than others.[148]

Additionally, it is interesting to note that when it is argued that the EU legal order can already be considered as stable and settled, it is also recalled that the Member States are already used to having "their" national judges voting independently and openly, since this already happens in numerous national settings as well as in the context of the European Court of Human Rights in Strasbourg (although, as said, not without allegations of undue influences and pressures).[149] And also, there are already scholarly efforts capable of piercing the veil of the apparent unanimity of Luxembourg—studying the patterns of the Court of Justice decisions and trying to establish the different preferences of individual judges.[150] Thus, the introduction of individual opinions should not be measured against a still fully fledged general perception of unanimity. In contrast, it would merely eliminate the task for scholars to second-guess individual judicial preferences using indirect indicators, with the risk of really endangering the judges' independence and also assuming mistaken conclusions.[151]

It has been suggested to look at the question of the authority of the CJEU at stake from two different perspectives: one focused on the quality of the Court's reasoning and the other, of course complementary, focused on the Court's formal role and position.[152] When prominent scholars suggested a turn for the Court towards judgements "not only authoritarian but also authoritative", with thoroughly reasoned decisions,[153] and a shift from a "command" model (in which the judgement has authority because it is formally a Court's order) to a "justification" model, where authority also rests on the quality and persuasiveness of the judgement's grounds,[154] such a change would be undoubtedly prompted by the adoption of individual opinions. These would arguably stimulate—at least in a first phase—more in-depth discussions among the judges thus leading to more authoritative and convincing decisions. But on the other hand, it is feared that the introduction of separate opinions merely to trigger a change in the style of the Court's decisions could amount to a disproportionate and hazardous reform, bringing more risks than benefits. Altering the decision-making process might be an excessive response to the need to improve quality and clarity in judgements, as well as a symptom of insufficient trust in the ability of the Court to evolve to respond to the needs of national courts and other claimants. This is an ability to evolve that has been much inspired, as will be seen, in the last years, by opposite concerns, especially in terms of streamlining and speeding up proceedings in front of the Court, in the constant search for better timing performances.

If these are the puzzling, debatable and debated aspects of the *legal* argument that still hampers a full open practice of the CJEU's deliberations, a clearer decisive *political* obstacle lies between the lines of the Treaties. A reform would particularly pose a problem in relation to the tralatitious renewable character of the mandate of the judges—already problematic per se because of their so-called "external" independence.[155] The possibility of issuing separate opinions could be easily distorted in its purpose with the current rules on the judge's appointment, and particularly with the option for reappointment. National authorities, which are still in charge of the initial selection of appointees, might be tempted to use the threat of not reappointing a judge to pressure him/her to publish a dissent in the case of decisions contrary to their national interest. This possibility would not be averted by the new procedures ex Article 255 TFEU that I already investigated above. In the actual configuration, the new European Panel would be powerless in this respect, and its actual practice is not even very much concentrated, admittedly, in the critical cases of reappointments. In this context, the paradigm of the Strasbourg Court seems to be particularly relevant: in that setting, while the members of the bench make use of the right to issue separate opinions, there have been reports of States trying to exercise pressure over their nominees,[156] so that a recent amendment to the appointment rules became necessary and the mandates were rendered longer, but non-renewable.[157] It should be noted that the same prominent authors who have always advocated for a more confrontational style of the Court of Justice and a reform in the transparency of opinions are the same who suggested a similar development for the CJEU appointment system, even before the Treaty of Lisbon's new rules.[158] The strength of such concerns is evident, yet doubts about the absolute necessity of comprehensive reform could have been raised. These include pointing to other possible avenues to preserve the judges' independence such as the forms of anonymous and separate opinions I already described (known in European national contexts such as Greece and international arenas such as the WTO system). In this respect, internal views tend to minimize the suggested interdependence of the non-renewability of the mandate and the independence of the individual judges. With the Court of Justice in mind, it is submitted that the Advocates' General example is particularly relevant, since their absolute and unchallenged independence in issuing their (individual) opinions seems not to be affected by the fact that they are appointed according to the same rules as judges, including the possibility of reappointment.[159] This last point leads us to the investigation of another aspect of the Court's transparency practices, which deserves an independent appraisal.

4.2.2 *The Advocates General and Their Role in the Transparency of the Court's Deliberations*

The last relevant argument against reform in the transparency practices of the Court of Justice, specifically towards the option of separate opinions, has always relied on the *status quo,* and specifically on a sort of *functional equation.* According to many, separate opinions of the Luxembourg judges would not be particularly useful or valuable, because there are already opinions issued by the Advocates General of the Court. These would perform a comparable function, also for what concerns the public appraisal of the judicial deliberations, their clarification, their intelligibility, their understandability.[160] These arguments deserve an independent investigation, not only because it is necessary to assess their veracity, but also because they lead me to the study of another essential original *comparative* inspiration of the structure and the organization of the Court.

First of all, it is interesting to note that the functional equation between the opinions issued by the Advocates General and the dissenting opinions of judges of other jurisdictions is not the only suggested by scholars in a comparative vein, to describe and understand this peculiar figure. Curiously, while a group of authors saw the AG as a substitute for individual opinions, others—especially until what is now the General Court came into existence—suggested its function "in a way as the first instance" of the judgement of the Court.[161] This is the sign of a certain discomfort of the literature delineating the traits of this peculiar figure. On the other hand, it is to be noted that what I call the functional equation with the role of dissenting opinions can be suggested directly by historical research. It is proven that the historical reason why the office of Advocate General was established was precisely to compensate for the lack of dissenting opinions, when these were discarded to protect the judges' independence from their national governments, potentially threatened by their short, renewable mandate.[162] There is historical evidence that the original proposal was made, here again, by the French delegation, with the express purpose of reproducing the same "*effets bienfaisants*" they provided in the French experience.[163] In the original Treaties, AGs were introduced into the institutional architecture of the newly established Court with an express reference to *commissaires du gouvernement* in the *Conseil d'Etat*: this was the spirit of the proposal advanced by Maurice Lagrange at the time, which he has repeatedly claimed,[164] and which he described as commonly accepted "*comme une sorte de contre-partie à l'interdiction du droit pour les juges de publier éventuellement leur opinion dissidente*".[165]

Still, in critically discussing the function of Advocates General for the openness and transparency of the Court's deliberation, a historical retrospective view on the original inspiration of the figure cannot be enough. The analysis may just start from the way in which the figure was imported, and from the textual reference upon which the European Advocates' General mandate is based. Indeed, the explicit mandate of the Advocates General, according to what is now Article 252 TFEU, is to *assist* the Court: its activity shall help to clarify the legal issues at stake in front of the bench by publicly issuing reasoned submissions on cases and doing so acting in complete impartiality and independence.

This can probably be intended as the explication of those general "*effets bienfaisants*" aimed at the internalization of the French influence.[166] However, it is also true that, through a minimal contextual historical analysis, one can see an ironic torsion of this concept of "beneficial effects" of such "*expérience essentiellement française*", to be emulated at the supranational level. Ironically, as it has been noted by scholars, also within French public law the function of the *commissaires du gouvernement* had been predominantly justified by their ongoing utility and by adherence to tradition.[167] The office was originally established for certain purposes and has mutated over time into something quite different; it was always confirmed, nonetheless, in its presence. Two basic justifications were behind its original appearance, in the first half of the nineteenth century.[168] There was, of course, an *internal* justification, which aimed at improving the quality of the discussion, of the deliberation and the decision drafting in the French administrative jurisdiction. The *commissaires* acted as critical readers and commenters of draft decisions of the judges and contributed to the internal debates both in the cases which foresaw the in-person presence of the parties and whenever that was not the case. But there was also a decisive, original *external* justification, retrospectively easy to understand but disappeared over the decades. The *commissaires* were prefigured to control, in some sense, on behalf of the state and therefore of the government, the members of the bench and their activities, and in this sense to defend in front of them the interest of the state, its administration and general public interest. As icastically said by Bobek, himself became an Advocate General, "(T)hat is why a fourth in the court was needed" originally: parties were seen "as pursuing just their own 'egoist' interests and judges (including those formally part of the administration) could not be trusted", as third parties of new configuration but still of not fully accepted independence.[169] When, in the years that followed, and surely by the mid-nineteenth century, the need for such external justification largely disappeared, and the *commissaires* emerged as a truly independent actor, questions arose in several respects on the part of the French doctrine and of the CdGs themselves on how to configure and justify the persisting presence of the figure. The *commissaires du gouvernement*, their name notwithstanding, were no longer bound by any advice from the executive or anyone else; they were magistrates themselves, as well as the judges they had to "overlook"; and also the views concerning judicial function and the creative role of the judge gradually changed, by replacing fears of arbitrary judicial legislating with the acceptance of judicial development of the law.[170] In this sense, the search for a rationalization of the figure became an "ongoing soul-searching activity",[171] often solved through negative definitions, describing this particular example of "fourth in the court" only for what it was not. Deep, ideological justifications for why it ought to be there became difficult to find: and existential explanations, in both academic writings as well as in the case law of the *Conseil d'État*,[172] simply relied on the actual work and the ongoing benefits the *commissaires* provide to the bench, as "*commissaire des lois*",[173] "*commissaire de la loi*",[174] or "*défenseur du droit*".[175]

Two interrelated phenomena are important for my purposes here. The first is that the mentioned historical evidence tells us that, in the context of the original European Coal and Steel Community Treaty and the setting up of its Court of Justice, a tralatitious, originally ill-defined figure was purposively imported, by only referring to its supposedly beneficial functions. The second is that, if one explores the functions performed by the historical antecedent directly and explicitly taken as paradigm, an original *external* function naturally had a short life, so that only an essentially *internal* justification remained: the French *commissaires du gouvernement*, as well as the European Advocates General, were meant to improve the quality of deliberations and decisions, and to bring discussion into a system in which the spaces for dialogue between the bench and the parties are rare and most of the decision-making is done *in camera*, behind closed doors. They were thought of as devices to supplement a perceived lack of external discourse and exchange, by actually enhancing internal discussion and built-in exchange, with a third pair of eyes and layer of analysis.[176] It is easy to see that this can also produce some external benefits for the public, for the observers, for the readers of the judgements: but, in looking for functional equivalence in terms of external openness and transparency of judicial institutions with the issuance of separate opinions, how can one not consider the inherent genetical difference? Opinions of Advocates General are *convergent* in nature, i.e. aimed at improving the elements leading, internally, to the judicial decision; separate opinions are *divergent* in nature, aimed at highlighting, externally, different elements than those taken into account in the main judicial dictum.

Given this significant historical insight, a real full appraisal of the capacity of the Advocates General in Luxembourg to make the Court's openness and transparency more pronounced must be supplemented by an analysis *in corpore vili*, on the actual practice of the institution. If the historical French "creation story"—the reliance on original French inspiration for the model of AG in the Court—cannot provide a fully fledged systemic justification for AGs and a clear link of their role to openness practices, one shall also investigate their present and ongoing uniqueness and utility.

In the EU law context as well, the literature first looked for relevant comparative reference points to describe the office. Early scholars generally sought to introduce the new institution by descriptively comparing its features with those of a *commissaire du gouvernement* in the French *Conseil d'Etat* (understandably, given the genetic history).[177] In a second phase, authors frequently tried to display the institution to the emerging non-francophone audience after the ongoing enlargements of the Union[178] until the final efforts to compare the professional figure (as realized in EU law) with other historical experiences of "fully independent fourth" parties in the court.[179] The other replicated *common lieu* has been to see, in a functional analysis of the Advocates General role, the detached representation of the "public interest" or the "interest of the law" within the Court of Justice.[180] This reading can be quickly criticized on the one hand because it implies a sort of strong, systemic, holistic idea of the "public" that could be admissible in the French administrative jurisdiction of the XIX century but hardly replicable in a supranational context. On the other hand, because it has been convincingly refuted by arguing that, should this be the case, "one should be able to position such public interest and AGs vis-à-vis the judges of the Court", with these last carrying a different interest.[181] It is well known that as per the Treaties' mandate, it is the European Commission's task to represent and uphold the interests of the Union as a whole and, by the way, for doing so the Commissioners swear an oath in front of the European Court of

Justice. In implementing this task, as a matter of policy, the Commission usually submits observations and appears in the disputes submitted to the Court, such as in almost every request for a preliminary ruling presented by national courts. In such proceedings, to which the Commission itself is not formally a party, one might say that it is, in fact, the executive branch, through its intervention, that represents the European "public interest" (if any exists) and functions as a veritable "*ministère public européen*", by pursuing its own agenda and usually advocating a pro-integration course in its observations. Therefore, in this context, it is arduous to identify an interest distinct from one of the judges as independent third parties and the Commission's one as representative of the Community to be attached to the AGs' figure. Also, in empirical terms, it should be taken into account that the AGs are present in the Court of Justice but not in the General Court where, according to Article 49 of the Statute, there is only an ad hoc possibility of the members of the General Court to be called upon to perform the task of AG in a particular case, where considered necessary or beneficial. But here again, one can find more proof of the merely *internal* justification for the assistance of the office, not aimed at making the Union court of first instance more open or transparent, but only to cooperate in its deliberations when internally desired: and in fact, the ad hoc appointment of an AG at the GC is very rare and examples of its use are by now aged.[182]

Against such background, also absent in the context of the EU is any original strong ideological justification for the office of AGs. What remains and has become commonly invoked for rationalization of its role is the argument of pragmatic internal and institutional utility. The Advocates provide an excellent service to the Court and, through it, directly or indirectly, to the outside world. However, perhaps there also lies the problem: how can one precisely draw the contours of the role of "assistance" (in the language of Art. 252 TFEU) AGs render to the Court, also to assess if there exists any real external spillover with a view to openness and transparency? A useful taxonomical effort has been recently provided in the literature—in particular by a renowned actual Advocate General[183]—which can be interestingly folded, for my purposes, to assess the inner workings and outer workings of such "assistance". In my view, it is important to reflect on how the possibly suggested definitions of "assistance" can or cannot have a real impact on the openness and the transparency of the Court. A first dimension of the assistance provided by AGs would be in their role of *framers*, of professionals who have the task of framing, of delineating the case and the legal arguments used in proceedings before the Court of Justice. If the first sketch of a future CJEU's decision is to be found in the *rapport préalable*, the preliminary report drafted by the judge Rapporteur given the Court's general meeting and the discussion therein, it is, in any case, the Advocate General who shapes, by developing the relative legal arguments, any later discussion: and its opinion, once published, will constitute the reference point in the light of which the Rapporteur, as well as other judges, will take their positions. In this sense, the framing function of the AGs is similar to what elsewhere, in other jurisdictions, is simply the role of the reporting judge, with the specificity of giving a precise shape to potentially extensive requests, especially in the case of preliminary rulings: she will base her work on the materials already presented before the court, prepare a report or a draft with comments for the benefit of the deciding formation, which shape the debate and the overall case. In this sense, albeit published at a certain point in the course of action, this task is clearly internally oriented, and internally justified. It is aimed at simply constituting a basis for the subsequent role of the college and not at making its further deliberations explicit. A second identified dimension of the assistance of AGs would be in their role as *controllers*. An AG provides, in fact, according to a unique institutional arrangement, a "second pair of eyes", performing as a sort of "second reporting judge", both in the analysis of possible procedural and substantive points of law to be raised and by asking questions with detailed knowledge of the file in the oral hearing. This is a role elsewhere performed by the presidents of chambers, who are nonetheless also present in the CJEU structure. In any case, it is another role more devoted to the internal functioning of the Court's works with no direct effect of externalization and thus no clear impact on the transparency of the Court's deliberation. The same negative remark can be attached, at least in part, to a third dimension of the assistance role, which is also a distinct feature of the style of the Advocates General: their attitude as *researchers*, which often makes the opinions issued a sort of precious summary and systematization of the previous case law of the Court, of the relevant academic debate, of the pertinent precedents of the ECtHR and possibly of other jurisdictions. This is surely an activity of internal documentation and clarification—often in fact assisted by the internal Research and Documentation Service of the Court—for seeking better comprehension of the entire bench. It is an activity surely fraught with important consequences; it is, still, very much related to the internal working of the college, with no capability of explanation of what is the actual deliberation in the single case. It is also rather linked to the other two dimensions of the assistance as per Bobek's proposed taxonomy, where the external aspect of the office is more evident. A fourth role of the assistance of AGs would be associated with them being *innovators*. It is acknowledged, again as a distinctive stylistic feature, that a good opinion of an AG is not only a mere summary of up-to-date case law; but, by relying on this and the other above-mentioned research activity, it often transcends the existing law and suggests its further development—not just the solution for a case at hand, but usually with a broader view.[184] In this respect, the AG is asked to see and describe the greater picture, context and further directions, in a dynamic way, "not tied by chamber-made compromises". But it is always important to note that this is done before the judges will give the final word, supported and maybe influenced by this potential source of inspiration; moreover, that in the actual structure of the CJEU, where, as will be seen in some more detail, more and more chambers and smaller formations of the court decide cases, the role of the Advocate General is more prosaically brought back at the necessity of keeping the case law consistent on the whole amongst such smaller formations—with some deprivation of the innovative or dynamic dimension. Thus, here as well, the external function does not seem preponderant and it is surely not aimed at "opening" the actual, coeval deliberation. Finally, a fifth role of assistance would be substantiated in the AGs' being *testers*. Their opinions could also be seen as testing balloons, also in an external dimension, being publicly available months before the decision of the Court. With the advantage of not being binding on anybody and not prejudicial to the parties, their peculiar function would be in the unique occasion to test potential reactions of various actors as far as the acceptability of certain legal solutions. Then the bench would have full power to correct the course by adding, subtracting, or also through radical change. In this sense, this aspect reminds us of the primitive comparative conceptualizations of the AGs as a first instance in relation to the final judgement of the Court I already mentioned above (the appellate systems performs a similar function in other jurisdictions).[185] But here as well, no particular relevance for the openness and the transparency of the deliberations of the Court is visible; quite on the opposite, the draft directed to the external dimension is explicitly devoted to an improvement of the internal conditions of better-informed decision-making and not to the disclosure of the effective judicial deliberation.

All these functional (and still precious) profiles are discrepant from the practices of openness and transparency of deliberations of separate judicial opinions. Advocates General opinions can provide the reader with more detailed arguments when confronted with the "cryptic, magisterial" decisions of the Court; they can even, occasionally, represent a dissenting voice in the otherwise externally "monolithic" Court.[186] After all, empirical research tells us that about 15% of the court's judgements are made contrary to the opinion of the advocates general.[187] But this is not done with a direct contribution to the valuable practice of transparency as far as the actual deliberations and the individual decisions of the Court are concerned. The Advocates General activity, in fact, has become first of all optional also in the context of the Court of Justice.[188] Furthermore, it can neither explain nor dissent from decisions the AGs never see in the course of action, but can only anticipate, in a more or less general or specific manner, topics that will be authoritatively expounded by the judges; whatever the common understanding is, the AG's opinion cannot *clarify* and make transparent the reasoning followed by the majority during the deliberation, since this takes place afterwards, logically and chronologically, but at most, it can only *contextualize* it. Therefore, not only is the course of action the other way around and it is the Court's judgement to be a follow-up of the AG's opinion, often worked by subtraction; but whenever the Court follows the substantial suggestions of the AG's opinion (which reportedly happens in a high percentage of cases, though not in all), the latter does not point to any possible alternative reasoning for an alternative decision which is still to be prefigured.[189] In this sense, there can be several options. In some cases, the Court departs from the AG's conclusions; in others, it follows the substance of its suggestions without fully endorsing their reasoning, and therefore, actually, with no function of transparency whatsoever. Often, this will not require an explicit rejection of the arguments brought by the AG but mere neglect of what is already stated. In these cases, it might be challenging to determine whether the court refused the argument, implicitly joined it, or just disregarded it; and the connection of the AG's opinions not only to dissents but to transparency practices in general becomes more and more blurred.[190]

There is no explanation of the deliberation or transparent dissent in the AGs' work, at least in individual cases. Their contribution to the external debate—not to be confused with a genuine openness of Court's deliberations—is simply at a systemic level. The opinions' arguments can only explain or disagree generally concerning directions of certain lines of case law or certain doctrinal interpretations. In a vein of stark realism and with a last appeal to functionality, this is, after all, the only source and dimension of confrontational style a court like Luxembourg can afford. "A more explicit drafting style, abundant reasons, a true account of judicial mentality and decision-making, allowing for dissents and open discourse"[191] represent the myth of academics and external observers who want and can (also in terms of resources, including time) compenetrate every single aspect of judicial decisions. But this ideal objective must always be balanced with the other values such as legal certainty (often represented by a line of case law which speaks concisely and in one voice) and celerity in the administration of justice. Seen comparatively, it has been remarked how the luxury of "lengthy and complex judicial opinions, containing extensive citations for almost every single proposition, dissenting in three parts and concurring in the other four"[192] is affordable only in systems where judgements to be given are counted in tens, not thousands per year, and on specific topics. And thus, the CJEU—an overburdened general jurisdiction precisely with thousands of cases to handle every year—can only afford the systemic explanation of its case law through the broadly oriented, peculiar, under-theorized activity of the Advocates General, with no openness of deliberations in the individual sense, if it does not want to collapse under the weight of its success and all the controversies brought to its knowledge.

4.3 Openness as Access to Court Documents

4.3.1 Access to Court Documents as a Second Dimension of Openness

We said that the debate on the separate judicial opinions is the traditional meaning attached to the concept of openness in the judicial activity. Still, there is a second dimension which is more and more linked to the idea of openness and transparency in the judicial functioning as well as in political and academic discussion: the possibility by third parties to access documents related to the courts' activity.

As it is well known, the general right of citizens to access to public information, in the form of "administrative transparency", is *en vogue* as a policy issue. However, it is by no means new. In the last two or three decades, a considerable number of legislative measures and administrative reforms have been put in place both in EU Member States and non-member States, often in the fashionable terms of so-called "Freedom of Information Acts".[193] This recent trend originates from several different factors. Administrative transparency has been recognized by various courts, constitutions and treaties as a fundamental individual right. More crucially, the promotion of the "right to know" of the people is increasingly perceived as an essential component of a democratic society, seen as the other side of the coin in freedom of expression, which includes the right to seek, receive and impart information and ideas. Liberal democracies, after all, are so intended because they are based and shaped on specific kinds of relationships between public powers and individuals.[194] The individual's right of access to information held by public authorities serves three primary purposes in this context. First, it helps private citizens to participate more closely in public decision-making processes. Second, it enables citizen control over the government and thus feeds the political circuit and prevents corruption and other forms of maladministration. Third, it provides the public administration with greater legitimacy in the eyes of individuals, as it becomes more transparent and accountable, i.e. closer to the often invoked "glass house" ideal-type.

The legislation on access to public information—born from the development of this debate—often formally relates to all the branches of public authority and therefore to the executive, legislative and judicial powers. However, traditionally, the judiciary as such, or at least legal proceedings and deliberations, has been exempt from the openness duties. The tendency, as said, has always been to use canonical arguments based on the protection of the authority and the impartiality of courts to create a presumption of "closeness" of judicial deliberations. It is typically claimed that in order to preserve the courts' independence and efficiency, it is necessary to apply specific, restricted publicity rules. The situation is nonetheless changing. Once one adds the so-called "soft" judicial accountability perspective to the traditional "hard" one—and therefore, as stated, the idea of judges scrutinized and held answerable for their professional functioning but also, more generally, for a perceived procedural transparency, representation and sensitivity regarding different interests and "needs of a changing social environment"—the same arguments on the protection of the authority and the impartiality of courts can lead to the opposite direction and therefore prompt openness of the judiciary. Nowadays, scholars in this vein support the view according that courts should also allow access to their files[195]; it is more and more submitted that, to promote transparency actively, courts should enable circulation of concerned documents beyond their walls.

The arguably emerging tendency within the EU and in the non-EU Member States is towards submitting the judiciary to respect the principle of transparency. One can say—and it has also been stated in official studies produced by the European Parliament[196]—that there is an incipient but clear emerging comparative trend to make the courts part of the transparency/"Freedom of Information" campaigns. Several countries have recognized the need for open and transparent courts, either through legislation or through practices and guidelines, which recognize the right for members of the public to access court files.[197] This has led to an interesting debate and certain partial but significant developments, also in the European Union and with specific regard to the European Court of Justice.

In general terms, the introduction of the problem cannot but start from the fact that, once the basis for a "right to know" is established by the individual vis-à-vis public powers, it is equally easy to understand that, just like any other fundamental right, the right of access to information is not unlimited and must be balanced with competing interests in its concrete application. Exceptions to the right of access to information represent the most sensitive part of Freedom of Information Acts regimes and *similia*.[198] They are aimed at striking a balance and ensuring that disclosure of information held by public authorities does not harm the relevant public or private interests. Of course, the risk is that the more the grounds for exemption are broadly defined and interpreted, the more the right to know maybe compressed or even repressed. Two main kinds of legitimate public interests are commonly contemplated in national and European regulations. The first includes the so-called "sovereign functions" of the state, including public interests such as defence and military matters, international relations, public security, public order or public safety, and the monetary, financial and economic policy of the government. The second group of justified exemptions typically includes information related to so-called "internal documents": documents relating to a matter where a final decision has not been taken as well as documents containing opinions for internal use as part of deliberations and preliminary consultations. These can encompass the conduct of investigations, inspections and audits, the formation of government decisions, and of course also court proceedings.

The application of such rationales to the activity of courts has peculiar forms. As previously stated, it constitutes an incipient, newly emerging legal discipline. In some states, it comes through as positive, written interventions (in laws or rules on the internal administration of national courts) while in other states, a similar trend is paving its way through decisions of (mostly) supreme or constitutional courts establishing the right of access to court documents through case law. Scholars have suggested that, in this respect, the accession in the European Union of Austria, Finland and Sweden in 1995 amounted to a new wave of comparative influences pressing on the supranational institutional organization: those "jurisdictions are committed to the principle of publicity of their legislative and administrative acts", yet "this principle is, at times, at odds with the tradition of administrative secrecy in France, Germany, and Britain, and it is clear that the Court will need to use its balancing powers to reconcile the proper functioning of administrative or judicial proceedings and the openness of such proceedings, depending on the historical context".[199] The comparative influence is in fact evident. In technical terms, the examples that are usually recalled in this respect come—in the absence of extensive academic studies on the specific point—particularly from two European Union Member states, Finland and Slovenia, and from Canada[200] (even though a recent official study of the Slovenian "Information Commissioner" included several other examples of continental national practices as a paradigm for its national reform).[201] Those mentioned are also the paradigms taken into account by an official Study commissioned by the European Parliament's Committee on Legal Affairs,[201] whose intention is precisely to examine national practices regarding access to court files and develop recommendations how to enable more comprehensive access by the general public to be achieved to the court files of the CJEU.

4.3.2 *The International Debate, the Comparative Paradigms*

Technical instruments employed, sources of law, and the degree of access to court documents vary across countries, but there is a clear trend towards transparency of judicial *interna corporis*.

In Finland, in particular, the first move has been to consider the general provisions of the Act on the Openness of Government Activities (621/1999) as applicable in relation to courts, unless provided otherwise in the *lex specialis* of the recent Act on the Publicity of Court Proceedings in General Courts (370/2007), entered into force on October 1, 2007. The main principle expressed by this provision is a general principle of publicity: "Court proceedings and trial documents are public unless provided otherwise (…)".[203] By "court proceedings" the Act labels all oral and written proceedings and deliberations by the courts; general publicity of those documents is intended as the principle according to which every person has an unconditional right to receive information from a public trial document, apart from absolute and relative types of exceptions pertaining to a *numerus clausus* of categories exhaustively listed (for instance, information which if made public, would probably endanger the external security of the State or sensitive information regarding matters relating to the private life, health, disability or social welfare of a person). It must be noted that internal *minutae* of judicial deliberations of the court also fall within this category. Specific law provisions and policies are devoted to the publication of documents on ad hoc databases and websites. The case law is made available through Finlex,[204] which consists of over ten databases about the precedents of the various Finnish jurisdictions. In addition, there are databases with the summaries of judgements of the European Court of Human Rights and the Court of Justice of the EU. The databases are also available in English and are accessible free of charge.

In Slovenia, one can find a similar approach and a comparable evolution of the applicable norms. The Judiciary of the Republic of Slovenia (*Sodstvo Republike Slovenije*) also has its own centralized and efficient webpage[205]—giving electronic access to all the courts and tribunals in Slovenia (general: civil and criminal; and specialized: labour, social and administrative), in all the instances (local, district, the Supreme court as well as the Constitutional Court of Slovenia). The webpage provides information on the entire Slovenian judicial system, types of procedures, lists of oral hearings, latest news, etc. All judicial decisions are available electronically while (unofficial) English translations are offered for key Supreme court judgements. Moreover, access to information detained by public authorities has been positively regulated by the Act on the Access to Information of Public Character (AAPI)[206]—another piece of regulation of the previous decade—which has introduced into the Slovenian context as well the principle of openness and transparency to all the three branches of the State: executive, legislative and judiciary. In this sense,

Slovenia has adopted a uniform regulation on access to public information, which exposes the judiciary as a whole to public scrutiny, not just its administration or so-called court management,[207] apart from some exceptions in some particular court proceedings,[208] provided that applicants demonstrate their legitimate interest.

These are just examples of a trend towards openness in judicial activity that is not confined to European countries. As stated, Canada has been, interestingly enough, considered as a third and significant world paradigm of courts' openness. In particular, it experienced a particularly developed debate on the point, which became a benchmark at the comparative level. In that legal order, the public right to open courts has been extensively discussed as an essential constitutional rule, considered as deriving from the fundamental right of expression which is guaranteed in the Canadian Constitution Act 1982 (Part I, Canadian Charter of Rights and Freedoms), Article 2.(b): "Everyone has the following fundamental freedoms: (…) (b) freedom of thought, belief, opinion and expression, including freedom of the press and other media of communication; (…)". Of course, as in other contexts, the right of an individual to privacy is also considered as a fundamental value. However, the adopted ideal of openness of judicial institutions outweighs the right to privacy.[209] As a result, in Canada, all court files are accessible to the public under the existing presumption that all court records are available to the public *in loco*. If technically feasible, the public shall also be entitled to remote access to court files. In Canada, court files are traditionally and generally accessible to the public in the courthouse. Therefore, the question of accessing them has just evolved in the last decade with the arrival of new technologies. Two aspects have been mainly explored and debated, so to make the Canadian case paradigmatic: the adoption of new information technologies for an enhanced realization of the open courts' principle; and on the other hand, the problem of unintended consequences of openness and therefore the possibility that unrestricted electronic access to courts' documents might facilitate some uses of information that are not connected to the underlying rationale for open courts and which might have a significant negative impact on values such as privacy, private and public security, the protection of confidential business information, the proper administration of justice and the timely conduct of judicial proceedings. In other words, there has been an open debate on the question of how to reconcile two fundamental values: the right of the public to transparency in the administration of justice and the individual right to privacy. A *Model Policy for Access to Court Records in Canada*, in the form of soft law measure, has been adopted by the Canadian Judicial Council in 2005, following a debate started some years before with a "Discussion Paper" entitled to "Open Courts, Electronic Access to Court Records, and Privacy", prepared by the local Judges Technology Advisory Committee (JTAC)[210] (putting forward thirty-three "conclusions" on different aspects of the "constitutional right" of the public to open courts, the connected right to privacy and policy, and logistical issues about access to court records if electronic and remote access is granted to the public). According to its definitions, "access" should be understood as "the ability to view and to obtain a copy of a court record"[211] and "court record" broadly includes "any information or document that is collected, received, stored, maintained or archived by a court in connection with its judicial proceedings", encompassing all the elements that constitute a "case file" such as pleadings, indictments, exhibits, warrants and judgements, docket information and documents in connection with a single judicial proceeding as well as other information. The Model Policy takes into account the progressive transition from paper records (traditional form of access in the courthouse) to digital documents (provided by new technologies), while stating the autonomy of each court in deciding which formats of access are provided to the public, e.g. paper, electronic, or both. In this sense, Rule 4.4 provides that "(m)embers of the public are entitled to access court records in the format in which they are maintained".[212] Moreover, the principle of open courts is further developed by stating a minimal requirement for openness, i.e. the public knowledge of the existence of documents. "Members of the public are entitled to know that a case file exists, even when a case file is sealed or subject to a non-publication order",[213] according to which it is not possible to disclose its content. As a faithful implementation of the Model Policy, the Supreme Court of Canada adopted its own access to court records policy in February 2009.[214]

All these national paradigms have been considered by the first few commentators on the matter,[215] and here again by an official Study commissioned by the European Parliament,[216] as the pioneering and possible models for the juridical treatment of a rising, always more relevant problem in the structural organization of courts. While all of them enable a very broad access to court files (the question of getting access to court files), the European national examples are peculiar for their direct legislative interventions and for the relevant questions they pose on the relationship between new regulations of judicial openness and classic instruments for public authorities' transparency. Moreover, they provide interesting elaborations on what kind of general or specific interests individuals should prove to have access to court documents and the counterbalancing interests and the type of exemptions that can be prefigured. The Canadian rules go even further in two respects. They are the examples of an autonomous, soft law measure made by an independent federal judicial council after an early example of open public debate on the matter. Additionally, it is an important example of encompassing regulation of the new frontier of judicial openness, i.e. the availability of remote access to the public via the Internet and technologies. In light of these important developments, it is interesting to have a look at how this debate—again, already officially started at the EU law level—is transposed in the special supranational context, also given that important policies have been developed in the "sister court" of the CJEU, the EFTA Court.[217]

4.3.3 *Openness as Access to Court Documents: The Debate in European Union Law*

The transposition of the debate on judicial institutions' institutional openness occurred in the European Union context with dynamics that are comparable to those seen in some national contexts. In this sense, one can notice that if the Court chose and maintained a certain institutional setting with regard to the traditional sense attached to the openness and transparency of deliberations, a change occurred in this second, more modern sense. First of all, there has been a significant evolution in the EU in terms of the general attitude about the right of access to documents with a number of major institutional and legislative changes over the years. The typical enlargement of public sensitivity concerning institutional openness also to the judicial sphere that has followed lately is coupled here again with scarce institutional and academic attention. However, there have been notable developments (not always in the extensive direction) and open debate on the European Court of Justice and its transparency practices, which I will investigate in the following pages.

In terms of general attitude towards the right of access to documents at the supranational level, it is essential to notice that the EU's predecessors, in the major institutional changes that have occurred over the years (the European Economic Community, the European Atomic Energy Community and the European Coal and Steel Community), definitely did not champion the ideas of administrative openness and transparency. On the contrary, they were essentially completely opaque in terms of information disclosure. Their "meetings were often held in secret and minutes were not published"; and public access to the relevant documents held by the Communities "was not generally regulated by rules, but was a matter of wide, often arbitrary, discretion".[218]

The Treaty of Maastricht represented the first significant change and an important step towards openness. It notoriously included a Declaration on the Right of Access to Information, which stated that "(T)he Conference considers that transparency of the decision-making process strengthens the democratic nature of the institutions and the public confidence in the administration. The Conference accordingly recommends that the Commission submits to the Council no later than 1993 a report on measures designed to improve public access to the information available to the institutions".[219] The Declaration was then, soon after, followed by the Commission and the Council's implementation, with the adoption of their Code of Conduct on public access to Commission and Council documents.[220] In it, the general principle according to which "(t)he public will have the widest possible access to documents held by the Commission and the Council" was affirmed; in a similar vein, the European Parliament adopted its own Decision on public access,[221] which provided that "(t)he public shall have the right of access to European Parliament documents pursuant to the conditions" specifically laid down. However, in terms of formal legal qualifications, it is relevant to note that neither the Declaration of 1992 nor the Code of Conduct (which was legally an internal regulation of administrative nature, not a proper binding EU legislation) explicitly conferred a legal right to access official information held by the EU institutions. The Court of Justice itself refused to read such a right in determining whether the Code was a challengeable act in front of itself.[222] Such recognition of a proper right, for any natural or legal person having its residence or registered office in a Member State, to have access to European Parliament, Council and Commission documents came years later with the fundamental Article 255 of the Amsterdam Treaty of 1998.[223] This time, its implementation arrived with a comprehensive Regulation on access to European Parliament and Council and Commission documents,[224] which replaced the Code of Conduct and the European Parliament rules on public access.

In the Lisbon Treaty, this provision of constitutional importance (now emphasized also by Article 42 of the Charter of Fundamental Rights of the European Union) became Article 15 TFEU. Not only has it been maintained, but its scope has been widened to reflect a concept of openness or transparency, which is broader than mere public access to official documents. Coupled with Article 1 TEU ("decisions are taken as openly as possible to the citizen"),[225] it provides, as said, that to promote good governance and to ensure the participation of civil society, not only the Union's institutions but also bodies, offices and agencies shall conduct their work as openly as possible—providing all the possible forms of active cooperation and communication between the institutions and the public typically entailing access to information. In this sense, the right of access to documents is very clearly linked to the principle of openness, which in turn requires transparency of institutions' actions to allow the exercise of the fundamental right of access to documents. Moreover, it is clear that the right to access documents is no longer confined to documents from political institutions such as the Parliament, the Council and the Commission, but generally aims to apply to all institutions, bodies and agencies.

In terms of secondary legislation, the Regulation 1049/2001 (which is currently under revision, and has been complemented by other legal standards in specific fields)[226] had the purpose of putting into effect the right of public access to documents and laying down general principles and restrictions to such access.[227] In principle, the Regulation states that all institutions' documents shall be accessible to the public, reinforcing in its preamble the holistic idea that openness prompts citizens to engage in the decision-making process closely and gives the administration greater legitimacy by being more effective and accountable to the individuals in a democratic system.[228] Openness contributes to strengthening the principles of democracy and respect for fundamental rights: a reading, after all, confirmed by the European Court of Justice case law in the seminal *Turco* case.[229] Currently, Regulation 1049/2001 applies to the large part of EU institutions, either through an extension via a separate legislative act or a unilateral adoption on a voluntary basis. In addition to the original institutions included, the Committee of the Regions, the European Economic and Social Committee, the European Central Bank, the European Investment Bank, the European Court of Auditors, Europol and Eurojust now all have rules that guarantee access to their documents which are identical or similar to the Regulation.

A notable exception in this evolution has always been represented by the EU Courts, which were not associated in this evolution, the general provision of today's Article 15 TFEU notwithstanding. In this sense, the EU corresponds to the typical phenomenology: the enlargement of public sensitivity concerning institutional openness also to the judicial sphere is following only later in time, and actually in our current days. Also typically, the growing public sensitivity in this regard has been oddly coupled, here again, with scarce institutional and academic attention about judicial institutions.[230] As has been noted,[231] this is particularly remarkable in the EU context, where the law scholarship as always been rather "Court-centered".[232] A sort of rationalization of the phenomenon has been interestingly offered, in the same vein,[233] by recalling the sarcastic words by J.H.H. Weiler, who depicted the legal actors of the European Union, custodians of the EU legal order, as a "conservative bunch",[234] recalcitrant to change; and with the accusations of authors like Rasmussen, who often observed that the European Court of Justice has entered an era of "bewildering silence",[235] lacking a policy of openness with regard to its internal functioning. Indeed, as openness and transparency progressively "became the modern buzzwords in debates on accountability and legitimacy of non-elected organizations", they also quickly became a "taboo subject" both within and outside the EU judiciary.[236]

In the literature, the studies focusing on transparency mainly looked at how the Court helped to introduce the principle within the EU legal order and encouraged its application, but only with regard to the other institutions.[237] As recently recognized,[238] the rich and evergreen literature on the EU judicial system does not seem to have explored the application of openness and transparency to the CJEU's own activity (with few exceptions)[239] by thus further consolidating the idea of a "taboo". Still, with some recent institutional reforms and some institutional and academic studies, the taboo was gradually toppled. This is not only coherent with comparative trends registered elsewhere, but is of particular importance within the realm of the EU.

We can surely say that CJEU is, in abstract terms, particularly exposed to the debate on the openness of its deliberations, not only in the general terms applicable to all courts that I already explained but for the inherently dialogical, *nomophylactic* function that it is assigned to. For instance, through the preliminary ruling procedure, as it is well known, the Court is meant to assist national courts in the application of EU law. In this respect, it was pointed out that a policy of openness and communication would be merely natural in the "dialogical" context of the EU judicial federal-like architecture and might enhance the legitimacy and the authority of the Court vis-à-vis national courts.[240] Smoother information flow between Luxembourg and national courts and players may serve not only to increase public knowledge about its judicial activities and to bolster the accountability and legitimacy of its outputs; it also would enhance mutual understanding and make compliance with EU case law more feasible. Given that, as said, Article 15 TFEU imposes on all EU institutions the obligation "to ensure that (their) proceedings are transparent", and requires them, at paragraph 3, to elaborate in their Rules of Procedure "specific provisions regarding access to documents, in accordance with the regulations" adopted by the European Parliament and the Council, an improved sensitivity emerged on how the CJEU can guarantee such a principle of openness, in its various forms of active cooperation and communication between the EU institutions and the public typically entailing access to information.

The Court has consistently guaranteed the principles of transparency of judicial proceedings and publicity of trial vis-à-vis the parties to a dispute as also stemming from Article 6 of the European Convention of Human Rights; but, according to various commentators, it has failed to provide a similar level of "openness" beyond the parties involved in its judicial activities.[241] This happened, in a rather typical way again, by emphasising the specificity of the judicial task with which the Court has been invested, vis-à-vis the work of the executive and legislative powers, to which the openness principle is considered to apply essentially. A sort of nominalistic debate is open here. Article 15 TFEU expressly extends the application of this principle to the activities of the CJEU. According to its third and fourth Paragraphs TFEU, the Court is nonetheless bound by an obligation to provide access to documents only when exercising its administrative tasks. However, the general obligation to conduct its tasks as openly as possible, stated with the Lisbon Treaty in Article 15(1), still applies. Therefore, even though it is undisputed that the judicial activity of the Court—being, by definition, non-administrative—is exempted from the safeguards of Article 15(3), this activity does not escape all requirements imposed by the principle of openness. Indeed, by extending the principle of openness to the CJEU, the Lisbon Treaty and Article 15(1) seems to suggest that there exists an autonomous area of openness that should be guaranteed regardless of the nature, administrative or non-administrative, of the activity undertaken by the CJEU.[242] The result of such overlapping of general and specific norms is that the Court is therefore called to gradually define this space when—based on Article 15(1) TFEU—it will be asked to determine the precise normative content of the principle of openness.

For a long time, no specific set of rules has been adopted on the openness and the transparency of the activity of the Court; on 11 December 2012,[243] pursuant to Article 15(3) of the TFEU, the CJEU has adopted for the first time rules in concerning public access to documents held in the exercise of its administrative functions; new sets of rules followed in October 2016[244] and then, recently, in November 2019.[245] With these interventions, now the Court of Justice has autonomously adopted its formal fully fledged regulation on the transparency of its activities at least where obliged, i.e. for its functions of administrative nature. In a constitutional perspective, this has been generally seen as a welcome and timely regulatory development that can bring the Court a step closer towards compliance with the transparency requirements dictated in Article 15 TFEU and more broadly, by Article 1 TEU; in the proposed perspective, it has also been recognized as a step of the Court in the direction of an internalization of modern comparative influences and trends registered in some Member States and elsewhere.

Moreover, again similarly to other comparative experiences, the Court website, CURIA, ensures access free of charge and has been progressively implemented, until recent developments. It firstly took the place of the papery European Court Reports, recently abandoned; and now its improved search engine, InfoCuria,[246] gives the possibility to research the case law of the European Courts, and had a strong impact in the transparency of output, when confronted with the previous fragmented versions of Eur-lex (for the judgements, orders and opinions issued before 1997) and Curia (for the judgements, orders and opinions issued after 1997). The website gives access to a whole bunch of information, including the list of members of the court (that now includes legal secretaries),[247] general information of its administration, annual Reports on the activity of the Court, press releases. The search engine gives access to all the conclusions submitted by the Advocates General and almost all the judgements issued by the Court. In 2019, this was complemented with the publication of all non-confidential documents coming from the database of the Judicial Network of the EU, i.e. the network created at the initiative of the President of the Court of Justice with the constitutional and supreme courts of the Member States in 2017, on the occasion of the Judges' Forum organized by the Court of Justice to celebrate the 60th anniversary of the signing of the Treaties of Rome. The Network was born as a private platform for exchange between the participating courts, with the view of enhancing judicial cooperation; the publication of part of its documents makes now available orders for reference for preliminary rulings made after 1 July 2018, at least in the language of the case, relevant decisions delivered by national courts that have been selected by the constitutional and supreme courts of the Member States on account of the interest they present for EU law, various scientific and educational documents stemming from research or monitoring works carried out by the courts participating in the JNEU, whether they be notes or studies, factsheets on EU case law or legal monitoring studies of the Court on national laws.

These last developments are important, given their potential relevance for the awareness of national operators and, therefore, for judicial cooperation in general. Previously, in terms of access to information on the very existence of a case, the Official Journal of the European Union just published a notice soon after the registration disclosing its date, the names of the parties, the subject matter of the proceedings, the form of order sought by the applicant, and a summary of the pleas in law and of the main supporting arguments. In the case of the preliminary ruling procedure, the notice also contains the identity of the referring court and the parties in the main proceedings, as well as a summary of the questions asked.[248] This publication represented the only information made available to the general public about pending cases, while, for instance, the EFTA Court publishes the case details on its website. Therefore, it was considered a development the choice of the final version of the new rules of procedure of the Court to discard the initial proposal of publishing "only when appropriate" the summary of the pleas in law and the supporting arguments.[249] But, in terms of references for preliminary rulings, the original version of the preliminary reference was only communicated by the Court to the Members States accompanied by a translation into the official language of the State to which it is addressed, also to make it possible for them to intervene: but these documents were never disclosed to the public.[250] And it was highlighted by scholars[251] that national courts could have benefitted from having access to the original order requesting the preliminary ruling as well as the final decision of national courts following the CJEU judgement; this is also true, on the other hand, for any observer who would like to know more about the Court's decisions based on specific substantial aspects, but also on certain relevant procedural ones, for instance the declaration of inadmissibility of national requests. Those transparency deficiencies were to a certain extent previously palliated by "other bodies than the CJEU",[252] i.e. by the practice of some Member States' courts to publish their own compilations of preliminary references from various Member States translated into their language,[253] or the practice of certain judicial networks or even of private companies to create databases sharing this type of case law.[254] But in this sense, such differentiation in the national practices of different Member States could only lead to further discrimination for the possibility of claimants, and ultimately in the uniform application of European Union law; while the CJEU established, through its Research and Documentation Service, Dec.nat, a first tentative summary of the case law of the courts and tribunals of the Member States concerning EU law.[255]

This is not to say that developments under this point of view draw a perfect picture. Some critical aspects remain.

As it was emphasized since the first Decision of 2012 was adopted by the Court,[256] the duty of openness is based on the critical and criticized distinction between administrative and judicial tasks of the Court, and its Decisions on the point has been considered as failing to clarify in a definitive way the line separating the two types of activities. Such *actio finium regundorum* between administrative and judicial tasks is undoubtedly difficult to draw and blurs the normative content of the openness requirement applicable to the EU judicial body; at the same time, it is true that the possibility to institute court proceedings against refusals to grant access can be interpreted "as streamlining the functional distinction existing between the CJEU as administrator and the same Court as a judicial body",[257] since the judges would assess the behaviour of administrative authorities of Luxembourg (such as the Director General whose service holds the document requested, the Head of Service, the Deputy Registrars) and indeed not their own actions; but the result can be read, nonetheless, as the Court becoming judge of itself.[258]

Another critical point raised in this respect is about the fact that, under the new Rules of Procedure of the CJEU, it is explicitly agreed that decisions concerning administrative issues are discussed and taken at the *general meeting* in which all court members take part[259]; but at the same time, this is (according to the same Rules) the important weekly meeting in which the Court also discusses pending cases and, in particular, adopts decisions upon the proposals contained in preliminary reports on the cases. Therefore, due to its "inherent judicial component",[260] the general meeting is not open to the public, and the agenda and output thereof are never published. In this sense, it can be discussed to what extent the whole current organizational structure of the Court of Justice concerning the exercise of its administrative tasks allows it to respond to the openness requirement as enshrined in Article 15 TFEU.

When talking of courts' submissions, procedural documents and supporting items filed in the EU Courts by the parties are not published but only entered in the Court's physical register.[261] Under the Rules of Procedure of EU Courts, third parties are free to consult this register and may obtain copies or extracts for a fee: but interestingly, scholars have highlighted how different specific rules are posed for the access to entries.[262] At the Court of Justice, simply "anyone" may consult the register[263]; at the General Court, only third individuals "having an interest" in the consultation can apply[264]; in the case of the Civil Service Tribunal, now suppressed, "a duly substantiated interest" was requested.[265] Again, if these differences are understandable and can be placed in the scale from the broad nomophylactic function of the CJ, where legal interpretation has the central role, to the specific, specialized and private nature of the CST, they are nonetheless sometimes considered incoherent and disproportionate, "as protecting private interests in cases might be done in a less restrictive manner by the Courts themselves, when classifying certain information".[266] Given the possibility of third parties to directly ask the parties of the proceeding to have access to the documents relevant to a dispute, this could be translated into an obligation for the EU institutions given the principle of free access to EU documents provided for in Regulation 1049/2001; however, the same Regulation recognizes that the refusal to grant access to institutional pleadings is justified if such access would undermine the protection of court proceedings unless there is an overriding public interest in the disclosure.[267] An exemption that was famously discussed, also in comparative terms, in the *API* cases in front of the General Court[268] and the Court of Justice some years ago,[269] where, in this respect, AG Maduro also noted that the "tendency seems to be that the more remote the judicial body, the greater its concern with the transparency of its judicial proceedings".[270]

In terms of proceeding before the Court, the abolition of the traditional report for the Hearing, a formal document prepared by the Judge Rapporteur of the case summarizing the various arguments of the parties and made public,[271] was met with considerable criticism by practitioners.[272]

Even the well-functioning CURIA website has some flaws, at least for what concerns the linguistic aspect and completeness in publication. The CURIA webpage ensures free access and the authenticity of the text of the decisions published in the language of the procedure. But if most of the judgements should be in principle translated in all official languages, while giving priority to the language of the case,[273] many cases are often not translated in languages other than French, the internal working language of the Court,[274] considerably restricting access for those who do not speak this language. This is due to the high number of cases treated in Luxembourg, and that require translation; backlogs and delays, also between the publication of the French and English versions of the orders and judgements, have been often registered,[275] so that after the 2004 EU enlargement, a policy of selective publication in the Courts' reports was decided.[276] At the Court of Justice, specifically, judgements (other than in preliminary ruling proceedings) delivered by Chambers of three judges, or delivered by Chambers of five judges ruling without an opinion from the Advocate General, as well as Court orders are exempt from publication, unless otherwise decided by the relevant Chamber[277]; similar rules are also present at the General Court. These formally unpublished acts are accessible on the CURIA website, always only in the language of the case and the language of deliberation, in this sense compounding the peculiar problem of the Court with its multilingual regime and relative burdens and consequences.

All in all, it must be in any case emphasized how the Court's institutional organization developed in the last two decades concerning this dimension of openness and transparency, and how, in particular, efforts were made to meet external needs (e.g. the need of national courts and counterparts) or even criticism (by scholars and practitioners). As usual, this has a lot to do with the Court's tension towards authority, by confronting "social expectations" using institutional and discursive resources to induce deference.

The described developments are coupled with the recent opening, in December 2015, of the archives of the Court to the public.[278] In the recent Regulation 2015/496, the Council established the deposit of the historical archives of the European institutions in a single location at the European University Institute in Florence with the purpose of making documents available for public consultation on-site after the expiry period of thirty years.[279] The same Regulation excepted the Court of Justice and the European Central Bank from such a duty. Still, the Court decided to comply on a voluntary basis, and started to move its archives to the EUI already in 2014. As it has been noted, the move was celebrated, also by the new President of the Court,[280] as the result of concerted efforts to overcome traditional fears regarding the loss of confidentiality and transparency.[281] A public access to the ancient *dossiers de procédure* is now possible, as well as an investigation in retrospect on affairs which were hitherto subject of oral testimony[282]; still, the Court retains the power to "blacken" in certain parts those *dossiers* because "under no circumstance shall access be given to documents relating to the secrecy of deliberation".[283]

4.4 Dimensions of Openness and the Authority of the Court of Justice

From the multi-dimensional analysis conducted throughout this chapter, it is possible to draw important conclusions, here again, on the ability of the Court of Justice to evolve from an institutional point of view and strengthen its own authority accordingly.

We saw that an initial traditional way to intend, and realize, the principle of openness of judicial deliberations is by looking at the admissibility (or non-admissibility) of the practice of separate/dissenting opinions by judges. According to a certain pre-comprehension of the topic, an open court, by allowing judges to express their view freely, would enhance its image of deliberative institution and, therefore, its authority. But a more traditional and realist reflection suggests that the fictitious collegiality invoked by not allowing the practice is primarily aimed at strengthening the authority of judicial institutions. In this way, courts always seem to speak with one voice—as authoritative mouthpieces of the only possible interpretation of the law, without contemplating any competing views. From a historical point of view, it was possible to note that (1) the design of the European Court of Justice, since the times of the ECSC, adhered to the model of collegiality prevalent in its original Member States, and that (2) such a model was explicitly aimed at protecting the "external" independence of the member judges and credibility of the institution, already in times in which the composition of the Court was yet to be clarified. In diachronic terms, it was also noticed that (1) the original prevalence of collegial judicial systems among the Member States is no more true since a majority of European systems now have separate opinions, and that (2) important doctrinal proposals for the adoption of dissenting at the CJEU's level flourished, often declined in terms of maturity reached in the EU legal order for such a change. Nonetheless, (3) it still seems to be the case that the need for protection of the authority of the CJEU in a multilevel, dialogical judicial system, in which a clear single voice of interpretation of EU law is desirable, is the strongest reason against a positive evolution in this respect, and (4) the critical, tralatitious mandate system of the CJEU's judges—renewable with a strong discretion of the Member States' governments—also prevents a change in the direction of a complete transparency over the court's deliberation. Thus, one can say that the institutional setting of the Court adheres to what is considered as the best way to protect and enhance its authority.

However, in terms of openness and transparency, it is possible to note how the CJEU has been recently able to evolve and change in another dimension, by internalizing a certain comparative influence also epitomized by some Member States: the Court was at the forefront of the new trend of openness intended as access by thirds to court documents. I analysed how this typically happened through the expansion of this specific part of the transparency debate from the realm of political bodies to judicial ones. I also mentioned some of the shortcomings denounced by the scholars in the Court's administration. Still, it is evident that by adopting this discipline—by its autonomous rulemaking, i.e. the series of Decisions of 2012, 2016, 2019—the European Court made important steps towards a progressive adherence with the "constitutional" principles of Articles 1 TEU and 15 TFEU, and with a modern idea of institutional governance aimed at fostering the perceived authority of the EU bodies. The same voluntary move was made in relation to compliance with Regulation 2015/496 and therefore with the deposit of the historical archives.

This can be conceptualized, as said, as *soft accountability*: a dimension of procedural transparency and a new relationship between institutions and "users", according to which the Court, open up to the public and creating possibilities of a dialogue with agents and social parts, becomes more *socially*—one could even say *politically*—legitimated. Here again, it is easy to see the connection with the authority of the Court vis-à-vis the public.

Notes

1. See J. Ferejohn, P. Pasquino, Constitutional Courts as Deliberative Institutions: Towards an Institutional Theory of Constitutional Justice, *op. cit.*, in the wake of J. Rawls, Political Liberalism, Columbia University Press 1993.
2. *Ivi*, at 24–25.
3. *Ibidem*.
4. *Ivi*, at 30.
5. But see also, authoritatively, the rich reflections of M. Cappelletti, The Judicial Process in Comparative Perspective, Clarendon Press 1989.
6. J. Ferejohn, P. Pasquino, Constitutional Courts as Deliberative Institutions: Towards an Institutional Theory of Constitutional Justice, *op. cit.*, at 30.
7. *Ivi*, at 36.
8. In the terms made famous by A.M. Bickel, The Least Dangerous Branch. The Supreme Court at the Bar of Politics, *op. cit.*
9. See A. Von Bogdandy, I. Venzke, In Whose Name? An Investigation of International Courts' Public Authority and Its Democratic Justification, *op. cit.*
10. *Ivi*, at 17.
11. *Ivi*, at 21.
12. *Ivi*, at 18.
13. *Ivi*, at 10.
14. Again in the words of J. Ferejohn, P. Pasquino, Constitutional Courts as Deliberative Institutions: Towards an Institutional Theory of Constitutional Justice, *op. cit.*
15. *Ivi*, at 24 *et seq.*
16. *Ivi*, at 24.
17. *Ibidem*.
18. In the sense of networks "of professionals with recognised expertise and competence in a particular domain and an authoritative claim to policy relevant knowledge within that domain or issue-area", according to the widely accepted definition offered by P. Haas, Introduction: Epistemic Communities and International Policy Coordination, in 46 International Organization, 1992, p. 1, at 3.
19. A. Von Bogdandy, I. Venzke, In Whose Name? An Investigation of International Courts' Public Authority and Its Democratic Justification, *op. cit.*, at 27.
20. *Ibidem*.
21. *Ibidem*.
22. Words of the United States Supreme Court Chief Justice Warren Burger in the well-known case Richmond Newspapers, Inc. v. Virginia 448 U.S. 555, 100 S.Ct. 2814, 65 L.Ed.2d 973 (1980).

23. W. Voermans, Judicial Transparency Furthering Public Accountability for New Judiciaries, in 3 Utrecht Law Review, 2007, p. 148, at 150.
24. *Ibidem.*
25. *Ibidem.*
26. See on this G.Y. Ng, Quality of Judicial Organisation and Checks and Balances, Intersentia 2007, p. 17.
27. This is a recurring critique to the EU debate on the topic: see for recent examples D. Curtin, Transparency, Audiences and the Evolving Role of the EU Council of Ministers, in J.E. Fossum and P. Schlesinger (eds.), The European Union and the Public Sphere: A Communicative Space in the Making?, Routledge 2007, p. 246; A. Alemanno, O. Stefan, Openness at the Court of Justice of the European Union: Toppling a Taboo, *op. cit.*, at 102.
28. According to the conceptualization of S. Cassese, Lezione sulla cosiddetta opinione dissenziente, in 4 Quaderni costituzionali, 2009, p. 973.
29. R. Raffaelli, Dissenting Opinions in the Supreme Courts of the Member States: Study. Report for the Directorate-General for Internal Policies, Policy Department C: Citizens' Rights and Constitutional Affairs of the European Parliament, available at the website http://www.europarl.europa.eu/studies (accessed 2 March 2020), at p. 2, with reference to E. Friesenhahn, Verhandlungen des 47. Deutschen Juristentages, Bd. II, München 1969, R 33, and C. Walter, La pratique des opinions dissidentes en Allemagne, in 8 Nouveaux Cahiers du Conseil Constitutionnel, 2000, available at the website http://www.conseil-constitutionnel.fr/conseil-constitutionnel/francais/nouveaux-cahiers-du-conseil/cahier-n-8/la-pratique-des-opinions-dissidentes-en-allemagne.52541.html (accessed 2 March 2020).
30. See some more reflections on the point in J. Malenovsky, Les opinions separées et leurs répercussions sur l'indépendance du juge international, in 3 Anuario Colombiano de Derecho Constitucional, 2010, p. 27, especially at 39 *et seq.*; K. Kelemen, Dissenting Opinions in Constitutional Courts, in 14 German Law Journal, 2013, p. 1345.
31. R. Raffaelli, Dissenting Opinions in the Supreme Courts of the Member States: Study, *op. cit.*, at 8.
32. See S. Cassese, Lezione sulla cosiddetta opinione dissenziente, *op. cit.*; J. Malenovsky, Les opinions separées et leurs répercussions sur l'indépendance du juge international, *op. cit.*, at 37.
33. See Y. Lécuyer, Le secret du délibéré, les opinions séparées et la transparence, in 54 Revue trimestrielle des droits de l'homme, 2004, p. 197.
34. Although the theoretical arguments appear to be very sound, research on the role of nationality in determining the judges' votes leads to more nuanced conclusions, especially in the context of regional tribunals. See

for details on this debate: M. Kuijer, Voting Behaviour and National Bias in the European Court of Human Rights and the International Court of Justice, in 10 Leiden Journal of International Law, 1997, p. 49; A.M. Smith, Judicial Nationalism, in International Law, in 40 Texas International Law Journal, 2005, p. 197; E.A. Posner, M.F.P. de Figueiredo, Is the International Court of Justice Biased?, in 34 Journal of Legal Studies, 2005, p. 599; E. Voeten, The Impartiality of International Judges: Evidence from the ECtHR, in 102 American Political Science Review, 2008, p. 417.

35. J. Malenovsky, Les opinions separées et leurs répercussions sur l'indépendance du juge international, *op. cit.*, at 38.
36. See D. Nicol, Lessons from Luxembourg: Federalisation and the Court of Human Rights, in 26 European Law Review, 2001, p.3.
37. F. Rivière, Les opinions séparées des juges á la Cour Européenne des Droits de l'Homme, Bruylant 2004, at 17.
38. See W. Mastor, Les opinions séparées des juges constitutionnels, Presse Universitaire d'Aix-Marseille 2005, pp. 19 and 289 in particular.
39. J. Azizi, Unveiling the EU Courts' Internal Decision-Making Process: A Case for Dissenting Opinions?, in 12 ERA Forum, 2011, p. 49.
40. D. Edward, How the Court of Justice Works, in 20 European Law Review, 1995, p. 557.
41. Actually after the first period of *seriatim* decisions, at least until the Marshall presidency in the first half of the XIX Century: see for all of this R. Bader Ginsburg, The Role of Dissenting Opinions, in 95 Minnesota Law Review, 2010, p. 1.
42. K. Kelemen, Dissenting Opinions in Constitutional Courts, *op. cit.*, at 1347.
43. K.H. Nadelmann, Non-Disclosure of Dissents in Constitutional Courts: Italy and West Germany, in 13 American Journal of Comparative Law, 1964, p. 268, at 272.
44. K. Kelemen, Dissenting Opinions in Constitutional Courts, *op. cit.*, at 1360; W.J. Brennan, In Defense of Dissent, in 37 Hastings Law Journal, 1986, p. 427.
45. Other institutional protections to shield judges from external influences would be usable: for instance, providing for longer, non-renewable mandates, eliminating the role of the executive in their appointment, and excluding any possibility of retaliations. See e.g. Y. Lécuyer, Le secret du délibéré, les opinions séparées et la transparence, *op.cit.*, at 205.
46. R. Bader Ginsburg, The Role of Dissenting Opinions, *op. cit.*, at 3: "there is nothing better than an impressive dissent to lead the author of the majority opinion to refine and clarify her initial circulation".
47. The reference here is obviously to the historical debate between R. Dworkin, Law as Interpretation, in 9 Critical Inquiry, 1982, p. 179 and

S. Fish, Working on the Chain Gang: Interpretation in the Law and in Literary Criticism, in 9 Critical Inquiry, 1982, p. 201.

48. For instance, the BVerfG, § 26(1) of the 1986 Geschäftsordnung des Bundesverfassungsgerichts, allows judges to request a reopening of the deliberations when a dissenting opinion has been issued.
49. C. L'Heureux-Dubé, The Dissenting Opinion: Voice of the Future?, in 38 Osgoode Hall Law Journal, 2000, p. 495.
50. J.H.H. Weiler, Epilogue: The Judicial Après Nice, *op. cit.*, at 225.
51. *Ibidem*; see also, extensively, V. Perju, Reason and Authority in the European Court of Justice, in 49 Virginia Journal of International Law, 2009, p. 308, at 323–325.
52. W. Mastor, Les opinions séparées des juges constitutionnels, *op. cit.*, at 74.
53. D. Edward, How the Court of Justice Works, *op. cit.*, at 557: "a disadvantage of the collegiate approach is that the judgement may simply cloak an inability to reach a clear decision. A camel is said to be a horse designed by a committee, and some judgments of the Court of Justice are camels".
54. I.e., as everybody knows, the Federal Constitutional Court.
55. M.T. Rörig, L'opinione dissenziente nella prassi del Bundesverfassungsgericht (1994–2009), available at the website http://www.cortecostituzionale.it/documenti/convegni_seminari/CC_SS_opinione_dissenziente_12012010.pdf (accessed 2 March 2020).
56. R. Raffaelli, Dissenting Opinions in the Supreme Courts of the Member States: Study, *op. cit.*, at 14.
57. W. O. Douglas, The Dissent: A Safeguard of Democracy, in 32 Journal of the American Judicature Society, 1948, p. 104, at 105.
58. See in particular H. Rasmussen, Present and Future European Judicial Problems after Enlargement and the Post-2005 Ideological Revolt, in 44 Common Market Law Review, 2007, p. 1661.
59. C. L'Heureux-Dubé, The Dissenting Opinion: Voice of the Future?, *op. cit.*, at 495; see also in this respect M. Cartabia, Europe and Rights: Taking Dialogue Seriously, in 5 European Constitutional Law Review, 2009, p. 5.
60. C. Bateup, The Dialogic Promise: Assessing the Normative Potential of Theories of Constitutional Dialogue, in 71 Brooklyn Law Review, 2006, p. 1109.
61. R. Raffaelli, Dissenting Opinions in the Supreme Courts of the Member States: Study, *op. cit.*, at 16.
62. Recently, see the debate between K. Kelemen, Dissenting Opinions in Constitutional Courts, *op. cit.*, and H. Rasmussen, L. Nan Rasmussen, Comment on Katalin Kelemen—Activist EU Court 'Feeds' on the Existing Ban on Dissenting Opinions: Lifting the Ban Is Likely to

Improve the Quality of EU Judgements, in 14 German Law Journal, 2013 as well, p. 1373.

63. R. Raffaelli, Dissenting Opinions in the Supreme Courts of the Member States: Study, *op. cit.*
64. See Art. 685 of the Codice penale, that criminalizes the publication of the names and votes of judges sitting in criminal cases; and tArt. 125(5), Codice di procedura penale, and Art. 131(2), Codice di procedura civile, as amended by Legge 13 aprile 1988, n. 117 and subsequently by the Corte costituzionale, judgement n. 18/1989.
65. Legge 11 marzo 1953, n. 87, Norme sulla costituzione e sul funzionamento della Corte costituzionale.
66. See in particular C. Mortati (ed.), Le opinioni dissenzienti dei giudici costituzionali ed internazionali, Giuffré 1964; and, very recently, S. Casssese, Dentro la Corte. Diario di un giudice costituzionale, Il Mulino 2015.
67. See in this respect G. Zagrebelsky, La pratique des opinions dissidentes en Italie, in 8 Nouveaux Cahiers du Conseil Constitutionnel, 2000, available at the website http://www.conseil-constitutionnel.fr/conseil-constitutionnel/francais/nouveaux-cahiers-du-conseil/cahier-n-8/la-pratique-des-opinions-dissidentes-en-italie.52545.html (accessed 2 March 2020); see also in a comparative perspective W. Mastor, Les opinions séparées des juges constitutionnels, *op. cit.*, at.
68. See the acts of the seminar held at the Corte costituzionale in 1993, published in A. Anzon (ed.), L'opinione dissenziente, Giappichelli 1995; and the papers of the *Seminario di Studio* held on 22 June 2009 available at the website http://www.cortecostituzionale.it/convegniSeminari.do (accessed 2 March 2020).
69. R. Raffaelli, Dissenting Opinions in the Supreme Courts of the Member States: Study, *op. cit.*, at 17.
70. See B. Nelissen, Judicial Loyalty Through Dissent or Why the Timing Is Perfect for Belgium to Embrace Separate Opinions, in 15 Electronic Journal of Comparative Law, 2011, p. 1.
71. See Conseil d'Etat, 17 nov. 1922, Lebon 1922 849, cited in J.P. Ancel, Les opinions dissidentes, available at the website http://www.courdecassation.fr/IMG/File/opinions_dissidentes_jp_ancel.pdf (accessed 2 March 2020).
72. *Ibidem*, with reference to Art. 448, code de procédure civile, and art. 6, ordonnance 58-1270 for the case of ordinary judges and art. 3, ordonnance 58-1067 portant loi organique sur le Conseil constitutionnel, 7 November 1958 for the members of the Conseil Constitutionnel.
73. R. Raffaelli, Dissenting Opinions in the Supreme Courts of the Member States: Study, *op. cit.*, at 19.

74. See R. Machacek, Die Einrichtung der "Dissenting Opinion" im internationalen Vergleich, in 7 Journal für Rechtspolitik, 1999, p. 1.
75. H. Mayer, Die Einführung der "Dissenting Opinion" am Verfassungsgerichtshof, in 7 Journal für Rechtspolitik, 1999, p. 30, giving account of the local parliamentary inquiry on dissenting opinions that took place in 1998, leading to the publication of a number of papers addressing this issue precisely in the Journal für Rechtspolitik n. 7/1999.
76. See e.g. F. Fernández Segado, La recepción del Sondervotum en Alemania, in 12 Revista Iberoamericana de Derecho Procesal Constitucional, 2009, p. 77.
77. K. Kelemen, Dissenting Opinions in Constitutional Courts, *op. cit.*, at 1347.
78. A. von Mehren, The Judicial Process: A Comparative Analysis, in 5 American Journal of Comparative Law, 1956, p. 197, at 209.
79. See for details P.W. Amram, The Dissenting Opinion Comes to the German Courts, in 6 American Journal of Comparative Law, 1957, p. 108; J. Luther, L'esperienza del voto dissenziente nei paesi di lingua tedesca, in 2 Politica del diritto, 1994, p. 241.
80. K.H. Nadelmann, Non-Disclosure of Dissents in Constitutional Courts: Italy and West Germany, *op.cit.*, at 272 in particular; K. Kelemen, Dissenting Opinions in Constitutional Courts, *op. cit.*, at 1347.
81. See § 30(2) of the Gesetz über das Bundesverfassungsgericht.
82. In the first year after the amendment, 17 separate opinions were issued out of a total of 72 judgements: see for details J. Luther, L'esperienza del voto dissenziente nei paesi di lingua tedesca, *op. cit.*
83. C. Walter, La pratique des opinions dissidentes en Allemagne, *op.cit.*; T. Rörig, L'opinione dissenziente nella prassi del Bundesverfassungsgericht (1994–2009), *op.cit.*
84. W. Mastor, Les opinions séparées des juges constitutionnels, *op. cit.*, at 132.
85. See for details also O. Due, Danish Preliminary References, in D. O'Keeffe, A. Bavasso (eds.), Judicial Review in European Union law, Kluwer 2000, p. 363.
86. See A.K. Koekkoek, Ireland, in L. Prakke, C.A.J.M. Kortmann, J.C.E. van den Brandhoff (eds.), Constitutional Law of 15 EU Member States, Kluwer Legal Publishers 2004, p. 465: according to Articles 26 and 34 of the Constitution, the Supreme Court, when exercising constitutional jurisdiction (upon the President's request or upon appeal) issues a single opinion, and no other opinion, "whether assenting or dissenting, shall be pronounced, nor shall the existence of any such other opinion be disclosed".

87. See G.P.J. McGinley, The Search for Unity: The Impact of Consensus Seeking Procedures in Appellate Courts, in 11 Adelaide Law Review, 1987, p. 203.
88. M. Kirby, Judicial Dissent—Common Law and Civil Law Traditions, in 123 Law Quarterly Review, 2007, p. 379; J. Lee, A Defence of Concurring Speeches, in 2 Public Law, 2009, p. 305.
89. *Ibidem*; see also J. Alder, Dissents in Courts of Last Resort: Tragic Choices?, in 20 Oxford Journal of Legal Studies, 2000, p. 221.
90. See the details provided by C. Hanretty, Dissenting Opinions in the UKSC, available at the website http://ukscblog.com/dissenting-opinons-in-the-uksc (accessed 2 March 2020).
91. Law no. 184/1975, Article 35(1). Also see the information provided by A. M. Mavčič, Importance of the Dissenting and Concurring Opinions (Separate Opinions) in the Development of the Constitutional and Judicial Review with a Special Reference to the Slovenian Practice, available at the website http://www.venice.coe.int/webforms/documents/default.aspx?pdffile=CDL-JU%282010%29016-e (accessed 2 March 2020).
92. K.H. Nadelmann, The Judicial Dissent: Publication v. Secrecy, in 8 American Journal of Comparative Law, 1959, p. 415, at 421.
93. Lei 28, 15 November 1982, Organização, Funcionamento e Processo do Tribunal Constitucional. See also C. Hanretty, Dissent in Iberia: The Ideal Points of Justices on the Spanish and Portuguese Constitutional Tribunals, in 51 European Journal of Political Research, 2012, p. 671.
94. T. Freixes, La pratique des opinions dissidentes en Espagne, in 8 Nouveaux Cahiers du Conseil Constitutionnel, 2000, available at http://www.conseil-constitutionnel.fr/conseil-constitutionnel/francais/nouveaux-cahiers-du-conseil/cahier-n-8/la-pratique-des-opinions-dissidentes-en-espagne.52543.html (accessed 2 March 2020) (with reference to the statute of the Constitutional Court of the Second Spanish Republic).
95. See Art. 260, Ley Orgánica 6/1985 del Poder Judicial.
96. W. von Eyben, Judicial Law making in Scandinavia, in 5 American Journal of Comparative Law, 1956, p. 112; W. Mastor, Les opinions séparées des juges constitutionnels, *op. cit.*, at 132.
97. K. Kelemen, The Road from Common Law to East-Central Europe: The Case of the Dissenting Opinion, in P. Cserne, M. Könczöl (eds.), Legal and Political Theory in the Post-National Age, Peter Lang 2011, p. 118, in particular at 130 *et seq.*
98. W. Mastor, Les opinions séparées des juges constitutionnels, *op. cit.*, at 142; K. Kelemen, The Road from Common Law to East-Central Europe: The Case of the Dissenting Opinion, *op. cit.*, at 127.

99. J. Laffranque, Dissenting Opinion in the European Court of Justice—Estonia's Possible Contribution to the Democratisation of the European Union Judicial System, in 9 Juridica International, 2004, p. 14.
100. *Ibidem.*
101. K. Kelemen, The Road from Common Law to East-Central Europe: The Case of the Dissenting Opinion, *op. cit.*, at 126.
102. L. Trosanyi, A. Horvath, La pratique des opinions dissidentes en Hongrie, in 8 Nouveaux Cahiers du Conseil Constitutionnel, 2000, available at the website www.conseil-constitutionnel.fr/conseil-constitutionnel/francais/nouveaux-cahiers-du-conseil/cahier-n-8/la-pratique-des-opinions-dissidentes-en-hongrie-les-opinions-individuelles-en-hongrie-une-institution.52544.html (accessed 2 March 2020).
103. W. Mastor, Les opinions séparées des juges constitutionnels, *op. cit.*, at 141.
104. Available (respectively) at the websites http://www.us-rs.si/media/constitutional.court.act.full.text.pdf and http://www.us-rs.si/media/the.rules.of.procedure-2012.pdf (accessed 2 March 2020).
105. R. Raffaelli, Dissenting Opinions in the Supreme Courts of the Member States: Study, *op. cit.*, at 25; A. Markides, The Republic of Cyprus, in C. Kortmann, J. Fleuren, W. Voermans (eds.), Constitutional Law of 10 EU Member States, Kluwer Law International 2006, p. 77.
106. Art. 59 of Law n. 47 of 1992 on the Organisation and Operation of the Constitutional Court: see K. Kelemen, Dissenting Opinions in Constitutional Courts, *op. cit.*, at 1350.
107. K. Kelemen, Dissenting Opinions in Constitutional Courts, *op. cit.*, at 1363.
108. See e.g. J. Malenovsky, Les opinions separées et leurs répercussions sur l'indépendance du juge international, *op. cit.*, at 53: «*il me paraît fondé de pouvoir constater, d'ores et déjà, l'existence d'une règle de droit international général de caractère permissif qui accorde à la magistrature internationale le pouvoir autonome de prévoir, dans le règlement de procédure d'une juridiction internationale, le droit de ses juges à une opinion séparée, même si un tel droit n'est pas expressément prévu par son traité constitutif*».
109. See, among the many, *ibidem*, at 31 *et seq.*, and organically D. Zimmermann, The Independence of International Courts. The Adherence of the International Judiciary to a Fundamental Value of the Administration of Justice, Nomos/Hart 2014; for interesting reflections cf. already R. P. Anand, The Role of Individual and Dissenting Opinions in International Adjudication, in 14 The International and Comparative Law Quarterly, 1965, p. 788.
110. See M. Manouvel, Les opinions séparées á la Cour Internationale, L'Harmattan 2004, at 67–69 in particular.

111. A. Zimmermann, C. Tomuschat, K. Oellers-Frahm (eds.), The Statute of the International Court of Justice: A Commentary, Oxford University Press 2006, at 1209.
112. *Ivi*, at 1210–1211.
113. See A.M. Smith, Judicial Nationalism, in International Law, *op. cit.*; E.A. Posner, M.F.P. de Figueiredo, Is the International Court of Justice Biased?, *op. cit.*
114. F. Rivière, Les opinions séparées des juges à la Cour européenne des droits de l'homme: essai d'analyse théorique, Bruylant 2004, at 81 *et seq.*
115. According to R.C.A. White, I. Boussiakou, Separate Opinions in the European Court of Human Rights, in 9 Human Rights Law Review, 2009, p. 37, at 50, in around 80% of the cases.
116. See for details K. Dzehtsiarou, European Consensus and the Evolutive Interpretation of the European Convention on Human Rights, in 12 German Law Journal, 2011, p. 1730.
117. See Protocol 14 to the ECHR (CETS No. 194) and its Explanatory Report, paragraph 50.
118. R. Raffaelli, Dissenting Opinions in the Supreme Courts of the Member States: Study, *op. cit.*, at 32; see Art. 24(3) of the Statute of the IACHR and Art. 28(7) of the Protocol establishing the African Court on Human and People's Rights.
119. As reported by J. Malenovsky, Les opinions separées et leurs répercussions sur l'indépendance du juge international, *op. cit.*, at 51. See for details C. Stahn, G. Sluite, Introduction: From 'Infancy' to Emancipation? A Review of the Court's First Practice, in *Eid.*, The Emerging Practice of the International Criminal Court, Brill 2009, p. 1, at 3.
120. See J. Flett, Collective Intelligence and the Possibility of Dissent, in 13 Journal of International Economic Law, 2010, p. 287. See on the relative exceptionality of the practice M. Kolsky Lewis, The Lack of Dissent in WTO Dispute Settlement, in 9 Journal of International Economic Law, 2006, p. 895.
121. See the details offered by A. Boerger-De Smedt, La Cour de Justice dans les négociations du traité de Paris instituant la CECA, *op. cit.*, at 17–18, and D. Tamm, The History of the Court of Justice of the European Union since Its Origin, *op. cit.*, at 18 in particular.
122. See, accordingly, A. Boerger-De Smedt, La Cour de Justice dans les négociations du traité de Paris instituant la CECA, *op. cit.*, at 17–18, and D. Tamm, The History of the Court of Justice of the European Union since Its Origin, *op. cit.*, at 18.
123. *Ibidem.*
124. A. Boerger-De Smedt, La Cour de Justice dans les négociations du traité de Paris instituant la CECA, *op. cit.*, at 20.

125. «*Le rôle qui leur revenait*», according to Paul Reuter, FJM, AMG 12/2/2, Reuter "Observations sur les problèmes politiques réservés aux entretiens directs entre gouvernements", 06.02.1951: see *ibidem*, at 21.
126. *Ibidem*: Paul Reuter talked of «*conversations d'ensemble sur les désignations à la Cour et à la HA, conversations où les satisfactions [pourraient] être négociées en faveur de tous les États membres*».
127. N. Catalano, Manuale di diritto delle Comunità europee, *op. cit.*, p. 63: «D'altro lato ciò che garantisce veramente l'indipendenza dei giudici è il segreto delle deliberazioni in camera di consiglio. Non è infatti prevista, come in certe giurisdizioni anglosassoni e come per la Corte internazionale di giustizia dell'Aja, la 'dissenting opinion'. I giudici prestano giuramento di osservare il segreto delle deliberazioni adottate in camera di consiglio. Le decisioni della Corte sono quindi decisioni del suo insieme, cioè della maggioranza o dell'unanimità dei suoi membri. L'opinione personale di ciascun giudice non è mai conosciuta. Ciò garantisce nella migliore maniera l'indipendenza dei giudici ed evita ogni pressione politica»; see also, accordingly, M. Lagrange, La Cour de justice des Communautés européennes du Plan Schuman à l'Union européenne, in 14 Revue trimestrielle de droit européen, 1978, p. 2, at 4–5.
128. G. de Búrca, The Principle of Subsidiarity and the Court of Justice as an Institutional Actor, in 36 Journal of Common Market Studies, 1998, p. 217, at 233.
129. J.H.H. Weiler, Epilogue: The Judicial Après Nice, *op. cit.*, at 225.
130. J.H.H. Weiler, Epilogue: Judging the Judges—Apology and Critique, *op. cit.*, at 252.
131. H. Rasmussen, Legal Opinion about the European Court of Justice's Competence Transgressions, Poor Reasonings and the Complete Non-transparency of Willensbildung, paper presented at the conference "National Judges and Supranational Laws: On the Effective Application of the EC Law and the ECHR", 15/16 January 2010, at the Scuola Superiore di Studi Universitari e Perfezionamento Sant'Anna, Pisa, already published as H. Rasmussen, Le pouvoir de décision politique du juge européen et ses limites, in 63 Revue française d'administration publique, 1992, p. 413.
132. V. Perju, Reason and Authority in the European Court of Justice, *op. cit.*, at 327 *et seq.*
133. G. Slynn, Introducing a European Legal Order, Stevens & Sons/Sweet & Maxwell 1992, at p. 162.
134. R. Raffaelli, Dissenting Opinions in the Supreme Courts of the Member States: Study, *op. cit.*, at 34.
135. As is the case, for instance, in Estonia and Latvia, and at the US Supreme Court: see *ivi*.

136. *Ibidem.*
137. In addition, the recital 7 of the preamble to the TEU declares the EU ambition "to enhance further the democratic and efficient functioning of the institutions so as to enable them better to carry out [...] the tasks entrusted to them". This idea is later confirmed by several articles of the TEU, especially in Articles 10 and 11 TEU.
138. J. Laffranque, Dissenting Opinion in the European Court of Justice—Estonia's Possible Contribution to the Democratisation of the European Union Judicial System, *op. cit.*, at 23; H. Rasmussen, Present and Future European Judicial Problems after Enlargement and the Post-2005 Ideological Revolt, *op. cit.*, at 1667; V. Perju, Reason and Authority in the European Court of Justice, *op. cit.*, at 309 and 327 *et seq.*
139. We echo the words of A. Alemanno, O. Stefan, Openness at the Court of Justice of the European Union: Toppling a Taboo, *op. cit.*, at 131.
140. See A. Alemanno, How Transparent Is Transparent Enough? Balancing Access to Information versus Privacy in Judicial Selection, *op. cit.*, at 211 *et seq.*
141. D. Edward, How the Court of Justice works, *op. cit.*, at 555–556.
142. *Ivi*, at 557.
143. R. Raffaelli, Dissenting Opinions in the Supreme Courts of the Member States: Study, *op. cit.*, at 14.
144. J.H.H. Weiler, Epilogue: The Judicial Après Nice, *op. cit.*, at 225.
145. See empirically N. Maveety, Concurrence and the Study of Judicial Behavior in American Political Science, in 8 Juridica International, 2003, p. 173; see also G.C. Rodríguez Iglesias, Entscheidungsfindung im Europäischen Gerichtshof, in 7 Journal für Rechtspolitik, 1999, pp. 27–28, and P. Jann, Entscheidungsbegründung am Europäischen Gerichtshof, in 7 Journal für Rechtspolitik, 1999, pp. 28–30, both with reference to the European context, and both claiming that the practice at the ECtHR supports such argument.
146. Most notably J.H.H. Weiler, Epilogue: The Judicial Après Nice, *op. cit.*, at 225; V. Perju, Reason and Authority in the European Court of Justice, *op. cit.*
147. See the reflections provided, also as practitioner in the field, by J. Azizi, Unveiling the EU Courts' Internal Decision-Making Process: A Case for Dissenting Opinions?, *op. cit.*, at 67.
148. S. Rodin, A Metacritique of the Court of Justice of the EU, in 2 Diritto dell'Unione europea, 2016, p. 191, at 196–197.
149. R. Raffaelli, Dissenting Opinions in the Supreme Courts of the Member States: Study, *op. cit.*, at 36.
150. See for a recent systematic example the work of M. Malecki, Do ECJ Judges All Speak with the Same Voice?, in 19 Journal of European Public Policy, 2012, p. 59.

151. In this sense also R. Raffaelli, Dissenting Opinions in the Supreme Courts of the Member States: Study, *op. cit.*, at 36.
152. *Ivi*, at 37.
153. J.H.H. Weiler, Epilogue: The Judicial Après Nice, *op. cit.*, at 225.
154. V. Perju, Reason and Authority in the European Court of Justice, *op. cit.*, at 338.
155. See the critical remarks by J.H.H. Weiler, Epilogue: Judging the Judges—Apology and Critique, *op. cit.*
156. See the allegations of J.F. Flauss, Brèves observations sur le second renouvellement triennal de la Cour Européenne des Droits de l'Homme, in 61 Revue Trimestrielle des Droits de l'Homme, 2005, p. 5; E. Voeten, The Impartiality of International Judges: Evidence from the ECtHR, *op.cit.*, at 421.
157. See again Protocol 14 to the ECHR (CETS No. 194) and its Explanatory Report, para. 50.
158. See notably H. Rasmussen, European Court of Justice, GadJura 1998, at p. 66; J.H.H. Weiler, Epilogue: The Judicial Après Nice, *op. cit.*
159. See for this argument D. Edward, How the Court of Justice Works, *op. cit.*, at 548–549.
160. See inter alia G. Grementieri. Il processo comunitario. Principi e garanzie fondamentali, Giuffrè 1973, p. 71; W. Feld, The Court of the European Communities: A New Dimension in International Adjudication, Martinus Nijhoff 1964, p. 100; U. Klinke, Der Gerichtshof der Europäischen Gemeinschaften – Aufbau und Arbeitsweise, Nomos 1989, p. 62.
161. See for this view e.g. O. Riese. Erfahrungen aus der Praxis des Gerichtshofs der Europäischen Gemeinschaft für Kohle und Stahl, Deutsche Richterzeitung 1958, p. 271; J.P. Warner, Some Aspects of the European Court of Justice, in 4 Journal of the Society of Public Teachers of Law, 1975, p. 15, at 18 in particular; A. Dashwood, The Advocate General in the Court of Justice of the European Communities, in 2 Legal Studies, 1982, p. 203, at 215; K.D. Borchardt. Der Europäische Gerichtshof: Besetzung, Anrufung, Zuständigkeiten, Vorabentscheidungen und einstweiliger Rechtsschutz. Kommentar zu den Art. 220–245 EGV mit Textanhang, Bundesanzeiger 2000, p. 59.

    See also the words of F.G. Jacobs, Advocates General and Judges in the European Court of Justice: Some Personal Reflections, in D. O'Keeffe, A. Bavasso (eds.), Judicial Review, in European Union Law: Liber Amicorum in Honour of Lord Slynn of Hadley, Kluwer 2000, p. 20: "The main justification for the institution of advocate general lies precisely in the fact that it introduces a two-stage process in which the advocate general provides an independent judicial appraisal of the case. ... [In most cases] we have to consider points of often great importance and difficulty without the assistance of a judgement from a lower court deciding the point, and with no appeal from our own decision. Only in the limited number of cases which come to the Court of Justice on appeal from the Court of First Instance [about 12% of ECJ cases according to recent statistics] do we have the luxury of a judgment to consider.".

162. See recently on the point M. Rasmussen, The First Advocate Generals and the Making of European Law, 1950–1958, paper presented at the Seminar of the Advocates General held at the European University Institute, Firenze, 16 September 2010; D. Tamm, The History of the Court of Justice of the European Union Since its Origin, *op. cit.*, at 18.
163. A. Barav, Le commissaire du gouvernement près le Conseil d'État français et l'avocat général près la Cour de justice des Communautés européennes, in 26 Revue internationale de droit comparé, 1974, p. 809, at 811: «*Le raport officiel de la délégation française était particulièrement net sur ce sujet en concluant que 'c'est avec la conviction qu'une telle institution procurera à la nouvelle Cour ses mêmes effets bienfaisants que nos partenaires ont accepté de la faire profiter des fruits d'une expérience essentiellement française'*"».
164. See M. Lagrange, La Cour de justice des Communautés européennes du Plan Schuman à l'Union européenne, *op. cit.*, p. 3, and his Discours prononcé par M. l'Avocat général Maurice Lagrange à l'audience solennelle de la Cour, le 8 octobre 1964, available at the website http://www.cvce.eu/obj/discours_de_maurice_lagrange_8_octobre_1964-fr-f2f00c1c-2587-497f-ace0-6890bf0cb85f.html (accessed 2 March 2020).
165. See M. Lagrange, Discours prononcé par M. l'Avocat général Maurice Lagrange à l'audience solennelle de la Cour, le 8 octobre 1964, *op. cit.*, p. 2: «*Une autre raison semble avoir milité en faveur de l'institution: celle-ci a été considérée comme une sorte de contre-partie à l'interdiction du droit pour les juges de publier éventuellement leur opinion dissidente. Il est certain, en effet, que l'exposé public par un magistrat d'une thèse qui sera ensuite confrontée avec l'arrêt peut utilement contribuer aux échanges d'idées et aux discussions doctrinales que provoque généralement la publication d'une opinion dissidente. D'autre part, que les conclusions soient 'conformes' ou 'contraires' à la solution adoptée, celle-ci se trouve éclairée et même confortée, que ce soit par analogie ou par opposition*».
166. A. Barav, "Le commissaire du gouvernement près le Conseil d'État français et l'avocat général près la Cour de justice des Communautés européennes", *op. cit.*, at 811.
167. M. Bobek, A Fourth in the Court: Why Are There Advocates-General in the Court of Justice?, in 14 Cambridge Yearbook of European Legal Studies, 2011–2012, p. 529, at 540.
168. *Ivi*, at 538.
169. *Ibidem.*

170. See on this R.C. van Caenegem, Introduzione storica al diritto privato, Il Mulino 2004, chapters five and six, and, specifically, L. Montazel, Entre faits et droit: histoire d'un pouvoir judiciaire. Les techniques de la cassation civile en France et en Allemagne au XIXème siècle, Klostermann 1998.
171. M. Bobek, A Fourth in the Court: Why Are There Advocates-General in the Court of Justice?, *op. cit.*, at 539.
172. Conseil d'Etat, 10 July 1957, Gervaise, Rec. p. 466; Conseil d'Etat, 29 July 1998, Eslatine, Rec. p. 320.
173. T. Sauvel, Les origins des Commissaires du Gouvernement auprès du Conseil d'État statuant au contentieux, in 55 Revue du droit public et de la Science Politique, 1949, p. 5, at 17.
174. R. Guillien, Les commissaires du gouvernement près les juridictions administratives et, spécialement, près le Conseil d'État français, in 71 Revue du droit public de de la science politique en France et à l'étranger, 1955, p. 281, at 297.
175. O. Dupeyroux, Le ministère public auprès des juridictions administratives, in Vv.Aa. (eds.), L'Évolution du droit public: Études offertes à Achille Mestre, Sirey 1956, p. 183.
176. See M. Lasser, The European Pasteurization of French Law, in 90 Cornell Law Review, 2004–2005, p. 995.
177. See for instance, as early contributions, C. Salcedo, La figura del abogado general en las Communidades Supranationales Europeas: naturaleza juridical y foncíon, in 12 Revista española de derecho international, 1959, p. 119; P. Gori, L'avocat général à la Cour de justice des Communautés européennes, in 12 Cahiers de droit européen, 1976, p. 375.
178. See in this sense A. Dashwood, The Advocate General in the Court of Justice of the European Communities, *op. cit.*; M. Vranken, Role of the Advocate General in the Law-Making Process of the European Community, in Anglo-American Law Review, 1996, p. 39.
179. M. Bobek, A Fourth in the Court: Why Are There Advocates-General in the Court of Justice?, *op. cit.*, at 545 *et seq.*
180. See in this sense D. Chalmers, C. Hadjiemmanuil, G. Monti, A. Tomkins, European Union Law: Cases and Materials, Cambridge University Press 2006, p. 123.
181. M. Bobek, A Fourth in the Court: Why Are There Advocates-General in the Court of Justice?, *op. cit.*, at 550–551.
182. Article 49 of the Statute of the Court of Justice reads as follows: "The members of the Court of First Instance may be called upon to perform the task of an Advocate-General. … A member called upon to perform the task of Advocate-General in a case may not take part in the judgment of the case".

See also *ivi*, at 551: the cases in which the at the time Court of First Instance made use of Art. 49 of the Statute and appointed an AG are limited in number ("slightly more than a dozen cases", e.g. Cases T-13/89; T-14/89; T-51/89; T- 120/89; T-24/90) and time, being all of them from the period at the turn of the 80s and 90s. The obsolescence of Art. 49 of the Statute is proven by the fact that in more complex or novel cases, the General Court relies in today's practice on a (more detailed) preliminary report presented by the reporting judge.

183. *Ivi*, at 552 *et seq*. See also, accordingly, L. Clément-Wiltz, La fonction de l'avocat général près la Cour de justice, Bruylant 2011, in particular at 53 *et seq*. with an interesting diachronic macro-distinction between «la fonction originelle» and «la fonction nouvelle» of the Advocate General.
184. See on this in particular L. Clément-Wiltz, La fonction de l'avocat général près la Cour de justice, *op. cit.*, at 231 *et seq.*, on the newly acquired functions of «mise à l'épreuve» and «mise en cohérence de la jurisprudence» by the AGs.
185. See the contributions already recalled above, Note 161 in this Chapter.
186. See the definition by I. Solanke, The Advocate General: Assisting the CJEU of Article 13 TEU to Secure Trust and Democracy, in 14 Cambridge Yearbook of European Law, 2012, p. 697, at 705.
187. J. Laffranque, Dissenting Opinion in the European Court of Justice—Estonia's Possible Contribution to the Democratisation of the European Union Judicial System, *op. cit.*, at 19, with reference to R. Streinz. Europarecht, 6th ed. C.F. Müller 2003, p. 127.
188. As well known, the Nice Treaty introduced for the first time the possibility for the ECJ to render judgements without an opinion from the Advocate-General in cases which do not raise new points of law: see Article 20 of the Protocol on the Statute of the Court of Justice as modified by the Nice Treaty, 2001 O.J. (C 80) 53, at its fifth paragraph: "Where it considers that the case raises no new point of law, the Court may decide, after hearing the Advocate-General, that the case shall be determined without a submission from the Advocate-General".
189. See e.g. J. Azizi, Unveiling the EU Courts' Internal Decision-Making Process: A Case for Dissenting Opinions?, *op. cit.*, at 59; J. Laffranque, Dissenting Opinion in the European Court of Justice—Estonia's Possible Contribution to the Democratisation of the European Union Judicial System, *op. cit.*, at 18–20; V. Perju, Reason and Authority in the European Court of Justice, in Virginia Journal of International Law, *op. cit.*, at 355–357; and the Comparative Remarks Given by M. Rosenfeld, Comparing Constitutional Review by the European Court of Justice and the U.S. Supreme Court, in 4 International Journal of Constitutional Law, 2006, p. 616, p. 640 *et seq*.

190. See in this respect the reflection and the examples from the case law provided by F. Dehousse, The Reform of the EU Courts (IV). The Need for a Better Focus on the European Court of Justice's Core Mission, Egmont Paper 96, September 2017, available at the website http://www.egmontinstitute.be/publication_article/reform-of-eu-courts-2/, pp. 14–15.
191. M. Bobek, A Fourth in the Court: Why Are There Advocates-General in the Court of Justice? *op. cit.*, at 558.
192. *Ibidem.*
193. Measures of the kind of "Freedom of Information Acts" (FOIA) have been enacted in Hungary (1992), Portugal (1993), Ireland (1997), Latvia (1998), the Czech Republic (1999), the United Kingdom (2000), Estonia (2000), Lithuania (2000), Poland (2001), Romania (2001), Slovenia (2003), Germany (2005), and at the European Union level (2001). See Organisation for Economic Co-operation and Development (OECD), The Right to Open Public Administrations in Europe: Emerging Legal Standards, 19 November 2010, Sigma paper no. 46, available at the website http://www.oecd.org/officialdocuments/publicdisplaydocumentpdf/?cote=GOV/SIGMA(2010)2/REV1&docLanguage=En (accessed 2 March 2020), at p. 7.
194. S. Bartole, Stato (forme di) (*ad vocem*), in Enciclopedia del diritto, Annali, II, 2, Milano, 2008, p. 1116.
195. See for example P. Leino, Just a Little Sunshine in the Rain: The 2010 Case Law of the European Court of Justice on Access to Documents, in 48 Common Market Law Review, 2011, p. 1215, at 1251–1252; W. Voermans, Judicial Transparency Furthering Public Accountability for New Judiciaries, *op.cit.*, at 149.
196. V. Naglič, National Practices with Regard to the Accessibility of Court Documents. Study, Directorate General for Internal Policies. Policy Department C: Citizens' Rights and Constitutional Affairs, 2013, available at the website http://www.europarl.europa.eu/studies (accessed 2 March 2020).
197. Open Society Justice Initiative, Report on Access to Judicial Information, March 2009 available at the website www.right2info.org (accessed 2 March 2020), at p. I and v: "Access to judicial records and to information about the judiciary is an important, yet often overlooked, aspect of transparency and access to information. While much legislative and scholarly attention has focused on promoting freedom of information and access to records with regard to the executive functions of government, much less has been done to secure or even evaluate access to judicial information (…) Seventy countries have developed a framework

for providing access to public information, and applying a comprehensive disclosure framework to the judiciary, while uniquely challenging, should be vigorously pursued".

198. See Note 193 above.
199. F. Nicola, National Legal Traditions at Work in the Jurisprudence of the Court of Justice of the European Union, in 64 American Journal of Comparative Law, 2016, p. 865, at 888.
200. V. Naglič, National Practices with Regard to the Accessibility of Court Documents. Study, *op. cit.*, at 20 *et seq.*
201. See N.P. Musar, Access to Court Records and FOIA as a Legal Basis—Experience of Slovenia, available at the website https://www.ip-rs.si/fileadmin/user_upload/Pdf/clanki/Access_to_court_records_and_FOIA_as_a_legal_basis_-_experience_of_Slovenia.pdf (accessed 2 March 2020), at 3.
202. V. Naglič, National Practices with Regard to the Accessibility of Court Documents. Study, *op. cit.*
203. Section 1 APCP. Unofficial English translation of this act is available at the website http://www.finlex.fi/fi/laki/kaannokset/2007/en20070370.pdf (accessed 2 March 2020).
204. Available at the website http://www.finlex.fi/en/oikeus (accessed 2 March 2020).
205. Available at the website http://www.sodisce.si (accessed 2 March 2020).
206. Zakon o dostopu do informacij javnega zna?aja (published in Official Gazette RS, No. 24/2003). English translation available at the website https://www.ip-rs.si/index.php?id=324 (accessed 2 March 2020).
207. See N.P. Musar, Access to Court Records and FOIA as a Legal Basis—Experience of Slovenia, *op. cit.*, at 1.
208. Article 6 AAPI, in its English translation mentioned above at Note 203, reads as follows: "Article 6 (Exceptions) (1) The body shall deny the applicant access to requested information if the request relates to:

    1. Information which, pursuant to the Act governing classified data, is defined as classified;
    2. Information which is defined as a business secret in accordance with the Act governing companies;
    3. Personal data the disclosure of which would constitute an infringement of the protection of personal data in accordance with the Act governing the protection of personal data;
    4. Information the disclosure of which would constitute an infringement of the confidentiality of individual information on reporting units, in accordance with the Act governing Government statistics activities;

5. Information the disclosure of which would constitute an infringement of the tax procedure confidentiality or of tax secret in accordance with the Act governing tax procedure;
6. Information acquired or drawn up for the purposes of criminal prosecution or in relation to criminal prosecution, or misdemeanors procedure, and the disclosure of which would prejudice the implementation of such procedure;
7. Information acquired or drawn up for the purposes of administrative procedure, and the disclosure of which would prejudice the implementation of such procedure;
8. Information acquired or drawn up for the purposes of civil, non-litigious civil procedure or other court proceedings, and the disclosure of which would prejudice the implementation of such procedures;
9. Information from the document that is in the process of being drawn up and is still subject of consultation by the body, and the disclosure of which would lead to misunderstanding of its contents;
10. Information on natural or cultural value which, in accordance with the Act governing the conservation of nature or cultural heritage, is not accessible to public for the purpose of protection of (that) natural or cultural value;
11. Information from the document drawn up in connection with internal operations or activities of bodies, and the disclosure of which would cause disturbances in operations or activities of the body.

(2) Without prejudice to the provisions in the preceding paragraph, the access to the requested information is sustained, if public interest for disclosure prevails over public interest or interest of other persons not to disclose the requested information, except in the next cases:

- For information which, pursuant to the Act governing classified data, is denoted with one of the two highest levels of secrecy;
- For information which contain or are prepared based on classified information of other country or international organization, with which the Republic of Slovenia concluded an international agreement on the exchange or transmitting of classified information.
- For information which contain or are prepared based on tax procedures, transmitted to the bodies of the Republic of Slovenia by a body of a foreign country;
- For information from point 4 of paragraph 1 of this Article;
- For information from point 5 of paragraph 1 of this Article, unless the tax procedure is final or the person liable for tax discovered the liability in the tax return and did not pay the tax in the prescribed time.

(3) Without prejudice to the provisions in the first paragraph, the access to the requested information is sustained:

- if the considered is information related to the use of public funds or information related to the execution of public functions or employment relationship of the civil servant, except in cases from point 1.0 and points 5.0 to 8.0 of the first paragraph and in cases when the Act governing public finance and the Act governing public procurement stipulate otherwise;
- if the considered is information related to environmental emissions, waste, dangerous substances in factory or information contained in safety report and also other information if the Environment Protection Act so stipulates.

(4) If the applicant holds, that information is denoted classified in violation of the Act governing classified data, he can request the withdrawal of the classification according to the procedure from the Article 21 of this Act.

(5) The body can choose not to provide the applicant with the requested information, if the latter is available in freely accessible public registers or is in another way publicly accessible (publication in an official gazette, publications of the body, media, professional publications, internet and similar), and can only issue instructions as to the location of the information.

(6) The body shall deny the applicant's request to re-use information if the request relates to:

1. Information from the paragraph 1 of this Article, or
2. Information protected by the intellectual property rights of third parties, or
3. information held by bodies performing public services of public radio-television or bodies performing public service in fields of education, research and cultural activities, or
4. Information, for which another Act stipulates accessibility only to authorized persons".

209. Model Policy for Access to Court Records in Canada, September 2005, available at http://www.cjc-ccm.gc.ca/cmslib/general/news_pub_techissues_AccessPolicy_2005_en.pdf (accessed 2 March 2020).

210. See the report prepared for the Judges Technology Advisory Committee (JTAC) entitled "Synthesis of the Comments on JTAC's Discussion Paper on Open Courts, Electronic Access to Court Records, and Privacy", available at the website http://www.cjc-ccm.gc.ca/cmslib/general/news_pub_techissues_Synthesis_2005_en.pdf (accessed 2 March 2020).

211. *Ivi*, at 3:
"1.3 Definitions
1.3.1 Access
"Access" means the ability to view and to obtain a copy of a court record".
212. *Ibidem*:
"4 Access
Format of Records
Members of the public are entitled to access court records in the format in which they are maintained".
213. *Ibidem*:
"4 Access
4.3 Existence of a Case File
Members of the public are entitled to know that a case file exists, even when a case file is sealed or subject to a non-publication order".
214. Supreme Court of Canada: Access to Court Records: Policy for Access to Supreme Court of Canada Court Records, available at the website: http://www.scc-csc.gc.ca/case-dossier/rec-doc/pol-eng.asp#s31 (accessed 2 March 2020).
215. A. Alemanno, O. Stefan, Openness at the Court of Justice of the European Union: Toppling a Taboo, *op. cit.*, at 117 *et seq.* in particular.
216. V. Naglič, National Practices with Regard to the Accessibility of Court Documents. Study, *op. cit.*
217. *Ivi*, at 47. See in this respect also C. Baudenbacher, M.J. Clifton, Courts of Regional Economic and Political Integration Agreements, in C. Romano, K. Alter, Y. Shany (eds.), The Oxford Handbook of International Adjudication, Oxford University Press 2014, p. 250, at 256 and 258.
218. V. Naglič, National Practices with Regard to the Accessibility of Court Documents. Study, *op. cit.*, at 38.
219. Annexed as Declaration 17 to the Final Act of the Treaty on European Union, signed in Maastricht on 7 February 1992 (OJ C 191, 29.7.1992).
220. 93/730/EC: Code of Conduct concerning public access to Council and Commission documents (OJ 1993 L 340, p. 41).
221. 97/632/EC, ECSC, Euratom: European Parliament Decision of 10 July 1997 on public access to European Parliament documents (OJ L 263, 25.9.1997, p. 27).
222. See the Judgement of 30 April 1996, Netherlands/Council (C-58/94, ECR 1996 p. I-2169) ECLI:EU:C:1996:171. The Kingdom of Netherlands brought an action to partially annul the Code of Conduct on public access to Commission and Council documents mentioned. The ECJ decided that the Code did not constitute an act having legal effects

and therefore it did not qualify as challengeable act. The Court emphasised that the Code merely reflected the agreement reached between the Commission and the Council on the principles governing access to the documents of the two institutions, while inviting the institutions to implement those principles by means of specific regulations, thereby not confining any right to individuals.

223. Article 255

1. Any citizen of the Union, and any natural or legal person residing or having its registered office in a Member State, shall have a right of access to European Parliament, Council and Commission documents, subject to the principles and the conditions to be defined in accordance with paragraphs 2 and 3.
2. General principles and limits on grounds of public or private interest governing this right of access to documents shall be determined by the Council, acting in accordance with the procedure referred to in Article 251 within two years of the entry into force of the Treaty of Amsterdam.
3. Each institution referred to above shall elaborate in its own Rules of Procedure specific provisions regarding access to its documents.

224. Regulation (EC) No. 1049/2001 of the European Parliament and of the Council of 30 May 2001 regarding public access to European Parliament, Council and Commission documents.

225. In addition, the recital 7 of the preamble to the TEU declares the EU ambition "to enhance further the democratic and efficient functioning of the institutions so as to enable them better to carry out [...] the tasks entrusted to them". This idea is later confirmed by several articles of the TEU, especially in Articles 10 and 11 TEU.

226. Such as by the Directive 2003/4/EC of 28 January 2003 on public access to environmental information, repealing Council Directive 90/313/EEC; Directive 95/46/EC of 24 October 1995 on the protection of individuals with regard to the processing of personal data and on the free movement of such data (data protection directive); Directive 2003/98/EC of 17 November 2003 on the re-use of public sector information.

227. Article 1 of the Regulation No 1049/2001, according to which "Article 1 Purpose The purpose of this Regulation is: (a) to define the principles, conditions and limits on grounds of public or private interest governing the right of access to European Parliament, Council and Commission (hereinafter referred to as 'the institutions') documents provided for in Article 255 of the EC Treaty in such a way as to ensure the widest possible access to documents; (b) to establish rules ensuring the easiest possible exercise of this right, and (c) to promote good administrative

practice on access to documents", and recital 4 of the same Regulation, which reads: "(4) The purpose of this Regulation is to give the fullest possible effect to the right of public access to documents and to lay down the general principles and limits on such access in accordance with Article 255(2) of the EC Treaty".

228. Recital 2 of Regulation 1049/2001: "(2) Openness enables citizens to participate more closely in the decision-making process and guarantees that the administration enjoys greater legitimacy and is more effective and more accountable to the citizen in a democratic system. Openness contributes to strengthening the principles of democracy and respect for fundamental rights as laid down in Article 6 of the EUTreaty and in the Charter of Fundamental Rights of the European Union".
229. See Judgement of 1 July 2008, Sweden and Turco/Council (C-39/05 P and C-52/05 P, ECR 2008 p. I-4723) ECLI:EU:C:2008:374. The Court rejected in here the arguments of the Council that the disclosure of an opinion of its legal service relating to a legislative proposal could lead to doubts as to the lawfulness of the legislative act concerned, with these clear words: "it is precisely openness in this regard that contributes to conferring greater legitimacy on the institutions in the eyes of European citizens and increasing their confidence in them by allowing divergences between various points of view to be openly debated. It is in fact rather a lack of information and debate which is capable of giving rise to doubts in the minds of citizens, not only as regards the lawfulness of an isolated act, but also as regards the legitimacy of the decision-making process as a whole" (paragraph 59).
230. With some exceptions, notably offered by members of the Court of Justice: see F.G. Jacobs, Recent and Ongoing Measures to Improve the Efficiency of the European Court of Justice, in 29 European Law Review, 2004, p. 823; C. Timmermans, The European Union's Judicial System, in 41 Common Market Law Review, 2004, p. 393; K. Lenaerts, The Rule of Law and the Coherence of the Judicial System of the European Union, in 44 Common Market Law Review, 2007, p. 1625; A. Rosas, L. Armati, EU Constitutional Law: An Introduction, Hart 2012, p. 138 *et seq*. Ultimately, for a comprehensive analysis, see A. Alemanno, O. Stefan, Openness at the Court of Justice of the European Union: Toppling a Taboo, *op. cit*.
231. A. Alemanno, O. Stefan, Openness at the Court of Justice of the European Union: Toppling a Taboo, *op. cit*., at 100.
232. J. Shaw, Introduction, in *Ead*., G. More (eds.), New Legal Dynamics of European Union, Oxford University Press 1995, p. 1.
233. A. Alemanno, O. Stefan, Openness at the Court of Justice of the European Union: Toppling a Taboo, *op. cit*., at 100.
234. J.H.H. Weiler, Epilogue: The Judicial Après Nice, *op. cit*., at p. 215.

235. See for instance H. Rasmussen, Present and Future European Judicial Problems after Enlargement and the Post-2005 Ideological Revolt, *op. cit.*, at 1687.
236. See in this sense A. Alemanno, O. Stefan, Openness at the Court of Justice of the European Union: Toppling a Taboo, *op. cit.*, at 100–101. See also in this respect the broad reflections of the Authors of the Symposium—The Future of Judicial Transparency, in 53 Villanova Law Review, 2008.
237. See K. Lenaerts, In the Union We Trust: Trust—Enhancing Principles of Community Law, in 41 Common Market Law Review, 2004, p. 317, at 318–319. See also on the principle of transparency J. Lodge, Transparency and Democratic Legitimacy, in 32 Journal of Common Market Studies, 1994, p. 343; D. Curtin, Betwixt and Between: Democracy and Transparency in the Governance of the European Union, in J.A. Winter, D. Curtin, A.E. Kellerman, B. de Witte (eds.), Reforming the Treaty on European Union: The Legal Debate, Kluwer 1996, p. 95; S. Peers, From Maastricht to Laeken: The Political Agenda of Openness and Transparency in the EU, in V. Deckmyn (ed.), Increasing Transparency in the European Union, European Institute for Public Administration 2002, p. 7.
238. A. Alemanno, O. Stefan, Openness at the Court of Justice of the European Union: Toppling a Taboo, *op. cit.*; V. Naglič, National Practices with Regard to the Accessibility of Court Documents. Study, *op. cit.*
239. See H. Rasmussen, Present and Future European Judicial Problems after Enlargement and the Post-2005 Ideological Revolt, *op. cit.*; M. Lasser, Judicial Deliberations: A Comparative Analysis of Judicial Transparency and Legitimacy, *op. cit.*; E. Sharpston, Transparency and Clear Legal Language in the European Union: Ambiguous Legislative Texts, Laconic Pronouncements and the Credibility of the Judicial System, in 12 Cambridge Yearbook of European Legal Studies, 2009–2010, p. 409; A. Stone Sweet, The European Court of Justice, *op. cit.*, at 146.
240. M. Bobek, Of Feasibility and Silent Elephants: The Legitimacy of the Court of Justice through the Eyes of National Courts, in M. Adams, H. de Waele, J. Meeusen, G. Straetmans (eds.), Judging Europe's Judges: The Legitimacy of the Case Law of the European Court of Justice, *op.cit.*, at 200 and 217 *et seq.*
241. A. Alemanno, O. Stefan, Openness at the Court of Justice of the European Union: Toppling a Taboo, *op. cit.*, at 97.
242. A. Alemanno, Unpacking the Principle of Openness in EU Law: Transparency, Participation and Democracy, in 39 European Law Review, 2014, p. 72.
243. See the Decision of the Court of Justice of the European Union of 11 December 2012 concerning public access to documents held by

the Court of Justice of the European Union in the exercise of its administrative functions (OJ C 38, 9.2.2013, pp. 2–4).
244. Decision of the Court of Justice of the European Union of 11 October 2016 concerning public access to documents held by the Court of Justice of the European Union in the exercise of its administrative functions (OJ C 445, 30.11.2016, p. 3).
245. Decision of the Court of Justice of the European Union of 26 November 2019 concerning public access to documents held by the Court of Justice of the European Union in the exercise of its administrative functions (OJ C 45, 10.2.2020, pp. 2–7).
246. Available at the website http://curia.europa.eu/juris/recherche.jsf (accessed 2 March 2020).
247. It was not the case until recently, and, given the importance of *référendaires* in the internal working of the Court, and that their appointment do not follow a common procedure being a prerogative of each member of the Court, the fact was criticized by scholars: see for instance A. Alemanno, O. Stefan, Openness at the Court of Justice of the European Union: Toppling a Taboo, *op. cit.*, at 101.
248. Article 21 (4) of CJ Rules of Procedure and Article 24 (6) of the GC Rules of Procedure.
249. Article 21 (4) of the Draft CJ Rules of Procedure, 25 May 2011.
250. A. Alemanno, O. Stefan, Openness at the Court of Justice of the European Union: Toppling a Taboo, *op. cit.*, at 119.
251. M. Bobek, Of Feasibility and Silent Elephants: The Legitimacy of the Court of Justice through the Eyes of National Courts, *op. cit.*, at 219–220.
252. A. Alemanno, O. Stefan, Openness at the Court of Justice of the European Union: Toppling a Taboo, *op. cit.*, at 121.
253. This is the case, for instance, of the Netherlands, the Czech Republic, Poland, Romania and Portugal (in this last case, the Portuguese Supremo Tribunal de Justiça, at its website http://www.stj.pt/jurisprudencia/tjue, accessed 2 March 2020, only lists the questions referred, and it does not offer translations of the whole preliminary reference).
254. See for instance JuriFast, a data base set by the Association of Councils of State and the Supreme Administrative Jurisdictions, available at the website http://www.juradmin.eu/fr/jurisprudence/jurifast_fr.html (accessed 2 March 2020); or CASELEX, a private website available at http://www.caselex.com (accessed 2 March 2020).
255. See the Dec.nat database, available at the website http://www.juradmin.eu/en/jurisprudence/jurisprudence_en.lasso (accessed 2 March 2020).
256. A. Alemanno, O. Stefan, Openness at the Court of Justice of the European Union: Toppling a Taboo, *op. cit.*
257. *Ivi*, at 112–113.

258. As it was denounced by a recent Report to the Ombudsman about Various Problems of Bad Administration in the European Court of Justice (available at the website https://www.linkedin.com/pulse/report-ombudswoman-various-problems-bad-european-court-dehousse?trk=portfolio_article-card_title) by the former Judge Fraklin Dehousse, who in personally sued the Court for a breach of its rights to transparency: see Judgement of 20 September 2019, Dehousse/Court of Justice de l'Union européenne (T-433/17, Publié au Recueil numérique) ECLI:EU:T:2019:632.
259. Article 25 of the Rules of Procedure of the CJ.
260. A. Alemanno, O. Stefan, Openness at the Court of Justice of the European Union: Toppling a Taboo, *op. cit.*, at 111.
261. Article 21 (1) of the CJ Rules of Procedure, Article 24 (1) of the GC Rules of Procedure, and Article 20 (1) of the CST Rules of Procedure.
262. A. Alemanno, O. Stefan, Openness at the Court of Justice of the European Union: Toppling a Taboo, *op. cit.*, at 121 *et seq.*
263. Article 22 (1) of the CJ Rules of Procedure.
264. Article 24 (5) of the GC Rules of Procedure.
265. Article 24 (5) of the CST Rules of Procedure.
266. A. Alemanno, O. Stefan, Openness at the Court of Justice of the European Union: Toppling a Taboo, *op. cit.*, at 122.
267. Article 4 (2) of the Regulation 1049/2001.
268. Judgement of 12 September 2007, API/Commission (T-36/04, ECR 2007 p. II-3201) ECLI:EU:T:2007:258.
269. Judgement of 21 September 2010, Sweden and others/API and Commission (C-514/07 P, C-528/07 P and C-532/07 P, ECR 2010 p. I-8533) ECLI:EU:C:2010:541.
270. See at the paragraph 26 of AG Maduro's Opinion in the case mentioned above.
271. See Article 20, sub-paragraph 4 of the Statute.
272. See in this sense the practical remarks by M. Patchett-Joyce, Barrister Outer Temple Chambers, London, in his Hearing on the Reform of the Court of Justice of the European Union before the Committee on Legal Affairs of the European Parliament, available at the website http://www.europarl.europa.eu/document/activities/cont/201305/20130521ATT66428/20130521ATT66428EN.pdf (accessed 2 March 2020), at p. 4 in particular.
273. See on this the remarks by K. McAuliffe, Language and Law in the European Union: The Multilingual Jurisprudence of the Ecj, in L.M. Solan, P.M. Tiersma (eds.), The Oxford Handbook of Language and Law, Oxford University Press 2012, p. 200, at 209 *et seq.*

274. See *ivi*, at 212 *et seq*., and M.A. Gaudissart, Le regime et la pratique linguistiques de la Cour de Justice, in D. Hanf, K. Malacek, E. Muir (eds.) Langues et construction européenne, PIE Peter Lang 2007, p. 137.
275. D. Edward, How the Court of Justice Works, *op. cit.*, at 548–549.
276. On this, specifically, M. Bobek, The Binding Force of Babel: The Enforcement of EC Law Unpublished in the Languages of the New Member States, in 9 Cambridge Yearbook of European Legal Studies, 2006–2007, p. 43.
277. See the relevant rules under the "Basis for publication" available at the website http://curia.europa.eu/en/content/juris/contenu.htm#principes (accessed 2 March 2020).
278. See Decision of the Court of Justice of the European Union of 10 June 2014 concerning the deposit of the historical archives of the Court of Justice of the European Union at the Historical Archives of the European Union (European University Institute), (2015/C 406/02).
279. Council Regulation (EU) 2015/496 of 17 March 2015 in OJEU L79/1.
280. Opening of the Historical Archives of the European Court of Justice, European University Institute—Historical Archives of the European Union: http://www.eui.eu/Research/HistoricalArchivesOfEU/News/2015/12-17-Official-opening-of-the-European-Court-of-Justices-papers.aspx (accessed 2 March 2020).
281. F. Nicola, National Legal Traditions at Work in the Jurisprudence of the Court of Justice of the European Union, *op. cit.*, at 872–873.
282. F. Nicola, Waiting for the Barbarians: Inside the Archive of the European Court of Justice, American University Washington College of Law Research Paper n. 2019-19, available at the website https://papers.ssrn.com/sol3/papers.cfm?abstract_id=3417267 and forthcoming in C. Kilpatrick, J. Scott (eds.) New Legal Approaches to Studying the Court of Justice, OUP 2020.
283. Decision of the Court of Justice of the European Union of 10 June 2014, Article 4.2.

CHAPTER 5

Docket Control at the Court of Justice

I mentioned in several respects throughout the dissertation the problem of the burden of cases that weighs on the Court of Justice's docket. I already said that it is a crucial and much-discussed aspect of its institutional structure and organization, collaterally related to other institutional problems of the body. This is another often neglected topic, at least in terms of academic attention. Still, it surely deserves an independent analysis for some coessential reasons.

The first one, to which I already hinted at, is that everyone who studies EU law is used to hearing about a European Court of Justice that is a "victim of its own success",[1] in this sense referring to the mass of cases that flow before the court; but a sort of general academic unconditional reflex is to study judicial bodies more through the lenses of grand theories of adjudication and talk about what they should do and how they should do it, rather than focusing on the equally important question of how many things they do and how they can do them better. As suggested in the previous chapter in talking about the practical possibility of fully open and transparent deliberations, this *quantitative* in addition to a *qualitative* study of judicial review is particularly relevant to understanding the reality of the Luxembourg Court. In the success of the inflow of cases and the practical problem of dealing with them effectively, one can see the issue of the authority of the Court of Justice very well symbolized vis-à-vis its interlocutors in its most concrete application.

L. Pierdominici, *The Mimetic Evolution of the Court of Justice of the EU*, https://doi.org/10.1007/978-3-030-47864-3_5

The second reason for concern on the topic is that the Court has known an essential institutional evolution. It has undergone, as in the other case studies I am investigating, the influence of the Member States' practices and different external comparative paradigms. In particular, as will be seen, this happened in the problem of conceptualizing the idea of docket control—which had become a necessity at a certain point—and in understanding the best solutions to tackle it, also given the specificities of the interface with different cultures and attitudes in the different national legal systems.

For docket control, one can generally refer to the basic institutional notion (and self-notion) that courts can decide, for capacity reasons, only a certain, limited fraction of issues generated in a legal system; and they are called to do so in a reasonable limit of time to offer an acceptable level of judicial protection to their users. The consequent institutional need for every court is to settle standards, doctrines and precedents, in the form of substantive choices to control the flow of litigation they receive in addition to the complementary need to isolate—through different expedients—among the cases and conflicts they receive, those which are to be dismissed as non-litigable from those which are admitted and dealt with a full judicial opinion on their merits. In general, judicial bodies need forms of control over the human and timing resources that they can spend in deciding cases.

In this, one can easily see a "*quantitative*" dimension of judicial review that can be juxtaposed to the somewhat typical "*qualitative*" analysis of the work of courts. When one reads that the dominant approach to the study of some specific areas of law has historically been "judicial review-centered"[2]—and the disciplines of constitutional law, European Union law and international law are all but exceptions—this means that the dominant scholarship has focused on the activity of courts by studying the different methods of interpretation deployed, relying on grand foundationalist/organic theories of judicial review, often trying to justify or to reject the practice of judicial review *in toto* and/or dictating its parameters. Behind such strong positions and the search for "first-best principles" of interpretation and judicial legitimacy[3] one can see a series of latent and intractable tensions, inherent in traditional constitutional theories of interpretation and adjudication: these tensions are, after all, the consequences of the unavoidably creative function of the judicial role. But for a complete and more realist understanding of the judicial function in its practical aspects and every broad discussion "of the advantages and disadvantages of the adjudicative process",[4] one should always consider its institutional, quantitative dimensions. Scholars of the discipline of so-called Comparative Institutional Analysis use to conceptualize the first problem as one of "competence": every court surely meets widespread problems in its relationships of power with other institutions, and has to face the related constraints. By competence, it is meant here the comparative ability of judges and courts (as composite institutions) as decision-makers: and therefore the ability to understand "highly technical issues and evidence in complex, large-scale litigation", the ability to handle complex and delicate issues concerning politically sensitive subjects, the ability to deal with large-scale social policy issues "where there are many conflicting interests and a continuing need for implementation and oversight".[5] However, the same scholars use to juxtapose and stress the importance of severe problems and constraints related to the "scale" of courts.[6] In this perspective, the focus is not so much on the inherent tensions due to the legitimacy of the judicial interventions but precisely on the fact that the very "physical capacity … of any institution"[7] is important in determining its ability, how it does whatever it is intended to accomplish. This is particularly true for courts, in comparison with other institutions; considerations of size, "in particular the implications of severe constraints on growth" in size of the tribunals, "play such an important role in the adjudicative process and so strongly affect inter-institutional choices that they require special consideration".[8] If one considers the market (intended, in economics jargon, as the aggregate of all the free individual transactions) and the political processes (as its mediate, delegated representation) as the opposite institutions in an ideal triangle, in relation to courts, it is easy to see to what extent a group of varying factors (demographic, economic, political, technological, among others) determine expansion in size and can lead to a significant increase in demand for adjudication. In the face of all this, the judicial bodies can hardly obviate with mere adjustments in size and are called to control such a relationship between demand and supply of justice in different ways.[9]

In this respect, the scarce comparative literature that tries to explore this neglected, "quantitative" dimension of judicial review (or at least try to call for new studies in the field) icastically makes a connection between "docket control and the success of courts".[10] Giving courts—particularly courts performing some form of review of constitutional significance—the ability to decide what to decide, or to manage in some ways their resources in deciding, proves crucial to what the scholars define as their "*success*". A court empowered to set or control—at least partially—its agenda, it is argued, is also a court that "can avoid excessive political conflict and ensure maximum compliance";[11] it is an institution able to better perform its basic tasks and in the condition to work more effectively. While it is almost universal for political actors to receive control not only over the decisions they make—something on which the courts will never have full discretion[12]—but also on the timing and resources employed for decisions, when it comes to judicial bodies the situation is different. In principle, they are called and obliged to devote the same efforts to all cases treated under the law with no discrimination. Still, for their "success", courts nonetheless need to manage and streamline the aspects of timing and resources employed—at least in a certain sense—through different means.

In the following pages, I will analyse, within a tentative taxonomy, the methods that the courts can employ to accommodate the supply and demand for adjudication and in general to control their docket and the related quantity and quality of judicial activity they engage in performing their task. I will situate in particular the analysis in the CJEU realm, by talking of its peculiar problems in controlling the flow of cases it receives. I will see, in particular, how the different concepts of docket control one can comparatively sketch correspond to the different phases in the debate on the CJEU's quantitative dimension of adjudication, and correspond to the various solutions that were contemplated under the comparative influence of Member States' practices and other external paradigms.

5.1 The European Court of Justice and Its Docket

In a sort of functional portrayal, the competences and the scope of adjudication of the Court of Justice may be summarily divided into three main areas[13]:

- *Arbitration of (Inter-)Institutional disputes*—where the Court, performing as a typical international tribunal,[14] decides on the types of actions that oppose Union institutions and/or the Member States primarily. These include, as it is known, infringement proceedings (Article 258 TFEU and its extension in Article 260 TFEU) and actions for failure to act (Article 265 TFEU). The remedy sought here is a declaration by the Court that a Member State or an EU institution failed to act or acted in violation of the Treaties.

- *(Proper) Judicial review*—where, inspired as seen by national administrative categories, the Court reviews, directly or on appeal, the legality of acts of Union institutions (Article 263 TFEU). The remedy sought is the annulment of the Union acts challenged. Jurisdiction falling under this head includes actions brought by the Member States directly to the ECJ, appeals against first instance decisions of the General Court in cases of all other applicants,[15] as well as an incidental review of the legality of EU acts emerging from other types of proceedings.
- *References for preliminary rulings*—where the Court hears the requests, submitted according to Article 267 TFEU by national courts, that seek either the authoritative interpretation or the assessment of the validity of an EU act. A decision rendered by the CJ forms part of the national proceedings—of which, as seen, this procedure is considered an "incident"—and will be applied by the referring court; it will then also bind other courts in the Member States.[16]

Although there are further kinds of relevant activities performed by the Court—such as the opinions rendered according to Article 218(11) TFEU on the compatibility with the Treaties of contemplated international agreements of the EU, or the claims for compensation based on non-contractual liability of the Community of Article 268 TFEU—the three mentioned categories can be considered as *main* areas of cognition precisely from a *quantitative* standpoint. They have always amounted to the vast majority of the judicial activity carried out in Luxembourg, in terms of cases treated, and therefore of time and resources employed. However, on the whole, the order in which I have described the three main types of CJEU activity also reflects, in ascending order, how strongly each category is represented within the overall docket of the Court today. In turn, this also reflects to what extent the Court has felt called to "control" and is capable of somehow "controlling" the flow of relative cases it receives, from the moment such control started to be deemed necessary.

Some data, observed in diachronic terms, are elucidative in this respect. In terms of relative numbers, in the last decades, and with an acceleration in the previous one, there was a distinct rise of the number of preliminary rulings, with a decline in direct actions; while their relationship in different stages of the history of the Court was inverse.[17] Such a phenomenon is nowadays so evident that, for instance, in the five years from 2007 to 2011, references for a preliminary ruling became more than half of the proceedings before the ECJ, while in the past five years, these amounted to about 2/3 of all cases decided.[18] The absolute numbers are even more telling. The judicial activity of the Court has, in fact, steadily increased over time. In the 1950s, when it was founded, the Court had less than 50 new cases each year; in the 1970s, usually between 100 and 200 new cases each year, still treated within a unique jurisdiction; in the 1990s, when the Court of First Instance had already been established, the apical Court of Justice alone had between 300 and 500 cases; and since 2001 there have been between 400 and 850 new cases each year, still generally on the increase despite the creation for some years of the European Union Civil Service Tribunal as an additional specialized branch (553 cases in 2009, 624 in 2010, 679 in 2011, 617 in 2012, 690 in 2013, 614 in 2014).[19] In 2018, 849 cases were brought before the Court of Justice, and 834 before the General Court of first instance.[20]

All this has happened for several important concurring reasons.[21] Some of them were evident and directly tangible, so to say. The first reason can be easily seen in the successive enlargements of the European Communities before and the European Union afterwards, with a progressive expansion from 6 to 28 States (before Brexit), which also meant a great expansion of the territorial validity of EU law. In turn, this led to an obvious expansion of the audience of potential applicants to the European jurisdiction and potential national judges exercising their "European mandate".[22] A second equally clear reason is in the constant parallel expansion of the European Communities' competences, epitomized, to name a few, in the succession of European Treaties, in the collapse of the "pillars" structure, ultimately in the recognition of the legally binding nature of the EU Charter of Fundamental Rights or the new Eurocrisis-law measures.[23] But there are also reasons that are less evident. A third factor can be traced back to the success of the supranational positive harmonization initiatives. These have always been one of the main tools in the arsenal of the European Communities aimed at fostering the creation of a truly single market through the removal of barriers to trade. But their success also depends upon the nature of the subject matter in question and the differences between the existing laws of the Member States[24]:

when a harmonization measure is enacted, it often generates new controversies and therefore new work for the EU judicial system, since any new piece of legislation, whether enacted at the supranational or the national level, will always contain important issues which require judicial clarification (also to understand the degree of discretion left in regulation at the different levels).[25] The harmonization of national trademark laws brought about by the Trade Marks Directive in 1989[26] and the subsequent introduction of the Community Trade Mark[27] are often cited as the most evident examples, since they led without a doubt to a relevant number of applications to the competent European authorities and then to a huge number of controversies, as it is well known assigned to the Court of First Instance. A fourth factor, again surely effective but of difficult appraisal, is the always growing awareness of EU law by practising lawyers and judges in the national contexts. At the inception of the Communities few knew much about EC law, and for a long time it remained "the preserve of a limited number of specialists",[28] a project led by the consciousness and the activism of a sort of intellectual elite.[29] Over decades and generations, this has undoubtedly changed, also thanks to specific programmes of instruction provided and subsidized by Brussels[30]: and it has become more and more natural for a lawyer to think about whether there is an EU law point in a case which comes before him. These rationales are listed without claiming to be exhaustive, and their single parts of contribution are debatable. Still, their combined effect was also acknowledged in several of the Courts' annual Reports, and in the famous, specific Due Report "on the future of the European Communities' Court System", requested to a Working Party of Wise Men by the Commission in 1999[31] (actually, the first of a series of institutional papers on the matter).[32]

While both the aforementioned numbers and factors can be considered as direct or indirect evidence of the success of the European integration project, the increase in the workload of the European judicial system has surely had an adverse effect on the CJEU's functionality. In particular, they had an impact on its ability to deliver its judgements within a short timeframe. Also, there were clear numbers that depicted the Court of Justice as the victim of such a success: in 1975, for instance, it took the ECJ an average of six months to deal with preliminary references, and nine months to deal with direct actions; in 1988, this time was no less than tripled, and the Court needed an average of 18 and 24 months, respectively; in 2003, the average period to obtain a preliminary ruling reached a peak of 25.5 months.[33] It is difficult and maybe speculative to try to single out a precise moment in which the phenomenon of inflow of cases assumed the characteristics of an emergency. Surely, one can say that a structured, plural debate on the matter started in the 1980s[34]; and that neither the emergency nor the search for solutions can be said to be concluded, if the previous President of the Court of Justice, Vassilios Skouris, in presenting one the last published Reports on the activity of the Court, wrote only some years ago that "(I)n 2013, the Court of Justice of the European Union experienced a striking increase in the pace of its judicial activity (…) the number of cases brought was the highest since the judicial system of the European Union was created (…) which indicates the confidence of national courts and of litigants in the judicature of the European Union. However, this intensification of judicial activity is liable, in the not necessarily distant future, to undermine the efficiency of the European Union's judicial system as a whole. For this reason, there is a constant and continuous need to seek means (…) of improving the efficiency of that judicial system".[35]

In light of all the above, one can realize how much what is defined as docket control is decisive for the institutional evolution of the Court of Justice. And for the specific purposes in this study, it is essential to notice first of all that the need for a quantitative streamlining of such inflow of cases had to face the specificity of the institutional position of the European Court of Justice. Quantitative concerns, although often neglected in academic studies, are common for every judicial body, as said; they are particularly so for supreme judicatures and higher courts, which are quintessential scarce resources, with particularly limited time and energy, and for which some rationing and targeting are essential.[36] Much is done elsewhere by the physiological functioning of the appellate systems, according to which the apical court of a pyramid-like structured judicial system is per se reached only by a minority of appeals, for both lack of reasons, interests, and economic resources of the parties.

But from this perspective, the European Court of Justice is placed in a peculiar institutional position. The taxonomical analysis of its previously mentioned main competencies illustrates the point. As it has been said in a comparative vein,[37] the Court can be considered as a "particularly salient exemplar" of the *sui generis* nature of EU law and its categories; and can be seen as a tribunal of hybrid nature, performing different tasks and in doing so assuming various forms. When dealing with its exclusive and mandatory jurisdiction on the controversies arising between the Member States of the EU (in rare cases), and those between the Member States and the EU in the infringement proceedings initiated by the Commission, the Court could be seen as a classic international court, albeit an "extraordinarily effective, sui generis one".[38] In annulment proceedings and in the preliminary proceedings on the validity of EU law under Article 267(b), where it is competent to review the legality of EU acts such as legislative acts and other acts adopted by the European institutions which are intended to have legal effects, the Court is on the other hand comparable to a constitutional court, in the Kelsenian terms in which it is called to enforce "a norm or a group of norms which are of the highest rank in a legal order in the sense that the validity of all other norms is measured on them"; and, again, it enjoys an exclusive competence, except for today's General Court, which is subject to review by the CJEU. Finally, thanks to the decisive powers it exercises in preliminary ruling proceedings on the interpretation of Community law under Article 267(a) TFEU, the Court has also assumed the role of a veritable supreme court to which every national court of every Member State refers questions of interpretation in case of any doubt on the meaning of EU law. With the widespread acceptance of the doctrines of the direct effect and supremacy of European law, the CJEU is de facto empowered to assess—by means of the preliminary ruling proceedings—not only the validity of EU law but also the conformity to EU law of Member States' legislation and practices,[39] in performing what I have repeatedly called a *nomophylactic* function typical of a supreme court. But it is always essential to remark that this could happen—thanks to the inner *genius loci* of the preliminary reference procedure[40]—by developing a constructive and mutual relationship (a "dialogue", as it has become customary to say) with the national courts, which means that the European and the national courts have collaborated in shaping the content and Community law "in action", without the need or the establishment of formal *hierarchical* relationship between themselves, nor the definition of an exclusive form of jurisdiction.

In recalling these well-known ingredients, one immediately sees their decisive role in the integration process and in the constitutionalization of the EU legal order, which put the Court of Justice at the forefront.[41] Still, it is equally evident for the reader—already in looking at the definition of these powers—the limited capability of the Court to autonomously determine its own workload. In fact, given its competences, the caseload of the Court depends primarily on factors that are external to the choices made in Luxembourg. This is true for the previously mentioned structural reasons that influence the potentiality of controversies such as the increasing size of the EU after the enlargements, the gradual but constant extension of EU competences into new policies areas, the growing constellation of economic, political and social interests involved in the enforcement of EU law, the general phenomenon of "*judicialisation*" (the tendency to a more significant presence of judicial institutions in political and social life), and so on. But it is also true for the technical reasons that influence the introduction of formal disputes when a controversy, in general terms, is already in place.

It suffices to think of the full discretion of the Member States and the Commission in the purely international, arbitral part of the jurisdiction of the Court, in which no spaces of discretion and no powers of control remain for the Court to streamline its docket: in particular, infringement proceedings are always initiated by the Commission which acts *motu proprio* or at the solicitation of individuals, businesses and associations, and which enjoys a full discretionary power to assess whether the action is appropriate and suitable from a political as well as legal point of view. In this respect, scholarly suggestions lean towards a move from trying to enforce an all breached approach to a more targeted approach by the Commission,[42] which, indeed, is trying to adopt the practice of pilot procedures to reduce the number of enforcement actions.[43]

In the context of annulment proceedings, the action can be brought by certain preferential plaintiffs (the Member States, the Council, the Commission, and the Parliament), by certain specialized bodies such as the Court of Auditors, the European Central Bank and the Committee of the Regions to protect their prerogatives, and directly by individuals with an interest in taking action against measures that address them or that directly and individually concern them. Also in this sense, for apparent political sensitivity and the "constitutional" rationality of the system, it was difficult to think of compressing the political discretion of institutions; and the possibility of individual actions has always been compressed and limited to rare, restricted cases of *individual concern*,[44] ignoring the suggestions and the opportunities for a reform of the *locus standi* requirements.[45] This last limitation—academic criticism based on the principle of access to justice notwithstanding[46]—has always been taken as a *datum*, and, though debated in both theory[47] and practice,[48] has never been questioned or reopened in the debate on the management of the workload of the Court, which took place simultaneously and evolved later.

In the context of interpretative preliminary rulings, precisely for the aforementioned heterarchical structure of the system, based on the ongoing voluntary dialogue with national courts, the more or less collaborative attitude of these can be fed and prompted, as will be seen, by the Court of Justice; but the related inflow of cases from national tribunals is also to be considered by the large part as an exogenous variable, to be critically taken into account when trying to contain the weight of the docket. These peculiarities notwithstanding, it is in this context that the debate on the docket control of the European Court of Justice has taken place, and it is interesting to note that it has been shaped around the contemplation of typical instruments. As anticipated, they can be fruitfully investigated in my perspective.

5.2 Docket Control as the Use of *Certiorari* and Procedural "Passive Virtues"

A policy of docket control has not been a special necessity of the European Court of Justice. Quantitative concerns on adjudication have been raised, and studied, and contemplated, in other jurisdictions as well, although to a lesser degree in comparison to what I called qualitative ones. Often, this happened before the relatively recent explosion of the problem at the EU level.

Notoriously, a sort of quintessential paradigm in this respect has been in the American system of "judicial federalism".[49] This became an example for several reasons. The Supreme Court of the United States is, as it is well known, the apical institution of a federal pyramid-like judicial architecture. In the past, it historically experienced serious problems in the management of its increasing caseload[50]; such issues were vastly debated and actively fought with peculiar solutions. The American system is not only, therefore, the one in which the observer can find the most traditional and highest degree of formalization in black-letter law or the case law of the relevant tools of docket control, but it is also the one in which one can find the highest degree of theorization on the use of these tools, in their broad constitutional implications, and the one in which more doctrinal efforts have been devoted to the matter. Not by chance, as will be seen with details, the vast majority of the first efforts in the European debate on docket control made specific reference to the American experience,[51] in search of previous and somewhat settled experiences as well as some lessons in comparative perspective.

The American experience is characterized, first and foremost, by the settlement and the instrumental employment of procedural tools for what has been generally labelled as the "selection of cases" to be heard by its apical Court. The United States Supreme Court is part of a typical pyramid-like structure, with 94 federal district courts at its broad base, 13 courts of appeals at its somewhat narrower middle section, and the "one Supreme Court" mandated by Article III of the US Constitution as its apex. It has, briefly said, ultimate appellate jurisdiction over all federal courts and state court cases involving issues of federal law, and original jurisdiction over a small range of cases: a rather traditional structure, only made special by the ample powers of docket control it enjoys. To make a long story short, concerns about the caseload of the Supreme Court emerged in the American context in different historical phases of its judicial system. Relevant organic studies of prominent scholars[52] have been devoted to the increase in the workload and its relative causes. Typically, they pointed to the growth of the Union, the growing mass of economic, political and social interests involved in its activity (notably after the Civil War fought from 1861 to 1865) and made particular reference to the parallel increase of federal competences and the expansion of federal legislative production.[53] The case submitted to the Court passed from a few hundred to thousands.[54]

Various efforts to keep the Court's docket under control were made. The one that rendered the US Supreme Court a paradigm in the debate is the procedural transformation of its jurisdiction from one in which the cases that could reach it were heard as a matter of right (and in which, therefore, the Court was required to issue a decision in each of those, and thus to review all properly presented appeals on the merits, hear oral argument, and write a judgement) to a mostly discretionary one. This had already happened in 1891 when after the physical expansion of the United States in the nineteenth century, the federal judicial system became increasingly strained—with the Supreme Court experiencing a backlog of several years.[55] The Judiciary Act of 1891, also known as the *Evarts Act* named after the name of its primary sponsor,[56] changed the whole architecture of the system. First, it created nine new courts, labelled the "United States circuit courts of appeals", and reassigned the jurisdiction of most routine appeals from the lower district and circuit courts to these appellate courts. The decisions in those cases were designed as usually final: in the majority of those, the Supreme Court could only review legal issues that a court of appeals certified to it (by voluntarily asking for an opinion on the question of law during the pendency of the case: a very infrequent procedure), and could also review the court of appeals decisions by *writ of certiorari*. The *certiorari* (the word is the present passive infinitive of the Latin verb *certioro*, *certiorare*—"to inform, apprise, show"—and thus translates "to be informed, apprised or shown") is in this system the writ that the Supreme Court, asked by a party through a "petition for writ of certiorari", issues to a lower court to review its judgement for legal error (reversible error) and review where no appeal is available as a matter of right. At the time, the change resulted in an immediate reduction in the Supreme Court's workload (from 623 cases filed in 1890 to 379 in 1891 and 275 in 1892). And it was confirmed, and even enhanced, by the subsequent *Judiciary Act* of 1925 and the *Supreme Court Case Selections Act* of 1988: the latter formalized in positive law the concept and the phrase of "selection of cases", then used also elsewhere, emphasizing the inherent discretion involved in the choice of *certiorare*. With these last measures, the same explicit aim of limiting the workload of the Supreme Court led to further reducing the cases of appeals as of right, and extending the system according to which appellants would file petitions for writs of certiorari with the Supreme Court, which would be accepted at the discretion of four of the nine Justices (the so-called rule of four).[57]

The shift from an appellate system—with an individual right of appeal and to a judgement and a parallel obligation of the Court—to a discretionary supervisory system was not only a formal matter. The US Supreme Court has made extensive use of its discretionary powers so that debates on a change in nature of its jurisdiction were already raised in the 1920s.[58] Without entering into too many details, it suffices to say that the American judges deny (in the present setting) the vast majority of petitions, thus leaving the relative decisions of the lower court to stand without review. They accept roughly 80 to 150 cases each term, out of thousands of petitions, with a grant rate that in the last years was around approximately 1 and 1.5% of appeals. The Supreme Court is generally careful to choose only cases over which the Court has clear jurisdiction and which the Court considers sufficiently important, such as cases involving deep constitutional questions, to merit the use of its limited resources. Moreover, while both appeals of right and certiorari petitions often present several alleged errors of the lower courts for appellate review, the Court usually only grants review of one or two questions presented in a certiorari petition, therefore choosing which of the questions to answer.

The Supreme Court sometimes grants a writ of certiorari to resolve a "circuit split", when the federal appeals courts in two (or more) circuits have ruled differently in similar situations (the so-called "percolating issues").

The introduction of the *certiorari*—the more radical, strong and quintessentially discretional tool for docket control—had a broad resonance, as previously said. Such resonance also shaped the comparative debate. Not only the United States' model became the yardstick against which to measure the attempts to control the docket of other (supreme) courts quantitatively; it was also cited and taken as a reference point for reform proposals in several contexts.[59] It is remarkable that this even happened for the European Court of Justice. The idea of "certiorari" has been repeatedly employed in looking for possible solutions to the massive workload and backlog of the European Union judicial architecture.[60] But in some of these references, it seems clear that the label "certiorari" is used in a non-specific manner, almost as a generic image, as a *synecdoche*, by referring to a part to represent a whole, to a species (the specific procedural tool) to intend a category (the idea of docket control in general), and therefore as a phrase to indicate all the possible usable tools for streamlining the inflow of cases.

First, this is true because the idea of "certiorari" is associated in certain EU law literature not to the adoption of the powerful instrument of discretionary admission of petitions by the apical court, but to other, not strictly comparable tools (which will be seen in the next pages) with a different nature and different effects.[61] But it is also true because sometimes there is no clear reflection on the fact that surely the writ of certiorari, with its broad discretional nature, would abruptly solve any problem of the workload of any judicial institutions in the pure quantitative terms of its workload, but it is also an instrument that clearly qualitatively change the nature of the jurisdiction of a particular institution and whose adoption should, therefore, be weighed carefully. As said, first of all, this comes at the price of making judicial discretion replace the concepts of obligation (by the court) and right (of the appellant) for a review of the appeal. It gives a court the possibility of streamlining the employment of its scarce resources by selecting from among the vast number of petitions those cases that most clearly invoke its essential functions. It also gives the possibility for a court to "set its own agenda", deciding which cases to decide, perhaps avoiding sensitive areas and surely aiming, with selective interventions, at preserving the integrity and the efficiency of judicial interpretation in a particular legal system as well as the quality of its judgements. Nonetheless, two essential features are to be considered. First, the certiorari system is clearly and inherently designed for the purposes of a traditional, pyramidal appellate system. Only with such an architecture, the denial of a grant for certiorari leaves, in any case, the judgement of the previous court alive, as *res iudicata inter partes* and as valid and unaltered precedent in point of law. Not by chance, its introduction in the US system came, as seen, in the context of an organic legislative measure (the Judiciary Act of 1891) that also restructured the appeals of lower court decisions and added a new layer of tribunals to the national system. Moreover, a system where a supreme court is endowed with such discretional powers of selection of cases is a system that envisages for the latter, more than a role of *corrector* of *any* possible error in the interpretation and the application of the law in the single cases, a different role of general *guidance* for lower courts for the correct and uniform application of the law, through few weighed interventions in selected areas of concern.

I already noticed, in brief, how these two aspects are of high and peculiar specificity, and sensitivity, within the legal realm of the EU. When talking of the EU judicial architecture, it is known that in some respects, in dealing with its "direct access" jurisdiction, the Court is bound to firstly satisfy the needs of the other EU institutions with no envisaged possibility of "selection". This is, after all, what still happens in the US system for the residual parts of the Supreme Court's "original jurisdiction". On the other hand, when speaking of preliminary references—the large part of the Court's docket where streamlining would be decisive and in abstract feasible—it is always important to remember that the structural organization of the system is very different from a pyramidal appellate system. A pyramidal appellate system of the kind, with the European Court of Justice at its apex, was interestingly envisioned but never applied under the European Defence Community Treaty in 1952.[62] But as well known, the system created by what is today Article 267 TFEU (and formerly was Art. 234 EC and Art. 177 EEC) is a different one: a heterarchical, cooperative and dialogical system which designs a different relationship between national and supranational judicial bodies. It is designed to foster an ongoing conversation between the Court of Justice and its interlocutors, all the national courts of the Member States, identified in Opinion 1/09 as joint guardians of the Union legal order alongside the ECJ.[63] The procedure, already in its original inspiration as seen in the first part of my analysis, was born to be an incidental parenthesis of the national proceeding, and therefore to offer an authoritative *ex ante* interpretation of the relevant European law to apply in relation to the final decision of the national judge. In such a system, often no previous judgement whatsoever, as *res iudicata* for the parties of the controversy, is available (if, as it frequently happens, the preliminary ruling is asked during a first instance trial); in any case, there is always an open proceeding which is ongoing at the national level, which must be eventually concluded with the application of the interpretative principle authoritatively stated in Luxembourg.

We already see in all this an essential and quite obvious problem of applicability of the real *certiorari* instrument for the case of the Court of Justice of the European Union. Not by chance, the most refined observers who suggested the application of a veritable discretionary system of selection of cases for the CJ—namely Jacqué and Weiler in a seminal reform proposal in 1990[64]—made it in the context of an overall reflection on a "New Judicial Architecture" for the European legal order, and notably by indicating a move strictly comparable to the one made in the United States with the Judiciary Act of 1891 which introduced the certiorari system. Their idea to tackle the increasing workload was to simultaneously restrict the possibility of direct access to the ECJ to major issues of Community law, expand the jurisdiction of (at the time) new Tribunal of First Instance and create four new Community regional courts. The European Court of Justice, remaining as the apical supreme court of the system, would in this pyramidal configuration settle divergent rulings of the regional courts and generally hear only the most important questions of Community law by discretionally selecting them through the use of writs of certiorari, at this point non-problematic.

As will be seen in the following pages specifically, the path of institutional reforms of the European judicial system took different directions. But for now, it is relevant to reflect on a second mentioned aspect and a second decisive problem of applicability of certiorari. It is the problem of the scope of powers of the Court of Justice as controller of the correct and uniform application of EU law, and the proper nature of its *nomophylactic* role. The reluctance to change the features of the preliminary ruling procedure is, in fact, understandable, in general terms. It is the reluctance to modify and distort a tool whose importance "is hard to exaggerate",[65] given its particularly profound influence on the Union's "constitutional" development. Once embraced by the national courts—prompted by individual parties, as per the decisive model of the "private attorney-general"[66]—the procedure enables the European Court to influence the way they apply Union law directly. It offers an opportunity to rule on a vast variety of issues and areas on which the Court might otherwise have been unable to pronounce, and provides a "detailed insight into the practical and legal problems (…) at the national level".[67] The procedure has been the vehicle through which the Court of Justice and the national judges educated each other "about the rules, principles, and methodologies of their respective systems"[68]; it led the CJEU to borrow and adapt principles and concepts of national law and in doing so it also bolstered the authority of Union law by ensuring that it was firmly rooted in the everyday practice of the legal systems of the Member States and merged with their underlying values.

But, from this sketched description of the ingenious, delicate dynamics of the preliminary reference procedure, it is clear that its success is measured against certain premises. First of all, since most national courts enjoy discretion in deciding whether to refer a case, the effectiveness of the procedure strictly depends on the willingness of the parties and most of all of the national courts to make use of it. Any practice that has the potentiality to breach such natural, eventually established inflow of references—including a practice of selection of cases at the supranational level, which would leave some of them unanswered—could also lead the national courts to stop making use of the procedure and to routinely resolve questions of Union law for themselves. This would be a direct problem for the CJEU, which would be deprived of the raw material of national cases it needs: and it needs it not only to engage in a productive, continuous dialogue with its national counterparts, but also to control the exact application of EU law at the national level. This leads to a second interrelated argument, which I also mentioned concerning the question of the transparency in the deliberations of the Court: the problem of the maturity of the EU legal order. Several observers think, as seen, that the general application of EU law in all the 27 internal legal systems of the Member States has not already achieved the necessary level of solidity and certainty to open its argumentation to a more plural, agonistic debate.[69] This is, even more, the case when talking about the dynamics of the preliminary ruling procedure. The general understanding is that the time is not yet ripe for a mere *supervisory* role of the Court of Justice, played, as per the *certiorari* mechanism, by selecting some cases in some selected areas of law, and by giving general *guidance* to lower courts by merely solving those few cases.[70] The correct and uniform application of EU law still needs the European Court of Justice to play a more organic, encompassing role of *corrector*, dealing with *any* possible error in the interpretation and the application of supranational law in all individual national cases. These concerns are so relevant in the EU legal order that they also hindered the adoption of the rational compromise solution advanced in the form of the so-called "green-light procedure".[71] According to this model, the cooperative system of the preliminary ruling procedure would be maintained and even prompted, but the workload of the Court at the same time would be alleviated, by encouraging/obligating national courts to include in their reference for a preliminary ruling an autonomous proposal suggesting the answer to be given. The Court of Justice may then dispose of a case by merely providing a "green light" to the proposal; or, otherwise, where on the opposite the Court would deem necessary a different or more elaborate answer, the case would be submitted for the ordinary procedure. The rationality of the idea is evident. The Court would be able to dispose in an agile way of a relevant number of references, with a good balance between the employment of internal resources for their solution and, on the other hand, the need for unity and consistency in the interpretation and development of EU law. A mix between what I called the role of controller and the role of supervisor by the Court would be found. But one should always note that in such an institutional setting doubts would arise not only about the value of the CJ's precedents; but also, importantly, about the possibility for Member States and the Commission to present, as usual, their views on the substance of the case; and the system would require in the national courts an already acquired good knowledge of EU law, also in specific fields, which is probably—at the actual level of maturity of the EU legal system—still not the case.[72] On the contrary, since such an acquired level of knowledge cannot be taken for granted, national courts could be in practice inhibited in their tendency to submit references and other players would be hindered in their possibility to opine before the Court on the interpretation of EU law—again an unacceptable result at this stage of EU integration.

5.3 The Possibility of Adopting Other "Passive Virtues" in Luxembourg

Certiorari, as said, has been historically considered as the quintessential, paradigmatic tool of docket control. This made the US system a point of reference in the debate. But, as also said, this came at the price of some confusion in the taxonomy of instruments capable of some streamlining of judicial workload: precisely because the US system, in its judicial and doctrinal elaboration, focused for the purpose also on other tools of procedural nature, and these fell in subsequent comparative reflection, even about the case of the European Court of Justice,[73] perplexingly under the same label of "certiorari". In particular, I am talking of the instrumental, purposive use of procedural tools linked to the technical admissibility of the cases in front of the bench. A precise categorization of those has been notoriously conducted in the US judicial system, *in primis* in the form of a jurisprudential elaboration of positive law, and in particular in the interpretation of the limit of the presence of a "*case of controversy*" posed by Art. III of the American Constitution to the power of adjudication of all federal courts. The existence of a veritable "*case of controversy*" in fact, as known, explicitly governs the "*justiciability*" of a case by American courts. From this acquired datum of positive law, a whole theorization on the nature and scope of the consequent "doctrines of justiciability" was developed, identifying the different procedural concepts of *mootness*, *ripeness*, *standing* and *political question*. These shall be used by American judges and the Supreme Court in particular to measure the admissibility of a certain case in front of them. As per the diffuse model of judicial review of the US system,[74] these concepts are ways for the courts to verify the *concreteness* of a certain case as a necessary feature for its solution: their presence ensures the existence of an adversarial proceeding with a real, active dispute. Respectively, they pertain to (1) the idea that further legal proceedings concerning a matter can have no effect, or events have placed it beyond the reach of the law; (2) the readiness of a case for litigation, "if it rests upon contingent future events that may not occur as anticipated, or indeed may not occur at all"; (3) the ability of a party to demonstrate to the court sufficient connection to and harm from the law or action challenged to support that party's participation in the case, and (4) the general question of whether or not the court system is an appropriate forum in which to hear the case.

The difference from the specific certiorari tool and the consonance with the general matter of the "selection of cases" are both evident. In the case of the Supreme Court, a case must first of all, from the logical point of view, be picked and accepted through the discretionary system of certiorari; then, only in rare though significant hypotheses, the Supreme Court can be in the situation to deem a particular case as inadmissible and therefore not decide it on the merits, with rapid use of scarce resources, through the use of those concepts. Nonetheless, the similarity is in the common use of all these procedural tools as a means of extreme self-restraint and as a way to decide not to decide. It is from here that the mentioned confusion among procedural tools for docket control arises. And it is by the way understandable since for non-local readers, these concepts were widely divulged, together, by the work of those leading constitutional theorists of the last century such as Alexander Bickel, who famously argued for an abundant use of all these tools as instruments of self-restraint by the Supreme Court in its constitutional adjudication, as organic forms of purposeful passivity that the Court has at its disposal.[75] The drafter of the even more notorious conceptualizations describing the driving forces behind constitutional adjudication such as the "counter-majoritarian difficulty",[76] or the distinction between the role of the elected branches and the judicature as being between "expediency" and "principle",[77] invented an equally memorable phrase for this common "quantitative" and "qualitative" idea of judging. Bickel put the certiorari and the "*doctrines of justiciability*", together, in the category of decisive "*passive virtues*" that the Supreme Court could instrumentally and strategically use. The common purpose was, of course, to streamline its docket, selectively pick and choose its interventions in sensitive areas and ultimately enhance its legitimacy and authoritativeness.[78] This idea of judicial "passive virtues" icastically merged the *certiorari* and the "*doctrines of justiciability*" in a same category of procedural tools to be strategically used.

So, when at a certain point in its historical evolution—actually coinciding with the years in which, as seen, its workload started to increase alarmingly—the European Court of Justice gave the impression of beginning to close the traditionally open doors of the preliminary reference procedure, this move was vaguely (and, as said, non accurately) compared to an incipient form of continental certiorari.[79] It was also naturally (and understandably) considered, in general terms, as a form of docket control and a form of exercised "passive virtue".

It must be noted that this happened in a context—the special, incidental configuration of the procedure of Art. 267 TFEU (ex 234 EC/177 EEC)—in which, in technical terms, the division or "separation" of functions[80] between Luxembourg and the national judges has always been clear, at least apparently. Some relevant criteria of admissibility, comparable in fact to the American "doctrines of justiciability", are present, as well known. There must be, here as well, a genuine dispute between the parties[81]; this must result in an action before a national court or tribunal[82]; in this context, a decision on the question of supranational law shall be "necessary" to enable the national court to give judgement.[83] Should this be the case, any court or tribunal "may" make a reference, and a "final" court or tribunal "shall" make a reference, as per the wording of the Treaty. But it is also true that the general understanding has always been that the assessment of the general criteria of justiciability should be the task of national courts in the context of the original proceedings. According to established teachings, it is for them— "which alone has direct knowledge of the facts of the case",[84] and "before which the actions are brought, and which must bear the responsibility for the subsequent judicial decision"[85]—to evaluate the relevance of the question of EU law to the outcome of the dispute, and therefore to decide whether a reference is necessary[86] and the pertinent content of the questions to be referred.[87]

Given this background, the resulting tasks of the Court of Justice should be to act in a way that does not discourage references from national courts, to receive cases, and solve them (since it is "in principle, bound to give a ruling")[88] being attentive to both provide enough guidance for the national judges to resolve the matter at hand and promote, in general terms, the correct and uniform application of EU law. It must be noted that in the entire first decades of European integration a "great willingness to receive references" was demonstrated by the Court, with almost no procedural limits and no judicial and doctrinal elaboration on the admissibility of the cases.[89] This was the phase of the tuning of the procedure, in which the Court had to defeat the natural reluctance of national courts (or at least of some national courts, in some Member States) to employ the new instrument; and it was also the phase in which the Court established, through the channels of Article 177 EEC, some of the fundamental tenets of Community law, including, as everybody knows, the concepts of primacy and direct effect.[90]

Evidence of such willingness could already be found in early, historical judgements like *Da Costa en Schaake*[91] and *Costa v. ENEL*.[92] In fact, in the first case, the Court—going against the opinion of the Commission that pleaded for the dismissal—explicitly accepted to rule on legal issues materially identical to those dealt with in *Van Gend en Loos* only some weeks before.[93] In the second case, it formally stated its "power to extract from a question imperfectly formulated by the national court those questions which alone pertain to the interpretation of the Treaty",[94] adding that "(S)ince (…) Article 177 is based upon a clear separation of functions between national courts and the Court of Justice, it cannot empower the latter either to investigate the facts of the case or to criticize the grounds and purpose of the request for interpretation".[95] In this respect, the much-discussed practice of the Court reframing/rewriting questions posed by national judges, "having regard to the facts in the main proceedings and in order to provide a helpful response to the national court",[96] could also be read as an element of such ample willingness to receive, to answer and to solve cases.[97] Given the tendency, in a second phase at least in the history of the Court, to receive more complicated references, "both because the issues themselves were becoming more complex and because the national courts were trying to be more sophisticated in what they asked",[98] the Court found itself in the necessity to rephrase some national court questions to better frame and answer the relevant issues. It is to be noted that this started to happen in early examples of imperfectly and inadequately formulated references[99] (which, at a later stage, have been treated differently): this gives the idea of a practice settled precisely not to declare the impossibility of an answer and aimed at avoiding the declining of jurisdiction at any cost.

Nonetheless, an opposite tendency began with an epiphany around the late 1970s and the early 1980s, arriving at a complete realization since the 1990s. The Court started to decline jurisdiction in Article 177 references and to put limits to the inflow of cases from national courts through a new interpretation of the admissibility/justiciability criteria. This altered attitude surprised the scholars, who started to wonder about a "changing face",[100] or a transformation in the "spirit",[101] of the preliminary reference procedure. The trend had its first episodes in the often disregarded *Mattheus v. Doego* case of 1978,[102] and in the (on the other hand) well-known *Foglia v. Novello (No. 1)* case of 1980,[103] in which for the first time the Court of Justice declined its jurisdiction in Article 177 references. In *Mattheus*, the Court refused to answer in a trivial episode where the requested interpretation related to measures not yet adopted by the Community institutions; but interestingly, it did so against an attempt by private parties to compel via their agreements both the national court of the Member State to request a preliminary ruling and the CJ to rule on a decisive matter, and by making an explicit reference to "the independent exercise of the discretion" and the spaces thereof provided by Article 177.[104] In a more disputable (and disputed)[105] move, in *Foglia v. Novello*, the Court did the same, and recognized the "artificial", fabricated nature of the dispute, in which two parties had merely used the device of a contractual clause to induce an Italian judge to refer a question on the validity of the French tax system, cleverly endangering "the whole system of legal remedies available to private individuals" in doing so.[106] Remarkably, it did so notwithstanding the danger implied in crossing the boundaries of the fact-finding domain, considered as a preserve of the referring courts.[107] In the following *Foglia v. Novello (No. 2)* case, raised by the same national court, the Court highlighted that by refusing jurisdiction it was not trespassing on the prerogatives of the national court, but was preventing the application of Article 177 to purposes other than those appropriate: in particular, it focused on the concreteness of the cases at hand and the unwillingness to offer mere advisory opinions.[108]

The second and much-discussed macroscopic episode came a couple of years later, in 1982, with the case *CILFIT Srl and Lanificio di Gavardo SpA v. Ministero della Sanità*.[109] At a time in which the Court "was already receiving about 100 references a year from nine Member States",[110] the Court introduced, according to the general understanding,[111] the doctrines of *acte clair* and *acte éclairé* into Community law: by interpreting the scope of the obligation for "national courts and tribunals against whose decisions there is no judicial remedy under national law" to refer questions concerning the interpretation of European law, it seemed to relax the unequivocal wording of paragraph three of Article 177 EEC and to exonerate "final" courts of the Member States in certain circumstances from what otherwise appeared to be an unconditional obligation to refer. In particular, it called them to an autonomous analysis on both whether the question posed in front of them could be irrelevant and also whether the Community provision in question had already been authoritatively interpreted by the Court of Justice (*acte éclairé*), or, whether the correct application of Community law is "so obvious as to leave no scope for any reasonable doubt" (*acte clair*). This not only has been read as the adoption of a certain civil law aptitude according to which the judge just intervenes to declare what the law already is[112]; but seemed to constitute a potential crack in the imperative of uniform protection since the Court was "replacing the mandatory wording of the Treaty with a formula which was open to judicial interpretation".[113] The Advocate General of the case, Francesco Capotorti, in his opinion,[114] and some scholars further underlined that by relaxing at least "psychologically" such obligation, and by drawing a "move from power (Article 177(2)) and obligation (Article 177(3)) to a perception of no absolute obligation",[115] the CJ was creating doubts as to the real necessity of making a reference even for lower courts, and frustrating years-long campaign for the inflow of cases and eventually for the uniform interpretation of Community law. The discussed trend went on and was corroborated by a series of cases in which—later in time, starting in the 1980s but with a sharp acceleration in the 1990s—with unprecedented moves, the Court declined jurisdiction, again by focusing on reasons strictly related to the admissibility and justiciability of the dispute. These amounted at more than 20 controversies,[116] and included for instance: cases such as where the procedure before the court making the reference for a preliminary ruling had already been terminated (and therefore the case, in the described American terms, was "moot")[117]; situations where the Court declared to have no jurisdiction under the EC Treaty over what it was asked to consider, in relation to the objects of the references (interpretation of national law[118]; references to Treaty articles on the objectives of the Union,[119] at least some of the disputes in which Community law does not apply *qua* Community law but is transposed into a national context by national law)[120]; situations where the Court was controlling, more closely than before, whether all the conditions for a reference laid down in Article 177 itself were satisfied, in particular about the nature of "*court or tribunal*" of the referring authority[121]; questions where the Court perceived that there was either no genuine dispute or that the issue is hypothetical,[122] or where it considered that inadequate information of fact and law had been provided,[123] or where it took the view that the questions referred had no connection with the dispute before the national court.[124]

These episodes can be read and were read in different ways, from different points of view. Some parts of the mentioned case law, which outlined important "new criteria for review of jurisdiction",[125] are considered nowadays as settled teachings of the Court of Justice. In some aspects, they were even incorporated in the black-letter law of the new *Guidance on References by National Courts for Preliminary Rulings* issued by the Court of Justice,[126] a soft law measure aimed at fostering the knowledge by national judges of the technicalities of the Art. 267 procedure. In historical perspective, a certain tendency towards an optimization of the procedure was evident, also given the transformation in size and quality of the EU integration process, of the EU legal order, of the Court's case law, and also, as previously said, of the national courts' references. In this sense, there was a symbolic value: the trend was the sign of a new phase of relative *maturity* acquired by the system, and I already pointed at how this concept could be relevant in the evolution of the Court and of the European judicial architecture, in several respects. But I also pointed at the fact that a part of scholars interpreted the trend as an evolution towards "European certiorari", or generally towards some form of docket control. Was this really the case? I already highlighted the comparative misunderstanding of taking the *certiorari* as a unified label for any procedural tool for the selection of cases. From my analysis, it is evident that several of the "new criteria for review of jurisdiction" forged by the European Court since the 1980s and 1990s coincided, in both their nature and their development, to the American "doctrines of justiciability", precisely aimed at assessing the concreteness of some instances in its various dimensions. Thus, it was tempting to see the same underlying dynamics theorized in the American context in those, and therefore describe a Court of Justice that—departing from its obligation to rule on preliminary references—changed the "spirit" of the procedure and moved towards quantitative and qualitative selections, also for strategic reasons.[127]

However, a diachronic analysis can also tell us more in this respect and disprove certain premises taken for granted. It is to be noted that these elements have often given a mere impression of a shift towards strategic docket control without being supported by coherent developments. For instance, *Foglia v. Novello* was, as previously said, the first widely discussed case of procedural inadmissibility (often considered the first that ever happened)[128]: and it provided a dismissal on a rather typical and central feature about the genuineness of the underlying dispute and the unwillingness to issue mere advisory opinions (an aspect of the "concreteness" of a case, in both the American jargon and the Italian theorization of constitutional incidental adjudication, as noticed the paradigm for Article 177 EEC). But in hindsight, the doctrine had not such a decisive application later on. The Court did not apply it in other later cases which probably would have merited the same treatment, even in the immediate aftermath.[129] In *Vinal*,[130] a case of the subsequent year, the Italian Government submitted that the controversy between the parties was artificial and only aimed to "impeach the Italian state in the absence of any actual dispute"[131]; but both the Advocate General[132] and the Court laconically distinguished[133] the case from *Foglia* and rejected the objection, pointing to the lack of decisive evidence of a "friendly suit", and that the facts were only sufficient to show "that the parties *may* have had a perfectly reasonable interest" in fabricating it.[134] The same happened later, in the cases *Rau*[135] and *Provide*,[136] where the facts of the cases could be dubious (in both, one party strangely refused to take delivery of the goods ordered by it and was sued by the other party in the national court), but the Court readily accepted the genuineness of the disputes. In *Delhaize*,[137] there was evidence that the parties were in agreement and that the action before the local judges was deliberately engineered in order to see whether Article 34 EEC forbade the application of a Spanish law prohibiting the export in bulk of wine protected by a certain designation of origin. The parties suggested identical solutions to the questions referred by the national court, even by expressly making a *renvoi* to the submissions of each other; and the action in the proceedings of origin was for specific performance, alternatively for damages "provisionally assessed at BF 1".[138] However, the Court, in here as well, did not refer to its (possible lack of) jurisdiction under Article 177.

The potential magnitude of the *CILFIT* case for the docket control is even more profound and debatable. The criteria set in the judgement surely importantly shaped, and are still part of, the fundamental division of labour in the EU judicial architecture, between the CJEU and the national courts. But a contextual comparative analysis of the case is again capable of putting it in a different light, in particular if one is tempted to interpret it as a major tentative quantitative streamlining of the inflow of cases. It has been recently written, against the general vulgate, that the Court in *CILFIT* indeed "rejected the doctrine of *acte clair*",[139] by, in a certain sense, simply reinforcing in a different historical phase its holding in *Da Costa*.[140] I already mentioned how in this latter judgement the Court of Justice accepted to rule on two questions materially identical to those of the *Van Gend en Loos* case, raised by the same Netherlands Tariefcommissie while it had not yet received an answer in the seminal proceeding. Already in 1963, the Court talked of the "unrestricted" nature of the obligation of Article 177(3); it simply went on in its reasoning and relied on the two concepts of the "authority" of its rulings and the "cause" of the national courts' obligation to refer. In *Da Costa*, the combination of these two concepts led the Court to state that the authority of a prior ruling of its own may at least in principle deprive the national obligation of its cause and so empty it of its substance[141]; however, not only this did not lead it to decline its obligation to rule in the individual case, but, when looking closer, this refined reasoning was nothing but an answer to other bolder and "dangerous" reconstructions. In fact, in *Da Costa*, the Commission argued for the dismissal of the case by the Court, for lack of substance; and the Advocate General Lagrange, relying on his own previous opinion in *Fédéchar*,[142] and on a French traditional argumentative *tòpos*, suggested that in similar cases, when the text of black-letter law is clear (or clarified) it would require no activity of "interpretation", and therefore could require no work by the Court (which is called for an *interpretative* preliminary ruling). Between the lines and the didactic tone of *Da Costa* (and before, in *Fédéchar*) laid the tentative application in Community law of the *acte clair* doctrine as per its derivation from French administrative law.[143] This doctrine, aimed at denying any role for a creative "interpretation" of law when a mere "application" was at stake, was originally forged by the *Conseil d'État* to historically circumvent the rule according to which the French executive had exclusive competence to interpret treaties. By holding that treaties could not require an active interpretation when their texts were clear, the French judiciary restricted the power of the government to interfere with its own role.[144] The Court of Justice, in its final judgement in *Da Costa*, departed from this view and the suggestions of the Advocate General by hinting at a more nuanced approach. But such a solution was surely not enough since, in the following years, the *acte clair* doctrine found its way in some Member States to circumvent the application of European law. This was the case of the *Conseil d'État* itself, already in 1964, which through that theory denied its obligation to request a preliminary ruling to the ECJ in the *Shell-Berre* case,[145] by arguing about the existence or not of a proper "question" as per the wording of Article 177 EEC.[146] The *Conseil* was then followed by other national jurisdictions such as Germany, in 1970 with the holding of the German Federal Social Court in the notorious *Widow's Pension* case[147] (and local scholars recognized the practice as a clear import of the French doctrine),[148] and in 1974 by the British judiciary.[149] Scholarly debates on the point flourished starring, among others,[150] former Advocate General Lagrange arguing in some articles on the perfect compatibility of the doctrine with the preliminary reference procedure,[151] in addition to other renowned scholars and even judges of the Court such as Pierre Pescatore[152] on more sceptical, critical positions. A Written Question in the European Parliament was even submitted on the point, with the Commission restating its positive attitude towards the autonomy of national courts.[153] It was against this factual, contextual background that the ECJ gave its ruling in *CILFIT*. The Advocate General Capotorti, as previously said, argued for a restrictive approach and a rejection of the practice and did so not only on refined theoretical grounds but also as an explicit reaction to the practical "abusive" employment made by the *Conseil d'État*. Interestingly, he also offered a reflection on how the concept of "*manifesta infondatezza*" ("manifestly unfounded nature" of a question raised) in the Italian incidental system of constitutional adjudication—as the original historical inspiration of Article 177—could be considered as a parallel but not anymore as a relevant point of reference, given "the specific formal and technical characteristics of Community law" as practically evolved as well as the "differences in the methods of interpretation adopted by the Court of Justice and those on which national courts rely, stemming from the differences between the legal spheres in which the former and the latter operate".[154] The judges, when confronted with all the above, chose not only to restate the words of the Treaty of Rome and the obligation therein provided, in a certain sense already breached in the early days of *Da Costa*. But they offered an important and cunning lesson that, in the wake of the Advocate General's opinion, took the specificity of the supranational legal order into account. The result was surely not, as per the general understanding, a plain adoption of the *acte clair* doctrine. Quite the opposite, the description of meticulous guidelines for the apical national courts (since then known as "*CILFIT criteria*")[155] were clearly aimed, in practice, at circumscribing and circumventing the scope of the doctrine. The Court of Justice famously ruled that national judges, who want to embrace the *acte clair* rationale, must be convinced that the interpretation would not lead to divergences in other Member States' courts and the Court of Justice; and importantly, the existence of this possibility must be assessed by them based on the characteristic features of EU law regarding interpretation, i.e. comparison of the different language versions, all equally authentic, the specificity of the Community law terminology, and the recourse to contextual/teleological interpretation. When Rasmussen famously observed, in the aftermath of the decision, that the Court appeared to be "giving" to the national courts but in reality it was "maintaining the *status quo*" because of the highly restrictive criteria imposed,[156] this was interpreted by many as a witticism of a famous dissenter: but in reality, his depiction was even limiting if one takes the obligations of exhaustive linguistic and jurisprudential comparison imputed on the national judges literally. In reality, the CILFIT criteria constitute a sort of *fictio iuris*, that *idem operatur, quod veritas*: the existence of a fact, i.e. the exhaustion of all those criteria, must be taken as occurred to make the foreseen legal consequences possible.

In the case of *CILFIT*, this nowadays includes a full linguistic and jurisprudential comparison among 27 legal systems and 24 languages, and many authors have already highlighted how technically impossible and disruptive a faithful obedience would be[157]; but already at the time of the judgement 10 legal systems and at least 7 languages were part of the European Communities, so that the nature of *probatio diabolica* of the criteria was already evident. Several neglected proposals[158] and several refused occasions[159] to relax the standards of *CILFIT* occurred in the following years, so that it is nowadays impossible to see the judgement, as originally done or feared, as a strategic technique for limiting the inflow of cases. *CILFIT* was read, in the aftermath of the Court's decision, as the proclamation of a docket control strategy[160]: but as previously seen, its historical and contextual meaning was different, influenced by the specific directions taken by some Member States' judiciaries; and, if any, its "strategy", as per the words of Rasmussen,[161] was actually the opposite.

Briefly, the same can be said for the requirement of adequate information in the order of reference, which was then also relaxed in practice by the possibility acknowledged by the Court to supplement the allegations with the material in the case file forwarded by the national court and the written observations submitted to the Court (especially with a view to the notice of governments and other interested parties)[162]; or by the supposed strategic filtering nature of the check of the existence of a proper "court or tribunal" asking for a ruling, since some of the components for such assessment were considered too lax even by internal members of the Court.[163]

In sum, one can surely conclude that if all the mentioned trends of new procedural *rigueur* by the Court of Justice could be technically similar to other courts' experiences, and could lead to comparative speculations on the adoption in Luxembourg of a sort of "European certiorari", in fact they did not amount—both in the original intention and in the actual practice—to techniques of docket control. As mentioned, they were signs of a new phase of relative maturity of the EU legal order and the functioning of its judicial architecture: per se, a relevant, maybe interrelated but different phenomenon. These choices had no practical quantitative or statistically relevant effects (nor even subtle, qualitative ones, as per the American example) in the streamlining of received cases.[164] For instance, empirical analysis has noted how, in a sample period of three years in recent times of massive workload, less than ten references were rejected as inadmissible.[165] The Court of Justice's institutional evolution did not pass through these bottlenecks; in this respect, it needed to take different paths.

5.4 Docket Control as a Result of Substantive Interpretative Choices, Delegation and Efficiency

Apart from the mentioned restriction posed in the *Plaumann formula* to the *locus standi* of individuals in annulment actions—then adopted and confirmed by positive law until actual Article 263(4) TFEU—the procedural tools for the "selection", admission, and treatment of cases, although typical instruments of docket control for several judicial bodies, have not been and could not be a decisive instrument in the hand of the Court of Justice, despite the perceived need of limiting the workload. The only abstractly workable solutions could be implemented in the preliminary reference procedure, but it was noted how strong the concerns not to change the dynamics of such a fundamental mechanism of dialogue among courts and development of the EU legal order have always been, given the risk of distorting it. It was also noted how this rationale also laid behind cases such as *Foglia v. Novello* or *CILFIT*, which a certain vulgate wanted to see as examples of a different attitude and a new awareness of its dimensional constraints by the Court, at a certain point of its historical evolution.

Some more relevant results—often neglected in the mainstream doctrinal analysis as generally the case for such quantitative matters—first came about from what one can define as substantive interpretative choices, addressed (not necessarily as their only reason) at regulating the inflow of disputes and "selecting" the cases devoting a full treatment and a comprehensive employment of resources. This is the most evident result of a general method of "internal" docket control, which comes in the form of a strategy of delegation of decision-making, decentralization and self-restraint, to make the employment of cognitive resources and time in the solution of a single case more efficient. This form of management of the workload, in the form of a better management of resources, would, in any case, result in aggregate benefits for all the "normative commitments" of the quality in judging, the preservation of correct and uniform application of law as well as timely and efficient access to the legal system.

We already talked of a traditionally higher-developed American doctrine concerning the quantitative aspects of judging. This is also the case in this respect, at least if one looks at the works of those scholars who advocate a "comparative institutional analysis" of the capacity and potentiality of different decision-making bodies.[166] From them came a call to conceptualize docket control not only through the lenses of *procedural* devices to formally admit (or not) a case in front of a court or for a full review on the merits. Also *substantive* choices and standards posed by courts in the different areas of law vastly influence the amount of litigation those courts will receive and the degree of review they will give to the cases. From this literature comes an invitation to consider that the underlying reasons for several judicial choices and standards of decision are also related, sometimes explicitly, sometimes not, to institutional concerns. Courts are naturally constrained for "scale" and capacity reasons to decide cases in a way that keeps the total volume of litigation below some threshold level; and in this sense, judges, sometimes more than scholars, would have a "general strong intuitive understanding of what kinds of decisions invite large volumes of litigation"[167]—also by evaluating and fostering the complexity of the relative substantive areas of law, their certainty or uncertainty, and consequently their tendency to produce disuniformity and new controversies.[168] Through this conceptual framework, some interesting developments in the "substance" of American constitutional law have been historically investigated and explained[169]: for example, in the field of the "constitutional rights revolution of the 1950s and 1960s, which generated an enormous volume of new litigation", and then asked for the setting of some more precise forms of standard of review to regulate and limit its inception[170]; or in the *Commerce clause* adjudication, where a somehow fictitious distinction between economic and noneconomic activity has been judicially constructed with the effect of keeping the incentives to challenge federal government regulation low,[171] given the well-known highly deferential rational basis test applied to the regulation of economic activity.

But in the same vein, one can fruitfully inspect and vindicate several choices of the European Court of Justice, also of fundamental and historically contested nature. Upon closer inspection, the Court seems to have used such techniques of deference towards other decision-makers and strategic setting of its standards of review to reduce the burden of its potential case law in the game of supply and demand for adjudication.

For instance, one can surely think of the judicial definition of certain complaints as "outside the scope of application" of supranational law. This definition is undoubtedly devoted to a proper allocation of competences and related institutional discretion in a federal-like system and to respect certain spheres of autonomy to the Member States. But it is also clearly aimed at closing the doors of the Court to the relative arising litigation. In thinking to established areas of review, this famously happened in *Keck and Mithouard*,[172] when the Court decided to "clarify" the scope of application of the free movement of goods rules concerning national restrictions on the ways goods were traded. This was done by establishing a category of measures that were not caught by Article 28 of the Treaty (now Article 34 TFEU) so that they did not have to be justified[173]: remarkably, this was done through the judicial introduction of a non-Treaty term, "selling arrangement", which became a concept for the national decision-makers to define.[174] As noted by its commentators,[175] the judgement wanted to prevent national traders from invoking Article 28/34 when their real complaint was not really about restrictions on interstate trade but merely about national trading rules: but in doing so, the judicial move was also doubtlessly intended to empower national courts to dismiss far-fetched attempts to deploy internal market law which was obstructing the European judicial system with the minutiae of purely local affairs[176]—having no adequate effect on intra-Community trade.

The same could also be said for other cases of "purely internal situations", i.e. those situations in which the Court finds all the facts confined within one Member State and no "cross-border element". In these cases, where no "connecting factor" or "connecting link" with "the situations envisaged by Community law" is found, the Court has consistently held that the market freedoms and the Treaty's protections do not apply (at least at the current stage) and has refused to intervene, even at the cost of "reverse discriminations" suffered by citizens. Thus, in several free movement cases under the preliminary reference procedure, this interpretation has critically led the Court to hold certain national measures illegal "only in so far as" they apply to cross-border situations, while such national measures remain valid in relation to purely internal situations, so that the same national measure is sometimes legal, sometimes illegal, depending on the underlying factual situation in which it is applied.[177] It is easy to see, also in this respect, not only an attention by the Court to the allocation of competences and the preservation of States' autonomy, but also concerns about both its physical resources and its own ability to investigate such questions.[178] The potential litigation that could arise in case of a more lenient interpretation would surely be massive.

But dynamics of delegation, decentralization and control of the burden of potential case law are not to be found only in these clear *actiones finium regundorum*. As previously said, a clarification of the intensity of judicial oversight can also lead to important effects, especially in controlling the incentives for litigation and inviting more or less high volumes of it. As suggested by Paul Craig,[179] this has been the technique that has been strategically employed by the Court of Justice when reviewing cases brought to it under the preliminary ruling procedure to contest the validity of Community acts which cannot be challenged directly through the annulment procedure, because of the mentioned limited *locus standi* rules for individual parties. Applicants who wish to challenge the validity of Brussels' action, given the difficulty to directly access the Court, will often have to do so through national courts and a request for preliminary ruling, "as to whether, for example, an agricultural measure was disproportionate and hence in breach of Article 34" (now Article 40 TFEU).[180] In any case, such a move amounts to a surreptitious circumvention of the standing rules and the Court—not to be overburdened by it—had to set a high standard for the success of a such a challenge: it will not readily find that the challenged Community norm is invalid, more especially in an area where the Commission and Council have broad discretionary power, and it made explicit that the applicant may well have to prove that the measure was manifestly disproportionate, or very obviously discriminatory.[181] In doing so, it is strategically limiting the inflow of actions from a whole category of potential actors.

A second example, again in an established area, could be seen in the rules created by the Court on the national remedies for the breach of European law.[182] The Court has notoriously mandated the existence of national remedies as means of enforcement of supranational law, has taken the view that they should be at least as good as those that apply for the *mise en œuvre* of national law; and also, has stated the requirement of their at least "effective" nature.[183] When English law rules, in a seminal case, were found not to be effective in providing a remedy, the CJ insisted on applying a standard of effectiveness based on principles built from the laws of Member States.[184] It did so by laying down precise criteria: the infringed rule of law must have been intended to confer rights on individuals, there was a sufficiently serious breach of Community law, and there was a direct causal link between the breach and the damage sustained. Such criteria delegate key issues of interpretation and fact to the national courts, in particular about the somewhat indefinite concept of "sufficiently serious" breach, and the approach has had an impact on the role of the Court in enforcement matters: to the extent that national judges have been encouraged to ensure that there are national-level remedies for the failure to implement EU law, this is said to explain why fewer enforcement cases are being brought at the supranational level.[185]

However, the most consistent practice of delegation, decentralization and control of employed resources by the Court of Justice rests somewhere else, again in the basic peculiarities of the preliminary ruling procedure: in particular, in the ambivalent nature of its interpretative version. It is well known that a judgement rendered according to what is today Article 267 TFEU is often an answer to an interpretative question raised by a national judicature. In this sense, its content serves two purposes simultaneously. First, the reply should give, in a specific vein, useful input to guide the referring body in solving the concrete case. Second, the interpretation should attempt universality and reach beyond the specific facts of the dispute at hand, providing insightful information for future cases that may arise in all the Member States.[186] In the above, I saw first-hand operative rules governing such inherent, precious ambivalence. The mandate and the division of labour provided by the procedure would ask at Luxembourg a mere *interpretation* of questions of law, thereby leaving the moment of the sequential *application* of the stated principle by the national referring judges. At the same time—and this may sound paradoxical—I saw how the Court of Justice is asking, formally as an admissibility requirement, the national judges to provide exhaustive information of the specificities of the cases, so to make a complete and fruitful answer possible: it emphasized in several occasions that it can only deal with references where the context is made clear.[187] Furthermore, I saw how the *CILFIT* judgement is an invitation, or almost a lesson, from Luxembourg to all the national judges to "think globally"—or better "comparatively/European"—by accepting a cooperative role and making the procedure work as a means to "*(...) assurer l'unité du droit communautaire, son efficacité, son dynamisme, son 'génie' propre, c'est-à-dire son originalité et sa conformité aux buts de la construction européenne*".[188]

The fundamental efficiency of the procedure is ensured by the coexistence in it of "abstractness and concreteness",[189] by its strategic relevance as a "way through which primary and secondary law find useful solutions for the present but also for the future".[190] Such double role ensures, or should ensure, what I have repeatedly called the *nomphylachia* of the Court, its role of φύλαξ, of guardian, of the νόμος, of the law: its *dicta* should ensure the correct application of European law in the individual cases and, in a proactive sense, simultaneously transcend them to "flirt with the conventional tasks of a rule-maker",[191] and ensure certainty and uniformity of interpretation in general terms. It is always important to consider that this ambivalence includes, in the ongoing process of the EU integration, a constructive, almost didactic role of the Court. Its judgements are intended to help national courts solve cases, and this should become, after the interpretative effort, "a job no harder than child's play"[192]; at the same time, the success of the device, its effects, the jurisdiction of the Court are almost totally dependent on the national courts' "good will",[193] on their willingness and capacity to refer questions—a feature that still needs to be constantly nurtured. In a nutshell, it could be said that the Court of Justice is constantly addressing, by calibrating the scope of its decisions, both a single interlocutor, the referring court, and a general audience, the wide array of individuals and institutions concerned by and bound to European law. As per a traditional adage, it is called to both give a fish and feed a man for a day, and teach to fish and feed him for a lifetime.[194]

Now, it is evident that playing such a double role is a considerable effort in terms of time and internal resources for the cognition and the solution of every interpretative question. In practice, this is particularly so given the tendency of the national courts to intend references for preliminary rulings not as abstract questions on the interpretation of the relevant primary or secondary EU law applicable to the case at hand, but on the contrary, commonly, as questions on the compatibility of internal national law with such supranational regulation or principles.[195] Accepting this partial, functional distortion of the procedure was a price to pay for the European Court, given its willingness to foster the precious dialogue with national judges. The mentioned tendency to reformulate the references, and answer to what "essentially" they mean, is major evidence of the phenomenon.[196] Over the years, the Court has been quite consistent in delineating and restating the basic division of labour with national courts. The activity of *application* of relevant national and supranational law is preserved for them; they are the only competent to assess the facts and the legality or proportionality of specific national measures. The teaching that "the court (has) no jurisdiction either to apply the Treaty to a specific case, or to decide upon the validity of a provision of domestic law in relation to the Treaty" was already part of the fundamental tenets of *Costa v. ENEL*[197]; and it was then also explicitly stated that "it is for the national court to apply the rules of Community law, as interpreted by the Court, to an individual case", since "(N)o such application is possible without a comprehensive appraisal of the facts of the case".[198]

Yet, the relationship of the CJEU with the facts is at least uncertain and multifaceted. For some observers, the Court is delivering judgements so specific that the case is effectively already decided, and therefore with unambiguous rulings on matters of fact, in more than two-thirds of the references.[199] Apart from statistics and aggregate percentages, this activity of the Court of Justice as a de facto "internal judge"[200] is surely evident in some well-studied areas of law. For instance, in the application of free movements rules, especially concerning goods, the abstract principles developed by the Court are quite simple and lean, ascribable to a limited set of standards; but the considerable, ever-growing body of relative case law is composed of repeated specific applications of such principles and standards in an iterative stream of formally similar cases. The most obvious example is the case law following *Cassis de Dijon*.[201] Everyone knows that this last judgement stated that Article 28 EC (now Article 34 TFEU) forbade the use of national standards to exclude imports unless those standards served some legitimate aim (and were not just protectionist) and their application to imports was proportionate (genuinely necessary for that aim, not going beyond what is necessary, and not resulting in disproportionately onerous disadvantages for the importer once compared with the claimed individual or aggregate benefits). Nonetheless, once stated these historical principles, the Court had to face a vast series of cases on standards and product rules, in which it was asked to consider a particular national measure in the light of those: and the reference was commonly phrased as an assessment of the proportionality of the national measure. Any sensible assessment of the kind, on whether a measure really goes beyond what is necessary, or what its effects are, obviously requires a factual investigation; and the Court would be neither abstractly competent nor actually able to seriously undertake it since it has often stated that the proportionality of a measure is a question of fact left the national courts.[202] Nonetheless, the Court has for instance investigated in an overwhelming series of cases the possible legitimate limitations based on consumer protection, with specific analysis of possible confusion induced by door-to-door sellers,[203] deceptive labels,[204] deceptive words,[205] with a sort of compulsion to repeat and to delve into the facts. In this vein, another relevant example concerns controversies over selling arrangements, before and after the distinction made in *Keck*. In early cases, when the Court still conceptualized them as obstacles to movement, it sometimes had to decide proportionality itself,[206] and sometimes it left it as a matter of fact to the national court.[207] Critically,[208] also after the historical "clarification", the Court found itself having to delve deeply into facts in order to assess whether there was an unequal effect provided by the arrangements on imported products.[209] The same can also be said of cases regarding discriminatory taxation, where Article 90 EC (now Article 110 TFEU) has led to great factual scrutiny on the concepts of "similar products", "indirect protection", "protective effect"[210]; or the even more detailed, notoriously debated[211] cases concerning common custom duties imposed on goods.[212]

All this tendency to distort the division of labour provided by Article 267, and to blur the distinction between the concepts and the moments of the interpretation and the application of EU law, has led scholars to invitations to reconsider the practice. This was suggested precisely to deal with the problem of workload.[213] In this view, the Court of Justice should rediscover its natural role of a reviewing court in questions that are supposed to be simply of law: it should restrain from examining fact too carefully and try to use its resources sparingly by evading the facts and their meticulous and time-consuming examination, and try to answer preliminary references by focusing on the broad, supervisory vision that is appropriate for the procedure. In this sense, it is also suggested that the more the Court of Justice continues to consider its mandate as a universal potential one, for which "any new fact set can be seen as requiring an interpretation" of the supranational norms,[214] the more it will devote time and energy to the analytical solutions of trivial and repetitive cases, it will face problem of workload attracting that minute and time-consuming species of references, and ultimately even discourage possible genuine references from national courts that, having discretion to refer and exercising it with an eye to cost and time, will prefer not to do it. In this sense, even the precious uniformity in the application of EU law, which the Court should protect as a major principle, could be endangered. Such circularity in the argument against the overburdened Court of Justice, which carries a great deal of truth, is also a mirror of the criticality of the situation.

In truth, the picture could also be worsened if one considers that, according to the opinion of insiders of the Court,[215] its tendency to a mere *arrêt d'espèce* with no breath and ambition to provide general guidance to the community of stakeholders is on the rise—prompted by the increasing workload and limited time for the examination of cases. In this sense, it is suggested that the Court is taking an opposite direction to the one proposed, in principle, above: a tendency not towards less better-theorized interventions, but towards numerous less-theorized ones. The tendency has been conceptualized as judicial *minimalism*, here again by borrowing and exporting American doctrinal insights on the practice of small, case-specific interpretations away from precedent, and narrowly applied.[216] It would be signalled, among other things, by the recent expansion of the use of formulas like "in the specific circumstances of the present case",[217] "in those precise circumstances",[218] or "taking into account all the relevant factors in the individual case",[219] also in cases of potential theoretical relevance involving questions such as the importance of the constitutional identity of Member States, the scope of the European citizenship provisions, the scope of the judicial cooperation in matters of parental responsibility. This could also be added to a more stratified inclination towards argumentatively impaired interventions in equally important areas such as direct effect of directives in relation to administrative authorities,[220] the scope of the duty to conform interpretation,[221] or again the scope of the European citizenship provisions.[222]

Such practice has been critically examined and rejected by the same scholar who has masterfully denounced it, for the inherent decline of the supervisory role of the Court it entails, and the possible paradoxical result of it can bring in terms of the invitation of new litigation in non-clarified areas of law. But it can also be seen, descriptively, as the last evidence of a sort of zero-sum game between "abstractness and concreteness" in preliminary reference procedures in the current stage of EU integration and development of EU law. This decisively involves the energy and time resources of the Court, which is forced to lean to one side and somehow leave the other in the alternative: a situation understandable only by looking closer at the influence of the national legal orders on the functionality of the system.

5.5 Preliminary Reference Procedure, *Unitas*, *Diversitas*

Our analysis has for now focused on two different, general methods of docket control, through the use of procedural and substantive devices. In investigating their applicability in the EU judicial architecture, the analysis has highlighted possibilities, evolutive paths and problems. Particularly concerning these latter problems, in one way or another, the report always seems to be compressed at a certain point by the peculiarity of the preliminary reference procedure, the preponderant form of action at the European Court of Justice and that on which efforts of streamlining are focused. Possible procedural devices are suggested but ultimately not used by the Court for concern of not distorting the procedure. Substantive devices are subject of intense thought and are sometimes indicated as evolutive paths by scholars and internal members of the Court, but eventually collide with the specificity of the Court's situation.

What lies behind these arguments? Indeed, the nature of the preliminary reference as a chain, as a binding element, between the European legal order and those of the Member States, with their specificities that cannot but shape the actual dynamics of the procedure. As previously said, several studies have been devoted to the success of the instrument, pointing to its positive reception by national courts. Almost all the fundamental tenets in the construction of the EU legal system have been shaped through preliminary references[223]; these have constantly, importantly raised over the decades, reaching the dangerous quantitative levels that I am discussing; refined, now classic reflections have indicated the reasons for such apparent enthusiasm of national judges, on which the preliminary rulings procedure decisively depends. These reasons include the "legalist"[224] perception of a particularly plausible legal reasoning employed by the Court of Justice, especially in its glorious early years, which persuaded their counterparts[225]; the incentives offered, in turn, in terms of reciprocity and cross-fertilization, for a better quality and authoritativeness of the national reasonings[226]; the pull represented by that "whole community of interests, by individuals, lawyers and courts which developed a stake—professional, financial and social—in the successful administration of Community law",[227] for which the national judiciary acted as an agency[228]; the dynamics of self-empowerment, perceived especially by the lower courts, in terms of facility to engage with the highest jurisdiction in the Community and innovative gain of a power of judicial review over executive and legislative branches "even in those jurisdictions where such judicial power was weak or non-existent"[229]; the confidence strengthened by its extensive programme of outreach activities, which enabled national judges to directly get in touch with the Court of Justice and learn about its activities, and by a growing body of initially all supportive specialist practitioners and academics.[230]

All these interesting reconstructions of an early history of success in the reception and in the structuring of the procedure cannot, in any event, be exempt from an appraisal on the following stages and the current one in the diachronic evolution. Whatever episodes of fundamental contribution one can enumerate and whatever general factors one might identify as liable to affect the willingness of national courts to use the procedure, it is becoming more and more common to read concerns on the general coverage capacity of the procedure concerning the whole abstract mass of cases decided at the national level in which EU law is applicable (and therefore, there are doubts on the actual overall level of use of the procedure).[231] Furthermore, the statistics show that there is a wide variation in national reference rates which cannot be explained with mere independent variables and "structural factors",[232] such as, as a more obvious example, population size (and therefore, there are also concerns on the specific level of use of the procedure in some Member States, compared to others). In other words, it has become evident that, next to satisfactory practices of "acceptance" and "embracing", there are still significant areas of ignorance and disregard[233]; and it is viewed with concern the fact that the likelihood that a reference will be made in any particular case may depend on the Member State in which it has been brought.[234] In fact, this means that the specific potentiality, inherent in the preliminary rulings, of cooperation and mutual education for the CJEU and the national courts about their respective systems and approaches is at least still to be nurtured, if not to be considered as in danger in the present setting; and that additionally, such potentiality is not being felt uniformly across the Union. In sum, there are dangers for both the *correct* and the *uniform* application of EU law: the first put in doubt by the general numbers on the acceptance of the preliminary reference procedure, and the second particularly by relative national ones. Still, both are relevant subjects of the *nomophylactic* mandate of the Court of Justice.

When talking of general numbers, it is usual in the literature to move from estimates of speculative though convincing nature, in the absence of significant empirical works on the point. The search is not for single, loud episodes of resistance against the teachings of the ECJ, but for aggregate data on the silent practices of national judges who, for whatever reasons, disregard them. For such a calculation, it has been suggested[235] to start from thinking to how many cases are decided by national courts of the Member States every year, in all their layers (possibly, tens of millions); then to consider what portion of national judicial decisions are nowadays rendered materially within the scope of application of EU law; and then, in contrast, to think to how many requests for preliminary ruling does this mass of national cases generate. Even if one considers in this operation, prudentially, the percentage of judicial application of EU law as sensibly lower than the percentage of overall amount of directly applicable norms and implementing legislation (in turn, esteemed not so far from the much-discussed Jacque Delors's 80% threshold),[236] and hypothesizes, soberly, that in one out of eight national cases (a percentage of approximately 15%) EU law is applicable, one would have in any case millions of cases potentially within the scope of application of EU law and jurisdiction of the CJEU before lower courts, with the opportunity to submit requests, and tens of thousands of them in courts of last instance, which would be bound to raise references in case of doubts.[237] Against such assumptions stand the annual statistics of the Court of Justice, to which I already referred, with their few hundreds of preliminary reference submitted (265 in 2007, 288 in 2008, 302 in 2009, 385 in 2010, 423 in 2011, 404 in 2013, 450 in 2013, 428 in 2014, 436 in 2015, 470 in 2016, 533 in 2017, 568 in 2018).[238] With millions of EU law cases before national courts and many thousands of them in supreme courts, almost five hundred preliminary references are annually generated. Those few hundreds are undoubtedly problematic with a view to the actual situation and resources of the Court of Justice, as said; but when seen in this light, compared with a potentiality which is in some sense also desirability for a proper check on the real correct and uniform application of law in the EU territory, they assume a different dimension, they seem a meagre outcome, they make the specialists talk of underemployment of the fundamental procedure or at least of a rather slow and just ongoing trend of improvement in this respect.[239] All these ideas embody an opposite tendency to the one for a pronounced docket control by the CJEU.

In dealing with the relative numbers, attention has been devoted to such aspects as the important variations in the number of references, the areas of law which they concern and the level of courts from which they originate in the various Member States. The fact that some areas of law create more litigation than others has been accepted or rationalized[240] and it is not a specificity of the EU legal order; the variations among lower or apical national courts were explained for both reasons of incentives[241] and in the natural functioning of appellate systems, some needed corrections notwithstanding.[242] Variations in Member States' use of preliminary references are, on the contrary, of utmost concern. Studies on the average number of preliminary references per year in the different EU Member

States, concerning, for instance, the last decade of considerable expansion, has illustrated that more than 60 of the mentioned hundreds of cases in the CJEU's docket came from Germany, more than 40 from Italy, more than 20 each from the Netherlands and Belgium, around 20 from France and the United Kingdom, more than 15 from Austria and Spain and less than 10 from all the other nations.[243] The statistics about the whole antecedent period of the Court of Justice's activities with the preliminary reference procedure, and therefore for the decades between 1961 (year of the first reference) and 2010, show no differences in the ratio.[244] The rates of preliminary references calculated per million inhabitants particularly highlight the role of the Benelux countries, yet, for the rest, simply normalizing the other data.[245]

As already hinted at, so-called structural factors are not considered as the only possible explanation for such diversity.[246] There is, of course, a trend related to differences in population size, since larger countries have more individuals, undertakings, and therefore more plaintiffs in static terms, but also a bigger market for exporters and more transnational activities.[247] Nonetheless, the difference between the attitude of German and Italian courts and that of French or British courts, more or less comparable "markets", would not be satisfied with such simplistic answer. There are historical differences in terms of general litigation rates: in some states, scholars could find a more pronounced tendency to resolve controversies through the judicial systems than by the use of other means,[248] patterns that tend to correlate in various ways with a high number of "courts and tribunals" as per Article 267 in the internal systems and with a larger number of preliminary references from the Member States in question.[249] A third basic structural factor has been seen in the level of Member States' internal application of EU law, compliance with their obligations under EU law, timely transposition of supranational legislation, all elements that can determine the likelihood that national legislation can be challenged in this sense before the local courts.[250]

Other factors have been categorized by scholars as "behavioural", since not related to the likelihood that a national court is faced with a question of EU law but on the following logical step of whether the judge, once so, will make an actual reference to the CJ.[251] These are particularly interesting for my perspective because linked to the inherent differences in the legal cultures of the Member States, more than other factors (such as the already discussed willingness to litigate, which are "structural" because they pertain to the existence of potential cases, but surely "behavioural" in terms of relation to psychological, social, cognitive factors), and linked to the influence that these cultural differences have in the development of the procedure. In this respect, a first interesting explanation of the mentioned divergencies came from those theories that link the use of the procedure with the Member States' constitutional traditions, in particular pertaining to the perception of the role of courts vis-à-vis the political branches.[252] It has been suggested that some Member States more than others have an institutional legacy of "majoritarian democracy", rooted in the notion of parliamentary supremacy or sovereignty[253]: this would be the base not only of a less intense familiarity of those with judicial review of legislative acts, but also to a certain reluctance in the adoption of a procedure which is similar to, and historically based on, judicial review of legislation, and also often directed at contesting public powers' choices.[254] In particular, this would be the case of the Nordic countries, Denmark, Sweden, Finland, and was the case of the United Kingdom until its recent exit. They all perform very poorly in terms of preliminary referrals, so as to be labelled as "reluctant Europeans".[255] UK, with more than 60 millions inhabitants, had an average of fewer than 20 cases raised per year in the last decade. The Nordic countries all have an average of less than 5. They all share traditions of strong conceptions of parliamentary sovereignty in which powers of legislative review have been for a long while downplayed (UK),[256] or formally recognized but rarely practised (Sweden and Denmark),[257] or even forbidden until very recent constitutional amendments (Finland).[258] Variants of this theory have been proposed, specularly, to point at the importance of the degree of perceived independence of national judges in relation to the political branches: at least in some countries, they would tend to strategically raise references to provoke certain outcomes and support desired substantive policies.[259] The same analysis of the traditional degree of independence of the judiciary would also serve to measure the tendency of lower courts to use the procedure as a mean of internal "inter-court competition", to circumvent and contest the practice of higher courts, for self-empowerment and the promotion of autonomous policy positions.[260] Also the tendency of national legal systems towards the creation of specialized judiciary—which is somewhere viewed with suspicion, essentially for historical reasons[261]—has been studied in its effects for preliminary references: highly specialized tribunals, for instance in tax or competition law, would tend to work more intensively with the relative EU law norms, be more competent and be more likely to make a reference.[262] Finally, the more or less stratified familiarity of the national judiciaries with European law would be an asset, though to be weighed with the massive programmes of specialized EU law education often directed to judges of newly accessed states and a certain tendency to post-accession "euphoria" in the use of the procedure.[263]

An investigation into the different legal cultures and national inclinations, in any event, does not only shed light on the likelihood of EU law cases to exist, or actual preliminary references to be raised. In having a look at these dynamics, one can better understand all the reluctance of the Court of Justice towards institutionally necessary practices of docket control in the procedural and substantive forms I have discussed. All the realist perspectives on Article 267 TFEU practical reality describe a procedure still in the process of consolidation, yet to be nurtured by Luxembourg, and describe risks of accentuating trends of discrepancy among the Member States.

A last reflection in this respect must be added, on the mentioned ambivalence of "abstractness and concreteness" of the procedure. This ambivalence is also significantly influenced by cultural differences, in a way that further frustrates the suggested idea of a recalibration between "facts and norms" of the Court's resources for docket control reasons. As already suggested by some scholars,[264] the preliminary reference procedure naturally takes different dimensions if seen through the lenses of the civil law and the common law lawyer. The first, at least in terms of habit, has no problems in conceptualizing the distinction between law and judgements and between interpretation and application of the law. In general terms, civil law's ideal type of uniformity of interpretation in a legal system consists precisely in the centralized identification of identical abstract rules, then to be applied in a decentralized way by all courts.[265] On the other hand, the second privileges in inductive terms, as a habit of mind, a discovering of law based on looking at what has been decided in individual cases and a process by analogy therefrom. It is not accustomed, for education, to form a conceptual distinction between interpretation and application, since interpretation, in his understanding, *is* also application; and tends to "leave posterity and lawyers to pronounce the principles which, with time, will surely emerge",[266] through stratification.[267] These fundamental conceptions have consequences on the practical use of the preliminary reference procedure: in particular, they have consequences on its described pendulum between "abstractness and concreteness". Civil lawyers and common lawyers are naturally tempted to use it in different ways. Civil lawyers are, in fact, naturally less concerned with autonomous interpretation and application of EU law, and this could also eventually be seen as not threatening the uniformity: judgements are not law. But they also tend to ask, idealtypically, to the Court of Justice to play a role it simply cannot, not only because of the current nature of the system described above, but for inherent reasons: by providing only pure abstract interpretations, given the fabric of EU primary and secondary law, the Court would add a new layer of abstract principles, generally applicable propositions, analytically indistinguishable from those of the legislator.[268] Their pendulum lean, generally, towards the abstractness. On the contrary, common lawyers tend to ask the Court precedents. By their references, which will also differ stylistically, they require judgements containing a fully argued analysis of the facts. Their pendulum leans towards the facts and the concreteness: they will easily follow the Court in the distinction between interpretation and application, but they will consider the uniqueness of every single case and will tend to ask (with all the conditions above) directly applicable solutions to Luxembourg. As it has been written, the common lawyer, "if the same robust sense that gave him the common law did not also incline him to a respect for consideration of cost and time", can be quickly become, for the Court, "a dangerous rich source of workload".[269]

It is possible to offer countless examples in this respect, by looking at the actual references for preliminary rulings raised by judges with different legal cultural backgrounds. In simply adopting a temporary criterium, it is easy to compare, for instance, the intricate questions for a preliminary ruling that the European Court had to answer in a notorious case such as Case C-446/03 *Marks & Spencer plc vs. David Halsey (HM Inspector of Taxes)*,[270] solved on December 13, 2005 and raised by the High Court of Justice (England & Wales), Chancery Division—a common law jurisdiction—and the questions solved *on the same day* in a case treated by the Grand Chamber (and therefore, of no triviality) such as Case C-411/03 *SEVIC Systems AG*,[271] raised by the German Landgericht of Koblenz—a civil law tribunal. The first common law court sent to Luxembourg the following reference:

1. In circumstances where:

.provisions of a Member State, such as the UK provisions on group relief, prevent a parent company which is resident for tax purposes in that State from reducing its taxable profits in that State by setting off losses incurred in other Member States by subsidiary companies which are resident for tax

purposes in those States, where such set off would be possible if the losses were incurred by subsidiary companies resident in the State of the parent company;

.the Member State of the parent company:

subjects a company resident within its territory to corporation tax on its total profits, including the profits of branches in other Member States, with arrangements for the availability of double taxation relief for those taxes incurred in another Member State and under which branch losses are taken account of in those taxable profits;

does not subject the undistributed profits of subsidiaries resident in other Member States to corporation tax;

subjects the parent company to corporation tax on any distributions to it by way of dividend by the subsidiaries resident in other Member States while not subjecting the parent company to corporation tax on distributions by way of dividend by subsidiary companies resident in the State of the parent;

grants double taxation relief to the parent company by way of a credit in respect of withholding tax on dividends and foreign taxes paid on the profits in respect of which dividends are paid by subsidiary companies resident in other Member States;

is there a restriction under Article 43 EC, in conjunction with Article 48 EC? If so, is it justified under Community law?

2.(a)What difference, if any, does it make to the answer to Question 1 that, depending on the law of the Member State of the subsidiary, it is or may be possible in certain circumstances to obtain relief for some or all of the losses incurred by the subsidiary against taxable profits in the State of the subsidiary?

(b)If it does make a difference, what significance, if any, is to be attached to the fact that:

.a subsidiary resident in another Member State has now ceased trading and, although there is provision for loss relief subject to certain conditions in that State, there is no evidence that in the circumstances such relief was obtained;

.a subsidiary resident in another Member State has been sold to a third party and, although there is provision under the law of that State for the losses to be used under certain conditions by a third party purchaser, it is uncertain whether they were so used in the circumstances of the case;

.the arrangements under which the Member State of the parent company takes account of the losses of UK resident companies apply regardless of whether the losses are also relieved in another Member State?

(c)Would it make any difference if there were evidence that relief had been obtained for the losses in the Member State in which the subsidiary was resident and, if so, would it matter that the relief was obtained subsequently by an unrelated group of companies to which the subsidiary was sold?[272]

In cases of the kind, it is evident that the Court of Justice is faced by a preliminary reference in the form of various questions asked, each one composed of different interpretative doubts, in a relationship of conditionality with each other, and with continuous reference to factual circumstances. It is likely that the judges simply reported in their reference the point raised by the parties in the national proceedings, with no autonomous activity of judicial *interpretation*. It is also evident that both the distinction between interpretation and application and the one between abstractness and concreteness of the procedure are blurred: the Court of Justice will be naturally prompted by this approach to become the judge of the facts of the case, with obvious major efforts implied in terms of internal resources in solving the case.

In the first example, the civil law tribunal of Koblenz raised a question like this in the Case C-411/03 *SEVIC Systems AG*, faced on the same day by the ECJ:

> *Are Articles 43 and 48 EC to be interpreted as meaning that it is contrary to freedom of establishment for companies if a foreign European company is refused registration of its proposed merger with a German company in the German register of companies under paragraphs 16 et seq. of the Umwandlungsgesetz (Law on transformations), on the ground that paragraph 1 (1)(1) of that law provides only for transformation of legal entities established in Germany?*[273]

In such a question referred, an autonomous activity of interpretation by the local judge is evident, in particular in its filtering effects vis-à-vis the factual details and the technicalities of the single case. Moreover, the reference is made in the form of a single, plain question. As a consequence, the distinction between interpretation and application and between abstractness and concreteness inherent in the procedure is respected, and the Court of Justice will be able to more easily focus on a general, *nomophylactic* response, with an explanatory potential for the single case but also the generality of the national cases on the matter.

For a more contextual approach, one can merge a temporary criterium like the latter with a thematic one, and therefore compare civil law and common law references solved on the same day, but also references solved in the same period of time and on the same area (and matter) of law. This allows us to understand whether the differences between the references' styles exist irrespective of the differences in the various areas of law, which may well affect the complexity of the questions referred. In adopting both the criteria, one can compare, again randomly, the questions for a preliminary ruling referred in the Case C-16/10—*The Number (UK) and Conduit Enterprises*,[274] solved on the February 17, 2011, and raised by the Court of Appeal (England & Wales) (Civil Division), a common law jurisdiction, the questions solved on the same day in a case raised by a civil law court (the *Cour d'appel de Rouen*) in the Case C-78/10—*Berel and Others*,[275] and the questions solved in the same period (just three months later) involving the same area of law and the same pieces of legislation of the first case but raised by a civil law tribunal (the *Bundesverwaltungsgericht* in the Case C-543/09 - *Deutsche Telekom*).[276] Here again, the questions posed by the common law judges read as follows:

> *Is the power afforded to Member States under Article 8(1) of Directive 2002/22/EC ("the Universal Service Directive"), read together with Article 8 of Directive 2002/21/EC ("the Framework Directive"), Articles 3(2) and 6(2) of Directive 2002/20/EC ("the Authorisation Directive"), and Article 3(2) of the Universal Service Directive and other material provisions of EC law, to designate one or more undertakings to guarantee the provision of universal service, or different elements of universal service, as identified in Articles 4, 5,6, 7 and 9(2) of the Universal Service Directive, to be interpreted as:*
>
> *(a) Permitting the Member State, where it decides to designate an undertaking pursuant to this provision, only to impose specific obligations on that undertaking which require the undertaking itself to provide to end users the universal service or element thereof in respect of which it is designated? Or*
>
> *(b) Permitting the Member State, when it decides to designate an undertaking under this provision, to place the designated undertaking under such specific obligations as the Member State considers to be most efficient, appropriate and proportionate for the purpose of guaranteeing the provision of the universal service or element thereof to end users, whether or not those obligations require the designated undertaking itself to provide the universal service or element thereof to end users?*
>
> *Do the above provisions, when read also in light of Article 3(2) of the Universal Service Directive, permit Member States, in circumstances where an undertaking is designated under Article 8(1) of the Universal Service Directive in relation to Article 5(l)(b) of that Directive (comprehensive telephone directory enquiry service) without being required to supply such a service directly to end users, to impose specific obligations on that designated undertaking:*

(a) to maintain and update a comprehensive database of: subscriber information;

(b) to make available in machine readable form the contents of a comprehensive database of subscriber information, as updated on a regular basis, to any person seeking to provide publicly available directory enquiry services or directories (whether or not that person intends to provide a comprehensive directory enquiry service to end-users); and

(c) to supply the database on terms which are fair, objective, cost oriented and non-discriminatory to such a person?[277]

On the other hand, the questions asked by the first civil law judge of this example read as follow:

Do Articles 213, 233 and 239 of the Community Customs Code prevent a joint and several co-debtor of a customs debt who is not the beneficiary of a decision to remit that debt from enforcing, against the administration responsible for collection, the decision to remit based on Article 239 of the Community Customs Code which that administration notified to another joint and several co-debtor, in order to be excused payment of the customs debt?[278]

The second civil law judge of this new comparison asked the following question, in the same period and on the same topic of her common law colleagues:

Must Article 25(2) of Directive 2002/22/EC of the European Parliament and of the Council of 7 March 2002 on universal service and users' rights relating to electronic communications networks and services (Universal Service Directive) be interpreted as meaning that Member States may require undertakings which assign telephone numbers to subscribers to make available data relating to subscribers to whom the undertaking in question has not itself assigned telephone numbers for the purpose of the provision of publicly available directory enquiry services and directories, in so far as that undertaking has such data in its possession?

If the answer to the previous question is in the affirmative:

Must Article 12 of Directive 2002/58/EC of the European Parliament and of the Council of 12 July 2002 concerning the processing of personal data and the protection of privacy in the electronic communications sector (Directive on privacy and electronic communications) be interpreted as meaning that the imposition of the abovementioned obligation by the national legislature is conditional upon the consent of, or at least the lack of any objection by, the other telephone service provider or its subscribers to the transmission of the data?[279]

Again, in this second example, one can see the tendency of the civil law judges towards a more concise and simple style of reference: this happens also in cases of technical difficulty and where more questions, in a logically subordinate relationship with each other, are needed. One also sees a filtering function performed, again, by the interpretative activity of the referring court. This is reflected in the evident minor importance given to the facts of the case in the structuring of the reference. These differences are the mirror of the mentioned ambivalence between concreteness and abstractness of the preliminary reference procedure. But they also explain how this ambivalence and the oscillation between the two extremes are culturally influenced, if not culturally shaped. The same existence of this conceptual ambivalence and the consequent distinct conceptualizations of the procedure is in itself a problem of workload for the European Court of Justice. As seen, the Court must face, hold together and meet very different demands in its practice. This is in itself a complicating factor for its activity.

The fact that these differences are culturally shaped, as highlighted, is the deciding factor for the impossibility of preparing common solutions towards a streamlining of the preliminary reference procedure and better management of internal cognitive resources. The Court—also given the described presence of further, numerical, differentiation in the use of the procedure—is not in the position to impose full rationalization, which could clash with the legal cultural background of belonging of certain national judges and fatally could go further to the detriment of its *nomophylactic* capabilities. The permanence of a still imperfect acceptance rate of the preliminary reference in the national legal orders forces the CJEU to accept its partial distortion, or even vilification. It is, in this sense, still forced to give answers and therefore analyse and spend its own resources (in terms of time and energy) to almost all the various forms of references it receives, with no possibility of ad hoc solutions in this respect. This leads, as previously said, to also receiving more and more cases, possibly specifying what already restated in precedents or just applying the same dicta to trivially different situations. Still, one can say that such a dynamic is surely and consciously accepted by the Court to strengthen its authority in the actual configuration of the EU judicial architecture and its maturity. It is in this perspective that the institutional evolution of the European Court of Justice throughout the decades must be read, as a continuous effort towards *neutral* institutional solutions, i.e. simply endogenous, without effects on its relationship with the other players of the EU federal judicial architecture.

5.6 Looking for *Neutral* Institutional Solutions

Sacha Prechal, a renowned EU law scholar who was already legal secretary at the Court of Justice and then became judge, recently wrote that: "(O)n the basis of some scarce and stray publications—where often some cautious allusions are made on the matter—personal experience and contact with the national judiciary, one comes to a somewhat perplexing conclusion, namely that the quality and capacity of the national courts to apply EC law and to do so correctly is a matter for serious concern. It seems that after several decades of EC membership national judges, even the "younger" generation, are rather still struggling with EC law than smoothly applying it".[280] One is tempted to compare this telling and authoritative vision, which seems to support the reflections above, with the one of another former member of the Court, Federico Mancini, who famously wrote in the early 1990s about the "inherent weakness of Article 177",[281] at times in which its mentioned success had already been ratified in the general understanding.[282] In substantiating his argument, Mancini wrote that "the outstanding feature of the procedure established by Article 177 of the EC Treaty is that it is entirely dependent on the goodwill of national courts"[283]: and that was already, in his view, perceived as a problem. He pointed first of all to the inhomogeneity inside the Community, since "the area (…) is enormous, the judges number tens of thousands and their ideological cohesion is zero", also because of decisive differences in their cultural backgrounds and the politicization of some of them[284] (in this sense, he anticipated some of the most relevant sociological/political reflections on the reasons for the different rates in preliminary references among the Member States). He then clearly stated the necessity of preserving as much as possible a role of "helmsman" conferred upon the Court by means of the preliminary ruling procedure, in terms of an accentuated "need for a central steering" as "the only way of preserving Community law from disintegrating as a result of divergent interpretations".[285] In this sense, he made interesting comparative remarks on the level of maturity of the EU legal order, which he described as "still in its adolescence, more or less as American constitutional law was in the age of Marshall and, like American constitutional law (…) suffering all the pangs of nation-building".[286]

If this last aspect of the direct comparability of the EU integration process with a nation-building one is, of course, disputable and has been authoritatively disputed for decades,[287] the power of the argument on the maturity of the legal architecture and its tools remains. As seen, in the current stage, with more significant numbers of employment of preliminary references, but all the divergences I have explored, one has just done a small step more, facing in any case the same problems of "inherent weakness".[288] This is confirmed first of all by the reluctance of the Court of Justice to deploy procedural instruments to streamline the inflow of references, given an evident concern to distort the still fundamental procedure. It is shown by the perceived obligation of the Court to answer nearly all the preliminary references, also of repetitive nature, also of accentuated analytical-factual nature, even beyond the theoretical division of labour of Article 267 TFEU. It is also shown by the perceived, accepted mandate to meet different, culturally shaped demands in the procedure, trying, by all means, to put together "abstractness and concreteness"—an always present need, even after Brexit, given the presence of other common law countries and the persistence of differences between the Member States. This is all done in view of keeping the doors and the channels of the procedure open and unaltered, since the Court, at the current stage of European integration, still seems to consider the didactic, constructive effects of Article 267 TFEU as essential.

The result of all this—in which an additional confirmation of the specific concerns on the dynamics of the preliminary rulings can be seen—is in the constant search for *neutral* solutions for the problem of the workload of the Court. This is the most evident characteristic of the institutional evolution of the Court in this respect. By neutral, I mean here that all the actual implemented solutions have been aimed, not by chance, at solving, or *rectius* at alleviating, the problem of the Court's workload via structural arrangements, with better management of the resources and the energies devoted at solving the cases and better efficiency in terms of timing. However, they were all inspired by the constant concern of taking no risk of distorting effects on the perceived possibility or opportunity for national courts for raising references, and in general for all the players of the EU judicial sphere to interact with Luxembourg.

This is true, of course, for the early creation by Council Decision 24 October 1988[289] of the Court of First Instance, then renominated General Court, with jurisdiction to deal with almost all cases against the institutions and the agencies of the EU, which alleviated the Court of Justice of a good part of the direct actions (and on whose decisions the ECJ has jurisdiction to hear appeals). The creation of such an autonomous court was explicitly aimed at rationalizing the judicial architecture and alleviating the apical Court of Justice of some of its burden.[290] In turn, it then became subject to severe problems of workload[291]; and its steady numerical expansion was decided in the very recent times after harsh debates.[292] This recent expansion is, in itself, the most evident solution of pure neutral nature: and, according to some observers, it was decided against the EU Parliament suggestion for an "external peer review in order to be provided with external instruments to identify possible solutions to the problems raised", and has no coherence with the actual needs of the EU judicial system.[293]

The same is true for the later creation of the Civil Service Tribunal as the only specialized court of the EU system—in existence since 2005 and then absorbed by the enlarged General Court in 2016—explicitly settled, at the time, to ease the workload of the General Court since only the appeals on its cases were heard by the latter.[294] The same debate on the opportunity of the creation of specialized courts for the EU judicial system is telling. Suggestions in this sense are common in the literature[295] and Article 256(2) TFEU already provides a legal basis, so to constitute a sort of preference in principle set by the Masters of the Treaties.[296] But they have never been implemented for the concern on decentralizing the treatment of preliminary rulings or, worst, for the risk of inhibiting their emergence in areas of supposed specialty but in which potential references of constitutional significance can in any case exist. In turn, this is also the reason why the possibility, stated in the Treaty, to decentralize Article 267 TFEU treatment also at the level of the General Court has always been resisted,[297] and it is still resisted by the Court of Justice itself, even after the recent sensitive enlargement of the first instance tribunal.[298]

In the same vein, the organization of the Court in small chambers of three or five judges, which deal with the majority of cases, and leave to the Grand Chamber or the even more rare Plenary treatment only the more relevant controversies, has been a decisive reform aimed at better use of human and therefore timing resources.[299] Recently, a little tuning, directly asked by the President of the Court, has been done to create the figure of the Vice-President,[300] and allow a more straightforward and smoother operation of such a chambers system. To rationalize the timing of the procedures, an opportunity to autonomously decide whether an oral hearing, with its employment of time and resources, is necessary in an individual case, given its complexity, has been attributed by Article 76(2) of the Courts' Rules of Procedure to the full College of Judges.[301] The same rationale is behind the possibility to reply "by reasoned order", according to Article 99 of the Rules of Procedure, "where a question referred to the Court for a preliminary ruling is identical to a question on which the Court has already ruled, where the reply to such a question may be clearly deduced from existing case law or where the answer to the question referred for a preliminary ruling admits of no reasonable doubt".[302]

Internal spaces of discretion for the treatment of preliminary references have also been recognized by the settlement of special separate procedures ("expedited preliminary ruling procedure" and "urgent preliminary ruling procedure") if the circumstances of the case show that "the nature of the case requires that it be dealt with within a short time" (Article 105 of the Court of Justice's Rules of Procedure),[303] or, when deemed necessary, in questions concerning the area of freedom, security and justice (Article 107 of the Court of Justice's Rules of Procedure).[304] All this is coupled with the possibility to use the standard procedure but with priority over other cases (where "special circumstances" according to Article 53(3) of the Rules of Procedure exist).[305]

All the mentioned aspects are remarkable reforms undertaken throughout recent decades in Luxembourg, which significantly changed the structure and the organization of the Court of Justice, had a substantial impact on its institutional evolution, and were often welcomed by commentators.[306] In particular, they had a decisive impact on the timing of the procedural activity of the Court, an improvement often emphasized in the recent Annual Reports.[307] From my perspective, it is relevant to highlight that they were also clearly influenced by a common rationale and had the same, only seemingly paradoxical effects. It is easy to see how all these moves were inspired by a continuous effort towards *neutral* institutional solutions of simply endogenous nature—aimed at rationalizing and improving the capabilities of the European Court in delivering justice. The constant attention was at the strengthening and streamlining of internal resources, with the creation of new sub-institutions, new procedures, new powers, new timings. On the other hand, it is essential to note that—given the described various, indented panorama of relationships with the other players of the EU federal judicial architecture, and in particular with national courts—each reform was very cautious in its *exogenous* effects and therefore in touching the though relevant interplay with other actors and their spillover on the resources of the Court. No risk of disentanglement within the still-to-be-nurtured EU judicial gameplay was even contemplated, as it would have been the case in hypotheses such as the mentioned ideas of radical reform of the judicial architecture[308] or even with the soft power of the green light procedure.[309] Not even the risk of forcing national judges to present their own solution (as per this last proposal) was accepted, as said: a simple invitation, deliberately not enforceable, to do so is contained in the mentioned *Guidelines* for the national tribunals,[310] which are also reassured at the same time that they will continue to see their references answered. Not by chance, an influent former member of the Court like Christiaan Timmermans acknowledged that, in this respect, the key challenge for the Court in the current times was and is still to "organize and maintain continuity".[311]

The same rationale seems to apply to the reforms that are developing at the moment. Following the changes made to the judicial architecture of the Union in 2015 and 2016 and the increase in the number of judges of the General Court, the Court of Justice proposes to transfer to its jurisdiction first instance adjudication in actions under Article 108(2) TFEU and in actions for failure to fulfil obligations under Articles 258 and 259 TFEU (subject to certain categories of these actions being reserved to the Court): but after the Commission opinion on such draft amendments to Protocol No 3 on the Statute of the Court of Justice,[312] the choice has been to postpone such delicate reform of constitutional relevance after the end of 2020 and a check on the efficiency of the General Court in the new composition.[313] In the same context, a discretionary filter in the hands of the Court has been finally provided[314]: but only for what concerns certain appeals before the Court of Justice where the seising of an independent administrative body is a prerequisite of an action being brought before the General Court (e.g. in the case of decisions taken by the European Union Intellectual Property Office or the European Chemicals Agency), so that a double degree of review is guaranteed and the Court can in any case decide whether significant issues in terms unity, consistency or development of EU law suggest its intervention.

In sum, when I referred to the seemingly paradoxical effects of such an institutional evolution, I pointed in fact to an even trivial result in light of my reflections but still not generally apparent in light of the debate on docket control of the last decades: all the mentioned reforms were aimed at control of docket but they were also very much concerned with resulting—and in fact resulted—in the enhanced inflow of cases and an efficient management of them. In turn, better and quicker treatment of cases eventually invited more actions and in particular preliminary references from the national courts: those national judges who have always historically/culturally restrained from making reference are still a matter of concern for the correct and uniform application of EU law, but those national professionals who have always used the procedure are now sure that they will face a Court with enhanced tools, attentive to a fast treatment of cases, with rationalized powers, and therefore they are prompted to make further use of the procedure.

5.7 The Evolution of Docket Control as a Form of Improvement of the Court's Authority

From the analysis conducted throughout this chapter, it is possible to draw, again, important conclusions on the ability of the Court of Justice to evolve from an institutional point of view. One can surely affirm that the problem of its docket control has emerged over time as a crucial aspect of its structure and organization. This coincided, as said, with the progressive entrenchment of the dynamics of the European federal-like judicial architecture in everyday life of national judges and other players, and therefore with the ECJ becoming more and more a "victim of its own success". The topic started at a certain point to become at the same time a symbol of the Court's acquired authority and crucial for its improvement over time.

We highlighted some main aspects in this respect. First, the debate on the conceptualization itself of the idea of docket control, and the possible solutions for the European Court of Justice, was very much influenced by comparative arguments, not always of refined quality. It had to confront the specificities of the heterarchical European judicial architecture where a simple transplant of foreign solutions could be particularly problematic. Moreover, important concerns came from the diversity of patterns of behaviour by national judges, often clearly influenced by culturally shaped factors. The appraisal of this complex phenomenon led the Court to necessarily evolve, given the situation of strain of its own resources, but evolve accordingly.

Still, serious concerns for the correctness, coherence and uniformity in the interpretation and the application of EU law in the current stage of EU integration, and therefore for the level of maturity of the EU legal system, are evidenced by data and research. There is still the need for a qualitatively unchanged, central role of the Court of Justice and the Article 267 TFEU procedure as a drive chain between the supranational and the national judges. The possible nature of "another infant disease" recognized by some in the procedure[315] must be confronted with the reality of a body not yet grown and fully developed. It is for this simple, but often overshadowed, reason that any reform involving the delicate relationship between the ECJ and the other players in the field was discarded; and the Court of Justice, forced and able to internalize the influences coming from the different culturally shaped behaviours of national judges, only evolved through rigorously *neutral* and *endogenous* reforms, by strengthening its own resources and capabilities but with a view at eventually maximizing its activity.

In the current setting, the authority of the CJEU as a capable guardian of the correct and uniform application of EU law throughout the continent surely rests on its power to solve cases efficiently and with a control of its resources of energy and time. Still, its authority also rests very much on its ability to attract cases, with the least possible risk of pockets of non-cooperation or compliance with its own work. And its evolution in dealing with docket control, by facing culturally shaped differences in the interplay with other actors, shows us that such a concept of authority has been of utmost concern.

Notes

1. The first author to use the phrase in a scientific article seems to be the already mentioned T. Koopmans, La procédure préjudicielle - victime de son succès? *op. cit*.
2. As for instance noted by J. Shaw, Introduction, *op.cit*., at 1.
3. In the words of N. Komesar, Imperfect Alternatives: Choosing Institutions in Law, Economics, and Public Policy, *op.cit*., at 53.
4. *Ivi*, at 138.
5. *Ivi*, at 139.
6. *Ivi*, at 142.
7. *Ibidem*.
8. *Ibidem*.
9. *Ivi*, at 143.
10. D. Fontana, Docket Control and the Success of Constitutional Courts, in T. Ginsburg, R. Dixon (eds.), Handbook of Comparative Constitutional Law, Elgar 2011, p. 624.
11. *Ibidem*.
12. Given at least the fundamental nature of the principle of *non liquet* and the prohibition of the denial of justice in judicial activity: see on this, in an interesting perspective linking national, comparative and international laws J. Kokott, The Burden of Proof in Comparative and International Human Rights Law: Civil and Common Law Approaches with Special

Reference to the American and German Legal Systems, Kluver Law International, 1998, p. 168 *et seq*.

13. I rely on the representation offered by M. Bobek, The Court of Justice of the European Union, in A. Arnull, D. Chalmers (eds.), The Oxford Handbook of European Union Law, Oxford University Press 2015, chapter 7. See, interestingly, for a similar taxonomy already N. Catalano, Manuale di diritto delle Comunità europee, *op. cit.*, at 72 *et seq*.
14. G. Itzcovich, The European Court of Justice as a Constitutional Court. Legal Reasoning in a Comparative Perspective, STALS Research Paper No. 4/2014, available at the website http://www.stals.sssup.it/files/itzcovich%204%202014.pdf (accessed 2 March 2020), p. 9.
15. See Art. 256 TFEU and its (partial) derogation in Art. 51 of the Statute.
16. See on the *inter partes* and/or *erga omnes* effects of the preliminary rulings, among the many, A. Trabucchi, L'effet erga omnes des décision préjudicielles rendues par la Cour de justice des Communautés européennes, *op. cit.*; F.G. Jacobs, The Effect of Preliminary Rulings in the National Legal Order, in M. Andenas (ed.), Article 177 References to the European Court—Policy and Practice, Butterworths 1994, p. 29; T. Tridimas, Precedent and the Court of Justice: A Jurisprudence of Doubt? in J. Dickson, P. Eleftheriadis (eds.), Philosophical Foundations of EU Law, Oxford University Press 2012, p. 307.
17. Detailed statistics concerning the judicial activity of the ECJ are available on the website of the Court, and published every year with rich and precious Reports commented by the President of the Court. See for details on the relative numbers of cases the statistics provided in its Annual Report on the institutional activity—Annual Report 2014, published in 2015, available at the website http://curia.europa.eu/jcms/upload/docs/application/pdf/2015-04/en_ecj_annual_report_2014_pr1.pdf (accessed 2 March 2020), at p. 113 in particular on the "General trend in the work of the Court (1952–2014)—New cases and judgments", and the last Annual Report on the institutional activity—Annual Report 2018, published in 2019, available at the website https://curia.europa.eu/jcms/upload/docs/application/pdf/2019-04/ra_pan_2018_en.pdf, p. 42.
18. *Ivi*, p. 114.
19. *Ibidem*.
20. Annual Report on the institutional activity—Annual Report 2018, published in 2019, available at the website https://curia.europa.eu/jcms/upload/docs/application/pdf/2019-04/ra_pan_2018_en.pdf, pp. 42–46.
21. On the multidimensional nature of the docket problems of the Court see P. Craig, The Jurisdiction of the Community Courts Reconsidered,

in 36 Texas International Law Journal, 2001, p. 555, at 561 *et seq.* (then published also in J.H.H. Weiler, G. de Burca, The European Court of Justice, *op. cit.*, chapter 6).

22. Again using here—in describing the task of national judges as fundamental players of the European judicial architecture—the well-known phrase by M. Claes, The National Courts' Mandate in the European Constitution, *op. cit.*
23. See generally on this point, with reference to the actual *zeitgeist*, B. Smulders, K. Eisele, Reflections on the Institutional Balance, the Community Method and the Interplay between Jurisdictions after Lisbon, in 31 Yearbook of European Law, 2012, p. 112, and M. Dawson, B. de Witte, E. Muir (eds.), Judicial Activism at the European Court of Justice, *op. cit.*
24. See P. Craig, The Jurisdiction of the Community Courts Reconsidered, *op. cit.*, at 561 *et seq.*
25. See on this, *in extenso*, I. Maletic, The Law and Policy of Harmonisation in Europe's Internal Market, Elgar 2013.
26. First Council Directive 89/104/EEC of 21 December 1988 to approximate the laws of the Member States relating to trade marks.
27. Council Regulation (EC) No. 40/94 of 20 December 1993 on the Community trade mark.
28. P. Craig, The Jurisdiction of the Community Courts Reconsidered, *op. cit.*, at 562.
29. See on this all the important contributions in P. Mbongo, A. Vauchez (eds.), Dans la fabrique du droit européen. Scènes, acteurs et publics de la Cour de justice des Communautés européennes, *op. cit.*, A. Vauchez, B. de Witte (eds.), Lawyering Europe, *op. cit.*; and, as *ante litteram* sociological legal studies on the point, E. Stein, Lawyers, Judges, and the Making of a Transnational Constitution, *op. cit.*, and H. Schepel, R. Wesserling, The Legal Community. Judges, Lawyers, Officials and Clerks in the Writing of Europe, in 3 European Law Journal, 1997, p. 165.
30. Such as the so-called "Jean Monnet Action" for the widespread teaching of European integration in national Universities, or the various projects for the training of judges.
31. Report by the Working Party on the Future of the European Communities' Court System for the European Commission, January 2000, available at the website http://ec.europa.eu/dgs/legal_service/pdf/due_en.pdf (accessed 2 March 2020).
32. See for other references the book "The Role and Future of the European Court of Justice", issued by The British Institute of International and Comparative Law in 1996; or the recent Report on "The Workload of the Court of Justice of the European Union" issued by European Union

Committee of the UK House of Lords, available at the website http://www.publications.parliament.uk/pa/ld201011/ldselect/ldeucom/128/128.pdf (accessed 2 March 2020).

33. See T. Millett, The Court of First Instance of the European Communities, Butterworth 1990, p. 2. Note that this has become a matter of concern not only debated in every Annual Report issued by the Court of Justice, but also in monographs on the Court's procedural law (see for instance M. Broberg, N. Fenger, Preliminary References to the European Court of Justice, *op. cit.*, at 23 *et seq.*) and even general EU law textbooks (see e.g. D. Chalmers, G. Davies, G. Monti, European Union Law, 2nd ed. Cambridge University Press 2010, at 178 *et seq.*).
34. See in fact F.G. Jacobs, Amendments to the Rules of Procedure, in 5 European Law Review, 1980, p. 52; H. Rasmussen, The European Court's Acte Clair Strategy in C.I.L.F.I.T.; Or, Acte Clair, of Course! But What Does it Mean? in 10 European Law Review, 1984, p. 242; F.G. Jacobs, Procedural Reform in the European Court, in J. Schwarze (ed.), Perspectives for the Development of Judicial Protection in the European Community, Nomos Verlagsgesellschaft 1987, p. 191; T. Koopmans, La procédure préjudicielle - victime de son succès? *op. cit.*; F.G. Jacobs, Proposals for Reform in the Organisation and Procedure of the Court of Justice of the European Communitites: With Special Reference to the Proposed Court of First Instance, in F. Capotorti, C. Ehlermann (eds.), Du droit international au droit de l'integration - Liber amicorum Pierre Pescatore, *op. cit.*, p. 287; J.H.H. Weiler, The European Court, National Courts and References for Preliminary Rulings—The Paradox of Success: A Revisionist View of Article 177 EEC, in H.G. Schermers, C.W.A. Timmermans, A.E. Kellerman (eds.), Article 177 EEC: Experiences and Problems, North-Holland 1987, p. 366.
35. As first sentences of the Foreword of the Annual Report for 2013, available at the website http://curia.europa.eu/jcms/upload/docs/application/pdf/2014-03/en_version_provisoire_web.pdf (accessed 2 March 2020), p. 1.
36. See generally D. Fontana, Docket Control and the Success of Constitutional Courts, *op. cit.*, and for reflections also on the CJEU, J. Bell, The Role of European Judges in an Era of Uncertainty, in P.J. Birkinshaw, M. Varney (eds.), The European Union Legal Order After Lisbon, Kluwer 2010, p. 277, at 281–282 in particular.
37. G. Itzcovich, The European Court of Justice as a Constitutional Court. Legal Reasoning in a Comparative Perspective, *op. cit.*, at 9. See, again, interestingly, for a similar taxonomy already N. Catalano, Manuale di diritto delle Comunità europee, *op. cit.*, at 72 *et seq*.
38. G. Itzcovich, The European Court of Justice as a Constitutional Court. Legal Reasoning in a Comparative Perspective, *op. cit.*, at 9.

39. See the well known studies by K. Lenaerts, Form and Substance of the Preliminary Ruling Procedure, in D. Curtin, T. Heukels (eds.), Institutional Dynamics of European Integration, Martinus Nijhoff 1994, p. 355, and S. Prechal, Direct Effect, Indirect Effect, Supremacy and the Evolving Constitution of the European Union, in C. Barnard (ed.), The Fundamental of EU Law Revisited, Oxford University Press 2007, p. 35, at 37 *et seq*, and the recent reflections by B. de Witte, The Preliminary Ruling Dialogue: Three Types of Questions Posed by National Courts, *op. cit*.
40. See in this respect, again, the recent authoritative summary by J.H.H. Weiler, The Political and Legal Culture of European Integration: An Exploratory Essay, *op. cit*., at 691: "the preliminary reference procedure is, overwhelmingly, a device for judicial review of member state compliance with their obligations under the treaties. It is ingenious for two reasons: First, it deploys individuals, vindicating their own rights, as the monitors and enforcers of Community obligations vis-à-vis the member states. It has been called the private-attorney-general model. And second, it deploys national courts. The judgement is spoken through the mouths of member state courts. The habit of obedience associated with national law is, thus, attached to European law. The gap between the rule of law and the rule of international law is narrowed, even closed" .
41. See the general reflections above, at Note 1 in Chapter 1 and Note 110 in Chapter 2.
42. See in this vein M. Smith, Enforcement, Monitoring, Verification, Outsourcing: The Decline and Decline of the Infringement Process, in 33 European Law Review, 2008, p. 777.
43. See the directions set forth in the Commission Staff Wording Document accompanying the 25th Annual Report on Monitoring the Application of Community Law (2007) Situation in the Different Sectors, EC Commission, SEC (2008), 2854, at p. 32 and p. 166 *et seq*.
44. See the well known Judgement of 15 July 1963, Plaumann/Commission of the EEC (25/62, ECR 1963 p. 95).
45. Namely, in particular, the Opinion of Advocate General Jacobs in Judgement of 25 July 2002, Unión de Pequeños Agricultores/Council (C-50/00 P, ECR 2002 p. I-6677) ECLI:EU:C:2002:462, the judgement by the Court of First Instance (CFI) in Judgement of 3 May 2002, Jégo-Quéré/Commission (T-177/01, ECR 2002 p. II-2365) ECLI:EU:T:2002:112, and the new wording of Article 263 (4) TFEU in the Lisbon Treaty.
46. For instance, F.G. Jacobs, Access to Justice as a Fundamental Right in European Law, in G.C. Rodríguez Iglesias et al. (eds.), Mélanges en hommage à Fernand Schockweiler, Nomos 1999, p. 197, and, recently, I. Pernice, The Right to Effective Judicial Protection and Remedies in the EU, in A. Rosas, E. Levits, Y. Bot (eds.), The Court of Justice and the Construction of Europe: Analyses and Perspectives on Sixty Years of

Case-law—La Cour de Justice et la Construction de l'Europe: Analyses et Perspectives de Soixante Ans de Jurisprudence, *op. cit.*, p. 381.

47. See *inter alia* A. Arnull, Private applicants and the action for annulment under Article 173 of the EC Treaty, in 32 Common Market Law Review, 1995, p. 7; D. Waelbroeck, A.M. Verheyden, Les conditions de recevabilité des recours en annulation des particuliers contre les actes normatifs communautaires: à la lumière du droit comparé et de la Convention des droits de l'homme, in 31 Cahiers de droit européen, 1995, p. 399; G. Vandersanden, Pour un élargissement du droit des particuliers d'agir en annulation contre des actes autres que les décisions qui leur sont adressées» , in 31 Cahiers de droit européen, 1995, p. 535; D. Boni, Il ricorso di annullamento delle persone fisiche e giuridiche, in B. Nascimbene, L. Daniele (eds.), Il ricorso di annullamento nel Trattato istitutivo della Comunità, Giuffrè 1998, p. 53, at 55–56.; E. Biernat, The Locus Standi of Private Applicants under Article 230 (4) EC and the Principle of Judicial Protection in the European Community, Jean Monnet Working Paper No. 12/03, especially pp. 15–16 *et seq.*
48. See in this sense the Opinions issued by Advocate General Slynn in Judgement of 10 June 1982, Lord Bethell/Commission (246/81, ECR 1982 p. 2277), by Advocate General Jacobs in Judgement of 16 May 1991, Extramet Industrie/Council (C-358/89, ECR 1991 p. I-2501) ECLI:EU:C:1991:214 and in Judgement of 9 March 1994, TWD/Bundesrepublik Deutschland (C-188/92, ECR 1994 p. I-833), by Advocate General Ruiz-Jarabo Colomer in Judgement of 12 December 1996, Associazione agricoltori della provincia di Rovigo and others/Commission and others (C-142/95 P, ECR 1996 p. I-6669) ECLI:EU:C:1996:493. See also the doctrinal contributions of members of the Court such as F. Schockweiler, L'accès à la justice dans l'ordre juridique communautaire» , in 25 Journal des tribunaux, Droit européen, 1996, p. 1; G.F. Mancini, The Role of the Supreme Courts at the National and International Level: A Case Study of the Court of Justice of the European Communities, in P. Yessiou-Faltsi (ed.), The Role of the Supreme Courts at the National and International Level, Sakkoulas 1998, p. 421; K. Lenaerts, The Legal Protection of Private Parties under the EC Treaty: A Coherent and Complete System of Judicial Review?, and A. Saggio, Appunti sulla ricevibilità dei ricorsi d'annullamento proposti da persone fisiche o giuridiche in base all'art. 173 quarto comma del Trattato CE, both in P. Alleva et al. (eds.) Scritti in onore di Giuseppe Federico Mancini, Vol. II, Giuffrè 1998, p. 591 e p. 879 respectively.

49. See D. Halberstam, Comparative Federalism and the Role of the Judiciary, in K. Whittington, D. Kelemen, G. Caldeira (eds.), The Oxford Handbook of Law and Politics, Oxford University Press 2008, p. 142.
50. See the historical analysis by G. Casper, R.A. Posner, The Workload of the Supreme Court, American Bar Foundation 1974.
51. See most notably J.P. Jacqué, J.H.H. Weiler, On the Road to European Union—A New Judicial Architecture: An Agenda for the Intergovernmental Conference, in 27 Common Market Law Review, 1990, p. 185; T. Kennedy, First Steps towards a European Certiorari? in 18 European Law Review, 1993, p. 121; L. Heffernan, The Community Court Post-Nice: A European Certiorari Revisited, in 52 The International and Comparative Law Quarterly, 2003, p. 907.
52. F. Frankfurter, J.M. Landis, The Business of the Supreme Court of the United States—A Study in the Federal Judicial System, Macmillan 1928; G. Casper, R.A. Posner, The Workload of the Supreme Court, *op. cit.*
53. G. Casper, R.A. Posner, The Workload of the Supreme Court, *op. cit.*, in particular at 27 *et seq.*
54. *Ivi*, at 20.
55. R.A. Posner, The Federal Courts, Harvard University Press 1996, at 53 *et seq.*
56. Judiciary Act of 1891 (26 Stat. 826).
57. See for details H.W. Perry Jr., Deciding to Decide: Agenda Setting in the United States Supreme Court, Harvard University Press 1991, at chapters 7 and 8 in particular.
58. The data collected by F. Frankfurter, J.M. Landis, The Business of the Supreme Court of the United States—A Study in the Federal Judicial System, *op.cit.*, persuaded the Authors that by 1925 the Supreme Court has ceased to be a "common law court": see *ibidem*, at p. 307.
59. D. Fontana, Docket Control and the Success of Constitutional Courts, *op. cit.*, at 625.
60. See above, Note 51, for the most explicit proposals in this sense.
61. See in particular T. Kennedy, First Steps towards a European Certiorari? *op. cit.*, and L. Heffernan, The Community Court post-Nice: A European Certiorari revisited, *op. cit.* On the other hand, as we will see later in detail, the work by J.P. Jacqué, J.H.H. Weiler, On the Road to European Union—A New Judicial Architecture: An Agenda for the Intergovernmental Conference, *op. cit.*, inserted (aptly) the certiorari tool in a more general and refined reform proposal of the EU judicial architecture.
62. D.G. Valentine, The Court of Justice of the European Coal and Steel Community, *op. cit.*, at 202.
63. See recently the reflections by A. Arnull, Judicial Dialogue in the European Union, in J. Dickson, P. Eleftheriadis (eds.), Philosophical Foundations of EU Law, *op. cit.*, p. 109, at 118.

64. J.P. Jacqué, J.H.H. Weiler, On the Road to European Union—A New Judicial Architecture: An Agenda for the Intergovernmental Conference, *op. cit.*, See for a discussion of this proposal A. Bzdera, The Court of Justice of the European Community and the Politics of Institutional Reform, in M.L. Volcansek (ed.), Judicial Politics and Policy-Making in Western Europe, Frank Cass 1992, p. 122.
65. A. Arnull, Judicial Dialogue in the European Union, *op. cit.*, at 118.
66. Once more in the recent authoritative words of J.H.H. Weiler, The Political and Legal Culture of European Integration: An Exploratory Essay, *op. cit.*, at 691, "the preliminary reference procedure is, overwhelmingly, a device for judicial review of member state compliance with their obligations under the treaties. *It is ingenious for two reasons*: First, *it deploys individuals, vindicating their own rights, as the monitors and enforcers of Community obligations vis-à-vis the member states. It has been called the private-attorney-general model*. And second, it deploys national courts. The judgement is spoken through the mouths of member state courts. The habit of obedience associated with national law is, thus, attached to European law. The gap between the rule of law and the rule of international law is narrowed, even closed" (emphasis added). See also in this respect J.H.H. Weiler, Revisiting Van Gend en Loos: Subjectifying and Objectifying the Individual, in Court of Justice of EU, 50th Anniversary of the Judgement in Van Gend en Loos 1963–2013, Conference Proceedings—Luxembourg, 13th May 2013, available at the website http://curia.europa.eu/jcms/upload/docs/application/pdf/2013-12/qd30136442ac_002.pdf (accessed 2 March 2020), p. 11, at 13.
67. A. Arnull, Judicial Dialogue in the European Union, *op. cit.*, at 118.
68. *Ibidem*.
69. See above, Chapter 4 in particular at paragraph 2.
70. See for a recent reflection on the point S. Prechal, National Courts in EU Judicial Structures, *op. cit.*, at 432–433.
71. On such a model see the Court of Justice's Report on "The Future of the Judicial System of the European Union (Proposals and Reflections)", 1999, published in A. Dashwood, A. Johnston, The Future of the Judicial System of the European Union, Hart Publishing 2001, p. 145, and the Report of the Working Party on the Future of the European Communities' Court System, 2000 (the so-called, already mentioned Due Report). In a resolution of the 9 July 2008 on the role of the national judge in the European judicial architecture (2007/2027(INI)), the European Parliament has pleaded for the consideration of the green-light procedure (see point 31: "31. Considers that, in a decentralized and mature Community legal order, national judges should not be marginalized but rather given more responsibility and further encouraged in their role as first judges of Community law; therefore

urges consideration of a "green light" system whereby national judges could include their proposed answers to the questions they refer to the Court of Justice, which could then decide within a given period whether to accept the proposed judgement or whether to rule itself in the manner of an appellate court"). See also F.G. Jacobs in his hearing before the House of Lords, European Union Committee, 14th Report of Session 2010–11, "The Workload of the Court of Justice of the European Union", available at the website http://www.publications.parliament.uk/pa/ld201011/ldselect/ldeucom/128/128.pdf (accessed 2 March 2020), pp. 31–32, advocating for such a reform.

72. See X. Groussot, C. Wong, A. Inghammar, A. Bruzelius, Empowering National Courts in EU Law, Swedish Institute for European Policy Studies, Report No. 3/2009, available at the website http://www.sieps.se/sites/default/files/541-2009-3-rapport.pdf (accessed 2 March 2020), at 26 *et seq*. in particular.
73. T. Kennedy, First Steps towards a European certiorari? *op. cit*.; L. Heffernan, The Community Court Post-Nice: A European Certiorari Revisited, *op. cit*.
74. See for concordant successful theorizations of the different existing models M. Cappelletti, Judicial Review in Comparative Perspective, in 58 California Law Review, 1970, p. 5; A. Brewer Carias, Judicial Review in Comparative Law, Cambridge University Press 1989.
75. A.M. Bickel, The Supreme Court, 1960 Term—Foreword: the Passive Virtues, in 75 Harvard Law Review, 1961, p. 40, then also in *Id*., The Least Dangerous Branch: The Supreme Court at the Bar of Politics, *op. cit*., at 111 *et seq*. For multidisciplinary comments on such influential perspective, see: E.A. Purcell Jr., Alexander M. Bickel and the Post-Realist Constitution, in 11 Harvard Civil Rights-Civil Liberties Law Review, 1976, p. 521; J. Moeller, Alexander M. Bickel: Toward a Theory of Politics, in 47 Journal of Politics, 1985, p. 113; A.T. Kronman, Alexander Bickel's Philosophy of Prudence, in 94 Yale Law Journal, 1985, p. 1567; T. Peretti, An Empirical Analysis of Alexander Bickel's the Least Dangerous Branch, in K.D. Ward, C.R. Castillo (eds.), The Judiciary in American Democracy: Alexander Bickel, the Counter-majoritarian Difficulty, and Contemporary Constitutional Theory, State University of New York Press 2005; and in a broad comparative sense, D. Fontana, Docket Control and the Success of Constitutional Courts, *op. cit*.
76. A. Bickel, The Least Dangerous Branch: The Supreme Court at the Bar of Politics, *op. cit*., at 16 *et seq*.
77. *Ivi*, at 24 *et seq*.
78. *Ivi*, at 169 *et seq*.
79. T. Kennedy, First Steps towards a European Certiorari? *op. cit*.

80. According to the wording of Judgement of 2 June 1994, AC-ATEL Electronics/Hauptzollamt München-Mitte (C-30/93, ECR 1994 p. I-2305) ECLI:EU:C:1994:224, at paragraph 17.
81. Judgement of 11 March 1980, Foglia/Novello (104/79, ECR 1980 p. 745) and Judgement of 16 December 1981, Foglia/Novello (244/80, ECR 1981 p. 3045); but see also Judgement of 9 February 1995, Leclerc-Siplec/TF1 and M6 (C-412/93, ECR 1995 p. I-179) ECLI:EU:C:1995:26, and recently Judgement of 22 November 2005, Mangold (C-144/04, ECR 2005 p. I-9981) ECLI:EU:C:2005:709 and Judgement of 7 July 2011, Agafiţei and others (C-310/10, ECR 2011 p. I-5989) ECLI:EU:C:2011:467.
82. See Judgement of 9 December 1965, Hessische Knappschaft/Singer et Fils (44/65, ECR 1965 p. 965); Judgement of 22 November 1978, Mattheus/Doego (93/78, ECR 1978 p. 2203); Judgement of 17 September 1997, Dorsch Consult Ingenieursgesellschaft/Bundesbaugesellschaft Berlin (C-54/96, ECR 1997 p. I-4961) ECLI:EU:C:1997:413; Judgement of 27 April 2006, Familiensache: Standesamt Stadt Niebüll (C-96/04, ECR 2006 p. I-3561) ECLI:EU:C:2006:254.
83. See Judgement of 16 June 1981, Salonia/Poidomani e Giglio (126/80, ECR 1981 p. 1563); Judgement of 16 July 1992, Lourenço Dias/Director da Alfândega do Porto (C-343/90, ECR 1992 p. I-4673); Judgement of 3 March 1994, Eurico Italia and others/Ente Nazionale Risi (C-332/92, C-333/92 and C-335/92, ECR 1994 p. I-711) ECLI:EU:C:1994:79; Judgement of 17 May 1994, Corsica Ferries/Corpo dei piloti del porto di Genova (C-18/93, ECR 1994 p. I-1783); Judgement of 13 December 1994, Grau-Hupka/Stadtgemeinde Bremen (C-297/93, ECR 1994 p. I-5535) ECLI:EU:C:1994:406.
84. See Judgement of 15 December 1994, Stadt Lengerich and others/Helmig and others (C-399/92, C-409/92, C-425/92, C-34/93, C-50/93 and C-78/93, ECR 1994 p. I-5727) ECLI:EU:C:1994:415, at paragraph 8.
85. Judgement of 28 November 1991, Durighello/INPS (C-186/90, ECR 1991 p. I-5773) ECLI:EU:C:1991:453, at paragraph 8.
86. See e.g. Judgement of 27 June 1991, Mecanarte-Metalurgica da Lagoa/Alfandega do Porto (C-348/89, ECR 1991 p. I-3277) ECLI:EU:C:1991:278, at paragraph 47; Judgement of 20 October 1993, Balocchi/Ministero delle finanze dello Stato (C-10/92, ECR 1993 p. I-5105) ECLI:EU:C:1993:846, at paragraphs 13 and 14; Judgement of 3 March 1994, Eurico Italia and others/Ente Nazionale Risi (C-332/92, C-333/92 and C-335/92, ECR 1994 p. I-711) ECLI:EU:C:1994:79, at paragraph 11; Judgement of 15

December 1995, Union royale belge des sociétés de football association and others/Bosman and others (C-415/93, ECR 1995 p. I-4921) ECLI:EU:C:1995:463, at paragraph 59; Judgement of 13 March 2001, PreussenElektra (C-379/98, ECR 2001 p. I-2099) ECLI:EU:C:2001:160, at paragraph 38.

87. See e.g. Judgement of 18 October 1990, Dzodzi/Belgian State (297/88 and C-197/89, ECR 1990 p. I-3763), at paragraph 34; Judgement of 8 November 1990, Gmurzynska-Bscher/Oberfinanzdirektion Köln (C-231/89, ECR 1990 p. I-4003) ECLI:EU:C:1990:386, at paragraph 19; Judgement of 2 June 1994, AC-ATEL Electronics/Hauptzollamt München-Mitte (C-30/93, ECR 1994 p. I-2305) ECLI:EU:C:1994:224, at paragraph 17.
88. See the same Judgement of 8 November 1990, Gmurzynska-Bscher/Oberfinanzdirektion Köln (C-231/89, ECR 1990 p. I-4003) ECLI:EU:C:1990:386, at paragraph 20; accordingly, Judgement of 16 July 1992, Meilicke/ADV-ORGA (C-83/91, ECR 1992 p. I-4871), at paragraph 24, and here again Judgement of 15 December 1994, Stadt Lengerich and others/Helmig and others (C-399/92, C-409/92, C-425/92, C-34/93, C-50/93 and C-78/93, ECR 1994 p. I-5727) ECLI:EU:C:1994:415, at is paragraph 9.
89. C. Barnard, E. Sharpston, The Changing Face of Article 177 References, in 34 Common Market Law Review, 1997, p. 1113, at 1117.
90. On the fundamental nature of the preliminary reference procedure for the construction of the basic tenets of the EU legal order see again Note 110 in Chapter 2.
91. Judgement of 27 March 1963, Da Costa en Schaake NV and others/Administratie der Belastingen (28 to 30-62, ECR 1963 p. 31).
92. Judgement of 15 July 1964, Costa/E.N.E.L. (6-64, ECR 1964 p. 585).
93. See Judgement of 27 March 1963, Da Costa en Schaake NV and others/Administratie der Belastingen (28 to 30–62, ECR 1963 p. 31), at 37–38, in which the Court recognized that "(…) the authority of an interpretation under Article 177 already given by the Court may deprive the obligation [to refer under Article 177(3)] of its purpose and thus empty it of substance. Such is the case especially where the question raised is materially identical (…)". Nevertheless, the Court also added that "(…) it is no less true that Article 177 always allows a national court, if it considers it desirable, to refer questions of interpretation to the Court again (…) The Court must, therefore, give a judgment on the present interpretation".
94. Judgement of 15 July 1964, Costa/E.N.E.L. (6-64, ECR 1964 p. 585), at 593.
95. *Ibidem.*

96. See Judgement of 7 March 1996, Merckx and Neuhuys/Ford Motors Company Belgium (C-171/94 and C-172/94, ECR 1996 p. I-1253) ECLI:EU:C:1996:87, at paragraph 15.
97. See on the practice D. Sarmiento, Poder Judicial e integración europea . La construcción de un modelo jurisdiccional para la Unión, *op. cit.* p. 206 *et seq.*, and U. Šadl, A. Wallerman, 'The Referring Court Asks, in Essence': Is Reformulation of Preliminary Questions by the Court of Justice a Decision Writing Fixture or a Decision-Making Approach? in 25 European Law Journal, 2019, p. 416.
98. C. Barnard, E. Sharpston, The Changing Face of Article 177 References, *op. cit.*, at 1120: they cite as early examples the procedures of Judgement of 31 March 1981, Jenkins/Kingsgate (96/80, ECR 1981 p. 911); Judgement of 16 February 1982, Burton/British Railways Board (19/81, ECR 1982 p. 554) ECLI:EU:C:1982:58; Judgement of 11 March 1981, Worringham and Humphreys/Lloyds Bank (69/80, ECR 1981 p. 767), this last also critically commented by A. Lester, The Uncertain Trumpet. References to the Court of Justice from the United Kingdom: Equal Pay and Equal Treatment without Sex Discrimination, in H.G. Schermers, C.W.A. Timmermans, A. E. Kellermann, J. S. Watson (Eds.), Article 177 EEC: Experiences and Problems, *op. cit.*, p. 164.
99. See for instance Judgement of 23 November 1989, Parfümerie-Fabrik 4711/Provide (150/88, ECR 1989 p. 3891), in which it was also stated, in paragraph 12, that "When ruling on questions intended to permit the national court to determine whether provisions of its national law are in accordance with Community law, the Court may provide the criteria for the interpretation of Community law which will enable the national court to solve the legal problem with which it is faced. The same is true when it is to be determined whether the provisions of the law of a Member State other than that of the court requesting the ruling are compatible with Community law".
100. C. Barnard, E. Sharpston, The Changing Face of Article 177 References, *op. cit.*
101. See D. O' Keeffe, Is the Spirit of Article 177 Under Attack? Preliminary References and Admissibility, in P. Alleva et al. (eds.), Scritti in onore di Giuseppe Federico Mancini, *op. cit.*, p. 695; the phrase "in conformity with the spirit of 177" was actually coined by AG Mancini in Judgement of 11 June 1987, Pretore di Salò/X (14/86, ECR 1987 p. 2545), at 2557, paragraph 5. See for a recent reflection on the same aspect X. Groussot, Spirit, Are You There? Reinforced Judicial Dialogue and the Preliminary Ruling Procedure, Eric Stein Working Paper No. 4/2008, available at the website http://papers.ssrn.com/sol3/papers.cfm?abstract_id=1279367 (accessed 2 March 2020).

102. Judgement of 22 November 1978, Mattheus/Doego (93/78, ECR 1978 p. 2203).
103. Judgement of 11 March 1980, Foglia/Novello (104/79, ECR 1980 p. 745).
104. Judgement of 22 November 1978, Mattheus/Doego (93/78, ECR 1978 p. 2203), at 2210.
105. See for instance G. Bebr, The Existence of a Genuine Dispute: An Indispensable Precondition for the Jurisdication of the Court under Article 177 EEC Treaty, in 17 Common Market Law Review, 1980, p. 525.
106. Judgement of 11 March 1980, Foglia/Novello (104/79, ECR 1980 p. 745), at paragraph 11.
107. D. Anderson, The Admissibility of Preliminary References, in 14 Yearbook of European Law, 1994, p. 170.
108. Judgement of 16 December 1981, Foglia/Novello (244/80, ECR 1981 p. 3045).
109. Judgement of 6 October 1982, CILFIT/Ministero della Sanità (283/81, ECR 1982 p. 3415).
110. C. Barnard, E. Sharpston, The Changing Face of Article 177 References, *op. cit.*, at 1125.
111. See the reflections on what he defined a "frequently misunderstood" judgement by D. Edward, CILFIT and Foto-Frost in Their Historical and Procedural Context, in L. Azoulai, L.M. Poiares Maduro (eds.), The Past and Future of EU Law. The Classics of EU Law Revisited on the 50th Anniversary of the Rome Treaty, *op. cit.*, p. 173.
112. As noted by R. Schütze, European Constitutional Law, 2nd ed., CUP 2018, p. 300.
113. C. Barnard, E. Sharpston, The Changing Face of Article 177 References, *op. cit.*, at 1125.
114. Judgement of 6 October 1982, CILFIT/Ministero della Sanità (283/81, ECR 1982 p. 3415), at 3437.
115. C. Barnard, E. Sharpston, The Changing Face of Article 177 References, *op. cit.*, at 1125.
116. See the caselaw cited by C. Barnard, E. Sharpston, The Changing Face of Article 177 References, *op. cit.*, at 1126–1127.
117. Judgement of 21 April 1988, Pardini/Ministero del commercio con l'estero (338/85, ECR 1988 p. 2041) ECLI:EU:C:1988:194, especially at paragraph 11.
118. For instance Order of 21 December 1995, Max Mara/Ufficio del registro di Reggio Emilia (C-307/95, ECR 1995 p. I-5083) ECLI:EU:C:1995:465, at paragraph 5.
119. For instance Order of 7 April 1995, Grau Gomis and others (C-167/94, ECR 1995 p. I-1023) ECLI:EU:C:1995:113.

120. For instance Judgement of 28 March 1995, Kleinwort Benson/City of Glasgow District Council (C-346/93, ECR 1995 p. I-615) ECLI:EU:C:1995:85.
121. For instance Judgement of 30 March 1993, Corbiau/Administration des contributions (C-24/92, ECR 1993 p. I-1277).
122. See for instance Judgement of 16 July 1992, Meilicke/ADV-ORGA (C-83/91, ECR 1992 p. I-4871), in particular at paragraph 24.
123. See for instance Judgement of 26 January 1993, Telemarsicabruzzo and others/Circostel and others (C-320/90, C-321/90 and C-322/90, ECR 1993 p. I-393); Order of 26 April 1993, Monin Automobiles (C-386/92, ECR 1993 p. I-2049) ECLI:EU:C:1993:153.
124. See for instance Judgement of 16 September 1982, ONTPS/Vlaeminck (132/81, ECR 1982 p. 2953) ECLI:EU:C:1982:294; Order of 26 January 1990, Falciola/Comune di Pavia (286/88, ECR 1990 p. I-191) ECLI:EU:C:1990:33.
125. C. Barnard, E. Sharpston, The Changing Face of Article 177 References, *op. cit.*, at 1141.
126. The last version of the *Recommendations to national courts and tribunals in relation to the initiation of preliminary ruling proceedings* [Official Journal C 257 of 20.7.2018], is available at the website https://eur-lex.europa.eu/legal-content/EN/TXT/PDF/?uri=CELEX:32018H0720(01)&from=EN (accessed 2 March 2020).
127. See the reconstructions given in this respect by T. Kennedy, First Steps towards a European Certiorari?, *op. cit.*; L. Heffernan, The Community Court Post-Nice: A European Certiorari Revisited, *op. cit.*; and recently by E. D'Alessandro, Il procedimento pregiudiziale interpretativo dinanzi alla Corte di Giustizia, Giappichelli 2012, at 22 *et seq.*
128. See e.g. R. Lane, Article 234: a Few Rough Edges Still, in M. Hoskins, W.Robinson (eds.), A True European: Essays for Judge David Edward, Hart Publishing 2004, p. 327, at 334.
129. C. Barnard, E. Sharpston, The Changing Face of Article 177 References, *op. cit.*, at 1123–1124.
130. Judgement of 14 January 1981, Vinal/Orbat (46/80, ECR 1981 p. 77) ECLI:EU:C:1981:4.
131. *Ivi*, at paragraph 5.
132. *Ivi*, at 98–99: "there is nothing in the conduct of the parties in concluding the contract which points inescapably to the conclusion that the contract was only intended to provide a pretext to call in question the Italian tax arrangements before the Court of Justice on the basis of a main action in the form of a friendly suit".
133. *Ivi*, at paragraphs 5–6.
134. *Ivi*, at 99, with original emphasis.

135. Judgement of 10 November 1982, Rau/De Smedt (261/81, ECR 1982 p. 3961) ECLI:EU:C:1982:382, in particular at paragraph 9.
136. Judgement of 23 November 1989, Parfümerie-Fabrik 4711/Provide (150/88, ECR 1989 p. 3891), in particular at paragraph 9.
137. Judgement of 9 June 1992, Delhaize Frères/Promalvin and others (C-47/90, ECR 1992 p. I-3669) ECLI:EU:C:1992:250.
138. See *ivi*, A.G. Gulmann, paragraph 14, I-3691.
139. D. Edward, CILFIT and Foto-Frost in Their Historical and Procedural Context, *op. cit.*, at 179.
140. See Note 93 above.
141. D. Edward, CILFIT and Foto-Frost in Their Historical and Procedural Context, *op. cit.*, at 179.
142. Judgement of 16 July 1956, Fédération charbonnière de Belgique/ECSC High Authority (8/55, ECR 1954-1956 p. 245).
143. X. Groussot, Spirit, Are You There? Reinforced Judicial Dialogue and the Preliminary Ruling Procedure, *op. cit.*, at 6; D. Edward, CILFIT and Foto-Frost in Their Historical and Procedural Context, *op. cit.*, at 175.
144. See in this respect the erudite reconstruction by Advocate-General Capotorti, Judgement of 6 October 1982, CILFIT/Ministero della Sanità (283/81, ECR 1982 p. 3415), at 3435.
145. Case Re Societé des Petroles Shell-Berre and Others, Conseil d'État, 1964-06-19, (1964) CMLR 462.
146. See for a survery of the Conseil d'État's approach M.F Conniff, The French Conseil d'État and Article 177 of the Treaty of Rome: A Case Analysis, in 12 Virginia Journal of International Law, 1972, p. 377.
147. Case BSG 1970-01-22, 4 RJ 109/69 (Re French Widow's Pension Settlement), (1971) CMLR 530.
148. See E. Schober, Die Lehre vom 'Acte Clair' im franzosischen Recht, in 19 Neue Juristische Wochenschrift, 1966, p. 2252.
149. Court of Appeal, 22 May 1974, HP Bulmer Ltd & Anor v. J. Bollinger SA & Ors (1974) EWCA Civ 14.
150. See for instance, in the pre-CILFIT literature, S.A. Kuipers, Pertinence et acte clair, art. 177 CEE. Observations sur Hoge Raad der Nederlanden, in Cahiers de droit europeen, 1967, p. 81, or G. Bebr, Development of Judicial Control of the European Communities, Brill 1981, at p 495 *et seq.*, and then N. Catalano, La pericolosa teoria dell'atto chiaro, in 1 Giustizia Civile, 1983, p. 3; G. Bebr, The Rambling Ghost of 'Cohn Bendit'. Acte clair and the Court of Justice, in 20 Common Market Law Review, 1983, p. 440; F. Capotorti, Sull'obbligo del rinvio alla Corte di giustizia per l'interpretazione a titolo pregiudiziale a norma del 3° comma dell'art. 177 del trattato Cee, in 1 Giurisprudenza italiana, 1983, p. 1008.

151. See M. Lagrange, Cour de Justice et Tribunaux nationaux. La theorie de l'acte clair pomme de discorde ou trait d'union, in 1 Gazette du Palais, 1971, and *Id.*, The Theory of Acte Clair: A Bone of Contention or a Source of Unity?, in 8 Common Market Law Review, 1971, p. 313.
152. See P. Pescatore, L' interpretation du droit communautaire et la doctrine de l'acte clair, in 33/34 Bullettin des juristes Européens, 1971, p. 49; *Id.*, Interpretation of Community Law and the Doctrine of 'acte clair', in 27 Legal Problems of an Enlarged European Community, 1972, p. 46.
153. Answer to Written Question by Mr. Krieg no. 600/78 (OJ 1979 C28), quoted under "Facts and procedure" in Judgement of 6 October 1982, CILFIT/Ministero della Sanità (283/81, ECR 1982 p. 3415), at 3425, and in extenso in D. Edward, CILFIT and Foto-Frost in Their Historical and Procedural Context, *op. cit.*, at 176.
154. Judgement of 6 October 1982, CILFIT/Ministero della Sanità (283/81, ECR 1982 p. 3415), at 3435.
155. X. Groussot, Spirit, Are You There? Reinforced Judicial Dialogue and the Preliminary Ruling Procedure, *op. cit.*, at 6.
156. See H. Rasmussen, The European Court's Acte Clair Strategy in C.I.L.F.I.T.; Or, Acte Clair, of Course! But What Does It Mean?, *op. cit.*.
157. See for instance M. Bobek, On the Application of European Law in (Not Only) the Courts of the New Member Sates: "Don't Do as I say"?, in 10 Cambridge Yearbook of European Legal Studies, 2007–2008, p. 1; X. Groussot, Spirit, Are You There? Reinforced Judicial Dialogue and the Preliminary Ruling Procedure, *op. cit.*, at 7.
158. See the proposals of the Report by the Working Party on the Future of the European Communities' Court System for the European Commission, January 2000 (the mentioned Ole Due Report), at 17 *et seq.*, and of the Report of the Working Group on the Preliminary Ruling Procedure, Association of the Councils of State and Supreme Administrative Jurisdictions of the European Union, The Hague, December 2007, available at the website http://www.juradmin.eu/seminars/Den Haag2007/Final_report.pdf (accessed 2 March 2020), at p. 11.
159. See Judgement of 15 September 2005, Intermodal Transports (C-495/03, ECR 2005 p. I-8151) ECLI:EU:C:2005:552 and Judgement of 15 July 2010, Gaston Schul (C-354/09, ECR 2010 p. I-7449) ECLI:EU:C:2010:439: in both the occasions, the Advocates General pleaded for a reconsideration of the CILFIT criteria. See e.g. the clear words in the Opinion of AG Stix-Hackl in C-495/03 Intermodal Transports, at paragraphs 99 and 100: "I take the view that the judgement in Cilfit cannot be intended to mean that the national court is required, for example, to examine a provision of Community law in every one of the official Community languages. That would place a practically intolerable burden on the national courts and would de facto reduce the – albeit

limited – delegation to national courts of last instance of questions of Community law which can be answered 'unequivocally' in accordance with the judgement in Cilfit to a lip service or a 'tactical move'. 100. It must therefore be concluded that the requirements set out in Cilfit cannot be regarded as a type of instruction manual on decision-making for national courts of last instance which is to be rigidly adhered to and on the basis of which an objective and clear dividing line can be drawn between questions of interpretation which may exceptionally be resolved by such courts themselves and questions of interpretation which must be referred to the Court of Justice. Those requirements cannot be used as a benchmark for establishing 'objectively' when the meaning of a Community provision is so obvious as to leave no scope for any reasonable doubt as to its interpretation".

160. See e.g. N. Catalano, La pericolosa teoria dell'atto chiaro, *op. cit.*; J.C. Masclet, Vers la fin d'une controverse? La Cour de justice tempère l'obligation de renvoi préjudiciel en interprétation faite aux juridictions suprêmes (art. 177, alinéa 3, CEE), in 26 Revue du Marché Commun, 1983, p. 363.
161. See H. Rasmussen, The European Court's Acte Clair Strategy in C.I.L.F.I.T.; Or, Acte Clair, of Course! But What Does It Mean? *op. cit.*
162. See for instance Judgement of 13 April 2000, Lehtonen and Castors Braine (C-176/96, ECR 2000 p. I-2681) ECLI:EU:C:2000:201.
163. See for instance the well-known flamboyant, critical remarks made by Advocate-General Jarabo Colomer in Judgement of 29 November 2001, De Coster (C-17/00, ECR 2001 p. I-9445) ECLI:EU:C:2001:651 (especially at paragraph 14 of the Opinion) about the liberal criterion employed by the Court to assess the judicial independence of the referring authority.
164. See P. Craig, The Jurisdiction of the Community Courts Reconsidered, *op. cit.*, at 565: "The Foglia principle, and the case law based upon it, will only serve to exclude *a limited number of references*" (emphasis added); T. Tridimas, Knocking on Heaven's Door: Fragmentation, Efficiency and Definance in the Preliminary Reference Procedure, in 40 Common Market Law Review, 2003, p. 9, at 22: "Despite fears to the contrary, the ECJ has not used its power to control the admissibility of references as a means of introducing certiorari by the back door", and at 47: "The Court's residual power to control the admissibility of references has been used in a cautious and measured way. This is correct as control of admissibility can be no substitute for the absence if a power of certiorari".
165. See the reconstruction made by T. Tridimas, Knocking on Heaven's Door: Fragmentation, Efficiency and Definance in the Preliminary Reference Procedure, *op. cit.*, at 22, on the period between 1998 and 2001, in which only the following cases were subject: Judgement of

12 March 1998, Djabali/Caisse d'allocations familiales de l'Essonne (C-314/96, ECR 1998 p. I-1149) ECLI:EU:C:1998:104; Order of 30 April 1998, Italia Testa and Modesti (C-128/97 and C-137/97, ECR 1998 p. I-2181) ECLI:EU:C:1998:187; Order of 8 July 1998, Agostini/Ligue francophone de judo et disciplines associées and Ligue belge de judo (C-9/98, ECR 1998 p. I-4261) ECLI:EU:C:1998:339; Order of 28 April 1998, Reisebüro Binder (C-116/96 REV, ECR 1998 p. I-1889) ECLI:EU:C:1998:169; Order of 21 April 1999, Charreire (C-28/98 and C-29/98, ECR 1999 p. I-1963) ECLI:EU:C:1999:188; Order of 11 May 1999, Anssens (C-325/98, ECR 1999 p. I-2969) ECLI:EU:C:1999:244; Order of 2 March 1999, Colonia Versicherung and others (C-422/98, ECR 1999 p. I-1279) ECLI:EU:C:1999:113; Order of 28 June 2000, Laguillaumie (C-116/00, ECR 2000 p. I-4979) ECLI:EU:C:2000:350. In some instances, the Court considered some of the questions referred irrelevant and thus refused to answer them, but accepted others: see Judgement of 13 July 2000, Idéal tourisme (C-36/99, ECR 2000 p. I-6049) ECLI:EU:C:2000:405.

166. N. Komesar, Imperfect Alternatives: Choosing Institutions in Law, Economics, and Public Policy, *op. cit.*; A. Coan, Judicial Capacity and the Substance of Constitutional Law, in 122 Yale Law Journal, 2012, p. 422.
167. A. Coan, Judicial Capacity and the Substance of Constitutional Law, *op. cit.*, at 453.
168. See accordingly N. Komesar, Imperfect Alternatives: Choosing Institutions in Law, Economics, and Public Policy, *op. cit.*, at 147–148, and R.A. Posner, The Federal Courts, *op. cit.*, at 90–91.
169. In the words of A. Coan, Judicial Capacity and the Substance of Constitutional Law, *op. cit.*
170. *Ivi*, at 438.
171. *Ivi*, at 443.
172. Judgement of 24 November 1993, Keck and Mithouard (C-267/91 and C-268/91, ECR 1993 p. I-6097).
173. *Ivi*, at paragraph 16: "By contrast, contrary to what has previously been decided, the application to products from other Member States of national provisions restricting or prohibiting certain selling arrangements is not such as to hinder directly or indirectly, actually or potentially, trade between Member States within the meaning of the Dassonville judgement (Case 8/74 [1974] ECR 837), so long as those provisions apply to all relevant traders operating within the national territory and so long as they affect in the same manner, in law and in fact, the marketing of domestic products and of those from other Member States".
174. See J. Bell, The Role of the European Judges in an Era of Uncertainty, *op. cit.*, at 288.

175. S. Weatherill, After Keck: Some Thoughts on How to Clarify the Clarification, in 33 Common Market Law Review, 1996, p. 885.
176. *Ivi*, at 885–886.
177. See the reflections by C. Ritter, Purely Internal Situations, Reverse Discrimination, Guimont, Dzodzi and Article 234, in 31 European Law Review, 2006, p. 690, at 691.
178. P. Caro de Sousa, Catch Me if You Can? The Market Freedoms' Ever-expanding Outer Limits, in 4 European Journal of Legal Studies, 2011, p. 162.
179. See P. Craig, The Jurisdiction of the Community Courts Reconsidered, *op. cit.*, at 564.
180. *Ibidem*.
181. See e.g. the well known Judgement of 7 February 2002, Weber (C-328/00, ECR 2002 p. I-1461) ECLI:EU:C:2002:91.
182. See J. Bell, The Role of the European Judges in an Era of Uncertainty, *op. cit.*, at 288.
183. See, *inter alia*, originally, Judgement of 15 May 1986, Johnston/Chief Constable of the Royal Ulster Constabulary (222/84, ECR 1986 p. 1651), Judgement of 15 October 1987, Unectef/Heylens (222/86, ECR 1987 p. 4097), Judgement of 3 December 1992, Oleificio Borelli/Commission (C-97/91, ECR 1992 p. I-6313), and, notably, after the formalization of the principle in Article 47 of the Charter of Fundamental Rights of the European Union, the recent Judgement of 22 December 2010, DEB (C-279/09, ECR 2010 p. I-13849) ECLI:EU:C:2010:811.
184. Judgement of 5 March 1996, Brasserie du pêcheur/Bundesrepublik Deutschland and The Queen/Secretary of State for Transport, ex parte Factortame and others (C-46/93 and C-48/93, ECR 1996 p. I-1029) ECLI:EU:C:1996:79.
185. J. Bell, The Role of the European Judges in an Era of Uncertainty, *op. cit.*, at 288; A. Arnull, The European Union and Its Court of Justice, 2nd ed., Oxford 2006, at p. 82 *et seq.*
186. D. Sarmiento, Half Case at a Time. Dealing with Judicial Minimalism at the European Court of Justice, in M. Claes, M. de Visser, P. Popelier, C. van de Heyning (eds.), Constitutional Conversations in Europe. Actors, Topics and Procedures, Intersentia 2012, p. 13, at 19.
187. See e.g. the cases mentioned in Note 123 above.
188. P. Pescatore, L'ordre juridique des communautés européennes. Etude des sources du droit communautaire, Presses universitaires de Liège 1975, at p. 215.
189. G. Davies, Abstractness and Concreteness in the Preliminary Reference Procedure, *op. cit.*

190. D. Sarmiento, Half Case at a Time. Dealing with Judicial Minimalism at the European Court of Justice, *op. cit.*, at 19.
191. *Ibidem.*
192. G.F. Mancini, A Constitution for Europe, in 26 Common Market Law Review, 1989, p. 595, at 606.
193. G.F. Mancini, D.T. Keeling, From CILFIT to ERT: The Constitutional Challenge Facing the European Court, in 11 Yearbook of European Law 1991, p. 1.
194. The image is suggested by G. Davies, Abstractness and Concreteness in the Preliminary Reference Procedure, *op. cit.*, at 233.
195. K. Lenaerts, Form and Substance of the Preliminary Ruling Procedure, *op. cit.*; M. Broberg, N. Fenger, Preliminary References to the European Court of Justice, *op. cit.*, 156 *et seq.*
196. See specifically on this practice U. Sadl, A. Wallerman, 'The Referring Court Asks, in Essence': Is Reformulation of Preliminary Questions by the Court of Justice a Decision Writing Fixture or a Decision-Making Approach?, in 4 European Law Journal, 2019, p. 416.
197. Judgement of 15 July 1964, Costa/E.N.E.L. (6-64, ECR 1964 p. 585), at 592-593.
198. Judgement of 8 February 1990, Staatssecretaris van Financiën/Shipping and Forwarding Enterprise Safe (320/88, ECR 1990 p. I-285), at paragraph 11.
199. H. Rasmussen, Remedying the Crumbling EC Judicial System, in 37 Common Market Law Review, 2000, p. 1071, at 1101. See also on this J.C. Cohen, The European Preliminary Reference and U.S. Supreme Court Review of State Court Judgements: A Study in Comparative Judicial Federalism, in 44 American Journal of Comparative Law, 1996, p. 421, at 429–430; G.F. Mancini, D.T. Keeling, From CILFIT to ERT: The Constitutional Challenge Facing the European Court, *op. cit.*, at 6 *et seq.*
200. To echo the words by G. Morelli, La Corte di Giustizia delle Comunità europee come giudice interno, in 41 Rivista di diritto internazionale, 1958, p. 3.
201. Judgement of 20 February 1979, Rewe/Bundesmonopolverwaltung für Branntwein (120/78, ECR 1979 p. 649).
202. See for instance Judgement of 26 November 1996, Graffione/Ditta Fransa (C-313/94, ECR 1996 p. I-6039) ECLI:EU:C:1996:450, paragraph 25; Judgement of 8 March 2001, Gourmet International Products (C-405/98, ECR 2001 p. I-1795) ECLI:EU:C:2001:135, paragraph 33; Judgement of 5 February 2004, Greenham and Abel (C-95/01, ECR 2004 p. I-1333) ECLI:EU:C:2004:71.
203. For instance Judgement of 16 May 1989, Buet and others/Ministère public (382/87, ECR 1989 p. 1235) ECLI:EU:C:1989:198.

204. For instance Judgement of 6 July 1995, Verein gegen Unwesen in Handel und Gewerbe Köln/Mars (C-470/93, ECR 1995 p. I-1923) ECLI:EU:C:1995:224.
205. For instance Judgement of 2 February 1994, Verband Sozialer Wettbewerb/Clinique Laboratories and Estée Lauder (C-315/92, ECR 1994 p. I-317) (SVXV/I-13 FIXV/I-13) ECLI:EU:C:1994:34.
206. See for instance Judgement of 16 December 1992, Council of the City of Stoke-on-Trent and Norwich City Council/B & Q Plc (C-169/91, ECR 1992 p. I-6635) (SVXIII/I-227 FIXIII/I-239) ECLI:EU:C:1992:519; Judgement of 28 February 1991, Marchandise and others (C-332/89, ECR 1991 p. I-1027) (SVXI/I-87 FIXI/I-99) ECLI:EU:C:1991:94; Judgement of 28 February 1991, Union départementale des syndicats CGT de l'Aisne/Conforama and others (C-312/89, ECR 1991 p. I-997) ECLI:EU:C:1991:93.
207. Judgement of 23 November 1989, Torfaen Borough Council/B & Q PLC (145/88, ECR 1989 p. 3851).
208. See N. Reich, The "November Revolution" of the European Court of Justice: Keck, Meng and Audi Revisited, in 31 Common Market Law Review, 1994, p. 459; S. Weatherill, After Keck: Some Thoughts on How to Clarify the Clarification, *op. cit.*
209. See Judgement of 15 December 1993, Hünermund and others/Landesapothekerkammer Baden-Württemberg (C-292/92, ECR 1993 p. I-6787) (SVXIV/I-467 FIXIV/I-515) ECLI:EU:C:1993:932; Judgement of 29 June 1995, Commission/Greece (C-391/92, ECR 1995 p. I-1621) ECLI:EU:C:1995:199; Judgement of 2 June 1994, Punto Casa and PPV (C-69/93 and C-258/93, ECR 1994 p. I-2355) ECLI:EU:C:1994:226; Judgement of 20 June 1996, Semeraro Casa Uno and others/Sindaco del Comune di Erbusco and others (C-418/93, C-419/93, C-420/93, C-421/93, C-460/93, C-461/93, C-462/93, C-464/93, C-9/94, C-10/94, C-11/94, C-14/94, C-15/94, C-23/94, C-24/94 and C-332/94., ECR 1996 p. I-2975) ECLI:EU:C:1996:242; Judgement of 23 October 1997, Franzén (C-189/95, ECR 1997 p. I-5909) ECLI:EU:C:1997:504; Judgement of 9 July 1997, Konsumentombudsmannen/De Agostini and TV-Shop (C-34/95, C-35/95 and C-36/95, ECR 1997 p. I-3843) ECLI:EU:C:1997:344.
210. See for instance Judgement of 14 January 1981, Chemial Farmaceutici (140/79, ECR 1981 p. 1); Judgement of 15 July 1982, Cogis (216/81, ECR 1982 p. 2701) ECLI:EU:C:1982:275; Judgement of 9 May 1985, Humblot/Directeur des services fiscaux (112/84, ECR 1985 p. 1367); Judgement of 4 March 1986, Walker/Ministeriet for Skatter og Afgifter (243/84, ECR 1986 p. 875) ECLI:EU:C:1986:100; Judgement of 17 September 1987, Feldain/Services fiscaux du département du

Haut-Rhin (433/85, ECR 1987 p. 3521); Judgement of 7 May 1987, Co-Frutta/Amministrazione delle finanze dello Stato (193/85, ECR 1987 p. 2085).

211. See H. G. Schermers, D. F. Waelbroeck (eds.), Judicial Protection in the European Union, *op. cit.*, at 238–239.
212. See for instance Judgement of 20 November 1997, Wiener/Hauptzollamt Emmerich (C-338/95, ECR 1997 p. I-6495) ECLI:EU:C:1997:552; Judgement of 7 February 2002, Turbon International (C-276/00, ECR 2002 p. I-1389) ECLI:EU:C:2002:88; Judgement of 7 March 2002, Biochem (C-259/00, ECR 2002 p. I-2461) ECLI:EU:C:2002:150.
213. J. Bell, The Role of the European Judges in an Era of Uncertainty, *op. cit.*, at 285; G. Davies, Abstractness and Concreteness in the Preliminary Reference Procedure, *op. cit.*, at 229.
214. G. Davies, Abstractness and Concreteness in the Preliminary Reference Procedure, *op. cit.*, at 229.
215. D. Sarmiento, Half Case at a Time. Dealing with Judicial Minimalism at the European Court of Justice, *op. cit.*
216. See for such reflections C.R. Sunstein, Legal Reasoning and Political Conflict, Oxford University Press 1996, and *Id.*, One Case at a Time: Judicial Minimalism on the Supreme Court, Harvard University Press 1999.
217. Judgement of 15 July 2010, Purrucker (C-256/09, ECR 2010 p. I-7353) ECLI:EU:C:2010:437.
218. Judgement of 29 April 2004, Faxworld (C-137/02, ECR 2004 p. I-5547) ECLI:EU:C:2004:267; Judgement of 7 December 2010, R. (C-285/09, ECR 2010 p. I-12605) ECLI:EU:C:2010:742; Judgement of 16 December 2010, Euro Tyre Holding (C-430/09, ECR 2010 p. I-13335) ECLI:EU:C:2010:786; Judgement of 22 December 2010, Sayn-Wittgenstein (C-208/09, ECR 2010 p. I-13693) ECLI:EU:C:2010:806.
219. Judgement of 23 November 2010, Tsakouridis (C-145/09, ECR 2010 p. I-11979) ECLI:EU:C:2010:708.
220. Judgement of 22 June 1989, Fratelli Costanzo/Comune di Milano (103/88, ECR 1989 p. 1839).
221. Judgement of 16 June 2005, Pupino (C-105/03, ECR 2005 p. I-5285) ECLI:EU:C:2005:386.
222. Judgement of 8 March 2011, Ruiz Zambrano (C-34/09, ECR 2011 p. I-1177) ECLI:EU:C:2011:124.
223. For a "bibliographic" evidence of such a fundamental nature see again Note 110 in Chapter 2.
224. A.M. Burley, W. Mattli, Europe Before the Court: A Political Theory of Legal Integration, *op. cit.*, at 45–46.

225. J.H.H. Weiler, The Constitution of Europe: 'Do the New Clothes Have an Emperor?', Cambridge University Press 1999, at 33 and 195 in particular.
226. J.H.H. Weiler, Journey to an Unknown Destination. A Retrospective and Prospective of the European Court of Justice in the Arena of Political Integration, *op. cit.*, at 424.
227. *Ibidem.*
228. A.M. Burley, W. Mattli, Europe Before the Court: A Political Theory of Legal Integration, *op. cit.*, at 45–46.
229. J.H.H. Weiler, Journey to an Unknown Destination. A Retrospective and Prospective of the European Court of Justice in the Arena of Political Integration, *op. cit.*, at 425; see also K. Alter, Establishing the Supremacy of European Law: The Making of an International Rule of Law in Europe, *op. cit.*, at 47; see M. Ovàdek, W. Wijtvliet, M. Glavina, Which Courts Matter Most? Measuring Importance in the EU Preliminary Reference System, in 12 European Journal of Legal Studies, 2020, for new empirical analysis on the point.
230. A. Arnull, Judicial Dialogue in the European Union, *op. cit.*, at 121. See on this sociological aspects also the organic works cited in Note 29 above.
231. See for a recent explicitation of this by a renowned academician and practictioner in the field S. Prechal, National Courts in EU Judicial Structures, *op. cit.*, at 432–433 in particular. See also, accordingly, A.W.H. Meij, Guest Editorial: Architects or Judges? Some Comments in Relation to the Current Debate, in 37 Common Market Law Review, 2000, p. 1039, at 1044–1045, J. Baquero Cruz, La procédure préjudicielle suffit-il à garantir l'efficacité et l'uniformité du droit de l'Union Européenne?, in L. Azoulai, L. Burgorgue-Larsen, *op. cit.*, p. 241, and the remarks in the Report by the Working Party on the Future of the European Communities' Court System for the European Commission, January 2000 (Ole Due Report), at 12 *et seq.*
232. M. Broberg, N. Fenger, Variations in Member States' Preliminary References to the Court of Justice—Are Structural Factors (Part of) the Explanation?, in 19 European Law Journal, 2013, p. 488.
233. In the words of M. Bobek, Of Feasibility and Silent Elephants: the Legitimacy of the Court of Justice through the Eyes of National Courts, *op. cit.*, at 212.
234. A. Arnull, Judicial Dialogue in the European Union, *op. cit.*, at 123; M. Broberg, N. Fenger, Preliminary References to the European Court of Justice, *op. cit.*, chapter 2.
235. M. Bobek, Of Feasibility and Silent Elephants: The Legitimacy of the Court of Justice through the Eyes of National Courts, *op. cit.*, at 209–210.

236. Notoriously, the former French European Commission President, speaking to the European Parliament in July 1988, soon after the enactment of the Single European Act, predicted that in ten years time the European Community would be the source of 80% of our economic legislation and perhaps even our fiscal and social legislation as well. The claim is sometimes considered as a "factoid in discussions of the EU", in the words of P.L. Lindseth, Power and Legitimacy: Reconciling Europe and the Nation-State, *op. cit.*, at 45, and, though not based on scientific data or methods, has gained momentum in the political debates since then. Several authors consider it as a reliable esteem: see e.g. S. Hix, The Political System of the European Union, Palgrave 1999, at 3. See, from a legal perspective useful for our arguments, M. Bobek, Of Feasibility and Silent Elephants: The Legitimacy of the Court of Justice through the Eyes of National Courts, *op. cit.*, at 210, with reference to A. Töller, Mythen und Methoden. Zur Messung der Europäisierung der Gesetzgebung des Deutschen Bundestages jenseits des 80-Prozent-Mythos, in 1 Zeitschrift für Parlamentsfragen, 2008, p. 3; T. Hoppe, Die Europäisierung der Gesetzgebung: Der 80-Prozent-Mythos lebt, in 6 Europäische Zeitschrift für Wirtschaftsrecht, 2009, p. 168; Y. Bertoncini, What Is the Impact of the EU Interventions at the National Level?, in Notre Europe—Jacques Delors Institute, Studies & Reports n° 73 May 2009.
237. M. Bobek, Of Feasibility and Silent Elephants: The Legitimacy of the Court of Justice through the Eyes of National Courts, *op. cit.*, at 210–211.
238. See the Annual Report of the CJEU for 2018, available at the website https://curia.europa.eu/jcms/upload/docs/application/pdf/2019-04/_ra_2018_en.pdf (accessed 2 March 2020), at p. 123 *et seq.*
239. See again S. Prechal, National Courts in EU Judicial Structures, *op. cit.*, at 432–433.
240. See the relative numbers in this respect given by the Annual Report of the CJEU for 2014, available at the website http://curia.europa.eu/jcms/upload/docs/application/pdf/2015-04/en_ecj_annual_report_2014_pr1.pdf (accessed 2 March 2020), at p. 102 *et seq.*
241. See again J.H.H., A Quiet Revolution: The European Court of Justice and Its Interlocutors, *op. cit.*, at 518 *et seq.* in particular.
242. Judgement of 30 September 2003, Köbler (C-224/01, ECR 2003 p. I-10239) ECLI:EU:C:2003:513.
243. M. Broberg, N. Fenger, Preliminary References to the European Court of Justice, *op. cit.*, at 35.
244. See M. Wind, D.S. Martinsen, G.P.Rotger, The Uneven Legal Push for Europe. Questioning Variation When National Courts Go to Europe, in 10 European Union Politics, 2009, p. 63, at 66.

245. *Ibidem.*
246. M. Broberg, N. Fenger, Variations in Member States' Preliminary References to the Court of Justice—Are Structural Factors (Part of) the Explanation?, *op. cit.* at 499 *et seq.*
247. A. Stone Sweet, T. Brunell, The European Court and the National Courts: A Statistical Analysis of Preliminary References, 1961–95, in 5 Journal of European Public Policy, 1998, p. 66.
248. M. Broberg, N. Fenger, Preliminary References to the European Court of Justice, *op. cit.*, at 40, with a reference to J. Blank, M. van der Ende, B. van Hulst, R Jagtenberg, Bench Marking in an International Perspective. An International Comparison of the Mechanisms and Performance of the Judiciary System, studied commissioned by The Netherlands Council for the Judiciary, available at the website http://siteresources.worldbank.org/INTLAWJUSTINST/Resources/Benchmarking.pdf (accessed 2 March 2020).
249. See M. Vink, M. Claes, C. Arnold, Explaining the Use of Preliminary References by Domestic Courts in EU Member States: A Mixed-Method Comparative Analysis, paper presented at the 11th Biennial Conference of the European Union Studies Association, Marina del Rey 24 April 2009, available at the website http://aei.pitt.edu/33155/1/vink._maarten.pdf (accessed 2 March 2020).
250. M. Broberg, N. Fenger, Variations in Member States' Preliminary References to the Court of Justice—Are Structural Factors (Part of) the Explanation?, *op. cit.*, at 497–498.
251. M. Broberg, N. Fenger, Preliminary References to the European Court of Justice, *op. cit.*, at 49.
252. See M. Wind, D.S. Martinsen, G.P.Rotger, The Uneven Legal Push for Europe. Questioning Variation When National Courts Go to Europe, *op.cit.*; M. Wind, The Nordics, the EU and the Reluctance towards Supranational Judicial Review, in 48 Journal of Common Market Studies, 2010, p. 1048; and M. Wind, D.S. Martinsen, When National Courts Go to Europe, in H. Koch, K. Hagel-Sørensen, U. Haltern, J.H.H. Weiler (eds.), Europe. The New Legal Realism—Essays in Honour of Hjalte Rasmussen, *op. cit.*, p. 479.
253. See M. Wind, D.S. Martinsen, G.P. Rotger, The Uneven Legal Push for Europe. Questioning Variation When National Courts Go to Europe, *op.cit.*, at 72.
254. J.H.H. Weiler, Deciphering the Political and Legal DNA of European Integration: an Explanatory Essay, in J. Dickson, P. Eleftheriadis (eds.), Philosophical Foundations of EU Law, *op. cit.*, p. 137, at 155.
255. See M. Wind, D.S. Martinsen, G.P.Rotger, The Uneven Legal Push for Europe. Questioning Variation When National Courts Go to Europe, *op. cit.*, at 72; see also T. Tridimas, Knocking on Heaven's Door:

Fragmentation, Efficiency and Definance in the Preliminary Reference Procedure, *op. cit.*, at 37–38.

256. See, with a view at the relationship with European affairs, D. Chalmers, The Positioning of EU Judicial Politics within the United Kingdom, in K.H. Goetz, S. Hix (eds.), Europeanised Politics. European Integration and National Political Systems, Frank Cass Publishers 2001, p. 169.
257. J. Nergelius, North and South: Can the Nordic States and the European Continent Find Each Other in the Constitutional Area—Or Are They Too Different?, in M. Scheinin (ed.), The Welfare State and Constitutionalism in the Nordic Countries, Nordic Council of Ministers 2001, p. 79.
258. *Ivi*, at 85.
259. See J. Golub, The Politics of Judicial Discretion: Rethinking the Interaction between National Courts and the European Court of Justice, in 19 West European Politics, 1996, p. 360; G. Tridimas, T. Tridimas, National Courts and the European Court of Justice: a Public Choice Analysis of the Preliminary Reference Procedure, in 24 International Review of Law and Economics, 2004, p. 125. See specifically K. Alter, J. Vargas, Explaining Variation in the Use of European Litigation Strategies: European Community Law and British Gender Equality Policy, in K. Alter, The European Court's Political Power, *op. cit.*, p. 159, at 180.
260. As per the theories of K. Alter, Explaining National Court Acceptance of European Court Jurisprudence: A Critical Evaluation of Theories of Legal Integration, in A. Slaughter, A. Stone Sweet, J.H.H. Weiler (eds.), The European Courts and National Courts—Doctrine and Jurisprudence: Legal Challenge in Its Social Context, *op. cit.*, p. 227, and W. Mattli, A.M. Slaughter, Revisiting the European Court of Justice, in 52 International Organisation, 1998, p. 177.
261. See e.g. the provisions of Article 102 of the Italian Constitution.
262. T. de la Mare, Article 177 in Social and Political Context, in P. Craig, G. de Bùrca (eds.), The Evolution of EU Law, 1st ed., *op. cit.*, p. 215, at 234.
263. All these aspects are critically discussed by M. Bobek, Of Feasibility and Silent Elephants: The Legitimacy of the Court of Justice through the Eyes of National Courts, *op. cit.*, at 210 *et seq.*
264. G. Davies, Abstractness and Concreteness in the Preliminary Reference Procedure, *op. cit.*, at 233 *et seq.* See also L.N. Brown, T. Kennedy, The Court of Justice of the European Communities, *op. cit.*, at 368 *et seq.*
265. See the general reflections by J.H. Merryman, The Civil Law Tradition, *op. cit.*, at 34 *et seq.*; R.C. van Caenegem, Judges, Legislators and Professors: Chapters in European Legal History, *op. cit.*, at 113 *et seq.*
266. G. Davies, Abstractness and Concreteness in the Preliminary Reference Procedure, *op. cit.*, at 235.

267. R.C. van Caenegem, Judges, Legislators and Professors: Chapters in European Legal History, *op. cit.*, at 127 *et seq.*
268. G. Davies, Abstractness and Concreteness in the Preliminary Reference Procedure, *op. cit.*, at 234; J.C. Cohen, The European Preliminary Reference and U.S. Supreme Court Review of State Court Judgements: A Study in Comparative Judicial Federalism, *op. cit.*, at 439 *et seq.* Cfr. with the various opinions of A. Toth, The Authority of Judgements of the European Court of Justice: Binding Force and Legal Effects, in 4 Yearbook of European Law, 1984, p. 1; F. Capotorti, Le sentenze della Corte di Giustizia delle Comunità Europee, in Vv.Aa. (eds.), La sentenza in Europa. Metodo, tecnica e stile, CEDAM 1988, p. 230; C. Nourissat, La jurisprudence de la Cour de justice des Communautés européennes: Un regard privatiste à partir de l'actualité, in Vv.Aa. (eds.), La création du droit par le juge, Dalloz 2006, p. 247.
269. G. Davies, Abstractness and Concreteness in the Preliminary Reference Procedure, *op. cit.*, at 236.
270. Judgement of 13 December 2005, Marks & Spencer (C-446/03, ECR 2005 p. I-10837) ECLI:EU:C:2005:763.
271. Judgement of 13 December 2005, SEVIC Systems (C-411/03, ECR 2005 p. I-10805) ECLI:EU:C:2005:762.
272. See the notice for the Official Journal available at the website http://curia.europa.eu/juris/document/document.jsf?text=&docid=50524&pageIndex=0&doclang=en&mode=lst&dir=&occ=first&part=1&cid=344217 (accessed 2 March 2020).
273. See the notice for the Official Journal available at the website http://curia.europa.eu/juris/document/document.jsf?text=&docid=52706&pageIndex=0&doclang=en&mode=lst&dir=&occ=first&part=1&cid=344351 (accessed 2 March 2020).
274. Judgement of 17 February 2011, The Number (UK) and Conduit Enterprises (C-16/10, ECR 2011 p. I-691) ECLI:EU:C:2011:92.
275. Judgement of 17 February 2011, Berel and others (C-78/10, ECR 2011 p. I-717) ECLI:EU:C:2011:93.
276. Judgement of 5 May 2011, Deutsche Telekom (C-543/09, ECR 2011 p. I-3441) ECLI:EU:C:2011:279.
277. See the notice for the Official Journal available at the website http://curia.europa.eu/juris/document/document.jsf?text=&docid=75430&pageIndex=0&doclang=en&mode=lst&dir=&occ=first&part=1&cid=344351 (accessed 2 March 2020).
278. See the notice for the Official Journal available at the website http://curia.europa.eu/juris/document/document.jsf?docid=82352&doclang=en&mode=&part=1 (accessed 2 March 2020).
279. See the notice for the Official Journal available at the website http://curia.europa.eu/juris/document/document.jsf;jsessionid=9ea7d2dc3

0ddd04f29bdeb794c4b90aada7affe91fcf.e34KaxiLc3qMb40Rch0SaxqTbhn0?text=&docid=79881&pageIndex=0&doclang=EN&mode=lst&dir=&occ=first&part=1&cid=1829 (accessed 2 March 2020).

280. S. Prechal, National Courts in EU Judicial Structures, *op. cit.*, at 432–433.
281. G.F. Mancini, D.T. Keeling, From CILFIT to ERT: The Constitutional Challenge Facing the European Court, *op. cit.*, at 1, then published also in G.F. Mancini, Democracy and Constitutionalism in the European Union. Collected Essays, Hart Publishing 2000, p. 17.
282. See again the first use of the phrase made by T. Koopmans, La procédure préjudicielle - victime de son succès? *op. cit.*
283. G.F. Mancini, D.T. Keeling, From CILFIT to ERT: The Constitutional Challenge Facing the European Court, *op. cit.*, at 1, and G.F. Mancini, Democracy and Constitutionalism in the European Union. Collected Essays, *op. cit.*, at 17.
284. G.F. Mancini, D.T. Keeling, From CILFIT to ERT: The Constitutional Challenge Facing the European Court, *op. cit.*, at. 6.
285. *Ibidem.*
286. *Ibidem.*
287. See the well known exchange between G.F. Mancini, Europe: The Case for Statehood, in 4 European Law Journal, 1998, p. 29 and J.H.H. Weiler, Europe: The Case Against the Case for Statehood, in 4 European Law Journal, 1998, p. 43.
288. Interesting empirical analysis has been recently provided by J.A. Mayoral, In the CJEU Judges Trust: A New Approach in the Judicial Construction of Europe, in 55 Journal of Common Market Studies, 2017, p. 551, T. Pavone, Revisiting Judicial Empowerment in the European Union: Limits of Empowerment, Logics of Resistance, in 6 Journal of Law and Courts, 2018, p. 303, and T. Pavone, R.D. Kelemen, The Evolving Judicial Politics of European Integration: The European Court of Justice and national courts revisited, in 25 European Law Journal, 2019, p. 352.
289. Council Decision of 24 October 1988 establishing a Court of First Instance of the European Communities.
290. See e.g. the clear words in the aftermath of the creation by G. Slynn, Court of First Instance of the European Communities, in 9 Northwestern Journal of International Law & Business, 1989, p. 542, and G. Vandersanden, A Desired Birth: The Court of First Instance of the European Communities, in 21 Georgia Journal of International and Comparative Law, 1991, p. 51.
291. See the recent Report on "The Workload of the Court of Justice of the European Union" issued by European Union Committee of the UK House of Lords, available at the website http://www.publications.

parliament.uk/pa/ld201011/ldselect/ldeucom/128/128.pdf (accessed 2 March 2020), at 18 *et seq*.

292. See for a first comment C. Curti Gialdino, Il raddoppio dei giudici del Tribunale dell'Unione: valutazioni di merito e di legittimità costituzionale europea, in 8 Federalismi.it. Rivista di diritto pubblico, comparato, europeo, 2015, available at the website http://www.federalismi.it/ApplOpenFilePDF.cfm?artid=29318&dpath=document&dfile=27042015190643.pdf&content=Il+raddoppio+dei+giudici+del+Tribunale+dell%E2%80%99Unione:+valutazioni+di+merito+e+di+legittimit%C3%A0+costituzionale+europea++-+unione+europea+-+dottrina+-+ (accessed 2 March 2020).
293. A. Alemanno, L. Pech, Thinking Justice Outside the Docket: A Critical Assessment of the Reform of the EU's Court System, *op. cit.*, with reference to European Parliament resolution of 29 April 2015 with observations forming an integral part of the decision on discharge in respect of the implementation of the general budget of the European Union for the financial year 2013, Section IV—Court of Justice (2014/2080(DEC)), para. 11.
294. See the 2004/752/EC, Euratom: Council Decision of 2 November 2004 establishing the European Union Civil Service Tribunal.
295. Notably, also by members of the Court: see e.g. P.J.G. Kapteyn, The Court of Justice of the European Communities after the year 2000, in D. Curtin, T. Heukels (eds.), Institutional Dynamics of European Integration, *op. cit.*, p. 135.
296. And in some Regulations such as Regulation 40/94/EC on the Community Trade Mark or Regulation 2100/94/EC on the Community Plant Variety Rights, both envisaging the creation of special Bords of appeals.
297. An option already envisaged by Article 256(3) of the TFEU, still not applied, and often discussed in the literature: for a summary, see K. Lenaerts, The Future Organisation of European Courts, in P. Demaret, I. Govaere, D. Hanf (eds.), European Legal Dynamics—30 Years of European Legal Studies at the College of Europe, Peter Lang 2007, p. 129, in particular at 144 *et seq*.
298. See the its Report submitted pursuant to Article 3(2) of Regulation (EU, Euratom) 2015/2422 of the European Parliament and of the Council of 16 December 2015 amending Protocol No 3 on the Statute of the Court of Justice of the European Union, available at the website https://curia.europa.eu/jcms/upload/docs/application/pdf/2018-01/en_2018-01-12_08-43-52_183.pdf.
299. For recent reflections on this see M. Malecki, Do ECJ Judges All Speak with the Same Voice?, *op. cit.*, and D. Kelemen, Selection, Appointment,

and Legitimacy: A Political Perspective, in M. Bobek (ed.), Selecting Europe's Judges, *op. cit.*, p. 244, at 254.

300. See 2012/671/EU: Decision of the Court of Justice of 23 October 2012 concerning the judicial functions of the Vice-President of the Court.
301. Article 76(2): "2. On a proposal from the Judge-Rapporteur and after hearing the Advocate General, the Court may decide not to hold a hearing if it considers, on reading the written pleadings or observations lodged during the written part of the procedure, that it has sufficient information to give a ruling" .
302. According to Article 99, this can happen "at any time, on a proposal from the Judge Rapporteur and after hearing the Advocate General" .
303. Article 105(1): "1. At the request of the referring court or tribunal or, exceptionally, of his own motion, the President of the Court may, where the nature of the case requires that it be dealt with within a short time, after hearing the Judge-Rapporteur and the Advocate General, decide that a reference for a preliminary ruling is to be determined pursuant to an expedited procedure derogating from the provisions of these Rules".
304. Article 107(1): "1. A reference for a preliminary ruling which raises one or more questions in the areas covered by Title V of Part Three of the Treaty on the Functioning of the European Union may, at the request of the referring court or tribunal or, exceptionally, of the Court's own motion, be dealt with under an urgent procedure derogating from the provisions of these Rules".
305. Article 53(3): "3. The President may in special circumstances decide that a case be given priority over others". See also the specular Article 56, on the "Deferment of the determination of a case": "After hearing the Judge-Rapporteur, the Advocate General and the parties, the President may in special circumstances, either of his own motion or at the request of one of the parties, defer a case to be dealt with at a later date".
306. See the authoritative remarks by K. Lenaerts, The Rule of Law and the Coherence of the Judicial System of the European Union, *op. cit.*, and M. Broberg, N. Fenger, Preliminary References to the European Court of Justice, *op. cit.*, at 396 *et seq.*
307. Just as an example, see the Foreword by the then President of the Court of Justice Vassilios Skouris at p. 5 of the Report for 2014, available at the website http://curia.europa.eu/jcms/upload/docs/application/pdf/2015-04/en_ecj_annual_report_2014_pr1.pdf (accessed 2 March 2020): "A new record was achieved in 2014 with a total of 1 691 cases brought before the three courts, that is to say, the highest number since the judicial system of the European Union was created. On the other hand, as 1 685 cases were completed, the institution's productivity

was likewise the highest recorded in its history. *This increased productivity also had its counterpart in the duration of proceedings, which was reduced*" (emphasis added).

308. J.P. Jacqué, J.H.H. Weiler, On the Road to European Union—A New Judicial Architecture: An Agenda for the Intergovernmental Conference, *op. cit*.
309. M. Broberg, N. Fenger, Preliminary References to the European Court of Justice, *op. cit*., at 28 *et seq*.
310. See already the Recommendations to national courts and tribunals in relation to the initiation of preliminary ruling proceedings (2012/C 338/01), available at the website http://eur-lex.europa.eu/legal-content/EN/TXT/PDF/?uri=CELEX:32012H1106(01)&from=EN, (accessed 2 March 2020) at paragraph 13: "13. Thus, a national court or tribunal may, in particular when it considers that sufficient guidance is given by the case-law of the Court of Justice, itself decide on the correct interpretation of European Union law and its application to the factual situation before it. However, a reference for a preliminary ruling may prove particularly useful when there is a new question of interpretation of general interest for the uniform application of European Union law, or where the existing case-law does not appear to be applicable to a new set of facts".
311. C. Timmermans, The European Union's Judicial System, *op. cit*., at 405.
312. Commission Opinion on the draft amendments to Protocol No 3 on the Statute of the Court of Justice of the European Union, presented by the Court of Justice on 26 March 2018—COM/2018/534 final.
313. See for some early reflections M. Condinanzi, Corte di giustizia e Tribunale dell'Unione europea: storia e prospettive di una "tribolata" ripartizione di competenze, in 3 Federalismi.it, 2018.
314. Regulation (EU, Euratom) 2019/629 of the European Parliament and of the Council of 17 April 2019 amending Protocol No 3 on the Statute of the Court of Justice of the European Union—PE/1/2019/REV/1 - OJ L 111, 25.4.2019, pp. 1–3, Article 2 in particular.
315. P. Allott, Preliminary Rulings: Another Infant Disease, in 25 European Law Review, 2000, p. 538, at 542, obviously with a provocative reference to the historical definition by P. Pescatore, The Doctrine of "Direct Effect": An Infant Disease of Community Law, in 8 European Law Review, 1983, p. 155; see also in this respect, recently, J. Baquero Cruz, La procédure préjudicielle suffit-il à garantir l'efficacité et l'uniformité du droit de l'Union Européenne?, *op. cit*.; J. Komarek, In the Court(s) We Trust? On the Need for Hierarchy and Differentiation in the Preliminary Ruling Procedure, in 32 European Law Review, 2007, p. 467.

CHAPTER 6

The Style of Court Decisions

In the final chapter of this work, I will focus on the style of the Court of Justice's decisions by looking at them in their specific nature of products and indicators of the judicial body's institutional setting. Similar to other chapters, I will also try to demonstrate how by looking at this last specific aspect of the Court's activity, at the judgements as its direct output, one can notice a diachronic influence played by the diverse environment of the European Union as well as by the interplay of its different legal cultures. As usual, I will also look at how this development was directly linked to the matter of the Court's authority, and at its strengthening.

In what sense can the style of the judgements be intended as a product and an indicator of the Court's institutional setting? One is tempted to look at the classic debates according to which judges are defined, also in modern settings, as "oracles of law".[1] In both historical experiences and modern usage and attitudes, they have been considered as ultimate depositaries of the law and its interpretation[2]; consequently, their activities and their decisions have always been carefully inspected and investigated as authoritative explanations and justification for the correct application of the law. Such investigation has been directed, with great efforts made by learned specialists of the law of any era,[3] to the substantial activity of interpretation made by judges in all the different areas of law and of their institutions, as well as to the argumentative tools thereby employed,

L. Pierdominici, *The Mimetic Evolution of the Court of Justice of the EU*, https://doi.org/10.1007/978-3-030-47864-3_6

with special characteristics in the different areas. But the same investigation has also been directed towards the judges' decisions per se, towards their style, their form, their discourse, their rhetoric. This study has never been considered secondary by scholars: on the contrary, its relevance has often been emphasized as a way to comprehensively understand the legal practice and the judicial role in a particularly given setting. It has been said that the judicial decisions' "form, discourse, and rhetoric combine to make implicit assertions about the process that produced the decisions. Judicial decisions, and judicial arguments generally, are therefore texts that offer representations of judicial practice and of the judicial role. These representations may be thought of as portraits: they are images of judging. Insofar as these portraits are produced by judges in judicial texts, they may be termed judicial self-portraits".[4]

6.1 The Style of the Court's Decisions Within the "Fabrication" Process of EU Law

The same idea of a "process" producing decisions—described by judicial forms, discourses and rhetoric combined—is reminiscent of those sociological, "ethnographic" theories that look at the judicial bodies as veritable "*fabriques du droit*".[5] This approach is explicitly aimed, by its adopters, at appreciating the importance of the textual materiality of law and understanding the channels through which such materiality is built and transported. As will be seen throughout the chapter, such industrialist metaphor can be particularly apt for my purposes since the same idea of a "fabrication" of European law—as it has been already suggested[6]—can lead to relevant reflections on the influences the Court can face and internalize in its material output. So, while recognizing that an analysis of the peculiar aspects of the Court's modalities of substantive interpretation of EU law, though interesting and remarkable also in terms of its evolution, is outside the reach of this study, I will embark on a stylistic analysis of its decisions, precisely intended as "judicial self-portraits" made by the Court and as the form of its external interaction. This will constitute the last chapter of my diachronic, comparative analysis of its institutional evolution, as the tentative appraisal—after an investigation of all the logically antecedent aspects in the structuring and the organization of the Court—of the characteristics of its ultimate "product": the judgement, in its morphological elements.

The comparative law literature has previously clarified what is relevant to study when taking the "style of the judicial decisions"[7] into account. This phrase is said to refer to a series of "morphological" elements, such as the syntactic structure, the language used by the courts, whether and how the facts of the case are presented, how issues to be decided are treated, the possible use of theoretical digressions or divagation, the reference to previous cases. The comprehension of all these elements is presented as a prerequisite for the understanding of the judgement itself; and it is also relevant to assess whether and to what extent the judgement can assume, according to these elements, the form of a veritable "precedent". In this definition, one can also see how the substantive/argumentative tools of judges' legal reasoning are considered as external elements to the concept of style of judicial decisions—or better, they are conceivable as independent elements which can be used and declined in all the possible formal styles with no decisive impact both from and on the machinery of the institution.

Focusing on the CJ, I already referred to the common accusation pertaining to the excessively concise, laconic nature of its judgements. According to the common doctrinal understanding, they would not merely, formally amount to a frequently invoked (and reproached) "cryptic, Cartesian style",[8] but they would, very much in practice, give serious problems of clarity and intelligibility, with a "pretense of logical reasoning and inevitability of results"[9] which is not beneficial for an envisioned "dialogue" with the other EU institutions, the national courts, a broader public. In Weiler's blunt words, the style of the Court's decisions would be "outmoded, does not reflect the dialogical nature of European Constitutionalism, and is not a basis for confidence-building European constitutional relations between the European Court and its national constitutional counterparts".[10] The problems of transparency and openness of the Court would thus not be confined to the limited possibility of access to information about its deliberations in the course of action, as discussed previously. They would result, even more relevantly and critically, in the final products and final output issued by the judges, affecting the institution's overall activity and, even more importantly, its inter-institutional relationships.

This result would be problematic for any judicial body per se. The quality of their decisions represents the first vector of legitimacy and authoritativeness for courts[11] since it is the inherent power of persuasion of their judgements that entitles courts to expect acceptance by those affected by the decisions. Reliance on the power of persuasion is particularly important in contexts such as the European Union legal order in which the means for enforcing judgements are limited and in which compliance with them ultimately depends on the recognition by all concerned that the common interest requires respect for the relative *dicta*.[12] Nonetheless, I also already referred to the opinions of who has depicted a certain formalism in the ECJ's judgements as a positive feature, at least in the glorious early years of the structuring of the EU legal order, when they nurtured the habit of obedience of other players and national courts in particular.[13]

In analytically examining all of this, this last chapter will try to investigate, from my usual perspective, the real and determinant factors of such denounced laconism and lack of explicitness. In particular, I will first explore the asserted determinant cultural factors in the shaping and the development of the style of the Court. I will then examine other factors of complication due to the specific machinery of the Court and shaped again by the peculiarity of the EU legal order and its plurality. I will then conclude by trying to understand, in an evolutive dimension, whether and why the situation has changed, is changing or is likely to change in the future. In all these, the relevance of the comparative element and the link to the strengthening of the Court's authority will be evident and emphasized.

6.2 The Style of the Court's Decisions as Culturally Shaped

The French model was not only preponderant in the structuring of the competences and the powers of the Court, as seen in detail in the first part of this study. As everybody knows, the importance of French culture in the XIX and the first half of the XX century was measured first and foremost in terms of radiation of the French legal forms in continental Europe (as well as in northern Africa and some specific areas of America), and from the French language being the recognized *lingua franca* of diplomacy and generally of learned layers of society during that whole period.[14] Therefore, it is not surprising that both the negotiations leading up to the Treaty establishing the European Coal and Steel Community and subsequent ones that resulted in the Treaty establishing the European Economic Community were conducted in French[15]; that the first ECSC Treaty contained an Article 100 stating that it was concluded and therefore only original in French; that on that basis the French delegates argued that since the Treaty was concluded in French, the judgements of the Court of Justice and the application rules should only be made public in French. Already at that early stage, the opposition of German delegates was the first step towards the multilingual nature of EU law. A compromise was found on the ECSC Treaty in declaring it as only authentic in French but in publishing official translations of all three languages[16]. The principle of equal value of all official languages of the European Communities (four, at the time) was then fully applied with the EEC Treaty (equally authentic in all of those) and with Regulation 1/58, which "determined" the authentic working languages "to be used by the European Economic Community".[17] As per specifically the Court of Justice, an apposite conference of the six original founding states of the European Coal and Steel Community in 1952[18] treated the question, and decided (for obvious reasons on fair accessibility to justice) the principle of plurilinguism of the proceedings of the Court[19]: a principle that is still in place today with twenty-four and not just four official idioms.[20]

Nevertheless, the internal working language of the Court to be used in the deliberation room and the drafting of judgements became French, as the quite obvious *lingua franca* among high-level lawyers and functionaries of the mid-XX century. As written by former Advocate General Francis Jacobs some years ago—echoing a series of famous witticisms by Oscar Wilde, George Bernard Shaw and Winston Churchill—"unlike the English and the Americans, who are divided by a common language, language differences in Europe do not prevent a common way of thinking"[21]: and surely the idea of a common way of thinking was also behind the choice of French, which was not only the more natural working language for a group of continental lawyers to facilitate internal communications, but also the more apt to facilitate the creation of an *esprit de corps*, a sense of togetherness. In any case, such a choice was also fraught with consequences. Languages are vehicles of cultural heritage and legal cultural heritage in particular. They have specific characteristics, which can shape the way of thinking and conceptualize law in a certain language, using a certain "toolkit". Being a decisive "morphological element", inevitably they shape legal documents written according to their codes.[22] This is also the case of judicial decisions. Already the first French scholars who commented in the 1950s on the "*problème de l'influence des droits internes sur la Cour de Justice de la Communauté Européenne du Charbon et de l'Acier*"[23] recognized, from their privileged point of view, the early adoption by the Court, in terms of "*technique juridictionelle*", of the same *imperatoria brevitas* of the French judiciary.[24]

As also noted by several other authors,[25] in the first three decades of its activity, the Court of Justice strictly adhered to a form of concise reasoning with a fixed and immutable structure. Each judgement opened with a brief summary of the case, followed by the description of the relevant supranational legal framework; the relevant national legal discipline; facts, procedure and presentation of the questions referred in case of preliminary references, or of the "conclusions of the parties" in other actions; "*moyens et arguments*" of the parties; judges' appraisal; and all these elements were always neatly packed in paragraphs and numbered.[26] The judgements all tended to be quite short and concentrated, with most of the facts and details being confined to the separately printed "report for the hearing". In this sense, the inspiration provided by the French drafting style was readily visible in both form and effects. The organization of the text took the typical form of a series of single paragraphs opened by the phrase "*attendu que*" ("considering that", "whereas-es").[27] This is considered one of the main specificities of the French heritage, traced back to the local tribunals of the fifteenth century[28]—a practice then followed in many continental countries including Belgium, Luxembourg, the Netherlands, Spain, Portugal and the Nordic countries.[29] It was, therefore, a technique not only shaped by the same choice of using French as a language, with its constraints and common usages; but also another example of "common way of thinking" around which the large part of the original members of the Court could quickly converge with their own background of practice, and new members could do the same progressively.

In turn, the "*attendu que*" structure has consequences on the rest of the "morphological elements" of the decisions and its "substance": after all, it was already clear for the first observers that "*(L)a substance même du raisonnement, son déroulement, se trouvent dans une large mesure commandés par la forme dans laquelle il se coule*".[30] This way of structuring the grounds of judgement leads, for instance, to writing using verbs in the indicative tense, with avoidance of conditional ones and hypothetical periods.[31] In general terms, it fosters the articulation of the judicial "*démarche intellectuelle*" in a contained and progressive way in which every argumentative step is a distinct, clearer and most obvious explanation of the antecedent.[32] In this sense, the early commentators already emphasized how this technique generally leads judges to "*s'expliquer*", to *explain* themselves and their deductive reasoning, more than to *justify* themselves and their choices, as typical of "*la forme 'dissertation'*".[33] This idea was then taken up and developed by recent comparative scholars who talked of a clear contrast between the transparent judicial opinions usual for a certain common law judiciary, in which a "unified or integrated decision making" is produced, on the one hand, and the "bifurcation" typical of the French legal infrastructure, on the other, in which the "*démarche intellectuelle*" leading effectively to a certain decision tends not to coincide—but quite the contrary to be contained, even cloaked, in the rigid pre-set forms of the official judgement.[34] It is at the weight of the French heritage that the scholars who have described the "succinct, syllogistic structure, with a dry tone" of the Court,[35] its "formal, terse and abstract" reasoning,[36] the nature of its judgements as "terse and opaque summary of the outcome and the reasons for it", expressed in a "strictly deductive form",[37] "carbon copy of the judgements of the great French courts",[38] all pointed. As a result, the Court indeed reached that kind of "stern, authoritarian style, expressed in a single-sentenced statement in which shines a single subject (the Court)" considered as typical of the French jurisdictions.[39]

But can one consider this purely the result of a deterministic choice, the obvious fruit of a fecund legacy? Probably this is only part of the story: not only for the inherent weakness of any "legal transplant", especially in peculiar contexts such as the supranational one, but also because differences and dissonances from the weighty paradigm of the past readily emerged, and other functional reasons were also present. The same early observers who highlighted the relevance of the general adoption of the "*attendu que* structure" also pointed to the first forms of hybridization.[40] A "lack of unity", also of "exterior unity", was already denounced in the early years of the ECSC Court of Justice. In some of its cases, the original rigid structure with separated, consequential paragraphs and single-sentence statements (the technique of the "*phrases unique*"),[41] was followed[42]; in others, it was disregarded[43]; while in others a sort of compromise solution with a general structure made of "*attendu que*", yet the whole «*motifs de droit*» grouped under the same unique "*attendu*" (so, with no "*phrases unique*"), was found.[44] Even judgements given in the same days presented stylistic dissonances of the kind.[45] Later members of the Court highlighted that the "concision and clarity" of the French style judgement was undoubtedly influenced by the "rigorous and terse" working language but also very much appreciated, in functional terms, for the univocity of the message that they were able to convey to "national judges whose knowledge of Community law and its bewildering intricacies" was "inevitably summary" (in this sense confirming Weiler's mentioned thesis of an early instrumental use of formalism); for the provided ease of translation in all the other official languages of the Communities, another connected practical factor often overlooked; for the possibility to mask, behind "the oracular tone" of a concise series of assertions, the inevitable dissonances and disagreements of single members obliged, with no separate opinions, to a joined collegiality.[46]

The development of a proper style of the Court was, therefore, a matter of stratification, surely strongly affected by a visible French basis but also open to other influences, and to purely functional, instrumental considerations of government of the *unitas in diversitate*. In one of the first studies devoted to the European Court of Justice with some comparative breadth,[47] Maurice Lagrange, another renowned former member of the Court from France, described, based on his own experience, a certain neutrality or better yet a *lassez-faire* practice in Luxembourg—especially when dealing with the drafting of judgements. Already in the mid-1960s, he recognized that "(T)he Court very wisely has refrained from interfering with the method of drafting with which each Justice is familiar, so that the drafter of each opinion, who usually is the 'reporter judge' (*juge-rapporteur*), has considerable latitude in form and style".[48] Lagrange put forward the example of the German judges, who, more than others, tended to move away from the primitive style of the Court: in an explicit contraposition with the style of the "French judge"—who tends to reach "his conclusions through a process of logical reasoning" and then to formulate "these conclusions in the dispositional part of his judgement", according to a historical scheme that I described—the "German judge" on the other hand was described as one that "first sets forth the specific decision in the case, and then supports it with as elaborate an explanation as possible, drafted informally without using 'in consideration of which' and 'whereas'; he endeavors to omit nothing and to make the judgement as convincing as possible".[49]

This internal stylistic plurality should not seem to be the result of mere perception or anecdotal: several commentators who ranged in the Court's college described it, and attributed it, precisely in terms of stratification of styles, to the different German cultural influence in the early days.[50] Its different and more "dissertational" style is generally seen as prompted by the lexical richness and the consequent ample range of conceptual distinctions made possible by all the languages of the Germanic branch.[51] It is surely commonplace to see this as an evergreen offspring of *Begriffsjurisprudenz*, as an innate German tendency to a "jurisprudence of concepts" in which law can be traced back to a logically organized system, or a pyramid, of dogmatic constructions.[52] On the other hand, it has been emphasized how a tendency towards legal thinking based on conceptual analysis, in which notions formally unknown to the EC Treaties of the time such as "good faith, good morals, proportionality, legitimate expectations etc." found a place, could not but lead to a "less deductive and apodictic" style.[53] Authoritative, internal opinions from the Court emphasized that "(A)s time moved on, German influences became visible in the Court's case law"[54]; and other scholars have suggested that an "examination of judgements in the 1960s and 1980s will reveal differences in the breadth of the Court's judgements and the tendency to be more discursive in its judicial style".[55] If one takes some of the judgements of that period in which, famously, some general legal principles often said to be derived by the German influence made their way, a certain tendency by the Court to be more discursive in its judicial style becomes evident. For instance, it is well known that the *Verhältnismäßigkeitsprinzip*, the principle of proportionality, which found its most achieved expression in German law, was already recognized by the European Court of Justice in early historical cases such as *Federation Charbonniere de Belgique*[56] and *International Handelsgesellschaft*,[57] as the general basic idea according to which "the individual should not have his freedom of action limited beyond the degree necessary in the public interest". The Court particularly elaborated on the principle when it had to decide how far Member States could go in limiting one of the market freedoms when the Treaties allows certain restrictions for specific purposes. For its analysis, in doing so, in a second phase, it worked out multipronged tests comparable to those of national jurisdictions.[58] With this passage, it surely and definitively broke the chains of any orthodox "*attendu que*" or "*phrases uniques*" structure for the elaboration of numerous dense paragraphs of detailed analysis of national regulatory policies. For instance, the famous *Italian vinegar case* ("*Aceto I*") of 1981 counted twenty-eight paragraphs of "*motifs de l'arrêt*", with a single central paragraph of proportionality analysis of fourteen lines.[59] The even more famous *German beer case* some years later counted no less than fifty-five paragraphs of "*motifs de l'arrêt*", of similar length and complexity.[60] Another example, among many, could be found in the *British fishery case*[61]: in this, the Court imported another principle of direct German (federal) influence, the notion of "*Bundestreue*", meaning something like loyal federal cooperation or federal comity, in adjudicating on a Treaty provision on the obligation of Member States to facilitate the achievement of the Community's tasks.[62] In adjudicating such principle of clear public policy nature (like proportionality after all), any velleity of contained, apodictic structure had to be abandoned and no "*attendu*" or "*phrases unique*" could find their place, and the Court used forty-four paragraphs of "*motifs de l'arrêt*" to find the United Kingdom as failing to fulfil its obligations under the EEC Treaty.

Of course, what I am discussing are only cultural influences, in the classic comparative sense of *formants*,[63] of one of several concurrent legal bases upon which legal institutions evolve. Other concurring ingredients can be enumerated. For instance, it is sure that the complexity of the Court's decisions has also gone hand in hand with the complexity of the set of EU norms it had to adjudicate. But the impact of the German conceptualizations—confirmed, as said, by several internal observers[64]—can also somehow be isolated if one notices that, in those same days of the mentioned case law, several judgements replicating the pure French style were still issued[65]: it seems therefore easy to point at certain specific judgements where the two ingredients were mixed, and some where they were not. After all, such a different way of thinking of legal arguments[66] and presenting them stylistically cannot but lead to a different way of "fabrication" of the law: the output, the textual materiality of the law, in this case of the judicial European law, could not but change after the graft in the assembly line of new and different treatment modalities.

The same discourse holds for the subsequently registered stratification of cultural influences, obviously seen in the mid-1970s accession in the ranks of the Court of judges from common law jurisdictions such as the United Kingdom and Ireland (and in some respect, also from a tradition different from the continental one like Denmark). Apart from the asserted enrichment of the EC law conceptual patrimony with substantive rules and notions drawn down from common law,[67] two main practical impacts on the style of the Court and, directly or indirectly, of its decisions, have been registered.

First, it has been acknowledged that the more traditionally adversarial culture of lawyers trained in the jurisprudential techniques of common law influenced "the style and the format of the hearings" of the Court.[68]

The Court's proceedings assumed a less formal atmosphere in the context of the encouragement of some sort of dialogue between judges and advocates,[69] which was absent in the past. Exchange of information and opinions between bar and bench became usual in addition to the practice of open questions put to the parties' agents or counsel, either in writing or orally at the hearing, also with interruptions and lively debates.[70] This surely went on at the advantage of the usefulness and liveliness of the hearings; but a better, *de visu* comprehension of the facts of the case and the submissions of parties and interveners could not but shape how those are translated in the judgements of the Court, by a clarification of the facts and of the intricacies of national and supranational law elements. Again, this is explicable in my metaphorical perspective of the "fabrication" of the law. The hearing is a decisive step in the assembly line of judge-made law, often forgotten or underestimated in academic commentaries on the CJEU precisely because it only had a development in a second phase of its historical evolution; but it is evident that a more dialogical and osmotic construction of the European legal fabric, with an enhancement of the parties' contributions, cannot but change the final output, the judgement, where a more multifaceted reality will be represented. In this sense, it is easy to think about how a different and better comprehension of the technicalities and intricacies of the relevant national law in European cases, conveyed by the more active role of the parties, began to play a role. In the same vein and with the same pursued effects of clarification, the new adversarial attitude led the Court to show (for the first time) a willingness to reopen a case for oral argument when it felt that it was possible to expedite a decision based on arguments which had not yet been discussed by the parties.[71]

Additionally, a renewed approach of the Court of Justice with regard to its earlier case law is often charged to the influence of common law judges. While (as also seen above in dealing with early cases such as *Da Costa*) it is no less than a myth that the Court never cited its previous decisions before the advent of common lawyers,[72] and while of course the development of a case law means that there is always more case law to refer to, some interesting developments indeed took place. First of all, not only did the reference to precedents become numerically usual if compared to the relative rarity of the 1960s and early 1970s[73]; but it became common for the Court the practice of declaring that it would follow a previous precedent because no new arguments had been advanced—a more structured adoption of consistent principled rules compared to the mere reference to some earlier case. In this sense, previous cases became used as the sole or the main argument for a decision,[74] by the employment of well-known formulas such as "it is established case law that...", or "as the Court already held in its judgement of...", or even "as the Court repeatedly held...", or the reference to a "settled case law of the Court".[75] This practice was coupled with the previously seen choice in *CILFIT* to talk of an incipient form of European ***stare decisis*** explicitly, a system in which cases started to be decided by reference to earlier ***dicta*** and by a gradual process of extending or reducing the scope of previous rulings,[76] and in which traces of the typical parallel "binding" and "persuasive" forms of authority of precedents started to be seen[77]—though probably under-theorized.[78] As said, such a move in *CILFIT* was relevant since it organized the crucial relationship between the Court and national judges around the existence of precedents. The complementary dimension of such an approach was seen in the first episodes of explicit overruling by the Court of its precedents, while the idea itself of acknowledging the existence of a conflict in its case law was probably unacceptable in the previous decades.[79] It was at the instigation of a British Advocate General, Sir Francis Geoffrey Jacobs, that the Court explicitly first took this bold step[80]; although the same attempt famously made some months later in ***Keck and Mithouard***, where the Court expressly stated its intention to overrule some of its earlier decisions, without formally indicating which ones, also made clear an under-theorization and a primitive nature of the practice—with severe risks for the correct and uniform application of EC law.[81]

6.3 The Style as Shaped by the Machinery of the Court and the Plurality of the EU Legal Order

A qualitative analysis of the style of the Court of Justice's decisions, especially if shaped around the critical evaluation of the common accusations of opacity and lack of argumentative openness, cannot be conducted only in terms of broad cultural influences. As seen, the ECJ's judgements are surely the products of mandatory collegiality that includes several different dynamics and cultural attitudes, and force to synthesize them. But other relevant factors linked to the machinery of the Court and of the EU legal order, to how the cases arrive in Luxembourg and how they are there treated and solved, shape the morphological elements of the decisions, and must be taken into account. Precisely by adopting an "industrialist" similitude in describing the work of the Court, one is forced to note that the judgement is only the "ultimate 'product'" of an "assembly line",[82] and that the Court, in such a process of "fabrication",[83] makes just the final intervention. It is to be noted in this respect that the Court is not the full master of the case and the textual material it employs: and that, as it has been said, it does not even work with raw material but with refined material, already with its specific characteristics.[84] There are several factors, exogenous and endogenous, that shape the Court's process of arriving at its decisions and limit, according to the critics, the extent to which it can develop truly coherent, ideal-typically convincing reasoning.[85]

Starting *ab origine*, by what has been categorized as the first of the "inputs" into the Court's judicial machinery,[86] one has to consider that the same legislative texts with which the European judges have to deal are of a peculiar nature. They are, as the simplification of the legal literature sometimes goes, the result of a fictitious "supranational legislator". However, behind such a label, in the institutional reality, it is known that occasionally those texts come from the Commission exercising delegated powers in minor legislation; but, more often, in the case of major acts, they are what results from an original Commission proposal, scrutinized and amended by negotiators from all the Member States' governments, then further scrutinized and amended by the elected members of the European Parliament, and finally accepted by the Council of Ministers soon before a not-so-obvious effort of translation in all the official languages of the EU. In technical terms, the EU drafting process is widely considered as a paradigm in quality, for which a *Quality of legislation team* is settled within the Legal Service Directorate of the Commission[87] and for which several soft law measures are set to assure clarity and simplicity—including an *Inter-institutional Agreement on common guidelines for the quality of drafting of Community legislation*[88] and a *Joint Practical Guide* "for persons involved in the drafting of European Union legislation" for its implementation.[89] Despite these efforts, it remains, as underlined by scholars,[90] a process often undertaken under strong timing and political pressure, in which a large number of different positions must converge into a single "product", often in the hands of people not working in their mother tongue, and subject to an essential work of internal translation of thousands of pages of EU legislation. In this reality, it is thus "virtually impossible to guarantee" the absence of "any infelicity, any ambiguity, any error".[91] It has also been emphasized how, in some borderline cases in front of the Court, the references for preliminary rulings have even been almost entirely prompted by the doubts on discrepancies between two linguistic versions of a certain contested regulation.[92] Already the first step of the process of "fabrication" of EU law, as refined material for the work of the Court, is thus a prime suspect for the accusations of lack of clarity.

The "assembly line" of the Court of Justice's decisions then has a second necessary phase, a second textual "input", when dealing with preliminary ruling procedures, in the production of national courts: the orders of reference. These are per se autonomous acts made under national procedural law and in compliance with internal rules. No standard supranational rule exists on how such orders for reference shall be drafted. There are only, as already recalled in the previous chapters, a series of "Recommendations to national courts and tribunals in relation to the initiation of preliminary ruling proceedings",[93] issued by the Court, and in particular by its *Rules of Procedure Committee*, which, "(S)ince the preliminary ruling procedure is based on cooperation", essentially aim at providing "guidance", "(I)n no way binding", to the national judges "as to whether it is appropriate to make a reference for a preliminary ruling, as well as practical information concerning the form and effect of such a reference".[94] Such detailed guidance, actually for both national judges and advocates who interact with the Court, is intended to supplement the Rules of Procedure of the Court of Justice (Articles 93–118). It is regularly updated to "reflect innovations introduced by those Rules which may affect both the principle of a reference for a preliminary ruling (..) and the procedure for making such a reference".[95] I already reflected on how certain cultural conceptions of differently trained national judges can affect the substantial use of the procedure and particularly on how preliminary rulings are expected to state on the abstract interpretation of relevant EU law and/or also on the factual *minutiae* of the cases at hand. In terms of formality as well serious discrepancies are registered, which make members of the Court suspect of a complete ignorance—voluntary or even merely on the very existence—of such recommendations by national lawyers.[96] Each national legal system is said to have, also in this sense, its irresistible conception of what "should" go into an order for reference and how this should be composed.[97] So, for instance, the "Recommendations" hasten to point out the average desirable length of the optimal reference ("(A)bout 10 pages is often sufficient to set out in a proper manner the context of a request for a preliminary ruling")[98]; they specify Article 94 of the Rules of Procedure in pointing at its necessary content ("That request must be succinct but sufficiently complete and must contain all the relevant information (…) a summary of the subject-matter of the dispute and the relevant findings of fact (…) or, at least, an account of the facts (…) the tenor of any national provisions applicable in the case (…) a statement of the reasons which prompted the referring court or tribunal to inquire")[99]; they underline its functional purpose ("must be succinct but sufficiently complete and must contain all the relevant information to give the Court and the interested persons entitled to submit observations a clear under- standing of the factual and legal context of the main proceedings")[100]; dare to give stylistic suggestions ("(O)wing to the need to translate it into all the official languages of the European Union, the request for a preliminary ruling should therefore be drafted simply, clearly and precisely, avoiding superfluous detail",[101] and "(I)n order to make the request for a preliminary ruling easier to read, it is essential that the Court receive it in typewritten form")[102]; beg for some efforts also in terms of solution for the case at hand ("If it considers itself able to do so, the referring court or tribunal may, finally, briefly state its view on the answer to be given to the questions referred for a preliminary ruling").[103] But, the confessed everyday practice, according to the same members of the Court,[104] seems to range from references in "1 1/2 pages of almost illegible judicial manuscript" with almost no indication of facts whatsoever, to fully fledged judgements of tens and tens of pages from which the Court is called the extract the needed indication; from hard conceptions of the principle of *jura novit curia* for which it be would for the ECJ to decide on the incompatibility of a certain internal measure, with reference to "10 separate (unconnected) Treaty articles 'or any other provision of Community law'", to precise efforts to solve the case by suggesting an application of the relevant EU provisions. In this sense, it is also suggested that while "some national traditions" would have no difficulty in thinking "in order for the national judge to set out his own tentative views on what the answers to those questions are (or should be)", others take the view that "if the judge thinks he may know the answers, he should not be asking the questions - so, if he *is* making a reference, it is improper for him to express any opinion".[105]

I already pointed at how the declarations of inadmissibility of references are rare, and for what good or at least understandable reasons. In such a process of "fabrication", the Court does not want to lose raw material for its refining activity. Therefore, almost all the ample latitude of stylistically spurious references are at the end of the day accepted, translated and notified to all Member States and the Commission, to constitute the basis of their observations in the proceedings before the Court. The possible uncertainty of EU law's textual fabric, filtered through the possible uncertain formalities of national references, thus propagates and becomes the basis of the submissions to the Court—the third source of its "inputs".[106] Not by chance, the submissions are also said to "vary enormously in their quality", some being mere political statements or expressions of belief, others "models of clarity and helpful research" in terms of relevant case law and policy choices, others "lengthy, repetitious, obfuscatory and virtually untranslatable"[107] in the working language in which judges and their assistants will actually discuss all this material: French. After all, the interveners can be puzzled over a certain interpretation and over the meaning of a certain reference just like anybody inside and outside the Court of Justice. And the quality itself of the submissions of the different Member States' agents can vary.

Only at this point, with this mass of material moulded by others' hands, after all this early process of "fabrication", comes the Court's activity. Also in the Court, texts are shaped by an ever-expanding multilingual, multicultural judicial machine, which in any case functions with a single working language. In its expansion, this machine passed, in the words of its professionals, from the nature of a relatively culturally and numerically homogenous "bit of a family" (in the previous days of the EC restricted composition) to the current state of "a bit of a factory".[108] Judges with different professional backgrounds and rooted cultural traditions discuss the cases in this context, in a common *lingua franca* of noble tradition but which is no longer—as it used to be—the *trait d'union* of the cultural experiences of all the members. Calls for a substitution of the "*langue de travail de la Cour*"—actually, a phrase that is not included in either the Treaties or in the Rules of Procedure of the Court—were raised recently by renowned former Judges,[109] who based their reflections on the changing statistics on the languages of the cases, determined for each action, and which describe English overtaking French in the last five years.[110] Still, the same author who recently pleaded for such reform acknowledges that the time is still not ripe, internally, institutionally, for such a momentous change in the organization of the Court,[111] which would have significant consequences on the composition of staff, recruiting and also the translation services and therefore on the budgetary allocations of the institution. Thus, French will continue to be the internal working language of the Court for several years, with relevant outcomes resulting from an organizational point of view.[112]

It has become usual to talk of an unequal situation among member judges so that the use of the working language would not only now be depleted of its original deep sense of commonality, but become nothing less than a source of power for some members over others. This would particularly happen at the moment of the common internal debates of the *projet de motif* (the draft judgement) presented in French among the judges and the *référendaires*, given the various levels of knowledge and interaction skills.[113] But there is something more about the linguistic aspect. Empirical research on the process of multilingual fabrication of the Court not only highlighted the specificity (also in this respect) of the EU and Luxembourg vis-à-vis other international organizations and jurisdictions, which function smoothly using only a few official languages.[114] It also emphasized the specificity of a process of "fabrication" in which deliberations are drafted in a language which is not native for the vast part of actual internal writers, in which these admittedly tend to think and reflect in their own mother tongue and then "translate" their reflections in French (instead of really "working in French"),[115] in which a sort of mechanical "Court French" ("alien to the 'real' French language") is fostered by such rudimental language regime[116] and even by the internal translation services of the institution, including technological ones,[117] leading to a stilted and rigid formulaic style in which adherence to previous dicta is prompted.[118] The results of all this process are then often put through the permutations of the Court's translation services to finally become part of the official "output" of the Court.

Apart from the decisive specificity of the language regime, it is also important to recall that cases are being assigned on a large scale, precisely since the times of the "industrialist" transformation, to Chambers of restricted compositions, with no stable presence of judges, and therefore with obvious increasing risks of internal divergences both at the substantive and at the formal stylistic level. Furthermore, the Court, as known, is forced to produce a single text signed by all participants to the single *délibéré*, with no possibility of majority and minority opinion, and therefore to "iron out", also with its drafting style, the possible differences. Moreover, it has been more and more working under intense time constraints (at least for a certain period, for the reasons investigated above) and this comes, deliberately, "often at the expense of quality".[119] Journalists even revealed that, in recent times, internal quarrels on the proposal to single out judges who do not draft their decisions on time took place.[120]

To this irrefutable *cahier de doléances*, it must be added that here again, for reasons that I already explored above, the idea of looking at the Opinions of the Advocate Generals, in academic terms, as a completely different drafting style—dissertational and confrontational—surely holds. Their Opinions are, in contrast to the somewhat anonymous, collegiate bench style, written in the first person, with a different breadth, openly addressed to possible inconsistencies in the case law of the Court, provided with a justificatory and not explanatory tone. However, "(I)n contrast to a popular myth",[121] they can hardly be thought of as part of the *ratio decidendi* of the Court,[122] and therefore a source of some additional clarity for the style of the Court, at least in terms of the appraisal of its single judgements. On the contrary, they are another intrusive factor that the Court's complex line of fabrication shall (not necessarily explicitly) take into account for its product.

6.4 The Style Decisions and the New Factors of Change

It was noted above that there have been substantial structural and organizational factors, also pertaining to cultural influences, that have shaped the often-invoked and reproached lack of clarity of the Court of Justice's style. But are judgements of today's Court still as cryptic as they used to be? Have there been recent new factors that can have led, or eventually can lead to a stylistic change? Some concluding, prognostic words are in order.

One is indeed faced with a mixed picture. On the one hand, in the 1980s, the Court abandoned, at least formally, the structure of the *attendus* to favour a more discursive style of argumentation.[123] This happened under the pressure of incipient different internal modalities of reasoning and drafting. Nonetheless, its judgements remained "strongly structured and somewhat rigid", characterized by the introduction of arguments in single and distinct paragraphs opened by standard, recurring phrases such as "it must be observed that", "it must be pointed out that", "it is clear that" and "it follows from the foregoing that".[124] According to the critics, such style is still oriented towards the production of "short, terse, and magisterial decisions" to "demonstrate tremendous interpretative confidence and suggest a certain logical compulsion".[125] And in this sense, in light of my reflections above, one would be tempted to observe that probably the Court still subjectively perceives some benefit in a certain *quid* of formalism, in the wake of a still-unsettled maturity of the EU legal system as a whole, and a need to clearly "instruct" its counterparts, as it was said to be in its early days.[126] Not by chance, a leading scholar recently reflected on how the Court's adjudication could become more "democratic", and how the Court could be more "responsive to its citizens": but he noticed that it is not in the habit of elaborating on hermeneutic alternatives, even to rebut them, so that one can get the impression (typical of the continental tradition) that the interpretation chosen is the only possible, while in fact different trends and phases in the Court's jurisprudence existed.[127]

One should also emphasize that what I already mentioned as a confessed exigency of the Court,[128] already in the first years—and therefore the idea that the judgements, though written in French, are then designed to be translated into every official language of the EU—has become even more pressing in the last decades of massive expansion. With this, there is no need to speculate. The consequences of such a "multilingual and multicultural"[129] mandate for the kind of prose that the Court can employ were not only recognized but somehow programmed/prefixed by authoritative past members. In his *Vade-mecum* for his colleagues at the Court, an influential judge like Pierre Pescatore explicitly recommended, already in the 1980s, to "(W)rite simple and uncluttered sentences, use the simplest possible vocabulary, avoid abstract and learned terms",[130] and argued that "legal reasoning, even when it is complicated, should eventually be reduced (...) to simple options that are compatible with the work of the machine".[131] In this sense, he remarkably anticipated the "industrialist" transformation of the Court and its necessities, the special need for replicable and translatable forms in the supranational setting, and also the more modern strategic choices for information retrieval in the age of database queries.

How the Court followed such recommendations would be evident not only in its actual tendency to avoid "rhetorically shaped, ornate language, elegant and brilliant prose, as well as abstract conceptualism and academic thoughtfulness".[132] An overall tendency towards "impersonality" would also be tangible in the ECJ's distinctive feature to use a formulaic language, made of fabricated, copy-and-paste quotations from the previous case law. Moreover, these rhetoric tools amount to specific means towards standardization, creation of consistency and redundancy and ultimately self-legitimation. As it has been noted,[133] the judgements of the Court become in this way "the result of a complex kind of 'collage' of judicial formulas", i.e. of doctrines and *rationes decidendi* formulated in landmark decisions and then repeated "to such an extent that in some cases it may seem as if it is the formulas which are speaking, instead of the Court and the preferences of its members".[134] In this phenomenon, an ever-present struggle of the Court of Justice is visible to maintain its interpretative authority over national judges: it started with certain strategic use of stylistic, structural formalism, and evolved in such a tendency towards standardization.

On the other hand, while it is maybe exaggerated to talk of a "stylistic earthquake" occurred in Luxembourg, as some authors do,[135] it is nonetheless true that, compared with the decisions of the early years, but also with those of the 1980s and the beginning of 1990s, the average length of the Court's judgements changed and "almost doubled".[136] The mere length of the decisions is certainly not to be linked directly with discursiveness or clarity: it also has to do with the nature of the proceedings, since the ECJ today also hears appeals against judgements of the General Court,[137] and it is also influenced by the rising complexity of EU law and its interrelationships with national laws. Moreover, even more than in the past, after the recent eastern enlargements, the Court of Justice has to deal primarily with Continental, civil law tribunals, whose expectations are certainly not for ample dissertational rulings but applicable products more similar to their own standards.[138]

Nonetheless, it is essential to add a reflection, at least as a conclusion of these pages, on the overall audience that the Court is now facing in its everyday activities. If direct counterparts of the Court are simply the EU institutions and national courts, words of truth and realism like those of Bobek—who stresses the nature of "academic dreams" of all the ideal types of ample, confrontational, discursive, judgements—are welcome.[139] Institutions and national judges value "reasonable conciseness" and coherence in the Court's case law more than any other principle, and for understandable, pragmatical reasons in their everyday practice of adjudication. I also saw how these concerns are behind several of the Court's internal choices in terms of the use of procedures, resources and control of its docket. However, if I was successful, in a study like this, to leave aside for many pages the celebrated, always present Eric Stein's words on the Court of Justice "tucked away in the fairy land Duchy of Luxembourg and blessed, until recently, with the benign neglect by the powers that be and the mass media",[140] one cannot but recall them now, and to state the obvious and thus say that those words are surely no longer valid. The Court is now an unmasked power, whose activities are openly and often critically debated,[141] well under the spotlight of the media,[142] and which, as seen, is evolving accordingly by openly facing the challenges of modernity. Did this have an impact on the Court's language? Any direct answer would be unmeasurable at best, apodictic and speculative at worst. But it would be impossible not to note that while the Court's initial audience was composed of few specialized Community lawyers, it nowadays includes many lawyers from many disciplines, also those that were initially foreign to Community law[143]; involves a more significant and plural academic community, now more accustomed to critical remarks on Luxembourg than to hagiography[144]; and that, given the social, political and economic impact of EU law, the Court is subject to a broad public scrutiny prompted by the unprecedented mediatism of some of its decisions.[145] Some new commentators, in light of this, go as far as to propose the introduction of *amicus curiae* participation in Luxembourg,[146] as it was recently the case of important national constitutional courts previously reluctant towards such kind of openness.[147] The Court of Justice, like any other judicial body, cannot answer to debates and criticism in the public arena; but it is evident, also in the academic discussion,[148] that there is an increasing perception of such new challenges from its ranks, and that the Court's style cannot in some sense be influenced, although not distorted.

6.5 The Evolution of Judgement Style as a Form of Improvement of the Court's Authority

From the analysis conducted throughout this chapter, it is possible once again to draw relevant conclusions on the ability of the Court of Justice to evolve from an institutional point of view, by internalizing external influences.

I defined the stylistic modalities of the Court's judgements as aspects of its structure and organization, as morphological elements of the final judicial output influenced by the institutional setting of the Court. It was noted how much they were influenced, throughout the decades of the Court's history, by the progressive osmosis with the legal cultures of the Member States. The original paradigm of the ECJ's judgements was clearly of French origin, and that impression also remained evident in their structural formalism in the following decades. Still, the stratification of the cultural influences led to relevant changes in the Court's practice and a renewed kind of formalism arose, easily linkable, as the original one, to the struggle of Luxembourg for an interpretative authority in the interplay with national counterparts. Both the original stern, authoritarian style and (although in a process of complication) its subsequent increasing formulaic approach have been traced back to the will to convey a univocal voice as much as possible with no possibility of misunderstandings given the complexity of the multilingual EU environment and its concerns.

The authority of the CJEU as an effective guardian of the correct and uniform application of EU law throughout the continent is also called in question in this case. Its stylistic modalities are, after all, a mirror of its unique role of final manufacturer in the assembly line of fabrication of EU law, where the Court is called to play an authoritative activity by working with raw material already influenced by the inherent complexity of the supranational legal order. My final speculative remarks of the new factors of change for the style of its decisions can only lead to a reflection on the role of the Court of Justice vis-à-vis the other powers of every nature, given the changed "political" environment in which it has to act and in which it is called to bring out its voice. Provocatively, one could say that the Court is asked to choose whether to adhere to its old role of clear addresser of domestic courts and counterparts or rather to interact in a more modern and dialogical way with the broader social audience emerging behind the EU legal order. A choice that is naturally influenced by the Court's attention to its authoritative presence, and will be shaped by it.

Notes

1. In the words of J.P. Dawson, The Oracles of the Law, *op. cit.*
2. See W. Blackstone, Commentaries on the Law of England, Clarendon Press 1765–1769, vol. I, p. 69, from whom Dawson's suggestive title is taken.

3. See R.C. van Caenegem, Judges, Legislators and Professors: Chapters in European Legal History, *op. cit.*, at 127 *et seq.*
4. M. Lasser, "Lit. Theory" Put to the Test: A Comparative Literary Analysis of American Judicial Tests and French Judicial Discourse, in 111 Harvard Law Review, 1998, p. 689, at 691–692.
5. See the fundamental work by B. Latour, La fabrique du droit. Une ethnographie du Conseil d'Etat, *op. cit.*
6. See the various contributions to P. Mbongo, A. Vauchez (eds.), Dans la fabrique du droit européen. Scènes, acteurs et publics de la Cour de justice des Communautés européennes, *op. cit.*
7. See the historical contribution by G. Gorla, Lo stile delle sentenze. Ricerca storico-comparativa, in 21 Quaderni de "Il Foro italiano" 1967, p. 291, actually coeval to the already mentioned J.P. Dawson, The Oracles of the Law, *op. cit.* See also the antecedent T. Sauvel, Histoire du jugement motivé, *op. cit.*, and, recently, in the Italian literature, L. Vacca (ed.), Lo stile delle sentenze e l'utilizzazione dei precedenti. Profili storico-comparatistici, Giappichelli 2000.
8. J.H.H. Weiler, Epilogue: The Judicial Après Nice, *op. cit.*, at 225.
9. *Ibidem.*
10. *Ivi*, at 219.
11. This is probably the basic teaching of comparative analysis like the one by M. Cappelletti, The Judicial Process in Comparative Perspective, *op. cit.*, at 15 *et seq.* in particular.
12. U. Everling, The Court of Justice as a Decision-Making Authority, in 82 Michigan Law Review, 1984, p. 1294, in particular at 1307 *et seq.*
13. J.H.H. Weiler, Journey to an Unknown Destination: A Retrospective and Prospective of the European Court of Justice in the Arena of Political Integration, *op. cit.*, at 424.
14. For both the aspects, see H.E.S. Mattila, Comparative Legal Linguistics. Language of Law, Latin and Modern Lingua Franca, Ashgate 2013, at p. 241 *et seq.*
15. See K. Loehr, Mehrsprachigkeitsprobleme in der Europäischen Union: Eine empirische und theoretische Analyse aus sprachwissenschaftlicher Perspektive, Peter Lang 1998, p. 50; M. Derlén, Multilingual Interpretation of European Union Law, Wolters Kluwer 2009, p. 3.
16. *Ibidem.*
17. EEC Council: Regulation No. 1 determining the languages to be used by the European Economic Community, Official Journal 017, 06/10/1958 P. 0385 – 0386.
18. D.G. Valentine, The Court of Justice of the European Coal and Steel Community, *op. cit.*, at 3 and 147.
19. Article 27 of the original Rules of Procedure of the Court of Justice.
20. Article 36 *et seq.* of the actual Rules of Procedure of the Court of Justice.

21. F.G. Jacobs, The European Court of Justice: Some Thoughts on Its Past and Its Future, *op. cit.*, at 7.
22. H.E.S. Mattila, Comparative Legal Linguistics. Language of Law, Latin and Modern Lingua Francas, *op. cit.*, at 87 *et seq.*
23. J. Rivero, Le problème de l'influence des droits internes sur la Cour de Justice, *op. cit.*
24. *Ivi*, at 297.
25. See, accordingly, *inter alia*, U. Everling, The Court of Justice as a Decision-Making Authority, *op. cit.*, at 1302 *et seq.*; T. Koopmans, The Birth of European Law at the Crossroads of Legal Traditions, *op. cit.*, at 500 *et seq.*; G.F. Mancini, D.T. Keeling, Language, Culture and Politics in the Life of the European Court of Justice, in 1 Columbia Journal of European Law, 1994–1995, p. 397, at 399 in particular (see also in G.F. Mancini, Democracy and Constitutionalism in the European Union. Collected Essays, *op. cit.*, p. 179); M. Lasser, Judicial Deliberations: A Comparative Analysis of Judicial Transparency and Legitimacy, *op. cit.*, at chapter seven in particular; G. Itzcovich, The European Court of Justice as a Constitutional Court: Legal Reasoning in a Comparative Perspective, *op. cit.*, at 42 *et seq.*; M. Bobek, The Court of Justice of the European Union, *op. cit.*, at 170.
26. M. Bobek, The Court of Justice of the European Union, *op. cit.*, at 169.
27. R. David, J.E.C. Brierley, Major Legal Systems in the World Today: An Introduction to the Comparative Study of Law, Free Press 1978, p. 129; H.E.S. Mattila, Comparative Legal Linguistics: Language of Law, Latin and Modern Lingua Francas, *op. cit.*, p. 258 *et seq.*
28. G. Gorla, Lo stile delle sentenze. Ricerca storico-comparativa, *op. cit.*, at 313; H.E.S. Mattila, Comparative Legal Linguistics. Language of Law, Latin and Modern Lingua Francas, *op. cit.*, at 259.
29. R. David, J.E.C. Brierley, Major Legal Systems in the World Today: An Introduction to the Comparative Study of Law, *op. cit.*, at 129–130.
30. J. Rivero, Le problème de l'influence des droits internes sur la Cour de Justice, *op. cit.*, at 298.
31. T. Krefeld, Das französische Gerichtsurteil in linguistischer Sicht. Zwischen Fach- und Standessprache, Studia Romanica et linguistica, Peter Lang 1985, at 107–109; H.E.S. Mattila, Comparative Legal Linguistics. Language of Law, Latin and Modern Lingua Francas, *op. cit.*, at 259.
32. J. Rivero, Le problème de l'influence des droits internes sur la Cour de Justice, *op. cit.*, at 298–299.
33. *Ivi*, at 299.
34. On such idea of «bifurcation» between internal and external discourse see notably M. Lasser, Judicial Deliberations: A Comparative Analysis of Judicial Transparency and Legitimacy, *op. cit.*, at 60 and 179 *et seq.* in particular.

35. G. Itzcovich, The European Court of Justice as a Constitutional Court: Legal Reasoning in a Comparative Perspective, *op. cit.*, at 32.
36. T.C. Hartley, The Foundations of European Community Law, 4th edn, Oxford University Press 1998, p. 74.
37. M. Wells, French and American Judicial Opinions, in 19 Yale Journal of International Law, 1994, p. 85, at 92 and 94; U. Everling, Reflections on the Reasoning in the Judgements of the Court of Justice of the European Communities, in J. Rosenløv et al. (eds.), Festskrift til Ole Due, Gads Forlag 1994, p. 55, at 59.
38. G.F. Mancini, D.T. Keeling, Language, Culture and Politics in the Life of the European Court of Justice, *op. cit.*, at 399 (see also in G.F. Mancini, Democracy and Constitutionalism in the European Union, *op. cit.*, at 179).
39. G. Gorla, Lo stile delle sentenze. Ricerca storico-comparativa, *op.cit.*, at 16.
40. J. Rivero, Le problème de l'influence des droits internes sur la Cour de Justice, *op. cit.*, at 298–299.
41. G. Gorla, Lo stile delle sentenze. Ricerca storico-comparativa, *op. cit.*, at 313.
42. See an example in Judgement of 13 June 1958, Meroni/ECSC High Authority (9/56, ECR 1957–1958 p. 133).
43. See an example in Judgement of 12 June 1958, Compagnie des hauts fourneaux de Chasse/ECSC High Authority (2/57, ECR 1957–1958 p. 199).
44. See as examples Judgement of 21 December 1954, France/ECSC High Authority (1/54, ECR 1954–1956 p. 1); Judgement of 21 December 1954, Italy/ECSC High Authority (2/54, ECR 1954–1956 p. 37); Judgement of 11 February 1955, Assider/ECSC High Authority (3/54, ECR 1954–1956 p. 63).
45. Compare Judgement of 12 June 1958, Compagnie des hauts fourneaux de Chasse/ECSC High Authority (15/57, ECR 1957–1958 p. 211) and Judgement of 13 June 1958, Meroni/ECSC High Authority (9/56, ECR 1957–1958 p. 133).
46. See for these points G.F. Mancini, D.T. Keeling, Language, Culture and Politics in the Life of the European Court of Justice, *op. cit.*, at 398.
47. M. Lagrange, The Court of Justice as a Factor in European Integration, *op.cit.*
48. *Ivi*, at 721.
49. *Ibidem*.
50. See for instance U. Everling, The Court of Justice as a Decision-Making Authority, *op. cit.*, at 1301–1302; G.F. Mancini, D.T. Keeling, Language, Culture and Politics in the Life of the European Court of Justice, *op. cit.*, at 399.

51. H.E.S. Mattila, Comparative Legal Linguistics: Language of Law, Latin and Modern Lingua Francas, *op. cit.*, at 218.
52. As done by H.E.S. Mattila, Comparative Legal Linguistics. Language of Law, Latin and Modern Lingua Franca, *op. cit.*, at 218. See H.P. Haferkamp, A. Nieschlag, Begriffsjurisprudenz/Jurisprudence of Concepts (*ad vocem*), in The Oxford International Encyclopedia of Legal History, 2009, for a taxonomy of the various meanings attached to such contested label.
53. T. Koopmans, The Birth of European Law at the Crossroads of Legal Traditions, *op. cit.*, at 502. In the same sense, see G.F. Mancini, D.T. Keeling, Language, Culture and Politics in the Life of the European Court of Justice, *op. cit.*, at 400; P. de Cruz, Comparative Law in a Changing World, Cavendish Publishing Limited 1999, p. 160.
54. T. Koopmans, The Birth of European Law at the Crossroads of Legal Traditions, *op. cit.*, at 501.
55. P. de Cruz, Comparative Law in a Changing World, *op. cit.*, at 161; for a similar remark, see M. Bobek, The Court of Justice of the European Union, *op. cit.*, at 168.
56. Judgement of 29 November 1956, Fédération charbonnière de Belgique/ECSC High Authority (8/55, ECR 1954–1956 p. 292).
57. Judgement of 17 December 1970, Internationale Handelsgesellschaft mbH/Einfuhr- und Vorratsstelle für Getreide und Futtermittel (11/70, ECR 1970 p. 1125).
58. See for recent accounts on this, among the many: M. Cohen-Eliya, I. Porat, American Balancing and German Proportionality: The Historical Origins, in 8 International Journal of Constitutional Law, 2010, p. 263; A. Stone Sweet, J. Mathews, Proportionality Balancing and Global Constitutionalism, in 47 Columbia Journal of Transnational Law, 2008, p. 73.
59. See Judgement of 9 December 1981, Commission/Italy (193/80, ECR 1981 p. 3019) ECLI:EU:C:1981:298, at the single paragraph 27: «Il n'est pas exclu, toutefois, que, suite a la mise en ouvre de la reglementation litigieuse, les consommateurs italiens se soient habitues à l'utilisation commerciale du terme 'aceto' pour le seuls vinaigres de vin. Dans ces conditions, la preoccupation du gouvernment italien de veiller à la protection du consommateur peut etre justifèe. Une telle protection peut cependant etre assurèe par d'autres moyens permettant un traitement egal des produits nationaux et des produits importes, et notamment par l'apposition obligatiore d'un etiquetage adequat concernant la nature du produit vendu, comportant les qualificatifs ou complements specifiant le type de vinaigre proposé à le vente, à la condition que cette prescription s'applique à tous les vinaigres, y compris

le vinaigre de vin. En effet, un tel procede permettrait au consommateur de fixer son choix en toute connaisance de cause et assirerait la transparence des transactions commerciales et des offres au pblic en indiquant la matière première employèe dans la fabrication du vinaigre».
60. Judgement of 12 March 1987, Commission/Germany (178/84, ECR 1987 p. 1227).
61. Judgement of 5 May 1981, Commission/United Kingdom (804/79, ECR 1981 p. 1045).
62. T. Koopmans, The Birth of European Law at the Crossroads of Legal Traditions, *op. cit.*, at 502.
63. R. Sacco, Legal Formants. A Dynamic Approach to Comparative Law, *op. cit.*, on which see Note 169 in Chapter 2.
64. See e.g. T. Koopmans, The Birth of European Law at the Crossroads of Legal Traditions, *op. cit.*, at 494 *et seq.*; U. Everling, The Court of Justice as a Decision-Making Authority, *op. cit.*, at 1302 *et seq.*; G.F. Mancini, D.T. Keeling, Language, Culture and Politics in the Life of the European Court of Justice, *op. cit.*, at 402.
65. See just for instance Judgement of 7 May 1981, Hansen/Hauptzollamt Flensburg (153/80, ECR 1981 p. 1165) ECLI:EU:C:1981:98, published just a couple of days after the mentioned British fishery case, replicating, in just sixteen paragraphs, the morphological elements of the judgements of the early years and of the French paradigm.
66. See the reflections of B. Latour, La fabrique du droit. Une ethnographie du Conseil d'Etat, *op. cit.*, on the influence of the specific French idea of «moyen» as compared to other modalities of construction of legal arguments.
67. In G.F. Mancini, D.T. Keeling, Language, Culture and Politics in the Life of the European Court of Justice, *op. cit.*, at 401, it is suggested that the important dicta of Judgement of 4 December 1974, Van Duyn/Home Office (41/74, ECR 1974 p. 1337) and Judgement of 5 April 1979, Ratti (148/78, ECR 1979 p. 1629) could be decisively influenced by the common law doctrine of *estoppel*; both T. Koopmans, The Birth of European Law at the Crossroads of Legal Traditions, *op. cit.*, at 502 and P. de Cruz, Comparative Law in a Changing World, *op. cit.*, at 161, suggest that the right to a fair hearing in the supranational decision making process before an administrative body or agency was prompted by the influence of the the English rule of *audi alterem partem,* see for instance Judgement of 23 October 1974, Transocean Marine Paint Association/Commission (17/74, ECR 1974 p. 1063).
68. See G.F. Mancini, D.T. Keeling, Language, Culture and Politics in the Life of the European Court of Justice, *op. cit.*, at 401. In the same sense, T. Koopmans, The Birth of European Law at the Crossroads of Legal Traditions, *op. cit.*, at 503; see in general on the influence of

common law and its adversarial character, R.D. Kelemen, Eurolegalism: The Transformation of Law and Regulation in the European Union, Harvard University Press 2011.

69. P. de Cruz, Comparative Law in a Changing World, *op. cit.*, at 161–162.
70. T. Koopmans, The Birth of European Law at the Crossroads of Legal Traditions, *op. cit.*, at 505.
71. This happened for the first time in cases such as Judgement of 18 May 1982, AM & S/Commission (155/79, ECR 1982 p. 1575), Judgement of 10 July 1980, Lancôme/Etos (99/79, ECR 1980 p. 2511); Judgement of 12 July 1983, Commission/United Kingdom (170/78, ECR 1983 p. 2265).
72. See in this respect, also the reflections of T. Koopmans, Stare Decisis in European Law, in D. O'Keeffe, H.G. Schermers (eds.), Essays in European Law and Integration, Kluwer 1982, p. 11, with reference in particular to H.G. Schermers, Judicial Protection in the European Communities, 2nd edn., Springer 1979, p. 123.
73. See G.F. Mancini, D.T. Keeling, Language, Culture and Politics in the Life of the European Court of Justice, *op. cit.*, at 402.
74. T. Koopmans, The Birth of European Law at the Crossroads of Legal Traditions, *op. cit.*, at 504.
75. See for instance Judgement of 17 June 1981, Commission/Ireland C-113/80, ECR 1981 p. 1625, at 1639.
76. See Lord Mackenzie Stuart and J.P. Warner, Judicial Decisions as a Source of Community law, in Va.Aa. (eds.), Europeische Gerichtsbarkeit und nationale Verfassungsgerichtsbarkeit, Festschrift H. Kutscher, Nomos 1981, p. 273; T. Koopmans, Stare Decisis in European Law, *op. cit.*, at 11.
77. T. Koopmans, Stare Decisis in European Law, *op. cit.*, at 20 *et seq.*
78. See the recent critical reflections by A. Arnull, The European Union and its Court of Justice, *op. cit.*, at 631; J. Komarek, Judicial Lawmaking and Precedent in Supreme Courts: The European Court of Justice Compared to the US Supreme Court and the French Cour de Cassation, in 11 Cambridge Yearbook of European Legal Studies, 2008–2009, p. 399; T. Tridimas, Precedent and the Court of Justice: A Jurisprudence of Doubt? *op. cit.*, p. 308; S.K. Schimdt, The European Court of Justice and the Policy Process, OUP 2018, Chapter 3.
79. See G.F. Mancini, D.T. Keeling, Language, Culture and Politics in the Life of the European Court of Justice, *op. cit.*, at 402.
80. See Judgement of 17 October 1990, CNL-SUCAL/HAG (C-10/89, ECR 1990 p. I-3711).
81. See for a recent comprehensive account E. Carpano (ed.), Le revirement de jurisprudence en droit européen, Bruylant 2012.

82. M. Bobek, The Court of Justice of the European Union, *op. cit.*, at p. 168.
83. Again in the words of B. Latour, La fabrique du droit. Une ethnographie du Conseil d'Etat, *op. cit.*, then adopted by L. Azoulai, La fabrication de la jurisprudence communautaire, *op. cit.*
84. L. Azoulai, La fabrication de la jurisprudence communautaire, *op. cit.*, at 158.
85. U. Everling, The Court of Justice as a Decision-Making Authority, *op. cit.*, at 1308.
86. E. Sharpston, Transparency and Clear Legal Language in the European Union: Ambiguous Legislative Texts, Laconic Pronouncements and the Credibility of the Judicial System, *op. cit.*, at 410–411.
87. See its webpage available at the site http://ec.europa.eu/dgs/legal_service/legal_reviser_en.htm (accessed 29 May 2015).
88. Inter-institutional Agreement of 22 December 1998 on common guidelines for the quality of drafting of Community legislation, [1999] OJ C 73/1.
89. The 'Joint Practical Guide: Guide of the European Parliament, the Council and the Commission for persons involved in the drafting of legislation within the Community institutions', available at the website http://eur-lex.europa.eu/content/pdf/techleg/joint-practical-guide-2013-en.pdf (accessed 2 March 2020).
90. E. Sharpston, Transparency and Clear Legal Language in the European Union: Ambiguous Legislative Texts, Laconic Pronouncements and the Credibility of the Judicial System, *op. cit.*, 411.
91. *Ibidem.*
92. See for instance the reference from the German Oberlandesgericht Frankfurt am Main in Judgement of 10 July 2008, Emirates Airlines (C-173/07, ECR 2008 p. I-5237) ECLI:EU:C:2008:400, cited by E. Sharpston, Transparency and Clear Legal Language in the European Union: Ambiguous Legislative Texts, Laconic Pronouncements and the Credibility of the Judicial System, *op. cit.*, 411, whose question referred was in fact the following: "Is Article 3(1)(a) of Regulation (EC) No 261/2004 of the European Parliament and of the Council of 11 February 2004 establishing common rules on compensation and assistance to passengers in the event of denied boarding and of cancellation or long delay of flights, and repealing Regulation (EEC) No 295/91, to be interpreted as meaning that 'a flight' includes in any event the flight from the point of departure to the destination and back in the case where the outward and return flights are booked at the same time?".
93. Recommendations to national courts and tribunals in relation to the initiation of preliminary ruling proceedings (2012/C 338/01), available at the website http://eur-lex.europa.eu/legal-content/EN/TXT/

PDF/?uri=CELEX:32012H1106(01)&from=EN (accessed 2 March 2020).
94. *Ivi*, at paragraphs 5 and 6.
95. *Ivi*, at 338/01.
96. See E. Sharpston, Transparency and Clear Legal Language in the European Union: Ambiguous Legislative Texts, Laconic Pronouncements and the Credibility of the Judicial System, *op. cit.*, at 411: "Judging by what sometimes arrives at the Court, either the very existence of these notes has escaped a significant proportion of the legal profession throughout the EU, or else they are known but usually ignored. (Either hypothesis is depressing if you happen, as I do, to sit on the Rules of Procedure Committee!)".
97. *Ivi*, at 413–414.
98. Recommendations to national courts and tribunals in relation to the initiation of preliminary ruling proceedings (2012/C 338/01), paragraph 22: "22. About 10 pages is often sufficient to set out in a proper manner the context of a request for a preliminary ruling. That request must be succinct but sufficiently complete and must contain all the relevant information to give the Court and the interested persons entitled to submit observations a clear understanding of the factual and legal context of the main proceedings. In accordance with Article 94 of the Rules of Procedure, the request for a preliminary ruling must contain, in addition to the text of the questions referred to the Court for a preliminary ruling: - a summary of the subject-matter of the dispute and the relevant findings of fact as determined by the referring court or tribunal, or, at least, an account of the facts on which the questions referred are based; - the tenor of any national provisions applicable in the case and, where appropriate, the relevant national case-law; - a statement of the reasons which prompted the referring court or tribunal to inquire about the interpretation or validity of certain provisions of European Union law, and the relationship between those provisions and the national legislation applicable to the main proceedings".
99. *Ibidem.*
100. *Ibidem.*
101. *Ivi*, at paragraph 21.
102. *Ivi*, at paragraph 25.
103. *Ivi*, at paragraph 24.
104. See E. Sharpston, Transparency and Clear Legal Language in the European Union: Ambiguous Legislative Texts, Laconic Pronouncements and the Credibility of the Judicial System, *op. cit.*, 413–414.
105. *Ivi*, at 413 (original emphasis).
106. *Ivi*, at 415.
107. *Ibidem.*

108. The reference is to the phrase used by Judge (and previously Legal Secretary) Sacha Prechal of the European Court of Justice in her Interview 'Part I: Working at the CJEU' of 18 December 2013, available at the website http://europeanlawblog.eu (accessed 2 March 2020).
109. K. Schiemann, La langue de travail de la Cour, in A. Tizzano, A. Rosas, R. Silva de Lapuerta, K. Lenaerts, J. Kokott (eds.), La Cour de justice de l'Union européenne sous la présidence de Vassilios Skouris (2003–2015). Liber amicorum Vassilios Skouris, Bruylant 2015, p. 563.
110. According to K. Schiemann, La langue de travail de la Cour, *op. cit.*, at 567–568, in the period 2004/2009 there were, at the Court of Justice, 500 cases in which the language of the procedure was French and 310 in which it was English; in the same period, at the Tribunal of first instance, there were 518 cases governed by French and 509 governed by English. In the subsequent period 2009/2014, at the Court of Justice 398 cases had French as language of the procedure, and 406 had English; at the General Court, 459 cases had French and 1019 had English.
111. *Ivi*, at 572–573.
112. See on the idea of a "French capture" of multinational judicial institutions M. Cohen, On the linguistic design of multinational courts: The French capture, in 14 International Journal of Constitutional Law, 2016, p. 498.
113. K. Schiemann, La langue de travail de la Cour, *op. cit.*, at 568.
114. See K. McAuliffe, Language and Law in the European Union: The Multilingual Jurisprudence of the ECJ, in P. Tiersma, L. Solan (eds.), The Oxford Handbook of Language and Law, *op. cit.*, at 201–202, who takes the EFTA as the major example of institution using, also in its judicial arm, English as an only foreign language for all of its four members.
115. *Ivi*, at 205, quoting the words of some interviewed *référendaires*: e.g. "I tend to *translate* what I want to say *into* French instead of *really* working *in* French… all of my own reasoning and thinking about the case is done in my own language and then put into French when I come to the writing stage" (interviewee's emphasis).
116. *Ibidem*: "The only référendaires who expressed any problems or difficulties (…) were 'francophones' who feel that the formulaic style of the ECJ judgements and the ensuing 'Court French' are almost as alien to the 'real' French language as English or German would be", quoting words such as "The mechanical French that is used at the Court is so far removed from 'proper' or 'real' French that it is almost like another language entirely" or "The French that is used at the Court is not 'real' French but a type of 'Court French'".
117. The reference is to the GTI, a computer software developed by the ECJ to aid and speed-up its translation process, which, still, seems to have its impact also on the style of the Court: according to the words

of a référendaire, "you are so bound to what has been said before that you can hardly even use a new verb or express the same thing in a slightly different way in case the GTI doesn't pick it up. Judgements are time-consuming but most are easy to draft because it has all already been said by the Court - maybe once in five or six years a case will come along that might have one single paragraph saying something completely new or different": see *ibidem*, at 206.

118. *Ibidem*: "Working in 'Court French' is actually *easier* than drafting in your own language – provided that you don't actually want to write anything on your own" (interviewee's emphasis).
119. E. Sharpston, Transparency and Clear Legal Language in the European Union: Ambiguous Legislative Texts, Laconic Pronouncements and the Credibility of the Judicial System, *op. cit.*, at 418; see in extenso her reflections on the point E. Sharpston, Making the Court of Justice of the European Union More Productive, in 21 Maastricht Journal of European of European and Comparative Law 2014, p. 763.
120. D. Seytre, Pour une liste de juges retardaires? in Le Jeudi (6 June 2013) p. 11 (citing from an internal memorandum), as remarked by C. Krenn, The European Court of Justice's Financial Accountability: How the European Parliament Incites and Monitors Judicial Reform through the Budgetary Process, in 13 European Constitutional Law Review, 2017, p. 453, at 467.
121. M. Bobek, The Court of Justice of the European Union, *op. cit.*, at p. 167. See also, specifically, L. Clément-Wiltz, La fonction de l'avocat général près la Cour de justice, *op. cit.*, at 614 *et seq.*
122. As, for instance, claimed by E. Calzolaio, Il valore di precedente delle sentenze della Corte di giustizia, in 1 Rivista critica del diritto privato, 2009, p. 41, at 50: «E' allora evidente che lo studio di ogni sentenza della Corte non può prescindere da una attenta considerazione delle conclusioni dell'avvocato generale, al fine di individuare in modo realistico e completo la *ratio decidendi*» (emphasis in the original text).
123. G. Itzcovich, The European Court of Justice as a Constitutional Court: Legal Reasoning in a Comparative Perspective, *op. cit.*, at 45.
124. *Ivi*, at 46.
125. M. Lasser, Judicial Deliberations: A Comparative Analysis of Judicial Transparency and Legitimacy, *op. cit.*, at 112.
126. As famously emphasized by J.H.H. Weiler, Journey to an Unknown Destination: A Retrospective and Prospective of the European Court of Justice in the Arena of Political Integration, *op. cit.*, at 423 and 427 in particular.
127. B. de Witte, Democratic Adjudication in Europe: How can the European Court of Justice be responsive to the citizens? in M. Dougan, N.

Nic Shuibhne, E. Spaventa (eds.), Empowerment and Disempowerment of the European Citizen, Hart 2012, p. 129.

128. See again G.F. Mancini, D.T. Keeling, Language, Culture and Politics in the Life of the European Court of Justice, *op. cit.*, at 398. See recently G. Itzcovich, The European Court of Justice as a Constitutional Court. Legal Reasoning in a Comparative Perspective, *op. cit.*, at 48 *et seq.*
129. In the words of J. Bengoetxea, Multilingual and Multicultural Legal Reasoning, *op. cit.*
130. P. Pescatore, Vade-mecum. Recueil de formules et de conseils pratiques à l'usage des rédacteurs d'arrêts, 1985, 3rd edn., Bruylant 2007, p. 46.
131. *Ivi*, at 28.
132. G. Itzcovich, The European Court of Justice as a Constitutional Court: Legal Reasoning in a Comparative Perspective, *op. cit.*, at 48–49.
133. L. Azoulai, La fabrication de la jurisprudence communautaire, *op. cit.*, at 163 *et seq.*
134. L. Azoulai, The Court of Justice and the Social Market Economy: The Emergence of an Ideal and the Conditions for Its Realization, in 45 Common Market Law Review, 2008, p. 1335, at 1339.
135. G. Martinico, Reading the Others: American Legal Scholars and the Unfolding European Integration, in 11 European Journal of Law Reform, 2009, p. 35, at 37.
136. M. Bobek, Of Feasibility and Silent Elephants: The Legitimacy of the Court of Justice through the Eyes of National Courts, *op. cit.*, at 204.
137. See for instance the paradigmatic 380 paragraphs and 29,000 words of the Judgement of 3 September 2008, Kadi and Al Barakaat International Foundation/Council and Commission (C-402/05 P and C-415/05 P, ECR 2008 p. I-6351) ECLI:EU:C:2008:461.
138. M. Bobek, Of Feasibility and Silent Elephants: The Legitimacy of the Court of Justice through the Eyes of National Courts, *op. cit.*, at 204–205.
139. *Ivi*, at 205–206 and at 214 *et seq.*
140. E. Stein, Lawyers, Judges and the Making of a Transnational Constitution, *op. cit.*, at 1.
141. See the general reflections on the doctrinal waves by J.H.H. Weiler, Hjalte Rasmussen - Nemo propheta in patria sua, *op. cit.*, at xiii *et seq.*; interesting remarks are also offered by S. Saurugger, F. Terpan, The Court of Justice of the European Union and The Politics of Law, *op. cit.*, p. 73 et seq., and S.K. Schimdt, The European Court of Justice and the Policy Process, *op. cit.*
142. See for recent remarks Editorial Comment—The Court of Justice in the Limelight Again, in 45 Common Market Law Review, 2008, p. 1571.
143. L. Azoulai, L.M. Poiares Maduro, Introduction, in L. Azoulai, L.M. Poiares Maduro (eds.), The Past and Future of EU Law: The Classics

of EU Law Revisited on the 50th Anniversary of the Rome Treaty, *op. cit.*, at p. xviii.

144. J.H.H. Weiler, Hjalte Rasmussen - Nemo propheta in patria sua, *op. cit.*, at xiii *et seq.*
145. L. Azoulai, L.M. Poiares Maduro, Introduction, *op. cit.*, at p. xviii.
146. C. Krenn, The European Court of Justice's Financial Accountability, *op. cit.*, at 469 *et seq.* in particular.
147. The Italian Corte costituzionale, with a reform in January 2020 of its rules of procedure and in particular of Article 4-ter of the Norme integrative per i giudizi davanti alla Corte costituzionale, opened its doors to amici curiae, third-parties interventions, technical expert hearing; for a long time, the Corte was an example of the opposite trend, see for instance P. Passaglia, L'intervento di terzi nei giudizi di costituzionalità concreti, Corte costituzionale – Servizio studi, area di diritto comparato, available at the website https://www.cortecostituzionale.it/documenti/convegni_seminari/Comp_213.pdf.
148. See E. Sharpston, Transparency and Clear Legal Language in the European Union: Ambiguous Legislative Texts, Laconic Pronouncements and the Credibility of the Judicial System, *op. cit.*, at 423.

CHAPTER 7

Conclusions

Summing up the reflections, one can say that throughout this book an attempt was made to highlight and investigate a particular and complex phenomenon. I argued that by looking at some specific aspects of the structure and the organization of the European Court of Justice—which form, however, a complete picture of its institutional setting—a specific history of its evolution can be read. In particular, I argued that the history of the European Court of Justice is a history of success not only in its role of shaper of the EU legal order, as a motor of the continent's integration and as a substantive interpreter of the inherent potentialities of the supranational political and legal construction, as the common narrative goes. It is a history of success in precise regards to its own institutional evolution as well—because of the capacity of the Court of Justice not to constitute a simple "unmoved mover" but to change as a living institution that made its way by both fostering and adapting to the different stages of a progressive integration. The evolution of the Court's structure and organization took place with specific characteristics. It evolved, in my view, by facing several organizational challenges and by solving them through a particular capacity of internalization of internal and external comparative lessons—stemming from the osmosis with its own Member states and their legal cultures and from the international debate. In this way, I also argued, the Court of Justice increased its authority within the EU legal order, particularly but not only within its federal-like judicial architecture.

L. Pierdominici, *The Mimetic Evolution of the Court of Justice of the EU*, https://doi.org/10.1007/978-3-030-47864-3_7

In substantiating this claim, I started *ab origine*, by saying that these dynamics already took place with the process of establishing a permanent European Court of Justice, and with its primitive institutional design. The very choice of establishing a permanent court, the design of its specific, decisive powers of adjudication—in particular its “administrative” powers and the preliminary reference jurisdiction—and even the first functional principles it happened to develop in its early jurisprudence decisively, were all based, as seen, on the institutional internalization of specificities coming from external influences—particularly by the decisive influence of the Member States’ legal cultures. As everybody knows, only in its nature of permanent jurisdiction and by playing such decisive roles with such decisive powers could the European Court of Justice emerge as a key actor of the supranational legal order.

In following a sort of “institutional building” roadmap, once looked into the structuring of the institutional position and the powers of the Court, I then looked at its composition and the choice of its members. Here, the evolution of the Court was also decisively influenced by the comparative conversation, in national and international environments: and the reform finally adopted with the Treaty of Lisbon (already previously discussed in several settings), which introduced an independent supranational panel for the screening of the national candidate European judges, has been decisive in the improvement of the Court’s authority, in several respects, not only related to the inherent quality of its composition but also its external image.

I could trace the same dynamics when I turned my attention to the problem of the deliberation of the Court as well as its transparency. In this respect, the original debate looked at the topic of the admissibility or not of the practice of separate/dissenting opinions by judges as well as the related role of collegiality as the crucial point. Here, it was noted that in its tralatitious adherence to the principle of forced collegiality, the Court’s institutional setting was influenced by the model of collegiality prevalent in its original Member States at the time of the ECSC, to which it adhered; and that such a choice was explicitly aimed at protecting the “external” independence of the member judges and the credibility of the institution—in times where the composition of the Court and the authoritativeness thereby implied were not still clarified. Although the comparative panorama has meanwhile changed, the need for protection of the authority of the CJEU in its legal order and of its judges in their professional mandates is an evergreen and robust reason against change in this respect. Still, it was noted how the Court was able to evolve in another relevant sense related to its deliberation and transparency. In internalizing a certain comparative influence, also epitomized by some Member States, the Court was invested by the new trend of openness intended as access by thirds to court documents. In doing so, it fostered its dimension of *soft accountability*: a dimension of procedural transparency and a new relationship between institutions and "users", according to which the Court, in becoming open up to the public and by creating the possibilities of a dialogue with agents and social parts, becomes more *socially*—one could even say *politically*—legitimated.

Once looked at its competences' design, composition and openness in deliberation, I then focused on the capacity of docket control of the Court, a well-known decisive aspect of its structure and organization. This became more and more debated with the progressive entrenchment of the dynamics of the European federal-like judicial architecture in everyday life of national judges and other players and therefore with the CJ becoming, as it has been said, more and more a "victim of its own success"; the topic has been simultaneously a symbol of the Court's acquired authority and crucial for its improvement over time, in several respects. Significant trends were visible from my perspective. The debate on the conceptualization itself of the idea of docket control and the possible solutions for the European Court of Justice was very much influenced by comparative arguments, not always of appropriate quality. Even more importantly, the solutions considered by the Court always had to confront the specificities of the heterarchical European judicial architecture, where a simple transplant of foreign solutions could be particularly problematic. The main concerns, for any possible solution, actually came from the diversity of patterns of behaviour by national judges, especially in the use of the preliminary reference procedure, often clearly influenced by culturally shaped factors. It was shown how the whole debate on the topic, and the choice to discard certain possible *endogenous* solutions and to adopt other "neutral" ones, were all influenced by the need to not put at risk the relationship between the Court and the other players in the field, precisely because of their culturally shaped behaviours.

Finally, I had a look at the style of the Court's judgements. It was highlighted how the stylistic modalities of the Court's decisions can be considered as final aspects of its structure and organization, as morphological elements of the final judicial output influenced by the institutional setting of the Court. It was also highlighted how much they were influenced by the progressive osmosis with legal cultures of the Member States in the original paradigmatic model and within the stratification of influences of the following decades. It was important to note that the Court is often the final manufacturer in a complex assembly line of fabrication of EU law, influenced yet again by the complexity of the EU legal order. I also stressed how its different waves of stylistic formalism were traceable to the will of Luxembourg to convey its univocal voice as much as possible and the struggle for an interpretative authority—a need that will probably also inspire the possible new changes ahead.

Already in the title of this dissertation, I proposed a definition for this specific, multifaceted modality of institutional evolution embodied by the European Court of Justice. I talked of *mimetism* and said that it can be considered as something peculiar about the project of supranational institutionalization of the EU. By *mimetism* I meant the capacity of the Court of Justice of the EU, as a supranational institution, to evolve by facing several organizational challenges and by solving them through a selective internalization of internal and external comparative lessons—therefore stemming from the osmosis with the legal cultures of its own Member states as well as the international conversation. In several respects, this has led to an enhancement of its authority in the EU legal space. The Court's institutional evolution was mimetic: made of a naturally utilitarian search for models that can guarantee advantages, in terms of fostering its authority in the EU public space. The peculiarity of this complex phenomenon is double-fold and leads us to a couple of final reflections that can meaningfully represent the conclusion of the research. The first, at the phenomenological level, is on the capacity of the Court of Justice to evolve with a hefty dose of institutional autonomy; the second, at the methodological level, is on how the researcher shall investigate this phenomenon.

7.1 The Autonomy and Authority of the Court in Its Evolution

It was noticed that the Court of Justice evolved, in its structure and its organization, by facing several organizational challenges, and I offered a panorama of relevant case studies. I emphasized its ability to face these challenges with a specific capacity of selective employment of internal and external comparative lessons, therefore coming from the osmosis with its own Member states and their legal cultures and from the international debate. I gave a definition to this specific capacity and I highlighted how it was relevant for the improvement of the Court's authority in its legal system—beyond the trite clichés on its "legitimacy" to perform as an institutional actor.

The story that I told, this story of *mimetic* evolution, also gives us the measure of how much and to what extent the Court of Justice has been *autonomous* in its development vis-à-vis other powers of its legal system. Its institutional evolution has always happened with a distinctive dose of self-determination, of autonomous negotiation: in a certain sense, this has been the logical premise for the particular forms of internalization that I described throughout the dissertation. It is relevant to reflect on this specific autonomous nature of the Court since it is peculiar for a judicial institution and it is also very much a characteristic of the most recent debates on its structure and organization. Not only the European Court of Justice is not an unmoved mover of the EU integration, and it is an institution able to evolve; it is important to notice that it has been capable of evolving autonomously, often with a large dose of independence from political powers—making itself a bearer and responsible of its own choices and positions.

One can notice this special institutional feature in several organizational aspects.

Interesting studies have been recently published about the Court's financial accountability, and therefore on how the Court budget is drawn up in a complex procedure laid down in Articles 314–319 TFEU and negotiated by the Court in its autonomy with the Parliament and the Council as co-legislators—with a certain pressure of the political power that tries to influence though this procedure that way in which "the European Court of Justice organises the institution and conducts the judicial process".[1]

More in general, it must be noted that, in the specific supranational environment, it happens that the judicial arm of the Community has its own Statute—containing the general traits of the institutional organization and the broader principles of its procedure—set by the High Contracting Parties "in a separate Protocol" of the Treaties, as per Article 281 Treaty on the Functioning of the European Union. The Statute is nowadays provided by Protocol no. 3 "on the statute of the Court of Justice of the European Union" attached to the TFEU.[2] Soon after that provision, Article 281 TFEU further provides that "The European Parliament and the Council, acting in accordance with the ordinary legislative procedure, may amend the provisions of the Statute, with the exception of Title I and Article 64. The European Parliament and the Council shall act either at the request of the Court of Justice and after consultation of the Commission, or on a proposal from the Commission and after consultation of the Court of Justice". Therefore, it is to be highlighted that already in setting the rules for the position and any reform of the Statute, a request or at least a consultation of the Court of Justice as an independent, separate entity is designed as necessary. Often, this request does not even come in the forms of a mere introductory act, but of a full-fledged policy proposal autonomously drafted by the Court.

It is then to be noted that the proper and specific "Rules of Procedure of the Court of Justice", as per Article 253 TFEU, are directly and autonomously established by the CJEU, and are just *ex post* approved by the Council. The idea and the extent of inherent self-determination in such an establishment are clear when reading, for example, the recitals of the act nowadays containing those Rules.[3] In the text in force today, before the introductory provisions, it is the Court of Justice itself—having regard to all the pertinent primary norms—to adopt its procedural devices advancing a vast series of broached "whereas". It explicitly links the perceived necessity for a reform to the changes in quantity and quality of the caseload[4]; it describes the experience acquired in the different procedures and, in light of this, the opportunity of a better differentiation among the various actions, the simplifications of some and the clarification of others[5]; it recalls the opportunity to dispose within a reasonable period of the cases brought before the judges and therefore to extend the opportunities for the Court to rule by reasoned order[6]; it emphasizes the interest in making the applied Rules easier to understand, to justify the necessity to delete some outdated or unapplied rules as well as the re-numeration and harmonization of the content in distinct paragraphs and headed articles.[7] All these (quite reasonable) arguments, in different settings, would be at the undisputed and unique discretionary disposal of political powers—yet this is not the case of the EU legal system where a significant role is played by the autonomous deliberations of the judicial institution.

The findings of my case studies throughout the dissertation are also relevant to this perspective. For instance, in following the proposed previous order, I recalled how the Court's originally conferred powers were decisively enhanced by some basic judicial, autonomous interpretative choices. I pointed to the fact that the idea to establish an independent panel for the screening of candidate judges was part of the proposals of some formal *cercles de discussion* composed of Court's members, and ended up in an institutional solution in which the applicable law came by the initiative of the Court and in which former members of the Court are involved. I noticed that the choice not to make its deliberation more transparent is part of a strategy of the Court itself, in the current state of the affairs of EU integration, and that, on the other hand, the recent choice to open up access to the Court's documents came again by autonomous Decisions of the Court itself, "in the exercise of its administrative functions",[8] and the consequent policies are subject to judicial scrutiny of the Court. It was shown how the necessity of docket control has been one of the significant topics debated internally, and it has always been measured against other self-determined priorities of the Court—first the preservation of its *nomophylactic* function—and I just recalled how this also explicitly inspired the last reform of the Rules of procedure. Finally, I analyzed how the Court's style reflects the natural, "organical" stratification of its autonomous internal practices governed by cultural and even individual leverage.

These findings are coherent with the traditional understanding of observers who have claimed that, in the EU, drafting and reforming the Court's procedural and organizational law has been a matter for a closed community, dominated by European Court of Justice members,[9] so that Ole Due, a Former President of the Court and the author of a report for its reform,[10] described the process of EU judicial reform as being akin to "a party of old schoolboys".[11]

In this perspective, it is impossible not to mention certain last important circumstances in which the high degree of autonomy of the Court of Justice has been expressed with particular clarity, and precisely in matters with strong structural and organizational implications.

The first episode is the procedure of accession of the European Union to the European Convention for the Protection of Human Rights and Fundamental Freedoms. As well known, the Court concluded two decades ago in its Opinion 2/94[12] that, under the existing treaty provisions, there was no competence for the Community to accede to the Convention. The Lisbon Treaty remedied this by amending Article 6(2) TEU and placed an obligation on the EU to accede. At the same time, a specific Protocol no. 14 of the ECHR was issued in June 2010, allowing the accession. In April 2013, a draft agreement on accession was agreed between the European Commission and the Council of Europe. Still, the Court of Justice, again exercising its *ex ante* jurisdiction now according to Article 218(11) TFEU, with a contested Opinion no. 2/13[13] and to the surprise of many[14] found the accession agreement incompatible with EU law. This is noteworthy for several compelling reasons. First of all, it is notable because the Court has been already accused of having masked, through the defence of the autonomy of EU law, the defence of its jurisdictional powers and its own autonomy vis-à-vis the European Court of Human Rights, threatened by perils such as the expansion of the latter's judicial review in matters of the common foreign and security policy, the procedure for the prior involvement of the Court of Justice in indirect actions concerning EU law brought in the courts of the member states and reaching Strasbourg without giving rise to a preliminary reference, the co-respondent mechanism needed when a responsibility of a Member State stems from the implementation of an action emanating from the EU.[15] Second, this (temporary?) negative outcome is even more noteworthy if one thinks that reliable sources have reported that the Court has constantly participated—in the person of its Registrar—in the negotiations between the High Parties leading to the draft agreement on the accession of 2013,[16] incidentally making tangible, once more, an autonomous, self-determined nature which is even difficult to justify or conceptualize.

A similar discussion is now emerging about the future role of the Court in the context of the Withdrawal agreement of the United Kingdom, in relation to the dispute settlement system through arbitration panel provided by.

A second relevant episode is the new exacerbated debate on the institutional reform of the Court of Justice taken as a whole, started in late 2014, to which I already referred at the end of Chapter five. It is, in fact, a renewed phase of the never-ending quarrel on the docket control of the Court, opened by a letter of the Italian Presidency of the Council of September 2014 directed to the judicial institution "to invite new suggestions regarding the procedures for increasing the number of judges at the General Court". The idea of increasing the number of members sitting in the EU tribunal of first instance was part of the legislative initiative to reform the Statute of the Court of Justice of the EU which the Court itself, according to the previously described procedure, submitted to the EU legislature in March 2011.[17] In doing so, it already showed how and to what extent it is the master of its own structure and organization. Such initiative was favourably received by the Commission and by the Parliament, where it was approved in a first reading; more difficulties raised in the Council, under the Greek Presidency of the first half of 2014, where the usual quarrels on any solutions involving fewer judges than the number of Member States (as also described) took place, also with reference to the Civil Service Tribunal, where such problems were already in order and in fact some appointments due at the end of 2014 were severely delayed. In light of all this, the Court of Justice of the EU—in the person of its then President Vassilios Skouris—submitted in October 2014 an official "response to the invitation of the Italian Presidency to present new proposals",[18] aimed at offering solutions to "reinforce the efficiency of justice at EU level". In the document, an extensive policy analysis was provided by the Court, including statistical analysis of the workload of the EU courts and the presentation of the first, heavy actions for damages in which the breach of the General Court's duty to adjudicate within a reasonable time was foreshadowed; and a detailed proposal to double the number of judges of the General Court was put forward, in a three-stage temporal programme including the transfer to the General Court of the EU civil service cases. The Court's proposal was so rich that it was not merely articulated in its temporal aspects but also discussed in its pro and cons, justified for the "lack of alternatives", and even accompanied by a financial statement showing the estimated costs of the various solutions. As documented, the proposal was strongly put forward, other suggestions from the EU Parliament notwithstanding.[19]

Here again, one can see the profound link between the discretional autonomy and the authority of the Court of Justice in the moves of an institution that directly and independently negotiates its own reform. And here again, there is something more to corroborate the argument. On the one hand, one can be tempted to speculate on the merits of the Court's autonomous proposals which—for good or bad reasons—in foreseeing an effacement of the Civil Service Tribunal, shift away from the preference of the Masters of the Treaties enshrined in Article 257 TFEU for specialized courts "attached to the General Court to hear and determine at first instance certain classes of action or proceeding brought in specific areas".[20] Such primary political preference can also be seen in the fact that the Treaty of Lisbon maintained the existing provisions on the possible establishment of specialized courts but introduced changes in relation to the procedures for the creation of such courts, namely that they can today be created in accordance with the ordinary legislative procedure rather than, as hitherto, by unanimity; in this sense, the proposal for a generalist jurisdiction made up of two judges per each Member State certainly goes in the opposite direction. Moreover, it happened that—following the President Skouris' initiative—the proposal was significantly opposed by many members of the General Court. The General Court took an explicit, contrary position with an official position paper of September 17, 2014, contesting some of the basic data; four of its judges then appeared before the European Parliament to object to the plan, explicitly explaining why "progressive, reversible and more economical solutions are far better" for a new reform of the EU judicial architecture.[21] They also made known that the President of the Court of Justice commenced a critical official disciplinary procedure against them "with the aim of preventing the communication of any previously uncensored information to the legislative authorities",[22] a fact that was then publicly discussed in the press in the terms of "EU judges at war".[23] The same disciplinary action was also reported to be taken against the then President of the General Court, Marc Jaeger, again for the public expression of a position contrary to the Court's unitarian one represented by its proposals (in a letter of response to the Italian Presidency's position), after having considered that it "seriously damages the Court's position in future budgetary negotiations".[24]

The initiative resulted in the now-completed expansion of the General Court, that absorbed the Civil Service Tribunal.[25] But from my point of view, apart from the folkloristic tone of such quarrels, it is evident that here again the idea of autonomy of the Court of Justice has been very much linked to that of its authority, so much that a real battle for the expression of such an autonomous position has been embarked on, and kept around the most typical structural/organization matters discussed throughout the proposed reflections. In this respect, some scholars even discuss of a "*réforme confisquée par la Court de justice*".[26]

7.2 Mimetism as Phenomenon and a Method in the Plurality of the EU Legal Order

A second, final reflection on the idea of *mimetism* in the institutional evolution of the Court of Justice links the phenomenological level to the methodological one. In my view, such peculiar nature of what I have studied can be traced back to both the described phenomenon of institutional evolution itself and the way in which, methodologically, the phenomenon should be investigated by the researcher.

It was noted that the adopted perspective of *mimetism* represents a peculiar syneresis of two main comparative approaches, the *functional* and the *culturalist*, considering this latter as a general category including comparative legal history, the study of legal transplants and the comparative study of legal cultures[27]—all "contextual" approaches that characterized my analysis throughout all the chapters. These are two schools of thought that are usually kept separate as antithetical in classic horizontal comparisons—intended as the typical comparisons "between legal systems or institutions belonging to the same level, both national (e.g. for comparative constitutional law) and international level (e.g. comparing international institutions)".[28] Still, one can say that in light of all of the above, the *functional* and the *culturalist* are two perspectives that naturally merge together in the evolutionary studies of the supranational legal context, in which both horizontal and vertical comparisons are in order. Only by looking at how different comparative influences have been faced and internalized by the structure and the organization of the Court of Justice, one can understand some of the "efficient secrets" of the functional evolution of the institution, able to develop and increase its authority in an increasingly plural setting and with a self-empowerment dynamic—often autonomously from other powers. Again, although the local specificities and the associated "cultural argument" have been deployed "in the specific European context (…) most often (…) in opposition to the possibility of achieving more legal Europeanisation", and in antithesis to the "edification of a community" and the construction of a "common legal culture", a more refined use of the "legal cultures" sensitivity, applied in the supranational environment, cannot but merge such an approach with the functional, evolutionary one.[29]

In the analysis of a whole series of decisive aspects of its structure and organization, it was shown how the institutional development of the CJEU has been wisely *culturally* influenced with the precise aim of being *functionally* efficient, to strengthen the authority of the Court. This happened in the structuring of the powers of the ECJ, to create a stable and decisively powerful institution; this occurred in the evolution pertaining to its composition, to create a more independent and legitimate body, certain original vices in the choice of its members notwithstanding; this happened concerning the openness of the Court's deliberation, with historical closures and new openings all linked to the need of strengthening the judicial authority; this happened concerning the problem of the docket control, with a specific attention to the peculiarities of the interrelation with national players not to erode the *nomophylactic* capacity of the ECJ; finally, this happened with the style of the Court, profoundly influenced by the progressive osmosis with legal cultures but always much aimed at conveying the clear voice of the Court. In all these moves, the cultural influence and the attention to the diversity of the EU legal space as well as the ability to create a *unitas in diversitate* proved crucial.

All this analysis is not only important, in my view, for the understanding of an interesting and relevant phenomenon. It is also naturally conducive to significant reflections on how the researcher should methodologically investigate this phenomenon and similar others, and with which approach and tools. Since the beginning, I clarified the plurality of references that inspired this work. It was explicitly *situated*, as said, at the crossroads of different important debates. I called them a discovery (or re-discovery) of historical studies of European Union law, a discovery (or re-discovery) of discussions on the legitimacy and the authority of international judicial review bodies, a discovery (or re-discovery) of debates on the cultural diversity in the supranational project and its role in the legal context.

It was also suggested that in looking in particular at the role of cultural diversity in the supranational project, a more refined approach should be adopted by striking a distinction—not always done in classic comparative law—between an external and an internal dimension of legal culture, and therefore by looking more specifically at the channels through which cultural elements have an impact on legal configurations. In this sense, the broad societal and the more specific professional ideas of legal culture—the latter linked to the way in which legal operators think about the law—should be kept separate.[30] While the often idealized societal perception of legal *culturalism* leads to the design of separated, fractured *families* of legal development,[31] with none or scarce permeability, a more realist appraisal of the higher degree of homogeneity within the professional legal operators,[32] who are also the actual actors of legal development, cannot but make us think of cultural differences even as an arsenal or a toolkit of solutions that can be used for functional purposes.

To analyse how and to what extent such degree of homogeneity was very much present and is still present in the process of integration and institutionalization of the EU—so that one can consider the institutional evolution of the CJEU as a single experiment of *unitas in diversitate*—a look at the new historiographical and sociological literature on the legal construction of the European Communities also proved decisive. It was all aimed at looking at how structural/cultural differences could also become, in the supranational setting and in Atlan's terms, functional factors of organization and re-organization for institutional evolution. My research, in this sense, was originally and explicitly intended to be eclectic in nature. This should not be read as an acceptance of an "anything goes methodology in a Feyerabendian sense",[33] as a methodological "anarchism" that "helps to achieve more progress in any one of the senses one cares to choose".[34] Quite the contrary, in a more modest way, it became clear that only by accepting the more recent calls for a "flexible understanding of methodology", capable of using different inspirations together in a "both-and", and not "either-or" perspective,[35] and by employing the tools offered by different professionals, "historians, sociologists, political scientists, linguists, and anthropologists",[36] though inserted in a technical perspective, a fruitful and original perspective on certain specific legal phenomena can be offered.

If this was the first way of dealing with the pluralism inherent in the study of the supranational legal order applied in my research, at least a second one was also adopted and was of utmost importance. I refer to the idea to expand, not only methodologically but also dimensionally, the boundaries of the comparative research. This is what is done when a vertical comparison—a comparison between systems or legal institutions which "do not belong to the same level"[37]—is added to a classic horizontal comparison, which "compare legal systems or institutions belonging to the same level, both national (e.g. for comparative constitutional law) and international level (e.g. comparing international institutions)".[38] A call for this multidimensional approach—as a way to deal with the problem of the "comparative methodology and pluralism in legal comparison in a global age"—came in recent times from several authors.[39] It has been suggested to expand the comparative research in a "top-down" vein to study the context of the *internalization* of international norms and regulations by national legal orders, whereby national law is required to incorporate international concepts into the national legal system[40]; and that the same expansion could also be directed in a "bottom-up" vertical comparison to analyse "the transposition of legal concepts, or the ideas behind them, from national to international level",[41] or the incorporation of national principles by international standards.[42] It is not a surprise that in these manifestos, the processes of globalization or regionalization—and the process of Europeanisation primarily—are taken as paradigmatic case studies: they are, according to many, de facto "challenging the mechanical understanding of methodology".[43]

Already in 1996, a heterodox scholar-like Ian Ward wrote that "(T)he law of Community cannot, and must not, be studied in splendid isolation. A proper understanding of the context of European Union law is vital. (…) European law, like any law, only exists in context. There is no such things as 'law'; it is not a discrete concept. Law only exists as a function of history, of politics, of society, of philosophy, of literature, and, perhaps most importantly in our particular context, of economics. Any attempt to study European law without a proper acknowledgment of this truth can only be described as insufficient, perhaps even dishonest".[44] In this sense, the methodological foundations of comparativism are said to be precisely "not only the comparative method" in itself, as mere juxtaposition, "but also the contrastive, systemic, functional axiological, synergetic, historical, and a number of other methods which are combined in the comparative approach"[45]; and its philosophy is found precisely in recognition of such contextual multiplicity, which reflects "the diversity of the world, a contemplation of the 'universal, general, different, and unique'" between different systems, and the possibility of a dialogue among them.[46] The proposed comparative perspectives on the institutionalization of the Court of Justice of the EU—which considered internal and external influences, vertical osmosis from Member States' legal cultures and experiences and inspiration from international debates, all in a functional perspective—are a modest contribution to this new research in an expanded area. What I called *mimetism* in the CJEU's evolution is not only, in itself, a fruit of the EU legal order pluralism. Also, it could only be read through the adoption of pluralism, as a methodological stance and as a broad perspective of research.

Notes

1. C. Krenn, The European Court of Justice's Financial Accountability, *op. cit.*, at 461 in particular.
2. Protocol (No. 3) on the statute of the Court of Justice of the European Union, available at the website http://curia.europa.eu/jcms/upload/docs/application/pdf/2008-09/statut_2008-09-25_17-29-58_783.pdf (accessed 2 March 2020).
3. Rules of Procedure of the Court of Justice. OJ L 265, 29.9.2012, pp. 1–42 (BG, ES, CS, DA, DE, ET, EL, EN, FR, IT, LV, LT, HU, MT, NL, PL, PT, RO, SK, SL, FI, SV).
4. *Ivi*, first Recital: "(1) Despite having been amended on several occasions over the years, the Rules of Procedure of the Court of Justice have remained fundamentally unchanged in structure since their original adoption on 4 March 1953. The Rules of Procedure of 19 June 1991, which are currently in force, still reflect the initial preponderance of direct actions, whereas in fact the majority of such actions now fall within the jurisdiction of the General Court, and references for a preliminary ruling from the courts and tribunals of the Member States represent, quantitatively, the primary category of cases brought before the Court. That fact should be taken into account and the structure and content of the Rules of Procedure of the Court adapted, in consequence, to changes in its caseload".
5. *Ivi*, third Recital: "(3) In the light of experience gained in the course of implementing the various procedures, it is also necessary to supplement or to clarify, for the benefit of litigants as well as of national courts and tribunals, the rules that apply to each procedure. The rules in question concern, in particular, the concepts of party to the main proceedings, intervener and party to the proceedings before the General Court, or, in preliminary rulings, the rules governing the bringing of matters before the Court and the content of the order for reference. With regard to appeals against decisions of the General Court, a clearer distinction must also be drawn between appeals and cross-appeals in consequence of the service of an appeal on the cross-appellant".
6. *Ivi*, sixth Recital: "(6) In order to maintain the Court's capacity, in the face of an ever-increasing caseload, to dispose within a reasonable period of time of the cases brought before it, it is also necessary to continue the efforts made to reduce the duration of proceedings before the Court, in particular by extending the opportunities for the Court to rule by reasoned order, simplifying the rules relating to the intervention of the States and institutions referred to in the first and third paragraphs of Article 40 of the Statute and providing for the Court to be able to rule

without a hearing if it considers that it has sufficient information on the basis of all the written observations lodged in a case".

7. *Ivi*, seventh Recital: "(7) In the interests of making the Rules applied by the Court easier to understand, lastly, certain rules which are outdated or not applied should be deleted, every paragraph of the present Rules numbered, each article given a specific heading summarising its content and the terminology harmonised".
8. Precisely echoing the words of the Decision of the Court of Justice of the European Union of 11 December 2012 concerning public access to documents held by the Court of Justice of the European Union in the exercise of its administrative functions (OJ C 38, 9.2.2013, pp. 2–4).
9. J.H.H. Weiler, Epilogue: The Judicial Après Nice, *op. cit.*, at 216; see for an organic reconstruction about the "judicial preferences" expressed M.P. Granger, The Future of Europe: Judicial Interference and Preferences, in 3 Comparative European Politics, 2005, p. 155.
10. The already mentioned Report by the Working Party on the Future of the European Communities' Court System for the European Commission, January 2000 (the mentioned Ole Due Report).
11. O. Due, Looking Backwards and Forwards, in Amicale des référendaires et anciens référendaires de la Cour de justice et du tribunal de première instance des communautés européennes (ed.), La Cour de Justice des communautés européennes 1952–2002: Bilan et perspectives, Bruylant 2004, p. 25, at 31; see also C. Krenn, The European Court of Justice's Financial Accountability, *op. cit.*, p. 474.
12. Opinion 2/94, of 28 March 1996 (ECR 1996 p. I-1759) ECLI:EU:C:1996:140.
13. Opinion 2/13, of 18 December 2014 (ECLI:EU:C:2014:2454).
14. See for instance the immediate critical responses issued in blog posts by renowned scholars such as S. Peers, The CJEU and the EU's accession to the ECHR: A clear and present danger to human rights protection, available at the website http://eulawanalysis.blogspot.co.uk/2014/12/the-cjeu-and-eus-accession-to-echr.html (accessed 2 March 2020); S. Douglas-Scott, Opinion 2/13 on EU accession to the ECHR: A Christmas bombshell from the European Court of Justice, available at the website http://www.verfassungsblog.de/opinion-213-eu-accession-echr-christmas-bombshell-european-court-justice/#.Vbj545Ptmkr (accessed 2 March 2020); and L.F.M. Besselink, Acceding to the ECHR notwithstanding the Court of Justice Opinion 2/13, available at the website http://www.verfassungsblog.de/en/acceding-echr-notwithstanding-court-justice-opinion-213/#.VJq5SFIM-U (accessed 2 March 2020), this last even arguing for a disobedience to the Court of Justice' Opinion.
15. All technical points touched by both the Draft Agreement and, critically, by the Opinion 2/13, of 18 December 2014 (ECLI:EU:C:2014:2454);

see on this point T. Lock, The European Court of Justice and International Courts, OUP 2015, p. 77 *et seq*; and S. Saurugger, F. Terpan, The Court of Justice of the European Union and The Politics of Law, *op. cit.*, p. 176.

16. I take this information by the oral intervention/interview of J.P. Jacqué in the workshop "The European Court of Justice Inside Out", organized in Florence, at the European University Institute, on the 26 May 2015, by the EUI, the Université Versailles Saint-Quentin en Yvelines and the Institut d'études politiques de Paris.
17. The proposals are available at the website http://data.consilium.europa.eu/doc/document/ST-8787-2011-INIT/en/pdf (accessed 2 March 2020).
18. The document is available at the website http://data.consilium.europa.eu/doc/document/ST-14448-2014-REV-1/en/pdf (accessed 2 March 2020).
19. See again A. Alemanno, L. Pech, Thinking Justice Outside the Docket: A Critical Assessment of the Reform of the EU's Court System, *op. cit.*, with reference to European Parliament resolution of 29 April 2015 with observations forming an integral part of the decision on discharge in respect of the implementation of the general budget of the European Union for the financial year 2013, Section IV—Court of Justice (2014/2080[DEC]), para. 11.
20. Article 257
    (ex Article 225a TEC)

    > The European Parliament and the Council, acting in accordance with the ordinary legislative procedure, may establish specialised courts attached to the General Court to hear and determine at first instance certain classes of action or proceeding brought in specific areas. The European Parliament and the Council shall act by means of regulations either on a proposal from the Commission after consultation of the Court of Justice or at the request of the Court of Justice after consultation of the Commission.
    > The regulation establishing a specialised court shall lay down the rules on the organisation of the court and the extent of the jurisdiction conferred upon it.
    > Decisions given by specialised courts may be subject to a right of appeal on points of law only or, when provided for in the regulation establishing the specialised court, a right of appeal also on matters of fact, before the General Court.
    > The members of the specialised courts shall be chosen from persons whose independence is beyond doubt and who possess the ability

required for appointment to judicial office. They shall be appointed by the Council, acting unanimously.
The specialised courts shall establish their Rules of Procedure in agreement with the Court of Justice. Those Rules shall require the approval of the Council.
Unless the regulation establishing the specialised court provides otherwise, the provisions of the Treaties relating to the Court of Justice of the European Union and the provisions of the Statute of the Court of Justice of the European Union shall apply to the specialised courts. Title I of the Statute and Article 64 thereof shall in any case apply to the specialised courts.

21. The report of the four General Court's Judges is available at the website http://g8fip1kplyr33r3krz5b97d1.wpengine.netdna-cdn.com/wp-content/uploads/2015/04/EP-Strasbourg-Summary-and-costs.pdf (accessed 2 March 2020).
22. *Ivi*, at 1: "Nevertheless, we are of the view that, in the interest of the Institution and the public interest generally, we should strive to find more efficient and less costly long term solutions to ensure the smooth running of the General Court. In that light, it is regrettable that the President of the Court of Justice has commenced an official disciplinary procedure against our court with the aim of preventing the communication of any previously uncensored information to the legislative authorities (which is also particularly difficult to accept given that we are independent judges charged, inter alia, with the duty of adjudicating upon the Court's administrative decisions)".
23. See for instance http://www.politico.eu/newsletter/playbook/politico-brussels-playbook-eu-judges-at-war-varoufakis-out-the-le-pens-top-twiplomats-spokespeople-shuffle/ (accessed 2 March 2020). See also, similarly, http://bruxelles.blogs.liberation.fr/2015/04/26/la-justice-europeenne-au-bord-de-la-crise-de-nerfs/ (accessed 2 March 2020).
24. See again http://www.politico.eu/newsletter/playbook/politico-brussels-playbook-eu-judges-at-war-varoufakis-out-the-le-pens-top-twiplomats-spokespeople-shuffle/ (accessed 2 March 2020) and, for details, http://blogs.ft.com/brusselsblog/2015/04/27/the-1st-rule-of-ecj-flight-club-is-about-to-be-broken/ (accessed 2 March 2020).
25. Regulation (EU, Euratom) 2015/2422 of the European Parliament and of the Council of 16 December 2015 amending Protocol No 3 on the Statute of the Court of Justice of the European Union OJ L 341, 24.12.2015, pp. 14–17; Regulation (EU, Euratom) 2016/1192 of the European Parliament and of the Council of 6 July 2016 on the transfer to the General Court of jurisdiction at first instance in disputes between the European Union and its servants OJ L 200, 26.7.2016, pp. 137–139;

see in this respect D. Sarmiento, The Reform of the General Court: An Exercise in Minimalist (but Radical) Institutional Reform, in 19 Cambridge Yearbook of European Legal Studies, 2017, 236.

26. C. Friedrich, Les vicissitudes de la jurisdiction européenne: une réforme confisquée par la Cour de Justice, in Review du Droit de l'Union européenne, 2017, p. 113; for critical remarks see also A. Arnull, The Court of Justice Then, Now and Tomorrow, *op. cit.*, p. 12; A. Alemanno, L. Pech, Thinking Justice Outside the Docket: A Critical Assessment of the Reform of the EU's Court System, *op. cit.*; F. Dehousse, The Reform of the EU Courts (II)—Abandoning the Management Approach by Doubling the General Court, Egmont Paper 83/2016, available at the website http://www.egmontinstitute.be/reform-of-eu-courts-2/ (accessed 2 March 2020).
27. As the "three main current approaches other than functionalism": see R. Michaels, The Functional Method of Comparative Law, *op. cit.*, at 339–340.
28. A. Momirov, A. Naudé Fourie, Vertical Comparative Law Methods: Tools for Conceptualizing the International Rule of Law, *op. cit.*; R. Scarciglia, Comparative Methodology and Pluralism in Legal Comparison in a Global Age, *op. cit.*
29. G. Comparato, New Voices: Challenging Legal Culture, *op. cit.*, at pp. 16–17 in particular.
30. *Ibidem*, with reference to L.M. Friedman, The Legal System: A Social Science Perspective, *op. cit.*, at p. 223.
31. See on the usual instrumentality of such design P.G. Monateri, *Geopolitica* del diritto: genesi, governo e dissoluzione dei corpi politici, *op. cit.*
32. Often "authoritatively created through legal education": see G. Comparato, New Voices: Challenging Legal Culture, *op. cit.*, at 17.
33. J. Husa, Methodology of Comparative Law Today: From Paradoxes to Flexibility? in 4 Revue Internationale de Droit Comparé, 2006, p. 1095, at 1096.
34. The reference is of course to the well known work by P. Feyerabend, Against Method: Outline of an Anarchist Theory of Knowledge, Verso ed. 1978, at p. 18.
35. J. Husa, Methodology of Comparative Law Today: From Paradoxes to Flexibility? *op. cit.*, at 1116 with reference to K.Å. Modeér, Östersjöområdets rättsliga kartor w rättskulturella konstruktioner i förändring, in J. Kekkonen et al. (eds.), Norden, rätten, historia: Festskrift till Lars Björne, Suomen lakimiesyhdistys 2004, at pp. 194–195.
36. J. Husa, Methodology of Comparative Law Today: From Paradoxes to Flexibility? *op. cit.*, at 1116.
37. R. Scarciglia, Comparative Methodology and Pluralism in Legal Comparison in a Global Age, *op. cit.*, at 45.

38. *Ibidem.*
39. *Ibidem*; A. Momirov, A. Naudé Fourie, Vertical Comparative Law Methods: Tools for Conceptualizing the International Rule of Law, *op. cit.*, at 295.
40. A. Momirov, A. Naudé Fourie, Vertical Comparative Law Methods: Tools for Conceptualizing the International Rule of Law, *op. cit.*, at 295.
41. *Ivi*, at 296; R. Scarciglia, Comparative Methodology and Pluralism in Legal Comparison in a Global Age, *op. cit.*, at 45.
42. H.E. Chodosh, Comparing Comparisons: In Search of Methodology, *op. cit.*, at 1038 in particular.
43. J. Husa, The Method Is Dead, Long Live the Methods! European Polynomia and Pluralist Methodology, *op. cit.*, at 252; R. Scarciglia, Comparative Methodology and Pluralism in Legal Comparison in a Global Age, *op. cit.*, at 45.
44. I. Ward, A Critical Introduction to European Law, Butterworths 1996, at pp. vii–viii.
45. A.D. Tikhomirov, Philosophical Problems of Legal Comparativistics, *op. cit.*, at 165.
46. *Ivi*, at 173.

Bibliography

All the references to relevant judicial cases, legislation, institutional material in general, are provided *in extenso* in the endnotes of the book chapters.

Monographs, Dissertations, Collected Volumes

M. Adams, H. de Waele, J. Meeusen, G. Straetmans (eds.), Judging Europe's Judges: The Legitimacy of the Case Law of the European Court of Justice, Hart 2013.

A. Albi, J. Ziller (eds.), The European Constitution and National Constitutions: Ratification and Beyond, Kluwer Law International 2006.

P. Alleva et al. (eds.), Scritti in onore di Giuseppe Federico Mancini, Vol. II, Giuffrè 1998.

K.J. Alter, Establishing the Supremacy of European Law: The Making of an International Rule of Law in Europe, Oxford University Press 2001.

K.J. Alter, The European Court's Political Power: Selected Essays, Oxford University Press 2009.

A. Anzon (ed.), L'opinione dissenziente, Giappichelli 1995.

H. Arendt, Between Past and Future: Six Exercises in Political Thought, Meridian 1963.

A. Arnull, The European Union and its Court of Justice, 1st ed., Oxford 1999.

A. Arnull, The European Union and its Court of Justice, 2nd ed., Oxford 2006.

A. Arnull, P. Eeckhout, T. Tridimas (eds.), Continuity and Change in EU Law: Essays in Honour of Sir Francis Jacobs, Oxford University Press 2008.

H. Atlan, Entre le cristal et la fumée. Essai sur l'organisation du vivant, Editions du Seuil 1979.

L. Pierdominici, *The Mimetic Evolution of the Court of Justice of the EU*, https://doi.org/10.1007/978-3-030-47864-3

D. Augenstein, Integration through Law Revisited: The Making of the European Polity, Ashgate 2012.
M. Avbelj, J. Komàrek (eds.), Constitutional Pluralism in the European Union and Beyond, Hart Publishing 2012.
L. Azoulai, L. Burgorgue-Larsen (eds.), L'autorité de l'Union européenne, Burylant 2006.
L. Azoulai, L.M. Poiares Maduro (eds.), The Past and Future of EU Law: The Classics of EU Law Revisited on the 50th Anniversary of the Rome Treaty, Hart 2010.
W. Bagehot, The English Constitution, Oxford University Press 1867, reprinted 2001.
B. Balassa, The Theory of Economic Integration, Homewood 1961.
B. Barbisan, Il mito di *Marbury v. Madison* e le origini della giustizia costituzionale negli Stati Uniti, Il Mulino 2008.
R. Barents, The Autonomy of Community Law, Kluwer Law International 2004.
V. Barsotti, L'arte di tacere: strumenti e tecniche di non decisione della Corte suprema degli Stati Uniti, Giappichelli 1999.
G. Bebr, Development of Judicial Control of the European Communities, Brill 1981.
G. Beck, The Legal Reasoning of the Court of Justice of the EU, Hart Publishing 2013.
J. Bell, Judiciaries within Europe: A Comparative Review, Cambridge University Press 2010.
J. Bengoetxea, The Legal Reasoning of the European Court of Justice, Clarendon Press 1993.
P. Bianchi, La creazione giurisprudenziale delle tecniche di selezione dei casi, Giappichelli 2001.
P. Biavati, Diritto processuale dell'Unione europea, 4a ed., Giuffrè 2009.
A.M. Bickel, The Least Dangerous Branch: The Supreme Court at the Bar of Politics, Yale University Press 1986.
R. Bin, A discrezione del giudice. Ordine e disordine. Una prospettiva «quantistica», Franco Angeli 2013.
W. Blackstone, Commentaries on the Law of England, Vol. I, Clarendon Press 1765–1769.
M. Bobek (ed.), Selecting Europe's Judges, Oxford University Press 2015.
S. Boccalatte, La motivazione della legge. Profili teorici e giurisprudenziali, CEDAM 2008.
A. Brewer Carias, Judicial Review in Comparative Law, Cambridge University Press 1989.
The British Institute of International and Comparative Law, The Role and Future of the European Court of Justice, 1996.

M. Broberg, N. Fenger, Preliminary References to the European Court of Justice, 2nd ed., Oxford University Press 2014.
G. Canivet, M. Andenas, D. Fairgrieve (eds.), Independence, Accountability and the Judiciary, British Institute of International and Comparative Law 2006.
F. Capotorti, C. Ehlermann (eds.), Du droit international au droit de l'intégration - Liber amicorum Pierre Pescatore, Nomos Verlagsgesellschaft 1987.
M. Cappelletti, La giurisdizione costituzionale delle libertà. Primo studio sul ricorso costituzionale (con particolare riguardo agli ordinamenti tedesco, svizzero e austriaco), Giuffrè 1955.
M. Cappelletti, Il controllo giudiziario di costituzionalità delle leggi nel diritto comparato, Giuffrè 1968.
M. Cappelletti, The Judicial Process in Comparative Perspective, Clarendon Press 1989.
M. Cappelletti, M. Seccombe, J.H.H. Weiler (eds.), Integration Through Law: Europe and the American Federal Experience, Vol. 1. Methods, Tools and Institutions, De Gruyter 1986.
E. Carpano (ed.), Le revirement de jurisprudence en droit européen, Bruylant 2012.
G. Casper, R.A. Posner, The Workload of the Supreme Court, American Bar Foundation 1974.
S. Cassese, Dentro la Corte. Diario di un giudice costituzionale, Il Mulino 2015.
N. Catalano, Manuale di diritto delle Comunità europee, Giuffrè 1962.
F. Cerutti, E. Rudolph (eds.), A Soul for Europe. Vol. 1: A Reader, Peeters 2001.
D. Chalmers, C. Hadjiemmanuil, G. Monti, A. Tomkins, European Union Law: Cases and Materials, Cambridge University Press 2006.
D. Chalmers, G. Davies, G. Monti, European Union Law, 2nd ed., Cambridge University Press 2010.
M. Claes, The National Courts' Mandate in the European Constitution, Hart Publishing 2006.
L. Clément-Wiltz, La fonction de l'avocat général près la Cour de justice, Bruylant 2011.
M. Codinanzi, R. Mastroianni, Il contenzioso dell'Unione europea, Giappichelli 2009.
L. Conant, Justice Contained: Law and Politics in the European Union, Cornell University Press 2002.
G. Conway, The Limits of Legal Reasoning and the European Court of Justice, Cambridge University Press 2014.
P. Curci, La Corte costituzionale: composizione, attribuzioni, funzionamento, Giuffrè 1956.

D.M. Curtin, D. O'Keeffe (eds.), Constitutional Adjudication in European Community and National Law, Butterworth 1992.

E. D'Alessandro, Il procedimento pregiudiziale interpretativo dinanzi alla Corte di Giustizia, Giappichelli 2012.

A. Dashwood, A. Johnston, The Future of the Judicial System of the European Union, Hart Publishing 2001.

R. David, J.E.C. Brierley, Major Legal Systems in the World Today: An Introduction to the Comparative Study of Law, Free Press 1978.

J.P. Dawson, The Oracles of the Law, Greenwood Press, 1968.

M. Dawson, B. de Witte, E. Muir (eds.), Judicial Activism at the European Court of Justice, Edward Elgar 2013.

G. de Búrca, J. Scott (eds.), Constitutional Change in the EU, Hart Publishing 2000.

G. de Búrca, J.H.H. Weiler (eds.), The European Court of Justice, Oxford University Press 2001.

G. de Búrca, J.H.H. Weiler (eds.), The Worlds of European Constitutionalism, Cambridge University Press 2012.

P. de Cruz, Comparative Law in a Changing World, Cavendish Publishing Limited 1999.

R. Dehousse, The European Court of Justice: The Politics of Judicial Integration, Macmillan 1998.

R. Dehousse, J.H.H. Weiler, The Dynamics of European Integration, Pinter Publishers 1990.

M. Derlén, Multilingual Interpretation of European Union Law, Wolters Kluwer 2009.

A. de Tocqueville, Democracy in America, Vol. 1, available at the website https://www.gutenberg.org/files/815/815-h/815-h.htm.

G. de Vergottini, Diritto costituzionale comparato, CEDAM 2013.

G. de Vergottini, Diritto costituzionale comparato, CEDAM 2019.

J. Dickson, P. Eleftheriadis (eds.), Philosophical Foundations of European Union Law, Oxford University Press 2012.

P. Duez, G. Debreyere, Traité de Droit Administratif, Dalloz 1952.

E. Fahey (ed.), The Actors of Post-national Rule Making: Contemporary Challenges of European and International Law, Routledge 2015.

W. Feld, The Court of the European Communities: A New Dimension in International Adjudication, Martinus Nijhoff 1964.

P. Feyerabend, Against Method: Outline of an Anarchist Theory of Knowledge, Verso ed. 1978.

G. Frankenberg, Comparative Law as Critique, Elgar 2016.

F. Frankfurter, J.M. Landis, The Business of the Supreme Court of the United States—A Study in the Federal Judicial System, Macmillan 1928.

L.M. Friedman, The Legal System: A Social Science Perspective, Russell Sage Foundation, 1975.

H.P. Glenn, Legal Traditions of the World, Oxford University Press 2014.
A.W. Green, Political Integration by Jurisprudence, A. W. Sijthoff 1969.
G. Grementieri. Il processo comunitario. Principi e garanzie fondamentali, Giuffrè 1973.
A. Grilli, Le origini del diritto dell'Unione europea, Il Mulino 2009.
E. Guinchard, M.P. Granger (eds.), The New EU Judiciary. An Analysis of Current Judicial Reforms, Wolters Kluwer 2017.
E.B. Haas, The Uniting of Europe: Political, Social, and Economic Forces, 1950–1957, Stanford University Press 1958.
H.R. Harré, Social Being: A Theory for Social Psychology, Blackwell 1979.
T.C. Hartley, The Foundations of European Community Law, 4th ed., Oxford University Press 1998.
T.C. Hartley, The Foundations of European Community Law, 6th ed., Oxford University Press 2007.
D. Hawkins, D.A. Lake, D. Nielson, M.J. Tierney (eds.), Delegation and Agency in International Organizations, Cambridge University Press 2006.
J. Hendry, Unitas in Diversitate: on Legal Cultures and the Europeanisation of Law, PhD dissertation, European University Institute, 2009, available at the website https://cadmus.eui.eu/handle/1814/12045.
S. Hix, The Political System of the European Union, Palgrave 1999.
S. Hoffman, The European Sisyphus: Essays on Europe, 1964–1994, Boulder: Westview Press 1995.
O. W. Holmes Jr., The Common Law, M. Howe ed. 1963.
T. Horsley, The Court of Justice of the European Union as an Institutional Actor: Judicial Lawmaking and Its Limits, Cambridge University Press 2018.
M.O. Hudson, International Tribunals: Past and Future, Carnegie Endowment for International Peace and Brookings Institution 1944.
J.W. Hurst, The Growth of American Law: The Law Makers, Little Brown and Company 1950.
G. Itzcovich, Teorie e ideologie del diritto comunitario, Giappichelli 2006.
L. Johns, Strengthening International Courts: The Hidden Costs of Legalization, University of Michigan Press 2011.
R.D. Kelemen, Eurolegalism: The Transformation of Law and Regulation in the European Union, Harvard University Press 2011.
H. Kelsen, General Theory of Law and State, Harvard University Press 1945.
A.L. Kjær, S. Adamo (eds.), Linguistic Diversity and European Democracy, Ashgate 2011.
U. Klinke, Der Gerichtshof der Europäischen Gemeinschaften Aufbau und Arbeitsweise, Nomos 1989.
H. Koch, K. Hagel-Sørensen, U. Haltern, J.H.H. Weiler (eds.), Europe: The New Legal Realism. Essays in Honour of Hjalte Rasmussen, Djøf Forlag 2010.
D. Kochenov, G. de Búrca, A. Williams, Europe's Justice Deficit?, Hart Publishing 2015.

N. Komesar, Imperfect Alternatives: Choosing Institutions in Law, Economics, and Public Policy, University of Chicago Press 1994.

N. Komesar, Law's Limits: Rule of Law and the Supply and Demand of Rights, Cambridge University Press 2001.

T. Krefeld, Das französische Gerichtsurteil in linguistischer Sicht. Zwischen Fach- und Standessprache, Studia Romanica et linguistica, Peter Lang 1985.

T. Kuhn, The Structure of the Scientific Revolutions, University of Chicago Press 1962.

E. Lambert, Le gouvernement des juges et la lutte contre la législation sociale aux État-Unis: l'expérience américaine du contrôle judiciare de la constitutionnalité des lois, M. Giard & Cie edition 1921.

M. Lasser, Judicial Deliberations: A Comparative Analysis of Judicial Transparency and Legitimacy, Oxford University Press 2004.

B. Latour, La fabrique du droit. Une ethnographie du Conseil d'Etat, La Découverte & Syros 2002.

R. Lecourt, L'Europe des juges, Bruylant 1976.

O. Lecucq (ed.), La composition des juridictions. Perspectives de droit comparé, Bruylant 2014.

E. Leferrière, Traité de la Jurisdiction Administrative et les Recours Contentieux, Berger-Levrault 1896.

K. Lenaerts, I. Maselis, K. Gutman, EU Procedural Law, Oxford University Press 2014.

B. Lincoln, Authority: Construction and Corrosion, University of Chicago Press 1994.

P.L. Lindseth, Power and Legitimacy: Reconciling Europe and the Nation-State, Oxford University Press 2010.

T. Lock, The European Court of Justice and International Courts, Oxford University Press 2015.

K. Loehr, Mehrsprachigkeitsprobleme in der Europäischen Union: Eine empirische und theoretische Analyse aus sprachwissenschaftlicher Perspektive, Peter Lang 1998.

R. Mackenzie, K. Malleson, P. Martin, P. Sands, Selecting International Judges: Principle, Process, and Politics, Oxford University Press 2010.

H. Maine, Ancient Law: Its Connection with the Early History of Society and Its Relation to Modern Ideas, Beacon Press 1963 (1st ed., London 1861).

I. Maletic, The Law and Policy of Harmonisation in Europe's Internal Market, Elgar 2013.

K. Malleson, The New Judiciary: The Effects of Expansion and Activism, Ashgate 1999.

K. Malleson, Peter H. Russell (eds.), Appointing Judges in an Age of Juducial Power: Critical Perspectives from Around the World, University of Toronto Press 2007.

G.F. Mancini, Democracy and Constitutionalism in the European Union. Collected Essays, Hart Publishing 2000.
C.J. Mann, The Function of Judicial Decision in European Economic Integration, Brill Academic Publishers 1972.
M. Manouvel, Les opinions séparées á la Cour Internationale, L'Harmattan 2004.
G. Martinico, L'integrazione silente. La funzione interpretativa della Corte di giustizia e il diritto costituzionale europeo, Jovene 2009.
G. Martinico, The Tangled Complexity of the EU Constitutional Process: The Frustrating Knot of Europe, Routledge 2012.
G. Martinico, O. Pollicino, The Interaction between Europe's Legal Systems: Judicial Dialogue and the Creation of Supranational Laws, Elgar 2012.
W. Mastor, Les opinions séparées des juges constitutionnels, Presse Universitaire d'Aix-Marseille 2005.
H.E.S. Mattila, Comparative Legal Linguistics: Language of Law, Latin and Modern Lingua Franca, Ashgate 2013.
P. Mbongo, A. Vauchez (eds.), Dans la fabrique du droit européen. Scènes, acteurs et publics de la Cour de justice des Communautés européennes, Bruylant 2009.
Y. Mény (ed.), Les politiques du mimétisme institutionnel, L'Harmattan 1993.
J.H. Merryman, The Civil Law Tradition, Stanford University Press 2007.
T. Millett, The Court of First Instance of the European Communities, Butterworth 1990.
P.G. Monateri, Geopolitica del diritto: genesi, governo e dissoluzione dei corpi politici, Laterza 2013.
C.L. de Secondat Montesquieu, De l'Esprit des Loix, Huart 1748.
A. Moravcsik, The Choice for Europe: Social Purpose and State Power from Messina to Maastricht, Cornell University Press 1998.
C. Mortati (ed.), Le opinioni dissenzienti dei giudici costituzionali ed internazionali, Giuffré 1964.
G. Napolitano (ed.), Diritto amministrativo comparato, Giuffrè 2007.
U. Neergard, R. Nielsen, L. Roseberry (eds.), The Role of Courts in Developing a European Social Model: Theoretical and Methodological Perspectives, Djøf Publishing 2010.
L. Neville Brown, T. Kennedy, The Court of Justice of the European Communities, 5th ed., Sweet & Maxwell 2000.
G.Y. Ng, Quality of Judicial Organisation and Checks and Balances, Intersentia 2007.
F. Nicola, B. Davies, EU Law Stories: Contextual and Critical Histories of European Jurisprudence, Cambridge University Press 2017.
N. Nic Shuibhne (ed.), Regulating the Internal Market, Edward Elgar Publishing 2006.

D. O'Keeffe, A. Bavasso (eds.), Judicial Review in European Union Law: Liber Amicorum in Honour of Lord Slynn of Hadley, Kluwer 2000.

C. Perelman, P. Foriers (eds.), La motivation des décisions de justice, Bruylant 1978.

I. Pernice, J. Kokott, C. Saunders (eds.), The Future of the European Judicial System in a Comparative Perspective, Nomos 2006.

H.W. Perry Jr., Deciding to Decide: Agenda Setting in the United States Supreme Court, Harvard University Press 1991.

V. Perju, Constitutional Transplants, Borrowing and Migrations, in M. Rosenfeld, A. Sajo (eds.), Oxford Handbook of Comparative Constitutional Law, Oxford University Press 2012, p. 1306.

P. Pescatore, L'ordre juridique des communautés européennes. Etude des sources du droit communautaire, Presses universitaires de Liège 1975.

P. Pescatore, Vade-mecum. Recueil de formules et de conseils pratiques à l'usage des rédacteurs d'arrêts, 1985, 3rd ed., Bruylant 2007.

W. Phelan, Great Judgments of the European Court of Justice. Rethinking the Landmark Decisions of the Foundational Period, Cambridge University Press 2019.

L.M. Poiares Maduro, We the Court: The European Court of Justice and the European Economic Constitution, Hart 1998.

R.A. Posner, Economic Analysis of Law, Little Brown, 2d ed. 1977.

R.A. Posner, The Federal Courts, Harvard University Press 1996.

L. Prakke, C.A.J.M. Kortmann, J.C.E. van den Brandhoff (eds.), Constitutional Law of 15 EU Member States, Kluwer Legal Publishers 2004.

H. Rasmussen, On Law and Policy in the European Court of Justice: A Comparative Study in Judicial Policymaking, BRILL 1986.

J. Rawls, Political Liberalism, Columbia University Press 1993.

M. Reimann, R. Zimmerman (eds.), The Oxford Handbook of Comparative Law, Oxford University Press 2006.

A. Riles (ed.), Rethinking the Masters of Comparative Law, Hart Publishing 2001.

F. Rivière, Les opinions séparées des juges à la Cour européenne des droits de l'homme: essai d'analyse théorique, Bruylant 2004.

A. Rosas, L. Armati, EU Constitutional Law: An Introduction, Hart 2012.

A. Rosas, E. Levits, Y. Bot (eds.), The Court of Justice and the Construction of Europe: Analyses and Perspectives on Sixty Years of Case-law - La Cour de Justice et la Construction de l'Europe: Analyses et Perspectives de Soixante Ans de Jurisprudence, T.M.C. Asser Press 2013.

W. Sadurski (ed.), Constitutional Justice, East and West, Kluwer Law International 2002.

D. Sarmiento, Poder Judicial e integración europea. La construcción de un modelo jurisdiccional para la Unión, Thomson Civitas 2004.

G. Sartori, Comparative Constitutional Engineering: An Inquiry into Structures, Incentives and Outcomes, New York University Press 1994.
S. Saurugger, F. Terpan, The Court of Justice of the European Union and The Politics of Law, Palgrave Macmillan 2017.
H.G. Schermers, Judicial Protection in the European Communities, 2nd ed., Springer 1979.
H.G. Schermers, C.W.A. Timmermans, A.E. Kellerman (eds.), Article 177 EEC: Experiences and Problems, North-Holland 1987.
H.G. Schermers, D.F. Waelbroeck, Judicial Protection in the European Union, 6th ed., Kluwer Law 2001.
S.K. Schimdt, The European Court of Justice and the Policy Process, Oxford University Press 2018.
R. Schütze, From Dual to Cooperative Federalism: The Changing Structure of European Law, Oxford University Press 2009.
R. Schütze, European Constitutional Law, 2nd ed., Cambridge University Press 2018.
A. Seibert-Fohr (ed.), Judicial Independence in Transition, Springer 2012.
J. Shaw, G. More (eds.), New Legal Dynamics of European Union, Oxford University Press 1995.
M. Shapiro, Courts: A Comparative and Political Analysis, University of Chicago Press 1986.
M. Shapiro, A. Stone Sweet, On Law, Politics and Judicialization, Oxford University Press 2002.
S. Shetreet, C. Forsyth (eds.), The Culture of Judicial Independence: Conceptual Foundations and Practical Challenges, Martinus Nijhoff–Brill Publishers 2012.
D. Siebert, Die Auswahl der Richter am Gerichtshof der Europäischen Gemeinschaften: zu der erforderlichen Reform des Art. 167 EGV, Taschenbuch 1997.
A.M. Slaughter, A. Stone Sweet, and J.H.H. Weiler (eds.), The European Court and National Courts, Doctrine and Jurisprudence. Legal Change in Its Social Context, Hart 1997.
G. Slynn, Introducing a European Legal Order, Stevens & Sons/Sweet & Maxwell 1992.
E. Steindorff, Le recours pour excès de pouvoir dans le droit de la Communauté européenne du charbon et de l'acier, Klostermann 1952.
G.G. Stendardi, La corte costituzionale: il giudizio di legittimità costituzionale delle leggi, Giuffrè 1955.
A. Stone Sweet, Governing with Judges: Constitutional Politics in Europe, Oxford University Press 2000.
C.R. Sunstein, Legal Reasoning and Political Conflict, Oxford University Press 1996.
C.R. Sunstein, One Case at a Time: Judicial Minimalism on the Supreme Court, Harvard University Press 1999.

D. Terris, C.P.R. Romano, L. Swigart, The International Judge, An Introduction to the Men and Women Who Decide the World's Cases, Oxford University Press 2007.

M. Tushnet, The Constitution of the United States of America: A Contextual Analysis, Hart 2009.

L. Vacca (ed.), Lo stile delle sentenze e l'utilizzazione dei precedenti. Profili storico- comparatistici, Giappichelli 2000.

D.G. Valentine, The Court of Justice of the European Coal and Steel Community, Martinus Nijhoff 1955.

R.C. van Caenegem, Judges, Legislators and Professors: Chapters in European Legal History, Cambridge University Press 1987.

R.C. van Caenegem, Introduzione storica al diritto privato, Il Mulino 2004.

F. van der Mensbrugghe, L'utilisation de la méthode comparative en droit européen, Presses universitaries de Namur 2003.

G. Vandersanden, A. Barav, Contentieux communautaire, Bruylant 1977.

A. Vauchez, B. de Witte (eds.), Lawyering Europe: European Law as a Transnational Social Field, Hart 2013.

A. Vedaschi, Istituzioni europee e tecnica legislativa, Giuffrè 2001.

R. von Jhering, The Struggle for Law, 2nd ed., Callaghan 1915.

A. von Bogdandy, J. Bast (eds.), Principles of European Constitutional Law, Hart Publishing 2010.

F. von Savigny, Of the Vocation of Our Age for Legislation and Jurisprudence, A. Hayward trans. London 1831, Arno Press reprint 1975.

I. Ward, A Critical Introduction to European Law, Butterworths 1996.

K.D. Ward, C.R. Castillo (eds.), The Judiciary in American Democracy: Alexander Bickel, the Countermajoritarian Difficulty, and Contemporary Constitutional Theory, State University of New York Press 2005.

A. Watson, Legal Transplants: An Approach to Comparative Law, University Press of Virginia 1974.

M. Weber, Economy and Society: An Outline of Interpretive Sociology, University of California Press 1978.

J.H.H. Weiler, The Constitution of Europe: Do the New clothes Have an Emperor?, Cambridge University Press 1999.

J.H.H. Weiler, M. Wind (eds.), European Constitutionalism Beyond the State, Cambridge University Press 2003.

J. Wigmore, A. Kocourek (eds.), Evolution of Law: Select Readings on the Origin and Development of Legal Institutions, Little Brown 1915–1918.

A. Williams, The Ethos of Europe: Values, Law and Justice in the EU, Cambridge University Press 2010.

A. Zimmermann, C. Tomuschat, K. Oellers-Frahm (eds.), The Statute of the International Court of Justice: A Commentary, Oxford University Press 2006.

D. Zimmermann, The Independence of International Courts: The Adherence of the International Judiciary to a Fundamental Value of the Administration of Justice, Nomos/Hart 2014.

K. Zweigert, H. Kötz, An Introduction to Comparative Law, Clarendon Press 1998.

Articles, Papers, Chapters (When Not Included in Collected Volumes Listed Above)

J. Alder, Dissents in Courts of Last Resort: Tragic Choices?, in 20 Oxford Journal of Legal Studies, 2000, p. 221.

S.A. Akkas, Appointment of Judges: A Key Issue of Judicial Independence, in 16 Bond Law Review, 2004, p. 1.

A. Alemanno, Unpacking the Principle of Openness in EU Law: Transparency, Participation and Democracy, in 39 European Law Review, 2014, p. 72.

A. Alemanno, O. Stefan, Openness at the Court of Justice of the European Union: Toppling a Taboo, in 51 Common Market Law Review, 2014, p. 97.

A. Alemanno, L. Pech, Thinking Justice Outside the Docket: A Critical Assessment of the Reform of the EU's Court System, in 54 Common Market Law Review, 2017, p. 129.

P. Allott, Preliminary Rulings: Another Infant Disease, in 25 European Law Review, 2000, p. 538.

K.J. Alter, The European Court's Political Power Across Time and Space, in 59 Revue française de science politique, 2009, p. 1.

G. Alpa, Comparazione e diritto straniero nella giurisprudenza della Corte di Giustizia dell'Union europea, in 32 Contratto e impresa, 2016, p. 879.

P.W. Amram, The Dissenting Opinion Comes to the German Courts, in 6 American Journal of Comparative Law, 1957, p. 108.

R. P. Anand, The Role of Individual and Dissenting Opinions in International Adjudication, in 14 The International and Comparative Law Quarterly, 1965, p. 788.

J.P. Ancel, Les opinions dissidentes, available at the website http://www.courdecassation.fr/IMG/File/opinions_dissidentes_jp_ancel.pdf.

S.S. Andersen, The Mosaic of Europeanization: An Organizational Perspective on National Recontextualization, ARENA Working Papers No. 04/11.

D. Anderson, The Admissibility of Preliminary References, in 14 Yearbook of European Law, 1994, p. 170.

A. Antoine, La Court de Justice de la C.E.C.A., in 6 Révue Génerale de Droit International Public, 1953, p. 234.

A. Arnull, Private Applicants and the Action for Annulment under Article 173 of the EC Treaty, in 32 Common Market Law Review, 1995, p. 7.

A. Arnull, A Constitutional Court for Europe? in 6 Cambridge Yearbook of European Legal Studies, 2003–2004, p. 1.
A. Arnull, Me and My Shadow: The European Court of Justice and the Disintegration of European Union Law, in 31 Fordham International Law Journal, 2007, p. 1174.
A. Arnull, The Court of Justice Then, Now and Tomorrow, in M. Derlen, J. Lindholm (eds.), The Court of Justice of the European Union: Multidisciplinary Perspectives, Hart Publishing 2018, p. 1.
M. Avbelj, Questioning EU Constitutionalisms, in 9/1 German Law Journal, 2008, p. 1.
M. Avbelj, The Pitfalls of (Comparative) Constitutionalism for European Integration, Eric Stein Working Paper 1/2008, available at the website http://ssrn.com/abstract=1334216.
J. Azizi, Unveiling the EU Courts' Internal Decision-making Process: A Case for Dissenting Opinions?, in 12 ERA Forum, 2011, p. 49.
L. Azoulai, Les garanties procédurales en droit communautaire, PhD dissertation, European University Institute, 2000, available at the website https://cadmus.eui.eu/handle/1814/4550.
L. Azoulai, The Court of Justice and the Social Market Economy: The Emergence of an Ideal and the Conditions for its Realization, in 45 Common Market Law Review, 2008, p. 1335.
L. Azoulai, The Future Constitutional Role of the European Court of Justice, in J. Baquero Cruz, C. Closa (eds.), European Integration From Rome to Berlin, Peter Lang 2009, p. 229.
R. Bader Ginsburg, The Role of Dissenting Opinions, in 95 Minnesota Law Review, 2010, p. 1.
A. Bakardjieva Engelbrekt, Comparative Law and European Law: The End of an Era, a New Beginning, or Time to Face the Methodological Challenges?, in 61 Scandinavian Studies in Law, 2015, p. 88.
J. Baquero Cruz, The Changing Constitutional Role of the European Court of Justice, in 34 International Journal of Legal Information, 2006, p. 223.
C. Baudenbacher, M.J. Clifton, Courts of Regional Economic and Political Integration Agreements, in C. Romano, K. Alter, Y. Shany (eds.), The Oxford Handbook of International Adjudication, Oxford University Press 2014, p. 250.
A. Barav, Le commissaire du gouvernement près le Conseil d'État français et l'avocat général près la Cour de justice des Communautés européennes, in 26 Revue internationale de droit comparé, 1974, p. 809.
C. Barnard, E. Sharpston, The Changing Face of Article 177 References, in 34 Common Market Law Review, 1997, p. 1113.
S. Bartole, Stato (forme di) (*ad vocem*), in Enciclopedia del diritto, Annali, II, 2, Milano, 2008, p. 1116.

C. Bateup, The Dialogic Promise: Assessing the Normative Potential of Theories of Constitutional Dialogue, in 71 Brooklyn Law Review, 2006, p. 1109.

G. Bebr, The Existence of a Genuine Dispute: An Indispensable Precondition for the Jurisdication of the Court Under Article 177 EEC Treaty, in 17 Common Market Law Review, 1980, p. 525.

G. Bebr, The Rambling Ghost of 'Cohn Bendit'. Acte clair and the Court of Justice, in 20 Common Market Law Review, 1983, p. 440.

J. Bell, European Perspectives on a Judicial Appointments Commission, in 6 The Cambridge Yearbook of European Legal Studies, 2003–2004, p. 35.

J. Bell, The Role of European Judges in an Era of Uncertainty, in P.J. Birkinshaw, M. Varney (eds.), The European Union Legal Order After Lisbon, Kluwer 2010, p. 277.

M. Bellocci, T. Giovannetti (eds.), Il quadro delle tipologie decisorie nelle pronunce della Corte costituzionale. Quaderno predisposto in occasione dell'incontro di studio con la Corte costituzionale di Ungheria. Palazzo della Consulta, 11 giugno 2010, available at the website http://www.cortecostituzionale.it/documenti/convegni_seminari/STU%20219_Tipologia_decisioni.pdf.

Y. Bertoncini, What is the impact of the EU interventions at the national level?, in Notre Europe—Jacques Delors Institute, Studies & Reports n° 73, May 2009.

L.F.M. Besselink, The Constitutional Duty to promote the Development of the International Legal Order, in 34 Netherlands Yearbook of International Law, 2003, p. 89.

L.F.M. Besselink, Acceding to the ECHR notwithstanding the Court of Justice Opinion 2/13, available at the website http://www.verfassungsblog.de/en/acceding-echr-notwithstanding-court-justice-opinion-213/#.VJq5SFIM-U.

A.M. Bickel, The Supreme Court, 1960 Term—Foreword: The Passive Virtues, in 75 Harvard Law Review, 1961, p. 40.

E. Biernat, The Locus Standi of Private Applicants under Article 230 (4) EC and the Principle of Judicial Protection in the European Community, Jean Monnet Working Paper No. 12/03.

F. Bignami, Rethinking the Legal Foundations of the European Constitutional Order: The Lessons of the New Historical Research, in 28 American University International Law Review, 2013, p. 1311.

J. Blank, M. van der Ende, B. van Hulst, R Jagtenberg, Bench Marking in an International Perspective: An International Comparison of the Mechanisms and Performance of the Judiciary System, studied commissioned by The Netherlands Council for the Judiciary, available at the website http://siteresources.worldbank.org/INTLAWJUSTINST/Resources/Benchmarking.pdf.

M. Bobek, The Binding Force of Babel: The Enforcement of EC Law Unpublished in the Languages of the New Member States, in 9 Cambridge Yearbook of European Legal Studies, 2006–2007, p. 43.

M. Bobek, On the Application of European Law in (Not Only) the Courts of the New Member Sates: "Don't Do as I say"?, in 10 Cambridge Yearbook of European Legal Studies, 2007–2008, p. 1.

M. Bobek, Learning to Talk: Preliminary Rulings, the Courts of the New Member States and the Court of Justice, in 45 Common Market Law Review, 2008, p. 1611.

M. Bobek, Quantity or Quality? Reassessing the Role of Supreme Jurisdictions in Central Europe, in 57 American Journal of Comparative Law, 2009, p. 33.

M. Bobek, A Fourth in the Court: Why Are There Advocates-General in the Court of Justice?, in 14 Cambridge Yearbook of European Legal Studies, 2011–2012, p. 529.

M. Bobek, The Court of Justice of the European Union, in A. Arnull, D. Chalmers (eds.), The Oxford Handbook of European Union Law, Oxford University Press 2015.

A. Boerger-De Smedt, La Cour de Justice dans les négociations du traité de Paris instituant la CECA, in 2 Journal of European Integration History, 2008, p. 7.

A. Boerger-De Smedt, Negotiating the Foundations of European Law, 1950–1957: The Legal History of the Treaties of Paris and Rome, in 21 Contemporary European History, 2012, p. 339.

A. Boerger-De Smedt, M. Rasmussen, Transforming European Law: The Establishment of the Constitutional Discourse from 1950 to 1993, in 10 European Constitutional Law Review, 2014, p. 199.

D. Boni, Il ricorso di annullamento delle persone fisiche e giuridiche, in B. Nascimbene, L. Daniele (eds.), Il ricorso di annullamento nel Trattato istitutivo della Comunità, Giuffrè 1998, p. 53.

A. Bredimas, Comparative Law in the Court of Justice of the European Communities, in 32 The Yearbook of World Affairs, 1978, p. 320.

M. Broberg, N. Fenger, Variations in Member States' Preliminary References to the Court of Justice—Are Structural Factors (Part of) the Explanation?, in 19 European Law Journal, 2013, p. 488.

A.M. Burley, W. Mattli, Europe Before the Court: A Political Theory of Legal Integration, in 47 International Organization, 1993, p. 41.

H. Brady, Twelve Things Everyone Should Know about the European Court of Justice, Paper of the Centre for European Reform no. 42/2014.

W. J. Brennan, In Defense of Dissent, in 37 Hastings Law Journal, 1986, p. 427.

A. Bzdera, The Court of Justice of the European Community and the Politics of Institutional Reform, in M.L. Volcansek (ed.), Judicial Politics and Policy-making in Western Europe, Frank Cass 1992, p. 122.

J.W. Cairns, Watson, Walton, and the History of Legal Transplants, in 41 Georgia Journal of International and Comparative Law, 2013, p. 637.

S.G. Calabresi, J. Owens, The Origins of Judicial Review, Northwestern Public Law Research Paper No. 14-05, available at the website http://ssrn.com/abstract=2391457.

P. Calamandrei, La Corte costituzionale e il processo civile, in F. Carnelutti et al. (eds.), Studi in onore di Enrico Redenti nel XL anno del suo insegnamento, Giuffrè 1951.

G.A. Caldeira, J.L. Gibson, The Legitimacy of the Court of Justice in the European Union: Models of Institutional Support, in 89 American Political Science Review, 1995, p. 356.

E. Calzolaio, Il valore di precedente delle sentenze della Corte di giustizia, in 1 Rivista critica del diritto privato, 2009, p. 41.

F. Capotorti, Sull'obbligo del rinvio alla Corte di giustizia per l'interpretazione a titolo pregiudiziale a norma del 3° comma dell'art. 177 del trattato Cee, in 1 Giurisprudenza italiana, 1983, p. 1008.

F. Capotorti, Le sentenze della Corte di Giustizia delle Comunità Europee, in Vv.Aa. (eds.), La sentenza in Europa. Metodo, tecnica e stile, CEDAM 1988, p. 230.

M. Cappelletti, Judicial Review in Comparative Perspective, in 58 California Law Review, 1970, p. 5.

P. Caro de Sousa, Catch Me If You Can? The Market Freedoms' Ever-Expanding Outer Limits, in 4 European Journal of Legal Studies, 2011, p. 162.

C.J. Carrubba, Courts and Compliance in International Regulatory Regimes, in 67 Journal of Politics, 2005, p. 669.

C.J. Carrubba, A Model of the Endogenous Development of Judicial Institutions in Federal and International Systems, 71 Journal of Politics, 2009, p. 55.

C.J. Carrubba, M.J. Gabel, Courts, Compliance, and the Quest for Legitimacy in International Law, in 14 Theoretical Inquires in Law, 2013, p. 505.

M. Cartabia, Europe and Rights: Taking Dialogue Seriously, in 5 European Constitutional Law Review, 2009, p. 5.

S. Cassese, Lezione sulla cosiddetta opinione dissenziente, in 4 Quaderni costituzionali, 2009, p. 973.

N. Catalano, La pericolosa teoria dell'atto chiaro, in 1 Giustizia Civile, 1983, p. 3.

D. Chalmers, The Positioning of EU Judicial Politics within the United Kingdom, in K.H. Goetz, S. Hix (eds.), Europeanised Politics. European Integration and National Political Systems, Frank Cass Publishers 2001, p. 169.

H.E. Chodosh, Comparing Comparisons: In Search of Methodology, in 84 Iowa Law Review, 1999, p. 1025.

M. Claes, The Europeanisation of National Constitutions in the Constitutionalisation of Europe: Some Observations against the Background of the Constitutional Experience of the EU-15, in 3 Croatian Yearbook of European Law and Policy, 2007, p. 1.

A. Coan, Judicial Capacity and the Substance of Constitutional Law, in 122 Yale Law Journal, 2012, p. 422.
A. Cohen, A. Vauchez, The Social Construction of Law: The European Court of Justice and its Legal Revolution Revisited, in 7 Annual Review of Law and Social Science, 2011, p. 417.
J.C. Cohen, The European Preliminary Reference and U.S. Supreme Court Review of State Court Judgments: A Study in Comparative Judicial Federalism, in 44 American Journal of Comparative Law, 1996, p. 421.
M. Cohen, On the Linguistic Design of Multinational Courts: The French Capture, in 14 International Journal of Constitutional Law, 2016, p. 498.
M. Cohen-Eliya, I. Porat, American Balancing and German Proportionality: The Historical Origins, in 8 International Journal of Constitutional Law, 2010, p. 263.
G. Comparato, New Voices: Challenging Legal Culture, in 7 European Journal of Legal Studies, 2014, p. 5.
M. Condinanzi, Corte di giustizia e Tribunale dell'Unione europea: storia e prospettive di una "tribolata" ripartizione di competenze, in 3 Federalismi.it, 2018.
M.F. Conniff, The French Conseil d'État and Article 177 of the Treaty of Rome: A Case Analysis, in 12 Virginia Journal of International Law, 1972, p. 377.
A. Corbin, The Law and the Judges, in 3 Yale Review, 1914, p. 234.
A. Corbin, Principles of Law and Their Evolution, in 64 Yale Law Journal, 1954, p. 161.
P. Craig, The Jurisdiction of the Community Courts Reconsidered, in 36 Texas International Law Journal, 2001, p. 555.
C. Curti Gialdino, Il raddoppio dei giudici del Tribunale dell'Unione: valutazioni di merito e di legittimità costituzionale europea, in 8 Federalismi.it. Rivista di diritto pubblico, comparato, europeo, 2015, available at the website http://www.federalismi.it/ApplOpenFilePDF.cfm?artid=29318&dpath=document&dfile=27042015190643.pdf&content=Il+raddoppio+dei+giudici+del+Tribunale+dell%E2%80%99Unione:+valutazioni+di+merito+e+di+legittimit%C3%A0+costituzionale+europea++-+unione+europea+-+dottrina+-+.
D. Curtin, Betwixt and between: Democracy and Transparency in the Governance of the European Union, in J.A. Winter, D. Curtin, A.E. Kellerman, B. de Witte (eds.), Reforming the Treaty on European Union: The Legal Debate, Kluwer 1996, p. 95.
D. Curtin, Transparency, Audiences and the Evolving Role of the EU Council of Ministers, in J.E. Fossum and P. Schlesinger (eds.), The European Union and the Public Sphere: A Communicative Space in the Making?, Routledge 2007, p. 246.
M.A. Damirli, Comparative Law Hermeneutics: Cognitive Possibilities, in 5 Journal of Comparative Law, 2010, p. 65.

P. Dann, Thoughts on a Methodology of European Constitutional Law, in 6 German Law Journal, 2005, p. 1453.
A. Dashwood, The Advocate General in the Court of Justice of the European Communities, in 2 Legal Studies, 1982, p. 203.
M. Dawson, How Does the European Court of Justice Reason? A Review Essay on the Legal Reasoning of the European Court of Justice, in 20 European Law Journal 2014, p. 423.
G. de Búrca, The Principle of Subsidiarity and the Court of Justice as an Institutional Actor, in 36 Journal of Common Market Studies, 1998, p. 217.
F. Dehousse, The Reform of the EU Courts (II)—Abandoning the Management Approach by Doubling the General Court, Egmont Paper 83, March 2016, available at the website http://www.egmontinstitute.be/reform-of-eu-courts-2/.
F. Dehousse, The Reform of the EU courts (IV). The Need for a Better Focus on the European Court of Justice's Core Mission, Egmont Paper 96, September 2017, available at the website http://www.egmontinstitute.be/publication_article/reform-of-eu-courts-2/.
R. Dehousse, Comparing National Law and EC Law: The Problem of the Level of Analysis, in 42 American Journal of Comparative Law, 1994, p. 761.
T. de la Mare, Article 177 in Social and Political Context, in P. Craig, G. de Bùrca (eds.), The Evolution of EU Law, 1st ed., Oxford University Press 1999.
U. de Siervo, L' istituzione della Corte costituzionale in Italia: dall'Assemblea costituente ai primi anni di attività della Corte, in P. Carnevale, C. Colapietro (eds.), La giustizia costituzionale fra memoria e prospettive. A cinquant'anni dalla pubblicazione della prima sentenza della Corte costituzionale, Giappichelli 2008, p. 49.
B. de Witte, Democratic Adjudication in Europe: How can the European Court of Justice be responsive to the citizens?, in M. Dougan, N. Nic Shuibhne, E Spaventa (eds.), Empowerment and Disempowerment of the European Citizen, Hart 2012, p. 129.
B. de Witte, The Preliminary Ruling Dialogue: Three Types of Questions Posed by National Courts, in B. de Witte, J. Mayoral, U. Jaremba, M. Wind, K. Podstawa (eds.), National Courts and EU Law: New Issues, Theories and Methods, Elgar 2016, p. 15.
W.O. Douglas, The Dissent: A Safeguard of Democracy, in 32 Journal of the American Judicature Society, 1948, p. 104.
S. Douglas-Scott, Opinion 2/13 on EU accession to the ECHR: A Christmas Bombshell from the European Court of Justice, available at the website http://www.verfassungsblog.de/opinion-213-eu-accession-echr-christmas-bombshell-european-court-justice/#.Vbj545Ptmkr.
T. Dumbrovský, The European Court of Justice after the Eastern Enlargement: An Emerging Inner Circle of Judges, paper presented at the EUSA Twelfth

Biennial Conference, Boston, March 2011, available at the website http://papers.ssrn.com/sol3/papers.cfm?abstract_id=2551211.

T. Dumbrovský, B. Petkova, M. Van Der Sluis, Judicial Appointments: The Article 255 TFEU Advisory Panel and Selection Procedures in the Member States, in 51 Common Market Law Review, 2014, p. 455.

O. Dupeyroux, Le ministère public auprès des juridictions administratives, in Vv.Aa. (eds.), L'Évolution du droit public: Études offertes à Achille Mestre, Sirey 1956, p. 183.

R. Dworkin, Law as Interpretation, in 9 Critical Inquiry, 1982, p. 179.

K. Dzehtsiarou, European Consensus and the Evolutive Interpretation of the European Convention on Human Rights, in 12 German Law Journal, 2011, p. 1730.

D. Edward, How the Court of Justice works, in 20 European Law Review, 1995, p. 557.

M. Egan, Toward a New History in European Law: New Wine in Old Bottles?, in 28 American University International Law Review, 2013, p. 1223.

E.D. Elliott, The Evolutionary Tradition in Jurisprudence, in 85:38 Columbia Law Review, 1985, p. 38.

U. Everling, The Court of Justice as a Decision-Making Authority, in 82 Michigan Law Review, 1984, p. 1294.

U. Everling, Reflections on the Reasoning in the Judgments of the Court of Justice of the European Communities, in J. Rosenløv et al. (eds.), Festskrift til Ole Due, Gads Forlag 1994, p. 55.

N. Fennelly, Legal Interpretation at the European Court of Justice, in 20 Fordham International Law Journal, 1996, p. 656.

F. Fernández Segado, La recepción del Sondervotum en Alemania, in 12 Revista Iberoamericana de Derecho Procesal Constitucional, 2009, p. 77.

S. Fish, Working on the Chain Gang: Interpretation in the Law and in Literary Criticism, in 9 Critical Inquiry, 1982, p. 201.

C. Flanders, Towards a Theory of Persuasive Authority, in 62 Oklahoma Law Review, 2009, p. 55.

J.F. Flauss, Brèves observations sur le second renouvellement triennal de la Cour Européenne des Droits de l'Homme, in 61 Revue Trimestrielle des Droits de l'Homme, 2005, p. 5.

J. Flett, Collective Intelligence and the Possibility of Dissent, in 13 Journal of International Economic Law, 2010, p. 287.

A. Follesdal, M. Wind, Introduction—Nordic Reluctance towards Judicial Review under Siege, in 27 Nordic Journal of Human Rights, 2009, p. 131.

D. Fontana, Docket control and the Success of Constitutional Courts, in T. Ginsburg, R. Dixon (eds.), Handbook of Comparative Constitutional Law, Elgar 2011, p. 624.

T. Freixes, La pratique des opinions dissidentes en Espagne, in 8 Nouveaux Cahiers du Conseil Constitutionnel, 2000, available at the website http://www.conseil-constitutionnel.fr/conseil-constitutionnel/francais/nouveaux-cahiers-du-conseil/cahier-n-8/la-pratique-des-opinions-dissidentes-en-espagne.52543.html.

Y. Galmot, Reflexions sur le recours au droit compare par la Cour de justice des Communautés européennes, in Revue française de droit administratif, 1990, p. 261.

G. Garrett, The Politics of Legal Integration in the European Union, in 49 International Organization, 1995, p. 171.

G. Garzòn Clariana, Le Parlement européen dans le développement de la CJCE, in N. Colneric, D. Edward, J.P. Puissochet, D.R. Colomer (eds.), Une Communauté de droit Festschrift per Gil Carlos Rodríguez Iglesias, Berliner Wissenschafts-Verlag 2003, p. 21.

M.A. Gaudissart, Le regime et la pratique linguistiques de la Cour de Justice, in D. Hanf, K. Malacek, E. Muir (eds.), Langues et construction européenne, PIE Peter Lang 2007, p. 137.

M.A. Gaudissart, La refonte du règlement de procedure de la Cour de justice, in 3 Cahiers de droit européen, 2012, p. 603.

M. Gilligan, L. Johns, B.P. Rosendorff, Strengthening International Courts and the Early Settlement of Disputes, 54 Journal of Conflict Resolution, 2010, p. 5.

H.P. Glenn, The Capture, Reconstruction and Marginalization of 'Custom', in 45 American Journal of Comparative Law, 1997, p. 613.

J. Goldschmidt, Merit Selection: Current Status, Procedures, and Issues, in 49 University of Miami Law Review, 1994, p. 1.

J. Goldsmith, D. Levinson, Law for States: International Law, Constitutional Law, Public Law, in 122 Harvard Law Review, 2009, p. 1791.

J. Golub, The Politics of Judicial Discretion: Rethinking the Interaction between National Courts and the European Court of Justice, in 19 West European Politics, 1996, p. 360.

P. Gori, L'avocat général à la Cour de justice des Communautés européennes, in 12 Cahiers de droit européen, 1976, p. 375.

G. Gorla, Lo stile delle sentenze. Ricerca storico-comparativa, in 21 Quaderni de "Il Foro italiano", 1967, p. 291.

A. Grilli, Moloch politico o governo dei giudici? Gli albori dell'Europa comunitaria, in P. Maffei, G.M. Varanini (eds.), Honos alit artes. Studi per il settantesimo compleanno di Mario Ascheri - Vol. III Il cammino delle idee dal medioevo all'antico regime. Diritto e cultura nell'esperienza europea, Firenze University Press 2014, p. 227.

A. Grimmel, Judicial Interpretation or Judicial Activism? The Legacy of Rationalism in the Studies of the European Court of Justice, in 18 European Law Journal, 2012, p. 518.

X. Groussot, Spirit, Are You There? Reinforced Judicial Dialogue and the Preliminary Ruling Procedure, Eric Stein Working Paper No. 4/2008, available at the website http://papers.ssrn.com/sol3/papers.cfm?abstract_id=1279367.

X. Groussot, C. Wong, A. Inghammar, A. Bruzelius, Empowering National Courts in EU Law, Swedish Institute for European Policy Studies, Report No. 3/2009, available at the website http://www.sieps.se/sites/default/files/541-2009-3-rapport.pdf.

C. Guarnieri, Judicial Independence in Europe: Threat or Resource for Democracy?, in 49 Representation, 2013, p. 347.

R. Guillien, Les commissaires du gouvernement près les juridictions administratives et, spécialement, près le Conseil d'État français, in 71 Revue du droit public de de la science politique en France et à l'étranger, 1955, p. 281.

A.T. Guzman, International Tribunals: A Rational Choice Analysis, in 157 University of Pennsylvania Law Review, 2008, p. 171.

P. Haas, Introduction: Epistemic Communities and International Policy Coordination, in 46 International Organization, 1992, p. 1.

H.P. Haferkamp, A. Nieschlag, Begriffsjurisprudenz / Jurisprudence of Concepts (*ad vocem*), in The Oxford International Encyclopedia of Legal History, 2009.

G. Hafner, Risks Ensuing from Fragmentation of International Law, in Official Records of the General Assembly, 55th Session, Supplement No. 10 (A/55/10), annex, the Report of the Study Group on Fragmentation of International Law, doc. A/CN.4/L.644.

D. Halberstam, Comparative Federalism and the Role of the Judiciary, in K. Whittington, D. Kelemen, G. Caldeira (eds.), The Oxford Handbook of Law and Politics, Oxford University Press 2008, p. 142.

G. Halmai, The Possibility and Desirability of Rule of Law Conditionality, in Hague Journal of the Rule of Law, 2018, p. 1.

C. Hanretty, Dissent in Iberia: The Ideal Points of Justices on the Spanish and Portuguese Constitutional Tribunals, in 51 European Journal of Political Research, 2012, p. 671.

C. Hanretty, Dissenting Opinions in the UKSC, available at the website http://ukscblog.com/dissenting-opinons-in-the-uksc.

O.A. Hathaway, Path Dependence in the Law: The Course and Pattern of Legal Change in a Common Law System, 86 Iowa Law Review, 2001, p. 101.

Justice Hedigan, The European Court of Human Rights: Yesterday, Today and Tomorrow, in 12 German Law Journal, 2011, p. 1716.

L. Heffernan, The Community Court post-Nice: A European Certiorari Revisited, in 52 The International and Comparative Law Quarterly, 2003, p. 907.

L. H. Helfer, A.M. Slaughter, Why States Create International Tribunals: A Response to Professors Posner and Yoo, in 93 California Law Review, 2005, p. 899.
C. Hen, La motivation des actes des institutions communautaires, in 13 Cahiers de Droit Européen, 1977, p. 54.
M. Hilf, The Role of Comparative Law in the Jurisprudence of the Court of Justice of the European Communities, in A.L.C. De Mestral et al. (eds.), The Limitation of Human Rights in Comparative Constitutional Law, Les éditions Tvon Blais 1986, p. 549.
F. Hoffmeister, Constitutional Implications of EU Membership: A View from the Commission, in 3 Croatian Yearbook of European Law and Policy, 2007, p. 59.
T. Hoppe, Die Europäisierung der Gesetzgebung: Der 80-Prozent-Mythos lebt, in 6 Europäische Zeitschrift für Wirtschaftsrecht, 2009, p. 168.
T. Horsley, Reflections on the Role of the Court of Justice as the 'Motor' of European Integration: Legal Limits to Judicial Lawmaking, in 50 Common Market Law Review, 2013, p. 931.
J. Husa, Methodology of Comparative Law Today: From Paradoxes to Flexibility?, in 4 Revue Internationale de Droit Comparé, 2006, p. 1095.
J. Husa, The Method Is Dead, Long Live the Methods! European Polynomia and Pluralist Methodology, in 5 Legisprudence, 2011, p. 249.
G. Itzcovich, The European Court of Justice as a Constitutional Court: Legal Reasoning in a Comparative Perspective, STALS Research paper no. 4/2014, available at the website http://www.stals.sssup.it/files/itzcovich%204%202014.pdf.
F.G. Jacobs, Amendments to the Rules of Procedure, in 5 European Law Review, 1980, p. 52.
F.G. Jacobs, The Member States, the Judges and the Procedure, in Institut D'Études Européennes. Université Libre de Bruxelles (ed.), La Cour de Justice des Communautés Européennes, Éditions de l'Université de Bruxelles 1981, p. 11.
F.G. Jacobs, Procedural Reform in the European Court, in J. Schwarze (ed.), Perspectives for the Development of Judicial Protection in the European Community, Nomos Verlagsgesellschaft 1987, p. 191.
F.G. Jacobs, The Effect of Preliminary Rulings in the National Legal Order, in M. Andenas (ed.), Article 177 References to the European Court—Policy and Practice, Butterworths 1994, p. 29.
F.G. Jacobs, The European Court of Justice: Some Thoughts on Its Past and Its Future, in 2 The European Advocate, 1994–1995, p. 2.
F.G. Jacobs, Access to Justice as a Fundamental Right in European Law, in G.C. Rodríguez Iglesias et al. (eds.), Mélanges en hommage à Fernand Schockweiler, Nomos 1999, p. 197.

F.G. Jacobs, Recent and Ongoing Measures to Improve the Efficiency of the European Court of Justice, in 29 European Law Review, 2004, p. 823.
F.G. Jacobs, The Evolution of the European Legal Order, in 41 Common Market Law Review, 2004.
F. Jacobs, Comparative Law and European Union Law, in M. Reimann, R. Zimmermann (eds.), The Oxford Handbook of Comparative Law, 2nd ed., Oxford University Press 2019, chapt. XIX.
J.P. Jacqué, The Principle of Institutional Balance, in 41 Common Market Law Review, 2004, p. 383.
J.P. Jacqué, J.H.H. Weiler, On the Road to European Union—A New Judicial Architecture: An Agenda for the Intergovernmental Conference, in 27 Common Market Law Review, 1990, p. 185.
P. Jann, Entscheidungsbegründung am Europäischen Gerichtshof, in 7 Journal für Rechtspolitik, 1999, p. 28.
C. Joerges, Unity in Diversity as Europe's Vocation and Conflicts Law as Europe's Constitutional Form, LEQS Paper No. 28/2010.
O. Kahn-Freund, On Uses and Misuses of Comparative Law, in 1 Modern Law Review, 1974, p. 1.
C. N. Kakouris, Use of the Comparative Method by the Court of Justice of the European Communities, in 6 Pace International Law Review, 1994, p. 267.
A.M. Kales, Methods of Selecting and Retiring Judges, in 11 Journal of the American Judicature Society, 1928, p. 133.
K. Kelemen, The Road from Common Law to East-Central Europe: The Case of the Dissenting Opinion, in P. Cserne, M. Könczöl (eds.), Legal and Political Theory in the Post-National Age, Peter Lang 2011, p. 118.
K. Kelemen, Dissenting Opinions in Constitutional Courts, in 14 German Law Journal, 2013, p. 1345.
R.D. Kelemen, The Court of Justice of the European Union: Changing Authority in the Twenty-First Century, in K.J. Alter, L.R. Helfer, M.R. Madsen (eds.), International Court Authority, Oxford University Press 2018, chapt. 10.
H. Kelsen, La garantie juridictionnelle de la Constitution (la Justice constitutionnelle), in 35 Revue du droit public et de la science politique, 1928, p. 197.
D. Kennedy, New Approaches to Comparative Law: Comparativism and International Governance, in 2 Utah Law Review, 1997, p. 545.
T. Kennedy, First Steps towards a European Certiorari?, in 18 European Law Review, 1993, p. 121.
T. Kennedy, Thirteen Russians! The Composition of the European Court of Justice, in A.I.L. Campbell, M. Voyatzi (eds.), Legal Reasoning and Judicial Interpretation of European Law: Essays in Honour of Lord Mackenzie-Stuart, Trenton Publishing 1996, p. 69.

S.J. Kenney, The Members of the Court of Justice of the European Communities, in 5 Columbia Journal of European Law, 1999, p. 101.
M. Kirby, Judicial Dissent—Common Law and Civil Law Traditions, in 123 Law Quarterly Review, 2007, p. 379.
J. Kokott, The Burden of Proof in Comparative and International Human Rights Law: Civil and Common Law Approaches with Special Reference to the American and German Legal Systems, Kluver Law International 1998, p. 168.
M. Kolsky Lewis, The Lack of Dissent in WTO Dispute Settlement, in 9 Journal of International Economic Law, 2006, p. 895.
J. Komarek, Federal Elements in the Community Judicial System: Building Coherence in the Community Legal Order, in 42 Common Market Law Review, 2005, p. 9.
J. Komarek, In the Court(s) We Trust? On the Need for Hierarchy and Differentiation in the Preliminary Ruling Procedure, in 32 European Law Review, 2007, p. 467.
J. Komarek, Judicial Lawmaking and Precedent in Supreme Courts: The European Court of Justice Compared to the US Supreme Court and the French Cour de Cassation, in 11 Cambridge Yearbook of European Legal Studies, 2008–2009, p. 399.
T. Koopmans, Stare Decisis in European Law, in D. O'Keeffe, H.G. Schermers (eds.), Essays in European Law and Integration, Kluwer, 1982, p. 11.
T. Koopmans, The Birth of European Law at the Crossroads of Legal Traditions, in 39 American Journal of Comparative Law, 1991, p. 493.
M. Koskenniemi, P. Leino, Fragmentation of International Law: Postmodern Anxieties?, in 15 Leiden Journal of International Law, 2002, p. 553.
C. Krenn, The European Court of Justice's Financial Accountability: How the European Parliament Incites and Monitors Judicial Reform through the Budgetary Process, in 13 European Constitutional Law Review, 2017, p. 453.
C. Krenn, Self-Government at the Court of Justice of the European Union: A Bedrock for Institutional Success, in 19 German Law Journal, 2018, p. 2007.
A.T. Kronman, Alexander Bickel's Philosophy of Prudence, in 94 Yale Law Journal, 1985, p. 1567.
M. Kuijer, Voting Behaviour and National Bias in the European Court of Human Rights and the International Court of Justice, in 10 Leiden Journal of International Law, 1997, p. 49.
S.A. Kuipers, Pertinence et acte clair, art. 177 CEE. Observations sur Hoge Raad der Nederlanden, in Cahiers de droit europeen, 1967, p. 81.
J. Laffranque, Dissenting Opinion in the European Court of Justice—Estonia's Possible Contribution to the Democratisation of the European Union Judicial System, in 9 Juridica International, 2004, p. 14.
M. Lagrange, The Court of Justice as a Factor in European Integration, in 15 American Journal of Comparative Law, 1966–1967, p. 709.

M. Lagrange, Cour de Justice et Tribunaux nationaux. La theorie de l'acte clair pomme de discorde ou trait d'union, in 1 Gazette du Palais, 1971.

M. Lagrange, The Theory of Acte Clair: A Bone of Contention or a Source of Unity?, in 8 Common Market Law Review, 1971, p. 313.

M. Lagrange, La Cour de justice des Communautés européennes du Plan Schuman à l'Union européenne, in 14 Revue trimestrielle de droit européen, 1978, p. 2.

M. Lagrange, The Court of Justice of the European Communities from the Schuman Plan to the European Union, in Mélanges Fernand Dehousse. Vol. 2, la construction européenne, Éditions Labor 1979, p. 127.

R. Lane, Article 234: A Few Rough Edges Still, in M. Hoskins, W. Robinson (eds.), A True European: Essays for Judge David Edward, Hart Publishing 2004, p. 327.

M. Lasser, "Lit. Theory" Put to the Test: A Comparative Literary Analysis of American Judicial Tests and French Judicial Discourse, in 111 Harvard Law Review, 1998, p. 689.

M. Lasser, The European Pasteurization of French Law, in 90 Cornell Law Review, 2004–2005, p. 995.

Y. Lécuyer, Le secret du délibéré, les opinions séparées et la transparence, in 54 Revue trimestrielle des droits de l'homme, 2004, p. 197.

J. Lee, A Defence of Concurring Speeches, in 2 Public Law, 2009, p. 305.

P. Legrand, The Impossibility of Legal Transplants, in 4 Maastricht Journal of European and Comparative Law, 1997, p. 111.

P. Leino, Just a Little Sunshine in the Rain: The 2010 Case Law of the European Court of Justice on Access to Documents, in 48 Common Market Law Review, 2011, p. 1215.

K. Lenaerts, Constitutionalism and the Many Faces of Federalism, in 38 American Journal of Comparative Law, 1990, p. 205.

K. Lenaerts, Form and Substance of the Preliminary Ruling Procedure, in D. Curtin, T. Heukels (eds.), Institutional Dynamics of European Integration, Martinus Nijhoff 1994, p. 355.

K. Lenaerts, Interlocking Legal Orders in the European Union and Comparative Law, in 52 International & Comparative Law Quarterly, 2003, p. 873.

K. Lenaerts, In the Union We Trust: Trust—Enhancing Principles of Community Law, in 41 Common Market Law Review, 2004, p. 317.

K. Lenaerts, The Rule of Law and the Coherence of the Judicial System of the European Union, in 44 Common Market Law Review, 2007, p. 1625.

K. Lenaerts, The Future Organisation of European Courts, in P. Demaret, I. Govaere, D. Hanf (eds.), European Legal Dynamics—30 Years of European Legal Studies at the College of Europe, Peter Lang 2007, p. 129.

K. Lenaerts, The European Court of Justice and the Comparative Law Method, in 25 European Review of Private Law, 2017, p. 297.

A.P. Le Sueur, Legal Duties to Give Reasons, in 52 Current Legal Problems, 1999, p. 150.
C. L'Heureux-Dubé, The Dissenting Opinion: Voice of the Future?, in 38 Osgoode Hall Law Journal, 2000, p. 495.
J. Lodge, Transparency and Democratic Legitimacy, in 32 Journal of Common Market Studies, 1994, p. 343.
M. Luciani, Costituzionalismo irenico e costituzionalismo polemico, in 2 Giurisprudenza costituzionale, 2006, p. 1643.
Y. Lupu, International Judicial Legitimacy: Lessons from National Courts, in 14 Theoretical Inquires in Law, 2013, p. 437.
I.S. Lustick, Institutional Rigidity and Evolutionary Theory: Trapped on a Local Maximum, in 2(2) Cliodynamics: The Journal of Theoretical and Mathematical History 2011, p. 3.
J. Luther, L'esperienza del voto dissenziente nei paesi di lingua tedesca, in 2 Politica del diritto, 1994, p. 241.
R. Machacek, Die Einrichtung der "Dissenting Opinion" im internationalen Vergleich, in 7 Journal für Rechtspolitik, 1999, p. 1.
R. Mackenzie, P. Sands, International Courts and Tribunals and the Independence of the International Judge, in 44 Harvard International Law Journal, 2003, p. 272.
Lord Mackenzie Stuart and J.P. Warner, Judicial Decisions as a Source of Community law, in Va.Aa. (eds.), Europeische Gerichtsbarkeit und nationale Verfassungsgerichtsbarkeit, Festschrift H. Kutscher, Nomos 1981, p. 273.
Lord Mackenzie-Stuart, Elogio funebre del sig. Nicola Catalano ex membro della Corte - udienza solenne 18 ottobre 1984, in Compendio delle attività della Corte di giustizia delle comunità europee 1984–1985 e udienza solenni 1984–1985.
G. Maggi, The Role of Multilateral Institutions in International Trade Cooperation, in 89 American Economic Review, 1999, p. 190.
M. Malecki, Do ECJ Judges All Speak with the Same Voice?, in 19 Journal of European Public Policy, 2012, p. 59.
J. Malenovsky, Les opinions separées et leurs répercussions sur l'indépendance du juge international, in 3 Anuario Colombiano de Derecho Constitucional, 2010, p. 27.
Lord Mance, Judges Judged, in European Advocate, in Journal of the Bar European Society, 2012, p. 2.
G.F. Mancini, A Constitution for Europe, in 26 Common Market Law Review, 1989, p. 595.
G.F. Mancini, The Role of the Supreme Courts at the National and International Level: A Case Study of the Court of Justice of the European Communities, in P. Yessiou-Faltsi (ed.), The Role of the Supreme Courts at the National and International Level, Sakkoulas 1998, p. 421.

G.F. Mancini, Europe: The Case for Statehood, in 4 European Law Journal, 1998, p. 29.

G.F. Mancini, D.T. Keeling, From CILFIT to ERT: The Constitutional Challenge Facing the European Court, in 11 Yearbook of European Law 1991, p. 1.

G.F. Mancini, D.T. Keeling, Language, Culture and Politics in the Life of the European Court of Justice, in 1 Columbia Journal of European Law, 1994–1995, p. 397.

G. Martinico, Reading the Others: American Legal Scholars and the Unfolding European Integration, in 11 European Journal of Law Reform, 2009, p. 35.

J.C. Masclet, Vers la fin d'une controverse ? La Cour de justice tempère l'obligation de renvoi préjudiciel en interprétation faite aux juridictions suprêmes (art. 177, alinéa 3, CEE), in 26 Revue du Marché Commun, 1983 p. 363.

W. Mattli, A.M. Slaughter, Law and Politics in the European Union: A Reply to Garrett, in 49 International Organization, 1995, p. 183.

W. Mattli, A.M. Slaughter, Revisiting the European Court of Justice, in 52 International Organisation, 1998, p. 177.

J.L. Maute, English Reforms to Judicial Selection: Comparative Lessons for American States, in 34 Fordham Urban Law Journal, 2007, p. 387.

A.M. Mavčič, Importance of the Dissenting and Concurring Opinions (Separate Opinions) in the Development of the Constitutional and Judicial Review with a Special Reference to the Slovenian Practice, available at the website http://www.venice.coe.int/webforms/documents/default.aspx?pdffile=CDL-JU%282010%29016-e.

A.M. Mavčič, Guarantees of Independence of the Judiciary: The Slovenian Experience, paper presented at the International Judicial Reform Symposium, 2–3 April 2012, Ankara, Turkey, available at the website http://www.concourts.net/lecture/Ankara%202012_1_.pdf.

N. Maveety, Concurrence and the Study of Judicial Behavior in American Political Science, in 8 Juridica International, 2003, p. 173.

H. Mayer, Die Einführung der "dissenting opinion" am Verfassungsgerichtshof, in 7 Journal für Rechtspolitik, 1999, p. 30.

J.A. Mayoral, In the CJEU Judges Trust: A New Approach in the Judicial Construction of Europe, in 55 Journal of Common Market Studies, 2017, p. 551.

P. McAuliffe, Selecting International Judges: Principle, Process, and Politics, in 11 International Criminal Law Review, 2011, p. 359.

K. McAuliffe, Language and Law in the European Union: The Multilingual Jurisprudence of the ECJ, in L.M. Solan, P.M. Tiersma (eds.), The Oxford Handbook of Language and Law, Oxford University Press 2012, p. 200.

G.P.J. McGinley, The Search for Unity: The Impact of Consensus Seeking Procedures in Appellate Courts, in 11 Adelaide Law Review, 1987, p. 203.

A.W.H. Meij, Guest Editorial: Architects or Judges? Some Comments in Relation to the Current Debate, in 37 Common Market Law Review, 2000, p. 1039.

A.W.H. Meij, Access to the European Union Courts: Standing in Direct Actions after Lisbon, in M. van Roosmalen (ed.), Fundamental Rights and Principles. Liber Amicorum Pieter van Dijk, Intersentia 2013, p. 141.

A.J. Menéndez, The Existential Crisis of the European Union, in 5 German Law Journal, 2013, p. 453.

J. Mertens de Wilmars, Le droit comparé dans la jurisprudence de la Cour de Justice des Communautés Européennes, in 110 Journal des Tribunaux, 1991, p. 37.

J. Moeller, Alexander M. Bickel: Toward a Theory of Politics, in 47 Journal of Politics, 1985, p. 113.

A. Momirov, A. Naudé Fourie, Vertical Comparative Law Methods: Tools for Conceptualizing the International Rule of Law, in 2 Erasmus Law Review, 2003, p. 291.

P.G. Monateri, La circolazione dei modelli giuridici e le sue conseguenze per l'Unione europea, in A.M. Petroni (ed.) Modelli giuridici ed economici per la Costituzione europea, Il Mulino 2001, p. 87.

P.G. Monateri, Il problema di una definizione di Europa: una questione di teologia politica?, in 1 Rivista critica del diritto privato, 2005, p. 3.

L. Montazel, Entre faits et droit: histoire d'un pouvoir judiciaire. Les techniques de la cassation civile en France et en Allemagne au XIXème siècle, Klostermann 1998.

A. Moravcsik, Preferences and Power in the European Community: A Liberal Intergovernmentalist Approach, in 31 Journal of Common Market Studies, 1993, p. 473.

G. Morelli, La Corte di Giustizia delle Comunità europee come giudice interno, in 41 Rivista di diritto internazionale, 1958, p. 3.

C. Mortati, La Corte costituzionale ed i presupposti per la sua vitalità, in Iustitia, 1949, p. 69.

N.P. Musar, Access to Court Records and FOIA as a Legal Basis—Experience of Slovenia, available at the website https://www.iprs.si/fileadmin/user_upload/Pdf/clanki/Access_to_court_records_and_FOIA_as_a_legal_basis_-_experience_of_Slovenia.pdf.

K.H. Nadelmann, The Judicial Dissent: Publication v. Secrecy, in 8 American Journal of Comparative Law, 1959, p. 415.

K.H. Nadelmann, Non-Disclosure of Dissents in Constitutional Courts: Italy and West Germany, in 13 American Journal of Comparative Law, 1964, p. 268.

V. Naglič, National Practices with Regard to the Accessibility of Court Documents. Study, Directorate General for Internal Policies. Policy Department C: Citizens' Rights and Constitutional Affairs, 2013, available at the website http://www.europarl.europa.eu/studies.

B. Nelissen, Judicial Loyalty Through Dissent or Why the Timing is Perfect for Belgium to Embrace Separate Opinions, in 15 Electronic Journal of Comparative Law, 2011, p. 1.
C. Nelson, A Re-evaluation of Scholarly Explanations for the Rise of the Elective Judiciary in Antebellum America, in 37 American Journal of Legal History, 1993, p. 190.
J. Nergelius, North and South: Can the Nordic States and the European Continent Find Each Other in the Constitutional Area—Or Are They Too Different?, in M. Scheinin (ed.), The Welfare State and Constitutionalism in the Nordic Countries, Nordic Council of Ministers 2001, p. 79.
T. Neumann, B. Simma, Transparency in International Adjudication, in A. Bianchi, A. Peters (eds.), Transparency in International Law, Cambridge University Press 2013, p. 436.
D. Nicol, Lessons from Luxembourg: Federalisation and the Court of Human Rights, in 26 European Law Review, 2001, p. 3.
F. Nicola, Critical Legal Histories in EU Law, in 28 American University International Law Review, 2013, p. 1173.
F. Nicola, National Legal Traditions at Work in the Jurisprudence of the Court of Justice of the European Union, in 64 American Journal of Comparative Law, 2016, p. 865.
F. Nicola, Waiting for the Barbarians: Inside the Archive of the European Court of Justice, American University Washington College of Law Research Paper n. 2019–19, available at the website https://papers.ssrn.com/sol3/papers.cfm?abstract_id=3417267.
C. Nourissat, La jurisprudence de la Cour de justice des Communautés européennes: Un regard privatiste à partir de l'actualité, in Vv.Aa. (eds.), La création du droit par le juge, Dalloz 2006, p. 247.
D. O'Keeffe, Is the Spirit of Article 177 under Attack? Preliminary References and Admissibility, in 23 European Law Review, 1998, p. 509.
P. Oliver, La recevabilité des questions préjudicielles: La jurisprudence des années 1990, in 37 Cahiers de droit européen, 2001, p. 15.
J. Olsen, Unity and Diversity—European Style, ARENA Working Paper No. 24/2005.
Open Society Justice Initiative, Report on Access to Judicial Information, March 2009, available at the website www.right2info.org.
Organisation for Economic Co-operation and Development (OECD), The Right to Open Public Administrations in Europe: Emerging Legal Standards, 19 November 2010, Sigma paper no. 46, available at the website http://www.oecd.org/officialdocuments/publicdisplaydocumentpdf/?cote=GOV/SIGMA(2010)2/REV1&docLanguage=En.

M. Ovàdek, W. Wijtvliet, M. Glavina, Which Courts Matter Most? Measuring Importance in the EU Preliminary Reference System, in 12 European Journal of Legal Studies, 2020.

R. Passos, Le Système juridictionnel de l'Union, in G. Amato, H. Bribosia, B. de Witte (eds.), Genèse et destinée de la Constitution européenne, Bruylant 2007, p. 565.

M. Patchett-Joyce, Barrister Outer Temple Chambers, London, Hearing on the Reform of the Court of Justice of the European Union before the Committee on Legal Affairs of the European Parliament, available at the website http://www.europarl.europa.eu/document/activities/cont/201305/20130521ATT66428/20130521ATT66428EN.pdf.

T. Pavone, Revisiting Judicial Empowerment in the European Union: Limits of Empowerment, Logics of Resistance, in 6 Journal of Law and Courts, 2018, p. 303.

T. Pavone, R.D. Kelemen, The Evolving Judicial Politics of European Integration: The European Court of Justice and National Courts Revisited, in 25 European Law Journal, 2019, p. 352.

L. Pech, The CJEU at 60: Still Fit for Purpose?, paper presented at the 50th Anniversary Jubilee Conference of the Common Market Law Review "Current Challenges for EU Law—New Views, New Inspirations", 26–27 April 2013, Noordwijk, Netherlands.

L. Pech, K.M. Scheppele, Illiberalism Within: Rule of Law Backsliding in the EU, in Cambridge Yearbook of European Legal Studies, 2017, p. 3.

S. Peers, From Maastricht to Laeken: The Political Agenda of Openness and Transparency in the EU, in V. Deckmyn (ed.), Increasing Transparency in the European Union, European Institute for Public Administration 2002, p. 7.

S. Peers, The CJEU and the EU's Accession to the ECHR: A Clear and Present Danger to Human Rights Protection, available at the website http://eulawanalysis.blogspot.co.uk/2014/12/the-cjeu-and-eus-accession-to-echr.html.

C. Penera, The Beginnings of the Court of Justice and its Role as a Driving Force in European Integration, in 1 Journal of European Integration History, 1995, p. 111.

A. Peri, La selezione dei giudici della Corte di giustizia. Poteri e limiti del comitato ex. Art. 255 TFUE, in 4 Diritto Pubblico Comparato ed Europeo, 2012, p. 1472.

V. Perju, Reason and Authority in the European Court of Justice, in 49 Virginia Journal of International Law, 2009, p. 308.

P. Pescatore, L' interpretation du droit communautaire et la doctrine de l'acte clair, in 33/34 Bullettin des juristes Européens, 1971, p. 49.

P. Pescatore, Interpretation of Community law and the doctrine of 'acte clair', in 27 Legal Problems of an Enlarged European Community, 1972, p. 46.

P. Pescatore, Le recours dans la jurisprudence de la Cour de justice des Communautés européennes, à des normes déduites de la comparaison des droits des Etats membres, in 32 Revue international de droit comparé, 1980, p. 337.

P. Pescatore, Les Travaux du 'Groupe Juridique' dans la négociation des Traités de Rome, in 34 Studia Diplomatica, 1981, p. 159.

P. Pescatore, The Doctrine of "Direct Effect": An Infant Disease of Community Law, in 8 European Law Review, 1983, p. 155.

T.R. Phillips, The Merits of Merit Selection, in 32 Harvard Journal of Law & Public Policy, 2009, p. 67.

A.E. Platsas, The Functional and the Dysfunctional in the Comparative Method of Law: Some Critical Remarks, in 12.3 Electronic Journal of Comparative Law, 2008, p. 1.

L.M. Poiares Maduro, Contrapunctual Law: Europe's Constitutional Pluralism in Action, in N. Walker (ed.), Sovereignty in Transition, Hart Publishing 2003, p. 502.

L.M. Poiares Maduro, Interpreting European Law: Judicial Adjudication in a Context of Constitutional Pluralism, in 1 European Journal of Legal Studies, 2007, p. 1.

P. Pollack, The New EU Legal History: What's New, What's Missing?, in 28 American University International Law Review, 2013, p. 1257.

R. Posner, Utilitarianism, Economics, and Legal Theory, in 8 Journal of Legal Studies, 1979, p. 103.

R. Posner, The Ethical and Political Basis of the Efficiency Norm in Common Law Adjudication, in 8 Hofstra Law Review, 1980, p. 487.

E.A. Posner, M.F.P. de Figueiredo, Is the International Court of Justice Biased?, in 34 Journal of Legal Studies, 2005, p. 599.

E.A. Posner, J.C. Yoo, Judicial Independence in International Tribunals, in 93 California Law Review, 2005, p. 1.

R. Pound, The Causes of Popular Dissatisfaction with the Administration of Justice, in 40 American Law Review, 1906, p. 729.

S. Prechal, Direct Effect, Indirect Effect, Supremacy and the Evolving Constitution of the European Union, in C. Barnard (ed.), The Fundamental of EU Law Revisited, Oxford University Press 2007, p. 35.

S. Prechal, National Courts in EU Judicial Structures, in 25 Yearbook of European Law, 2007, p. 429.

E.A. Purcell Jr., Alexander M. Bickel and the Post-Realist Constitution, in 11 Harvard Civil Rights-Civil Liberties Law Review, 1976, p. 521.

C. Radaelli, Whither Europeanization? Concept Stretching and Substantive Change, European Integration online Papers (EIoP), 2000.

R. Raffaelli, Dissenting Opinions in the Supreme Courts of the Member States: Study. Report for the Directorate-General for Internal Policies, Policy

Department C: Citizens' Rights and Constitutional Affairs of the European Parliament, available at the website http://www.europarl.europa.eu/studies.
H. Rasmussen, Why is Article 173(2) Interpreted against Private Plaintiffs, in 5 European Law Review, 1980, p. 112.
H. Rasmussen, The European Court's Acte Clair Strategy in C.I.L.F.I.T.; Or, Acte Clair, of Course! But What Does it Mean?, in 10 European Law Review, 1984, p. 242.
H. Rasmussen, Le pouvoir de décision politique du juge européen et ses limites, in 63 Revue française d'administration publique, 1992, p. 413.
H. Rasmussen, Remedying the Crumbling EC Judicial System, in 37 Common Market Law Review, 2000, p. 1071.
H. Rasmussen, Present and Future European Judicial Problems after Enlargement and the Post- 2005 Ideological Revolt, in 44 Common Market Law Review, 2007, p. 1661.
H. Rasmussen, Legal Opinion about the European Court of Justice's Competence Transgressions, Poor Reasonings and the Complete Non-transparency of Willensbildung, paper presented at the conference "National Judges and Supranational Laws: On the Effective Application of the EC Law and the ECHR", 15th/16th January 2010, at the Scuola Superiore di Studi Universitari e Perfezionamento Sant'Anna, Pisa.
H. Rasmussen, L. Nan Rasmussen, Comment on Katalin Kelemen—Activist EU Court 'Feeds' on the Existing Ban on Dissenting Opinions: Lifting the Ban is Likely to Improve the Quality of EU Judgments, in 14 German Law Journal, 2013, p. 1373.
M. Rasmussen, The Origins of a Legal Revolution—The Early History of the European Court of Justice, in 2 Journal of European Integration History, 2008, p. 77.
M. Rasmussen, The First Advocate Generals and the Making of European Law, 1950–1958, paper presented at the Seminar of the Advocates General held at the European University Institute, Firenze, 16 September 2010.
M. Rasmussen, Rewriting the History of European Public Law: The New Contribution of Historians, in 28/5 American University International Law Review, 2013, p. 1187.
M. Rasmussen, Revolutionizing European Law: A History of the Van Gend en Loos Judgment, in 12 International Journal of Constitutional Law 2014, p. 136.
N. Reich, The "November Revolution" of the European Court of Justice: Keck, Meng and Audi Revisited, in 31 Common Market Law Review, 1994, p. 459.
D. Reiling, Technology in Courts in Europe: Opinions, Practices and Innovations. In 4 International Journal for Court Administration, 2012, p. 11.

D. Ritleng, The Independence and Legitimacy of the European Court of Justice, in Id. (ed.), Independence and Legitimacy in the Institutional System of the European Union, Oxford University Press 2016.
C. Ritter, Purely Internal Situations, Reverse Discrimination, Guimont, Dzodzi and Article 234, in 31 European Law Review, 2006, p. 690.
J. Rivero, Le problème de l'influence des droits internes sur la Cour de Justice de la Communauté Européenne du Charbon et de l'Acier, in 4 Annuaire français de droit international, 1958, p. 295.
F. Rivière, Les opinions séparées des juges á la Cour Européenne des Droits de l'Homme, Bruylant 2004, at 17.
S. Rodin, A Metacritique of the Court of Justice of the EU, in 2 Diritto dell'Unione europea, 2016, p. 191, at 196–197.
G.C. Rodríguez Iglesias, Entscheidungsfindung im Europäischen Gerichtshof, in 7 Journal für Rechtspolitik, 1999, p. 27.
M.T. Rörig, L'opinione dissenziente nella prassi del Bundesverfassungsgericht (1994–2009), available at the website http://www.cortecostituzionale.it/documenti/convegni_seminari/CC_SS_opinione_dissenziente_12012010.pdf.
M. Rosenfeld, Comparing constitutional review by the European Court of Justice and the U.S. Supreme Court, in 4 International Journal of Constitutional Law, 2006, p. 616.
P. Rubin, Why Is the Common Law Efficient?, in 6 Journal of Legal Studies, 1977, p. 51.
D.W.P. Ruiter, A Basic Classification of Legal Institutions, in 10 Ratio Juris 1997, p. 357.
P.H. Russell, Judicial Recruitment, Training, and Careers, in P. Cane, H. Kritzer (eds.), The Oxford Handbook of Empirical Legal Research, Oxford University Press, 2010, p. 522.
R. Sacco, Legal Formants: A Dynamic Approach to Comparative Law, in 39 American Journal of Comparative Law, 1991, p. 1.
U. Sadl, A. Wallerman, 'The Referring Court Asks, in Essence': Is Reformulation of Preliminary Questions by the Court of Justice a Decision Writing Fixture or a Decision-Making Approach?, in 4 European Law Journal, 2019, p. 416.
C. Salcedo, La figura del abogado general en las Communidades Supranationales Europeas: naturaleza juridical y foncíón, in 12 Revista española de derecho international, 1959, p. 119.
D. Sarmiento, Half Case at a Time. Dealing with Judicial Minimalism at the European Court of Justice, in M. Claes, M. de Visser, P. Popelier and C. van de Heyning (eds.), Constitutional Conversations in Europe. Actors, Topics and Procedures, Intersentia 2012, p. 13.
D. Sarmiento, The Reform of the General Court: An Exercise in Minimalist (but Radical) Institutional Reform, in 19 Cambridge Yearbook of European Legal Studies, 2017, p. 236.

T. Sauvel, Les origins des Commissaires du Gouvernement auprès du Conseil d'État statuant au contentieux, in 55 Revue du droit public et de la Science Politique, 1949, p. 5.
T. Sauvel, Histoire du jugement motivé, in 61 Revue du droit public, 1955, p. 5.
R. Scarciglia, Comparative Methodology and Pluralism in Legal Comparison in a Global Age, in 6 Beijing Law Review, 2015, p. 42.
F. Schauer, The Politics and Incentives of Legal Transplantation, in J. Nye Jr., J. Donahue (eds.), Governance in a Globalizing World, Brookings Institution Press 2000, p. 253.
H. Schepel, R. Wesserling, The Legal Community: Judges, Lawyers, Officials and Clerks in the Writing of Europe, in 3 European Law Journal, 1997, p. 165.
H.G. Schermers, The European Court of Justice: Promoter of European Integration, in 22 The American Journal of Comparative Law, 1974, p. 444.
K. Schiemann, La langue de travail de la Cour, in A. Tizzano, A. Rosas, R. Silva de Lapuerta, K. Lenaerts, J. Kokott (eds.), La Cour de justice de l'Union européenne sous la présidence de Vassilios Skouris (2003–2015). Liber amicorum Vassilios Skouris, Bruylant 2015, p. 563.
T. Schilling, Multilingualism and Multijuralism: Assets of EU Legislation and Adjudication?, in 12 German Law Journal, 2011, p. 1460.
E. Schober, Die Lehre vom 'Acte Clair' im franzosischen Recht, in 19 Neue Juristische Wochenschrift, 1966, p. 2252.
F. Schockweiler, L'accès à la justice dans l'ordre juridique communautaire», in 25 Journal des tribunaux, Droit européen, 1996, p. 1.
M. Shapiro, Comparative Law and Comparative Politics, in 53 Southern California Law Review, 1980, p. 537.
M. Shapiro, The European Court of Justice, in P. Craig, G. de Búrca (eds.), The Evolution of EU Law, 1st ed., Oxford University Press 1999, p. 321.
M. Shapiro, Judicial Independence: New Challenges in Established Nations, in 20 Indiana Journal of Global Legal Studies, 2013, p. 253.
E. Sharpston, Transparency and Clear Legal Language in the European Union: Ambiguous Legislative Texts, Laconic Pronouncements and the Credibility of the Judicial System, in 12 Cambridge Yearbook of European Legal Studies, 2009–2010, p. 409.
E. Sharpston, Making the Court of Justice of the European Union More Productive, in 21 Maastricht Journal of European of European and Comparative Law 2014, p. 763.
G. Slynn, Court of First Instance of the European Communities, in 9 Northwestern Journal of International Law & Business, 1989, p. 542.
G. Slynn, What Is a European Community Law Judge?, in 52 Cambridge Law Journal, 1993, p. 234.
A. M. Smith, 'Judicial Nationalism' in International Law, in 40 Texas International Law Journal, 2005, p. 197.

M. Smith, Enforcement, Monitoring, Verification, Outsourcing: The Decline and Decline of the Infringement Process in 33 European Law Review, 2008, p. 777.

B. Smulders, K. Eisele, Reflections on the Institutional Balance, the Community Method and the Interplay between Jurisdictions after Lisbon, in 31 Yearbook of European Law, 2012, p. 112.

I. Solanke, Diversity and Independence in the European Court of Justice, in 15 Columbia Journal of European Law, 2008, p. 89.

I. Solanke, The Advocate General: Assisting the CJEU of Article 13 TEU to Secure Trust and Democracy, in 14 Cambridge Yearbook of European Law, 2012, p. 697.

A. Somma, Giochi senza frontiere. Diritto comparato e tradizione giuridica, in 8 Ars Interpretandi, 2003, p. 317.

E. Stein, Uses, Misuses - and Non-Uses of Comparative Law, in 2 Northwestern Law Review, 1977, p. 198.

E. Stein, Lawyers, Judges, and the Making of a Transnational Constitution, in 75 American Journal of International Law, 1981, p. 1.

E. Stein, The European Coal and Steel Community: The Beginning of Its Judicial Process, in 55 Columbia Law Review, 1995, p. 985.

A. Stone Sweet, The European Court of Justice and the Judicialization of EU Governance, in 5 Living Reviews in European Governance, 2010, available at the website http://www.livingreviews.org/lreg-2010-2.

A. Stone Sweet, The European Court of Justice, in P. Craig, G. de Búrca (eds.), The Evolution of EU Law, 2nd ed., Oxford University Press 2011, p. 121.

A. Stone Sweet, T. Brunell, The European Court and the National Courts: A Statistical Analysis of Preliminary References, 1961–95, in 5 Journal of European Public Policy, 1998, p. 66.

A. Stone Sweet, J. Mathews, Proportionality Balancing and Global Constitutionalism, in 47 Columbia Journal of Transnational Law, 2008, p. 73.

C.R. Sunstein, Practical Reason and Incompletely Theorized Agreements, in 51 Current Legal Problems, 1998.

Symposium—The Future of Judicial Transparency, in 53 Villanova Law Review, 2008.

G. Teubner, Rechtsirritationen: Zur Koevolution von Rechtsnormen und Produktionsregimes, in G. Dux, F. Wetz (eds.), Moral und Recht im Diskurs der Moderne: Zur Legitimation gesellschaftlicher Ordnung, Leske + Budrich 2001.

A.D. Tikhomirov, Philosophical Problems of Legal Comparativistics, in 5 Journal of Comparative Law, 2010, p. 159.

C. Timmermans, The European Union's Judicial System, in 41 Common Market Law Review, 2004, p. 393.

A.V. Tkachenko, Functionalism and the Development of Comparative Law Cognition, in 5 Journal of Comparative Law, 2010, p. 71.
A. Töller, Mythen und Methoden. Zur Messung der Europäisierung der Gesetzgebung des Deutschen Bundestages jenseits des 80-Prozent-Mythos, in 1 Zeitschrift für Parlamentsfragen, 2008, p. 3.
A. Toth, The Authority of Judgments of the European Court of Justice: Binding Force and Legal Effects, in 4 Yearbook of European Law, 1984, p. 1.
A. Trabucchi, L'effet erga omnes des décision préjudicielles rendues par la Cour de justice des Communautés européennes, in 10 Revue trimestrielle de droit européen, 1974, p. 56.
G. Tridimas, T. Tridimas, National Courts and the European Court of Justice: A Public Choice Analysis of the Preliminary Reference Procedure, in 24 International Review of Law and Economics, 2004, p. 125.
T. Tridimas, The Role of the Advocate General in the Development of Community Law: Some Reflections, in 3 Common Market Law Review, 1997, p. 1349.
T. Tridimas, Knocking on Heaven's Door: Fragmentation, Efficiency and Defiance in the Preliminary Reference Procedure, in 40 Common Market Law Review, 2003, p. 9.
T. Tridimas, Constitutional Review of Member State Action: The Virtues and Vices of an Incomplete Jurisdiction, in 9 International Journal of Constitutional Law, 2011, p. 737.
L. Trosanyi, A. Horvath, La pratique des opinions dissidentes en Hongrie, in 8 Nouveaux Cahiers du Conseil Constitutionnel, 2000, available at the website www.conseil-constitutionnel.fr/conseil-constitutionnel/francais/nouveaux-cahiers-du-conseil/cahier-n-8/la-pratique-des-opinions-dissidentes-en-hongrie-les-opinions-individuelles-en-hongrie-une-institution.52544.html.
S. Turenne, Constitutional Adjudication and Appointments to the UK Supreme Court, in S. Shetreet (ed.), The Culture of Judicial Independence, Brill 2014, p. 396.
W. Twining, Diffusion of Law: a Global Perspective, in 49 Journal of Legal Pluralism & Unofficial Law, 2004, p. 1.
G. Vandersanden, A Desired Birth: The Court of First Instance of the European Communities, in 21 Georgia Journal of International and Comparative Law, 1991, p. 51.
G. Vandersanden, Pour un élargissement du droit des particuliers d'agir en annulation contre des actes autres que les décisions qui leur sont adressées, in 31 Cahiers de droit européen, 1995, p. 535.
W. van Gerven, The Role and Structure of the European Judiciary Now and in the Future, in 21 European Law Review, 1996, p. 211.

M. Van Hoecke, M. Warrington, Legal Cultures, Legal Paradigms and Legal Doctrine: Towards a New Model for Comparative Law, in 47 The International and Comparative Law Quarterly, 1998, p. 495.

K. Van Leeuwen, On Democratic Concerns and Legal Traditions: The Dutch 1953 and 1956 Constitutional Reforms 'Towards' Europe, in 21 Contemporary European History, 2012, p. 357.

H.F. van Panhuys, The Netherlands Constitution and International Law, in 47 American Journal of International Law, 1953, p. 537.

H.F. van Panhuys, The Netherlands Constitution and International Law: A Decade of Experience, in 58 American Journal of International Law, 1964, p. 88.

A. Vauchez, The Force of a Weak Field: Law and Lawyers in the Government of the European Union (For a Renewed Research Agenda), in 2 International Political Sociology, 2008, p. 128.

A. Vauchez, The Transnational Politics of Judicialisation: Van Gend en Loos and the Making of EU Polity, in 16 European Law Journal, 2010, p. 1.

I. Venzke, Understanding the Authority of International Courts and Tribunals: On Delegation and Discursive Construction, in 14(2) Theoretical Inquiries in Law, 2013, p. 382.

B. Vesterdorf, A Constitutional Court for the EU?, in 4 International Journal of Constitutional Law, 2006, p. 607.

M. Vink, M. Claes, C. Arnold, Explaining the Use of Preliminary References by Domestic Courts in EU Member States: A Mixed-Method Comparative Analysis, paper presented at the 11th Biennial Conference of the European Union Studies Association, Marina del Rey 24 April 2009, available at the website http://aei.pitt.edu/33155/1/vink._maarten.pdf.

W. Voermans, Judicial Transparency Furthering Public Accountability for New Judiciaries, in 3 Utrecht Law Review, 2007, p. 148.

E. Voeten, The Impartiality of International Judges: Evidence from the ECtHR, in 102 American Political Science Review, 2008, p. 417.

E. Voeten, The Politics of International Judicial Appointments, in 9 Chicago Journal of International Law, 2009, p. 389.

M.L. Volcansek, Appointing Judges the European Way, in 34 Fordham Urban Law Journal, 2006, p. 363.

A. von Bogdandy, The European Lesson for International Democracy: The Significance of Articles 9 to 12 EU Treaty for International Organizations, in 23 European Journal of International Law, 2012.

A. von Bogdandy, The Democratic Legitimacy of International Courts: A Conceptual Framework, 14 Theoretical Inquiries in Law, 2013, p. 361.

A. von Bogdandy, European Law Beyond 'Ever Closer Union'—Repositioning the Concept, Its Thrust, and the ECJ's Comparative Methodology, in 22 European Law Journal, 2016, p. 591.

A. von Bogdandy, I. Venzke, Beyond Dispute: International Judicial Institutions as Lawmakers, in 12 German Law Journal, 2011, p. 979.
A. Von Bogdandy, I. Venzke, In Whose Name? An Investigation of International Courts' Public Authority and Its Democratic Justification, in 23 European Journal of International Law, 2012, p. 7.
T. von Danwitz, The Rule of Law in the Recent Jurisprudence of the ECJ, in 37 Fordham International Law Journal, 2014, p. 1311.
W. von Eyben, Judicial Law Making in Scandinavia, in 5 American Journal of Comparative Law, 1956, p. 112.
A. von Mehren, The Judicial Process: A Comparative Analysis, in 5 American Journal of Comparative Law, 1956, p. 197.
M. Vranken, Role of the Advocate General in the Law-Making Process of the European Community, in Anglo-American Law Review, 1996, p. 39.
D. Waelbroeck, A.M. Verheyden, Les conditions de recevabilité des recours en annulation des particuliers contre les actes normatifs communautaires: à la lumière du droit comparé et de la Convention des droits de l'homme, in 31 Cahiers de droit européen, 1995, p. 399.
N. Walker, Legal Theory and the European Union: A 25th Anniversary Essay, in 25 Oxford Journal of Legal Studies, 2005, p. 581.
C. Walter, La pratique des opinions dissidentes en Allemagne, in 8 Nouveaux Cahiers du Conseil Constitutionnel, 2000, available at the website http://www.conseil-constitutionnel.fr/conseil-constitutionnel/francais/nouveaux-cahiers-du-conseil/cahier-n-8/la-pratique-des-opinions-dissidentes-en-allemagne.52541.html.
J.P. Warner, Some Aspects of the European Court of Justice, in 4 Journal of the Society of Public Teachers of Law, 1975, p. 15.
S. Weatherill, After Keck: Some Thoughts on How to Clarify the Clarification, in 33 Common Market Law Review, 1996, p. 885.
J.H.H. Weiler, The Transformation of Europe, in 100 Yale Law Journal, 1991, p. 2403.
J.H.H. Weiler, Journey to an Unknown Destination: A Retrospective and Prospective of the European Court of Justice in the Arena of Political Integration, in 31 Journal of Common Market Studies, 1993, p. 417.
J.H.H. Weiler, A Quiet Revolution: The European Court of Justice and Its Interlocutors, in 26 Comparative Political Studies 1994, p. 510.
J.H.H. Weiler, Europe: The Case against the Case for Statehood, in 4 European Law Journal, 1998, p. 43.
J.H.H. Weiler, On the Distinction between Values and Virtues in the Process of European Integration, paper of the Institute for International Law and Justice, International Legal Theory Colloquium Spring 2010, available at the website http://iilj.org/courses/documents/2010Colloquium.Weiler.pdf.

J.H.H. Weiler, The Political and Legal Culture of European Integration: An Exploratory Essay, in 9 International Journal of Constitutional Law, 2011, p. 678.

J.H.H. Weiler, Revisiting Van Gend en Loos: Subjectifying and Objectifying the Individual, in Court of Justice of EU, 50th Anniversary of the Judgment in Van Gend en Loos 1963–2013, Conference Proceedings, Luxembourg, 13 May 2013, available at the website http://curia.europa.eu/jcms/upload/docs/application/pdf/2013-12/qd30136442ac_002.pdf.

J.H.H. Weiler, J. Trachtman, European Constitutionalism and Its Discontents, in 17 Northwestern Journal of International Law & Business, 1997, p. 354.

M. Wells, French and American Judicial Opinions, in 19 Yale Journal of International Law, 1994, p. 85.

R.C.A. White, I. Boussiakou, Separate Opinions in the European Court of Human Rights, in 9 Human Rights Law Review, 2009, p. 37.

M. Wind, The Nordics, the EU and the Reluctance Towards Supranational Judicial Review, in 48 Journal of Common Market Studies, 2010, p. 1048.

M. Wind, D.S. Martinsen, G.P. Rotger, The Uneven Legal Push for Europe. Questioning Variation when National Courts go to Europe, in 10 European Union Politics, 2009, p. 63.

E.M. Wise, The Transplants of Legal Patterns, in 38 American Journal of Comparative Law, 1990, p. 1.

G. Zagrebelsky, La pratique des opinions dissidentes en Italie, in 8 Nouveaux Cahiers du Conseil Constitutionnel, 2000, available at the website http://www.conseil-constitutionnel.fr/conseil-constitutionnel/francais/nouveaux-cahiers-du-conseil/cahier-n-8/la-pratique-des-opinions-dissidentes-en-italie.52545.html.

M. Zürn, M. Binder, M. Ecker-Ehrhardt, International Authority and Its Politicization, in 4 International Theory 2012, p. 69.

All the abovementioned websites were accessible on 2 March 2020.

Index

L. Pierdominici, *The Mimetic Evolution of the Court of Justice of the EU*, https://doi.org/10.1007/978-3-030-47864-3

The manufacturer's authorised representative in the EU is Springer Nature Customer Service Centre GmbH, Europaplatz 3, 69115 Heidelberg, Germany. If you have any concerns regarding our products, please contact ProductSafety@springernature.com

Printed and bound by CPI Group (UK) Ltd, Croydon, CR0 4YY
30/09/2026
02225649-0016